Keep this book. You will need it and use it throughout your career.

MANAGING SERVICE
in
FOOD AND BEVERAGE
OPERATIONS

Educational Institute Books

HOSPITALITY FOR SALE
C. DeWitt Coffman

UNIFORM SYSTEM OF ACCOUNTS AND EXPENSE DICTIONARY FOR SMALL HOTELS, MOTELS, AND MOTOR HOTELS
Fourth Edition

RESORT DEVELOPMENT AND MANAGEMENT
Second Edition
Chuck Y. Gee

PLANNING AND CONTROL FOR FOOD AND BEVERAGE OPERATIONS
Third Edition
Jack D. Ninemeier

STRATEGIC MARKETING PLANNING IN THE HOSPITALITY INDUSTRY: A BOOK OF READINGS
Edited by Robert L. Blomstrom

TRAINING FOR THE HOSPITALITY INDUSTRY
Second Edition
Lewis C. Forrest, Jr.

UNDERSTANDING HOSPITALITY LAW
Second Edition
Jack P. Jefferies

SUPERVISION IN THE HOSPITALITY INDUSTRY
Second Edition
Raphael R. Kavanaugh/Jack D. Ninemeier

SANITATION MANAGEMENT
Second Edition
Ronald F. Cichy

ENERGY AND WATER RESOURCE MANAGEMENT
Second Edition
Robert E. Aulbach

MANAGEMENT OF FOOD AND BEVERAGE OPERATIONS
Second Edition
Jack D. Ninemeier

MANAGING FRONT OFFICE OPERATIONS
Third Edition
Michael L. Kasavana/Richard M. Brooks

STRATEGIC HOTEL/MOTEL MARKETING
Revised Edition
Christopher W. L. Hart/David A. Troy

MANAGING SERVICE IN FOOD AND BEVERAGE OPERATIONS
Anthony M. Rey/Ferdinand Wieland

THE LODGING AND FOOD SERVICE INDUSTRY
Third Edition
Gerald W. Lattin

SECURITY AND LOSS PREVENTION MANAGEMENT
Raymond C. Ellis, Jr., & the Security Committee of AH&MA

HOSPITALITY INDUSTRY MANAGERIAL ACCOUNTING
Second Edition
Raymond S. Schmidgall

PURCHASING FOR HOSPITALITY OPERATIONS
William B. Virts

THE ART AND SCIENCE OF HOSPITALITY MANAGEMENT
Jerome J. Vallen/James R. Abbey

MANAGING COMPUTERS IN THE HOSPITALITY INDUSTRY
Second Edition
Michael L. Kasavana/John J. Cahill

MANAGING HOSPITALITY ENGINEERING SYSTEMS
Michael H. Redlin/David M. Stipanuk

UNDERSTANDING HOSPITALITY ACCOUNTING I
Second Edition
Raymond Cote

UNDERSTANDING HOSPITALITY ACCOUNTING II
Second Edition
Raymond Cote

MANAGING QUALITY SERVICES
Stephen J. Shriver

MANAGING CONVENTIONS AND GROUP BUSINESS
Leonard H. Hoyle/David C. Dorf/Thomas J. A. Jones

HOSPITALITY SALES AND ADVERTISING
Second Edition
James R. Abbey

MANAGING HUMAN RESOURCES IN THE HOSPITALITY INDUSTRY
David Wheelhouse

MANAGING HOUSEKEEPING OPERATIONS
Margaret M. Kappa/Aleta Nitschke/Patricia B. Schappert

CONVENTION SALES: A BOOK OF READINGS
Margaret Shaw

DIMENSIONS OF TOURISM
Joseph D. Fridgen

HOSPITALITY TODAY: AN INTRODUCTION
Rocco M. Angelo/Andrew N. Vladimir

MANAGING BAR AND BEVERAGE OPERATIONS
Lendal H. Kotschevar/Mary L. Tanke

POWERHOUSE CONFERENCES: ELIMINATING AUDIENCE BOREDOM
Coleman Lee Finkel

ETHICS IN HOSPITALITY MANAGEMENT: A BOOK OF READINGS
Edited by Stephen S.J. Hall

HOSPITALITY FACILITIES MANAGEMENT AND DESIGN
David M. Stipanuk/Harold Roffmann

MANAGING HOSPITALITY HUMAN RESOURCES
Robert H. Woods

FINANCIAL MANAGEMENT FOR THE HOSPITALITY INDUSTRY
William P. Andrew/Raymond S. Schmidgall

HOSPITALITY INDUSTRY FINANCIAL ACCOUNTING
Raymond S. Schmidgall/James W. Damitio

MANAGING SERVICE
in
FOOD AND BEVERAGE OPERATIONS

Anthony M. Rey, CFBE, CHA
Ferdinand Wieland, CFBE, CHA

Contributing author: Jack D. Ninemeier, Ph.D., CHA

EDUCATIONAL INSTITUTE
of the American Hotel & Motel Association

Disclaimer

This publication is designed to provide accurate and authoritative information in regard to the subject matter covered. It is sold with the understanding that the publisher is not engaged in rendering legal, accounting, or other professional service. If legal advice or other expert assistance is required, the services of a competent professional person should be sought.

—From the Declaration of Principles jointly adopted by the American Bar Association and a Committee of Publishers and Associations

The authors, Anthony M. Rey, and Ferdinand Wieland, are solely responsible for the contents of this publication. All views expressed herein are solely those of the authors and do not necessarily reflect the views of the Educational Institute of the American Hotel & Motel Association (the Institute) or the American Hotel & Motel Association (AH&MA).

Nothing contained in this publication shall constitute a standard, an endorsement, or a recommendation of the Institute or AH&MA. The Institute and AH&MA disclaim any liability with respect to the use of any information, procedure, or product, or reliance thereon by any member of the hospitality industry.

Library of Congress Cataloging in Publication Data

Rey, Anthony M.

    Managing service in food and beverage operations.
    Includes index.
    1. Food service management. I. Wieland, Ferdinand.
    II. Ninemeier, Jack D.   III. Title.

TX911.3.M27R48   1985   647'.95'068   85-12962

ISBN 0-86612-023-8

Editor: Donna M. Paananen

Contents

Preface xi

PART I
Preparing for Dining Service

1 Introduction 3

Defining Terms.. 6
Types of Food and Beverage Operations in a Hotel 10
The Manager of Dining Service 14
Service: The Marketing Perspective... 17
Quality in Dining Service.. 18

2 Personnel Administration 21

Employee Recruitment and Selection Procedures 21
Orientation and Training Programs.. 24
Principles of Supervision 28
Motivation and Morale.. 32
Evaluation Procedures 34
Employee Discipline Programs... 37

3 Menu Planning 41

Menu Planning Objectives... 41
Menu Planning Procedures 44
Basic Types of Menus... 46
General Menu Planning Considerations....................................... 46
Menu Planning Constraints.. 50
Health and Wellness: New Concerns in Menu Planning 51
The Menu and the Food Service Operation.................................... 52
The Menu and the Service Plan.. 54
Designing the Menu 55

4 Food Production Systems **59**

Coffee Shops 60
Room Service 60
Banquet Operations 61
Timing Food Orders 63
Facilitating Communication Between Production and Service Personnel 64
Service Staff in Production Areas 65

5 Dining Service Supplies and Equipment **69**

Purchasing 69
Receiving and Storing 86
Issuing 88
Controlling Dining Service Supplies 89

6 Dining Service Methods and Procedures **95**

American or Plate Service 95
French or Cart Service 96
Russian or Platter Service 100
English or Family Service 101
Buffet Service 102
Salesmanship in the Dining Room 106

7 Controlling Service Labor Costs **111**

Establishing Performance Standards 111
Incorporating Fixed Labor Requirements 112
Developing the Staffing Guide 115
Forecasting Food Service Sales 116
Scheduling Employees 120
Measuring Productivity 128
Putting It All Together to Control Labor Costs 134

8 Sales Income Control Systems **139**

Manual Guest Check Procedures 139
Rules for Guest Checks 140
Cash Handling Equipment 140
Income Control Procedures 142
Income Theft: Methods and Precautions 145
Accepting Noncash Payments 156
Planning for Cash Income Control 158

Closing Procedures 159
Recordkeeping Requirements and Income Control 164
Security of Income Collected. 166

PART II
Delivering Dining Service

9 Coffee Shop Service 173

Personnel. 173
Coffee Shop Service Procedures. 176
Forecasting and Employee Scheduling 181
Supplies and Equipment 181
Control Procedures 181
Special Concerns 182

10 Room Service 193

Personnel. 193
Room Service Procedures. 196
The Room Service Menu 204
Forecasting and Employee Scheduling 206
Supplies and Equipment 207
Income Control Procedures 207

11 Dining Room Service 211

Personnel. 211
Dining Room Service Procedures. 221
Reservation Systems 232
The Dining Room Menu 236
Supplies and Equipment 240

12 Banquet Service 243

Banquet Business Markets 243
Organization of a Banquet Department 243
An Overview of Banquet Duties and Responsibilities. 244
Pricing Banquets. 268
Banquet Contracts 269
Protocol for Banquets 272
Banquet Income Control. 273

13 **Other Dining Services** **277**

    Vending Machine Services.. 277
    Cafeteria Food Service 278
    Employee Dining Arrangements 283
    Off-Site Catering Operations..................................... 286
    VIP Dining Rooms.. 287
    Club and Show Operations....................................... 288
    Miscellaneous Food Services 298

PART III
Supportive Functions for Dining Service

14 **Beverage Service**..**303**

    Personnel.. 304
    Procedures for Beverage Service................................ 307
    Purchasing Beverage Service Supplies and Equipment..... 319
    Bar Design 321

15 **Sanitation, Safety, and Security** **325**

    Sanitation... 325
    Safety 333
    Security.. 344

16 **Dining Room Design, Decor, and Maintenance** **353**

    Planning an Effective Design 353
    Dining Room Decor and Ambience............................. 362
    Maintenance of Dining Areas 365

    Appendix A - Selecting Table Linens 373
    Appendix B - Preparing for Kosher Service 383

Index **387**

Educational Institute Board of Trustees **393**

Preface

Managing Service in Food and Beverage Operations is clearly a major contribution to the hospitality industry. It is an up-to-date, comprehensive text that discusses thoroughly the procedures necessary to plan for and manage effectively the delivery of food and beverage products to guests in outlets ranging from employee cafeterias and coffee shops to room service, banquet areas, and high-check-average gourmet dining rooms. This text has been developed by a team of experts who have had years of experience in food and beverage service management. It presents basic service principles with the emphasis and focus constantly where they belong—on the guests. It not only provides forms for implementation of procedures but also checklists to ensure that standards are met. In addition, it offers dozens of creative ideas that can be adapted by properties throughout the United States and the world.

Managing Service in Food and Beverage Operations has been written for a variety of readers—those already in the hospitality industry and those who may become part of it. Heads of food and/or beverage departments; restaurant and lounge managers; all those who supervise service in dining outlets; employees who wish to get a foot on the food service career ladder (or wish to climb higher on it); students; and laypersons who want to find their niche in this vast and growing industry will find a great deal of "food for thought" in this text.

Food and beverage service managers will want to keep and consult this textbook throughout their careers, for it is a primary reference for those seeking to grow and develop in the profession. This textbook can also be used as a training tool for service staff members. In addi-

tion, it can be used as a basis for a major course in two- and four-year college and university hospitality management curricula, in individualized learning and group study programs (it is supplemented with student/instructor materials), and in local Educational Institute chapter programs.

As is true with all textbooks published by the Educational Institute, this book was written by the industry for the industry. While it is virtually impossible to recognize all those who have provided necessary information and critiqued the manuscript as it was being developed, we would like to acknowledge the other members of the American Hotel & Motel Association's Food and Beverage Steering Committee who devoted their talents, as well as tireless hours of their time, toward the publication of this text during the many months it took to produce it. The committee members are: Gary Budge, Area Food and Beverage Director, Sheraton Washington Hotel, Washington, D.C.; Joseph Gardiner, CFBE, Senior Vice President, Food and Beverage, Hilton Hotels Corporation, Beverly Hills, California; Rudy Mazzonelli, CFBE, Executive Vice President, Food and Beverage, Resorts International, Inc., Atlantic City, New Jersey; and Rod Stoner, Executive Food Director, The Greenbrier, White Sulphur Springs, West Virginia. Finally, we would like to thank George R. Conrade, CHA, Director of Educational Programs, Educational Institute of AH&MA; Jack D. Ninemeier, Ph.D., School of Hotel, Restaurant, and Institutional Management, Michigan State University; and Donna M. Paananen, Writer/Editor, for their contributions to this book.

Anthony M. Rey, CFBE, CHA
Senior Vice President, Community Relations
Resorts International, Inc.
Atlantic City, New Jersey

Ferdinand Wieland, CFBE, CHA
General Manager
Hotel du Pont
Wilmington, Delaware

Part I
Preparing for Dining Service

1
Introduction

Managing dining service is a relatively new concept in food and beverage operations throughout the world. In the nineteenth century, even those people who could afford to eat out generally did not. They dined privately in their own or others' homes, and dining service was often a "below-the-stairs" function. The domestic staff, usually under the supervision of the lady of the house, would serve a wide variety of meals, complete with the correct beverages—sometimes from early morning until late in the evening.

In America, this situation started to change in 1827 when the Delmonico brothers from Switzerland opened a pastry shop and cafe in New York City.[1] After they opened their first restaurant a few years later, the art of food service began to be recognized as an important part of the dining experience. No longer was it enough simply to serve good food in a public place; it also had to be served courteously and graciously, accompanied by the finest of wines in the pleasantest of surroundings.

The arrival on the hotel scene of another Swiss man—Cesar Ritz—did much to alter attitudes toward public dining in Europe.[2] In the latter part of the 1870s, he became the general manager of the Grand Hotel National in Lucerne, Switzerland, and soon aristocratic ladies enthusiastically began to support his special fetes in the July and August "season." These were the same duchesses and countesses who would not appear in public dining rooms and ballrooms in London or Paris at the time.

When Ritz met Auguste Escoffier in 1880, the scene was set for European dining fashion to change.[3] Like Ritz, Escoffier (called the king of chefs and the chef of kings) had exacting standards. Because of their reputation for superb cuisine impeccably and stylishly served, Escoffier and Ritz were followed by their clientele, including royalty, wherever they went. Public dining gained in respectability, and by the turn of the century, it had become proper, even among the staid upper class in London, for gentlemen to dine in a public place with their wives. These changes came about mainly because of Ritz's extraordinary management of people and service and Escoffier's unmatchable menus. Years later, Madame Ritz was to write of their association as well as of proper dining management:

> The association of Ritz and Escoffier, which began at Monte Carlo, was one of the most fortunate things that ever happened in either of the two men's lives. During the first years Ritz had spent at the Grand Hotel National in Lucerne he had evolved almost completely his ideas of what a *de luxe* hotel could and should be, and had been convinced of the importance in such a hotel organization of superb cuisine. Until he met Escoffier he had not yet been able perfectly to apply his ideas in that realm. As to Escoffier,

---

[1] For a history of the Delmonico family and their restaurants, consult Lately Thomas's *Delmonico's: A Century of Splendor* (Boston: Houghton Mifflin, 1967).

[2] Much of the material about Ritz in this book was adapted from Marie Louise Ritz's biography of her husband, *Cesar Ritz: Host to the World* (Toronto: Lippincott, 1938).

[3] In addition to Escoffier's own books *Le Guide Culinaire, Le Livre des Menus, Les Fleurs en Cire*, and *Ma Cuisine: Traite de Cuisine Familiale*, consult *Georges Auguste Escoffier* (London: Practical Press, 1955), written by his pupils and "literary executors"—Eugene Herbodeau and Paul Thalamas.

A Continuing Case Study...
Managing Service at the Hotel Columbia
Page One

The Midtown Hotel had not been doing well financially for several years, so it came as no surprise when the hotel's owners decided to actively seek buyers. Fortunately, a great package was put together and the Midtown Hotel changed hands. The new investors were convinced that a first-class, deluxe hotel would do well and would provide for unmet needs in the marketplace. After months of strategic planning, developing projected financial statements, and negotiating with lending institutions, the plan was given the go-ahead. The Midtown Hotel became the new Hotel Columbia. The change would require more than $50,000,000 in remodeling costs and several million additional dollars to market the new hotel.

After a thorough search, the owners selected the Hotel Columbia's first president and managing director, Clifford Mansford, who was immediately charged with finding a strong management team. Because the quality of the food and beverage services offered by the hotel would be a critical component of the hotel's image, the Hotel Columbia's top executive knew that it was imperative that he find the right person to head the food and beverage department. The owners believed that if that department were operated correctly, it could contribute approximately 50% of the total revenue generated by the hotel.

At long last the right person was found. Lewis Scott became the vice president for food and beverage at the Hotel Columbia. He was brought on board ten months before the property opened in order to develop the many systems and procedures required to run a large, complex, first-class hotel operation.

Lewis Scott was well qualified for his new position. He was a graduate of a major hotel school with an excellent reputation. After graduation, he had advanced from his first job as an assistant beverage manager in a relatively small resort to a position of corporate responsibility for food and beverage operations in a hotel management company with 30 units. During his 20-year career, Lewis had worked in almost every type of hotel food and beverage operation—both in the United States and abroad. He had also worked for one year as a special consultant to a restaurant chain that wanted him to develop dining service procedures and training programs.

Lewis knew that he could do the work; he had ten months before the opening. Fortunately, he could anticipate some excellent help from the hotel's purchasing, accounting, and sales/marketing departments; personnel had been hired in these key areas and would take some of the burden of pre-opening planning off his shoulders. While all areas of the operation were important, Lewis knew that the management of dining service had to be given a great deal of attention. After all, the Hotel Columbia deserved nothing less than the very best food and beverage operation—both from the property's perspective and that of the guests.

until he met Ritz no one had fully appreciated his talents nor given him full scope to exercise them. For if the success of a hotel is dependent upon its kitchens and its table—as it is—the kitchens and the restaurant in their turn are dependent upon the hotel management. If the management is progressive, imaginative, daring, generous, if it can attract fashionable, wealthy and discriminating people to its doors, then the chef has the equipment, the supplies, and the clientele worthy of his genius. And what is good food if it is not finely served? (Marie Louise Ritz, 1938)

With increased affluence among many segments of society, the expansion of cities, and the growth and development of the travel and hospitality industries, restaurants of all kinds have multiplied in this century. According to Horwath & Horwath International, in lodging properties worldwide, food and beverage sales brought in approximately 39% of the total revenue generated in these properties in the mid-'80s.[4] Expenditures on food and beverages consumed in lodging properties and restaurants

---

[4] See *Worldwide Lodging Industry* (New York: Horwath & Horwath International, 1984), the 14th annual report on international hotel operations.

Service in the tradition of Ritz and Escoffier in Le Palais Restaurant, Resorts International Casino Hotel, Atlantic City, New Jersey.

have risen almost constantly. In America alone, according to Department of Commerce estimates, over $1.7 billion was spent on such food and beverages in 1935; in 1958, more than $8 billion was spent, and in the early '80s, food service industry sales were over $90.5 billion.

In its annual "Restaurant Guide Index" (RGI), the periodical *Restaurant Business* indicated that, in the early 1980s, food and beverage sales in American hotels and motels annually amounted to approximately $9.4 billion.[5] Its prediction for the latter part of the decade was that over $13 billion per year would be spent for food

and beverages in lodging properties. Given such sales figures and projections, it is understandable that the lodging industry is paying increased attention to management of its food and beverage operations.

The National Restaurant Association (NRA) in its *Restaurant Industry Operations Report '81* stated that in the past when sales have fallen due to recessions or other reasons, the industry has always "tried harder" to get the customers back.[6] The NRA asserts,

---

[5] For more information, consult both the 16th and 17th annual restaurant growth indices in *Restaurant Business* (Sept. 15, 1983, and Sept. 20, 1984).

[6] See the *Restaurant Industry Operations Report '81 for the United States* (Washington, D.C.: National Restaurant Association, 1981), which is prepared in cooperation with Laventhol & Horwath, the international accounting firm.

The hallmark of today's, and tomorrow's, successful restaurant operation is growing professionalism exemplified by efforts to improve service and offer customers increased value for their dollars. As competition intensifies, quality operations will do better than average because they will deliver the all important price/value relationship today's sophisticated consumer is shopping for. A premium will, therefore, be placed on the well run operation. . . .

The restaurant industry is preparing itself for the future and its more sophisticated patron. It is learning from its past how to avoid future mistakes and how to take advantage of the changing environment it will be operating in throughout the 1980s.

Most of us are familiar with the expansion and changes in food and beverage service for all segments of society in recent years. But what of the future?

John Naisbitt in his *Megatrends: Ten New Directions Transforming Our Lives* predicts that as industrial societies shift to those that predominantly provide services and information, there will be unprecedented diversity.[7] America has, according to Naisbitt, already gone from being an "either/or" world to one with multiple options. He concludes his book, in part, as follows:

> . . . We have finally abandoned the myth of the melting pot and learned to celebrate ethnic diversity. The new languages, ethnic food and restaurants, and the additional layer of foreign cultures all around us seem to fit the multiple-option mood. This new openness enriches us all. (John Naisbitt, 1982)

Alvin Toffler, author of *Future Shock* and other works, has also noted that our mass society is now becoming "de-massified"—thus moving toward a more advanced and complex form of social order.[8] What these trends will mean to managers of dining service, no doubt, is a movement away from mass-produced foods prepared to serve the masses. As the end of the twentieth century approaches, we will see a return to many of the practices of such entrepreneurs as Escoffier and Ritz. Even in fast-food operations, the accent will be on giving the individual exactly what he or she would like—within the limits of the establishment. In high-check-average operations, service personnel will more and more be trained by management to make each guest as satisfied as possible with all aspects of the dining experience—whether it is the perfect presentation of the uniquely garnished first course or the unobtrusive service of the freshly brewed after-dinner coffee accompanied by a superb cognac.

It is with this future in mind that this book has been written. What makes this book unique is its emphasis on the management of dining service. Furthermore, the focus in our study of managing service is constantly on the guest.

Unfortunately, restaurant managers have sometimes neglected to consider the guest when they have developed operating policies and procedures. Sometimes policies have little direct impact on the guest (e.g., decisions regarding the quantities of food and beverages to have in storage). At other times, however, the guest is directly affected (e.g., when a manager defines quality requirements for food products and develops them into purchase specifications). Even professional restaurant managers with years of experience have sometimes forgotten the guest when they have undertaken planning, supervising, controlling, and other management activities. To be successful in the future, managers of dining service operations must constantly focus first on the guest, then on other aspects of management. This focus is central not only to this chapter but to this entire book.

Defining Terms

Let's look more closely at the hospitality industry and some of the terms associated with it. The first term to define is **hospitality** itself. The *Oxford English Dictionary* (OED) defines hospitality as "the reception and entertainment of guests, visitors, or strangers, with liberality and good will." Such a reception invariably includes providing a pleasant environment. Can you envision the innkeeper of several hundred years ago extending a hand of welcome to guests seek-

---

7 See John Naisbitt's *Megatrends: Ten New Directions Transforming Our Lives* (New York: Warner Books, 1982). Ronald F. Cichy discusses each of Naisbitt's ten trends in relation to its potential impact on food service and lodging operations in his book *Sanitation Management: Strategies for Success* (East Lansing, Mich.: Educational Institute of the American Hotel & Motel Association, 1984), pp. 13-18.

8 Alvin Toffler, "Reordering Industry as the Era of the Masses Passes," *Wall Street Journal*, June 16, 1983.

What's the Difference Between a Customer and a Guest?

Some food service managers use the terms **customer** and **guest** interchangeably. There is, however, an important difference. When we think of a **customer**, we emphasize the purchase of a product or service. A **guest** is someone whom we entertain in our own homes—someone whom we desire to please.

The concept of hospitality as we know it today began when innkeepers literally invited travelers and other guests into their homes and shared their food and accommodations with them. Today the managers of dining service should continue to focus on hospitality toward guests rather than the need to collect money from customers.

ing a meal and overnight accommodations as they arrive weary after a day's dusty travel by horse or coach? The modern dining room manager greeting guests at the entrance to an elegant hotel restaurant accented with plants, polished mahogany, leather, crystal, or chrome, offers the same kind of welcome. But no matter how grand or simple the environment or accommodation is, the most important aspects of the hospitality industry are a welcome reception and cordiality.

The word **hotel** in its original French meant "a large private residence, a town mansion." Mansions in which rooms or apartments could be rented by the day, week, or longer were called **hotel garni**. According to the OED, in the late eighteenth century a hotel came to be known by English speakers as "a house for the entertainment of strangers or travelers, an inn; especially one that is, or claims to be of a superior kind." In this text, the word **hotel** is used generically to include motels, motor hotels, and inns.

Restaurant, meaning "a public establishment where refreshments or meals may be obtained," is a fairly modern term in English. It was slowly adapted into the English language after 1765 when Boulanger, a Frenchman in Paris, served soups that he called "restaurants," which in English meant restoratives.

The person in charge of the dining room is often called the **maitre d'hotel**; other titles for this person could be the **headwaiter/headwaitress**, the **director of service**, or the **dining room** or **restaurant manager**. In his *Larousse Gastronomique*, Prosper Montagne writes, "In the past, in royal, princely, and other noble households, the office of *maitre d'hotel* was always held by persons of the highest rank, sometimes princes of the royal blood." Montagne concludes his definition by

saying that a modern maitre d'hotel ". . . is usually a man of distinction, good education and, most essential, a master of his art, for service at the table is as much an art as cooking."[9]

As we examine more closely the food service segment of the hospitality industry, we realize we must define **service**. The OED's discussion of service covers nearly four pages, but the meaning applicable here is "an act of helping or benefiting; an instance of beneficial or friendly action" and "conduct tending to the welfare or advantage of others." While the fourteenth century definition relates service to being a "servant," that is far from the role of service personnel in our modern hospitality industry. One's own personal worth is not diminished in the least as one goes about the task of helping others.

Other Definitions. The term **a la carte** traditionally means offering food items that are priced separately on a menu. In contrast, **table d'hote** (literally, the table of the host) pricing offers an entire meal at a fixed price (*prix fixe*). Guests may have a choice of the main entree but little or no choice about the other items served. Exhibits 1.1 and 1.2 show menus with a la carte and table d'hote pricing.

Throughout this book we shall discuss many concepts that you should consider as you develop guest service systems for commercial food and beverage operations. **Commercial food and beverage operations** are those that are planned to yield a profit, such as hotel or restaurant operations. (**Institutional food services** are not-for-profit dietary services in health care,

---

[9] Prosper Montagne, *Larousse Gastronomique* (New York: Crown, 1961), p. 605.

Exhibit 1.1 Example of Table d'Hote or Prix Fixe Menu

WINSTON'S

Les Entrees	Les Soups
La Galatine de Canard	La Bisque d'Homard
L'Homard Parisienne	Le Glace de Pêche
Le Ris de Veau Favorite	Le Consomme au Fumet de Carre
Les Oyster Pie Nouvelle Orleans	Crab and Corn Chowder

Salade Cecile
Main Course

Le Filet de Boeuf aux Morilles
Succulent slices from the beef tenderloin, roasted whole, sliced to order and served with imported French morels

Le Carré d'Agneau en croute
A New Zealand lamb rack completely deboned, wrapped in puff pastry with a mint and fresh tarragon duxelle

Le Suprême de Canard Montmorency
Long Island Duckling roasted whole, deboned and sliced, finished with sauce Bigarde with fresh cherries

La Sole A L'Encienne
A fresh dover sole sauteed in butter, deboned, laced with sauce au Vin Blanc, garnished with julienne of fresh apples and celery

La Côtellete de Veau En Papillote
A large Provimi Veal Chop, stuffed with a prociutto ham duxelle, sauteed in butter finished en papillote served with sauce Beurre Blanc

Les Crevettes Etouffé
Jumbo shrimp sauteed in butter, deglazed with a rich cajun sauce, finished with green onions and sweet bell pepper. A New Orleans favorite

Trois Legumes de La Saison
Les Desserts
Le Soufflé glacé Arlequin
Le Soufflé ala poire Williams
Les Pêches Flambeé Au Sabayon

"Some Items may vary as our Chef takes full advantage of the Seasons, offering you only the Finest Ingredients"

Menu Prix Fixe $26.95	Service Non Compris
(Complete Dinner)	(Service Not Included)

Le Maitre De Cuisine – Louis Chatham
Le Maitre D'Hotel – Fernando Barahona
New Orleans Hilton and Towers

Exhibit 1.2 Example of an A la Carte Menu

Les Hors d'Oeuvres

	Prix
Pâté Maison – The specialty of our chef.	xxx
Huitres Grilés – Marinated oysters, deep fried until golden.	xxx
Escargots à la Bourguignonne – Classic snail dish.	xxx
Coquilles Saint Jacques – Scallops and mushrooms in a white wine sauce	xxx

Les Potages

Potage Crème d'artichauts – Creamy artichoke soup.	xxx
Potage Julienne – Four vegetables in our best beef bouillon	xxx
Potage Royal de Tomates – Cold tomato soup fit for a king or queen.	xxx

Les Poissons

Truite en Papillot – A perfect way to serve trout – in a case.	xxxx
Turbot à la Granvillaise – Lightly poached turbot in a white wine sauce.	xxxx
Sole à la Normande – Lightly poached sole garnished with mussels, oysters, mushrooms, and shrimp.	xxxx

Les Viandes

Escalope de Veau Farcies aux Champignons – Veal cutlet in a light sauce, garnished with stuffed mushrooms.	xxxx
Entrecôte Forestiere – Club steak, pan broiled, in a mushroom and wine sauce with a hint of bacon.	xxxx
Tournedos Rossini – Twin fillets with artichoke hearts, foie gras, truffles and Madeira sauce.	xxxx
Côtelettes de Mouton Panées – Two marinated and lightly breaded lambchops, grilled to your order.	xxxx
Brochettes de Côtelettes d'Agneau – Lamb mixed grill.	xxxx
Fois de Veau aux Pommes – Calf's liver with apples, flamed with apple brandy.	xxxx

Les Legumes

Haricots Verts à la Française	xxx	Petites Courgettes Farcies	xxx
Asperges à la Polonaise	xxx	Ratatouille	xxx
Carrottes à la Vichy	xxx	Pommes de Terres Anna	xxx
Epinards aux Champignons	xxx	Gratin de Pommes de Terre Gréy	xxx

Les Salades

Salade de Cresson aux Noisettes	xxx
Salade de Tomates aux Haricots Verts	xxx
Salade de Jardin	xxx

Les Entremets

Soufflé Glacé aux Frambroises	xxx
Babas au Rum	xxx
Soufflé au Chocolat (this dessert takes approximately 50 minutes)	xxx
Crêpes Suzette	xxx

What Are the Elements of Successful Dining Service?

Regardless of the type of dining service you offer, there are two basic elements for success: courtesy and efficiency. Courtesy stems from a genuine concern of dining service staff to do all that is reasonably possible to meet the needs and wants of guests while they are visiting a food and beverage establishment. Efficiency results from the way that you organize the food service operation to deliver required food products effectively. Efficiency may mean almost instant service in a fast-food operation; or it may refer to well-paced service at the guests' leisure in a high-check-average, a la carte dining operation. Efficiency also means minimizing the waste of expensive resources, for higher-than-necessary costs incurred during the delivery of dining service will ultimately be translated into higher costs for guests and/or lower profits for the operation.

Dining service employees must be just as professional as any other staff members. They must be committed to the highest standards of performance at all times, be dedicated to the goal of putting guests first, and be aware that there is always something new to learn. One of the goals of any food service manager should be to provide opportunities for service employees to improve themselves professionally and to advance in the profession. The guests will not only appreciate this approach, but the operation itself will also benefit.

educational, and other facilities.) It cannot be emphasized enough: The design and implementation of guest-oriented service procedures must be accompanied by a philosophy or attitude of service held by all food service personnel.

Types of Food and Beverage Operations in a Hotel

The food and beverage department in a large hotel today is very complex. (You will find an example of an organization chart for such an operation in the case study at the end of Chapter 2.) The large hotel's food and beverage department can offer several different types of dining facilities ranging from low-check-average outlets such as a coffee shop or a family-oriented restaurant to high-check-average outlets such as a plush, intimate dining room specializing in *haute cuisine* or a roof-top restaurant with an incredible view and top-notch food and service. In addition, the department can operate clubs featuring happy hours, nightly entertainment, and dancing; banquet and catering operations; an employee cafeteria with vending services; room service; and a variety of bars and lounges. It may even offer take-out food services, a delicatessen, snack kiosks, poolside fast-food counters, morning coffee in the main lobby, or afternoon tea in the hotel's garden. Almost any type of food

service operation can be found in one lodging property or another. As we examine these food service outlets in more detail, remember that the same principles of efficient production and service apply as much to freestanding commercial operations as they do to the food service outlets that are a part of a lodging property's food and beverage operation.

Low-Check-Average Table Service Outlets

Coffee Shop Operations. In many hotels the coffee shop offers a low-check-average or family-type menu. Convenience is a major concern of guests. Coffee shops offer fast service and relatively low prices; therefore both guests and non-guests of many lodging properties enjoy them. While service must be swift, it must also be correct, which requires careful attention to procedures that will ensure guest satisfaction. (For complete information on service in coffee shops, see Chapter 9.)

Family-Oriented Operations. These dining outlets frequently offer a wide variety of menu items at very reasonable prices in pleasant surroundings. Guests in family-oriented operations appreciate novelties to keep children busy (e.g., crayons, puzzles, comics) and special menu items that children will enjoy. Guests value good

---

Principles of Excellence

Service personnel in all types of dining operations must:

1. Be knowledgeable about the food service operation.
2. Know how to perform all the duties required of them.
3. Consistently greet every guest with a smile and a warm welcome; practice the spirit of hospitality.
4. Be able to answer all questions posed by guests.
5. Be neat, clean, and well groomed.
6. Be able to handle all potential conflicts with tact and skill.
7. Be alert to any guest who needs assistance.

These principles of excellence in dining services can be summed up by the phrase: "Treat the guest the way that you would want to be treated if you were the guest."

---

food, reasonably sized portions, and, above all, low prices.

Family-oriented outlets may be open 24 hours daily or from early morning until late evening. Such less-than-desirable working and eating times suggest that service staff must have the ability to remain hospitable and give excellent service—no matter what time of day the guests arrive. Incidentally, some family-oriented restaurants are moderate-check-average operations.

Moderate-Check-Average Dining Outlets

Specialty or Theme Dining Rooms. Food service operations that emphasize a total dining experience might provide appropriate food and beverages consistent with a unique setting. Some examples are a medieval banquet in a great hall, wild west food and drinks in a Gay Nineties saloon, traditional American food (like specialty hamburgers and chocolate malts) in a Fabulous Fifties diner, or Polynesian food and beverages served in a South Seas "village." Whether the theme is the Roaring Twenties or the twenty-first century, in these operations, service employees generally contribute to the dining experience offered. Staff may wear creative uniforms, repeat appropriate sayings or expressions to guests, and even help provide imaginative entertainment. Interaction with service staff becomes an aspect of what the guest buys. Of course it should be

noted that some specialty operations could be low- or high-check-average rather than moderate.

High-Check-Average Dining Outlets

First-Class Dining Rooms. These are dining outlets that offer high-class dining services to the quality-conscious diner, but they don't consider themselves "gourmet." They might specialize in seafood, steaks and chops, or regional foods in season. Because the costs of products, service, and atmosphere that make up the dining experience are very high, they must be passed on to the guests. For example, such an outlet might use very expensive china, glassware, and silverware or provide specialty serviceware such as soup or dessert trolleys or, perhaps, offer live entertainment. The ratio of service staff to guests is often excellent; these staff members must be able to provide first-class service to guests who will spend a great deal of money and expect much in return for it. Guests in high-check-average dining rooms purchase far more than fine food and beverages. The service of the entire meal is so important that it may mean the difference in whether or not guests will visit the establishment again.

Gourmet Dining Rooms. The focus in traditional gourmet dining outlets is on food, beverages, and service. While ambience is, of course, important, guests in a gourmet operation are generally there to enjoy dishes of the highest possi-

---

What Does the Guest Want?

Why does a guest visit a food service operation? An obvious answer is to obtain food and beverages in order to appease hunger and thirst. However, this answer is only partially correct. Depending upon the situation, the guest is also seeking service, cleanliness, atmosphere, prestige—all elements of a total dining experience.

Fast-food and other low-check-average operations usually emphasize their specialties: reasonably priced food and quick service. Specialty, high-check-average, and other establishments can offer more than just products and services. For instance, some operations can gratify guests with the knowledge that "there is no better food in town." Others can provide a casual atmosphere that appeals to an informal, relatively young professional crowd. Still others can offer a traditional dining area and an upscale dining experience. Food service personnel can help satisfy guests' wants and needs in a variety of ways including remembering their names, listening carefully to what they say, and providing attentive service.

The professional dining room manager knows that no single component—food, service, or atmosphere—can be emphasized alone. Rather, the combined effect of all these components will ultimately influence guest satisfaction.

---

ble quality prepared according to imaginative—but often labor-intensive—recipes that bring out the best in the choicest and freshest of ingredients. The service provided to the guests must complement to the fullest the foods and beverages being served. Service staff must be extremely knowledgeable about every item on the menu, preparation procedures, ingredients used, and other topics of concern to the guests. Often food servers actually prepare some food and beverage items at tableside. Such preparations could occur at any time from the beginning to the end of the meal (e.g., mixing a specialty cocktail, creating a salade gourmande, sauteing veal and other ingredients for a dish like escalopes de veau a la duxelles, flaming a dessert such as crepes suzette, or preparing an after-dinner drink such as Gaelic coffee). While knowledge of wines and spirits as well as the service of them is important in other kinds of restaurants, it is crucial in gourmet food service operations. The selling price in gourmet operations is high; so are guest expectations. Because gourmet restaurants are places where special events such as anniversaries or birthdays take place or where business discussions are held, service problems can be disastrous. Management must make every effort to ensure that all dining room staff are well trained to perform their various duties flawlessly. (For complete information on table service in a variety of dining rooms, see Chapter 11.)

Room Service and Banquet Service

Room Service. Room service is a usual operation in many lodging properties. The manager of room service must develop procedures that best meet the unique demands of such an operation and improve on those procedures as necessary. For instance, because guests usually give their food and beverage orders over the telephone—not on a face-to-face basis as is true with other service styles—the manager must organize a system that ensures that such orders are taken correctly and completely. If a system in use doesn't always work, then it must be studied thoroughly to discover its weak points so it can be revamped and improved. Furthermore, in order to make certain that high-quality food is consistently presented to guests, the manager must plan the timing of order production and delivery carefully. Managers must also recognize when delivery personnel need special training in such areas as beverage service (e.g., pouring a beer properly, removing a cork from a wine bottle correctly) or in serving an entire evening meal in the suite of a corporate executive who has chosen to conduct a business meeting over dinner.

Room service standards must always focus on the guests first—then on the difficulties that must be faced by the property itself. By focusing on the guests, many managers have, through innovative methods, resolved a wide variety of operating problems. (For a complete discussion of room service procedures, see Chapter 10.)

Banquets. Many lodging properties offer banquets and cater receptions on-site for groups ranging from fewer than ten to several thousands of people. Such services can be generated in-house (e.g., a Mother's Day buffet deluxe), but most frequently they are requested by those who need the services (e.g., parents of the child who is having a bar mitzvah, convention planner, tour group operator). They can be as informal as an outdoor, poolside barbecue for those attending a conference or as elegant as a $500-a-plate, black-tie fund-raiser for a political party. Furthermore, banquets and catering services can feature table service, buffet service, or a combination of the two. Nearly any type of service style that is possible in a dining room operation is also possible for banquets.

The responsibility for planning the banquet or reception rests with the catering director (banquet manager) who works in conjunction with the chef. They should be constantly aware that the keys to the success of the function they plan are coordination and communication. As stressed throughout this book, banquet service staff must practice procedures which, from each guest's perspective, will yield as satisfactory a dining experience as is possible. (For complete information about banquet service, see Chapter 12.)

Other Food and Beverage Operations in Lodging Properties

Other food and beverage operations that could be offered by a large property range from vending machines and fast-food outlets to full-service dining, complete with entertainment, in a private club affiliated with the property.

Many lodging properties provide snack and/or dining services for staff members. These can include both machine (vending) and manual (cafeteria) services. When vending machines are used, the food products offered can either be prepared on-site or purchased from companies that provide such products.

Cafeterias (or buffets, as some properties that offer elaborate presentations refer to them) can offer a wide variety of food products at reasonable prices and can serve many individuals within a short time. Service staff in cafeterias must be able to work quickly under pressure. As with fast-food and family-oriented food service operations, the guests' focus is more often on the food than on the performance of service employees. When problems occur, however, they are more often due to shortcomings in the service staff rather than with the food. Thus, cafeterias need to have as effectively trained service staff as any other food service operation.

Some properties offer off-site catering services. Meals prepared in hotel kitchens have been served in almost any place imaginable: in railroad cars, in helicopters, on yachts, after football games, and during the intermissions of operas. Many of the problems faced by room service operations are of even greater concern to off-site catering services.

Most large lodging properties offer guests at least one bar or lounge. Guests visit these facilities for a variety of reasons including to relax, to be entertained, and to discuss business. Some guests visit bars and lounges before and/or after dining. Others frequent these facilities during such times as happy hours and rarely, if ever, visit the dining rooms. Many properties successfully market their products to two separate clientele bases—those who use nearly all the services of the property and those who desire only beverage and snack services in lounge areas.

The food and beverage operations discussed briefly here are just a few of the many types offered by lodging properties. For complete discussions of managing service in such food and beverage operations, see Chapters 13 and 14.

Self-Contained Operations

To this point, we have been reviewing dining services in large and complex hotel operations. However, commercial properties other than hotels also offer these services and require the same management practices to operate them effectively. Like the lodging industry, the commercial (for profit) restaurant industry also features fast-food operations, cafeterias, family-style food operations, specialty or theme restaurants, high-check-average restaurants, gourmet restaurants, banquet and catering services, and more.

In addition, institutional (nonprofit) food services such as those in health care, educa-

What Is Service?

Smiles for everyone.
Excellence in everything we do.
Reaching out to every guest with hospitality.
Viewing every guest as special.
Inviting guests to return.
Creating a warm atmosphere.
Eye contact that shows we care.

tional, military, and other facilities provide food and beverage products to patients, residents, students, and others. Many decisions made in these food service operations are based on a consideration for the individual who is served.

Whether the food service operation is in a hotel, self-contained restaurant, or institution, that operation requires the services of a professional food service manager who can assess the clientele's wants, needs, and expectations and ensure that they are met. He or she must be able to incorporate basic service procedures, adapted to fit the specific needs of the operation, into food delivery plans. Furthermore, service staff must know and consistently practice the principles of service that the facility has developed. Because more similarities than differences exist among food service operations in lodging properties, restaurants, and institutions, this text's discussions of principles of dining service management in a hotel will also apply to all other types of quantity food service operations.

The Manager of Dining Service

Someone in the dining service operation must be responsible for service-related tasks; typically, this person is the manager of each dining service outlet. Whether the person is the coffee shop, room service, gourmet dining room, or banquet manager, he/she must not only be concerned about dining service but also about a wide range of other work-related activities. First of all, this official must supervise the operation of the dining area itself. He/she must decide who will orient and train new service staff, develop and implement training procedures that will pre-

pare service staff to meet the required performance standards, plan maintenance and housekeeping schedules for equipment within the dining facility, and handle guest complaints. Managers are likely to help with menu planning for their outlets, are usually responsible for the labor costs and supplies that apply to the specific outlet, and often are responsible for marketing programs to build repeat business. It is critical, of course, that dining service managers develop and maintain strong working relationships with the outlet's food production managers.

Managers usually supervise one or more assistants who, in turn, supervise others. You may wish to refer to the organization chart shown in the case study at the end of Chapter 2 to review the reporting relationships that exist within a particular food and beverage department.

You should understand that managers must utilize a great deal of knowledge and skill to plan, organize, execute, and evaluate dining service. They must provide persuasive and persistent supervision to ensure that service staff continually achieve the required performance standards. In order to anticipate and provide personalized attention to individual guest needs, managers and their staff must be consistently thoughtful, creative, and concerned about the guests. A number of personal and professional traits are necessary to be an effective manager of dining service. Exhibit 1.3 focuses on the dining service manager and lists many of the managerial, operational, and personal/professional skills and abilities the position requires.

In order to render the degree of service required to make guests comfortable, managers must be dedicated to the profession and must constantly pay attention to details. In fact, they

Exhibit 1.3 Qualifications and Responsibilities of Dining Service Managers

A. Managerial Skills and Responsibilities

1. Leadership
2. Employee relations
3. Employee motivation
4. Oral communication
5. Employee training
6. Human relations
7. Staff coordination
8. Guest relations
9. Short-range planning
10. Delegation of responsibilities
11. Goal orientation
12. Written communication
13. Team development
14. Problem solving
15. Staff time management
16. Discipline maintenance
17. Personal time management
18. Interdepartmental relations
19. Policy and procedure implementation
20. Stress management
21. Long-range planning
22. Employee control (turnover and absenteeism)
23. Production time management
24. Recognition of industry trends
25. Employee grievance resolution
26. Personnel evaluation appraisal
27. Interviewing
28. Recruitment

B. Operational Skills and Responsibilities

1. Cost control
2. Food merchandising
3. Employee scheduling
4. Marketing (sales & public relations)
5. Cash control
6. Business forecasting
7. Menu pricing/planning
8. Financial planning
9. Food preparation
10. Wine merchandising
11. Menu design
12. General accounting
13. Banquet service
14. Product specifications
15. Accident prevention and safety
16. Portion control
17. Sanitation requirements
18. Union relations
19. Buying (purchasing)
20. Wine service procedures
21. Receiving
22. Room service procedures
23. Bartending procedures
24. Product storage
25. Fire regulations
26. Dining room space utilization
27. Industry laws
28. Credit procedures
29. Culinary terms
30. Tableside cooking
31. Product issuing
32. Facility design
33. Private function planning

C. Personal and Professional Traits

1. Honest
2. Quality-conscious
3. Profit-minded
4. Cost-minded
5. Responsive to employee needs
6. Responsible
7. Consistent
8. Responsive to guest needs
9. Creative
10. Action-oriented
11. Adaptable to change
12. Loyal to property
13. Energetic
14. Diplomatic
15. Willing to work long hours
16. Ambitious
17. Clean
18. Upwardly mobile
19. Businesslike appearance
20. Desires long-term employment
21. Systems-oriented
22. Adheres to deadlines
23. Experienced

Why Do Food and Beverage Operations Fail?

The statistics are shocking! Ninety percent or more of the restaurants that open each year are forced to close their doors within five years.* Relative to the amount of risk and hard work required to make them work, many operations that do remain open generate very little, if any, profit. Why is this true?

Many food and beverage operations are not successful because of the owner's inability to generate the capital required to purchase/remodel facilities, acquire equipment, and meet the responsibility of initial operating expenses. Another frequently cited reason for failure is the manager's inability to manage. If the manager cannot effectively control each available resource (food and beverage products, employees, time, money, equipment, and more), a financial disaster is likely.

The initial decision to build or expand a food service operation is made based on the answer to the question: What do the guests want and need? That question also affects decisions regarding methods for building a strong guest base, generating repeat business, and continually pleasing the guests so that growth and financial health will result.

As you can see, the management of dining service is part of the "recipe" for the success of a food service operation. We must always place the guests' concerns at the forefront of our decision-making process. This is true for all phases of the food service operation but is especially important when dining service decisions are made.

*Gerald W. Lattin, *Modern Hotel & Motel Management*, 3rd ed. (San Francisco: Freeman, 1977), p. 117.

set the pace for service staff if they constantly strive for perfection. Good managers usually adopt some version of the following statement:

"The possible we will do immediately; the impossible takes just a little more time."

You can begin to see that managers are responsible for maintaining the agreed upon standards of the property. This task is difficult because it requires a manager to accommodate both the guests' and the property's concerns simultaneously. For instance, experienced dining service managers in high-check-average dining rooms practice, and ensure that their service staff practice, such principles as the following:

1. We always provide the highest quality products and services.

2. We always practice true courtesy.

3. The rule of the house is quiet efficiency.

4. The dining area is always orderly.

5. We always make a sincere effort to please guests.

6. We undertake every effort to satisfy the personal preferences of patrons with sophisticated tastes.

Managing dining service is a difficult job. To do the job effectively, you must have an extensive amount of formal training and/or education. In addition, you must supplement your technical knowledge of food, beverages, wine, and proper service with on-the-job experience. You must have a strong personal commitment to high standards of service and quality, and you must have already demonstrated the leadership abilities needed to command a sizable service staff, including captains, food servers, dining room attendants, bartenders, and others. You must be a strong administrator with the desire and capability to train employees and carry out the detailed planning required to operate a successful dining outlet. You will need to be innovative, to develop and implement sales and cost budgets, and to promote dining room sales. You must also have an extensive knowledge of marketing principles as they apply to pleasing guests and building sales and repeat business. You must have effective communication skills and be able to prepare coherent written reports. Finally, you must greatly enjoy contact with guests and be able to use their suggestions creatively to improve your overall operation.

Service: The Marketing Perspective

Throughout this chapter we have emphasized the need to consider the guests' wants and needs as decisions are made about dining services. This is known as **marketing** dining services. The term **marketing** can be defined as "business from the perspective of the guest." The guest can be a patron in a hotel or restaurant or a patient or resident in an institutional facility. It makes no difference. Managers must focus on the guests and, whenever possible, meet their needs and wants as they receive food and beverage services. Food service managers who do well recognize that as they show concern for individual guests, others with the same desires or needs may also benefit. As a result, the number of guests served will increase as the quality of the food service operation becomes known throughout the marketplace.

One goal of marketing deals with the initial attraction of guests and the ability to please them during their first dining experience. Another goal focuses on generating repeat business, which is the key to the success of almost any food service operation. A more detailed discussion of marketing is beyond the scope of this book.[10] However, if management has developed operating procedures and associated performance standards and trains and continually supervises service staff to ensure that those standards are met, many marketing concerns will be addressed as the operating procedures are carried out.

Food service managers must consider marketing (guest-related) concerns as they develop and evaluate department plans. The following questions help place the proper emphasis on the guest:

1. What are your current and future guest objectives?

2. In your judgment, how well does your organization meet these objectives?

3. Who are the competitors to whom guests compare your operation?

4. How do you rate the quality of services provided by your competitors? (Be specific.)

5. What are the quality and service demands of your guests?

6. What trade-offs are your guests prepared to make? (For example, what price will they pay for service and quality?)

7. How do you market the quality and service differences between your operation and your competitors? How do you educate your guests about these differences?

8. How do you educate your employees about the quality and service differences between your operation and your competitors?

9. How do you respond to guest suggestions/complaints?

10. Is your pricing policy consistent with guest objectives for quality and service?

11. Do you know the cost of errors? If so, what are your programs to correct errors?

12. Do you have a program to offset higher quality in products and services with reductions in peripheral costs?

13. To what extent does your operation exceed the competition's standards in quality and service? (Be specific.)

14. What are the known weaknesses in your operation?

15. What are the measurable quality standards in your operation? How do you audit for quality?

16. How would you form and use a quality assurance committee to continually evaluate the quality of your products and services? (The objective is to solve problems so that they do not recur under high stress conditions.)

17. What are your short- and long-range goals for improving quality? Are these goals

---

[10] See, for example, David A. Troy, *Strategic Hotel/Motel Marketing* (East Lansing, Mich.: Educational Institute of the American Hotel & Motel Association, 1985) and Robert L. Blomstrom, ed., *Strategic Marketing Planning in the Hospitality Industry: A Book of Readings* (East Lansing, Mich.: Educational Institute of the American Hotel & Motel Association, 1983).

What About Complaints?

For every complaint that a dining operation receives, an average of 26 additional guests have complaints.* That means approximately 96% of all complaints are never heard. Guests who do not complain while they are still in the restaurant are not only the least likely group to patronize a business again, but they can also cause that outlet considerable damage by complaining to friends, family members, business associates, and other acquaintances. Therefore, it is important that food service managers develop feedback systems to learn how guests feel so that any identified problems can be quickly and completely resolved.

*Source: Direct Selling Education Foundation, 1983.

commensurate with your guests' expectations for future price levels?

Quality in Dining Service

You know that a successful food service operation must provide products and services of the proper quality to its guests, but what is **quality**? A working definition of quality for the lodging industry is the "consistent delivery of services and products based on standards established by individual properties or chains." Quality involves setting, communicating, and maintaining appropriate performance standards for all of the activities offered by the property to meet the needs of its guests. **Quality service** is the result of an operation's effort to discover exactly what guests want. Once those needs and desires are known, procedures are implemented to deliver those wants effectively and consistently. When an operation meets guests' expec-

tations, it is providing quality service. No one can deny that food service employees contribute to the success or failure of a dining operation. The old saying "Courtesy costs nothing, but it's worth everything" has merit. If service personnel interact well with guests and make the guests want to come back to the operation again, they are helping to provide quality service.

Some properties have **quality assurance programs** that are directed by a **quality assurance director** and **committee**. Committee members are often such employees as department managers, assistant department managers, and other key personnel. While quality assurance programs differ from property to property, reducing costs and increasing productivity is compatible with their goals to maintain quality standards. **Quality assurance** does not mean higher costs; it means better use of existing resources. Virtually every aspect of a quality assurance program depends upon people, not expensive equipment or materials.

Managing Service at the Hotel Columbia
Page Two

Over the years, Lewis had learned a great deal about the management of dining services. His plan was to modify this information to meet the unique needs of the Hotel Columbia and give himself a head start on his efforts to have a first-class staff trained and ready for the grand opening.

Lewis knew that the specific procedures for delivering service would come together after a great deal of planning and work. His real concern, however, was finding service employees who, in addition to doing their assignments correctly, had the philosophy of quality guest service that is so critical to the success of a first-class lodging property. He decided, therefore, to consistently emphasize quality assurance as the "common thread" that would tie all aspects of dining service together.

Very soon after he accepted his new position, Lewis took the time to develop a preface for the hotel's dining service manual. He wanted the preface to establish an overall dining service management philosophy within the Hotel Columbia. This is how it read:

Let's look closely at the fundamentals of a quality assurance program for dining service. A quality assurance program depends upon individuals; the image projected by the food and beverage department depends upon you—its employees. The personal appearance, actions, and attitudes of all people directly associated with the food service operation have a far greater impact on the department's success than advertising and public relations activities. While managers are responsible for guest service and also play an important role in the process of building an image, the ultimate success of an operation depends upon the efforts made by all its employees to attain quality goals. The quest for quality is our philosophy—not just a policy or procedure—and constantly requires a 110% effort by all the service employees.

Our image contributes to the guests' expectations for our operation; the extent to which those expectations are met will influence the level of guest satisfaction. Clearly, the development of reasonable, realistic, and attainable images, goals, and operating plans is an integral part of our quality assurance program.

Developing and communicating performance standards for our property comprise the second phase of our quality assurance program for dining services. Marketing principles play a major role in the development of our performance standards and operating plans. We must know who our guests are and what they need.

At the Hotel Columbia, the development and implementation of standards is the joint responsibility of the management team and the employees who use them. Records, performance appraisals, and guest feedback are used regularly to ensure that our standards are consistently maintained. We take seriously our personal contacts with our clientele, the information written on our guest comment cards, and other suggestions we receive from the guests. The Hotel Columbia has definite procedures to deal with both positive and negative guest feedback, and all employees are kept informed about our guests' reactions to the services we provide. We believe that it costs five times as much to earn a new guest as it does to *keep* an existing one. Determining what the guests want, providing them with products and services of the highest quality possible, and evaluating the success of our quality assurance program all receive a high priority at the Hotel Columbia.

Lewis Scott looked at the preface he had developed. How could he justify spending the time he had spent writing it? "Easy," he thought. "We're going to have excellent dining services here at the Hotel Columbia. We must start with and state an operating philosophy that will guide us throughout the development of all our other procedures. Our subsequent supervision and evaluation efforts must also reflect this philosophy. Where is a better place to make this statement than in the hotel's dining service manual, the first orientation and training tool that our service staff will receive? We are going to emphasize quality dining service here at the Hotel Columbia. Everything that we do will take the guest into account. Proper guest service is our philosophy, a goal, a strategy, and an operating plan, and it dictates all the procedures that we will use."

2
Personnel Administration

Food and beverage managers must recruit, select, orient, and train the very best service staff they can locate because guests often judge an operation by the contact they have with its employees. It is ironic that service employees, who are often undertrained and incorrectly supervised, have such an important effect on guests' reactions as well as their desire to return to the property.

Most dining service tasks are very labor-intensive and require employees who really care about doing them well. Technology has not discovered effective ways to replace service staff with equipment—nor would many food service managers want to replace people with machines. While vending service operations have in some cases replaced a few service employees with equipment, the impersonal aspects of this service style are frequently a source of complaints. In fact, many large vending service operations employ a food service attendant who is available on-site during times of high use to refill machines, keep service areas clean, restock condiments, and provide assistance to guests.

Some people are much more able to please guests than others. Dining service managers must be able to recognize and hire these applicants who are willing and able to care about guests. In order to accomplish this task, managers must be fully acquainted with employee recruitment and selection procedures.

Employee Recruitment and Selection Procedures

Training and supervision procedures will produce effective service employees only if qualified applicants are hired. In large properties, a separate personnel department may initially recruit and screen job applicants. The most desirable applicants are then referred for further consideration to the manager of the dining outlet which requires the new employee. In smaller organizations, which are unlikely to have a personnel department, the recruitment and selection of employees may be the responsibility of the restaurant manager.

The process of recruiting applicants for a particular job must begin with answering the question, "What does the employee in that position do?" The answer to that question is often expressed in a job description such as the one shown in Exhibit 2.1.

Managers, assisted by supervisors and personnel actually filling positions within the department, should develop and frequently update job descriptions. Often, a task force of several restaurant managers within a property may meet to update job descriptions for all food service positions, including service staff.

Restaurant managers frequently complain about the quality of applicants referred to them by the personnel department. Many employees are either unable to do the work or quit soon after they are hired. Such situations may result from the personnel department's recruiting methods—perhaps they are using job descriptions that do not accurately reflect the work currently done by employees occupying these positions. If job descriptions are out-of-date or inaccurate, new employees may fit the job description, but they won't be right for the job as it currently exists. Other new employees may have been misled by a job description, and, being disappointed with the actual work that they must

Managing Service at the Hotel Columbia
Page Three

The food and beverage department that Lewis Scott is organizing for the Hotel Columbia is extensive. The hotel will feature a gourmet restaurant, a high-check-average specialty restaurant, a coffee shop, room service, and a take-out deli bar. In addition to the beverage service units in the gourmet and specialty restaurants, the Hotel Columbia will have three lounge/bar outlets. The catering department will handle an extensive banquet business from the local community as well as from conventions being held within the property. Finally, the hotel will offer employee dining services.

The main production kitchen will have to be large enough to accommodate most of the food requirements for the dining outlets as well as for the banquet and catering business. Additionally, the hotel will operate an on-site bakery where the bread and pastry products served in all the culinary operations will be prepared. Small satellite kitchens will be responsible for specialty items served in only one dining operation.

Lewis understood how and why managers organized food service operations in specific ways. He knew that communication must flow effectively among many departments in the organization, and he wanted to design a food and beverage department that would best suit the Hotel Columbia. Lewis realized that he had to consider many aspects of the operation other than just delivery of service. He asked himself, "What type of system should I develop to control cash income? How should I organize recordkeeping responsibilities? How should I develop the income statements and other financial documents that I know are important to effective planning and control? Who should manage the storeroom? Who should purchase the food and beverage products?"

As Lewis considered these and related questions, he realized that he should give immediate attention to the design of an effective organizational system. He knew that once the structure of the food and beverage department was in place, it would be easier to identify functions and allocate responsibilities.

---

do, soon resign from their positions. In either case, an accurate job description which adequately informs the personnel department and the applicants about current job requirements would help eliminate many misunderstandings.

Job specifications are a second useful tool in personnel administration. Education, experience, and the ability to work with specialized equipment are examples of factors you should consider including in a job specification. Notice that in Exhibit 2.1 the job specifications are referred to as **position prerequisites** and are actually a part of the job description. Restaurant managers must carefully consider and objectively determine the personal qualities that are important for the successful completion of tasks assigned to each position. While the list of factors which you need to address in a job specification will be unique to each property, some common concerns include:

1. Education

2. Experience

3. Job knowledge

4. Personal hygiene and physical requirements

5. Skills

6. Minimum training requirements

When developing job specifications, you need to ensure that the personal qualities listed are actually required for the successful performance of the job. Sometimes managers use such artificial requirements as family status, distance from work, type of transportation available, and others. Not only do these requirements restrict the number of applicants for vacant positions, they may also violate state laws or the Equal Employment Opportunity Commission's (EEOC) regulations which protect applicants from discrimination based on race, religion, sex,

Exhibit 2.1 Job Description: Banquet Headwaiter/Headwaitress

Position Prerequisites:

Must have basic knowledge about food and beverage industry; minimum of two years experience as a Banquet Captain.

Purpose:

To supervise banquet setups, breakdowns, and service according to the standards established by the property. To coordinate banquet service in conjunction with other departments involved. To make up weekly schedules for banquet staff and housepersons.

Duties and Responsibilities:

1. Scope of work: Responsible for service of all banquet functions as well as outside catering jobs.

2. Supervision Exercised:
   A. Positions Directly Supervised:
      Banquet service staff and housepersons.
   B. Positions Indirectly Supervised:
      Enginering staff (microphone, lighting effects, spotlights, etc.), bartenders, and stewards.

3. Supervisor: Director of Catering

4. Responsibilities and Authority:
   A. Employee and Client Relations:
      Works directly with clients, as well as banquet, kitchen, setup, and beverage personnel.
   B. Materials or Products:
      Responsible for economical use of food, beverages, and equipment.
   C. Money Management:
      Banquet payroll and customer billing; issue weekly paychecks to banquet service staff.
   D. Tasks:
      1. Supervise employees engaged in the performance of banquet service according to Banquet Event Order (BEO) sent by catering office.
      2. Report daily payroll.
      3. Set up work schedules and job requirements.
      4. Report daily to Director of Catering to evaluate functions, equipment needs, and problems related to food, beverages, and service.
      5. Review in advance each function's needs to ensure the proper delivery of service according to contract negotiated with client as outlined on BEO. Hold daily BEO meetings with Banquet Chef. Hold pre-function meetings with banquet service staff.
      6. Maintain accurate inventories and records.
      7. Carry out all reasonable job assignments or requests of the Director of Catering.

Supervisors and the Selection Process

Large hospitality operations may have personnel departments to help recruit and select dining service employees. Smaller properties may use department heads for this activity. In an operation of any size, the person who will supervise the new employee should actively participate in the selection process. It is important for supervisors to have a chance to interview the applicants. Similarly, a prospective employee likes to know what to expect from the new boss. Supervisors are more likely to accept new employees and work effectively with them if they have had some role in the actual selection process.

or national origin.[1]

Employee recruitment is the process of seeking applicants and initially screening them to assess their suitability for vacant positions. The process essentially involves announcing job vacancies through various sources and using initial evaluation tools to determine which applicants should receive further consideration. You can recruit applicants for dining service positions in a variety of ways. For example, you can:

1. Promote current employees.

2. Send vacancy notices to vocational/secondary schools, colleges, and universities that have food service education or similar hospitality-related training programs.

3. Contact governmental and other groups that sponsor training programs in order to hire trained handicapped and/or financially disadvantaged individuals.

4. Advertise vacancies in newspapers and/or use public and private employment agencies.

5. Notify current employees about vacancies so that they can notify friends and relatives.

You must have some method to obtain basic information from those that apply for your vacant positions. Most properties use job application forms followed by personal interviews to collect this information. If possible, staff from the personnel office, as well as the line supervisor and his/her immediate supervisor, should interview applicants. Good employment practices also include checking applicant references and conducting selection tests.

As you design and use application forms, check references, interview applicants, and use various selection tools, you must be certain that you are always within the letter of the law (e.g., do not include questions on an application form that would lead to charges that you are discriminating against someone because of race, religion, sex, or national origin; never ask a female applicant whether she is planning to have a family; don't ask an applicant what his/her religion is). Whenever you are in doubt about job application wording or questions that can legally be asked during an interview, consult your attorney for clarification.

Throughout the entire selection process, remember that your primary objective is to find people who have the potential to become competent employees. If you select carefully, you will generally find that it will be easy to train, coach, and supervise these new members of your staff effectively.

Orientation and Training Programs

Much employee turnover occurs within the first few weeks or months of employment. Therefore, the employee selection process and orientation programs, which are the property's first contacts with new staff, are very important. When dining service employees take a new position, they are generally very enthusiastic and

---

[1]   For more information, consult Chapter 13 "Laws Against Discrimination in Employment" in Jack P. Jefferies' *Understanding Hotel/Motel Law* (East Lansing, Mich.: Educational Institute of the American Hotel & Motel Association, 1983).

Social Skills of Applicants

It is easy to say that applicants for dining service positions must be able to get along with people. However, it is much more difficult to determine objectively whether or not applicants for these positions possess, or can develop, the social skills which are necessary to please guests.

How do you tell whether or not applicants have the philosophy or attitude toward service that would make them good employees? During the interview, the supervisor can ask them these and similar questions: What would you do if a guest who was not in your work station had an obvious problem? How would you react to a guest who is angry about the food or service? What would you do if the guest was obviously wrong to complain about something? What would you do if you saw a guest put a serving piece in his pocket or her purse? The applicants' answers will not only lead to their being hired (or turned down for the job) but will also help the supervisor determine the amount of training that they will need to meet the service requirements of the property.

Some of the social skills which dining service employees must have include:

1. An ability to recognize faces and remember names.

2. An ability to be a good listener.

3. An ability to make the guest feel important.

4. An ability to be attentive and tend to every request of the guest.

5. Courtesy. (They should help guests with coats, chairs, or dropped items, and use such words as "please," "thank you," and "excuse me" with the genuine concern which they imply.)

6. Honesty. (They should never deceive the guest or the food service operation.)

7. An ability to work quietly.

8. A sensitivity to the guest's wants and needs, and an ability to meet them.

9. An ability to know when to speak and when to listen.

10. Tact. (They should say or do the *right* thing at the *right* time without offending others.)

highly motivated. They want to do their jobs well and meet their supervisor's expectations. Managers should build on their employees' initial desire to please. One of the ways to do so is to offer new employees a well-organized orientation program.

Orientation programs are designed to make the employee feel welcome, comfortable, and eager to learn the new job. They help new employees realize that their employer does care about them and that they have found a good place to work. Exhibit 2.2 outlines a sample orientation program for dining service staff in a large property that has a number of new employees beginning work at approximately the same time.

In a smaller property which has added only a few new members of staff, the supervisors of the new employees are usually in charge of orientation. In this situation, once the new employee has completed forms required by the government and/or the property (e.g., tax withholding statement, health and dental benefit applications), the supervisor and his/her employee should review the job requirements together. Employees should understand thoroughly the specific tasks of their jobs as outlined in current job descriptions. They should also know about promotion opportunities. Success stories of current employees are helpful, and a review of career progression possibilities is also in order. Give new employees a tour of the property and introduce them to other good service staff members. Point out the location of all the necessary equipment, define work stations, and make available any uniforms, tools, or other small equipment which employees will need and which the property provides.

When the supervisor completes his/her pri-

Exhibit 2.2 Sample Orientation Program Outline for Dining Service Staff

Topic	Time Allowed	Topic	Time Allowed
I. Introduction	(30 minutes)	3. Emergency Evacuation Plan	
		F. Bomb Threat Procedures	
A. Welcome			
B. Company History & Background		VI. Break	(10 minutes)
C. Organization Chart			
D. Officers & Divisions		VII. Customer Relations	(25 minutes)
E. Other Introductory Information			
		A. Introduction to Courtesy	
II. Benefits	(20 minutes)	Awareness Programs	
		B. Courtesy Principles	
A. Salary		and Practices	
B. Meals			
C. Parking		VIII. Credit Union Information	(10 minutes)
D. Discounts			
E. Training		IX. Labor Relations for New	(25 minutes)
F. Credit Union		Union Employees	
G. Savings Bonds			
H. Job Advancement		A. Role of the Labor Relations Department	
		B. Probationary Period	
III. Employee Services	(20 minutes)	C. Attendance Policy	
		D. Role of the Union Representative	
A. Sports and Fitness Programs		E. Disciplinary Actions	
B. Community Affairs		F. Grievance Procedure	
1. Bloodmobile		G. Benefits Determined by the Labor Agreement	
2. United Way			
3. March of Dimes		**Room Setup**	
C. Personnel Reports			
D. Counseling		Adequate classroom seating	
E. Employee Recognition Programs		Small display table in front of room	
		Small table for projector	
IV. Company Policies	(15 minutes)	Blackboard	
		Flip chart	
A. Gambling		Screen	
B. Drugs/Alcohol		Carousel projector	
C. Use of Facilities		16-mm projector	
D. ID Badges		Extension cord	
E. Uniforms and Locker Facilities			
V. Safety	(10 minutes)		
A. Safety Committee			
B. Accident Prevention			
C. Accident Reports (Employees and Guests)			
D. Health Care Facility			
E. Fire Prevention	(15 minutes)		
1. Use of Fire Extinguishers (Locations)			
2. Fire Alarm Boxes			

Training Dining Service Employees

Some restaurant managers may have the mistaken impression that the personnel department is responsible for training their employees. In fact, this responsibility rests with the officials of the food and beverage department. The food and beverage director must place a high priority on training. He/she must develop and implement high-quality training and educational experiences for staff members at all organizational levels in order to provide high-quality guest services.

In a large property, the food and beverage director, working with restaurant managers, may develop general training programs for service staff. These programs can include such basics as guest relations, sanitation and safety, and work methods. However, each restaurant manager must also develop specific training information relative to his/her dining outlet/service. For example, table setting, service, and food pickup procedures are likely to *differ* in coffee shops, room service, and high-check-average dining rooms; therefore, specific information to supplement the generalized training is necessary to address these topics.

In many properties, supervisory staff and employees help develop training programs. After all, these staff members encounter problems and potential solutions on a daily basis. They might have creative suggestions about procedures which management should incorporate into standard operating plans. Often, supervisors and staff members are also involved in the actual training activity. The restaurant manager might delegate to a supervisor the responsibility for orienting new front-of-house staff members. Experienced employees might also provide on-the-job training experiences for new staff members.

Regardless of the specific training plans your property uses, it is important to give training a high priority and involve the restaurant manager in both the design and implementation of training experiences for dining service staff.

---

mary role in the orientation, an experienced employee who will work closely with the new staff member may take over. This staff member should show the new employee exactly what to do. Patience and understanding are needed at this point. If at all possible, the supervisor should visit with the new staff member at the end of the first workshift to answer questions and express concern about the new employee's well-being and future with the company.

Training programs are usually necessary for both new and current employees. These programs may be used to teach or improve job skills, broaden knowledge, and/or develop attitudes. Job-related problems such as guest dissatisfaction, waste of dining service supplies, excessive employee grievances, or accidents may point to the need for training or retraining.

New employees must be given training to bring them to the level of competency of others in similar positions. Immediately placing a new employee in a work station to let him/her watch what is happening, and then, with little supervision, putting the employee right to work is not effective training. Furthermore, constantly telling a new employee what to do or correcting

his/her errors in front of guests is not only unprofessional but also embarrassing for the employee as well as unpleasant for the guests.

Developing and using a proper training program is not difficult. However, it requires time and money. Employees in training are less productive, will require more supervision, and probably will make more mistakes than those already trained. However, effective training programs are worthwhile since trained employees eventually become very productive and competent to do their work well.

Staff members who train other employees should have a desire to teach, a thorough working knowledge of the job, and an enthusiasm for training. Trainers must have the respect of other employees as well as the trainees themselves. They must possess patience and a sense of humor and the ability to convey information. It is most important that they are given the *time* necessary to train new employees; often trainers with other things to do place a low priority on training because of the pressure to finish their required duties.

Trainers should follow a sequence when they undertake training activities for new employees. First of all, you must define your training needs. Use preliminary observations, testing devices, and employee interviews to assess an employee's pretraining performance levels. Prepare a job list which notes all the tasks that the employee must perform as a part of his/her job. Exhibit 2.3, a sample job list for a food server, shows a format that you can use to present job tasks. It also provides examples of tasks that you might want to include on a job list for a typical dining service employee.

Once you develop a job list, you need a job breakdown which outlines the exact procedures employees should follow as they undertake each task. Exhibit 2.4 is a sample job breakdown that illustrates the detail that might be necessary to explain the standard procedures for assisting guests with their food and beverage selections.

After you complete job breakdowns for all tasks, you must define broad training goals. Normally, you should design training around the ability *to do* something rather than the ability *to know* something. Therefore, when an employee completes the training, he/she should be able to perform adequately each required task on the job list.

In order for both the trainers and the trainees to know the performance levels which are expected after the training is over, you need to give some attention to quality standards. Exhibit 2.5, a sample of job performance standards for a food server on the lunch shift, illustrates measurable, objective factors that help define how well an employee should perform each task.

Once you develop a well-planned training program, you must implement it. Frequently, managers use on-the-job training (OJT) programs. In these programs, employees work with an experienced staff member to learn the required procedures by watching, talking with, and helping this person. However, these programs still require adequate training preparation. Additionally, good training programs combine presentation, practice, and follow-through activities to help ensure that the trainees understand correct job procedures.

You can also use group training activities such as lectures, discussions, seminars, conferences, and related methods to train dining service staff. These strategies are most frequently implemented when you must train a large number of people to perform relatively common job procedures within a short period of time.

After your employees have completed their training, you must evaluate the program to ensure that it has fulfilled your training objectives and to improve future training programs. Follow-up coaching is another step in the training process. This one-on-one technique requires supervisors to review training information with employees when they observe job-related difficulties.

While complete details of the training process are beyond the scope of this chapter, you should be aware that good training for dining service staff is absolutely critical to effective job performance.[2] Restaurant managers have to decide what employees must do as they perform their work and then provide the training and necessary resources for the employees to fulfill those requirements.

Principles of Supervision

Restaurant managers must be good leaders. They must know something about the art and science of directing employees and must consistently practice principles of personnel management.[3] In fact, they help provide guidelines for employees by their own demeanor—their warmth, knowledge, and personality.

Leadership involves the ability to attain objectives by working with and through people—both individual employees and employee groups. An effective restaurant manager must have more than just power. Not too long ago a leader could tell employees what to do; if they did the work, the leader was successful. Today, however, this strategy is unlikely to work. Therefore, the concepts of leadership, direction, and supervision often imply the need to *influence* and *request*, rather than to tell employees to per-

[2] Interested readers are referred to Lewis C. Forrest, Jr., *Training for the Hospitality Industry* (East Lansing, Mich.: Educational Institute of the American Hotel & Motel Association, 1983).

[3] Interested readers are referred to John Daschler and Jack D. Ninemeier, *Supervision in the Hospitality Industry* (East Lansing, Mich.: Educational Institute of the American Hotel & Motel Association, 1984).

Exhibit 2.3 Sample Job List for a Food Server

JOB LIST*

Position: Food Server   **Date Prepared:** 00/00/00
Tasks: Employee must be able to perform the   **J. B. Number****
      following tasks courteously and efficiently:

1. Greet and seat restaurant guests	32
2. Serve water; light candles	33
3. Take beverage orders and serve drinks	34
4. Present the food menu and beverage list	35
5. Assist guests in making food and beverage selections	36
6. Place orders in the kitchen (using the call system)	37
7. Serve food and clear table between courses	38
8. Serve wine and champagne	39
9. Collect sales income; make change	16
10. Remove stains from dining room carpets	19
11. Set tables	21
12. Clean pantry and service station areas	27
13. Other	

*This is a partial job list. The list developed for a specific property should include all tasks to be performed by the employee.
**Job Breakdown Number. This number refers to the specific job description that breaks down the task into its identifiable, specific activities. The task and the appropriate job breakdown can apply to and appear in the job list for more than one position. For example, the Host/Hostess may also "Greet and seat restaurant guests." If so, the job breakdown number (32) for the Food Server position would also apply to the Host/Hostess position.

Source: Adapted from Lewis C. Forrest, Jr., *Training for the Hospitality Industry* (East Lansing, Mich.: Educational Institute of the American Hotel & Motel Association, 1983), p. 41.

Exhibit 2.4 Sample Job Breakdown

Job Breakdown # 36: The ability to assist guests in making food and beverage selections.
Equipment needed: Guest check, pen. (Guests will already have menus and wine list.)

WHAT TO DO	HOW TO DO IT	ADDITIONAL INFORMATION
1. Approach the table.	1. Stand erect. Look at the guests, smile, and greet them pleasantly. Introduce yourself. If you know their names, use them when you greet them. Be courteous.	1. You <u>win</u> the table with your first contact when you are pleasant and personable.
2. Take cocktail order.	2. Ask if guests would like a cocktail or appetizer wine. Be sure to get the complete details of the order, such as on-the-rocks, straight up,	2. Most guests know which drinks they prefer. Be prepared to make suggestions, if appropriate. Do not push your personal preferences.

Source: Adapted from Forrest, pp. 45-46.   continued

Exhibit 2.4 Sample Job Breakdown, continued

	or extra olives. Remember which guest ordered each cocktail.	Do not act surprised when a guest orders some nonstandard drink.
3. Serve cocktails.	3. Place a cocktail napkin in front of each guest. Serve all beverages from the right with the right hand, when possible. Place cocktail glasses on napkins. Do not ask who ordered each drink. (You must remember.) As each drink is served, state what it is, such as Scotch and water, double martini, or Scotch-on-the-rocks.	3. Knowing who ordered what shows that you care about the order. Guests feel special when you repeat their order as you serve their drinks.
4. Check back for a second cocktail order.	4. Be courteous and bring the second round, if ordered, following the same procedure as the first round. Remove all first round empty glasses and napkins. Put down new napkins and serve the drinks.	4. Check back when drinks are approximately two-thirds consumed.
5. Take the food order.	5. Ask the guests if they are ready to order. Explain the chef's specialty and answer any questions about the food. Take orders beginning with the women, when possible. Suggest appetizers, soup, or salads, as appropriate, to help them plan a complete meal. Proceed to the male guests. Be sure to inform the guests of the approximate cooking times of their selections. Communicate with the guest during this very important step. It is more than taking orders. It should be **menu planning.**	5. Guests expect you to know about the food. When you are asked a question and do not know the answer, do not bluff. Go to the kitchen or manager and find out the answer. Then go back and tell the guest. Suggesting menu items helps a hesitant guest make a decision he/she really wanted especially if they may require some wait.
6. Take the wine order.	6. Ask, "Have you chosen a wine?" When you are asked to help, ask whether, the guest prefers red or white, dry or semi-sweet, and other questions to get some idea of his/her preferences. Then point out two or three choices that fall within the characteristics described. The guest can choose according to price or other factors. Excuse yourself from the table and assure the guests that you will be right back with the first course.	6. Know the wine list. Always be careful to recognize the timid guest who is a novice at selecting wines. Be prepared to coach them through a selection process that will meet their needs. Experienced wine drinkers will usually know what they want to order and will not expect much assistance. This is not the time to feed your ego by demonstrating your techniqal wine knowledge and intimidating the guest. Be confident, but be courteous.

Exhibit 2.5 Sample Job Performance Standards for Food Server: Lunch Shift

---

PERFORMANCE STANDARDS

A food server's performance in taking care of assigned tables for the lunch shift is considered good when the server:

1. Arrives at the dining room by 11:00 a.m. rested and ready for work with hands washed, nails clean, hair tidy, and is in a clean uniform.

2. Has all assigned tables fully set up with tablecloths, napkins, glasses, silverware, condiment sets, ashtrays, and matches by 11:45 a.m.

3. Learns the specials of the day before service begins and checks with the kitchen to ensure that everything listed on the menu is available. Can help guests with their selections when they order.

4. Greets guests cordially. Approaches the table as soon as the guests are seated to provide necessary service.

5. Stays to take order or is back within five minutes of greeting to take beverage and food orders. Suggests cocktails while guests decide on menu.

6. Is able to wait on a minimum of four tables (each seating a party of four) without generating complaints about service or delays.

7. Fills out bar and kitchen orders legibly. Picks up and delivers orders promptly.

8. Serves wines, drinks, and food dishes properly (according to prescribed methods and placement).

Source: Adapted from Forrest, p. 57.

form specific tasks. The restaurant manager acts more as a facilitator (one who assembles resources and provides guidance) than as a dictatorial taskmaster.

Managers are generally consistent in the way that they direct their staff members. It is unlikely that a domineering person will use one approach to supervise some employees and an entirely different approach to supervise others. The combination of factors which you use to manage employees is known as leadership style. While the topic is complex, let's take a brief look at the usual styles of leadership.

Autocratic Leadership. The manager who practices the autocratic style of leadership makes decisions without getting ideas from staff members. He/she gives orders without explanation or defense and expects employees to obey them. Frequently, these managers use a structured set of rewards and punishments to help ensure compliance with their orders. Autocratic managers are task-oriented; they emphasize getting the work done. The wants and needs of the employees are second to those of the food service organization and the manager.

Democratic (Participative) Leadership. The democratic or participative leadership style is the reverse of the autocratic style. The democratic manager shares decision-making responsibilities with those he/she supervises and solicits their input in resolving problems which affect them. This manager keeps his/her employees informed and tries to appeal to their wants and needs. The democratic manager also tries to emphasize the employees' role in the organization and provides opportunities for employees to find fulfillment on the job.

Laissez-Faire (Free-Rein) Leadership. The laissez-faire or free-rein leadership style refers to a hands-off approach in which the manager actually does as little leading as possible. Laissez-faire managers delegate all authority (power) to those they supervise. Staff members themselves establish goals, make decisions, and resolve problems. The employees are, in effect, leaderless; they have the greatest amount of freedom possible.

Bureaucratic Leadership. The manager who uses a bureaucratic leadership approach relies on the

Personnel Management Practices and Quality Concerns

In hotels with reputations for high quality, certain management practices are common. Among these practices are the following:

1. Employee orientation is emphasized. The turnover of employees is greatest where the orientation lasts only two hours or less. It is lowest where the orientation is comprehensive.
2. Turnover reports are emphasized. Managers receive daily or weekly reports about turnover. They recognize the correlation between low employee turnover and high quality in a food service operation.
3. Interaction with employees is structured. Managers don't meet with employees randomly; rather, they conduct scheduled meetings. Managers see to it that communication barriers don't arise between them and their employees.
4. Guest comment cards are taken seriously. Managers of dining rooms with excellent reputations put great stock in guest comment cards and other means of obtaining evaluations of their services and products from guests.
5. Performance evaluations are structured. Most general managers of quality operations rate their evaluation programs as effective tools in communicating and maintaining high standards.

property's rules, regulations, policies, and procedures to make decisions. Bureaucratic leadership is, in effect, "management by the book." The manager becomes an officer who enforces rules and relies on higher levels of management to make decisions about problems not covered in "the book."

Most restaurant managers do not follow any of the preceding leadership styles exclusively. Ideally, they would adapt the leadership style that best fits the needs of the specific employee and his/her work environment. That is seldom possible, however. After all, restaurant managers are only human. They develop attitudes, feelings, and personalities based on their own unique background. They also have wants and needs which they hope their jobs will fulfill. Those factors generally limit their ability to switch leadership styles.

Researchers disagree with one another about managers' abilities to modify their leadership styles to fit various needs in the work environment. Some researchers believe that managers cannot make adaptations in styles; others believe that it is possible to modify, at least slightly, leadership approaches over time. Some managers seem able to study a situation and effectively use the applicable leadership style. Consider, for example, the restaurant

manager who has an employee who is eager to learn and advance within the organization; she constantly asks questions about how to do things better. The same manager has another employee who cares little about the job and his future with the organization. Can't the restaurant manager use a democratic leadership style with the first employee and an autocratic style with the second?

Motivation and Morale

Motivation is a force within a person that makes him/her act in a certain way to achieve some goal. Since restaurant managers must encourage and/or influence employees to take necessary actions, they must understand principles of employee motivation. While employees come to their jobs motivated to attain personal goals, an organization cannot effectively attain its goals unless employees work together as a team.

Morale, simply defined, is the way an employee feels about all aspects of his/her job (the actual work, supervisors and peers, the organization and working environment, and more). Proven relationships exist between morale levels

Qualities of Successful Managers

Successful managers set the tone for their operation by projecting an image not only outwardly to the guests and the public, but also inwardly to their employees. They are often actively involved in civic functions in their communities. They have a broad background in all phases of hospitality operations. Their greatest objective in managing their property is guest satisfaction, and they believe that a quality operation will undoubtedly yield profits.

Successful managers consider employee satisfaction equally important to guest satisfaction. They make employee training and development a priority so that staff members can reach their fullest potential.

Effective managers utilize well-defined standards for each phase of the operation. They use current technology to help solve their problems, and they budget for well-structured capital preservation or improvement programs. They use a visible, easily accessible style of management.

and absenteeism, turnover, and accidents.[4] As morale improves and fewer employees are absent from or quit their jobs, the food and beverage operation should benefit from lower recruitment and hiring costs, reduced orientation and training expenses, and decreased problems with work quality. Similarly, as absenteeism problems dwindle, managers should see fewer scheduling and emergency problems, lower overtime costs, and other benefits. As accidents decrease, personnel-related problems and insurance costs will also decrease. Obviously, the level of employee morale has an impact on organizational success. Employees whose wants and needs are being satisfied on the job generally have good morale. This positive attitude, in turn, affects their motivation.

Clearly, managers need to consider, to the extent possible, the personal goals of each member of their dining service staffs and work to ensure that the goals of the employee and the food service operation are compatible. When employees want to accomplish the same things that the employer does, they will find the work interesting and challenging; they will be more likely to do the work that the organization desires.

Restaurant managers can do a great deal to develop motivated employees. For example, they can attempt to provide a climate in which employees will want to work with, rather than against, the food service operation. Because restaurant managers influence job security, working conditions, the performance of job tasks, and the quality of the work itself, they must realize how these factors directly influence the staff. Restaurant managers interact with employees throughout every workday. They, along with the employees' immediate supervisors, are likely to influence how their employees feel about their jobs.

Managers must listen closely to their employees in order to determine how to motivate them. Put yourself in your employees' place to assess what they as individuals need; consider how you can meet those needs on the job. If you have an employee whose behavior prevents him/her from working to meet organizational goals, discover, if you can, what is causing that employee to act in this manner. If one employee is worried about emergency bills she must immediately deal with, perhaps you can assign more work to her so she can earn more income. If another employee believes he has not been given any chance to advance in the profession, perhaps you can suggest further training to help him achieve his goals. If still another employee is feeling overburdened by classes she is taking while feeling obligated to work overtime in the dining outlet, perhaps you should ask if she needs some time off. Recognize the different approaches that you can use to motivate staff members. If one approach does not work, try another.

The use of proper communication techniques is a basic motivational strategy. You can

---

[4] Ross A. Webber, *Management: The Basic Elements of Managing Organizations*, rev. ed. (Homewood, Ill.: Irwin, 1979), p. 175.

satisfy, at least to some extent, such employee desires as those for security, recognition, or a sense of belonging by using effective communication techniques. Show appreciation for the employees' work by giving praise where it is due, involve employees in decisions that affect them, emphasize their importance to the organization, discuss how employees in the past have received merit rewards, reinforce the benefits to them of insurance programs, and listen to their suggestions for improving service.

One of the easiest-to-use motivational tools available to managers is the career ladder. With it managers can show employees how they can advance in an organization. For that matter, managers themselves can see the challenges, responsibilities, and excitement that lies ahead for them as they advance in an organization.

Many employees leave a specific hospitality operation because they have no place to which they can advance, or they are bored with repetitive jobs. Experienced employees are often highly motivated to perform well when they know that the food and beverage operation will give them greater responsibilities and higher wages/salaries in return for quality work. Since each food service operation is unique, it must develop its own routes of advancement (career ladders) which can serve as guides for training, job rotation, and job enlargement programs within the organization.

The career ladder for hotel food and beverage positions (Exhibit 2.6) outlines a possible professional advancement program for dining service employees. Of course, job descriptions listing the required tasks that must be performed by each position should accompany the chart. In addition, job specifications which list the personal skills, experience, and other qualifications required for each position must also be developed. When a career ladder plan is used, employees know where they are in the organization and can develop a structured plan to advance within it. In Exhibit 2.6 the route to the top can go through the beverage operation, food operation, or cashier/accounting positions. It may also be possible to include employees from the hotel's sales and housekeeping departments since, at least at higher organizational levels, transfers between these departments do occur.

Evaluation Procedures

Evaluating employees is an important part of a manager's job. Some evaluation takes place informally on a daily basis when the manager interacts with the employee and makes decisions about the adequacy of the work performed. However, a more formal evaluation process—a performance review—is needed to provide a structure for informing employees about how they are doing and, when necessary, how they could improve.

The evaluation process should include five distinct elements that apply not only to the evaluation of employees but also to the evaluation of any other aspect of the food service operation:

1. Someone must be responsible for the evaluation.

2. Standards used to measure and define satisfactory performance must be established (see Exhibit 2.7).

3. Personnel involved in the appraisal process must know what they are supposed to do and must be given all the necessary resources to do it.

4. Actual performance must be assessed.

5. A comparison between what should be (the standard) and what is (the present condition) is the actual evaluation activity.

Since a performance review must focus on the performance of individual employees, it is necessary to know the tasks which each employee must perform and the definition of an acceptable performance for those tasks. The specific tasks are included in job descriptions and job lists (Exhibits 2.1 and 2.3). Managers should spell out the required performance levels for these tasks (Exhibit 2.5) as they develop their training programs. As you can see, the information developed as you recruit and select staff members and plan training programs can also be used for subsequent performance reviews. All employee appraisal systems should focus on performance factors that distinguish a good staff member from a poor one. Programs which fail to do this do not help employees become better

Exhibit 2.6 Career Ladder for Food and Beverage Positions

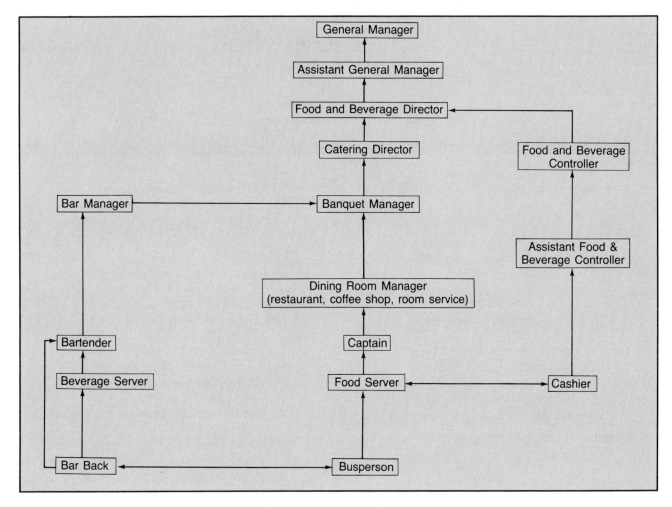

staff members. The basic steps for designing an effective performance review program include:

1. Establishing objectives for the performance reviews.

2. Identifying factors important to judging employee performance.

3. Properly training the people who will conduct the performance reviews.

4. Determining the frequency of the performance reviews. Normally, these reviews should occur at least twice a year.

5. Developing procedures for employee participation.

6. Establishing appeal procedures so that employees who believe that their review was administered unfairly will have an opportunity to discuss perceived problems with higher management levels.

7. Drafting follow-up plans to indicate what will happen after a performance review is completed.

8. Developing procedures to inform employees about the performance review.

Let's look for a moment at the relationship between performance reviews and employee potential, which is the highest level at which an employee can perform. Often, an employee's actual work falls short of this optimal perform-

Exhibit 2.7 The Development of Performance Standards for Dining Service

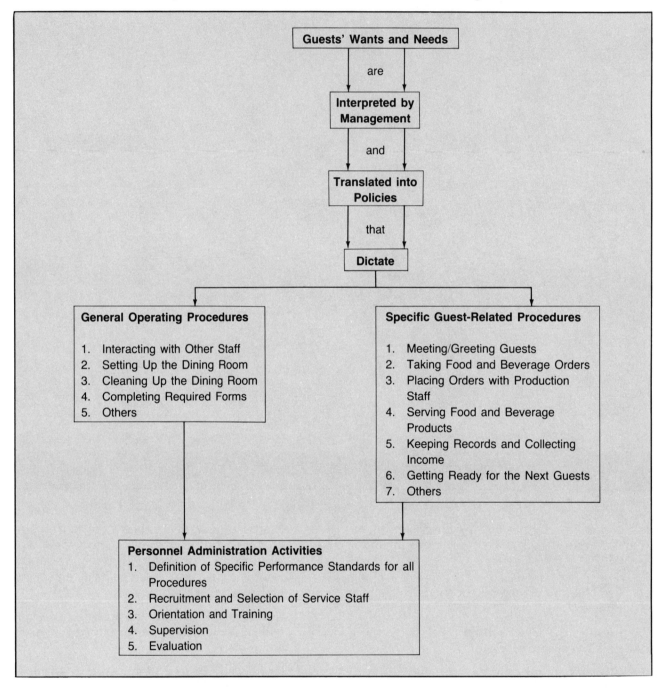

ance level. Restaurant managers who evaluate employees must be able to assess whether or not those who do substandard work (that which does not meet the operation's quality and/or quantity requirements) can actually perform better. Most can, and the performance appraisal process is the first step toward identifying prob-

lems and ultimately yielding better employees.

When performance reviews indicate that employees are not performing up to their potential, the restaurant manager should practice principles of motivation to encourage employees to improve their work. In fact, the manager who determines that employees are capable of doing better work has already taken the first step toward understanding employees. Many times, a manager assumes that employees always work to the best of their abilities. The manager then attributes substandard performance to the employees' inability to carry out tasks rather than to factors in the job environment which inhibit work.

Opportunities for promotion also affect employee potential. Giving employees additional responsibilities and working closely with them to design their career development programs are examples of activities that can evolve from the performance appraisal process (see Exhibit 2.6).

Employee Discipline Programs

Discipline is any attempt to modify employee behavior. While we often think of discipline as punishment, a more positive view is to regard it as an activity designed to correct, strengthen, and improve employee performance. Discipline requires individuals to follow rules, policies, and procedures. In effect, it is a positive process similar to coaching.

In order to be effective, restaurant managers must develop skills in disciplining employees. Many managers are able to do this quite well; they have a special ability to deal with people and know how to work with employees to foster cooperation. Other managers always seem to resort to punishment (negative discipline) as the only way to gain cooperation. Some rule with an iron hand and, in effect, dare employees to break the rules so that they can dispense punishment. In between these extremes are managers who do nothing when rules are broken.

Many hospitality operations have replaced the "big stick" approach to discipline with positive approaches. Union movements that have helped present the employees' point of view to management, competition for employees, and an increasing trend toward involving employees in the decision-making process have all helped to focus on the positive aspects of discipline programs.

Managers should recognize one serious drawback to negative discipline: frequently, it only achieves the minimum performance level necessary for employees to avoid punishment. The goal of avoiding punishment is the reverse of what managers should attempt to instill in

their employees. Instead, they should foster a desire to cooperate and help develop plans and procedures to attain organizational goals.

How can you use positive approaches to employee discipline? The process begins with the use of the necessary leadership skills to develop a spirit and an attitude of cooperation among employees. As this occurs, staff members are more likely to follow reasonable rules and procedures. Employees will follow requirements because they want to—not because they fear punishment. For example, have you ever thought a manager was using a principle of discipline when he/she praised the employees for the good job they did? According to our definition of positive discipline, that's exactly the principle that was used.

In order for any type of discipline program to be effective, employees must know what their job requirements are. Using orientation, training, coaching, supervision, and personal example, managers can make these requirements known. Rules and other requirements must be fair, reasonable, and consistent. Managers must plan policies and procedures regarding discipline for all aspects of the operation—not just on a by-department basis.

Whenever possible, representatives of management and labor should work together to plan such policies and procedures. Once you develop these organizational tools, you should put them in writing. Include them in employee handbooks and provide oral explanations of them during orientation and supervision activities.

If punishment becomes necessary, you should administer it consistently. You must not only require all employees to follow the rules, but also, whenever possible, you must provide equal punishment for the same offense. However, be certain to take into account all the circumstances related to a specific situation. A good manager should attempt, for example, to determine whether the offense was a result of the purposeful actions of an employee or if it was, at least in part, beyond the employee's control.

Managers should also design and incorporate appeal procedures into the discipline process. After managers make a disciplinary decision, the route of appeal is normally through the manager's immediate supervisor. Of course, in unionized operations the bargaining agreement often covers the appeal process and other aspects of the disciplinary program.

Managing Service at the Hotel Columbia
Page Four

Lewis gave immediate priority to developing an organization chart for the Hotel Columbia's food and beverage department. He had previously studied textbook organization charts and had conferred with his immediate supervisor, the president and managing director of the hotel. His active involvement in the American Hotel & Motel Association had also paid off; he had met many people who could provide high-quality advice, and they were willing to do so because he was a colleague in the lodging industry.

The results of his study and research are shown in the organization chart for food and beverage services at the Hotel Columbia. Lewis planned to employ five directors whom he would supervise himself: a catering director, a director of culinary operations, an executive steward, a beverage director, and a director of restaurant operations.

As delineated in the chart, the catering director would supervise both the banquet sales man-

ager (who would direct the work of the banquet sales representatives) and the banquet manager. (The latter would direct the operation of the property's banquets.) A head houseperson would direct the banquet setup; a banquet steward would organize the china, glassware, flatware, and other tabletop arrangements. Finally, a banquet captain would handle the banquet's service and supervise the banquet servers.

The director of culinary operations would supervise an executive chef. Three positions would report directly to the executive chef: a banquet chef who would work closely with the banquet manager, a sous chef (an assistant to the executive chef) who would supervise the kitchen production staff, and an executive pastry chef who would manage the bakery operations.

The executive steward would supervise an assistant executive steward, who would, in turn, manage the stewards. Essentially, stewards would

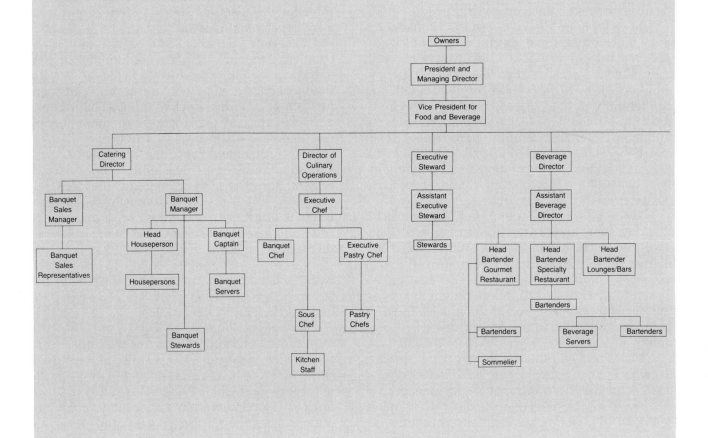

Managing Service at the Hotel Columbia
Page Four (continued)

handle sanitation and cleaning responsibilities at the Hotel Columbia. Because the head executive felt that it was important to separate the activities of purchasing, storing, and production in the Hotel Columbia, he had already assigned the storage of food and beverage products to the accounting department, not the steward's department as is usual in some properties. In addition, a separate purchasing department would procure food and beverage products.

The beverage director would supervise an assistant beverage director who, in turn, would supervise the head bartenders in the hotel's gourmet and specialty restaurants and the lounge/bar operations. The various head bartenders would each supervise employees with varying titles as shown in the chart.

The director of restaurant operations would supervise the managers of the gourmet and specialty restaurants, the coffee shop, room service, the take-out deli bar, and the employee cafeteria. Miscellaneous positions, as depicted on the chart, would round out service in each of the hotel's dining outlets.

Lewis carefully reviewed the proposed organization chart. "Yes," he thought, "some changes may be necessary as we get going. However, this organization chart will give us a good basis for segregating duties, helping the flow of communication throughout the department, and planning the most effective delivery of service to guests at the Hotel Columbia."

Lewis realized that other lodging properties would use other organizational patterns, perhaps with different terminology and allocation of authority. "When it comes right down to it," Lewis concluded, "the ultimate purposes of such patterns are a concern for the guests and the development of the best methods to deliver services to them."

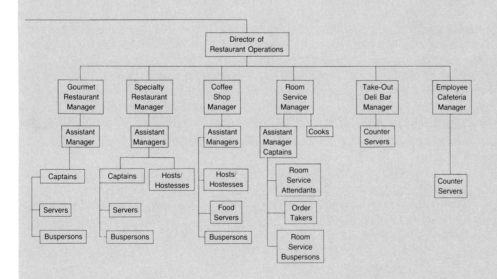

3
Menu Planning

The word **menu** comes to us from French and, according to the OED, means a "detailed list of the dishes to be served at a banquet or meal; a bill of fare." A restaurant's menu is not only a very important marketing tool in that it tells guests about products and prices, but it also dictates many back-of-house management activities. Because dining service managers often help develop menus for their outlets, the discussion that follows covers both menu planning procedures and the impact that menus have on dining service.

Menu Planning Objectives

Before you can produce an effective menu for your dining outlet—one that will both please guests and help achieve the goals of the lodging property itself—you should consider just what the objectives are that should be met by your menu.

The menu must satisfy guest expectations. Because guest satisfaction is a byword of dining service management, your menu must, above everything else, reflect your guests' tastes and preferences—not the chef's, the food and beverage director's, nor those of the manager of the particular dining outlet.

You must plan a menu from the guests' perspective and discover exactly what it is that they want. How can you ascertain their needs? Sometimes guests express their preferences by their choice of a particular type of dining outlet. Guests eating breakfast in a motel coffee shop located near a major expressway certainly have different expectations from those having a lei-

surely dinner in a city hotel's revolving rooftop restaurant. (In these two cases, guest preferences could range from having a relatively inexpensive, quickly served meal to impressing someone with unique cuisine in an exotic environment.)

You can sometimes pinpoint guests' preferences by their ages or socio-economic status. Whether your outlet attracts mostly young families, a singles crowd, or a high percentage of senior citizens, if you wish to continue to attract that particular group, your menu should reflect the kinds of foods and beverages that they enjoy.

Another way to identify guest needs and desires is by recognizing what kind of overall appeal your property has for guests. If your operation is part of a "destination" property (e.g., a resort) and most of your guests are with you for a week or two, no doubt their desire would be for an interesting, varied diet, and they'd be pleased with either a vast menu or one that changes regularly, even daily.

The menu must attain marketing objectives. While part of marketing is discovering what guests want, another important aspect is providing for their needs at convenient locations and times and at prices that they are willing and able to pay. In some cases, excellent product development, pricing, and promotion will convince guests that you have what they desire—even if up until now they never knew what it was that they'd been looking for. Some good examples of specific food items that have been developed and promoted across America over the years include pizza, specialty hamburgers, fish and chips, a vast array of ice cream flavors, fried chicken, variety pancake and crepe dishes,

Managing Service at the Hotel Columbia
Page Five

Lewis Scott had hired Don Jackson, who was well-qualified to be director of restaurant operations; he readily understood what the investors had in mind when they made their commitment to the property. Don had worked for ten years in another first-class hotel in the city and had moved up in that property to become manager of several of its restaurants. During the interview, Don had admitted that the director of restaurant operations in his present situation seemed uninterested in responding to the changing dining preferences of guests. "I know the market is out there for a gourmet restaurant of the first order," he told Lewis, "and a well-run specialty restaurant will particularly attract the young professionals who work and live in this part of the city. Furthermore, the Hotel Columbia's coffee shop and take-out deli bar will be the only facilities of their kind for blocks around."

Lewis was pleased that his new director was enthusiastic about planning dining experiences for both the guests staying at the hotel and those from the city and surrounding suburbs. The Hotel Columbia's midtown location was excellent. In addition to high-rise office and apartment buildings, the hotel was near the civic center, an art museum, and a metropolitan theater which regularly drew in huge crowds for concerts, plays, operas, and ballet.

As Lewis and his new employee discussed the types of guests the Hotel Columbia would attract and their probable dining needs and desires, they also focused on the various dining outlets that had already been allocated space by the planners: La Terrasse, the gourmet restaurant; The Eagle Room, an American specialty restaurant; Round the Clock, the coffee shop; room service; the employee cafeteria; and the take-out deli bar.

Both managers had extensive menu collections which they decided to review to get some ideas for the Hotel Columbia's dining operations.

As they looked at the wide range of menus before them, Lewis and Don discussed the image that a particular menu would help to create in each Hotel Columbia dining outlet. They knew that if labor-intensive food items became specialties in the property, they would have to consider the equipment and employees that would be needed to prepare and serve the items. Lewis pointed out that some food items would be selected because they would be prepared on-site in the bakery. Other items would appear on the menu because the ingredients are available fresh year-round and/or the low cost of the raw food would keep down the costs to the operation. Both wanted to have balanced menus throughout the property— menus that would offer foods with pleasing taste combinations, colors, sizes, and textures. They didn't want to overlook vegetarian diners, weight-conscious guests, nor those concerned with the nutritional contents of food. Both Lewis and his director of restaurant operations agreed that menu planning was a challenge, but one that they both found appealing.

---

quiche, baked potatoes with variable toppings, nachos, croissant sandwiches, stuffed potato skins, and pita bread sandwiches. Marketing objectives when these items first appeared on menus may have varied from giving the customer a delicious, nutritious, take-away lunch to introducing the guests to a new, gourmet taste treat. Regardless of the marketing techniques you use, the menu must help bring guests back to your operation; guests won't return if their perceived expectations aren't met.

The menu must help achieve quality objectives. Quality concerns are closely related to marketing concerns. It is important that you clearly understand all aspects of quality requirements and develop menus that incorporate these standards into your food items. Consider the following examples:

- You are planning a menu for a cafeteria line, buffet, or special banquet. Because of preparation and holding difficulties for such menu items as fluffy omelets, veal marsala, or sole vin blanc, it would simply not be practical for you to include these items on the menu.

- You wish to place a number of prepared-to-order food items on the menu (e.g., broiled steaks and chops, fish en papillote, stir-fried vegetables). However, you have a large dining room that regularly has a high guest count. You must decide if you have the work space and the production employees needed to prepare a large volume of high-quality, prepared-to-order dishes. Also you must decide which are not practical for your operation.

High quality and good nutrition go hand-in-hand. While institutional operations such as those in hospitals, schools, and the military must provide nutritionally well-balanced meals on their menus, commercial operations have no such requirement. Yet the expert commercial dining service manager knows that while people want attractive, good tasting dishes, most are also interested in the nutritional quality of those foods. Therefore, a menu that helps achieve quality objectives would also offer enough choices to the guests so that they can order a nutritionally well-balanced meal.

Other aspects of food quality include flavor, texture, color, shape, consistency, palatability, flair, and guest appeal. As you plan the menu, remember to balance it so that textures, colors, shapes, and flavors aren't repetitious. An example of an unbalanced banquet menu would be cod in cream sauce, mashed potatoes, and cauliflower—an all-white meal with little variation in texture. Remember too that some guests can't eat or don't care for highly spiced or garlicky foods while others can't get enough of them. The latter guests would be most unhappy if your menu offered only bland foods. Because there is a growing trend toward low-fat, high-fiber diets, serving dishes that are both low in fat and high in fiber might attract customers; if these dishes suit vegetarian guests as well, you'll add to your potential clientele.

Again, look at your menu from the guests' perspective. What do they want? How can you provide for their needs? Your work is not over until you have produced a menu that not only helps the operation meet quality objectives but also meets the needs of your market.

The menu must be cost-effective. Both commercial and institutional food service operations should plan menus that recognize financial re-

straints. Generally, commercial properties cannot attain their profit objectives unless their product costs, which the menu often dictates, fall within a specific range. In institutional food service operations, minimizing costs is also the menu planner's responsibility. Whether you plan a menu for a commercial or an institutional operation, you must select menu items that are within the operation's budget (its estimate of allowable food expenses).

The menu must be accurate. You are responsible for telling the truth when you formulate menus. You must not mislabel a product, describe it inaccurately, or deceive the guest by your menu presentation. Some examples of misleading menu descriptions include:

- Offering "fresh Gulf shrimp" when the product is actually frozen Pacific Ocean shrimp or Wyoming beef in lieu of "Colorado beef"

- Describing a grilled cheese sandwich as "cheddar" when it is actually made with processed cheese food

- Calling an item "homemade" when it was purchased ready-to-heat

- Labeling a steak "USDA Choice" when it is actually USDA Good

- Stating that a food item is served with "butter" or "cream" and actually serving margarine or milk (or a nondairy whitener)

Truth-in-menu laws exist in some localities. However, you should not need a law to recognize the obligation you have to inform the guests accurately about the items you offer.

The menu is a powerful advertising tool. It can influence what guests order and their expectations. If your food service operation does not deliver the type of products that your menu represents, your guests may feel cheated and never return. Furthermore, you could find yourself in court, trying to defend yourself against a charge of fraud.[1]

---

[1] See Jack P. Jefferies, *Understanding Hotel/Motel Law* (East Lansing, Mich.: Educational Institute of the American Hotel & Motel Association, 1983), pp. 60–62.

Exhibit 3.1 Menu Planning: Focus on the Guest

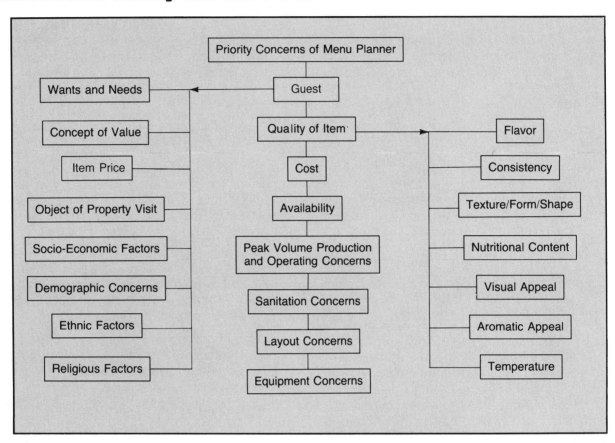

Source: Jack D. Ninemeier, *Principles of Food and Beverage Operations* (East Lansing, Mich.: Educational Institute of the American Hotel & Motel Association, 1984), p. 115.

Menu Planning Procedures

Once you have reviewed the objectives that should be met by your menu, you are ready to begin the process of menu item selection. Exactly how should you go about this process? As always, begin by focusing on your guests. Exhibit 3.1 graphically displays major factors that motivate guests and help determine their wants and needs. It also prioritizes the concerns of the menu planner. Note that quality is so important to the menu planner that it is broken down into its constituent parts. Quality concerns range from the flavor of the served product to the sanitary handling of it through various stages—from storing through preparation to serving.

Even with all the other concerns of the menu planner, the starting point—certainly in the commercial sector and as often as possible in the institutional environment—is "What do the guests want?" Once the planner has begun creating the menu by focusing on the guests, the process then becomes one of elimination. Of all the items the guests might want, some must be eliminated for a number of reasons including:

- Difficulty of developing and retaining adequate product quality levels
- High cost of ingredients
- Unavailability of ingredients
- Not enough personnel and/or inadequately skilled personnel
- The image of the particular menu item conflicts with the operation's image
- Inadequate equipment and/or space to prepare an item

Carnival Menu

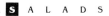

A P P E T I Z E R S

SAUSAGE GUMBO
*Homemade Andouille and Boudin Cajun Sausages
with essence of Fresh Herbs, Vegetables and Sassafras*

CRAWFISH PIE
*Crawfish tails panfried with minced vegetables
and slowly baked in a Tartlette Shell*

STUFFED MIRLITON
*Creole Squash lightly poached and filled
with Beef, Shrimp, and double breaded*

SEAFOOD REMOULADE
Shrimp and Crab with a traditional Remoulade

S A L A D S

AMERICUS
Prepared tableside with the Chef's ingredients

CHICKORY
*Endive with Pearls of Melon.
Raspberry Fennel Vinaigrette*

OLD FASHIONED WILTED SALAD
*Mixed Greens, Beef Steak Tomatoes,
Herb Vinaigrette Dressing*

E N T R E E S

SHRIMP
Prepared in triple fashion
Cajun Barbeque Style *— steeped in Olive oil, Butter
and Fresh Herbs*
Etouffé *— with minced Vegetables and Wine in a stew fashion*
Creole *— Zesty Tomato Sauce with Vegetables*

BEEF
*Medallions of beef tenderloin, panfried
"Merchants" Wine Sauce*

REDFISH COURTBOUILLON
*From the waters of Louisiana Gulf, poached and
accompanied by a zesty Tomato Sauce*

Complete Dinner — $17.95
Includes your choice of Appetizer, Salad and Entree
Accompanied by Americus Vegetable Selection

D E S S E R T S

AMERICUS SOUFFLE
A light and airy delicacy
4.25

RICE CUSTARD
A creole tradition
2.25

BANANAS FOSTER
*A Brennan's discovery, with
homemade creole Cream Cheese Ice Cream*
3.50

DOBERGE CAKE
*An intricate seven layer cake
with essence of Chocolate*
2.75

BREAD PUDDING
*A blend of Bread, Fruit and Custard
topped with a Rum Sauce*
2.25

PECAN CAKE
*Candied Pecan Cake layers
frosted with a Pecan Icing*
2.75

SWEET POTATO PIE
*Fresh Sweet Potatoes blended with Spices
and baked in a sweet Crust*
2.25

Sheraton Washington Hotel
2660 WOODLEY ROAD AT CONNECTICUT AVENUE, N.W. • WASHINGTON, D.C. 20008
328-2922

Menu from Americus Restaurant which offers a prix fixe meal with the guest's choice of appetizer, salad, and entree. The dessert menu is a la carte. (Courtesy of Sheraton Washington Hotel, Washington, D.C.)

As you develop a menu, never overlook the fact that planning the right one for a particular dining outlet will take time. An appropriate menu is probably the single most important tool you can use to attain all of your operation's objectives. Never put off menu creation till tomorrow if you can plan your menu today. Certainly don't procrastinate until a few days before it is scheduled to arrive at the printers.

Since the task of menu planning is fairly complex, find a workplace that is free from interruptions and distractions and gives you plenty of elbowroom. Some of the aids that you will want to have close at hand as you develop your menu include:

- Copies of old menus, including the menu you currently use in your operation

- Standard recipes[2]

- Inventory information and lists of seasonal foods, best buys, etc.

---

[2] For over 800 standard recipes, plus other valuable information about food production and menu building, see Wayne Gisslen, *Professional Cooking* (New York: Wiley, 1983). It is available from the Educational Institute of the American Hotel & Motel Association, 1407 S. Harrison Road, East Lansing, Mich., 48823.

- Cost per portion or similar information
- Sales history
- Production records
- Regular dictionary, menu dictionary, or, if you will be using non-English names for dishes, a glossary of menu terms in the applicable language

Basic Types of Menus

You can classify menus in several ways. For example, you can differentiate them according to the type of food service outlet in which they appear (e.g., coffee shop menus, room service menus, specialty restaurant menus), or according to meal periods (e.g., breakfast, lunch, dinner).

Another way to classify menus is to determine whether they are fixed or cyclical. A fixed menu does not change from day to day, although it may feature daily specials in addition to regular items. A cyclical menu, on the other hand, changes daily for a certain number of days until the menu cycle repeats itself.

Another popular classification utilizes the pricing structures of menus. Many food service operations use an *a la carte* menu which offers and prices each food item on an individual basis. The guest may select from a variety of different salads, entrees, vegetables, desserts, and beverages—all individually priced. Suggestive selling is an important task of service staff in outlets using a la carte menus.

In contrast, a *table d'hote* (fixed price or *prix fixe*) menu generally provides less choice for guests. This menu usually offers an entire meal with several courses at one price. Guests often have little or no choice regarding individual courses. Some gourmet and other high-check-average properties use this type of menu; banquets are often served table d'hote. The server's main role in properties using a fixed price menu is proper service; beverages and desserts, however, can sometimes be "merchandised."

Finally, some dining rooms feature a basic a la carte menu, then combine selections from it to offer a table d'hote menu as well.

General Menu Planning Considerations

The complexity of planning a menu varies according to the type of operation. Obviously, table service restaurants usually offer menus that vastly differ from cafeteria or buffet menus. Thus, you need to consider the type of food service outlet that you are developing the menu for, its check average (the amount spent by one person on a meal), and the overall marketing concerns of your property. Furthermore, you should consider the items that your competitors offer. After all, they are trying to attract the same guests. What are guests purchasing in other properties? Why? What can you do to make your products special and more attractive to potential guests? If your restaurant has an ethnic theme such as French, Italian, or Mexican, or has an unusual decor such as that of an old English pub or the dining room on a luxury cruise ship, your menu should reflect that theme and/or atmosphere.

When building a menu, begin with the entrees. Keep in mind not only the various types you could offer, but also their cost, their preparation methods, and, where applicable, their adherence to the theme and atmosphere of your operation. You can offer a large number of entrees or only four or five. If you feel that you should have something for everyone and provide a wide range of entrees, you should know that you may be faced with some back-of-house problems. For instance, you will have to order, receive, store, issue, and prepare a great number of food products, and you will need sufficient equipment and personnel to perform these activities. Your operating costs will probably increase and production/service problems will likely rise compared with offering only a small number of entrees. You should know that the trend in the United States today is toward specialty/theme restaurants that offer relatively few entrees. These restaurants not only reduce their marketing costs by focusing on a specific segment of the market (e.g., guests who desire specialty steaks or seafood dishes, guests who prefer whole grain or "health" foods), but they also minimize their production and serving problems.

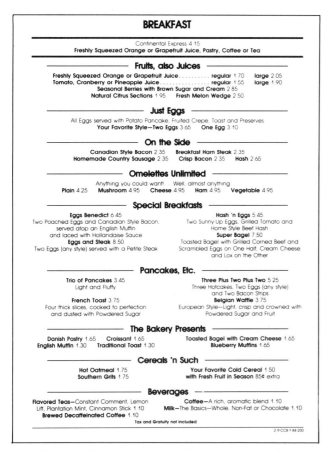

A coffee shop breakfast menu that combines a la carte items with special breakfast combinations. (Courtesy of Sheraton Washington Hotel, Washington, D.C.)

After you select your entrees, determine the complementary items that will fill each of the remaining categories on your property's menu pattern. A common procedure is to select appetizers and/or soups, followed by high-starch foods and vegetables (if not part of the entree), then salads. Finally, you should plan the other menu components such as salads served as entrees, desserts, breads, and beverages.

Planning Coffee Shop Menus

What items should the coffee shop menu feature? Such concerns as access to necessary equipment and availability of required labor must be considered when any type of menu—including that for the coffee shop—is planned. Special marketing concerns of the coffee shop operation must also be addressed. Consider, for example, that coffee shops generally offer guests convenience, fast service, and relatively low-priced food service; additional food service outlets may be available to serve guests with differing needs and preferences. However, in other properties alternative food services may be unavailable or available for limited hours of service only; the coffee shop in this property must serve a wider variety of guest needs.

Coffee shop menus are of two basic types—California-style and meal specific.

- A California-style menu features items typically offered for breakfast, midday, and evening meals during the entire time that the coffee shop is open. In this type of operation, a guest can order scrambled eggs or french toast at midnight.

- When menus are meal specific, the operation offers separate menus to feature items traditionally served at a single meal period; there will be, then, different menus for morning, midday, and evening meal periods. In such a coffee shop, a guest could not order a hamburger at 7:00 a.m., generally because the restaurant's one grill is being used for such foods as egg dishes.

Regardless of the type of menu used, it is necessary to consider perceived guest preferences. If alternative food service outlets are available, the menu might be designed with a limited variety of items that can be prepared quickly at a relatively low selling price. However, if the coffee shop is the only food service outlet available, it is likely that variety, preparation times, and selling prices may need to focus on a wide range of guest preferences.

Many coffee shops have limited food preparation equipment. Food items requiring extensive equipment and/or production labor are then prepared in a central kitchen for transport, holding, and service at the coffee shop location. Obviously, as menus are planned for these operations, quality, feasibility, and cost concerns of each menu item are very important.

The basic procedures for coffee shop menu planning differ very little from those used for other food service operations. Concerns for

One page from a room service menu that emphasizes catering for small groups, luncheons, and late suppers, and hours of dining service throughout the property. (Courtesy of The Greenbrier, White Sulphur Springs, West Virginia)

meeting guest needs must be matched with the ability of the property to deliver products of acceptable quality at a selling price judged to be a value by the guest.

Planning Room Service Menus

Room service menus generally offer more expensive food items and frequently provide less variety than dining room menus. Often, you can plan the room service menu around regular menu items that can maintain their quality during transportation to rooms. In other instances, you must plan special room service menus featuring items not found on your regular menu. Some operations use both their dining room and coffee shop menus as a basis for the room service menu, then supplement it with fast-food items.

Regardless of the approach you use, you must be sure that the items you offer will meet your property's quality requirements. Such items as french fries and other hot products may become soggy, cold, or otherwise suffer a loss of quality if they are held for long time periods between production and subsequent service in the guest's room. Likewise, egg souffles are a poor choice for most room service menus. Other items, such as chicken breast in a wine sauce, tournedos vert-pre, or beef saute a la Deutsch could require tableside preparation which room service employees may not be able to perform.

Some properties have special room service kitchens. Others use the same preparation facilities for all food outlets. In either case, the food and beverage manager, chef, and room service manager must work together to develop a room service menu that provides products of the proper quality for guests in their rooms.

Planning Buffet Menus

A buffet, whether restaurant or banquet, features a large variety of food attractively arranged. Ice carvings, tallow (fat) sculptures, flowers, fruit, or other decorations often enhance the food's presentation. Buffets may also offer novelty foods. If you feature buffets daily and have guests who dine with you regularly, you must change your menu selections. Since you can offer an extensive number of items on a buffet, it is generally easy to maintain an adequate variety.

Factors to consider when you plan buffet menus include the following:

- Total per portion costs
- Production feasibility/ease
- Popularity of alternate items
- Quality retention, especially during long meal periods
- Portioning problems
- Proper serving equipment, especially to maintain the temperature of hot and cold foods

- Sneeze-guards or other equipment to prevent the contamination of food
- Additional service staff to portion/serve some menu items, especially if you want better control of your costs
- Use of leftovers

You should select entrees first when you plan your buffet menu. Naturally, you should base your selections on the price you charge for the buffet. Inexpensive buffets usually include various cold cuts, entree salads, chicken, ham, casseroles, and other dishes. In contrast, expensive buffets usually offer an extensive variety of meats, seafoods, and gourmet dishes.

The popularity of specific buffet items will obviously affect your costs. If high-cost food items are popular, your guests will probably choose them before low-cost items. You must carefully consider sales history information (the actual quantity of each menu item sold during a specific time period spanning several weeks) in order to assess the approximate cost of the buffet items that your guests consume.

After you select the entrees, you should choose hot food accompaniments such as high-starch items and vegetables. These items must fit in with the other food offerings; their colors, textures, flavors, costs, and other factors must be considered. After you have selected your hot foods, select salads of all types: vegetable, fruit, and gelatin-based. Breads and rolls are essential and can help you control your costs if guests select them over more expensive food items. Finally, choose desserts and beverages that complement the other food items.

Determining a menu's selling price is more difficult with buffets than with other service styles that give properties more control over guest selections. Some hotels develop pricing plans based on their anticipated patronage. For example, if a property expects 200 guests at a buffet charge of $10 per person, it can anticipate approximately $2,000 income from its buffet. Most hotels allocate a specific percentage (usually 50%) of their buffet income to cover the buffet's food costs. Using this information, the menu planner can select food items for the buffet menu within the range of the property's allowable costs.

Other properties plan their buffet menus

first, calculate their estimated costs, then establish a selling price based on a markup factor. For example, if a property felt that food costs should be 50% of the buffet income, the menu planner would first establish the per person food costs of the buffet menu, then double that figure to determine the selling price.

Restaurant managers must consider several other costs besides food costs when they plan buffet service. Capital costs for purchasing buffet serving equipment are important. In addition, the need to keep buffets looking fresh and wholesome during service often requires a "runner" or other staff member to tend to the buffet through the entire meal period. (The use of runners can eliminate the savings on labor costs that properties usually realize when guests help themselves.) Other buffet costs include staff time for setting it up and tearing it down, carpet wear in buffet traffic aisles, additional cleaning time required when food preparation is done on the buffet line, and increased ventilation to eliminate food odors.

Planning Banquet Menus

One of your first considerations in developing a banquet menu is the type of service that you will provide: table service, buffet, or a combination of the two. The type of banquet service you use should reflect your property's image and quality requirements. If your client requires table service, then any of the service styles described in Chapter 6 would be appropriate. Typically, banquets are served with the food already plated and garnished. The server's main responsibility is to present the plated courses to the guests as efficiently as possible.

Many hotels use established banquet menus (see Chapter 12). Sometimes these menus can be "sold" to prospective guests as they are. At other times, you may need to modify them or develop an entirely new menu to fit the specific needs of a group. Because some guests will want to host an extravagant affair and incorporate their own food and beverage preferences into a banquet menu, you should decide whether your operation can accommodate such requests. If you are willing to let guests design their own banquets, then you should be able to point out to them such details as the cost of their choices of menu items, what impact their menu will have on

speed of service, and the number of trips the service staff will have to make to the tables.

Some hotels offer products and services similar to those provided in first-class a la carte restaurants to groups of 15 or more. Again, you will have to decide whether your operation could handle meals of this caliber. If you will provide such products and services, your staff may need training in addition to what they already have received to give them the professionalism required.

Further details of banquet planning are discussed in Chapter 12. Information on accommodating kosher banquet functions appears in Appendix B.

Menu Planning Constraints

The menu is affected by the resources available to the food service operation. You must recognize that these resources are constraints as you plan the menu. Consider the following:

Facility Layout/Design and Equipment. You must have the space and equipment available to produce all the items offered on the menu. If not, your staff may need to prepare convenience foods.

Available Labor. You must hire an ample number of employees with the required skills to manage, prepare, and serve all the items on the menu. If skilled labor is not available to prepare menu items, you may need to implement training programs or reconsider including such items on the menu.

Ingredients. Before you make your final selections, choose the standard recipe which your production staff will use. Also, make certain that all the ingredients required by each recipe will be available during the life span of the menu. You may not want to include on your menu items that require ingredients such as fresh seafoods which are not always available. If you include items on your menu that require seasonal ingredients (e.g., strawberries, asparagus, watercress, melon), you should realize that you will pay a premium price for those ingredients during the off-season.

Marketing Implications. Guest preferences should be a primary concern when you plan the menu. Even though certain menu items may be practical to serve from your property's standpoint, if your guests do not care for them, you should eliminate them from further consideration. Because for many people dining out is an experience that meets their social and psychological needs (as well as their physiological needs), foods listed on the menu should complement their dining experience.

Another marketing concern of menu planning deals with the meal period involved. Typically, breakfast and lunch menus focus on nutrition and fast service. Dinner menus, however, are designed to offer leisurely dining because most dinner guests prefer a relaxed and festive meal.

Quality Levels. You must know what level of quality the guests expect and how to incorporate quality requirements into the food items offered on the menu. If, for any reason, your operation cannot provide menu items with the desired degree of quality, you should not serve them. The level of your employees' skills and knowledge and the availability of equipment and specific ingredients all affect the quality of food items.

Costs. Food items that are expensive to prepare should be priced at a level which compensates for their high costs. You must know the cost of preparing specific menu items and their possible selling prices. If the cost of a menu item is excessive, you may decide not to offer it.

Health and Wellness: New Concerns in Menu Planning

Traditionally, menu planners in hotels and other commercial food service operations have considered nutrition and health as private, individual concerns which the guests, not the property, should address. Today, however, that philosophy is quickly changing. People recognize the important role that proper eating habits play in the maintenance of their good health. They are watching what they eat, both in their homes and in the hotels and restaurants they visit.

Each year nearly 1.5 million Americans have a heart attack and more than 550,000 of them die. Diet-related problems are important factors in many of these cases. The American diet features foods high in saturated fats, such as fatty meats and dairy products, and high-cholesterol foods, such as egg yolks and organ meats. Such a diet can, over time, increase the development of fatty deposits in the arteries; these deposits can interfere with the circulation of oxygen-rich blood to the heart muscle. An interruption in the blood supply can cause a heart attack.

Polyunsaturated fats tend to reduce the level of cholesterol in the blood. Whenever possible, substitute these fats for saturated fats; consider using vegetable oils and margarines in your food service operation.

High blood pressure is another health problem that increases the risk of heart attack and other illnesses. Doctors often advise patients to reduce the level of their sodium intake and the number of calories they consume to control high blood pressure.

Many Americans are improving their dietary habits and want certain foods available in hotels and restaurants to help them meet their health-related goals. Increasingly, commercial menu planners are recognizing these health issues and are addressing them. They are designing menus that offer alternative food production techniques and that allow guests to make healthful food selections. Many restaurants offer menu items that are broiled or baked rather than fried and are low in sodium and saturated fat. There has been a dramatic rise in the number of health food restaurants. Guests planning banquets are also more frequently requesting broiled fish, poultry, and veal.

Americans also recognize that obesity can contribute to health-related problems. Dieting has always been practiced by many segments of the population. But today, it is no longer a fad; it is becoming a way of life. Wise menu planners recognize the need to offer low-calorie alternatives to the weight-conscious guest. Some properties even list on the menu the milligrams of specific nutrients found in their food items. Facilities that offer buffets may list information about each product on table tents; some even provide hand-held calculators that help guests determine the caloric content of the products they select from the buffet line.

Examples of how commercial menu planners recognize health-related concerns abound. The point is that nutritional concerns are likely to increase. In an effort to please the guest and remain competitive, those who develop menus for their properties must increasingly address issues of health and wellness.

The Menu and the Food Service Operation

During the menu selection process, the menu planner has been constantly aware of the guests' preferences, the objectives of the operation, and the variety of constraints placed upon the menu item selection. While the menu's impact on both front- and back-of-house procedures has been kept in mind as the menu was being created, once the menu is finalized, it should be studied in depth so that all service needs will be met with as little difficulty as possible. Let us look more specifically at how a finalized menu defines many of the property's dining service needs.

The menu helps determine staffing needs. As the variety and complexity of menu items increase, the number of personnel who are required to produce the items will also increase. Conversely, the use of convenience food products, which have some or all of the labor that is normally provided on-site built-in, would reduce the number of back-of-house personnel required in an operation. The number of service employees needed is also affected by the menu. Obviously, a fast-food operation in which employees portion some or all menu items prior to guests placing orders needs fewer service employees than a high-check-average dining room in which a number of items are cooked or carved tableside.

The menu dictates production and service equipment needs. If your restaurant offers such a service as tableside carving of roasts, you must make the required equipment (e.g., carving utensils, carving board) available to your staff so that the service is as effective as possible. Other examples of special equipment that might be required because of items on the menu include soup tureens, souffle dishes, suzette pans, fondue sets, large wooden salad bowls, and an espresso machine. (The wheeled cart used in dining rooms that offer tableside cookery is called a *gueridon*; its heating unit is a *rechaud*. The heated cart from which such entrees as roast beef or leg of lamb are served is called a *voiture*.)

The menu dictates dining space. A take-out sandwich or pizza operation would require no dining space whatsoever, and the amount of square feet required per person in the service area where guests order or collect the food items would be minimal. On the other hand, if a restaurant offers a huge salad buffet, dessert selection from a pastry cart, or an after-dinner-drink trolley, wide aisles would be needed between tables to allow guests ease of movement between their tables and the buffet or to accommodate moving equipment.

Purchase specifications may be dictated by the menu. If the menu offers such items as USDA Choice New York strip steaks, quarter-pound lean beef burgers, grade AA eggs, freshly squeezed Florida orange juice, or vine-ripened tomatoes, back-of-house procedures will not only include receiving, storing, issuing, and producing the menu items but also purchasing the specific products described. (When such factors as grade and portion size are not dictated by the menu, managers and chefs must determine purchase specifications and related quality factors for the property.)

The menu dictates how and when items must be prepared. To stimulate guest interest, the menu planner may offer a dish prepared in a variety of ways. For example, a fish fillet could be poached, broiled, or batter-dipped and deep-fried, and the guest could choose the preparation method that most appeals. Obviously, if the menu offers only one method of cookery for an item, the finished product must be prepared using that method. You cannot serve fried chicken to a guest who has ordered roast chicken or braised vegetables when the menu stipulated steamed or sauteed vegetables. Some items lend themselves to cooking in small quantities, or "batch cooking," in which a small amount of an item is produced immediately before service (e.g., pancakes, hot shrimp dishes, most vegetables). (In a traditional system, you produce the full quantity of a product needed at one time.)

SHERATON WASHINGTON HOTEL

Elegance In Black and White

This exciting banquet theme is designed to dramatize the pristine look of black and white. Poised against reflective candlelit surfaces, the effect comes from the mirrored table tops, which appear to float above black floor length tablecloths. With white napery and crystal serviceware the look has been described as "incredibly stunning" and "a must for your next special event." The following is a suggested dinner menu:

Ballotine of Salmon
Watercress Sauce

෯ඥ෯

Bibb Lettuce, Chopped Walnuts
Shredded Gruyere, Dark Grapes
Red Wine Vinaigrette

෯ඥ෯

Champagne Sorbet

෯ඥ෯

Sliced Tenderloin of Beef
garnished with Fresh Seasonal Vegetables
and Potato

෯ඥ෯

French Rolls, Lahvosh, Grissini
Butter

෯ඥ෯

Charlotte Russe

෯ඥ෯

Demi-tasse

$35.00 per person

Your catering executive will be most pleased to quote prices relative to mirrored top presentation, specialty linen, clear serviceware, lighting, room decor, centerpieces and wines to accompany your meal.
TAX AND GRATUITY ADDITIONAL

An established banquet menu offering dishes designed to be the focal point of a theme of elegance. (Courtesy of Sheraton Washington Hotel, Washington, D.C.)

Cooking food on an as-needed basis often results in higher quality products; therefore, you should use such a method whenever possible. However, most menus offer items that generally aren't or can't be batch cooked immediately before service (e.g., breads, pastry-based dishes, soups, dishes made from dried legumes, curried foods, casserole-type pasta dishes such as lasagne). Because some items prepared in quantity lend themselves to creative use as leftovers and many others do not, the quantity needed must be carefully determined before preparation. Costs obviously increase when leftovers cannot be utilized.

Finally, the menu is a factor in the development of cost control procedures. The restaurant manager must control food and beverage, labor, and equipment/facility costs. As the menu requires more expensive food items and more extensive labor or capital (equipment) needs, the property's overall expenses and the procedures to control them will reflect these increased costs.

You can see how important the menu is to both the guest and the food service operation. It is also critically important to the food and beverage server.

The Menu and the Service Plan

You already know some of the menu's implications on dining service, but there are more that should be discussed. Because the menu affects the development of a property's entire dining service plan, restaurant managers must answer the following questions for *each* food item:

- On what type and size of dinnerware (plates, bowls, etc.) should each menu item be served?

- What type of flatware (knife, fork, spoon, etc.) will the guest need?

- Who will place the garnish (service or production staff)?

- What are the timing requirements for ordering the product?

- Must you use any additional dining service supplies to serve this item? (Examples include lobster bibs, chopsticks, finger bowls, etc.)

- Does the item require any special serving procedures? (For example, will the server portion the vegetables for the individual guests from a common platter? Will a cheese appetizer be flamed before service?)

- Must guests receive any special information when they order the item, such as the time required to prepare the item or a reminder that an item is available either "regular" or "spicy"?

If the menu offers items which require tableside food preparation, the manager must answer another set of questions:

- Who will prepare the item?

- What preparation equipment will they need?

- Who is responsible for setting up the *mise en place* (all equipment and food required for preparation)?

- What recipe will be used?

- How much preparation time will be required?

- What impact will tableside food preparation have on other dining service procedures?

Many aspects of personnel administration play a role in the answers to these questions. Since the menu lists the items that you serve, it also establishes the framework within which you must train your service employees. Restaurant managers must determine the exact service procedures which their properties will require.[3] In many operations, the restaurant manager, the food and beverage director, and the chef make these decisions jointly. Since dining service procedures often affect the presentation, preparation, and quality of the menu items, the chef

---

[3] For more information on this subject, readers are referred to Jack D. Ninemeier, *Principles of Food and Beverage Operations* (East Lansing, Mich.: Educational Institute of the American Hotel & Motel Association, 1984).

should help handle the food-related aspects of dining service.

After you develop specific procedures, you must develop performance standards for each procedure. How long should it take to serve each item? How many guests can one employee serve? What is the definition of a *good job* when an employee serves a specific menu item? Your training programs must address these issues and yield trained dining service employees who can perform at the expected level of service quality.

Designing the Menu

After you plan, price, review, and finalize your menu, you must organize it into a format that your service employees can present to the guests. Whether it is placed on a menu board, etched into a cleaver, or printed on expensive parchment, you should use basic principles of menu design. (Please note the distinction between "menu planning" and "menu design." The former refers to selecting food items to include on the menu. The latter relates to designing a method to inform the guests of the menu selections.) When designing a menu, remember the following:

1. The menu is the most important in-house marketing tool your property uses to represent the operation to the guests. Because first impressions are always important, remember that the entire menu should complement the operation's theme and that the menu cover is just as important as its interior.

2. The menu planner (restaurant manager)— not the menu printer—should make the most important menu design and merchandising decisions.

3. Creativity helps make the menu memorable. One creative aspect of any menu is its layout. Exhibit 3.2 shows examples of menu styles that use different numbers of pages/panels. Once you know how many items will be listed on your menu and the sequence that your staff will follow to take orders, you can select the menu size, shape, and fold that is most appropriate for your operation.

4. The type of material on which you print the menu is important. You can use inexpensive paper if the guests use the menus only once. (An example is a disposable placemat with the menu printed on it.) If you plan to use your menus for a long time, select high-quality paper. Durable menu covers and treated papers that resist tears, discoloration, and soil help protect menu pages.

5. Color gives the menu variety. Since production costs increase as you add colors to the menu, try to work within the constraints of two colors. Usually, dark ink on a white or light-colored paper makes the menu easier to read.

6. The menu should not appear crowded. Some designers like to allow approximately 50% of the menu for blank space (wide borders, and/or space between menu listings). Common mistakes on menus include type styles that are too small, lack of descriptions of food items, spelling errors, and limited use of design techniques to set off items that the house wants to sell.

7. The type style and/or lettering used on the menu can add to or detract from its effectiveness. The size, color, style, and background of a menu affect its readability. Because the lighting in many dining rooms is much dimmer than in office areas where you design menus, be certain to take that fact into consideration when selecting type style, size, and color.

8. The menu copy is important; guests must be able to understand the names of food items. Descriptions of menu items must generate both interest and sales. Any general information which the menu provides about the food service operation must complement the operation's desired image.

9. Frequently, the items at the top of a list of food items in a specific menu division are the most popular (e.g., the first meat, poultry, or seafood selections, the desserts named first). Once you know the items you most wish to sell, place them at the head of the list, put a box around them, or otherwise set them apart on the

Exhibit 3.2 Menu Designs:

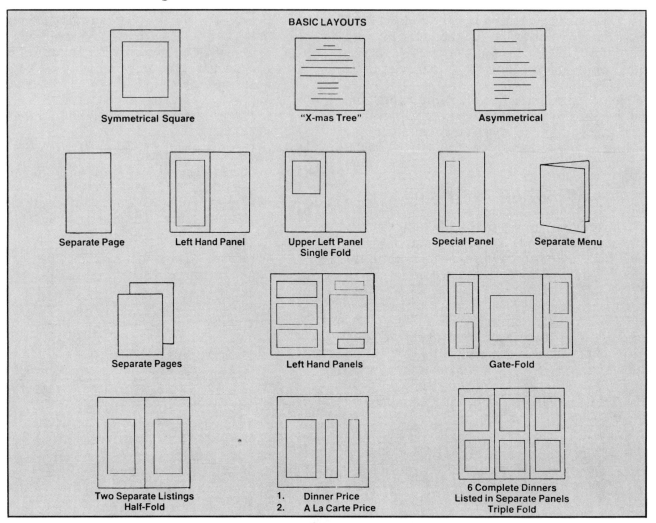

Source: Ninemeier, p. 115.

menu. Items on the right-hand page of a two-page, side-by-side menu may sell the best; the middle panel in a three-panel menu is also a good location for food items that you wish to promote.

10. Some operations use clip-ons, inserts, or blank spaces in their menus to note daily specials.

11. The operation's address, telephone number, and hours of operation should appear on the menu. Some guests may want to take their menus home, which may be acceptable if your menus are inexpensive. If you use expensive menus, you

might consider making smaller, "take home" versions available for your guests.

12. If your operation serves cocktails, wine, and related items, say so on the menu.

13. It is possible, but often not practical, to offer separate menus for each meal period. Some operations also offer such separate menus as beverage, dessert, children's, or dieter's menus. To make separate menus more practical, you could use a permanent menu cover and simply insert different menus for the changing meal periods or clientele. You could also lay out the menu according to meal peri-

Tasty Beginnings

Shrimp Toast—Deviled Shrimp rolled in Sesame Seeds, fried and served
with a Mustard Plum Sauce 3.95

BBQ Ribs—Lightly smoked and basted
with our own Zinger of a BBQ Sauce 4.25

Potato Skins—Fried and covered with chopped Bacon Bits,
Grated Cheese and a Sidecar of Sour Cream 3.35

Chicken Drummettes—Breaded and rolled in Sesame Seeds,
served with Plum Sauce 3.45

Creole Popcorn—Fried Baby Shrimp and Crayfish Tails
with the devil's Red Sauce 5.25

Lobster Au Gratin—Morsels of Lobster in a delicate
Cheese Sauce wrapped in a Crepe 5.95

Baked Brie—Wedge of Brie Cheese rolled in Crushed Almonds
with a Cranberry Preserve Sauce 3.45

Real Soups

All of our soups are made fresh each day . . .

Soup of the Day 2.25   Hearty Vegetable 2.25   Senate Bean 2.25

Soup, Salad and Sandwich 4.95

Cup of Soup—Your choice of the offerings

Salad—Cafe Salad with choice of dressing

Sandwich (A half)—Egg, Tuna & Cheddar, Chicken or Shrimp Salad

Ask about our kid size specials from Sherwood Forest

COURTYARD CAFE

The Sandwich Maker

Smoked Turkey, Corned Beef, Salami, Roast Beef, Baked Ham,
Egg Salad, Tuna and Cheddar or Shrimp Salad
on Rye, Whole Wheat, White or Pumpernickel Bread,
Bagel, Kaiser or Onion Roll, or Croissant
(P.S. We'll add free cheese if you like . . .) 5.25

Salads and Such

Tijuana Madness—A huge Tostada Shell, filled with Tangy
Beef and a not-so-traditional Mexican filling 6.65

Sumptuous Fresh Fruit—The Best the Season has to offer,
accompanied by Cottage Cheese or Homemade Fruit Sorbet with
Poppy Seed Dressing 6.35

Shrimp Salad—Baby Shrimp blended with our own sauce and crunch,
embellished with a special touch 7.65

Zorba—A huge bowl of Greens with Sliced Peppers, Tomatoes,
Cauliflower, Red Onions, Olives, Feta Cheese, Eggs
and a Lemon Dressing 6.25

The Sunburst—Slices of Avocado with Citrus Sections
and Sprouts on a bed of crisp Greens with Smoked Julienne Duck
and Poppy Seed Dressing 6.50

Tom's Best—Lightly smoked Breast of Tom Turkey blended with
Apples, Raisins, Walnuts and Celery with a Cranberry Relish 6.45

The Trio—A sampling of Egg, Chicken, and Tuna and Cheddar Salads
with all the appropriate fixins 6.45

Cafe Salad—Romaine, Iceberg, Spinach, Escarole, Mushrooms, Cherry
Tomatoes, Red Onions, Croutons and your choice of Dressing 2.05

COURTYARD CAFE

The Traditionals

The Reuben—Open Faced and Grilled Shaved Corned Beef
on Rye with Swiss Cheese, Sauerkraut and
Thousand Island Dressing 5.15

The Hoagie—Thinly sliced Beef grilled with Onions and topped
with Grated Cheese on French Bread 5.40

The Italian—Plump homemade Italian Sausage with Marinara Sauce,
Sautéed Onions and Green Peppers with melted Provolone
on a Roll 5.35

The Club—Ham, Turkey, Swiss Cheese and Mayonnaise on a
Baguette Roll 5.45

The Plain and Simple Burger—if you want Cheese, just ask! 4.95

The Daily Burger—An original trip through Fantasia 5.25

More Food

Cincinnati Chili—An original dish of Spaghetti and Chili
with all the toppings 5.95

Skillet Fried Chicken—A half disjointed Chicken, dusted with
Pecan Flour and Honey and fried to a golden brown 6.25

Frittata—Eggs and Cream blended together and served as an
open omelette with Fresh Vegetables and a blend of Jack
and Cheddar Cheeses melted 5.45

Bagel Benedict—A toasted Bagel split with Grilled Corned Beef,
Poached Egg and Hollandaise 5.75

Lasagne—If you think Mom's is good, wait till you try this! 6.50

Stir Fry Combinations—Shrimp and Scallops with Mushrooms,
Pea Pods and more . . . stir fried and served on Oriental Rice 7.50

Crabcakes—Prepared in the Maryland tradition,
served with Tartar Sauce 7.15

Steak—A generous 8 oz. Ribeye broiled to your liking with
Sautéed Mushrooms 8.85

COURTYARD CAFE

Sugar and Spice

Pies, Pies and More Pies 2.05

Cheesecake 2.25

Carrot Cake 2.15

Chocolate Fudge Cake 2.15

Banana Cake 2.15

Strawberries and Cake—
Pound Cake split and filled with
fresh Whipped Cream and Strawberries 2.35

The Ice Cream Endings—

All of our Ice Cream is made here in our kitchens.
We guarantee a 17% Butterfat content with the freshest ingredients
available. Inquire about our ever-changing selections.

One Scoop 1.95   Double Header 2.45   Triple Header 2.80

And if that doesn't suit your fancy, try . . .

Pie A La Mode or Fudge Brownie A La Mode 3.25

(With Hot Fudge or Strawberry Sauce if you like . . .)

Beverages

Milk—Whole, Non-Fat or Chocolate 1.10

Sodas—Cola, Orange, Root Beer or Diet 1.35

Flavored Teas—Plantation Mint, Cinnamon Stick, Lemon Lift
or Constant Comment 1.10

Coffee 1.05

Wine-By-the-Glass—Red or White 2.10

COURTYARD CAFE

A creative menu that merchandises items offered with lively descriptions and commentaries. (Courtesy of Sheraton Washington Hotel, Washington, D.C.)

ods, and list the time periods during the day that such meals are served. If you use a California-style menu, which allows guests to order any item while the property is open (often 24 hours a day), you would list items according to type (e.g., egg dishes, salads, entrees, desserts).

14. It is better to replace menus than to scratch out old prices and insert new, higher prices. To resolve this problem, menu designers may indicate "market price" on items with fluctuating costs. You can also have a large quantity of menus printed without prices. As prices change, you can discard the old menus and neatly write the new prices on new menus.

15. Some high-check-average restaurants and clubs provide only the host/hostess at the table with a menu that has prices listed. The guests of the person picking up the tab receive menus that list no prices. A major reason for such a service is to let guests select exactly what they would like without being concerned about what the host/hostess must pay for their choices. Another reason is to allow the host/hostess the chance to recommend favorites on the menu without causing guests to feel that price is in any way part of the recommendation.

Managing Service at the Hotel Columbia
Page Six

After consulting the various menus in their collections and discussing at length the goals of the various dining outlets at the Hotel Columbia, Lewis Scott and Don Jackson drew up a number of guidelines to be passed on to the individual restaurant managers when they were hired.

They decided that La Terrasse would feature traditional French cooking but with the lighter sauces and subtle, unusual combinations of flavors used in the *nouvelle cuisine*. A number of dishes would be prepared at tableside by the captain.

The Eagle Room would specialize in the best of American foods in season; guests could expect steaks and chops grilled to perfection as well as regional favorites such as barbecued spare ribs, Virginia ham, southern fried chicken, Long Island duckling, and Maine lobster. Vegetable and dessert offerings would also be traditionally American— from fresh corn on the cob and stuffed acorn squash to apple, pumpkin, and blueberry pies.

The main feature of the Round the Clock coffee shop would be the availability of quick-to-prepare-and-serve breakfast items 24 hours a day. The menu would also include items that coffee shop customers expect from such an operation—hamburgers, deli sandwiches, soup of the day, and homemade pies. Some of the items served in the coffee shop could also appear on the menu elsewhere in the property—at lunch in the Eagle Room, for example, or at the take-out deli bar.

Because the Hotel Columbia's room service department would not only serve guests in their rooms but also in hospitality suites and private dining rooms, Lewis and Don realized the room service manager would have to plan several different kinds of menus. "Our room service manager will have to work closely with our catering director on menus appropriate for hospitality suites," Don Jackson commented.

"Right," Lewis replied, "and the doorknob menu must reflect the fact that food orders from 2:00 a.m. until 6:00 a.m. will be prepared in the coffee shop." Both men agreed that room service should offer a selection of alcoholic beverages by both the drink and the bottle.

The take-out deli bar would not have a printed menu; instead, it would display specials and other items in a prominent place on the wall above the service counter. The employee cafeteria would use a similar method to alert the staff about each day's offerings and prices.

Lewis wanted to make certain that his dining outlet managers wouldn't think their menus would be cast in stone. Rather, the managers would need to study them in use to ensure that they satisfied the guests and also recognized the hotel's concerns—particularly profitability.

4

Food Production Systems

Food production employees use many methods to prepare food and make it available to the service staff. In older properties it is common to find individual, self-contained kitchens for each food outlet. That is, each service area may have its own food preparation area. However, certain food items, especially those requiring specialized equipment or a significant amount of hand labor (e.g., bread products, pastries), might be made in one production unit for use in other outlets.

Another popular food production system uses one preparation center for the regular dining outlets (including room service), and a second, remote kitchen for banquet operations. The high cost of labor, space, equipment, and borrowed money (interest) involved in designing or remodeling lodging properties has increased the need for a more creative, centralized production operation in which all the food for each dining outlet in the property could be prepared for service. Dining room managers should be aware that service is affected by centralized food preparation areas. Simply put, as the site of food service becomes more distant from the area of production, the transportation of food becomes more critical.

A wide variety of equipment is available to transport food. For example, bulk food can be placed in 12″ x 20″ x 4″ steam table pans. Special equipment heated by electricity and/or canned fuel is available to move such pans of food from the kitchen to the site of service. Cabinets are also available which can hold more than one steam table pan. (Some hotels use food transportation equipment that is only insulated, not heated.)

Other equipment is especially designed for moving portioned meals. Plates for banquet service can be stacked on racks which are then placed in heated, transportable chests. Or, you can place heated covers on plates and then place them on racks or stack them on top of one another. Again, you need mobile equipment to transport the portioned meals to the point of service. Styrofoam, aluminum foil, plasticized paper, plastic, and other types of containers (either washable or disposable) can be used to transport and serve portioned meals. It is always wise to be aware of all options. Only then can you make a wise decision about the type of service most appropriate for your specific property.

The same principles of food transportation and delivery to a remote site within a lodging facility apply to the transportation of meals to buildings other than the one housing the central kitchen (commissary). Some institutional commissaries are located in buildings that house patients, students, residents, or other members of the institution; food is then served in those facilities and possibly in other buildings as well. Other institutions use a separate building entirely for food production. The staff produces food in the centralized facility and then later further prepares it, brings it to serving temperature, and serves it at the remote property (sometimes many miles away).

Some large, multi-unit commercial food service operations also use commissary facilities. They may have food products produced in a centralized location for shipment to retail units over a wide geographic area. From the perspective of each individual unit, the products that it receives are convenience foods, which need very little on-site labor to make them ready to be served.

Managing Service at the Hotel Columbia
Page Seven

Lewis Scott's experience in food services had taught him that work flow patterns were very important. The time required for service employees to make extra trips to and from soiled dish return areas, pantry counters, hot food pickup stations, and other areas was time that they could spend more effectively providing service to guests in the dining outlets.

The Hotel Columbia's owners had hired a team of architects and kitchen consultants to de-sign the food production areas. However, Lewis and his staff would have to live with the facilities once construction was complete. "Now is the time," he thought, "to be certain that traffic flow patterns will make it easy for service employees to maximize their time with the guest and, at the same time, enhance the communication and working relationships between service and production personnel."

Hotels with off-site catering businesses operate, in effect, commissaries when they produce meals for catered functions. As a result, many commercial hotel properties use the basic systems found in institutional food service programs.

How is food service affected by centralized and commissary kitchens? Some operations are not affected at all: the food is available for portioning/serving, and the server's role is no different than if the items were prepared immediately before service at the site. In other operations, however, there are obvious effects upon dining service. Consider, for example, servers in a school food service operation who must reheat portioned meals before serving them to the students. Or, hotel service employees who must transport food to dining sites before it can be prepared and served. More important, consider that when the preparation area is removed from the serving site, communication and coordination problems may increase.

Coffee Shops

A variety of food production systems may be found in coffee shop operations. In some properties the production staff prepares all food items in a special kitchen located adjacent to the coffee shop. In other facilities the production staff prepares food items that require a significant amount of hand labor and/or sophisticated equipment in the main or central kitchens; the food is then transported to the coffee shop and held in heated serving counters or refrigerated equipment. With this system, the staff may use microwave or other fast-heat ovens to quickly bring food products to serving temperatures. In still other coffee shops, production employees prepare much of the food in public view behind service counters. Even some high-check-average properties feature "display cooking" as part of their dining atmosphere—the guests watch the chef, see their food prepared, smell the aromas, and hear the sounds of cooking—all of which may add enormously to the sensory enjoyment of their meal.

Some hotels design small kitchens for use by both coffee shop and room service operations. These mini-kitchens often receive some products from central kitchen areas, and their production employees perform only short-order grilling, deep-frying, and related cooking procedures.

Room Service

Room service kitchens may be either separate from or part of the property's main food preparation area. In some operations the room service kitchen is actually little more than a facility equipped to handle short orders. Usually, it is designed near the room service office and adjacent to an elevator.

Some hotels have experimented with the use of an elevator that houses a minimal amount of food storage and preparation equipment for the production of room service orders. Orders are transmitted to the cook (or cook-server) and as the elevator moves between the floors where the food is needed, the server arranges the items appropriately on a tray (e.g., continental-type breakfasts, sandwiches, salads, and related products that require little or no preparation prior to service). A second employee, the food server, actually delivers completed trays to the rooms requiring service. The limited variety of products which can be served with this system has, in the past, minimized its application in many properties. But, with equipment becoming more compact and with creative ventilation and refrigeration equipment becoming increasingly available, this system may soon enjoy wider use.

Banquet Operations

The banquet kitchen may be a separate area used to prepare meals for special functions; however, it is often a mini-kitchen located close to the banquet rooms. In some mini-kitchens the staff merely portions banquet food which they have transported in bulk from preparation areas. In other facilities, equipment such as that used to heat food before it is plated, as well as the plates themselves, is available in the banquet kitchen. Exhibit 4.1 highlights the advantages and disadvantages of the two main kinds of banquet plating. When considering your plating options, remember that plate presentation often affects a property's image.

Roll-in refrigerators are frequently used to store salads and other refrigerated items which production employees prepare in advance of actual banquet service needs. Coffee urns and ice-making machines are also found in banquet kitchens, and dishwashing facilities are sometimes located adjacent to banquet halls.

A banquet kitchen moves most food preparation tasks close to the point of service, which provides significant advantages for banquet operations. Less time and equipment are needed to transport food, the variety of menu items that can be effectively served increases, food quality may improve, and labor may be reduced.

Some properties use banquet kitchens for activities other than preparing food or plating food shipped in bulk from a central kitchen. For example, staff in some banquet kitchens prepare and/or portion food items that require little, if any, production equipment and/or hand labor

Production employees plating banquet meals. (Amway Grand Plaza Hotel, Grand Rapids, Michigan)

Equipment used to transport pre-portioned meals. (Amway Grand Plaza Hotel, Grand Rapids, Michigan)

Exhibit 4.1 Where Should Banquet Foods Be Plated?

Alternative	Potential Advantages	Potential Disadvantages
Plate meals in the production area; transport to service area.	1. Kitchen is close for last minute needs. 2. Closer supervision by the chef is possible. 3. Better facilities. 4. Sanitation control may be better. 5. Fewer employees may be needed. 6. Utilities, such as water, are readily available.	1. Possible temperature problems with prolonged holding. 2. Presentation may become unappetizing en route to the serving area. 3. Staff may need to make extra trips to the kitchen. 4. Harder to time delivery. 5. Expensive transportation equipment is needed.
Transport food in bulk to service area; plate meals in the service area.	1. Better temperature control. 2. Food may have fresher appearance. 3. Plate counts are easier when the food is portioned closer to the dining area. 4. Fewer equipment needs.	1. Need extra employees and equipment at plating site. 2. Staff must make extra trips to the kitchen if quantities are insuffficient. 3. Facilities in the service kitchen may be inadequate. 4. Noise may create problems for the guests.

(e.g., salads, appetizers, cakes). Staff can then portion food in either the central kitchen or the service kitchen, and place it in this equipment until the time of service.

Portion-control tools help maintain consistency in the size of menu items served to guests. For instance, employees should use a scale when learning to portion the correct amount (weight) of beef on each plate and to randomly check the accuracy of portions as plating continues. A slicer could be used to slice the beef and produce uniform cuts. Employees can also use portion scoops, slotted spoons, and ladles to portion various other food items. Of course, the staff must practice basic sanitation principles to ensure that guests receive high-quality, safe food.

The chef or his/her representative should be a member of the banquet planning team, because no one knows better what can go wrong in banquet food production. (For example, the chef knows which items must be kept under refrigeration when not being prepared.) When banquet menus are being created, consultations with the chef and other food production staff members will yield reduced operating problems later. When considering changes in established banquet menus, it is also imperative to involve the production staff. Experienced catering representatives share the chef's concerns about selling such delicate items as veal cutlets, rare roast beef, Yorkshire Pudding, and flaming desserts to large groups. Some hard-to-prepare items such as roast duckling or rack of lamb do not lend themselves to preparation in large quantities. Also, some products may not meet acceptable levels of quality or freshness during certain times of the year. You should also consider the chef's concerns as you plan buffets. While stews, casseroles, and items in sauces may maintain their quality on buffet lines, what about such items as a seafood mousse, most plain, hot vegetables, or individual cuts of broiled meats without sauces?

Timing Food Orders

Service staff in dining rooms must closely and constantly interact with food production personnel. This interaction is never more important than when service staff turn in food orders for production. The dining room manager, working closely with the chef, must develop procedures which specify exactly when service staff should place food orders. Once developed, these procedures must be incorporated into ongoing training programs for both service and production personnel.

Let's take a look at a typical situation. Three people are seated together in a moderate-check-average dining room. One orders a well-done filet mignon, which in that outlet takes 15 minutes; the second person orders deep-fried chicken, which takes 10 minutes; the third guest orders moussaka, which is already prepared. In that outlet, servers inform guests when an order will take an exceptional amount of time to prepare (as with a cheese souffle) or when one order will take longer than the others (as with the filet mignon). (Lengthy preparation times are also noted on the menu.) When the server tells the first guest how long the preparation time will be for the filet mignon, the guest says that she doesn't mind. At that point all three tell the server they want a very relaxed evening with no hurried service. Since the servers in that dining room turn in orders immediately after taking them but are responsible for letting the cook know when to begin preparing them, the server can time the production of the orders so that the guests will have the unhurried service they desire.

Other dining room procedures require servers to turn in orders when guests leave their tables to go to the salad buffet. In still other outlets, servers routinely turn in the order when guests *begin* their salad courses. The point is that a prior agreement must exist between the production staff and the service attendants about when orders should be turned in and who is responsible for timing the preparation of them.

Many factors can complicate the production of food orders even after standard operating procedures are developed. For example, orders can get backed up and thus, during extremely busy times, take longer. If production employees must prepare several very large orders at the same time, they may be delayed in the preparation of smaller orders. If servers place an unusually large number of orders at the same time for grilled, deep-fried, or sauteed items, production staff in those work stations might get behind. Obviously, as equipment malfunctions, or servers return food to the kitchen because of mistakes, production and service delays will arise.

Some food service operations break up the order by stations. For example, service employees place orders for entrees at one site. (Large operations may require servers to break down entree orders by fry station, grill station, saute station, and others.) Orders for dessert items or cold items are placed elsewhere. Some items may be self-service; others may be portioned and/or picked up by the service employees themselves.

In other facilities, all food orders go through an expediter who coordinates the placement and pickup of food orders and facilitates communication between the service and production staff. Effective expediters answer a wide range of questions as they manage the flow of service orders to production personnel and prepared food to the service staff. Some of these are:

- When should servers call in orders?
- When should production staff begin preparing an order?
- When should servers pick up the food? How long has the production staff had the order?
- Which order should be put up first?
- How do we know when we're out of a specific product?
- When *exactly* is the kitchen open?
- When is the kitchen closed?

While overall systems and procedures used by different operations vary, a clearly defined set of specific procedures by which servers order

Placing Food Orders

In the past, standard operating procedures required food and beverage servers to walk back to production areas to place an order. Today, remote printers wired into precheck registers or into electronic cash registers automatically print orders for the production center. These units can increase productivity, for they alleviate the need for service staff to make a trip to the kitchen or bar to place an order.

Control also increases. Servers cannot place orders unless they enter items into the equipment, which automatically records sales information and assigns responsibility for income collection to a specific server. With this plan, management has better control of guest checks and a more accurate assessment of the sales income which the servers collect.

Remote printers also reduce communication problems. Many food service operations use an abbreviation system that eliminates the need for dining service staff to completely write out the names of menu items. Sometimes, however, these shortcuts can cause problems. What does "TUR" mean? Is it a turkey sandwich or a turkey dinner? If abbreviations are not standardized within the operation, service problems are likely. A machine-printed order clearly indicates requested items and lessens the possibility of communication problems.

and pick up food is absolutely necessary. The time to invent procedures is not when you have a full dining room. You should not assume that there will always be a problem when you are busy. Rather, you should carefully analyze and design procedures to move food items efficiently from production to service personnel. Above all, you should anticipate and forestall service problems before they can occur.

Facilitating Communication Between Production and Service Personnel

Our discussion about timing orders gave you some idea about the importance of effective communication between food service staff and production personnel. Service employees have many ways to communicate with production personnel. Let's review some of them.

Guest checks or remote printing slips are important communication tools. Order placement problems can be substantially reduced when servers correctly complete guest checks or correctly enter information into the remote printing device. Illegible handwriting, the use of wrong abbreviations, incorrect completion of a guest check, and mistakes in writing an order are examples of basic and routine problems that

hinder the communication process. Exhibit 4.2 shows some food service standards and abbreviations for a number of items served in one property.

All too frequently, personal relationships between production and service employees also have an impact on their ability to communicate effectively. At one extreme is the antagonistic relationship between production and service employees which ultimately hinders production and service. At the other extreme is the close personal relationship which results in favoritism toward a specific production or service person. Again, this relationship may adversely affect guest service.

Dining room managers in some properties request that production personnel attend training meetings for service staff. During these sessions production employees can explain what they do and why it is important for service staff to comply with basic procedures. As food servers begin to understand some of the problems which confront production personnel, especially those which service employees bring about themselves, they will begin to appreciate the importance of consistently following procedures. Similarly, if restaurant managers attend cooks' meetings, they can air problems from the service staff's perspective. The result of this increased flow of communication between service and production personnel often yields positive benefits for the guests.

Exhibit 4.2 Sample Food Service Standards and Abbreviations

COURTYARD CAFE FOOD SERVICE STANDARDS			
ITEM	**HOW SERVED**	**ABBREVIATION**	**GENERAL DESCRIPTION**
Smoked Turkey Sandwich	Oval Platter	Tur	ALL SANDWICHES ARE 4 OZ. ON CHOICE
Roast Beef Sandwich	Oval Platter	RB	OF BREAD WITH MAYO, SL TOMATO,
Baked Ham Sandwich	Oval Platter	Ham	SHREDDED LETTUCE, CHEF GARNISH,
Shrimp Salad Sandwich	Oval Platter	Sh San	CHIPS
Rye		Rye	
White		White	
Pumpernickel		Pump	
Whole Wheat		WW	
Pasta del Giorno	Black Skillet	Pasta	Changes daily
Shrimp & Scallops	Black Skillet	Sh/Scallop	3 oz. ea. shrimp/scallop w/oriental veg. and fried rice w/watercress
Rib Eye	Oval Platter	Rib Eye	10 oz. rib eye w/2 oz. mushrooms, pot., veg.
T-Bone	Oval Platter	T-Bone	16 oz. T-Bone w/2 oz. mushrooms, pot., veg.
Pork Chops	Oval Platter	Pork	Two 4 oz. center chops w/apples, pot., veg.
Lamb Chops	Oval Platter	Lamb	Three loin chops, w/pot., veg., mint demiglaze

Courtesy of Sheraton Washington Hotel, Washington, D.C.

If you have ever been in a service/pickup area during a busy period, you are aware of how hectic it can become. Noise, numbers of people, and the many activities going on increase the need for effective communication. Bar areas can also be very busy during rush periods. Coordinating order/pickup procedures is just as critical in bars and lounges as it is in dining rooms.

Income control procedures should also be mentioned here (see Chapter 8). Each property must develop and use specific procedures to ensure that it receives income for all products served. Generally, these procedures are essential aspects of the entire communication process; you frequently waste time and effort when you use separate steps for income control. You should understand that the way in which the service staff communicates with production personnel influences the income control procedures which you use.

You also lessen your reliance on spoken or written communication when you put in place and consistently use standard operating procedures for placing and picking up food orders. Yes, problems may still arise, but their incidence and impact will be minimized when such procedures are used.

Service Staff in Production Areas

Areas commonly used by all employees of the food service operation include the employee restrooms, dining rooms, and time clock locations. Some other areas should generally be off limits to all but authorized personnel. These areas include receiving, storing, and food production areas.

If food service areas are properly designed, service employees will have easy access to soiled dish return and to food and beverage pickup

The Server's Role

What role should the food server play in picking up food and beverage products? A range of possibilities exists. In some operations, food servers may do nothing more than put down a service tray when the order is plated and wait for a production staff member to put the garnished plate on the tray. In other operations, they must place the garnish, wipe up spills, and otherwise ensure that the presentation meets the property's standards.

Servers perform a greater range of tasks in beverage production systems than in food production systems. In some properties the beverage server selects the glass, fills it with ice, and after the bartender has portioned the beverage, adds any needed filler (water, tonic, soda). The server may also add the garnish, swizzle stick, or other items. Other properties delegate few of these duties to the service personnel. However you design the server's role, remember that wise dining room managers look for bottlenecks during busy periods and attempt to resolve problems creatively to speed the flow of service.

areas, and they will have less reason to go behind the bar or into food preparation and food storage areas. Space in these areas is usually limited. Also, floors may be wet, other employees may be in these areas, the areas may be hot, and many safety hazards may exist. Food, beverage, and income control problems can arise when employees are in areas where their presence is not required.

In many operations the service staff is responsible for obtaining prepared salads from refrigerators, additional condiments from storage areas, additional serviceware from dishwashing areas, etc. Generally, these responsibilities should be assigned to production personnel so that service staff may spend as much time as possible where they belong—in the dining areas with the guests. When emergencies or rush periods arise, service staff may need to help out with preparation tasks in order to expedite orders. However, standard operating procedures should not require the presence of service staff in these areas.

Managing Service at the Hotel Columbia
Page Eight

Lewis obtained a schematic of the proposed layout for the food preparation and pickup areas in the main kitchen. He noted that the kitchen consultants had done their job well.

"First of all," he thought, "separate entrances and exits facilitate a good traffic flow and there is no backtracking required. Service staff can go to separate areas within the kitchen to deposit soiled dishes, to pick up required food items, and to perform other necessary tasks in the pickup areas. The need for service employees to cross paths as they travel between pickup areas in the kitchen is minimal."

Lewis felt comfortable about the effectiveness of the kitchen plans after he had reviewed the traffic flow pattern his service staff would use. However, he also wanted to address the relationship between the production and service staffs. He made a few telephone calls to chefs and restaurant managers with whom he had once worked and in whom he placed a great deal of confidence. As a result of his conversations, Lewis developed a list of concerns that he would incorporate into the training programs for both production and service personnel:

1. An effective food service operation requires close, cooperative teamwork. Production and service personnel must work in a harmonious and cooperative manner.
2. The vice president for food and beverage should hold routinely scheduled meetings with the director of culinary operations, the director of restaurant operations, the executive chef, and the various dining outlet managers. This group would attempt to resolve immediately any problems creating conflict or inhibiting communication between production and service employees.
3. At the Hotel Columbia, the chef's responsibility for the appearance, temperature, and flavor of the food will extend beyond the kitchen to the dining areas themselves. If problems arise about the food in the dining rooms, their correction is the responsibility of the chef, not the restaurant manager.
4. The exact responsibilities of both production and service employees when food orders are being picked up must be determined by the restaurant managers and the executive chef. The decisions must be put in writing and must be adequately addressed during initial and ongoing employee training sessions.

Schematic of Server Traffic Flow Pattern

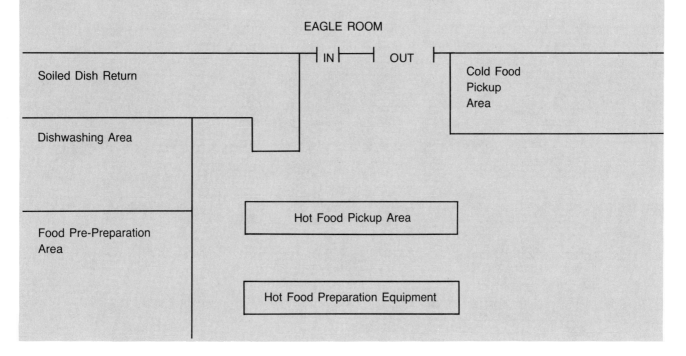

EAGLE ROOM

IN   OUT

Soiled Dish Return

Cold Food Pickup Area

Dishwashing Area

Hot Food Pickup Area

Food Pre-Preparation Area

Hot Food Preparation Equipment

5

Dining Service Supplies and Equipment

Food service operations of any type require a variety of supplies and equipment in order to serve guests properly. The management of dining service supplies and equipment begins with the development of purchase procedures and continues with receiving, storing, issuing, and controlling procedures. This chapter will focus on basic management principles which you should practice as you undertake each of these activities.

Purchasing

Purchasing is more than just picking up the phone and calling in an order. It is very important to purchase the *right* product at the *right* time from the *right* supplier for the *right* price. Planning for the purchase of supplies actually begins as the operation determines its goals. In Chapter 1, we stressed the importance of determining what guests want and assessing how an operation can best provide for those wants. The type and quality of supplies and equipment that you use will affect the provision of quality dining service to your guests. Just as you would not use expensive china in a fast-food operation, you would not use disposable dinnerware in a high-check-average restaurant. Beyond these obvious points, how should you plan the purchase of dining service supplies and equipment?

Some food service operations have a purchasing department that serves an advisory role to the restaurant manager and his/her staff. While the purchasing department may be re-

sponsible for obtaining bids from suppliers, the restaurant manager determines purchase specifications. In some properties, either the general manager does the purchasing or department heads purchase supplies for the needs of their department. In either case, the person responsible for dining service should be involved in making purchasing decisions for the department.

Some of the major purchases for any dining outlet are such common items as eating utensils, plates, beverage containers, and napkins, which can be either disposable or reusable. These dining service supplies are frequently maintained at what is known as par inventory levels. When a property uses the par inventory method, the restaurant manager must set the correct par levels. If supplies are overstocked, problems with cash flow, theft and pilferage, or wasted storage space can occur. In contrast, if quantities are insufficient, you may need to change your operating procedures or face guest dissatisfaction.

It is extremely difficult to generalize about the specific par inventory levels which should be maintained in the wide range of food and beverage outlets available at hotels. The manager must try to establish specific needs for the operation based on the type of outlet he/she is in charge of, the number of seats, the hours of operation, the different kinds of supplies needed, the availability of supplies, the frequency and style of dishwashing procedures, and the availability of an on-site laundry. The manager must also decide how low the par inventory should be allowed to go before an order must be placed to build the inventory up to its

Managing Service at the Hotel Columbia
Page Nine

Lewis Scott had enjoyed talking with the interior decorators who were designing the Hotel Columbia's restaurants and lounges. He was generally very pleased with their ideas, for they were able to carry through the theme of the outlets into the physical surroundings. He was certain that without their professional assistance, the Hotel Columbia would not be able to attain its goal of providing a high-quality dining experience for its guests.

However, Lewis did have one overriding concern that would have an impact on the design of each food and beverage outlet in the hotel. He was concerned about the selection of china, flatware, glassware, linen, and other necessary items which each outlet would use. As he selected these items, he needed to consider not only how they would fit into the design of the outlet, but also how they would work as a part of such procedures as food preparation, service, and dishwashing.

Since the purchase of a separate inventory of all these items for each outlet would require a large amount of money, Lewis could easily justify taking special note of these tabletop items.

established par level.[1] Once you establish par inventory levels for your outlet, you must also re-evaluate them frequently to accommodate any changes in business conditions. Some rules of thumb follow to help managers establish their own par levels for various supplies.

Par Inventory Levels for China

The china inventory should permit one complete setup in the dining room, one complete setup in process (in the dish room, in transit, etc.), and one complete setup in reserve (storage). When you open a new restaurant, the following guidelines can help you establish order quantities:

1. Dinner plates—2 to 3 times the number of seats

2. Salad plates (underliners)—3 to 4 times the number of seats

3. Bread and butter plates—3 to 4 times the number of seats

4. Cups—3 to 4 times the number of seats

5. Saucers—3 to 4 times the number of seats

6. Fruit dishes/bowls—2 to 3 times the number of seats

   Sugar containers—½ to 1 times the number of seats[2]

You can recognize the significant expense which you can incur by purchasing dinnerware for a food and beverage operation. If your lodging property has a number of food and beverage outlets, each with its own china pattern, you can easily see how expenses can get overwhelming. In addition, the use of different china patterns in each outlet can create sorting problems in a common dishwashing area. For these reasons, many managers prefer to use one china pattern throughout a property.

Of course, you must consider the cost of holding large quantities of dining service supplies in inventory. Frequently, high inventory costs are a distinct disadvantage to the selection and use of china. Some properties, however, feel that the higher quality and the unique atmosphere/presentation experiences which these special supplies make possible justify their

---

[1] Details related to establishing and ordering products according to par inventory levels are beyond the scope of this book. Interested readers are referred to Jack D. Ninemeier, *Planning and Control for Food and Beverage Operations* (East Lansing, Mich.: Educational Institute of the American Hotel & Motel Association, 1982), pp. 66-67.

[2] This information is from *Questions and Answers*, American Restaurant China Council, Inc., no date.

Centralized Purchasing

Many food service professionals point to advantages in centralized purchasing. Rather than permitting all the department heads in the organization to do their own purchasing, this task becomes the responsibility of one or a very small number of staff members. With the increase in popularity of one-stop shopping (a distributor carries a wide range of different products), the concept of centralized purchasing is even more useful. Several suppliers serving the food service operation may carry food, small equipment, dining service supplies, and other required products. You can often eliminate much paperwork if you place one order with one supplier rather than separate orders with a number of suppliers. However, because a one-stop vendor may not have as good a price as a specialist vendor, you should know that an advantage of competitive bidding may be lost.

high purchase prices as well as the long wait between placing the order for them and taking delivery.

Par Levels for Glassware and Flatware

A rule of thumb that the hospitality industry uses for flatware or silverware is three place settings per seat. A rule for glassware is to have a par inventory per seat of three of the most frequently used glasses (e.g., water glass, white wine glass, and red wine glass). Obviously, many factors may alter this recommendation. For example, if the glassware carries a specific logo and silverware carries a special embossed design or if a property has high breakage (glassware) or losses (flatware), it will need higher inventory levels.

Par Levels for Uniforms and Linen

It is imperative that the dining service staff and dining area equipment are immaculately clean at all times. Your policies regarding the purchase, inventory, and subsequent laundering of uniforms and linen will affect this standard of cleanliness. Many hotel food and beverage facilities make three complete uniforms available to each service staff member. With this plan, the employee can store one, launder another, and wear the third. You must also make some provision for employees whose uniforms become soiled during the shift; they may require a uniform change in order to maintain the sanitation and quality requirements of the food service outlet.

Par inventory levels for linen (tablecloths and napkins) are frequently set higher than those for uniforms. Many properties use a par inventory level of four times the number of tablecloths and napkins used during a busy shift. With this system, one set is in use, a second set is in the laundry, a third set is on the shelf, and a fourth set is "resting." Linen needs to "breathe" between uses in order to maintain high quality and long life.

Quality and the Purchase Specification

It is crucial to consider the guests, as well as applicable operating restraints, as you make decisions about quality. Purchasing department personnel can help you with your decision-making by obtaining information from eligible dining service suppliers, discussing alternatives with representatives of these companies, and bringing samples to user departments for further analysis and consideration.

Other restaurant managers might offer excellent advice for incorporating quality concerns into the purchase decisions made about dining service supplies and equipment. Similarly, ideas and suggestions from the guests themselves help greatly as you establish quality requirements for these items.

In some hotel operations, a concern about quality prompts the executive council to make decisions about dining service supplies and equipment. (The executive council in many hotels comprises department heads, assistant and resident general managers, the general manager, and other top-level management officials.) Management uses this approach because it recognizes that quality decisions made in the food and

Exhibit 5.1 Format for Purchase Requirements

Purchase Requirements

Royale Room
(Name of food and beverage outlet)

1. *Product name:* Tablecloths

2. *Product used for:* Tables in our gourmet restaurant, the Royale Room

3. *Product general description:*
   (Provide general quality information about desired product.)

   To be made of cotton damask, weighing 6¼ oz. per square yard.

4. *Detailed description:*
   (Purchaser should state all factors that help to clearly identify desired product. Examples of specific factors, which vary by product being described, include brand name, color, materials composed of, and style.)

   Material to have approximately 170 threads per square inch; thread count should be 91 (warp) and 79 (weft). Cloth should be 72" x 72" and shrink less than 10% (warp) and 5% (weft). Color to be white, non-fading (see attached sample for color/sheen).

5. *Product test procedures:*
   (Test procedures occur at time product is received and as/after product is used.)

   Sample cloth will be laundered by laundry manager immediately upon receipt to check shrinkage and durability.

6. *Special instructions and requirements:*
   (Any additional information needed to clearly indicate quality expectations can be included here. Examples include bidding procedures, if applicable, labeling and/or packaging requirements and delivery and service requirements.)

   Bids should include price for 150 tablecloths, a sample cloth, and estimated delivery date. (Delivery date to be within 4 months of order.) All bids to be returned in 30 days; chosen bidder to be notified by phone.

beverage department have an impact on the image of the entire hotel.

After you have a general idea about the level of quality required, you must do a great deal of research. Studying brochures, talking with sales representatives, and reviewing sample products are techniques that you can use to assess quality requirements. Whenever possible, consider manufacturers' brands which are available from more than one supplier. Competitive price quotations on the same product may yield lower costs for your property. If you decide to purchase a brand carried by only one supplier, you have less of a chance to negotiate prices, especially when you reorder products with patterns or imprints.

As you make decisions about quality requirements, write the details down in a format similar to that shown in Exhibit 5.1. In large properties, details of quality requirements often are sent to the purchasing department. In smaller properties, a manager might use the details to fill out the property's purchase specification form. After the form is completed, it should be sent with a cover letter to all eligible suppliers. Since the specification details the minimum quality requirements for the products you need, chances are good that all suppliers will quote prices for the same quality of product, thus making it easier for you to make a selection based on cost.

After receiving bids and making a purchase decision, record the appropriate information on a purchase record (Exhibit 5.2). Food service personnel are very busy; it is unlikely that you will recall the item, quoted purchase price, and quantity which you ordered. The purchase record documents this information and is useful when you receive the products. (Large hotels use a purchase order—an external document authorizing the purchase and detailing the requirements of the purchase.)

Other Selection Factors

There are a number of other important factors that restaurant managers must address as

Exhibit 5.2 Purchase Record Form for Small Hotels

Date: _____ Supplier: _____

Delivery Date: _____ Order Taken By: _____

Freight charge confirmation: _____
(e.g., prepaid, COD, truck shipment)

Item	Purchase Unit	Cost per Purchase Unit	Amount	Total Cost

they develop purchase specifications for dining service supplies and equipment. These range from whether or not to use any disposables to how to select the most suitable chairs for a dining room. Following are some specific aspects to consider as you purchase china, glassware, flatware, uniforms, linens, service equipment, and furniture.

China. It can cost thousands of dollars to purchase an initial china inventory and to replace items as breakage and theft occur. Therefore, it is very important to analyze all factors before making purchase decisions. The pattern you choose will likely "lock in" the property for years to come. The significant cost makes pattern switching impractical, even if you find other products which better meet the quality requirements of your property and harmonize more closely with the decor.

Commercial-quality china is available that is fairly resistant to breaking, chipping, and scratching. In many cases, breakage occurs due to the improper handling of china during wash-

Warehousing Supplies

Wise restaurant managers recognize that frequently a long lead time exists between ordering and receiving dining service supplies. For example, it may take one year to receive "signature" (specially designed) table linen; a six-month lead time is common for many types of glassware. Special orders for china can also take many months.

As the lead time for the purchase of these and related products increases, higher inventory levels must be maintained. When managers store supplies in a warehouse, they buy the necessary products in large quantities and issue them either into storage areas to replace reduced par inventory levels or into service as additional quantities are required. A number of managers have found that computerizing inventories aids the control of stock and helps maintain specified inventory levels.

ing and storage. Because it is reported that 75% to 80% of all breakage occurs in the soiled dish area,[3] good supervision in this area is absolutely essential. Since china is expensive, durability is an important selection factor. If possible, test samples of products which you are considering. Part of your analysis must include an assessment of the durability of the china design. Wise managers wash sample pieces of china many times and observe the ability of the samples to withstand the standard dishwashing procedures. This helps assure managers that the products will maintain their appearance in the operation. Examining the competitions' supplies can also provide you with information about the practicality of the items you are considering.

Heavy or thick china, which is most often used in fast service outlets, will hold heat more efficiently, but it is not necessarily more durable than other products. It may also make serving awkward and may require extra storage space.

How do restaurant managers know which china is best for their properties? We have discussed durability, thickness, and weight. Additional considerations include how well it cleans and holds heat, whether or not it can be used in microwave ovens, and whether or not the design will scratch or fade. When selecting coffee cups, managers often select mugs for low-check-average dining outlets and graceful cups with comfortable-to-hold handles and matching saucers for high-check-average outlets. Also, china plates are often selected on the basis of how food

will look on them. Most professional managers recommend selecting china with a narrow rim so that food will not have to "spill over" onto the rim. These managers know that the appealing presentation of food on the correct china can be as important to guests as the flavor of the food. In brief, the size, shape, thickness, pattern, and color of an outlet's china must harmonize with the atmosphere and theme of the dining room.

You can purchase china products of almost any quality from domestic or foreign sources. As a result, an additional selection factor—national pride—may be important in the purchase decisions made at some operations. Although it may have only very subtle image implications for

Gueridon Unit

[3] Raymond J. Goodman, *The Management of Service for the Restaurant Manager* (Dubuque, Iowa: Brown, 1979), p. 79.

properties in some areas of the country, overt theft and/or breakage problems can arise in other properties when brands or patterns of china stir the emotions of the guests.

Some high-check-average restaurants use service plates (show plates) to heighten the elegance of their tabletop appointments and their service. These plates are frequently works of art, custom-designed for the specific property. Generally, you must special-order them, and they require a great deal of care and control to ensure that they are not damaged, broken, or stolen. Typically, employees handwash them in the dining or pantry area, never in the kitchen.

Restaurant managers who want to change the china in their operations must consider a great deal more than the cost:

1. Many orders require a long lead time (typically, six months or more).

2. Long waiting periods between the discontinuation of present items and the arrival of new products can have an impact on purchase; sufficient lead time is required.

3. The size of the new products must be compatible with existing self-leveling equipment, storage units (such as side stands), conveyors, and service trays.

4. Food presentation procedures and the placement of garnishes may be affected by new china. In addition, you may need to purchase new plate covers. (Made of either plastic or metal, plate covers keep foods warm and facilitate the stacking of plates for transport to service areas. They need to be the correct size for the china they are used with.)

5. New items frequently become "collectibles," and you can expect an increased amount of pilferage or theft when you get new china, especially when a logo or other identifying mark is imprinted on it.

Obviously, the china you select must be compatible with the other service items you use. It is ridiculous to use a high-quality china with low-quality glassware and flatware. In addition to the need for supplies of similar quality, the total presentation must be harmonious; china has an obvious impact on the total appearance of the dining room.

Normally, open-stock china (commonly stocked or readily available from one or more suppliers) is more feasible than a custom-made, special-order product. However, some properties believe that their logo or other special imprint on the china adds to the image which they are trying to portray, and they are willing to pay additional costs for these products.

While the continuity of a china design cannot be ensured, the wise purchasers make certain that the pattern they are considering won't be discontinued. Even with the best storage and handling practices, breakage is likely. Because quality food and beverage operations should never use mixed china patterns in the same outlet, they must be certain that their chosen design will be available continually.

Disposables. Some hotels use disposable dinnerware items in their fast-food, take-out, and delicatessen operations. Disposables are a useful alternative in these outlets since they cost less, are consistent with the guests' desired quality of service, and allow guests to consume products off-site. They also reduce the cost of labor needed to clean dinnerware items.

Because the environment concerns all of us, you must also consider the ecological implica-

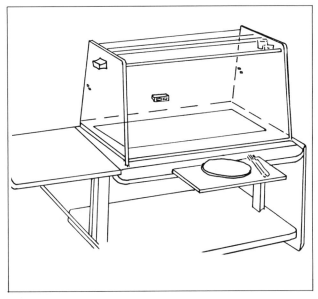

Mobile Food Cart

More Details About China Specifications

China for your food service operation should have a complete glazed cover. China with a rolled edge is better reinforced than china without the edge and reduces chipping. China patterns should be under the glaze. China comes in different strengths and, all other factors being equal, china of strong construction will last longer than china of lower quality. Undecorated china is less expensive than decorated items, and the type of design (spray-on, print, decal, or hand-decorated) also affects the cost. Most food service operations do not use bone china because it is very expensive and very fragile.

tions of disposables if you decide to use them. You must be certain that no environmental problems will arise and that no legal or other problems governing the disposal of these products will create difficulties for your property. (Sometimes, the cost of disposing of disposables is about as much as the cost of their initial purchase.)

In deciding what type of dinnerware to use, you need to calculate the different costs associated with permanent ware and disposables. However, before you calculate these costs, ask yourself this important question, "What type of serviceware do the guests expect in our food and beverage operation?" If it is clear that the guests desire permanent ware, you have little need for a cost analysis. Do a cost analysis only when it appears that both types are potentially useful.

Of course, a wide variety of quality levels is available in permanent ware and disposable products. Some permanent ware items are relatively inexpensive, and you can justify the cost in many types of food service operations. For example, if you want permanent ware, and problems with breakage, theft, the pricing structure, and/or the value expectations of the guests warrant it, inexpensive permanent ware is a wise choice. Some upscale properties may decide to use a high-quality disposable item.

As we have said then, the decision to use disposable products or permanent ware is generally a marketing decision. What does the guest want? While cost implications are important, you can generally pass higher costs on to the guests if their expectations warrant such a policy.

Glassware. Many of the factors important to making purchase decisions about china also ap-

ply to the purchase of glassware. Breakage is certainly a factor; therefore, you must consider replacement as well as initial purchase costs. Because the typical glassware supplier offers a wide range of glassware styles, the manager of dining service needs to know a great deal about glassware before he/she makes a choice for a particular outlet.

As is true with china, the selection of glassware has marketing implications. First, your glassware must be compatible with the theme and atmosphere portrayed in your property. Similarly, the type and style of glass in which you serve a drink greatly affect its presentation. Some properties have begun to use the same style of glassware for several different beverages. This practice reduces the variety of glassware which they require in their inventories. However, other properties like the presentation/marketing implications of fancy glassware and use a wide variety of styles.

Open-stock glassware is less expensive than its custom-made counterpart. However, just as with china, many properties desire logo imprints on their glasses.

Mass-produced glassware is generally thick and may have imperfections not found in fine, expensive products. However, this type of glassware is quite acceptable in the vast majority of food service operations which consider value, not cost alone, an important factor. Rolled edges and rims on glasses reduce problems with chipping and cracking. Selecting glassware with rolled edges, thick glass, and specific shapes can also reduce breakage.

Stemmed glassware is more susceptible to breakage, although some designs are harder to tip over than others. However, a good wine glass should have a stem for guests to hold so that the

Know the Definitions of Tableware Alternatives

POTTERY—The term pottery properly applies to the clay products of primitive people or to decorated art products made of unrefined clays and by unsophisticated methods. As a generic name, pottery includes all fired clayware. As a specific name, pottery describes the low-fired porous clayware which is generally colored.

Ceramic products acquire strength through the application of heat. The chemical composition of the materials used determines, with the heat applied, the strength, porosity, and vitrification of the fired product. Primitive pottery, often baked in the sun and composed of one or more unrefined clays, has little strength and is quite porous.

EARTHENWARE—A porous type of ceramic product fired at comparatively low temperatures, producing an opaque body, not as strong as stoneware or china, and lacking the resonance of those products when struck. The product may be glazed or unglazed.

CROCKERY—A term, often synonymous with earthenware, used to describe a porous opaque product for domestic use. Because of its permeability, it is normally glazed.

STONEWARE—A nonporous ceramic product made of unprocessed clays, or clay and flux additives, fired at elevated temperatures. It is quite durable but lacks the translucence and whiteness of china. It is resistant to chipping and rings clearly when struck. It differs from porcelain chiefly in that it produces colors other than white. These result from the iron or other impurities in the clay.

IRONSTONE WARE—A historic term for durable English stoneware. The composition and properties of this product are similar to porcelain, except that the body is not translucent and is off-white. In more recent times, this term has been used to describe a number of other products.

COOKING WARE—A broad term applied to earthenware, stoneware, porcelain, and china designed for cooking or baking as well as serving. It has a smooth, glazed surface and is strong and resistant to thermal shock.

FINE CHINA—A term applied to a thin, translucent, vitrified product, generally fired at a relatively high temperature twice: first, to mature the purest of flint, clay and flux materials; second, to develop the high gloss of the beautiful glaze. It is the highest quality tableware made for domestic or retail trade.

PORCELAIN—A term used frequently in Europe for china. European porcelain, like china, is fired twice. In this country, porcelain may be fired in a one- or two-fire process. Porcelain has a hard, nonabsorbent, strong body, which is white and translucent. European porcelain is made primarily for the retail market.

BONE CHINA—A specific type of fine china manufactured primarily in England. The body contains a high proportion of bone ash to produce greater translucency, whiteness, and strength. Like fine china, it is made primarily for the retail trade.

RESTAURANT CHINA—A uniquely American blend of fine china and porcelain, designed and engineered specifically for use in commercial operations. The body was developed in the United States to give it great impact strength and durability, as well as extremely low absorption which is required of china used in public eating places. Decorations are applied between the body and the glaze, thereby protecting the decoration during commercial use. Most of this tableware is subject to a high temperature during its first firing and a lower temperature during its second. However, some of it is fired in a one-fire operation during which the body and glaze mature at the same time. Like fine china, American restaurant china is vitrified.

Source: *Questions and Answers*, American Restaurant China Council, Inc., n.d.

heat of their hands does not affect the temperature of the wine when they taste it.

Many properties have begun to use shatterproof glassware. While shatterproof items are initially more expensive than other glasses, over time they become a very reasonable expense. Shatterproof glassware helps prevent glass particles from contaminating food products and is very useful in many kitchen areas.

Quality food operations typically use clear rather than colored glasses, with the possible exceptions of Hock glasses, which have brown stems the color of Hock bottles, and Moselle glasses, which have green stems the color of

---

Price and the Purchase Decision

Wise purchasers want to buy needed products at the lowest possible price. They know that product quality is a primary factor which determines the price. The use of a purchase specification form helps ensure that the quality of products for which suppliers will quote prices will be similar. In other words, price differences between vendors are not likely to be caused by differences in the quality of the products they offer.

Wise purchasers know that more than just the products themselves are purchased from the supplier. Along with dining service supplies and equipment, suppliers also provide intangibles such as the resolution of problems or help in developing purchase specifications and in evaluating the operation's market. Timely delivery is also important. A lowered price for products that a supplier does not deliver on time may cause problems for the food service operator. Credit provisions can also cause a manager to choose one supplier over another, for having an extended period of time to pay for the products might be worth a higher price.

Some suppliers offer a discount for volume purchase or timely payments. Two percent of a $5,000 bill could produce $100 in savings; the food and beverage operation with a profit margin of 10% of sales must generate $1,000 in sales to equal the $100 savings which price negotiations with the supplier might produce.

It is important to consider all the products and services which eligible suppliers offer as you make your purchase decisions. Even if the quality of products is the same, the lowest price is not always the best.

Moselle bottles. The size of glassware is also important. The glass must be large enough to hold the size of drink for which it is intended. Some food service operations like to use oversized glasses because they enhance the presentation/marketing possibilities. Consider, for example, a colorful cordial in an oversized brandy snifter, or an exotic specialty drink in a large hurricane glass. Some banquet operations use small wine glasses so that one bottle of wine will serve eight guests.

Food service operations that stress high quality use crystal. To minimize breakage of expensive crystal, these properties use a racking system; employees take crystal to and from dishwashing areas in racks to prevent the items from coming in contact with each other or any other piece of serviceware that can cause breakage. When practical, the use of a racking system is also wise for other types of breakable glassware.

Exhibit 5.3 illustrates some of the different shapes and styles of glassware which many hotel food and beverage operations use.

Flatware (Silverware). Washable flatware items, such as forks, knives, or spoons, are typically made of stainless steel. True silverware is prohibitively expensive for almost all food service operations; however, some elegant food service operations use a "hotel plate" (silverplated) flatware.

Most properties prefer to use stainless steel eating utensils of good quality rather than lower quality silverplate because the plating on the latter can chip and peel. In addition, commercial-grade stainless steel flatware is durable and difficult to bend, dent, scratch, or stain; it does not tarnish or rust and will not require replating.

You can buy flatware from a wide range of prices and styles to suit almost any requirement. Less fancy flatware is more popular than specific patterns because it is less expensive and easier to clean. Several grades are available. Higher priced items generally incorporate alloys of various metals which provide greater durability, grain, and luster than lower priced items. A finish can be highly polished, dull, or matte. In addition to the traditional knife, fork, and spoon, a vast array of specialty items to use with such products as asparagus, oysters, corn on the cob, lobster, butter, and grapes is available. Flatware manufacturers want to meet the varied needs of the food service industry and have made a seemingly endless selection of products available to suit almost any purpose.

To reduce theft, restaurant managers must carefully control some small flatware items, such as demitasse spoons, corn-on-the-cob holders, and any flatware with logo imprints. Basic tech-

Exhibit 5.3 Types of Glasses Available in One Line of Stemware

Courtesy of Libbey Glass

Exhibit 5.3 Types of Glasses Available in One Line of Stemware, continued

Tableware for Exquisite Dining (Reprinted by permission of Oneida Ltd.)

niques for controlling theft include such common-sense procedures as promptly removing items from the table when guests have finished with them and issuing only the number of items required for service.

Exhibit 5.4 illustrates some of the flatware serving pieces that fine dining operations use.

Uniforms. Uniforms for dining service employees are an important part of the atmosphere and theme which food service operations want to portray for their guests. As you might imagine, the range of uniform styles, designs, colors, and fabrics is almost endless.

Appearance and style are important, but so are such factors as comfort, practicality, durability, and ease of maintenance. Above all, uniforms should be functional.

Should uniforms have short or long sleeves? Short sleeves can contribute to burn and splash problems. Long sleeves can get in the way as employees use their arms. Long sleeves can also brush serviceware or food, causing obvious sanitation, appearance, and other problems.

When selecting uniforms, get samples. Ask employees of all shapes and sizes to try them on. Frequently, a uniform can look very attractive on some employees and most unattractive on others; try to find a uniform that makes *all* your employees look good.

Try to find uniforms that employees can wear year-round. With air conditioning, year-round uniforms are seldom a problem except for door attendants and bellhops. Of course, when you make these decisions, it is important to consider the employees' comfort as well as their safety. Involve employees in the uniform-selection process; they are more likely to accept uniforms that they help select. If employees like their uniforms and are comfortable in them, they are likely to have a positive attitude about their work. If they do not like their uniforms, their feelings can have a negative effect on their work habits.

Custom-designed uniforms can reflect the image that your food service operation wishes to portray; however, the costs of such uniforms can be excessive. Custom designs take a great deal of time to make for both initial orders and reorders. On the other hand, customized accessories such as special belts, hats, or neckties can make open-stock service uniforms "special."

High personnel turnover rates in food service operations generally require the availability of a wide range of uniform sizes. However, properties often purchase a large number of uniforms for the most common sizes.

When you purchase uniforms, you always make trade-offs between aesthetic and practical concerns. Comfort is important because food servers must balance food trays, reach, lift, and

Exhibit 5.4 A Selection of Serving Pieces for Fine Dining

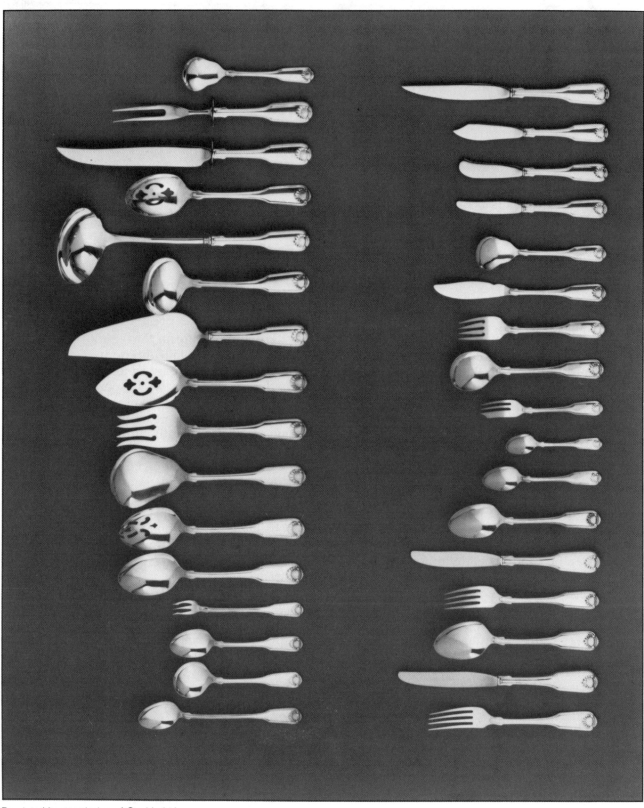

Cost, Quality, and the Purchase Decision

Restaurant managers who buy products for some operations are not concerned about cost. They are only interested in the highest quality product available; they know that their guests will pay the price. At the other extreme, some managers desire the least expensive product available and will accept low quality. They are reacting to guests who are less concerned about quality and want products at the lowest possible price. In between these extremes is the vast majority of restaurant managers who are value-conscious. When they make purchase decisions, they are concerned not only with price, but also quality. They first define the quality which they require, then they shop around for the best possible price.

Perhaps the difference between the four-ply, linen-finish, disposable napkin and the one-ply, rough-finish napkin can serve as an example. The quality-conscious buyer will purchase the former; the price-conscious buyer may purchase the latter. Value-conscious buyers will look at weights, thicknesses, a multitude of finishes, and sizes. They will consider buying in large quantities to take advantage of discounts and will also be alert to a wide range of factors which fulfill required quality standards *and* influence the final purchase price.

stretch to do their work. Because uniform pockets are frequently used to carry pencils, guest checks, and related dining room necessities, inside pockets are often best in order to present a more "crisp" appearance. Zippers or Velcro strips are much more convenient than snaps or buttons. Belts may add to the uniform's appearance, but are easily lost unless they are attached in some fashion. Shoes are seldom, if ever, part of the uniform which the property purchases; however, some thought to basic requirements (e.g., color, lacing, and closed toe) is generally in order.

While the initial purchase price of uniforms can be significant, you must also consider maintenance and replacement costs as you make your selection. Uniforms made of modern, permanent press or other synthetic fabrics should last for a long time if they receive the proper care. As you might suspect, proper laundering is also important to the durability of uniforms. Regardless of whether you have your uniforms laundered on-site or by a laundry service, you must keep them properly cleaned so that they look good and remain in service for a long time.

You also need to control uniforms carefully during their distribution, use, and storage. Professional managers suggest that the most satisfactory method of controlling clean uniforms is to require employees to turn in a soiled uniform in exchange for a clean one. While further details

are beyond the scope of this book,[4] you incur excessive costs if you do not maintain control over your uniforms.

Linens (Napery). Fabric tablecloths and napkins (serviettes) must be compatible with the operation's design and atmosphere. When restaurant managers select linens, they must consider quality requirements. (A detailed discussion of linen selection factors is found in Appendix A.) Seasoned banquet managers recommend a selection of colored napery to accommodate guests' decor requirements.

Many properties undertake cost studies that demonstrate that on-site laundry facilities would reduce their operating costs. However, restaurant managers must be sure to maintain the proper quality of finished napery in the dining room. Sometimes, you need special procedures and exotic cleaners to remove food and beverage stains. When cleanliness and presentation are primary concerns, using napery that contains nonremovable stains is an unacceptable strategy. Incidentally, some napkin folds require very heavy starch which on-site laundries often find difficult to process.

Other Dining Service Equipment. The typical

---

[4] For additional information, interested readers are referred to Georgina Tucker and Madelin Snyder, *The Professional Housekeeper*, 2nd ed. (Boston: CBI, 1982).

Mobile Dessert Cart

dining service operation must use a wide range of service equipment. Examples include hollowware (e.g., creamers, serving dishes, vases, and pitchers), hot plates, coffee makers, toasters, water pitchers, food server trays, tray stands, bus boxes, cash registers, data processing equipment, and more.

When you offer buffet service, you also need a wide range of chafing dishes, serving trays, and other service items. Banquet functions often require mobile transport equipment.

Some high-check-average food service outlets also use special equipment for exquisite dining service. Common examples include the gueridon and various types of dessert, beverage, and other display carts. Typically, a gueridon is a rectangular table mounted on wheels with work space, shelves, and a heating device known as a rechaud. A large number of manufacturers produce these and related items.

Consult the checklist of dining room accessories (Exhibit 5.5) for suggestions for equipment your operation might need. To help make appropriate purchase decisions, study advertising brochures available from suppliers, review possible products (e.g., at trade shows), and draw

on your own and your staff members' experience.

As with any product, questions you should consider when you select these pieces of equipment include:

1. Are they needed?
2. Are they able to serve the purpose for which you need them?
3. Do they satisfy the other unique needs of the facility?
4. Does their quality (value) justify the cost?
5. Are they safe and sanitary?
6. Does their appearance and design fit into the dining environment?
7. Does their size accommodate aisles, doorways, and other areas through which they will be moved?

Dining Room Furniture. Dining room furniture can help create almost any atmosphere the designer wishes the outlet to have. However, because dining room furniture is very expensive, you must match its costs with the level of quality and the image that your operation wishes to

Mobile Utility Serving Cart

Exhibit 5.5 Checklist of Dining Room Accessories

☐ Menu boards	☐ Water pitchers	☐ Pens	☐ Cheese trays
☐ Cutting boards	☐ Plate covers	☐ Mobile transport carts	☐ Tip trays
☐ Ashtrays	☐ Serving ladles	☐ Bus carts	☐ Pastry carts
☐ Flower vases	☐ Pie servers	☐ Utility carts	☐ Wine carts
☐ Bottle openers	☐ Napkin dispensers	☐ Bus boxes	☐ Salad carts
☐ Condiment holders	☐ Silverware bins	☐ Dish storage carts	☐ Pepper mills
☐ Coffee creamers	☐ Food server trays	☐ Ice tongs	☐ Service plates
☐ Sugar bowls	☐ Cocktail server trays	☐ Table numbers	☐ Wine decanters
☐ Napkin holders	☐ Tray stands	☐ Coffee servers	☐ Food service towels
☐ Butter dishes	☐ Baby chairs	☐ Oil and vinegar cruets	☐ Menus
☐ Candles	☐ Chafing dishes	☐ Relish dishes	☐ Utility buckets
☐ Salt and pepper shakers	☐ Corkscrews	☐ Wine cooler stands	☐ Side towels
☐ Teapots	☐ Flashlights	☐ Side stands	☐ Serving utensils
☐ Coffee warmers			

portray. You must carefully calculate how much your operation can afford to spend and purchase furniture in a price range that fits your budget.

When selecting furniture, remember that the comfort of your guests is one of the most important factors to consider. (The only exception to this statement might be in fast-food operations which use less than comfortable seats to encourage fast guest turnover.) The elbow room at tables and the amount of space between tables and chairs are important concerns. When interior designers or decorators select the furniture for a dining outlet, they may allow the ambience and decor of the facility to have precedence over guests. This should never happen; compatibility with the decor should always take second place to the guests' comfort. Other factors to consider when selecting furniture include the size of various groups you will host, the total number of meals you plan to serve, available space, and required aisle widths.

Wood is perhaps the most commonly used material in dining room furniture. Various types of woods and wood grain finishes are available, so blending a particular wood with a specific dining theme is generally not a problem. Wood is strong, rigid, and able to resist wear and stains.

Metals, including aluminum, steel, and brass, are also becoming popular in dining areas as are plastics, fiberglass, and vinyl. Wood and glass tabletops with metal bases are examples of how manufacturers use different materials together to make attractive, modern furniture. If your property uses placemats or runners rather than tablecloths, give careful attention to the tabletops you select. Constant use can create problems with appearance and sanitation. Materials used for tabletops should be easy to clean and long-wearing.

You must also make some decisions about table size and shape. Tables must match the chairs, provide the proper height between the tabletop and the seat base (30 inches), and complement other tables in the dining area. When making your selection, keep in mind that guests are often more comfortable seated at tables with pedestals rather than legs.

Tabletop size is an important consideration because more space permits greater comfort. Frequently, a variety of shapes and sizes is useful to accommodate different group sizes and enhance your dining room's appearance. For example, a two-top table might be the same width as a four-top table. (The term "top" is used in the industry to represent a guest; a "four-top" table seats four guests.) You could then combine these two tables to accommodate six people. Of course, when you move tables in this manner, you need to ensure their stability as a single unit.

Round tables frequently have drop sides; they are square when the sides are down. You can put up the sides to accommodate large groups when necessary. If you use these tables correctly, you can frequently serve a maximum number of people in a minimal amount of space.

Dining Service Supplies for Employee Cafeterias

Should food service operations use washable or disposable dining service supplies in their employee cafeterias? While each property must answer this question based on its specific needs, consider the following:

1. Some employees may feel like "second-class citizens" if they work in a high-check-average property that uses china, glass, and silver for guests and inexpensive, disposable items for staff. Morale problems may result.

2. If you use washable items for your employees, select inexpensive but durable products.

3. The same concerns and analyses of cost-effectiveness that help you select washable/disposable dining service supplies for the front of the house should also be used when you make decisions about supplies for employee dining areas.

Folding tables are essential for banquets and meeting purposes, and you can purchase them in many shapes and sizes. These tables should be movable and stackable for convenient storage. Such units often have padded tops so that you can place tablecloths directly on them. However, improper handling during setup and teardown can frequently damage these pads.

All chairs should be durable, easy to clean, and appropriate for the existing decor. If you select furniture containing any fabric, you should be aware of potential fire hazards. Some furniture is made of fabrics that burn more quickly than others; some fabrics will smolder and give off dangerous fumes. Also, some fabrics are longer wearing and resist stains better than others. Generally, when selecting chairs containing a fabric, purchasers check to see whether the fabric has been treated with a fire retardant and a stain resistant/waterproof solution. Because synthetic fabrics can cause perspiration and discomfort, properties with low turnover should not use chairs made with such fabrics.

In some cases, modern chairs are designed more for fashion than safety. For that reason, select chairs with chair backs and legs that do not stick too far out into traffic aisles. Check the angle of the chair legs to ensure that they will not trip your guests or employees. Also, select rigidly constructed chairs with bracing to prevent breakage and possible injury to your guests. These suggestions apply no matter what type of chair you select, including stackable or lightweight chairs.

While chairs with arms may be the most comfortable from the guest's perspective, they are likely to take up more space than chairs without arms. Many properties use arm chairs at round tables.

Typically, tables and chairs for banquets must withstand a great deal of wear and tear; therefore, strength and durability are central concerns when you develop purchase specifications for them.

Receiving and Storing

The process of receiving and storing dining service supplies can be summarized as follows:

1. Check incoming products against the purchase record (Exhibit 5.2). This document reminds the receiver of the commitments made at the time of purchase. If, for example, you order five dozen soup spoons of a specific brand and style at a specific price, the purchase record will help ensure that the proper quantity and quality of spoons are delivered at the agreed upon price. An actual count is essential for costly items.

2. Check incoming products against the purchase specification form (Exhibit 5.1). If you

have put quality factors in writing and given them to suppliers, you can review incoming products against these quality requirements to ensure that you receive the correct product.

3. Check incoming products against the delivery invoice. The supplier provides a delivery invoice which a representative of the food service operation must sign. Since this document is the basis for the charges from the supplier, it is important that the type and quantity of products you receive match those for which the supplier will bill the property.

4. Record, in writing, any variances between what has been received and what was ordered. Also record any errors in price. Write credit memorandums for both price corrections and unsatisfactory or damaged goods returned.

5. Remove items to secure storage areas. Dining service items which you receive should not be left unattended in general product receiving areas. Rather, they should be brought under strict storeroom control as quickly as possible to prevent employee theft, damage, or other problems.

In large food service operations, it is generally wise to split the responsibilities for product purchasing and product receiving. For example, personnel in the purchasing department can purchase the products, and personnel in the accounting department can receive and store the products. Dividing these duties reduces possibilities of employee theft.

Small food service operations may not be able to assign different personnel to purchase and receive supplies. Frequently, the owner/manager will handle both duties. Alternatively, whoever is closest to the back door may do product receiving. However, the product receiving procedures previously outlined suggest that someone with specialized training is necessary, no matter the size of the operation.

Typically, dining service supplies are purchased less frequently than food and beverage products—generally, to re-establish par inventory levels. Therefore, it may be possible, even in

the smallest facilities, to keep dining service supplies under lock and key. If so, someone with keys must always be available to receive, or at least store, the supplies. That person may be the restaurant manager. However, incoming products may be delivered when he/she is unavailable. When that happens, special precautions should be taken to help ensure that the appropriate employees are at hand.

Many food service operations use the "precious room" concept for storing expensive dining service supplies such as china, flatware, and serving dishes. This plan entails the use of a locked storage area *within* the locked storeroom to protect these items from employee theft.

Of course, you have no reason to maintain locked storage facilities unless you use key control procedures. Simply stated, only those employees with a need for storeroom keys should have access to them. At all times, the official responsible for the storage area should have the keys on his/her person. When he/she is off duty, the property should keep the keys under lock. Alternatively, some properties keep keys under lock at all times; they use a control form to keep track of *who* issues the keys at *what* time. Locks should be changed when staff members who have access to the keys leave the employ of the property. Likewise, keys should not specifically identify the locks which they open. Should unauthorized employees find such keys, they might misuse them.

Entering the quantity of incoming products into a perpetual inventory record (Exhibit 5.6) helps keep a running balance of products in stock. This plan is especially important for controlling products when you use par inventory levels. Simply put, when the inventory balance of an item reaches a predetermined order point, you purchase additional quantities. A perpetual inventory record shows the quantity of supplies actually in the inventory at any given moment. It helps determine usage rates by indicating when and how many supplies are withdrawn (issued) from the inventory.

Periodically, you must verify that the quantity of products listed is the amount actually available. A physical inventory serves a dual purpose. It verifies the perpetual inventory quantity, and you can use it to assess the inventory's value. This information is important to the balance sheet, which lists the value of the

---

Caring for Dining Service Supplies and Equipment

Dining service supplies are expensive. They also have an impact on the total dining experience of guests who visit the food and beverage operation. Therefore, you must carefully maintain these items to ensure that the quality specified at the time of purchase is still apparent at the time of service to promote guest satisfaction.

How do bent tines on forks affect the customer? What about dried-on food on spoons or stains on linens? What about chipped china, or unpolished silverware, dirty condiment containers, dusty wall hangings, or squeaky wheels on mobile serving carts?

The point is that purchasing supplies and equipment of the proper quality is only the beginning. Dining service employees must follow through with effective cleaning, maintenance, and repair procedures. Managers, using ongoing supervision techniques, must ensure that the dining service supplies and equipment consistently reflect the desired image of the property.

---

food service operation's assets, including its dining service supplies.

Issuing

Dining service supplies must be transferred from storage areas to dining areas as you need them. This process is called issuing, and you need specific control procedures to regulate the issuing activity.

Exhibit 5.7 illustrates an issue requisition which you can use during the issuing process. List items which you need for dining services on the form. Record the unit size (for example, a box of 50 candles) and the quantity (such as two boxes). Depending on the operation, the issue requisition might be completed by the restaurant manager, assistant manager, host/receptionist, or other individual. In large operations, a subordinate staff member might complete it and then would need authorization from the restaurant manager before he/she could receive the products from storage.

The issue requisition form shown in Exhibit 5.7 is a general one which other departments in the operation may also use to remove food and beverage products from storage.

You have learned that you often purchase dining service supplies to build up pre-established par inventory levels. The use of par inventory levels in dining rooms can also help you assess the quantity of supplies to issue to dining service areas. For example, it may be determined

that each shift, day, or other period requires a specific number of boxes of paper goods, sugar packets, matches, and novelties for children. The issuing plan would involve building the available supply of these products in each dining service area to the required par level. Bars use a similar system; supplies of behind-bar liquors, beers, and other products are constant, and employees use the issue process to build par inventory levels back to predetermined maximums.

Space for the storage of supplies in dining areas is generally limited. Therefore, managers must ensure that the proper quantities of dining service supplies—and no more are available in these areas. Besides wasting valuable dining space with excessive storage, dining service supplies become more susceptible to employee pilferage when they are not in central storage areas. Likewise, when larger-than-average quantities are readily available, some employees may have the attitude, "There's plenty; we can waste a little."

However, running out of necessary dining service supplies will affect service speed and subsequent guest reactions. The term **mise en place**, which literally means "put in place," applies equally well to dining service. While it is commonly used when assembling tools, preparing raw ingredients for cooking, and preparing equipment, the concept of *mise en place* is applicable when stocking areas with dining service supplies before the start of service. It is a job that should never be ignored.

Exhibit 5.6 Perpetual Inventory Record

					Par Levels			
Item: _____				Minimum			Maximum	
Specification Number: _____								
Balance Carried Forward: _____				Balance Carried Forward: _____				

Date	In	Out	Balance		Date	In	Out	Balance

Controlling Dining Service Supplies

You have learned that dining service supplies are expensive and aid in attaining your property's guest satisfaction goals. Therefore, you must properly control them and have them readily available for use during dining service times. Unlike food and beverage products which can spoil, primary control problems with dining service supplies revolve around misuse, waste, breakage, and theft. Let's take a look at each of these potential problems.

Misuse. Have you ever seen dining room employees using napkins as potholders or food service towels? Have you ever noticed properties using prepackaged condiments such as sugar envelopes to level tables? These and similar examples illustrate the fact that there are management problems in the property.

Employees should always have the necessary supplies and equipment available to them.

Exhibit 5.7 Issue Requisition Form

Date: _____		Dept.: _____		
Item	Unit Size	Quantity	Cost per Unit	Total Cost
Authorized By: _____				
Issued By: _____				

Often, creative employees improvise when they don't have the materials they need to do their work effectively. To help prevent misuse of supplies in dining areas, restaurant managers should provide proper tools, develop specific procedures, and train and supervise employees effectively.

Waste. Product waste is a second way that properties misuse dining service supplies. Giving guests handfuls of matches, throwing away unopened prepackaged condiments such as jelly or mustard, discarding washable supplies because it's easier than sorting them, and accidentally discarding silverware into garbage receptacles or folding it into dirty linen to be sent to the laundry are wasteful practices. Some employees may think that the costs of these items are so low it doesn't make a difference. Other employees simply may not care. Regardless of the reason, you cannot tolerate the waste of supplies. Training and supervision help reduce the problem. Useful techniques to reduce the waste of supplies in dining areas include developing proce-

---

Keep Service Stations Neat

Since many dining service stations are in public view, special care of these areas is necessary to give guests the impression that the food service operation is professional and well organized. An unsightly service station with spilled food and beverages and items in disarray does not support such an image. Such problems, which usually occur when the outlet is extremely busy, can be reduced by organizing and supplying the service station properly, using correct staffing levels, and training staff members to work effectively at all times. Even when they are not in public view, clean and organized work stations promote efficient work and are indicative of well-trained employees.

---

dures to improve employee attitudes, utilizing opportunities for employee motivation, and building a team of employees whose goals are compatible with those of the organization.

Breakage. Breakage of china, glassware, and other dining service supplies is a third potentially serious problem. You must train employees to properly handle those items. Proper stacking of used china on trays and clean china in storage areas or on dish carts helps reduce breakage as does proper handling of stemmed glassware and proper unloading of dishes in dishwashing areas. For example, dishwashers can set up a decoy system with dishes of each type; you can train service staff to stack similar dishes on top of these decoys to help prevent stacks of unsorted dishes that often topple and cause breakage.

Theft. Theft of dining service supplies is another potential problem. Some guests like to take home items with a logo. Some employees also like to take items from the property. Whatever the reason, the result is the same: costs of dining service supplies increase. Some food service operations implement employee package inspection programs in which management inspects all packages that employees bring into or take out of the property to help detect the theft of dining

service supplies and other items. Check with your attorney to determine whether such a procedure is legal in your area. You should also train food servers to remove empty glassware and other items when they serve a second drink or an additional course. This practice not only gives the guests more room, but it also makes dinnerware available for reuse and helps prevent theft. A number of food and beverage operators have reduced problems of theft by offering dining service supplies for sale. With this approach, guests who desire these items have an opportunity to obtain them.

Special problems with the control of supplies become especially evident in bar and lounge areas. Not only are the beverage products themselves susceptible to theft or misuse, but bar supplies, garnishes, and cash are also easily stolen. Many of the same principles discussed earlier in this chapter, including the proper stocking of bar areas, the development of specific operating procedures for subsequent staff training, and supervision to ensure that employees follow the required procedures, help minimize these potential problems. However, because of the increased possibilities of theft in bar areas, management must give special attention to these areas.

Managing Service at the Hotel Columbia
Page Ten

Lewis did not want to interfere with the interior designers as they designed each of the food and beverage outlets for the Hotel Columbia. However, he wanted functional tabletop items that would address operating as well as aesthetic concerns. He therefore decided to give the director of restaurant operations, the beverage director, and the catering director the opportunity to make suggestions about the tabletop appointments that they would like to use in their outlets. Lewis decided to make a list of specific factors that the interior designers, the three directors, and the purchasing department should consider as they made decisions about the hotel's tabletop items. He drafted the accompanying memo.

Memorandum

TO: Interior Designers, Director of Restaurant Operations, Catering Director, Beverage Director, and Purchasing Staff
FROM: Lewis Scott, Vice President for Food and Beverage
SUBJECT: Selection of tabletop items for food and beverage outlets in the Hotel Columbia

We want our tabletops to contribute to guest expectations about our food and beverage outlets. The tabletop must accurately project the level of service, the type and quality of food, and the price range which guests will encounter in the outlet. All items for the tabletop must go well together and must blend with the decor of the outlet. We want the guests to recognize instantly the amount of care that we have given to their dining experience. We want our tabletops to be interesting and creative; however, we don't want to clutter them with too many unusual things.

In order to meet these goals, a great deal of thought must go into the selection of our tabletop appointments. A definite relationship must exist between the foods and beverages we serve and the items in/on which we serve them. As we select our tabletop items, we should consider the following:

1. Everything must be practical. If we can use multi-purpose items, we should. Items must not be too delicate; they must be able to withstand reasonable handling in dishwashing, food preparation, and service station areas.
2. We must stay within our budget. We want and will pay for high-quality items, but we simply will not accept extremely expensive items. If we search long enough, I'm sure we can find what we want in the way of design and function at a reasonable price.
3. The tabletop must complement the surrounding. If we have a complex and busy dining room, we'll want a simple tabletop.
4. Some relationship must exist between the dining area and the colors of the tabletop appointments.
5. Whenever possible, something should customize our tabletops. While not every piece of china, glassware, and/or flatware needs to have our logo or emblem on it, some things should. After all, it only costs a little bit more and helps our guests realize how unique we are.
6. We must make sure that items we consider for purchase will be available for a number of years, especially if we buy items from open stock. If we buy custom-made items, we need to order enough items initially to compensate for the long lead times we may have to face when ordering additional products.
7. When selecting glassware, we need to think about:
     commercial durability,
     style and good looks,
     temperature resistance,
     breakage resistance, and
     compatibility with glassware racks used in the dishwashing area.

Memorandum, continued

8. When selecting china, we need to think about:
   stackability,
   eye appeal,
   heat retention attributes,
   durability,
   shape,
   size, and
   color.

9. We need to have some ideas about the food items we will serve. The china, glassware, and flatware patterns will be around for a long time; our menus are likely to change fairly frequently. However, we want to serve our menu items in the right manner. We will not serve an excellent, high-quality food or beverage product in the wrong serviceware or without the proper serving tray or utensil. In addition, the size of the dish or glass must fit the portion size of the food item or beverage. If we wish to use an oversized piece of serviceware as part of the presentation (for example, a large brandy snifter to serve a cordial), it shouldn't be so large that it dwarfs the portion served.

10. The napkin fold makes an impression on the guests as they are seated. While it does not need to be elaborate or complicated, the napkin fold we use should be neat and attractive. Again, we want our napkins to create the impression that we have given careful thought and consideration to every element of the dining experience we offer our guests.

11. Small flowers or plants are welcome additions to tabletops. Let's consider their use in the tabletop designs we plan.

12. Manufacturers and/or sales personnel can help us. Let's call them in, make use of their ideas, obtain samples from them, and take advantage of their expertise. Advertising brochures, magazine articles, and publicity concerning the winning contestants in trade journals and at restaurant shows are other sources of ideas for our tabletop designs.

6

Dining Service Methods and Procedures

While the food service industry offers many variations in the procedures and techniques it uses to serve food to guests, only four main styles of table service exist. They are quite different, and dining room managers should know the details about each style.

One style in the United States, appropriately named **American service** and also known as **plate service**, is very common; most commercial food service operations use variations of this method. **French** or **cart service** and **Russian** or **platter service**, while less common in the United States, are frequently used in the international hospitality industry. The fourth style, **English** or **family service**, is sometimes used for banquets, in institutional food service operations, and in clubs.

In addition to these table service styles, some properties are increasingly using buffets. Other operations give guests a choice between ordering from the menu or selecting from the buffet. Still other properties offer a special buffet only at certain times such as on weekends or holidays (e.g., Mother's Day, Easter, or Thanksgiving). In the United States, the Sunday buffet is very popular and can represent a significant percentage of a property's business. Some operations also offer buffets in banquet service. Therefore, catering and banquet service managers must understand the basics of buffet service as well as the basics of each table service style.

American or Plate Service

American or plate service is the most common style of table service found in restaurants in the United States. Generally, production employees portion food onto service plates in the kitchen. In some properties, service employees garnish the food and/or plate items such as soup, salad, and vegetables that simply need portioning. Generally, the server who takes the order is responsible for picking up the plates and delivering them to the guests' tables.

This plan has many variations. For example, some properties use runners to take food from the kitchen to a side stand so that the server can present the orders to the guests. Other properties use employees whose only job is to deliver, not take, food orders. Still other properties use a team system; one server takes the order and maximizes his/her time spent in the dining area, and a second team member delivers the order, maximizing his/her time spent in the kitchen and on food pickup duties. Managers who use runners or team server systems emphasize these advantages: food service employees can spend more time in the dining areas with the guests; food is served when it's ready—not when the food server is ready; and because food service is prompt, the employees can serve more guests in a shorter period of time. If you use one of these plans, however, you must develop very detailed order-taking procedures so that service staff unfamiliar with the guests' orders will be able to serve the food without asking, "Who gets what?"

Before looking at the details of American service, let's discuss some of the advantages and disadvantages of this service style. One important advantage is that quality rests with the chef. The policy in many properties is that the chef has sole responsibility for food quality in the kitchen as well as its presentation and quality in dining areas. American service easily accommodates the policy that production employees must prepare and portion food products totally under the chef's direction. A second advantage to American service is that food presentation is consistent because the chef and one or more production employees control the plating of food. A further advantage of American service is the prompt service which it permits. While it is never proper to rush guests, those who desire fast service in a dining room outlet are more likely to receive it with American service than with the other service styles. American service also does not require servers with as much experience and training or as many skills as other service styles do. Finally, this service style has low equipment costs since it does not require elaborate serving trays, carts, or other expensive dining room equipment.

However, American service does have disadvantages. For example, the dining activity loses some of the flair and elegance that other service styles offer. Also, except when menus state that different portion sizes are available, American service makes it difficult to modify portions to meet the specific desires of the guest.

With American service, the rule of plating the food in the kitchen is sometimes broken for the sake of convenience or speed or to provide a marketing tool for the property. For example, servers might present small loaves of bread, a bread board, and a bread knife to guests so that they may cut slices for themselves, or guests might select their desserts from a trolley and the server then plates them in full view of the guests.

In addition to plate service, some American service dining rooms also offer tableside food preparation or soup and salad bars from which guests help themselves. Frequently, restaurant managers discover that they must combine elements of several different table service styles in order to fit the specific needs of their properties and the guests they serve.

A well-designed, well-stocked service station for food servers is an absolute must for American service. (See Exhibit 6.1.) The dining area must be designed so that service employees have convenient access to the service stations. At the same time, these stations should not offend guests seated near them—there should be no excessive noise, unattractiveness, and/or traffic jams caused by service personnel. When possible, use partitions or other devices to keep service stations out of your guests' view.

When an outlet offers American service, tables are usually already set before the guests arrive with all but the plates required for each course. Bread and butter plates, water and wine glasses, napkins and flatware, and other items are often already on the table. Some properties, especially high-check-average and gourmet food service operations, also use a **show plate** which is already on the table before guests are seated. Often ornately designed with the property's logo and/or made of fine china, pewter, or other attractive material, this plate enhances the table presentation when guests first arrive at the table.

Normally, products which either production or service personnel have portioned are placed on food service trays for delivery to the dining area. Most properties use plate covers to

Exhibit 6.1 A Well-Stocked Service Station

Amway Grand Plaza Hotel, Grand Rapids, Michigan

keep food products warm and to facilitate the stacking of plates. Upon reaching the dining area, food servers place the trays on food service stands, remove the plate covers, and then serve the guests. In some properties, service rules dictate that guests are served all food items from the left and beverage items from the right. In other properties, guests are served everything from the right. In still other properties, especially those that have booths, the rule is "serve with the least inconvenience to the guests." After the guest is finished eating, the server typically removes everything from the right.

Servers generally wait on several tables simultaneously. The actual number depends upon how much experience the servers have, the distance from their service stations to the food pickup area, the menu itself, and the number of guests which can be seated at the tables in their stations. (Generally, it is easier to wait on three 4-top tables than six 2-top tables even though both sections seat 12 guests.) Many other factors also determine the number of guests that one food server can handle. For example, food servers in this style of service who are also responsible for some tableside food preparation cannot wait on the same number of guests as servers without these responsibilities. Other factors, such as whether or not the food server must serve drinks

or a food service attendant (busperson) is available to help with table clearing and setup, also affect the number of guests which a single food server can accommodate. In some operations, special beverage servers (e.g., sommelier or wine steward, cocktail server) provide drinks for guests in the dining room.

When a property offers American service, food servers normally clear the emptied plates and the used flatware from each course before they serve the next course—unless the guest prefers otherwise. For example, if a guest has soup or salad as a first course, the service employee should remove the dishes and soup spoons or salad forks before serving the entree. These procedures are not only common sense from the guest's perspective, but they also reduce the need for a large inventory of dishes because soiled dishes can be cleaned and put back into service more quickly. These procedures also help minimize the chance that guests will take home as souvenirs such items as flatware engraved with the property's logo.

French or Cart Service

In the United States, the term **French service** describes the dining service style by which meals are prepared at tableside by service employees using service carts. Thus, this service is also known as **tableside** or **cart service**. In France, incidentally, this service is known as Russian service. Relatively few restaurants or hotel food and beverage operations use French service; those that do are generally gourmet and high-check-average dining outlets. Properties considering using this high-priced and labor-intensive service need to undertake detailed feasibility studies to confirm the existence of a clientele sophisticated enough to support it.

French service costs are high for several reasons. First, enough dining room space is needed to provide for the wide aisles required to move preparation carts to tables. One writer estimates that compared with a similar sized, 150-seat restaurant not using cart service, a property using French service needs an additional 450 square feet of dining space.[1]

[1] Raymond J. Goodman, *The Management of Service for the Restaurant Manager* (Dubuque, Iowa: Brown, 1979), p. 62.

Matching Guests with Their Orders

In order to remember which guest ordered which items, some servers use a focal point technique that identifies all guests in relationship to some point in the dining room, such as the main entrance, a fireplace, a specific picture on the wall, or a service station. Then, regardless of the sequence in which the guests order, food servers are able to write the order on the guest check in such a way that they can easily recall "who gets what" when they deliver the order.

One method used in server training sessions by experienced managers is to have servers mentally identify one seat at every table as number 1; then, all other seats are numbered sequentially counterclockwise. When the server takes first course orders, for example, he/she would begin with the woman closest to the number 1 seat. In our example, she is in seat number 2. If she orders the chef's pate, the server would write down "pate 2." If the person in seat 3 also orders pate, the server needs only to add "3" to the pate listing. When the person in seat 4 orders shrimp cocktail, the server would similarly write "shrimp cocktail" (or an approved abbreviation) on the order form, followed by "4." Finally, when the man in seat number 1 orders pate, the server simply adds "1" to the other two pate orders. With this simple and time-saving system, the server always knows who ordered what dish or beverage. If a "runner" system is used, that individual would also have no difficulty knowing who should be served which order.

In addition to the costs of providing extra space, higher capital costs are incurred because of the extensive amount of serving and preparation equipment required. Typically, serviceware for French service is very elegant; ornate serving pieces such as silver platters are often used. Operating costs are also higher; a large number of staff members are required to serve a few guests, and table turnover is much slower than in other service styles. In order to generate enough income to cover labor and other costs, food and beverage prices in operations using French service must reflect those costs.

In addition to high costs, it is difficult to find professionally trained service employees who understand and can follow all the procedures required for effective tableside food preparation; a maitre d' hotel who know the intricacies of French service is required to supervise the dining room, seat guests, and perform other duties.

French dining service typically makes use of a **sommelier**. In some facilities, this individual not only helps guests select wines, serves them their wines, and resolves any operating/serving problems, but he/she may also manage the wine inventory, make purchasing decisions, and provide wine-related training for the dining service staff.

In a very large and busy dining room, it may be difficult for one sommelier to approach each table to suggest, sell, and serve wine. In this instance, the property may use a head wine server with a staff of several assistants. There is also a growing trend toward training all service employees in the essentials of wine and its service so that they can perform this task. However, traditional French service restaurants continue to use sommeliers and adhere to the many rituals of wine service. (Chapter 14 has a detailed discussion of wine service.)

At least two food service staff members are needed in each dining station: the **chef de rang** and the **commis de rang**. The chef de rang is generally responsible for taking orders, serving drinks, preparing food at the table, and collecting the sales income. He/she must be very experienced and versatile. In the absence of a sommelier, he/she may serve dinner wines. Normally, production personnel partially prepare the food in the kitchen; then the chef de rang finishes it at tableside. He/she must be able to cook or flame a wide variety of menu items at tableside, carve meat, and bone fish and poultry. The chef de rang also knows how to use a fork and spoon to transfer prepared food to plates and knows how to garnish food effectively.

The commis de rang assists the chef de rang. He/she is responsible for taking food orders to the kitchen, placing the orders, picking up food in the kitchen, and bringing it to the tableside

Setting the Table in American Service

Professional dining room managers recognize that attractive tabletop appointments can complement the decor and carry through the theme of the outlet. They plan every detail of the tabletops carefully, whether it is an attractive napkin fold or unusually shaped glassware. They select decorations, including flowers, candles, or other centerpieces, with the guests' pleasure in mind.

Many properties consider the marketing and suggestive selling possibilities of table settings. For example, some operations place wine glasses on the table to suggest that guests order wine and/or in anticipation of their wine orders. Table tents (colorful advertising messages printed on heavy paper, folded, and placed on the table in an inverted "V" shape) are also examples. Other facilities have messages or "The Chef's Suggestions" printed on their placemats.

Professional restaurant managers realize how necessary it is to set the tables in their outlets properly. They develop procedures to ensure that the table settings will enhance guests' dining experiences. They make the appropriate dining service supplies available to their servers, and train them not only to use proper table setting procedures but also to make a last-minute check of each tabletop in their station before guests arrive.

Attractive tabletop settings must be carefully planned to ensure that they consistently and appropriately represent your food service operation to the guest. In some properties, when the tables are cleaned and reset after one set of guests leaves, receptionists are required to check them carefully to ensure nothing is out of order before the next set of guests is seated.

While properties will vary in the details of setting the table for plate service, generally the standard cover is as follows: the napkin is folded and placed in the center of the cover, the fork is to the left of the napkin (tines up), and the knife to the right with blade facing in. Often dining room attendants are instructed to place cutlery a specific distance from the edge of the table (such as an inch). Such a standard procedure helps guests avoid knocking cutlery off the table when they are seated. The water glass or all-purpose wine glass is set above the tip of the knife or slightly to the right. When there is a cup, it is to the right of the knife. Whenever there is a pattern on the china, servers must make certain the pattern never appears upside down to guests.

cart, often on silver trays. Since the chef de rang is busy with preparation duties, the commis de rang also delivers drink orders and serves food to the guests.

French service requires a cart or **gueridon** which holds a portable heating unit (**rechaud**).[2] To serve soup, for instance, the server brings it into the dining room in a service bowl and places it on the cart's rechaud unit. He/she then places an empty, hot soup bowl on an underliner. The chef de rang portions the item, and the commis de rang serves it.

Many special and detailed rules of courtesy, etiquette, and tradition are also components of traditional French service; however, they go be-yond the scope of this book.[3] From management's perspective, it is important to understand that the spin-off effects of French service are vast. For example, the use of French service changes the configuration of the food preparation area; production personnel do not handle plates, and food is finished at the table. Since it requires specialized service employees, they normally cannot be used for other purposes. Furthermore, the guests who desire and pay for French service won't accept mistakes. This service style also must fit the environment; it is not possible to implement French service in an inadequately planned dining room. The furniture, fixtures, and equipment in the room must be compatible with the elegant service style offered.

2   See Joseph F. Durocher and Raymond J. Goodman, Jr., *The Essentials of Tableside Cookery* (Ithaca, N.Y.: School of Hotel Administration, Cornell University, 1979).

3   Readers interested in detailed information about French service are referred to *The Essentials of Good Table Service* (Ithaca, N.Y.: School of Hotel Administration, Cornell University, 1971), pp. 20-25.

Table set with fine linen, silverware, and china for serving dessert and coffee. Guests will long remember dining in such pleasant surroundings. Note the underliner beneath the dessert plate and the variety of accessory pieces. (Courtesy of Mayer China)

Some hotels have found it profitable to lease space to an independent operator for a French service restaurant because of the large number of special problems associated with this exacting/demanding style of service.

Russian or Platter Service

Russian or **platter service** is another basic serving style. It is popular in many of the best international restaurants and hotels, and some food service operations in the United States, particularly banquet operations, also use it. In France, this service is known as French service or silver service.

When Russian service is offered, the food production employees generally prepare, and if necessary, precut food in the kitchen. They then arrange it attractively on service platters which food servers deliver to the dining room. Generally, service employees use a team approach; one server carries the entree, and a second carries the vegetables. They line up in the kitchen and, at the appropriate time, parade into the dining area. After presenting (showing) the food to the

guests, they place the platters on waiter side stands to keep foods warm while they position a very hot, empty dinner plate in front of each guest. The platter is held in the server's left hand while he/she transfers the food to the plates by manipulating a fork and spoon held in the right hand. Service employees have an important duty to ensure that the platter retains its attractiveness until the last guest is served. When guests in dining rooms that use platter service order soup, one way in which they are served is as follows: the server places a hot soup bowl on an underliner and positions it in front of the guest. The server brings to the table a service bowl of soup, which is then ladled into the soup bowl.

How much food should servers provide to the guests? Typically, they can use their own discretion and provide the guest with an amount which they judge sufficient. Of course, it is important to ensure that the last guest served receives an adequate portion. In many properties the servers pass items twice; any food remaining on the platter must be discarded.

Russian service can be as elegant as traditional French service, but it is much more practical because it is faster and less expensive. Rus-

One table-setting style used in an elegant dining room. (Courtesy of Libbey Glass)

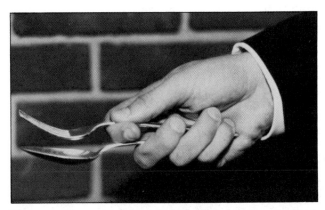

The correct manipulation of fork and spoon—used primarily in French and Russian service. (Kellogg Center, Michigan State University)

sian service can provide a special touch and still allow the manager to control labor and product costs closely.

The restaurant manager considering the use of Russian service should recognize the need for an initial capital investment in service platters. Because service problems can result when guests order a wide variety of items, food servers may need to bring several different platters to the table concurrently. For this reason, some properties use Russian service only at banquets because all the guests receive the same menu items.

Service Rules Make the Difference

Many traditions have become part of the French and Russian service styles. For example, in French service the food server nearly always serves the plate with the right hand to the guest's right side. The only exceptions occur when the server is left-handed and when there are side plates such as those for bread and butter or salad, which are placed to the left of the guest.[4] In Russian service, the food server holds the serving platter in the left hand at the guest's left side so that he/she can transfer the food with fork and spoon held in the right hand. Service in this way proceeds around the table counterclockwise.

These and other rules are used because they are easy for the server and convenient for the guests. They illustrate a basic management prin-

ciple emphasized throughout this text: restaurant managers must first decide exactly what procedures their properties will use. They must then provide their service employees with the necessary equipment and supplies to implement the procedures and train their service employees to use the correct procedures consistently.

When French and Russian service styles are used, highly skilled and experienced service staff are needed. Since food servers in Europe must complete a three-year apprenticeship, it is highly unlikely that inexperienced personnel can be quickly trained to use difficult serving procedures. Rather, service employees need formal training in a culinary school and many years of experience before they can comply with the procedures dictated by almost 200 years of tradition.

English or Family Service

English service, also known as **family-** or **butler-style service**, is the fourth type of dining service. The primary characteristic of English service is that servers bring all food to the table on serving platters or in serving bowls. They present the food to the host guest, who then passes it "family-style" around the table; guests help themselves to the amount that they desire.

This service style is relatively easy to implement, for service employees do not need to be highly skilled. In fact, they generally put more effort into clearing tables than presenting and serving the food. In effect, each of the disadvantages of French service can be countered with the advantages of English service. English service requires relatively little dining room space and special equipment (except serving platters); service time and table turnover can also be rapid. Additionally, exceptionally high prices need not be the norm since there are reduced equipment and labor costs.

One possible disadvantage of English service is that it is difficult to implement portion-control procedures. If, however, the initial amount of food employees place on the platter is relatively generous, and the selling price of the menu item is based on this amount, a direct relationship will exist between the amount of food presented to the table and its established selling price.

The homelike atmosphere of English service

---

[4] *The Essentials of Good Table Service*, pp. 20-25.

A buffet at the Hotel du Pont, Wilmington, Delaware, that is as appealing to the eye as to the palate.

could possibly become a major disadvantage if guests don't feel that they are receiving special attention. If guests are especially seeking a great deal of contact with dining room personnel in their dining experience, they may not find English service acceptable.

Buffet Service

In properties that offer buffets, food is displayed on counters or tables and guests help themselves to as many of the items as they wish to eat. Some buffets feature steamship rounds of beef, large hams, and other roasts which servers carve as guests request a portion. Such items as crepes and omelets are sometimes made to order by the kitchen staff. Buffets can range from a simple offering of several food items to elaborate presentations that appeal to guests with sophisticated, gourmet tastes. Buffets have obvious marketing implications; when food items are attractively displayed, the products will sell themselves.

When is buffet service useful? It depends on the desires of the guest. However, some properties use buffets to provide service and a great variety of foods to a large number of guests within a relatively short period of time. In addition, a buffet allows guests to obtain food at their leisure and in the quantities they desire. Prospective banquet clients should be informed about the potential advantages of buffet service because, for many occasions, buffets are an excellent alternative to table service.

Planning the layout for a buffet requires special attention to the number of guests expected, the size and shape of the room, and the amount of time available for service. As a rule of thumb, some managers plan that 75 guests are the maximum number that one buffet line in a banquet setting can serve; an event for 150 guests would therefore require two buffet lines.

Several potential difficulties must be considered when planning buffets. For instance, the overall cost of buffet service can be high. The proper service equipment (e.g., serviceware, centerpieces, food presentation trays), which is relatively expensive, must be available in adequate quantities in order for service to flow smoothly. Carpet wear can also be a problem (and an expense) when large numbers of guests frequently travel through the same area of a room. Odors and grease can also soil furnishings. (This is especially true for buffets that feature some cooking on the line.)

Buffet service requires a system to maintain cleanliness and order. Service employees must consistently keep containers full, quickly attend to food spills on and around the buffet line, properly attend to the tables in the dining areas, and efficiently remove soiled serviceware from the room.

Dining tables in operations that use buffet service must receive special attention. The manager must select appropriate centerpieces, for instance, and make decisions regarding such services as the following:

- Will tables be set with flatware and napkins or will guests pick up these items on the buffet line?

- Will crackers, breads, or other items be placed on the tables so that guests who do not go through the buffet line immediately will have some food items available to them?

- What provisions, if any, should be made for guests who do not want to go through a buffet line or, for some physical or other reason, cannot?

Some properties use a scramble type of buffet system. The term **scramble system** was first used to describe cafeteria line operations in which guests go to separate stations rather than wait in a single line. For example, hot foods are at one station, beverages at another, and desserts and salads are in additional areas. Using this plan for buffets, cold foods could be placed on one buffet table, hot foods on a second, and foods prepared to order on a third. This system allows guests to limit their trips through the buffet line to those areas where self-service is fastest. While requiring more setup space than other buffet service styles, the scramble system does yield faster service since it lessens bottlenecks. If you do select the scramble system and set up several service stations offering different food items around the room, you may need to give guests special instructions so they will know how to find everything they would like to have.

There are many popular layouts for buffet service that can be used in place of the traditional straight-line shape; however, when you set up buffet lines, you must address the issue of guest flow. See Exhibit 6.2 for some illustrations of popular buffet arrangements.

As buffet lines are developed, effective presentation of foods should receive a great deal of attention. For instance, an ice or tallow (fat) sculpture, fresh flowers, or edible vegetable or fruit centerpieces can be attractive focal points. Decorative service platters or bowls may enhance many presentations. Because almost any

Exhibit 6.2 Some Popular Buffet Arrangements

Photos courtesy of The Greenbrier, White Sulphur Springs, West Virginia

Sanitation and Buffet Service

A basic rule of sanitation is to "keep hot foods hot, cold foods cold, or don't keep foods at all." Sanitation problems can arise in buffet service when potentially hazardous foods—particularly those of animal origin or that contain large amounts of foods of animal origin such as milk, milk products, eggs, meat, poultry, fish, and shellfish—are not maintained at the correct temperatures. Hot foods should be kept at temperatures above 140°F (60°C); cold foods should be kept below 45°F (7°C).

Special serving equipment should be used to keep hot foods hot. Ice may be necessary to keep foods chilled. In other cases, servers will bring only small quantities of food to the buffet line to be served quickly and replenished. Establishments that offer buffet service must comply with all applicable laws and ordinances, including the provision of sneeze-guards. (**Sneeze-guards** are protective panels that prevent guests from breathing, sneezing, or coughing on foods while going through the buffet line.)

food item is more appealing when decorated with such items as radish roses, accordion pickles, carrot curls, or turnip lilies, close attention to placement of garnishes is necessary.[5]

The manager must constantly keep in mind the fact that efforts to create an attractive buffet are often defeated when the buffet is left unattended during service. Spills, almost-empty food pans, and unsightly, burned food left in hot chafing dishes can easily ruin a buffet's visual appeal.

Typically, the chef plans the buffet menu since his/her responsibility for the food extends into the dining area.[6] However, concerns such as the placement of the buffet, the control of guests as they pass through the buffet line, and related front-of-house details are generally the responsibility of the dining room manager.

When an outlet offers a buffet every day, fewer service staff members are usually required than when buffets are offered only once a week or less often. Because the work of servers in such an outlet is limited, service labor costs may be lower. (Servers typically just remove soiled dishes, reset tables, provide beverage service, and perform related tasks.) Also, since food can be produced over a longer period of time, and items do not need to be portioned, production labor costs may be reduced. However, additional

kitchen employees may be required to prepare such items as centerpieces and the large quantities and varieties of buffet food.

The required serviceware must be constantly available during the buffet period. When plates are not available or when serving utensils have been dropped into food products, guests have a right to complain. Who would want to place chilled foods on hot plates that have just come from the dishwashing machine? These and related examples help illustrate why food service staff need to pay constant attention to buffet lines to ensure that they meet the quality standards of the property.

Many buffets have themes that are suggested by holidays and other special occasions. When managers plan buffets for special groups or want to emphasize special foods, they may select a theme that provides consistency among the elements of food, service, and atmosphere. For instance, a group's logo or insignia could be used as a unifying theme for their buffet. When emphasizing certain foods, the highlighted foods can themselves serve as the unifying feature.

Typically, foods are placed in the following order: salads and other chilled meal accompaniments, hot vegetables, meats, poultry, fish, and other hot entrees. Such items as sauces, dressings, and relishes should be placed close to the menu item which they accompany.

Many variables affect the speed of buffet serving lines. Among them are the variety of available menu items, whether or not items are prepared to order, and even the beauty of the buffet presentations. (Guests may pass through

---

[5] Interested readers are referred to Frederic H. Sonnenschmidt and Jean F. Nicolas, *The Art of Garde Manger* (Boston: CBI, 1982).

[6] See George K. Waldner and Klaus Mitterhauser, *The Professional Chef's Book of Buffets* (Boston: CBI, 1971).

Safety and Buffet Service

Dining room managers must be concerned about safety when they plan and execute buffets. Potential safety hazards include lighted candles which may drip wax, hot water baths which may splash, heat lamps which may burn, and sharp knives which may cut. Because guests' attention is focused on carrying food to their tables, they may trip on unprotected electric cords used to provide power to serving equipment or improperly maintained carpeting or other floor coverings. Buffet tables can collapse if they are overloaded or if the weight is distributed poorly on them. Ice carvings can drip onto the floor. Liquid fuels used to keep foods hot can burn table coverings and people. Guests and employees can be burned during the transportation of hot food to the buffet tables.

The list of potential safety problems is endless. However, the point is simple: safety must come first. The dining room manager must practice safety management, and the buffet must meet safety requirements while satisfying the guests.

---

lines slowly to maximize their view of center-pieces and other items of visual appeal.) Therefore, it is difficult to develop statistics about the average serving line speed. One's own experience in a specific property eventually becomes the best guide for deciding the shape, length, and number of buffet lines required to accommodate a specific number of guests.

Buffets generally have a higher food cost percentage (cost of food divided by sales income) than banquets or food outlets using the traditional American service plan. However, if buffets are popular, their contribution margins (total income minus total food costs) can be higher than those of other service styles.

It is obviously important to consider the buffet's selling price when menu items are selected. When it is desirable to keep the selling price low, low-cost entrees that incorporate such items as ground beef and poultry can be used. In contrast, roast beef, leg of lamb, shrimp, and other seafoods can be offered as the selling price warrants. Professional dining room managers realize that low-cost buffets need not look inexpensive; the presentation and layout of a buffet have a great deal to do with its success.

Salesmanship in the Dining Room

In some dining outlets, the job of the food server is not only to serve the food and beverage products that guests desire but also to take an active role in helping guests make their selections. In these outlets, food servers do more than ask, "What do you want?" and then provide it; they are also salespeople. Most guests appreciate information, suggestions, and polite assistance. Let's see what salesmanship means in the dining room.

Know What You Want to Sell

Many guests know which food and beverage products they wish to order. Some guests go to a specific dining outlet just so they can enjoy their favorites. Many others, however, have not made up their minds before they arrive. They want to look at the menu, and they often appreciate suggestions and comments from the service staff.

What items does the food service operation want to sell? Generally, dining room managers are not directly responsible for establishing the selling prices of menu items. The food and beverage director, working in conjunction with the chef, typically performs that task. However, because dining room managers are responsible for profitability, they should realize that some food items are more profitable than others.

One way to view profitability is in terms of the food item's contribution margin, which is the difference between the item's selling price and the cost of its ingredients. If, for example, you sell a steak dinner for $12.00, and the ingredients cost $5.50, the contribution margin is $6.50

($12.00 income - $5.50 food cost = $6.50 contribution margin). If managers know the contribution margin of each item, and they should, they then can develop strategies to sell the items that are the most profitable. A system of menu analysis called **menu engineering** determines which menu items are both profitable and popular.[7]

Food service professionals refer to the term **suggestive selling** when they discuss procedures designed to influence the guest's purchasing decisions. They are quick to point out, though, that guests should be served the items they desire. Suggestive selling is used only to help guests who are uncertain about their preferences.

How does suggestive selling work? Perhaps it starts with the advertisement in the newspaper which says, "Come in and try our specialty." Suggestive selling continues when the guest enters the property and sees a menu board or other device which promotes the product's sale. Table tents or other table decorations, pictures, displays, and buttons or banners on the uniforms of service personnel can all have a subtle effect on guests.

Suggestive selling continues with the design of the menu itself. (See Chapter 3 for a discussion of an item's location on a menu and its impact on the frequency of sale.) The way in which the food server takes the order can also influence sales. Such comments as "Everything here is delicious, but the chef says the canard bigarade is especially good tonight," or, "I really recommend the duckling a l'orange," can help guests make up their minds and, at the same time, help the property sell the most desirable items. Obviously, servers must assess their guests carefully, and if it appears that guests would be annoyed by a server trying to sell them something they don't want, the server would change the tenor of his/her recommendations, or in some cases, make none at all.

Suggestive selling can also be used for items other than entrees. The manner in which the food server suggests before-dinner drinks,

---

[7] Readers interested in detailed information about determining the popularity and profitability of menu items are referred to Michael Kasavana and Don Smith, *Menu Engineering* (East Lansing, Mich.: Hospitality Publications, 1982).

wines, desserts, and after-dinner drinks can affect the sale of all these items.

Presentation also affects sales. Many guests will notice the sizzling steaks, flaming shish kebab, beautifully presented baked Alaska, or seven-liqueur "rainbow" after-dinner drinks served at another table and will wish to try these products, too.

Perhaps the food service outlet is offering a new product. Free samples brought to the table with an accompanying commentary by the server may help sell a full portion of the item on the first visit or help guests recall and order the item during their next visit. (The accompanying commentary is also valuable to forestall guests' anxiety; they should know without question that they will not be charged for something that they did not order.)

Wine sales certainly lend themselves to suggestive selling. Even though wine consumption is increasing in the United States and many people are familiar with the "art and science" of tasting and enjoying wine, some guests are still intimidated by wines and their service. Offering complimentary samples, perhaps at a wine tasting bar or by means of a mobile wine cart, can help sell wines. Suggesting specific wines with the dinner, either by listing them on the menu or having food servers mention them as they take the food orders, is another helpful technique.

Some managers train their food servers never to ask questions which can be answered "No." For example, "Would you like dessert?" may yield a negative response from the guest. In contrast, the question "Our apple turnovers, napoleons, and eclairs are all homemade; which would you prefer?" is more likely to produce a dessert sale. Food servers should be aware, however, that this latter approach may annoy some guests. Making guests feel "cheap" in front of their companions may yield a sale during their initial visit, but certainly reduces the likelihood of repeat business.

Radiation Advertising

How does a food and beverage operation advertise? Many people believe that the best approach is to develop a budget and allocate funds to the external media (newspaper, radio, television, etc.).

However, **radiation advertising** is also very

useful. In addition to involving management officials concerned with marketing, it has a direct impact on the dining room manager and the service strategies used in the dining areas. The concept of radiation advertising suggests that a specific part of the advertising budget should be spent in-house. For example, you could give guests with reservations some unexpected extra such as matchbooks with the property's logo and their own last names on them, or everyone could receive opera mints when presented with the bill. These extras cost relatively little but can produce a great deal of goodwill. When you use radiation advertising, your guests are likely to leave your property happy; they will tell others with whom they come in contact about the property, and new business—probably repeat business—can result.

A team composed of the sales manager, chef, food and beverage manager, and dining room manager should make the decisions regarding radiation advertising. These administrators can develop the who, what, why, and how aspects of procedures which provide the unexpected extras to guests. They then must train service employees to use these procedures properly. Finally, dining room managers themselves should help evaluate the effectiveness of this type of advertising campaign.

Managing Service at the Hotel Columbia
Page Twelve

Lewis Scott and Don Jackson, the director of restaurant operations, were discussing the important role that the food and beverage operation would play in representing the property to the guests. They agreed that it was important that the service styles and procedures used in the various food and beverage outlets feature salesmanship where appropriate, elegance where required, and always a special concern for meeting the wants and needs of the guests visiting the property.

"Well," Don said, "the service style that is appropriate for La Terrasse, our gourmet French restaurant, is cart service combined with platter service for such items as the accompanying vegetables. It is an expensive service style; it requires a very well-trained food service staff, a wide array of costly service utensils and equipment, and wide aisle spaces to accommodate the gueridons. Of course, that will reduce the number of tables that we can place in the restaurant as well as the number of guests we can serve. We will need to compensate for that by charging a high price for the meals in that restaurant. Our feasibility studies suggest that our potential guests recognize high quality products, service, environment, and dining experiences and are willing to pay a high price for them."

Lewis readily agreed, for he had expected the gourmet restaurant to feature this service. He was more interested in learning some of the details of the service styles planned for the other outlets.

Don suggested that plate service be used in the Eagle Room, modified as necessary to accommodate the menu items being served. The kitchen staff would prepare and plate most of the food items for service by the servers. However, a wide array of exceptions would contribute to a unique dining experience for the guests. For example, the dining room would feature self-service stations for soup and salad ingredients during lunch and salad and dessert items at dinner.

They both knew that space would be available in the dining area to set up a buffet line for special occasions or for a Sunday brunch, if desired. The buffet station could also offer breakfast items, if necessary. "The design of the Eagle Room offers flexibility so that space is available for whatever menu, service plan, or special catered event is desired," Lewis commented.

Initial plans called for the property's banquets to feature either plate or platter service. The property would advise potential clients that the latter service provided something special. Lewis felt that the payback period for the service trays and related items that platter service requires would be relatively short, especially since the Hotel Columbia's catering staff would emphasize the high quality of service which the property could provide for special occasions.

Butler service would be available from room service as well as for small catered events in hospitality suites. Both Don and Lewis believed that the guests of the hotel would indeed be special and, therefore, alternative service styles that recognized the property's desire to give the guests high priority were in order.

The coffee shop would use traditional counter service and modified American service at the tables and booths. The take-out deli, located near the coffee shop, would have a special take-out counter. (A special menu of take-out items that lend themselves to almost instant delivery would be available to speed service in this area.)

The Hotel Columbia's employee eating area would have a cafeteria line. To set up the cafeteria line, Don would follow procedures similar to those used to establish and maintain the buffet service lines in the public areas. Vending machines would also be available for employee use. In addition, food vending machines would be located in several places on each of the guest floors—most likely where the ice and soft drink machines were located.

"Well," said Lewis, "it appears that the Hotel Columbia will have a wide array of food service operations and service styles available to meet the needs of a wide range of guests. I'm glad because, as you know, our motto is to do everything we reasonably can to meet the needs of our guests. I think our dining operations will do just that."

"Yes," Don agreed. "Running our dining operations will be a big job. However, it is also going to be very exciting. It will require the very best management, production, and service staff to consistently provide quality service. I'm sure, however, that our initial planning will yield dining operations in which we can take pride and that will satisfy our guests."

7

Controlling Service Labor Costs

Control activities are an essential part of the dining service manager's job. Controlling service labor costs begins when the manager establishes performance standards and continues when he/she assesses the actual number of work hours and/or labor dollars spent. It concludes when the manager makes comparisons, takes necessary corrective actions, and then evaluates the success of those corrective actions.

How do you begin to control labor costs? You begin by assessing your standard labor requirements (the number of labor hours or dollars required if nothing goes wrong). The labor standards which you use must reflect your property's quality requirements. For example, you could decrease service labor costs if you assign more tables to one food server; however, is the cost savings acceptable if the quality of service to the guest decreases?

Establishing Performance Standards

Management should determine exactly what tasks service employees must perform and exactly how they should do them. Dining outlet managers must work with the food and beverage director, the chef and production staff, and other personnel as they establish minimum quality levels. Managers must then build those quality requirements into the property's standard operating procedures which specify how employees will perform tasks in the operation.

All work should have a standard against which actual performance can be measured. Many times the manager knows how long it should take to perform a particular job in a manner which meets the property's existing quality standards. In this case, it is only necessary to formalize the knowledge by putting it in writing. However, in many operations the restaurant manager does not have that knowledge. Perhaps no one has analyzed the job recently, or perhaps management has changed the work procedures since the last analysis.

Exhibit 7.1 demonstrates how you can develop a performance standard that incorporates quality requirements. Let's assume that the restaurant manager, working with the receptionist and other selected front-of-house personnel, has defined expected levels of quality for service to guests in the dining room at lunch. For example, they have established the tasks which buspersons and food servers will perform. They have also outlined a sequence of activities (greeting the guests, approaching the table, providing beverages, salad, entree, and dessert, and more), and they have established all other aspects of the property's quality requirements. They then set up an observation period during which they instruct the employees to follow all policies and procedures. They supervise the staff during this time period and assess job performance by closely observing a better-than-average food server. The supervisor can then answer questions such as the following:

Managing Service at the Hotel Columbia
Page Thirteen

Lewis Scott knew that he needed to ask the rooms department manager for her forecasts concerning the Hotel Columbia's occupancy rates. Although many people within the Hotel Columbia would need this information, Lewis was well aware that the food and beverage department would rely heavily on accurate occupancy forecasts to schedule production and service staff.

"Certainly," he thought, "it will take awhile before our occupancy forecasts become meaningful indicators of anticipated food and beverage activity in the hotel's dining outlets. Over time, however, this information will help us meet our service labor performance standards. Similarly, occupancy forecasts will help us control labor costs by developing meaningful personnel schedules."

Lewis planned to train his restaurant managers to use scheduling procedures that would meet the needs of the guests, the hotel, and the service staff. He recalled a very useful training aid that he had used in other properties and asked his secretary for a copy of it.

1. Is the server providing the required level of service?

2. Does the server seem rushed or overworked?

3. Could the server do more work and still maintain the required quality standards?

4. How many guests are served during the shift?

5. How many more guests could be served, or how many fewer guests should be served in order to meet performance standards?

6. How long should it take for a new employee to perform at the same skill level as an experienced employee?

After close analysis of several servers during several shifts, it will be possible for you to determine a labor performance standard for the food service position. Since menus and service styles may change between meal periods and may require different tasks, you should complete position performance analysis forms for each position during each shift. You should also draft these forms for positions in each food service outlet because the work responsibilities for the same position in different types of dining outlets will vary.

In Exhibit 7.1 the manager observed the food server over five lunch shifts. For each shift the manager recorded the number of guests served and hours worked, then calculated the number of guests served per labor hour. For example, 38 guests were served during a four-hour work period on April 14. That means 9.5 guests were served per labor hour (38 guests divided by 4 hours = 9.5 guests served per labor hour).

You can make a similar position performance analysis for other service-related positions and develop performance standards for all positions under your supervision. After you define your quality standards and incorporate them into performance standards, you will be able to develop an effective staff planning program to help control labor costs.

Incorporating Fixed Labor Requirements

Labor Staffing Guide

A labor staffing guide matches the number of guests you plan to serve with the number of labor hours you need to provide your property's required levels of product and service quality.

Fixed Versus Variable Labor

Before you can develop staffing guides, you must understand the difference between fixed

Exhibit 7.1 Position Performance Analysis Form

Position Performance Analysis

Position: _____Service_____   Name of Employee _____Joyce_____

Shift: _____AM—Lunch_____

	4/14	4/15	4/16	4/17	4/18
No. of Guests Served	38	60	25	45	50
No. Hours Worked	4	4	4	4	3.5
No. of Guests/Labor Hour	9.5	15	6.3	11.3	14.3
Review Comments	Even Workflow; no problems	Was really rushed; could not provide adequate service	Too much "standing around"; very inefficient	No problems; handled everything well	Worked fast whole shift; better with fewer guests

General comments

Joyce is a better than average server; with all the tasks that service personnel must do in our restaurant, approximately 10 guests per labor hour can be served by one server. When the number of guests goes up, service quality decreases. When Joyce really had to rush, some guests waited longer than they desired. When the number of guests several per labor hour dropped and Joyce was not busy, there was a lot of unproductive time.

Suggested Meals/Labor Hours
(for this position): _____10_____

Performance Review by: _____W. Brown_____
Restaurant Manager

Adapted from Jack D. Ninemeier, *Planning and Control for Food and Beverage Operations* (East Lansing, Mich.: Educational Institute of the American Hotel & Motel Association, 1982), p. 180.

and variable labor. **Fixed labor** is the minimum amount of labor required to operate the property regardless of business volume. For instance, if the dining room is open from 6:00 a.m. to 11:00 a.m. for breakfast, there must be at least one server on duty during that time. One server may work the entire five-hour shift or he/she may work until 9:30 when another server takes over until 11:00. Regardless of the schedule pattern, there is a fixed labor requirement of five hours of service labor for the breakfast shift.

Above some specific level, however, additional labor hours are necessary. This incremental labor is referred to as **variable labor**. It fluctuates according to the volume of business activity. Therefore, as you produce more meals and serve more guests, you will need additional production and service labor hours.

The amount of fixed labor is a benchmark—the minimum labor required to operate your food

service outlet properly. Thus, when you develop staffing guides, you must incorporate this minimum number of labor hours into your staffing plans.

A sample variable labor staffing guide for a hotel food service outlet is shown in Exhibit 7.2. You will note that management increases the number of labor hours when more guests are forecasted. Based on this forecast information, the manager calculates the number of allowable hours for each position in the department.

Remember that each food service outlet has fixed labor requirements (the minimum amount of labor hours needed regardless of business volume) that dictate a minimum staffing level.

Because the amount of fixed labor significantly affects both the labor control program and the level of labor costs, fixed labor should be established specifically for each food service outlet. Dining room managers must designate the

Exhibit 7.2 Variable Labor Staffing Guide

Variable Labor Staffing Guide: Dinner

Number of Guests Served

Position	50	75	100	125	150
Food Server	8.5 5:00–9:30 7:00–11:00	9.5 5:00–9:30 6:30–11:30	16.0 5:00–9:30 6:30–10:00 7:00–10:00 7:30–12:30	16.0 5:00–9:30 6:30–10:00 7:00–10:00 7:30–12:30	19.0 5:00–10:00 6:00–11:00 6:00–11:00 7:30–11:30
Bartender	9.0 5:00–12:00 6:00–8:00	9.0 5:00–12:00 6:00–8:00	9.0 5:00–12:00 6:00–8:00	9.0 5:00–12:00 6:00–8:00	9.0 5:00–12:00 6:00–8:00
Cocktail Server	6.5 4:30–11:00	6.5 4:30–11:00	6.5 4:30–11:00	6.5 4:30–11:00	6.5 4:30–11:00
Cook	7 4:00–11:00	14 3:00–10:00 5:00–12:00	14 3:00–10:00 5:00–12:00	14 3:00–10:00 5:00–12:00	16 3:00–11:00 4:00–12:00
Steward	6.5 5:00–11:30	6.5 5:00–11:30	9.0 4:00–6:00 5:00–12:00	9.5 4:00–6:00 5:00–12:30	9.5 4:00–6:00 5:00–12:30
Busperson	—	2 7:30–9:30	4 7:30–9:30 7:30–9:30	5 7:00–9:30 7:30–10:00	7 7:00–9:30 7:30–10:00 7:30–9:30
Host/Hostess (Manager serves as host on slow evenings.)	—	3 6:00–9:00	3.5 6:00–9:30	4.0 6:00–10:00	4.0 6:00–10:00

To understand the staffing guide, examine the position of food server. When 50 dinners are forecasted, 8.5 food server labor hours should be scheduled. The 8.5 labor hours represent the meals per labor hour standard based upon study of the position and completion of the position performance analysis form (Exhibit 7.1). The 8.5 labor hours do not specify how many food servers or which food servers, but only the total labor hours required. Times listed "5:00–9:30" and "7:00–11:00" are suggested staff schedules. The standard, 8.5 labor hours, equals the **total hours allowed** for 50 meals to be served.

Source: Ninemeier, *Planning and Control*, p. 182.

amount of fixed labor that they judge necessary; however, they know that assessment is always open to review. Managers should reassess their levels of fixed labor several times a year. Factors such as changes in quality requirements, operating procedures, and guest expectations influence the amount of fixed labor required.

Fixed Labor Needs Constant Analysis

You need to carefully analyze the work performed by your fixed labor staff to ensure that these employees are as productive as their situation permits. For example, on an average slow shift (when most labor is fixed), how much of the employees' time is spent on work normally expected of the position? As the amount of idle time increases, it is important to answer the following questions:

1. Must we continue to provide the service? Will quality standards permit adjusting the hours of dining room service? (If you can make an operating change, you might be able to reduce labor costs. However, it is always important to recall the service standards which the property has established.)

2. Can we adjust the tasks performed by the fixed staff? (A server who can perform some other duty such as folding napkins for the following shift may reduce the amount of variable labor staff you will need during subsequent shifts.)

3. Can we combine work so that salaried labor can perform some service tasks during slow periods? (For example, you could station a salaried assistant restaurant manager at the host stand during the early and late dining periods. Reservation calls and occasional seating duties usually do not significantly interfere with the paperwork required of the assistant manager. Therefore, you would not require fixed labor employees, who must be paid a wage, at the host stand during these slow times.)

Developing the Staffing Guide

When developing staffing guides, remember two important points: first, the concept of economy of scale suggests that efficiency per unit of output increases as business volume increases. For example, you do not need to schedule twice as many labor hours to serve 200 guests as you do to serve 100 guests. In Exhibit 7.2 the staffing guide calls for 8.5 labor hours to serve 50 guests; it requires only 16 labor hours to serve 100 guests. (In large part, the number of labor hours you will require per 100 guests depends on *when* your guests are scheduled to arrive.) Therefore, the percentage of fixed labor that you will require and the labor cost per guest are greater

for low levels of business volume than during periods of peak business volume.

Second, if your property has an operating budget (and it should!), your staffing guide must not produce higher labor costs than the budget permits. Conversely, if you use the staffing guide to develop the labor costs for the operating budget, you must first determine the number of guests you expect to serve, then calculate the number of labor hours you will require to serve those guests. Multiply the total number of labor hours by the hourly wage to determine your budget (allowable) expense for labor.

You can use the variable labor staffing guide (Exhibit 7.2) to record labor performance standards for each position. For example, according to Exhibit 7.2, you should schedule 8.5 hours of service labor if you anticipate 50 guests for dinner and you should schedule 19.0 food server hours if you have forecasted 150 meals. The guide also provides suggestions regarding how to divide up the allowable number of hours among your employees. You should determine actual workshifts, based in part on reservation records and other information that suggest times during which you need a specific number of servers.

When unionized employees work in your dining room outlets, you must incorporate a wide range of other restrictions into your variable labor staffing guide. It is not uncommon, for example, for a labor contract to stipulate the hours which a server can work per shift (minimum and maximum). Some unionized operations have a specific ratio of seats or guests which one staff member can serve. You may also need to consider overtime restrictions for unscheduled labor hours and the number and timing of coffee breaks. Another basic part of many union contracts is the exact definition of tasks which union members in each position can and cannot perform. For example, if food servers cannot clear tables, the variable labor staffing guide should exclude the time required to perform this task from the server's labor hours and include it under the labor hours for buspersons.

Even with these and a wide range of other complicating factors, you can begin to see how dining room managers can incorporate quality and quantity requirements into employee work schedules. You can also see how easy it is to follow up and assess the actual number of hours each staff member works in order to determine whether or not a control problem exists. (By our definition, excess labor hours are a type of overtime and occur when the actual number of labor hours exceeds the standard, allowable number of labor hours. A more common definition only considers the hours employees work in excess of those permitted by applicable wage and hour laws.)

Perhaps the most important lesson to learn from this discussion of labor control is *not* the exact procedure that you should use; rather, it is the fact that you *can* control labor. Obviously, the manager should play a major role in the process of controlling labor costs. Simplified procedures do exist for establishing labor performance standards, assessing actual labor costs, and taking corrective action. (Review the reference cited for Exhibits 7.1 and 7.2 for more detailed information.)

Forecasting Food Service Sales

The variable labor staffing guide can be a useful tool for scheduling service labor. However, to use it properly, the restaurant manager must first forecast food sales, then use those forecasts to schedule labor based on the **total hours allowed** which the staffing guide dictates.

Sound sales forecasts are crucial to many areas of a restaurant's operation. Back- and front-of-house staff members must know the estimated number of meals that they will serve. Production staff must purchase, receive, store, issue, and produce products in sufficient quantities to serve the estimated number of guests. Managers must schedule employees to produce and serve the necessary number of meals; to do this, restaurant managers must know approximately how many people to expect and when they will arrive.

Of course, some properties do not need to develop and implement a sales forecasting system because of the consistency in their business from day to day or week to week. More typically, however, business fluctuates and is affected by a variety of factors:

Holidays. Mother's Day and Easter are the busiest days of the year for many dining outlets. Such summer holidays as Independence Day and Labor Day may be slow for high-check-average properties because families schedule outdoor activities but very busy for fast-food and other operations that cater to the traveling public. (Properties taking reservations for holidays must prepare their reservation books early so that no confusion results from guests making holiday reservations weeks in advance of the date.)

Weather. During snowstorms in the winter and very hot days in the summer, business may be slow. However, imagine how snowstorms can improve business in properties located near major expressways. Not only will snowbound travelers stay in the lodging property, they will no doubt eat all their meals in the property's dining outlets.

Community activities. Community-wide sales, celebrations, and other events may bring more people into a local food service operation.

Other factors. Food service operations in college towns and resort areas, properties catering to business travelers who generally do not travel nor stay in a lodging property on weekends, and restaurant outlets affected by catered events for in-house guests are examples of properties dealing with other factors which influence their business.

How Forecasting Helps the Dining Room Staff

Obviously, accurate forecasting aids the production staff, but how does it help the dining outlet manager? As we have already mentioned, the manager must match the estimated number of guests to the number of dining service labor hours required to provide them with quality service. In addition, the manager must ensure that employees supply service areas with an adequate beginning inventory of items to reduce the possibility of service bottlenecks. Sound forecasting helps the manager ensure that personnel and work stations are ready for guest service at the start of the service period.

In some properties, dining service employees must do some preparation work. Filling portion containers with condiments, preparing butter chips, slicing bread, portioning sour cream, preparing iced tea, and wrapping flatware in napkins are among the tasks that these employees may perform. The number of meals the manager expects to serve will obviously affect the quantity of these items that service employees must make ready for service.

Some properties find a correlation between the total number of guests they expect to serve and the number of two-person, four-person, or other sized groups. Use of a forecasting system can help them determine how to set up dining room tables to accommodate these groups.

In some properties, experience has shown that a rush of guests without reservations will often occur early or late in a shift. If an accurate sales forecast system is in place, schedule planners may be able to determine not only how many server labor hours to schedule but also the number of servers and when they must begin their shifts. Managers can also dispense guest checks and server cash banks, if necessary, with more ease when they know the estimated number of guests.

Procedures for Developing Sales Forecasts

Each property needs specific procedures to develop sales forecasts. However, as an important first step, pre-production planning sessions should be regularly scheduled with the staff to review special menus, anticipated problems, and other items. For example, in a small operation the manager, head cook, and head server may meet every Wednesday to review plans for the week beginning the next Friday.

Exhibit 7.3 illustrates a sales history record that reviews sales on a specific day over a five-week period. Each day's sheet shows the number of items sold and the percentage of the total guests who ordered each item. (In this particular case, every guest ordered an entree, so the calculation is also based on percentage of entrees sold.) With this form, management can track the sales of items over an extended period of time and identify trends useful in predicting future sales.

In Exhibit 7.3, column 1 lists the number of each menu item ordered. You calculate column 2 by dividing the number of each item sold by the total number of guests served. For example, during the previous 80 days, the property served an average of 46 orders of shrimp cocktail; 27.4% of 168 guests ordered this appetizer (46 items sold divided by 168 total guests = 27.4%).

Information from the previous Tuesday (4/13/00) is listed in columns 3 and 4. Forty-nine of 177 guests ordered the shrimp cocktail on that date. That represents 27.7% of all the guests (49 items sold divided by 177 total guests served = a percentage trend of 27.7%).

Once you estimate the total number of guests for the next Tuesday, you can use the percentage trend to estimate the number of portions of each menu item which will be required. Assume an estimate of 200 guests. If you use the percentage trend of guests who previously ordered this appetizer, you can calculate the estimated number of servings (200 guests multiplied by 27.4% = 55 servings) needed next Tuesday. Repeat this process to calculate the estimated production requirements for all other menu items on that day (Tuesday) and for all other days in the period covered by the forecast.

Exhibit 7.3 Sample Sales History Record

Date	Previous 80 Day Average		4/13/00		4/20/00		4/27/00		5/4/00		5/11/00	
	No. Sold	% of Total	No. Sold	% of Total	No. Sold	% of Total	No. Sold	% of Total	No. Sold	% of Total	No. Sold	% of Total
Items	1	2	3	4	5	6	7	8	9	10	11	12
Appetizers												
Shrimp Cocktail	46	27.4	49	27.7								
Fruit Cup	17	10.1	18	10.2								
Marinated Herring	16	9.5	15	8.5								
Half Grapefruit	6	3.6	8	4.5								
Soup du Jour	27	16.1	31	17.5								
Total Appetizers	112	66.7	121	68.4								
Entrees												
Sirloin Steak	26	15.5	29	16.4								
Prime Rib	58	34.5	62	35.0								
Lobster	28	16.7	26	14.7								
Ragout of Lamb	22	13.1	21	11.9								
Half Chicken	34	20.2	39	22.0								
Total Entrees	168	100.0	177	100.0								
Vegetables & Salads												
Whipped Potatoes	51	30.4	57	32.2								
Baked Potatoes	108	64.3	119	67.2								
Asparagus Sprs.	111	66.0	108	61.0								
Half Tomato	48	28.6	49	27.7								
Tossed Salad	102	60.7	107	60.5								
Hearts of Lettuce	57	33.9	64	36.2								
Total Veg. & Sal.	477	283.9	504	284.8								
Desserts												
Brownie	19	11.3	21	11.9								
Fresh Fruits	9	5.4	10	5.6								
Ice Cream	33	19.6	36	20.3								
Apple Pie	19	11.3	25	14.1								
Devil's Food Cake	14	8.3	10	5.7								
Total Desserts	94	55.9	102	57.6								
Total Guests Served	168	100.0	177	100.0								

Sales History Record Showing Percent of Total Guests Sales Information — Day *TUESDAY*

Source: Carl H. Albers, *Food and Beverage Cost Planning and Control Procedures,* rev. ed. (East Lansing, Mich.: Educational Institute of the American Hotel & Motel Association, 1976), p. 67.

Exhibit 7.4 Food Production Planning Worksheet

Date: 7/16/00

Shift: PM

Item	Portion Size	Portions Required	Portions Available	Amt. To Prepare	Recipe Number	Employee	Remarks	Portions Left	Portions Served
1	2	3	4	5	6	7	8	9	10
Fruit Cup	5 oz.	75	25	50	107	Joe	Substitute pears for peaches	10	65
Marinated Herring	2½ oz.	15	5	10	112	Sally	Make full recipe (15)	0	20

General Comments: Out of herring at 9:00 p.m.

You can also use the sales history records of popular and unpopular dishes to produce a food production planning worksheet (Exhibit 7.4). When reviewing this worksheet, you should note that the form adjusts and transfers the estimates of production *needs*, derived from the study of sales history records and similar information, into production *plans*. Food production personnel can then use this form to determine raw material requirements. For example, the food production manager (or chef) estimates that 75 portions of fruit cup will be needed for the evening shift. There are already 25 portions available, so 50 portions must be prepared. The manager instructs Joe to prepare the required number using recipe #107. However, since the operation has no fresh peaches (they were refused because they did not meet quality requirements), the employee is told to substitute pears for peaches. At the end of the shift, there are 10 portions remaining because 65 servings were served.

Similarly, the manager estimates that 15 portions of marinated herring are needed. Since five portions are available, ten must be prepared. However, because the standard recipe yields 15 servings and the items will keep well under refrigeration, the employee (Sally) is instructed to fix 15 portions. The amount available will then be 20 servings.

$$\underset{\substack{\text{Portions} \\ \text{Available}}}{5} + \underset{\substack{\text{Amount} \\ \text{Prepared}}}{15} = \underset{\substack{\text{Amount} \\ \text{Available}}}{20}$$

Contrary to the estimate, all portions are sold. The manager makes a note that the item ran out at 9:00 p.m. Future production forecasts may be increased based upon this information.

Staff in a pre-production planning meeting must consider other matters such as scheduling labor based on estimated production needs. Also, any equipment scheduling problems can be resolved at this meeting. For example, perhaps a special catered event requires the production of items in especially large quantities or involves equipment not normally used by production staff.

After the pre-production planning meeting, you should know the required number of portions of each menu item. You can then fill out food issue requisition forms—at least for most days and items and for all catered events (if these costs are charged to a separate revenue/cost center).

You can see how the sales history record can provide helpful information to both production officials and to the restaurant manager. Estimating, for example, that you will serve approximately 175 guests on a specific shift can help you implement action plans to schedule employees and prepare for dining room service during that shift.

Special Forecasting Procedures for Lodging Operations

Derived demand affects food and beverage operations in many lodging properties; the occupancy rate of the hotel influences the sale of food and beverages. You should understand that the number of guests staying at a property is especially likely to affect its level of breakfast and dinner business. (Lunch service may be less affected since many guests who do not attend in-house meetings may not be in the hotel at midday.) Of course, most hotels do not rely entirely on transient guest business to support their food service operations. They know they must generate substantial business from the community and surrounding area.

Typically, food and beverage sales forecasts in hotels are based on estimates of room sales. As is true with other food service operations, sales history information and a subjective evaluation based on experience also play roles in the development of sales forecasts.

You can use the form shown in Exhibit 7.5 to record sales estimates for the guests you expect to serve in your hotel. Information about the previous three days allows current business trends to influence your decisions for the future week. Again, data in this forecast may need revision as the week evolves.

In a hotel, food and beverage outlets depend on good information from the rooms and sales departments. Food and beverage outlets also need to know what events the banquet department has scheduled and whether they are local or convention-related. For example, the coffee shop and room service will expect less business if breakfast is served in the banquet rooms for an in-house group. Once restaurant managers have the required room information, a list of banquet/catering activities, and other sales history records, they can use forecasting formulas to estimate the number of guests they expect to serve on a given day or during a specific meal period.

Exhibit 7.5 reflects food sales only since many properties estimate beverage sales by applying a percentage factor to the forecasted food sales. The percentage factor is obtained by dividing the total food and beverage revenue figure into the total beverage revenue figure for the same time period. Exhibit 7.6 shows how a manager can estimate food covers and beverage sales for a dining outlet.

The successful development of an accurate business forecast depends in large measure on the historical information that restaurant managers use. Wise managers make use of all available sales history information.

Just as the forecasting system for room sales must be updated by assessing the differences between forecasts and actual sales, you must also examine the differences between actual and forecasted food covers. You should determine reasons for the differences and adjust the forecasting system to increase the accuracy of future sales forecasts.

After you estimate your business volume, you can schedule your staff. You should note that you have followed a planned sequence of activities. First, you determined the level of required labor based on the property's minimum quality and productivity standards and adjusted for various volumes of business. This information is summarized on a labor staffing guide. Second, you forecasted your business volumes. The next logical step is to match up the required labor with your sales forecasts.

Scheduling Employees

Once you have a forecast of the number of guests you expect to serve during a given shift on a specific day, you return to the staffing guide to determine the number of allowable labor hours you can schedule. If your property rarely exceeds the standard number of labor hours listed on the staffing guide, you have some assurance that the service personnel work efficiently and that the dollars spent for actual hours worked will be within your property's budget. If you frequently exceed the standard number of allowable hours, you will need to re-evaluate

Exhibit 7.5 10-Day Volume Forecast: Food

TEN-DAY VOLUME FORECAST—FOOD

Motor-Hotel _____
(Location)

Date Prepared _____
Week Ending _____

FOOD DEPARTMENT	DATE																					
	DAY	THUR.		FRI.		SAT.		SUN.		MON.		TUES.		WED.		THUR.		FRI.		SAT.		Totals
		Previous Week																				
		F	A	F	A	F	A	F	A	F	A	F	A	F	A	F	A	F	A	F	A
Dining Room																						
Breakfast																						
Lunch																						
Dinner																						
Total D.R. Covers																						
Coffee Shop																						
Breakfast																						
Lunch																						
Total C.S. Covers																						
Banquet																						
Breakfast																						
Lunch																						
Dinner																						
Total Banquet Covers																						
Room Service																						
Total R.S. Covers																						
TOTAL FOOD COVERS																						

SPECIAL COMMENTS
(i.e. types of groups—V.I.P. etc.)

F = Forecast
A = Actual

Source: David L. Balangue, "Payroll Productivity (Part IV: Staff Planning)," *Lodging,* November 1978, p. 39.

your staffing guide as well as your employees' performances.

Using the Labor Staffing Guide

Specific procedures for using the staffing guide to schedule labor hours are as follows:

Set a time frame for scheduling personnel. For example, every Thursday you could schedule required labor hours for the following week (Monday-Sunday). Depending on the needs of the outlet, managers may develop personnel work schedules for longer or shorter time periods.

Exhibit 7.6 Estimating Food Covers and Beverage Revenue

Assume that the total occupancy rate for a hotel is estimated to be 255 guests for the day and the property has only one food outlet. Knowing this and other factors from experience, the restaurant manager can estimate food covers and beverage sales.

Estimates of Food Covers

Breakfast: 20% of house guests plus 65 walk-in guests

255		20%		51		65		116
number of house guests	×	percent	=	breakfasts for house guests	+	walk-in guests	=	estimated breakfast covers

You must also figure factors which affect lunch and dinner volumes such as events in the hotel, conventions in the city, and related statistical history into the forecasts.

Lunch:

105		$4.55		$477.75
number of lunches	×	check average	=	lunch sales

Dinner:

160		$8.55		$1,368.00
number of dinners	×	check average	=	dinner sales

Beverage Revenue

Based on experience, beverage sales are approximately 22% of the lunch and dinner sales. No relationship between breakfast sales and beverage income has been discovered.

$477.75		$1,368.00		$1,845.75		22%		$406.07
lunch sales	+	dinner sales	=	total sales	×	beverage income percent	=	estimated beverage revenue

This property will base the scheduling of labor for this day on breakfast, lunch, and dinner covers of 116, 105, and 160 meals, respectively. The allowable labor listed on the staffing guide for the beverage section is based on an estimated beverage revenue of $406.07.

Estimate the number of meals you expect to serve. Since the staffing guide has been developed by planning the range of meals normally served, you must know the estimated number of meals that your property will serve on a specific shift. The sales history information which you use for such purposes as ordering food and scheduling salaried labor will help you here.

Some properties develop sales income forecasts and schedule service labor based on sales estimates rather than the number of guests they expect to serve. (We will review this approach later in this chapter.)

Schedule labor hours on the basis of the number of forecasted meals. For example, if you

Derived Demand Affects Food and Beverage Sales

Many hotels can estimate a base level of food and beverage business in various outlets from their occupancy rates. For example, experienced restaurant managers may know that a specific percentage of guests will consume their breakfasts on-site. They can also translate the number of hotel guests into a base of guests who will wish to order lunch and/or dinner.

You should be aware, however, that many factors affect these rules of thumb; experienced dining service managers wisely adjust estimates based on house counts to accommodate the following variables:

1. Will a large percentage of the hotel guests attend a pre-arranged breakfast as part of a convention or other large group event? If so, reduce the number of guests you expect for breakfast in the dining room(s).

2. In the preceding example, does the convention offer an open breakfast period on one day of its meetings? If so, you can expect more people for breakfast in the dining room(s) than you would otherwise anticipate. This factor would be of special concern when the group's first activity is scheduled relatively early.

3. Are pre-arranged evening banquets planned for in-house guests? Such events will have the same impact on the anticipated amount of business in the dining room as breakfast meetings have on expected early morning business.

In an effort to develop more accurate estimates of derived demand, some properties deduct the number of guests in the house who attend large group meetings; the reduced occupancy rate then forms the basis of business estimates for the food and beverage outlets. Property managers then consider the impact that the group's scheduled activities has on those estimates.

---

expect to serve 150 meals during the evening shift on Thursday, and the staffing guide indicates that 19 service labor hours are necessary to handle this number of meals, then schedule 19 labor hours. If you schedule less than 19 labor hours, the quality of service is likely to decrease since personnel will be rushed and the quality standards of your property will not be met. If you schedule more than 19 labor hours, service staff will not work efficiently; labor costs will be higher, and productivity will be lower than the labor performance standards permit. Incidentally, scheduling more than 19 labor hours will not guarantee that quality standards will be met.

In this example, you can allocate the 19 hours as necessary. One food server may work six hours doing initial dining room setup work and finish the shift at the end of the rush period. Another food server might work eight hours, coming in when the evening rush begins and staying until closing time; a third food server may work five hours during the rush only. Regardless of how you shuffle the 19 labor hours, you will control your labor costs if the property

actually serves the number of forecasted meals and if you do not exceed the number of standard labor hours listed on your staffing guide.

Exhibit 7.7 is a schedule worksheet to help determine *when* a property needs employees. When reviewing this form, note that the 19.0 standard labor hours for food servers are spread among three employees. You can also see that the total number of hours that the three employees are scheduled to work does not exceed the number of labor hours recommended by the staffing guide. However, occasionally managers must knowingly schedule additional hours, even though they will not adhere to the labor performance standards. You may require additional labor when employee training occurs, equipment breaks down, and/or nonroutine cleaning is done.

After you develop the employee schedule, post the standard number of labor hours required for each position on a weekly labor hour report (Exhibit 7.8). Use this form to record the actual labor hours worked by each employee, then compare those hours with the standard

Exhibit 7.7 Schedule Worksheet

Schedule Worksheet

Day: *Monday* Estimated Guests: Section: *Food service*
Date: *8/1/00* Position *Food Server*
Shift: *PM*

AM	PM
	150

Position/Employee	6:00a	7:00a	8:00a	9:00a	10:00a	11:00a	12:00p	1:00p	2:00p	3:00p	4:00p	5:00p	6:00p	7:00p	8:00p	9:00p	10:00p	11:00p	12:00p	1:00a	2:00a	3:00a	4:00a	5:00a	Planned Total Hours
Joe											├──					──┤									6.0
Sally												├──						──┤							8.0
Brenda														├──				──┤							5.0
																									19.0

Position: *Food Server*
Standard Labor Hours: *19*
Planned Labor Hours: *19*
Difference: *0*

Source: Ninemeier, *Planning and Control*, p. 186.

(allowable) labor hours. (The form's role in service labor control will be discussed later in this chapter.)

Techniques for Scheduling

Restaurant managers should consider the following when scheduling personnel to meet labor performance standards:

Schedule staff to fit work needs. It is *not* generally a good idea to have all the staff begin and end workshifts at the same time. Rather, schedule employees as the volume of work requires. This is called "staggered scheduling." As a simple example, schedule one person to begin work one hour before the dining room opens. The employee can use the time to check and/or set up tables in the dining room or to do other miscellaneous setup work. Bring in a second service employee 30 minutes before opening to perform similar duties. Both employees are then ready to serve guests when the dining room opens. Schedule other service personnel so that the required number of employees are available to serve the volume of meals expected at different hours. The first employee who checks in may be the first employee to leave; staggered quitting times are also important to ensure maximum worker efficiency.

Exhibit 7.8 Weekly Labor Hour Report

Week of: 7/14/00   Section: Food Service   Supervisor: SANDRA

Shift: PM

Position/ Employee	7/14 Mon	7/15 Tues	7/16 Wed	7/17 Thurs	7/18 Fri	7/19 Sat	7/20 Sun	Total Labor Hours Actual	Total Labor Hours Standard
DINING ROOM									
Jennifer	7	—	7	6	7.5	6	—	33.5	31.0
Brenda	—	7	6.5	7	5	8	5	38.5	38.5
Sally	—	5	8	8	7	10	—	38.0	36.0
Patty	8	6	6	—	4.5	—	6	30.5	31.0
Anna	4	4	6.5	—	4.5	—	5	24.0	22.0
Thelma	6	5	7.5	—	7.5	—	—	26.0	24.0
ELSIE	6	4	—	—	8	8	8	34.0	34.0
								Total 224.5	216.5

Remarks: 7/18– Jennifer, Sally, and Elsie given extra hours to learn tableside flaming

7/19– Sally stayed 2 extra hours— special cleaning

Difference +8.0

Source: Adapted from Ninemeier, *Planning and Control*, p. 190.

Use creative schedule plans. Since the workflow may not be constant and a property frequently has less rush time than normal or slow time, you should schedule personnel accordingly. Staggered scheduling frequently decreases the need for full-time personnel. To the extent that only a few management tasks exist to justify full-time positions, you might want to develop such titles as "head food server." In this manner, a full-time job involves both management and nonmanagement tasks. The head food server might have such management duties as supervising personnel, writing cleaning schedules, and others. However, the position may also involve the nonmanagement task of waiting on tables.

Set salary or wages on the basis of reasonable pay for all the work performed so that both the operation and the employees benefit from the arrangement. Hire part-time staff to work short shifts (three, four, or five-hour periods). If some of these staff members want longer hours, and you do not need to consider union and/or wage problems, you might want to arrange split shifts (two short shifts in one day separated by a nonworking time period).

You can also use temporary employees. Managers in many properties know people who don't want steady work, but who do like to work occasionally. If a special event, an employee illness, or a similar circumstance creates the need for temporary assistance, these people, who are carried on the payroll for infrequent work, can be very helpful. Of course, if any union restrictions exist, you must consider them as you develop your staffing plans.

Restrictions in unionized operations may temper the usefulness of many staffing suggestions. For example, the current union bargaining agreement may influence the use of on-call systems, which allow management to call certain service employees if a rush occurs, or it may influence the minimum number of hours a property must pay employees if they report to work. You must consider these and other scheduling restraints as you develop employee schedules for your property.

Consider personnel preferences whenever possible. Use schedule request forms which allow employees to indicate, *several weeks in advance*, days/shifts when they do not want to work. Food service officials should honor these requests whenever possible.

Recall policies that are applicable to employee scheduling. For example, your property may have requirements for rotating the arrival time of staff members or assigning kitchen cleanup tasks at closing time. Past experience in allocating labor hours to each employee is generally the best information you can rely on when you are scheduling personnel.

Inform employees about the schedule. After you develop the schedule worksheet (Exhibit 7.7), you know the hours each employee is set to work. Compile these hours on an employee schedule and post it for employees to review and use. An employee schedule is pictured in Exhibit 7.9. Note that the schedule indicates for each food server the days and hours that he/she will work for an entire week. Knowing his/her work schedule allows the employee to make personal plans that will not conflict with his/her job.

The total of all labor hours scheduled for all employees should not exceed the labor performance standard hours listed on the schedule worksheet (Exhibit 7.7). However, both the restaurant manager and the employees must understand that things do not always go according to plan; you may need to make changes on the schedule as employees call in sick, no-shows occur, or the volume of meals produced indicates that you need more or fewer labor hours. The posted schedule is an attempt to provide employees with the best possible advance notice of their workshift requirements.

Hourly Guest Counts

Some restaurant managers track the number of guests seated hourly and use this information when they schedule dining service employees. If records show that the number of guests seated during the early or ending hours of a meal period is small, fewer service employees are needed at those times. However, during the busy hours, more staff should be scheduled. Keeping track of this information on a formal basis helps avoid problems which can arise when managers *think* that they know about the flow of guests through the property but actually they have never tracked guests on paper.

Exhibit 7.9 Employee Schedule

Week of: 7/14/00

Shift: PM

Section: Food Service

Position: Food Server

Supervisor: Julie

Employee	7/14 Monday	7/15 Tuesday	7/16 Wednesday	7/17 Thursday	7/18 Friday	7/19 Saturday	7/20 Sunday
Joe	12:00–7:00 (5/6)*	—	12:00–7:00 (—)	1:00–7:30 (—)	—	12:00–7:00	—
Ann	—	12:00–7:00 (5/6)	1:00–7:30 (—)	12:00–7:30 (—)	—	—	12:00–7:00 (—)
John	3:00–8:00 (7/8)	1:00–5:00 (—)	3:00–8:00 (—)	—	—	1:00–7:30 (5/6)	1:00–7:30 (—)
Sue	—	3:00–8:30 (7/8)	12:30–8:30 (5/6)	12:30–7:30 (—)	12:00–7:00 (—)	—	—
Myron	12:30–6:30 (—)	12:30–6:00 (—)	—	—	3:00–7:30 (—)	3:00–8:00 (7/8)	3:00–8:00 (—)
Stacey	3:00–7:00 (—)	3:00–7:00 (—)	3:00–7:30 (—)	3:00–7:30 (7/8)	—	—	12:30–8:30 (5/6)
Paul	1:00–5:00 (—)	1:00–5:00 (—)	—	—	3:00–8:00 (—)	12:30–8:30 (—)	3:00–7:00 (7/8)
June	1:00–7:00 (—)	—	—	1:00–7:00 (5/6)	1:00–8:30 (—)	3:00–7:00 (—)	—
Stan	—	—	3:00–8:00 (7/8)	1:00–7:00 (—)	3:00–7:30 (—)	—	1:00–6:00 (—)
Karen	1:00–7:00 (—)	1:00–7:00 (—)	—	—	1:00–5:00 (5/6)	1:00–6:00 (—)	2:00–7:00 (—)
Betty	—	—	3:00–7:00 (—)	3:00–8:00 (—)	3:00–7:00 (7/8)	2:00–7:00 (—)	—

*Numbers in parentheses refer to required setup/cleanup activities noted in Chapter 11, Exhibit 11.7. Since this is a PM shift, there are fewer setup and cleanup duties than would be required during early morning or late evening shifts.

Hourly guest counts also help back-of-house staff. Obviously, the number of guests served will affect the scheduling of employees who work on production/serving lines during hours of operation. Since you can also use guest counts to establish basic sales history data, they help forecast the amount of food to produce. They also suggest when you should set your operating hours and influence the total amount of production and serving time that back-of-house personnel will require. Finally, you can measure the productivity of employees working on the service lines by tallying the number of meals produced within a specific time period.

Some operations use guest counts to measure productivity. Following is an example of how productivity is calculated from guest counts. Assume that four dining service employees (servers only) work between 7:00 and 8:00 p.m. and 30 guests are seated:

$$\underset{\substack{\text{Number of}\\\text{Guests}}}{30} \div \underset{\substack{\text{Number of}\\\text{Server}\\\text{Hours}}}{4} = \underset{\substack{\text{Guests}\\\text{Served}\\\text{per Hour}\\\text{(Server}\\\text{Productivity)}}}{7.5}$$

Once you know the productivity rate (the number of guests served per hour), you can compare the rate with previous periods and assess the impact that alternative staffing plans have on productivity.

Hourly guest count information can be used to establish the hours of operation. For example, if relatively few people are seated before or after a specific time, perhaps you should adjust the hours of operation. However, you should also consider that serving only a few guests may still benefit the property. For example, the income generated during these slow periods may cover all direct costs, including service labor, and also contribute toward the indirect or fixed costs. Or, you could use a marketing campaign to introduce meal specials during these early or late periods. A comparison of the hourly guest counts before and after the marketing campaign can help you evaluate the effectiveness of such promotions.

Hourly guest counts have still another potential benefit; they can help managers factor reservation counts into the estimates of the total meals they expect to serve. For example, a dining outlet might generally take about 25 reservations between 8:00 and 9:00 p.m. on a typical Saturday evening. If a study of the hourly guest counts shows that you seat approximately 50 guests during that hour, you can begin to predict that the reservation count will normally represent about 50% of the total guests eventually seated during that time period. Obviously, this information will help you develop production and service schedules.

Exhibit 7.10 illustrates a form that can be used at the entrance to the dining area to manually tally the number of guests seated each hour. Hourly time intervals are shown in the left-hand column. The host/hostess or cashier enters a tally mark on the form each time a guest is seated during the hour. Also, the food server can record the guest's time of arrival on the guest check (manual system), or record it when he/she first enters the guest check into the precheck register or other machine (automated system). The bookkeeper or other staff members can then tally this information at the time of the guest check audit. You use the right-hand columns of the hourly guest count worksheet (Exhibit 7.10) to total the number of guests seated during the hour and to record reservation information. (Some electronic units automatically calculate hourly guest counts and include them on a routine printout of sales summary information.)

Exhibit 7.11 illustrates an hourly guest count record that summarizes information from the hourly guest count worksheet (Exhibit 7.11) for the month. Note that information about the number of guests with reservations and the actual number seated (from Exhibit 7.10) is transferred to this record; applicable information from other dates can also be recorded so that planners can easily note trends and make estimates. Completed for several months, the hourly guest count record can help restaurant managers schedule staff effectively, consider changes in the hours of operation, assess productivity, and make other decisions.

Measuring Productivity

Some properties collect sales income information on an hourly basis. The procedures to do this are relatively easy when electronic registers

Exhibit 7.10 Hourly Guest Count Worksheet

Date: ___8/1/XX___   Prepared By: _____

TIME	TALLY	TOTAL Reservations	Actual
5:00 p.m.	||||| |||	3	8
6:00 p.m.	||||| ||||| ||||| ||||| ||||	8	24
7:00 p.m.	||||| ||||| ||||| ||||| ||||| ||||| ||||| ||||| ||||| ||||	22	49
8:00 p.m.	||||| ||||| ||||| ||||| ||||| ||||| ||||| ||||| ||||| |||||		36	51
9:00 p.m.	||||| ||||| ||||| ||||| ||||| ||||| ||||| |||||	14	40
10:00 p.m.	||||| ||||| ||||| ||||	10	19
11:00 p.m.	||||| |||	0	8

Exhibit 7.11 Hourly Guest Count Record

Prepared By: _____

Date	5–6 p.m.		6–7 p.m.		7–8 p.m.		8–9 p.m.		9–10 p.m.		10–11 p.m.		11 p.m.–12 midnight	
	Res.	Actual	Res.	Actual	Res.	Actual	Res.	Actual	Res.	Actual	Res.	Actual	Res.	Actual
8/1	3	8	8	24	22	49	36	51	14	40	10	19	0	8
8/2	3	6	10	25	30	55	38	55	10	30	10	25	5	6

generate this information as part of sales history recaps.

You can use information about the amount of sales generated per hour of service time to measure productivity. **Productivity** is a measure of output relative to input. For example, if four dining service employees work between 7:00 and 8:00 p.m., and $115 in sales income is generated, you can calculate the sales income per hour ($115 in sales divided by 4 server hours = $28.75 in sales per server hour). In this example, sales income of $28.75 (output) is generated for each server hour (input).

Dining room managers can compare this income productivity rate to similar statistics from earlier periods. They also use it to schedule service staff. For example, if an income productivity rate indicates that each server labor hour generates $30 of dinner income for a shift, and you forecast 200 meals with a dinner check average of $15, then you can determine the allowable number of service hours to schedule:

Step 1: Calculate expected sales income.

200	x	$15	=	$3,000
Number of Meals		Check Average		Estimated Income

Step 2: Determine the number of allowable service hours.

$3,000	÷	$30	=	100
Estimated Income		Hourly Income Standard		Number of Allowable Service Hours

Managers know that they can use no more than 100 hours of service labor as they develop the schedule for the specific shift. The next step in the actual labor scheduling process is to translate the allowable labor hours into the number of employees needed for each hour of operation. For example, perhaps you need only five staff members early in the meal period and have another four employees report to work stations later in the shift. As you develop the actual schedule, however, you must limit your employees to a total of no more than the 100 labor hours allowed by the sales income productivity standard.

Employee Time Records

Dining room managers must keep accurate records of the number of hours which their employees work since waged employees are paid on the basis of hours worked. Applicable fair wage and hour laws require the payment of overtime (generally, 1 to $1\frac{1}{2}$ times the hourly rate) when the hours employees work exceed specific maximums. These and other laws may also require overtime pay for nonexempt salaried employees as well.

Calculating payroll and other taxes and withholding or deducting other amounts from employee paychecks are not normally the responsibilities of the dining outlet manager. Usually, the accounting department in a large property or the manager, bookkeeper, or off-site accounting/bookkeeping service in a small operation performs those duties. However, keeping track of and recording the number of hours each employee works are frequently the responsibility of the dining room manager.

How should you develop information about the hours that employees work? In very small operations you can use an employee sign-in sheet, which you can either entirely complete, or at least sign, to confirm the accuracy of the information. Exhibit 7.12 illustrates an employee time log. Note that you can tally information for two periods within the workshift; this may be necessary when you schedule an unpaid break during the employee's shift. Some properties use a modification of the employee time log we have just described. Rather than use a separate page for each employee, these properties use a single sheet which lists the hours all the employees work each day or week. Exhibit 7.13 is an example of this form. Note that in Exhibit 7.13 the first employee was scheduled to work 29.5 hours and actually worked only 27.5. She may, for example, have come to work two hours later (or left two hours early on Tuesday); she would, of course, not be paid for this time. (This form shows the total time the employee is scheduled to be at the property and includes an unpaid break of one-half hour.)

Properties of almost any size can justify the use of a time clock. Employees punch in and out of work by inserting a card into the time clock which prints the precise time on the card. Management collects the cards at the end of each

Exhibit 7.12 Employee Time Log

Department: _____ Payroll Number: _____

Employee: _____

DATE	TIME IN	TIME OUT	TOTAL HOURS	TIME IN	TIME OUT	TOTAL HOURS	DAILY TOTAL HOURS

week or other time period and calculates the hours each employee works for payroll purposes. If you do use time clocks, you must develop policies regarding the use of them and explain these policies to your employees. Supervision is important to ensure that the employees consistently follow such policies as "no employee may punch in more than five minutes before his/her shift begins" and "no employee may punch in another employee."

Large properties may be able to justify the cost of using very sophisticated time clocks (electronic data machines) which, in addition to recording hours worked, calculate and print out a wide variety of information used for payroll and control purposes. The payroll functions of these machines can include: summarizing hours worked; calculating payroll deductions; and

completing various forms used to report payroll information to state, federal, and local governments for tax purposes. The control functions of these units may provide information about the hours worked and labor costs incurred by department, shift, and position—information which would otherwise require an extensive amount of time to develop manually.

Managers can use this equipment to determine labor hours and costs and to evaluate the effectiveness of employee schedules and staffing plans. Given their versatility, these machines could eliminate a significant number of hours that payroll employees work, thus justifying their purchase. Exhibit 7.14 illustrates an automatic time clock printout and some of the different data which this equipment can generate.

Exhibit 7.13 Alternate Employee Time Log

Work Schedule   From: 7/1   To: 7/7

Clock No.	Name	Sched-uled: Mon.	Actual Hours Worked	Sched-uled: Tues.	Actual Hours Worked	Sched-uled: Wed.	Actual Hours Worked	Sched-uled: Thurs.	Actual Hours Worked	Sched-uled: Fri.	Actual Hours Worked	Sched-uled: Sat.	Actual Hours Worked	Sched-uled: Sun.	Actual Hours Worked	Sched-uled Hours*	Actual Reg.** Hours	OT*** Hours
5432	Sally Johnson	—	—	7:00–2:00	4.5	8:00–1:30	5.0	8:00–1:30	5.0	7:00–2:00	6.5	7:00–2:00	6.5	—	—	29.5	27.5	—
5433	Joe Jones	—	—	8:00–5:00	8.0	8:00–5:00	8.0	8:00–5:00	8.0	8:00–5:00	8.0	8:00–5:00	8.0	—	—	40.0	40.0	—

*   Scheduled hours include an unpaid break of 30 minutes.
**   Reg. = Regular
***   OT = Overtime

Exhibit 7.14 Automatic Time Clock and Printout

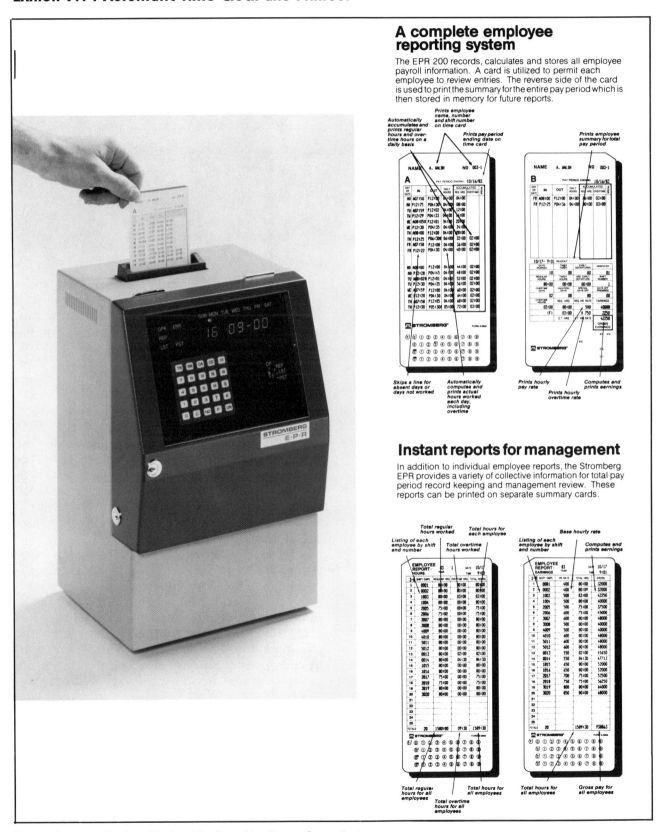

A complete employee reporting system

The EPR 200 records, calculates and stores all employee payroll information. A card is utilized to permit each employee to review entries. The reverse side of the card is used to print the summary for the entire pay period which is then stored in memory for future reports.

Instant reports for management

In addition to individual employee reports, the Stromberg EPR provides a variety of collective information for total pay period record keeping and management review. These reports can be printed on separate summary cards.

Source: Stromberg Products Division, Mite Corp., New Haven, Connecticut.

Putting It All Together to Control Labor Costs

The variable labor staffing guide (Exhibit 7.2) dictates the number of allowable labor hours for each position according to various business volumes (guests to be served); in other words, it establishes labor performance standards. Daily and weekly employee time logs (Exhibits 7.12 and 7.13) show the actual hours employees worked. Management must review standard and actual hours worked in order to discover deviations between performance standards and actual results. Generally, you can tolerate some deviations. For example, if the labor performance standard for service labor permits 300 hours for the lunch shift in a dining outlet for a specific week (based on the forecast of business volume for that time period), you might permit a variance of 1 to 2% (up to 6 hours). The amount of variance that you can tolerate before corrective action becomes necessary depends on:

The extent to which restaurant managers permit actual labor hours to exceed the standards. For example, the managers are likely to allow only small deviations if they believe that the standards are reasonable, and especially if some tolerance is already built into them.

Whether or not larger control problems exist in other areas. Corrective action should focus on the greatest variances that reflect the largest loss of profits.

Whether or not restaurant managers can explain the variances. It is one thing when labor hours are excessive because a new employee is in training. It is another matter when hours are consistently excessive and the supervisor does not know why.

Since the weekly labor hour report (Exhibit 7.8) recaps standard and actual labor hours worked so that top management can review such data, it can also provide the means for restaurant managers to explain reasons for variances. If these officials can explain the variances which occur, there is probably little or no need for corrective action. On the other hand, if the actual hours exceed the standard hours, and managers have no defensible reason for the difference—a

problem has been identified.

Regardless of whether variances are explainable or unexplainable, top management and dining outlet managers must work out plans to resolve problems:

1. Is the performance standard expressed in the staffing guide incorrect? If so, should it be adjusted?

2. Is a piece of equipment broken? If so, when will it be fixed?

3. Is a new employee in training? If so, how long will it take for that employee to be as efficient as others? Can scheduled hours be reduced as the trainee becomes more proficient?

Using a question and answer process, these and other concerns should be addressed until an acceptable plan is reached that will reduce variances between standard and actual labor hours.

Excessive Costs Represent Potential Savings

When the actual labor hours worked by employees exceed the standard labor hours indicated on the variable labor staffing guide, the property incurs unnecessary wage costs for the additional hours. Those unnecessary costs represent potential savings to the property; each dollar spent for labor hours beyond the required maximum takes one dollar of profit away from the bottom line.

You can calculate potential savings by comparing standard and actual labor hours. For example, note that the property in Exhibit 7.8 used 224.5 actual labor hours during the week in the dining room. That figure represents eight hours more than the 216.5 hours suggested by the staffing guide. The excess number of hours multiplied by the average hourly rate (including fringe benefits) for the position yields the approximate amount of lost profit (potential savings). To arrive at the exact amount, you can multiply the number of additional hours each dining room employee worked by the employee's hourly rate (including fringe benefits).

As the variance between standard and actual labor hours increases, the amount of potential savings becomes larger. As the amount of potential savings grows, corrective action becomes more necessary. Comparing standard and actual labor hours enables you to see the results of your labor control efforts and assess whether corrective action is necessary.

Let's assume that you compare actual labor hours with standard labor hours and identify the need for specific corrective action. If you discuss the problems causing the variances with other managers, the immediate supervisor, affected employees, and others, you will often be able to identify possible alternatives for reducing incurred labor hours. Dining room managers must analyze those options to assess where the problem is actually occurring and which alternative is most likely to resolve it. When selecting a corrective action plan, consider:

- **The probability of success.** You must assess whether or not you can reduce the variance by using a particular alternative and, if so, by how much.

- **Estimates of cost.** You must carefully calculate the cost of implementing each alternative.

- **Past experience.** Knowing what actions have and have not resolved similar problems in the past can help you.

- **Feasibility.** Is it possible to implement successfully the alternative that you choose? While this may seem obvious, some restaurant managers waste time wishing things were different instead of accepting the situation as it is and working within its constraints.

- **Operating restraints.** Such factors as your property's quality standards, equipment, and layout and design may prevent you from correcting some problems with variances between standard and actual labor hours.

- **Compromise.** The best plan to resolve a labor control problem is often a compromise between two or more possible solutions.

- **Experimentation.** Sometimes you can test an alternative. One employee or one shift could evaluate revised procedures by using them.

- **Learning from others.** A study of similar hospitality operations, a review of hospitality literature, and conversations with management staff with similar responsibilities may help identify ways to reduce labor problems.

After you have developed a corrective action plan, you should be aware of several important points before you implement it:

- Service staff affected by corrective action often resist changes. They may defend the status quo by saying, "We have always done it this way." As these employee concerns arise, restaurant managers can best resolve them by explaining and defending the need for the changes and, when possible, telling the employees how the changes will make things better for them.

- You must train employees to use the new procedures. Too often, restaurant managers are in a hurry. They show their employees new procedures only once; then they forget about the need for additional training, reinforcement, and coaching.

- Employees should clearly understand what you expect of them; restaurant managers must carefully communicate their expectations to the staff.

- You must make available all tools and equipment required to perform the revised work.

- Employees require supervision both during training and when they start to use the revised procedures.

After you have defined and implemented the corrective action plan, you must evaluate the results to ensure that you have reduced the variance between the standard and actual labor hours. It is also necessary to ensure that the revised procedures have not created spin-off problems in other areas. When evaluating the results of corrective action, you should consider the following:

- The analysis should take place over a

long period so that the observed results adequately reflect the changes which you have implemented. Staff members also need some time to learn what they are supposed to do.

- If corrective action plans significantly tighten up the labor control program, you may need to revise the staffing guide.

- Evaluation should continue over several fiscal periods. Often, changes may produce positive results temporarily but, for some reason, problems recur.

- The evaluation process must be continuous. Begin with a review of the differences between standard and actual labor hours, follow up with corrective action, and conclude with evaluation; then start the process all over again. The effective dining outlet manager is constantly alert for ways to increase employee output and maintain or improve the quality of work which employees perform.

Managing Service at the Hotel Columbia
Page Fourteen

Lewis's secretary handed him the "Dining Room Scheduling Exercise" he had asked for. Lewis knew that this training aid, while fairly simple, was an effective way to help managers consider a wide range of factors when they schedule employees. "I'll show it to my director of restaurant operations." (The exercise accompanies this case study.)

After Don Jackson studied Lewis's scheduling exercise, he decided that it could be used to help the Eagle Room manager:

1. Determine the number of servers necessary to staff the dining room.
2. Assess the number of servers to be scheduled for the week.
3. Determine the number of servers needed each day.
4. Develop a schedule of servers' workdays.

Dining Room Scheduling Exercise

You are the manager of a high-check-average hotel dining room that seats 250 guests. Most of the food is served plated. One of your many responsibilities is to prepare a weekly work schedule for your servers. Some specific factors to consider in drafting next week's schedule include:

1. The restaurant does not serve lunch but is famous for its Sunday brunch which is served plated.

2. The hours of operation are:

Monday–Thursday	5:00 p.m.–10:30 p.m.
Friday–Saturday	5:00 p.m.–11:30 p.m.
Sunday Brunch	11:00 a.m.–3:00 p.m.

3. The variable labor staffing guide suggests that one server assist 13.5 guests at one time.

4. The restaurant averages 2.5 turnovers per table per shift.

5. The daily meal averages from previous months are:

Monday	400	Thursday	570
Tuesday	470	Friday	620
Wednesday	495	Saturday	630
		Sunday	618

6. This week the convention center will host a Shriner's Convention beginning on Monday. Estimates are that the restaurant will serve 160 additional guests on Monday and 100 more on Tuesday.

7. The week has a holiday on Friday which begins a three-day weekend. The holiday is expected to reduce Thursday evening business by 100 guests.

8. The majority of the service staff is off only two shifts weekly.

9. You have several schedule requests for this week:
   • Margaret is in a wedding and needs Saturday/Sunday off.
   • Cindy is a part-time student with classes on Monday and Wednesday nights until 9:00.
   • Jack has asked to work as many hours as possible—tuition is due.
   • Linda needs Sunday off for a family outing.
   You assume all other servers are reasonably flexible as far as the schedule is concerned.

Step 1: Determine the number of servers necessary to staff the dining room.

250	÷	13.5	=	18.5
Total seats		Maximum number of guests per server		Maximum number of servers needed for shift

Step 2: Assess the number of servers to be scheduled for the week.

18.5	×	7	=	129.5
Servers needed daily		Number of Days Open		Total server shifts

129.5	÷	5	=	25.9
Total server shifts		Number of weekly shifts per full-time server		Maximum number of servers to be scheduled for the week

Step 3: Determine the number of servers needed each day.

13.5	×	2.5	=	33.75
Total guests per server		Number of table turnovers		Maximum total guests served per server shift

	Estimated guests to be served						
Day	Regular	Special Event	Total	÷	% Maximum total guests served per server shift	=	Number of servers needed daily*
Mon	400	160	560	÷	33.75	=	17
Tues	470	100	570	÷	33.75	=	17
Wed	495	—	495	÷	33.75	=	15
Thurs	570	(100)	470	÷	33.75	=	14
Fri	620	—	620	÷	33.75	=	18
Sat	630	—	630	÷	33.75	=	19
Sun	618	—	618	÷	33.75	=	18

*Rounded. (When controlling labor costs, you should always calculate the effects of rounding off any numbers. For example, in this exercise, the dining outlet will be overstaffed by .57 for the week.)

Step 4: Develop a schedule of servers' workdays.

Employee Name		Monday	Tuesday	Wednesday	Thursday	Friday	Saturday	Sunday
				Server Scheduling Worksheet				
Margaret	1	ON	ON	ON	ON	ON	—	—
Cindy	2	—*	ON	—	ON	ON	ON	ON
Jack	3	ON	ON	ON	X	X	ON	ON
Linda	4	ON	ON	X	ON	ON	ON	—
Sally	5	ON	ON	X	X	ON	ON	ON
Bill H.	6	ON	ON	X	X	ON	ON	ON
Phil	7	ON	ON	X	X	ON	ON	ON
George	8	ON	ON	X	X	ON	ON	ON
John	9	ON	ON	X	X	ON	ON	ON
Stacey	10	ON	ON	X	X	ON	ON	ON
Ray	11	ON	ON	X	X	ON	ON	ON
Mary	12	ON	ON	—	—	ON	ON	ON
Karen	13	ON	ON	ON	ON	X	X	ON
Mike D.	14	ON	ON	ON	ON	X	X	ON
Sam	15	ON	ON	ON	ON	X	X	ON
Betty B.	16	ON	ON	ON	ON	X	X	ON
Betty C.	17	ON	ON	ON	ON	X	X	ON
Don	18	ON	X	ON	ON	X	ON	ON
Joy	19	X**	X	ON	ON	ON	ON	ON
Glenda	20	X	X	ON	ON	ON	ON	ON
Brenda	21	X	X	ON	ON	ON	ON	X
Mike F.	22	X	X	ON	ON	ON	ON	X
Marj	23	X	X	ON	ON	ON	X	X
Bill J.	24	X	X	ON	X	ON	ON	X
Whitey	25	X	X	ON	X	X	ON	X
Blake	26	X	X	X	X	ON	ON	X
Total Server Shifts		17	17	15	14	18	19	18

*Dash indicates server cannot work that day.
**"X" indicates server is not needed that day.

8

Sales Income Control Systems

Restaurant managers must develop procedures to help ensure that all sales income is collected. Unfortunately, some restaurant managers have a tendency to think that every food service employee is honest, or that problems of dishonesty occur someplace else. One of the first steps to take in developing sales income control procedures is to recognize that theft can and does occur. In fact, loss of income because employees have stolen it is not unusual in the industry. Therefore, the restaurant manager must understand basic principles of sales income control that can help reduce the incidence of theft.

Who should design the income control procedures? Actually, management staff at all organizational levels, along with dining service and other employees, have important roles to play. In hotel and restaurant operations, the profits generated from food and beverage sales help to meet the property's economic goals; therefore, everyone working for the property should be concerned that profit levels do not suffer because of inattention to required sales income control procedures. A commitment to head off problems before they can occur must come from top-level managers.

Restaurant managers should have a special concern for income control. After all, they are responsible for achieving the food service outlet's economic goals. They have a difficult time accomplishing those goals when income is stolen; therefore, they must ensure that the operation *does* receive all sales income which it has generated. At the same time, restaurant managers must address the marketing issue and ensure that cumbersome income collection procedures do not inconvenience guests.

Dining service employees must follow the income collection procedures which restaurant managers develop. Service employees should be concerned about the income control procedures which their property uses because these procedures protect them from allegations of theft. Only effective control systems can provide such protection.

Sales income control systems are designed in much the same way as control systems for any other resource (food or beverage products, labor, energy, etc.). First, you must know the amount of expected (potential) income that your property should generate. Second, you must assess the amount of actual income your employees collect. When the expected and actual income amounts vary, you may have identified a problem. Let's look more closely at procedures to establish anticipated income levels for dining room operations.

Manual Guest Check Procedures

Guest checks are central to the sales income control system in many operations. If you implement procedures that require food servers to write all food and beverage orders on guest checks, and if production employees are not allowed to prepare a food or beverage order without a guest check, you can control income by controlling the guest checks. The total sales income reported on guest checks—after you have accounted for *all* of them—represents your potential sales income.

The control of guest checks begins when you issue them to the service staff. These checks should be numbered sequentially (e.g., 5001, 5002, 5003). Exhibit 8.1 shows a form that you

Managing Service at the Hotel Columbia
Page Fifteen

Lewis Scott was very concerned about the sales income control procedures the restaurant managers would use in the food service outlets at the Hotel Columbia. He had had experience with both cashier and server banking systems. In the former system, cashiers or other register operators collect monies from the guests and/or service staff, then become responsible for all income collected. In the latter system, service employees retain all income collected until the end of their shifts. Lewis thought that he could use cashier banking in the dining outlets and a server banking system in the lounges/bars.

Lewis believed that the individual restaurant managers should contribute to the initial design of the sales income control systems that they would use in their outlets. He would provide them with state-of-the-art electronic data machines offering precheck registers and/or remote printing devices, but he knew they could use guidelines for designing sales income control systems.

"I know I have some general information about the design of sales income control systems," Lewis thought. "With that information, the restaurant managers can get a head start in designing effective income control systems."

can use to record the beginning and ending numbers of all guest checks given to servers. In the presence of a management official, servers can note that they have, in fact, received all the guest checks; their signature on the form confirms that they have received and are responsible for each guest check.

At the end of each server's shift, you must account for all his/her guest checks. Depending on the income control system you use, a check will have been (a) used and retained by the server or cashier, (b) unused and retained by the server, or (c) left in process. If the check is left in process because the server's shift has ended, then another food or beverage server is assigned to the check. After you have accounted for all the guest checks, you can add up the various amounts guests paid for food and beverages to determine the total amount of sales income which the server generated.

Rules for Guest Checks

In most sales income control systems, you should treat guest checks like money. In fact, if employees misuse them, they can create a large and unnecessary expense for the food service operation.

In addition to being numbered sequentially, guest checks should be unique to the property so that dishonest servers cannot purchase them in a restaurant supply store, replace their assigned checks with them when serving customers, and then keep the revenue that should have gone to the property. Also, you should not leave unused guest checks lying around. If you do, dishonest employees can obtain them and use them to bypass the sales income control system.

Duplicate (or triplicate) guest checks are often useful. After food servers take the order from the guests and ring it through a precheck register, they turn one copy into the kitchen and retain the second. The kitchen staff should retain the duplicate copy; many properties use a locked box for this purpose. At the end of the shift, you can match copies to ensure that employees did not tamper with the guest checks to reduce the amount of sales income owed to the operation.

Other common sense rules apply to guest check control. For example, employees should use pens, not pencils, to fill out guest checks. They can cross out mistakes rather than erase them. Management, controller, and/or clerical audits of guest checks are also important on a routine but random basis.

Cash Handling Equipment

Unfortunately, some food service operations use equipment that is almost as antiquated

Exhibit 8.1 Guest Check Number Log

| Date | Shift | Type Check | | Server Name | Guest Check No. | | Signature |
		Food	Bev.		Begin	End	

Source: Adapted from Jack D. Ninemeier, *Food and Beverage Security: A Systems Manual for Restaurants, Hotels, and Clubs* (Boston: CBI, 1982), p. 167.

as the cigar box. Equipment that provides a great deal of income control and financial information is available; frequently, even relatively small operations can justify its cost.

Modern cash registers are really electronic data machines. Depending on how you program them, these units can provide you with such statistics as the total number of guests served, the amount of sales income generated by each food server (use a separate clerk key for each server), the number of guests served and/or income generated during certain time periods, the number of each menu item sold, the income received from these sales, and a wide variety of financial information that you can use for your property's recordkeeping system.

In addition to cash handling equipment, many properties use a precheck register, which is similar to a cash register but does not have a cash drawer. After service employees take orders, they log the guest checks on the precheck register. The machine prints information onto the guest check which serves as an authorization for the food production staff to prepare the menu items.

Some precheck registers use a remote printer. As servers enter guest check information into the precheck register, it automatically prints

order information on a remote device in the production area. Such a system not only saves food servers trips to the production area, but it also reduces the possibility that servers will place orders without entering the information into the machine.

Again, depending on the equipment and the way you program it, precheck registers can tally sales information on a by-server basis. Some units have preset keys; they automatically tabulate the number of items ordered. If production employees know the number of orders that servers have placed for each menu item, they can better control the number of portions they prepare. (The difference between the orders produced and served and the products available in the opening inventory should represent the number of items left in the inventory at the end of the shift.)

Prenumbered guest checks are not necessary for some precheck registers. Rather, a server enters an unnumbered guest check into the unit which automatically assigns a control number to the check; the unit also records the guest check number in its memory. Later, when the server enters the guest check for additional orders, or the guests are ready to leave, the precheck register carries forward previous bal-

Guest Checks and Issuing Procedures

Generally, checks should not be part of the issuing procedures for dining service supplies. Some food service operations keep supplies of guest checks in dining service supply areas for easy access by service personnel. Unless the guest checks do not have check numbers (numbers assigned to them as part of an automated data machine process), this is normally a very poor control procedure. Guest checks are like money. If dishonest service employees gain access to them, they can use them to steal from the property and/or guests. Therefore, management should generally keep guest checks secure and issue them to individual servers on a by-shift as-needed basis only. Servers can verify receipt of their guest checks when they sign a control form.

ances. The machine also enters taxes (and any other necessary charges) both onto the guest check and into its own memory, thus facilitating later statistical tabulation.

Some properties use another interesting variation of precheck register control. For example, beverage servers in the lounge may enter guest check information into the precheck register in that area. The machine then automatically transfers that information to the precheck register at the server, cashier, or checker station. When a guest moves from the lounge to the dining room, units in the food serving area already know how much the guest has spent in the lounge, which, of course, is the amount due to the property at that point.

Income Control Procedures

There are two basic types of sales income collection systems. Either the food or beverage servers collect and retain income from the guests during their entire shift (server banking system), or the bartender, receptionist, or cashier collects income from the guests (cashier banking system). The server banking system is a popular method throughout Europe and is gaining in popularity in the United States. In some operations, servers keep the income they collect on their person; a pouch, pocket, or other device is an integral part of their uniform. More commonly, however, a locked cashier box which is only available for the server's use is located in a server station or other convenient place.

When a property uses a server banking sys-

tem, income verification is very easy. The restaurant manager first accounts for all the guest checks, then totals them to determine the amount of sales income due from the server. Often, he/she can verify that amount with the precheck register.

If a property uses the cashier banking system, the restaurant manager should, if possible, assign each food server a separate clerk key on the cash register. When the cashier collects income, he/she can ring the server's guest check on that server's specific key. At check-out time, after the restaurant manager accounts for all the server's guest checks, he/she can then confirm that the amount of sales income which the cashier rung on the food server's key does, in fact, represent the total income reported on the server's guest checks.

Procedures for Food Servers

As you have already learned, income control procedures for food servers begin with methods for issuing guest checks to servers. To use the checks, a server writes guest orders directly onto them. When the server completes the guest checks, identification numbers (or special keys for food servers) allow him/her to enter information into the precheck register. Some systems require servers to enter information about items and their prices manually; when properties use preset keys, the machine automatically enters this information. Once the machine prints this information on the guest check, the server then takes it to the food production area and gives one copy to the food production staff. Busy operations frequently make use of an expediter to coordinate the activities of the service and production employees. At the end of the meal, the guest receives the check and the server (server banking system) or the cashier (cashier banking system) performs income collection activities.

Procedures for obtaining drinks at the bar are frequently similar to procedures for ordering food; servers write the orders on the guest check, often using the back of it. Many systems require beverage servers to enter the order into a pre-check register before giving the guest check to the bartender for drink preparation. An intermediate step may require the bartender to mark the guest check after preparing the drinks so that he/she will know if a server has failed to enter orders for second and third rounds into the pre-check register.

Some operations use a multiple guest check system. With this plan, servers use separate guest checks for each round of drinks and each meal course. The property provides wall slot-racks or pigeonholes to hold all the guest checks for each table. When guests wish to leave, the servers total these individual guest checks and present them for payment.

Normally, guests pay for both food and beverage products at the same time—typically, at the end of the meal. However, a few properties collect payment when servers take the orders. For some, this procedure is a matter of tradition; properties even capitalize on the unique way that their service system operates. With other properties, this method eliminates the *dine and dash* problem. Some facilities implement this pay-in-advance policy only during late night hours or other specific times.

When food servers complete their shifts, the restaurant manager must account for all guest checks assigned to them and must compare the guest check totals with the register control totals and the actual collections. When a property uses a server banking system, a precheck register becomes even more important; it is often the only way to double-check the amount of income due from food servers.

Management can also use daily physical inventories of the property's food products to verify that the number of menu items sold (from the precheck register tallies) is correct. If inventory records indicate that the production department received 25 steaks and 3 remain, the precheck register tallies should confirm that 22 steaks

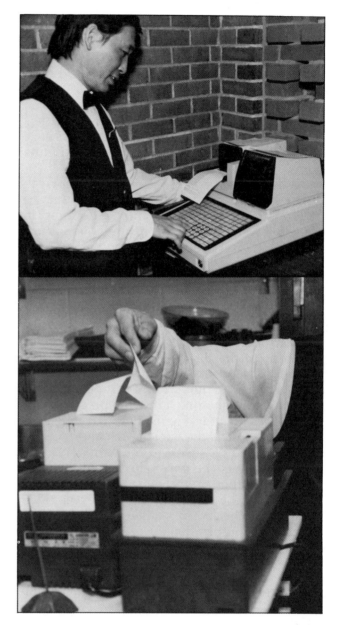

Server using point-of-sale register to send order to kitchen, and expediter removing printout from kitchen remote printer. (University Club, Michigan State University)

were served. Of course, adjustments for burns, returns, and other situations will be necessary.

Procedures for Beverage Servers

Normally, beverage servers are responsible for providing service to guests in lounge areas. However, in some food service operations, they also provide beverage service in the dining areas. When properties use this latter method, requirements for ordering and serving beverages and for controlling sales income should be identical in both the dining room and lounge areas.

Sometimes, beverage servers are also responsible for serving food in lounge areas. For example, they might serve appetizers or even light meals. In such operations, beverage servers would follow the same kind of income control procedures as are used in the property's dining rooms.

When the bartender is responsible for collecting sales income from the beverage server, the actual process of serving beverages in lounges is very similar to our previous discussion of food service in the dining room. For example, beverage servers take drink orders and ring them through a precheck register. They give the printed guest check to the bartender. The bartender prepares the drinks, perhaps rings the guest check through an "accounts receivable" function on the bar cash register, then returns the check to the beverage server. (Again, the bartender should mark the guest check to ensure that a server does not order a second round of drinks without entering it into the precheck register.) When the guest is ready to pay, the beverage server totals the guest check and takes it, along with the payment, to the bartender. The bartender enters the guest check into the cash register and rings up the sale.

You may have noted that employees must handle guest checks several times. To simplify the process, some operations use a server banking system in the lounge. With this system, beverage servers pay the bartender for the drinks when they pick them up—just like a paying guest would. The guest's payment then replenishes the server's bank. You can develop procedures to handle large groups, payments with credit cards, and even transfers of charges between the lounge and dining room areas so that this system is quite workable. When you use it, you eliminate some potential areas of employee abuse.

Some operations permit guests to run a tab in the lounge area or at the bar. Beverage servers keep a record of the guest's orders so that the guest only needs to pay once for all drinks (rounds) which he/she has received. An advantage to this plan, of course, is its convenience for the guest. Disadvantages include the additional effort required to keep track of the number of drinks served and the possibility that guests will leave without paying their tab. Typically, the decision about whether to permit the running of a tab rests with the beverage servers. After all, they are responsible for sales recorded in the precheck register and on guest checks. Or, if they have to pay cash to the bartender at the time they pick up the drinks, they will want to ensure that they receive payment from the guests to replenish their cash banks.

In contrast, some properties establish policies that require payment as employees serve each round of drinks. While this policy may be easier for the property and more convenient for the service staff, it may irritate the guests.

Some properties implement policies that permit the running of a tab during all but the busiest times. During those periods, guests must pay for each round of drinks as it is served. To avert potential guest complaints, well-trained service staff can explain the property's policies when they first take the guest's orders.

Procedures for Bartenders

Income control at the bar is a constant management challenge. Perhaps no other food service employee requires as much constant supervision and surveillance as the bartender because he/she is responsible not only for taking orders from guests at the bar, but also for preparing and serving drink orders, collecting income, and recording sales information on the cash register. When you cannot assign production, service, and income collection duties to several employees, you have an increased potential for employee theft.

An increasing number of properties use a beverage cashier to work with the bartender. This person collects income for products sold and rings it up on the bar cash register in much the same way as the food cashier in the dining area. Some properties view this employee as unnecessary; others believe that they can justify the small amount they pay for such an employee in terms of reduced potential for bartender theft.

What system should you use to control sales income generated by the bartender? When practical, you should use a guest check system similar to the one designed for food servers. Typically, you need only a single-copy guest check. With this plan, you issue numbered guest checks to the bartender. He/she records on the guest checks the orders from guests seated at the bar, then prepares the drinks. The bartender places the guest check face down in front of the guest when he/she serves the drink. When the guest wishes to pay, the bartender puts the guest check in the cash register. After ringing up the sale on the guest check, the bartender places it in a locked guest check box. While employees can misuse this system and it may be impractical during busy times, once management accounts for and totals all the bartender's guest checks, the total can be double-checked with the amount of sales rung up on the bartender's cash register.

Management has at least one additional tool to help ensure that bartenders follow the required sales income control procedures—a shopping service. When a property uses this service, people who are not employed by the property visit the bar, pose as guests, and report their findings to management. This evaluation technique is especially effective when bartenders are aware that the property plans to use a shopping service on a frequent but random basis.

Procedures for Cashiers

While many of the procedures designed to control income generated by the bartender also apply to the cashier (since both use a cash register), specific procedures are needed when you have cashiers in dining areas.

First of all, you should develop a detailed set of operating procedures for the use of the cash register and require cashiers to follow them at all times. Exhibit 8.2 describes procedures that specific properties might find useful. As is true with bartenders, cashiers must be responsible for their beginning cash bank and for all sales income that they collect; you must use some method to double-check the amount of income which is in the register at the end of each shift.

There are two basic methods of tallying sales information. In using the first, cashiers manually abstract information from each guest check. Exhibit 8.3 illustrates a form which they could use. This form not only determines, by food server, the amount of income generated from each product (food, liquor, wine, and beer/soda), but also represents a source of information about anticipated income. It also provides a source document to manage the payment of charged tips.

When servers are paid tips that have been charged to guests' credit cards, they initial column 11.

Managers use the second method when checking out cashiers at the end of their shifts. Exhibit 8.4 illustrates a form that managers can use to (a) take sales information from the "X" and "Z" register readings (Part I); (b) determine sales income collected from a physical count of all currency, checks, and charge vouchers (Part II); and (c) recap by comparing total sales with actual amounts turned in (Part III). (It is not necessary to use *both* the cashier's guest check sales record and the cashier's department sales record to tally sales information when using the cashier banking method; one form is sufficient.)

Income Theft: Methods and Precautions

There are numerous ways in which dishonest employees attempt to steal sales income. The discussions that follow list possible types of employee theft and precautions which management can take to reduce the possibility of theft by these methods.[1]

Bartender Theft

Type of theft: Violating procedures used for cash register operation, including bunching sales (adding two or more sales together and ringing up the total), no rings (money is collected but isn't put into the cash register), and making change from the tip jar.

Precaution: Ensure through close supervision that bartenders consistently follow procedures similar to those listed in Exhibit 8.2 each time they operate the cash register.

Type of theft: Underpouring drinks and pocketing cash from the sale of the extra drink. If bartenders underpour drinks by 1/4 ounce, they could pocket the sales from every fifth drink without affecting the established beverage cost percentage.

---

[1] Adapted from Jack D. Ninemeier, *Food and Beverage Security: A Systems Manual for Restaurants, Hotels, and Clubs* (Boston: CBI, 1982), pp. 75-88.

Exhibit 8.2 Sample Cash Register Operating Procedures

Cash Bank:

At the beginning of each shift, personnel who will operate a cash register are given a cash bank. The amount of money in the bank will be set by management and will not vary from shift to shift. A minimum amount of currency to ensure that change can be made throughout the shift should be determined. For example, in a lounge with drink prices set on a twenty-five-cent graduated basis ($1.25, $1.50, $1.75, etc.) the following amounts for a $200 cash bank may be very effective.

NUMBER	UNIT	TOTAL DOLLARS
50	$ 1.00	$50.00
2	10.00	20.00
15	5.00	75.00
2 ROLLS	.25	20.00
1 ROLL	.10	5.00
2 ROLLS	.01	1.00
2 ROLLS	.05	4.00

The balance ($25.00) will be composed of dollar bills and "broken roll" change.

As a minimum, currency in the amounts shown will be needed to make up the cash bank. Responsibility for securing change should be assumed by management, who will be able to obtain change from the bank when deposits are made. Cashiers and bartenders should not be permitted to bring in their own change. The bank should remain intact. No IOUs, no petty cash receipts, personal loans, or other deductions from the cash balance will be carried in the bank.

Personnel receiving a cash bank should sign a document showing that they have done so. (A sample form is shown in Exhibit 8.5.) From that point, personnel will be responsible for their own cash bank until the end of their shift. The employee should be permitted to count the beginning bank in the presence of management to make sure that the correct amount of cash is in the beginning bank.

At the end of the shift, the value of the beginning bank should be counted out first. The remaining funds in the cash drawer should, of course, equal the value of sales income necessary to satisfy register tape and/or guest check and precheck register totals. Register operators will be liable for any shortages in cash banks or sales income.*

Specific Register Operating Procedures:

The cash drawer is to be closed when not in use.

Each ticket must be rung up separately. At no time should two or more tickets be totaled in the bartender's head and rung as a total. Each ticket will be closely checked to ensure that the printed ring-up agrees with the total charge due from the guest.

At no time is the bartender's tip jar to be near the cash register. The tip jar should be located away from the cash register to eliminate the possibility of the bartender making change from it or removing money from the register to the tip jar.

Bills over $20.00 should be placed under the currency tray. Bills collected from the customer should remain on the register shelf until the transaction is acceptable to the guest. When making change, count from the amount of the sale to the amount of money given by the customer. Call the manager on duty if there are any questions regarding cash collection or change making.

Only the bartender or cashier should have access to the register. No employee other than the one with responsibility should use, enter, or otherwise have any contact with the cash register for any reason whatsoever. Management may, of course, conduct spot audits of tapes and currency as believed necessary.

The appropriate department key must be depressed to record the type of transaction represented by the guest check being rung up. All procedures in register ring-up should be designed to provide sales information on a department basis for greater accuracy in financial accounting.

*Restaurant managers should check with their attorney or other officials to determine the legality of requiring employees to make up cash register shortages.

Exhibit 8.2, continued

Separate cash drawers (or separate cash registers) should be used by each person having access to the cash register.

The register user should not be able to read or total the machine. Information regarding total sales should not be made known to the cashier/bartender.

Cashiers/bartenders should begin each shift with a new bank.

Each register user should have a separate key to the register. A separate identification number should be used to identify transactions on cash register tapes.

Each sale must be rung up in proper sequence, in the proper amount, and without "bunching" or totaling tickets. Each ticket or transaction must be rung separately.

Each register user should have a written copy of procedures for use of the cash register.

Register users, when practical, should call out the price of items being rung on the register.

The cash drawer should only be opened by depressing the sales price or "no sale" key. It should not be possible to enter the machine by use of a lever or other mechanical device, except in case of power outage.

Detail tapes should be replaced before they run out (there is generally a colored strip or other marking which becomes noticeable as the tape supply diminishes).

Registers should be empty, unlocked, and left open when not in use (or drawers should be removed) to prevent damage to machine during possible theft attempts.

Voids, overrings, or other problems should be reported to management as soon as possible after they occur.

Surprise cash register audits, including the counting of money in the drawer(s), should be made on a random basis.

Management should watch the cash register and its operation closely as part of its ongoing supervisory responsibilities.

Detail tapes should be studied on a random basis to uncover possible fraud.

Cashiers are not allowed to accept postdated checks or IOUs in payment or as collateral for loans.

Only a minimum number of supervisory personnel should have access to cash register keys.

Register banks should be counted and exchanged at each change in cashiers; cash register tapes are read or totaled and cleared at this time.

All checks accepted from employees are immediately marked "FOR DEPOSIT ONLY." Forms should be available to record, by shift, sales from each register (point-of-sale) for food and beverage service for the entire day (or other period).

Register balances should be reconciled with cash receipts at least once each shift.

Cash income from miscellaneous sales (vending proceeds, grease, returnable bottles, etc.) must be properly recorded in business accounts if it is first deposited in a cash register.

Cash register bell, alarm, or buzzer systems should not be bypassed; a noise should be heard each time the cash drawer is opened.

The cash register should be located in a position visible to guests, employees, and management.

If a register is used by a food cashier who collects sales revenues directly from guests, the machine should be located close to the exit.

Exhibit 8.2, continued

Cash registers should be kept locked during service periods when the register operator is not at the machine.

Audits of detail tapes should ensure continuity in transaction numbers. The first transaction number for a new shift should be in sequence with the last transaction number from the previous shift's detail tape.

Constant cash overages should be investigated. (The register user may be underringing and removing only part of the money to avoid a shortage which might alert management.)

Random and unexpected audits should be made of the cash register. The machine should be read to determine the amount of sales during the shift. This sales income plus the amount of the beginning cash bank should be in the register. If there is more money in the machine, it may be because the operator has "not rung" or has underrung sales and has not had time to remove the cash.

Cash register readings should not be made by the cashier/bartender.

No money should be paid out of cash register funds without the approval of management, and then only with the writing up of a paid-out slip; if applicable, an invoice or sales slip should be attached.

The cash register should not be used as an imprest petty cash fund.

All employees who handle cash should be bonded.

Source: Adapted from Ninemeier, *Food and Beverage Security*, pp. 67-70.

Precaution: Require bartenders to prepare all drinks using a shot glass or jigger; do not permit free pouring. Use shoppers regularly to ensure compliance with sales income control procedures.

Type of theft: Bringing in personal bottles and preparing drinks from these bottles.
Precaution: Mark bottles and use a subsequent visual inspection program to help eliminate this practice. Keep bottle stamps (property identification tags) secure (e.g., in a safe) so that employees cannot misuse them.

Type of theft: Accumulating the individual drink sales made with one liquor until the entire bottle is used, recording a bottle sale (usually at a lower sale price than the individual drinks), and pocketing the difference.
Precaution: Use shoppers, implement effective cash register operating controls, closely su-

pervise employees, and require bartenders to record all drinks served on guest checks.

Type of theft: Selling drinks for cash and recording them as spilled, returned, or complimentary.
Precaution: Do not allow bartenders to give out free drinks or discard returned drinks without management approval. You must also retrain and more closely supervise bartenders or other employees who have excessive spillage or other high pouring costs.

Type of theft: Diluting liquor and keeping income from extra sales.
Precaution: Use shoppers to watch the bartender. Investigate frequent guest complaints about beverage quality. Gin and vodka may become cloudy when you add water or soda to them; other liquors turn a lighter color.

Exhibit 8.3 Cashier's Guest Check Sales Record

DATE: __10/01/00__   Name of Cashier: __James Frank__

SHIFT: __PM__

Food Server Name (check one)					Amount of Sale						Type of Sale			Tip	
Helen	Cindy	Phyllis	John	Guest Check No.	Food (1)	Tax (2)	Liquor (3)	Wine (4)	Beer/ Soda (5)	Total Sale (6)	Cash (7)	Charge (8)	Room Charge (9)	Tips Paid Out (10)	Server Initials (11)
✓				211780	15.83	.63	—	—	1.25	17.71	✓				
	✓			211388	32.20	1.29	—	9.50		42.99		✓		6.50	CA
	✓			211389	45.95	1.84	4.00	8.75		60.54			✓	10.00	CA
TOTALS					Col. 1	Col. 2	Col. 3	Col. 4	Col. 5	Col. 6					

Source: Adapted from Ninemeier, *Food and Beverage Security*, p. 185.

Type of theft: Serving a low-quality brand when guests request a call brand and pocketing the extra cash (substitution).

Precaution: Require bartenders and cocktail servers to write all drink orders on a guest check; the amount rung and printed on the guest check should equal the total charge on the guest check.

Type of theft: Working in collusion with a cocktail server so that the property does not receive income for drinks prepared and served; the bartender and server split the income earned.

Precaution: Rotate employee shifts. Management should also be alert to gossip about employee relationships and use control systems to monitor beverage cost percentages.

Type of theft: Writing a lower sales income value on the guest check and ringing it into the register (undercharging).

Precaution: Make routine audits of guest checks to ensure that pricing "errors" do not occur.

Type of theft: Trading liquor with the cook for food products.

Precaution: Enforce all eating and drinking policies. Management employees should stay alert for signs of eating and drinking, such as

Exhibit 8.4 Cashier's Department Sales Record

DATE: *1/15/00* SHIFT: *PM* NAME OF CASHIER *Jane Fenimore*

Part I—Cash Register Key Totals:

KEY #1 ___*Food*___ (Dept.)
Sales $ *961.91*
add underrings* $ —
less overrings* $ —
TOTAL SALES $ *961.91*

KEY #2 ___*Tax (Food)*___ (Dept.)
Sales $ *38.48*
add underrings* $ —
less overrings* $ —
TOTAL SALES $ *38.48*

KEY #3 ___*Liquor*___ (Dept.)
Sales $ *240.10*
add underrings* $ *1.00*
less overrings* $ —
TOTAL SALES $ *241.10*

KEY #4 ___*Wine*___ (Dept.)
Sales $ *282.80*
add underrings* $ —
less overrings* $ *2.00*
TOTAL SALES $ *280.50*

KEY #5 ___*Beer/Soda*___ (Dept.)
Sales $ *98.25*
add underrings* $ —
less overrings* $ —
TOTAL SALES $ *98.25*

TOTAL SALES $ *1620.24*
(ALL DEPTS.)

*Approved by manager.

Part II—Sales Income Collected:

Cash in Drawer	$ *1309.92*
Less Beginning Bank	$ *(200.00)*
Cash Sales	$ *1109.92*
Charge Sales	$ *+500.00*
Check Sales	$ *+12.32*
Total Sales Income	$ *1622.24*
Turned In	$

Part III—Recap

Total Sales (Part I)	$ *1620.24*
Actual Sales Income Collected (Part II)	$ *1622.24*
CASH OVER	$ *2.00*
CASH SHORT	$

Comments:

Source: Adapted from Ninemeier, *Food and Beverage Security*, p. 187.

plates and glasses in the restrooms or items hidden at work stations.

Type of theft: Using stolen checks to replace cash.

Precaution: Do not allow bartenders to accept checks without management approval.

Type of theft: Using own guest checks to collect sales income.

Determining How Much Income to Collect

Many restaurant managers take an unfortunate shortcut when they assume that everything is fine if the income rung on the cash register equals the income in the cash drawer, or when the amount turned in by the server seems to be all right. Restaurant managers should establish a system to determine the amount of income they should collect. Follow-through procedures then become important to ensure that the income they collect does, in fact, match the anticipated income level.

Restaurant managers should develop income control systems which provide at least two, if not three, ways to double-check income amounts. For example, when using a precheck register in a cashier banking system, the sum of the guest checks should equal the amount rung on the precheck register. Both of these totals should agree with the total rung on the cash register. Further, managers should be sure to reconcile register control totals taken at the end of each shift with the master control meter that is a feature on most cash register systems. You cannot reset this meter, so no one can clear the machine without authorization.

Precaution: Use unique, hard-to-duplicate guest checks in your property.

Type of theft: Mingling sales income with tips.

Precaution: Do not permit the location of tip jars in areas close to the cash register.

Type of theft: Using counterfeit bottle stamp or other property identification tag to mark personal bottle.

Precaution: Use unique, hard-to-duplicate bottle stamps in your property. Keep identification tools and supplies secure.

Type of theft: Bringing in personal jigger to aid in over/underpouring.

Precaution: Routinely check the portion control tools in use. Bartenders should use only the portion tools provided by the facility.

Type of theft: Taking cash from the cash drawer.

Precaution: Use a basic sales income control system to determine exactly how much money should be in the cash drawer; where legal, make the bartender liable for all cash shortages.

Type of theft: Borrowing from the cash bank.

Precaution: Check the cash bank at the beginning and end of each shift. The amount of cash in the bank should remain constant.

Type of theft: Giving away drinks to friends to promote a bigger tip.

Precaution: Do not allow bartenders to provide complimentary drinks without management approval. Guest checks should be in front of each guest at all times. Use shoppers to spot these and similar problems.

Type of theft: Reusing paid guest checks. (The bartender serves a guest and collects the sales income but does not ring it up. He/she then uses the guest check for other orders of the same type.)

Precaution: Require bartenders to ring up all tickets when they receive cash and deposit them in a locked box to which only management has access.

Type of theft: Ringing sales on another bartender's key, causing another bartender to come up short, and pocketing the income from the sales.

Precaution: If possible, assign each bartender a separate register, or at least use separate cash drawers. If you cannot, keep a record of shortages that occur when each bartender is working.

Food/Beverage Server Theft

Type of theft: Receiving food from the kitchen and/or beverages from the bar without

Facts About Employee Theft

Did you know that a food service operation that has a 10% profit margin (10% of gross sales is profit) must generate $10 of income for each dollar stolen in order to overcome that loss? So, while the theft of $1 doesn't seem significant, the loss of $10 in sales income certainly is. Many hospitality operations lose thousands of dollars each year because of employee theft. That translates into tens of thousands of dollars in wasted sales annually. No hospitality organization can afford that.

Did you know that the purpose of sales income control systems is *not* to catch thieves? Rather, it is to help keep honest employees honest; effective sales income control systems help reduce employees' temptation to steal.

Did you know that a correlation may not exist between an employee's length of service and his/her desire to steal? Often, properties do not require experienced employees to follow established income control procedures. However, the restaurant manager's belief that experienced employees are honest may actually permit them to bypass the same income control procedures which safeguard revenue from theft by new employees.

recording them on the guest check and pocketing the income received from these products.

Precaution: Do not allow production personnel to give food or beverages to service personnel without a copy of a guest check unless, as in the case of cocktail servers, service personnel pay cash for the drinks when they pick them up.

Type of theft: Collecting cash from a guest without a guest check and pocketing the cash.

Precaution: Same as previous precaution.

Type of theft: Reusing a paid check, or collecting cash from one guest with a guest check that has already been presented to another guest.

Precaution: Record all guest checks given to food servers by number and match them up with their duplicates. Do not allow servers to take food or beverages out of the preparation area without submitting a duplicate check.

Type of theft: Collecting cash and destroying the guest check.

Precaution: Same as previous precaution.

Type of theft: Underadding the check or omitting items for friends to influence the amount of tip.

Precaution: Audit guest checks to check arithmetic; match up original and duplicate copies.

Type of theft: Collecting cash with personal guest checks.

Precaution: Use guest checks unique to your restaurant.

Type of theft: Providing high-priced items to friends and recording them as low-priced items.

Precaution: Use and match up duplicate checks to ensure that items which servers picked up from the kitchen or bar are, in fact, the items for which they received payment.

Type of theft: Collecting sales income from guests and alleging that a guest walkout occurred.

Precaution: Closely supervise all dining areas to minimize walkout problems; all food and beverage servers should keep a record of walkouts that do occur. You should retrain and more closely supervise any server with more than an infrequent rate of walkouts.

Type of theft: Collecting for a beverage transfer from the lounge to the restaurant, destroying the ticket, pocketing the cash, and claiming that the transferred guest check was never received.

Precaution: Use a method for processing beverage transfers that involves a ticket mark-off system along with the physical presentation of a transferred check by the host or hostess to the food server.

Employee Lockers: A Potential Source of Trouble

Many food and beverage operations provide locker room facilities for employees. This fringe benefit can often be very expensive for the property, especially when employees use locker facilities to store stolen items until they can remove them from the building. At least two design features can be built into lockers that can help prevent theft and abuse. First, a wire mesh (screen) door front promotes air circulation and permits management staff to easily view the insides of lockers. Second, tall lockers can be built with slanted tops that eliminate the surface on which stolen items are sometimes placed out of sight. (Slanted top lockers also eliminate dust buildup and other unsanitary conditions.)

It is important for managers to develop policies regarding locker inspections. Consult your attorney to learn what steps you can legally take; for example, can you inspect the inside of employee lockers at least once a week to discourage employees from using them as hiding places for pilfered goods?

Another good control measure is to require all employees to leave through the same exit and to conduct regular checks at this exit. Any employee who leaves by other than the designated exit is automatically suspect. Again, consult with your attorney to learn whether you have the right to set up such a control measure.

Type of theft: Collecting sales income, destroying the ticket, claiming the ticket was lost, and turning in the alleged correct amount which is lower than income collected.

Precaution: Where legal, assess servers a charge for lost checks. Keep records of lost checks, and retrain and more closely supervise servers with more than an infrequent number of lost checks. Also, examine duplicate checks to verify the alleged value of food items on the lost check.

Type of theft: Collecting sales income for a ticket, deleting items because of alleged returns, and pocketing the cash.

Precaution: Require servers to report all returns, burns, and other problems of this nature to management as they occur.

Type of theft: Serving guests, collecting sales income, deleting some items because a guest allegedly didn't eat or have a drink, and pocketing the cash.

Precaution: Match up original and duplicate copies of guest checks.

Type of theft: Serving items (coffee, desserts, etc.) to which servers help themselves, charging guests for the items, deleting them from the check before submitting check to the management, and pocketing the cash.

Precaution: Whenever possible, do not allow food servers to help themselves to items which they will serve.

Type of theft: Eating food and drinking beverages that were not paid for by the server.

Precaution: Consistently enforce all policies regarding eating and drinking.

Cashier Theft

Type of theft: Collecting cash with a guest check and recording the check as void.

Precaution: Match guest checks with their duplicates; require cashiers to report all voids to management.

Type of theft: Collecting cash with a guest check and recording it as a charge.

Precaution: Require cashiers to consistently follow all procedures regarding the use of credit cards.

Type of theft: Collecting cash and recording the transaction as a guest walkout.

Precaution: Require cashiers to keep a record of all walkouts; retrain or reassign any employee with more than a very occasional walkout.

Type of theft: Removing cash and indicating a shortage.

Precaution: Use an effective sales income control system to indicate the amount of sales income that should be in the cash register. Remove any employee with excessive shortages from the cashier's position.

Type of theft: Using invoices for personal expenses as pay-outs from the register.
Precaution: Require prior management approval for all pay-outs and make them from petty cash funds.

Type of theft: Underadding cash sheets at the end of the shift.
Precaution: Allow only management staff to make all calculations determining sales income; others should audit those calculations. Compare the cash sheet totals to the guest check totals after you have accounted for all the guest checks.

Type of theft: Failing to record cash income from returning bottles, selling grease to a renderer, vending machine proceeds, and other miscellaneous sales.
Precaution: Allow only management staff to accept payment for such miscellaneous income.

Type of theft: Underringing the check, bunching tickets, using no-ring transactions, manipulating the register sales journal tape, stealing from the cash drawer, and more.
Precaution: Require cashiers to follow at all times the property's procedures regarding the use of the cash register.

Type of theft: Ringing up sales on another cashier's key, thereby making that cashier short of income, and pocketing the cash.
Precaution: If possible, assign each cashier a separate register. At least use separate cash drawers activated by separate register keys.

Type of theft: Collecting sales income from guests and indicating guest dissatisfaction or refusal to pay.
Precaution: Do not allow cashiers to give complimentary meals without management approval.

Type of theft: Receiving cash, destroying the guest check, and claiming that the check was never received.
Precaution: This method implicates the food or beverage server as the guilty party. If the

problem occurs more than very occasionally, require food servers to bring their checks to the cashier who then initials a separate guest check record indicating that he/she has received the checks. You may also want to consider the use of a food server banking system, which would eliminate the cashier.

Type of theft: Changing the ticket to show a reduced amount owed and pocketing the cash.
Precaution: Require cashiers to ring up guest checks at the time that they collect the cash. Do not allow tickets to be erased. Also, match up duplicate checks.

Type of theft: Adding a tip to the charge voucher and pocketing the cash.
Precaution: Require cashiers to follow all procedures involving the acceptance of credit cards. Do not permit changes on credit card slips. If an error occurs during the original write-up of the charge voucher, make the cashier re-write it.

Type of theft: Taking money from the cash drawer and replacing it with a stolen check or fabricated charge slip.
Precaution: Require cashiers to follow all procedures regarding the acceptance of checks and credit cards and supervise them closely to see that they do so.

Guest Theft

Restaurant managers must develop systems to ensure that guests pay what they owe the operation. The following list, while not complete, describes some types of theft by guests and possible precautions against such theft.[2] You can guard against guest theft by designing preventive measures and training employees to carefully and consistently follow required procedures.

Type of theft: Failing to note errors in arithmetic on guest checks that favor the guest.

Precaution: Require service employees to work carefully and to use an adding machine or cash register to total guest checks.

---

2 Ninemeier, *Food and Beverage Security*, pp. 87-88.

Type of theft: Passing worthless checks and/or using a voided credit card.

Precaution: Train employees to follow at all times the required procedures regarding the acceptance of checks and the use of credit cards.

Type of theft: Leaving without paying the bill, or leaving only a partial payment (a walkout).

Precaution: Train food servers, cashiers, and other personnel to notice when guests are getting ready to leave. They should present bills promptly. Food servers must give constant attention to all guests. Management should keep records of walkouts to determine whether any server or cashier is responsible for more than an infrequent number.

Type of theft: Paying only part of the total bill when the server presents more than one check to the party.

Precaution: Staple all checks together, include the total of all checks on the front of the top check, and total all checks on an adding machine. (Attach the tape to the ticket.)

Type of theft: Disclaiming charges for beverages served in the lounge and transferred to the dining room.

Precaution: Have guests sign beverage checks in the lounge before they move into the dining room. Since beverage transfers require more processing work, you might want to discourage, but not prohibit, guests from transferring charges.

Type of theft: Passing worthless currency or traveler's checks.

Precaution: For advice regarding the identification of worthless currency, contact the property's security department or the local police. Generally, employees can easily identify all but extremely professional counterfeiting if they are even marginally observant. Many counterfeiters reproduce currency on low-quality paper with inks and inferior processes that quickly reveal their lack of authenticity. Do not return such currency to the passer; rather, notify your security department who will detain the passer and notify police if that is the procedure used in your operation. While the passer is probably not the counterfeiter, he/she may be able to trace the source of the bill(s). When guests present bills in denominations of $100 or more, you may want to require employees to obtain management opinion regarding the worth of such currency.

Type of theft: Failing to point out omissions of food or beverages from guest checks.

Precaution: Require servers to enter all food and beverage charges on guest checks *before* they receive the food or beverages.

Type of theft: Claiming that the cashier or bartender made an error in making change.

Precaution: Train cashiers to leave the currency they receive on the register ledge until the guest is satisfied with the accuracy of the transaction.

Type of theft: Disclaiming credit card charges listed on one's subsequent credit card statement.

Precaution: Have the guests sign their guest check, as well as the charge voucher, whenever they make a payment with a charge card.

Type of theft: Stealing glassware or flatware, restaurant furnishings, and other items.

Precaution: Train dining service personnel to remove all soiled serviceware as soon as possible. For example, if guests order a second drink, the servers should remove the first glass as they present the second drink. Service employees should also look for items missing from the table as guests leave. They should contact management (rather than accuse the guests themselves) if they suspect a problem.

Type of theft: Changing the amount of total sales on the guest check.

Precaution: Attach an adding machine tape showing all the charges on the guest check. Have the cashier compare the tape amount and total guest check amount when the guest pays the bill.

Type of theft: Claiming sickness, damage to garments, or personal injury after leaving the property.

Precaution: While these may not be examples of theft, money losses to the facility can result from such allegations. Contact the property's insurance company and/or attorney for instructions to follow in the event of such circumstances. Train employees to notify management immediately when such allegations occur; make certain they know that under no circumstances are they to make any statements or take any actions other than to contact management immediately.

Accepting Noncash Payments

A complete sales income control program must also include procedures that help ensure that income is not diverted by guests committing fraudulent acts at the time of payment. Restaurant managers should make procedures for accepting checks and credit cards important parts of their income control plans.[3]

Check Acceptance Procedures

The acceptance of personal and business checks can be a potential source of great loss to restaurant operators. Checks have advantages: employees are less likely to steal checks than cash and, unlike credit cards, there are no discounts to pay on checks. But the fact remains that checks may be worthless. Therefore, as a minimum control, consider using the following procedures for each check presented:

Have management approve all checks. Unless the employee accepts responsibility and will reimburse the restaurant for a check which is returned NSF (nonsufficient funds) or "Account Closed," management must approve the acceptance of all checks. This rule should have no exceptions. Checks should be initialed by the employee accepting them.

Make a list of all bad checks. Management should develop and make accessible a list of all people and businesses whose checks should not be honored. This list should include the names of all guests whose current checks are outstanding.

Customers using checks for payment must have proper identification. Before you accept a

check, request two pieces of identification (e.g., driver's license, major credit card, state I.D.). Compare the names and addresses. Do not accept a check without the bearer's name printed on it by the issuing bank.

Management should use check approval services. If a national check approval service is available, consider using it. This service generally requires approval from the company before you can honor a check. If the bank does not honor an approved check, the check approval service will reimburse the restaurant for the bad check. A discount fee is charged for the service.

Put returned checks on "Hold." Turn over checks returned NSF to the bank to arrange "Hold for Collection" procedures. Essentially, "Hold for Collection" is a process by which the bank will use any money deposited into the account within a specific period of time to honor the property's NSF check.

Report "Account Closed" checks. Without exception, report checks written on closed accounts to local police officials. In some municipalities, police will assist properties with the collection of lost revenue and the prosecution of guilty individuals. If you cannot recover the amount of the check, consider securing the services of a collection agency. Generally, these agencies levy a service charge based on a percentage of the bad debts collected. If the restaurant manager is certain that the check writer will not reimburse the restaurant for the value of the bad check, hiring a professional collection agency may be the only solution to the problem.[4]

Accept checks for the exact amount of purchase only. If you allow guests to write checks for larger amounts than they owe, you are essentially giving them a cash advance. Accept only those checks that are written for the exact amount of purchase; do not make additional advances.

---

[3] Ninemeier, *Food and Beverage Security*, pp. 64-70.

[4] For further information about setting up a system for collecting overdue accounts and/or employing a collection agency, consult Donna M. Paananen's *Successful Credit and Collection Techniques* (East Lansing, Mich.: Educational Institute of the American Hotel & Motel Association, 1981), pp. 28-34.

Management should refuse postdated checks. Do not accept postdated checks for any reason; the restaurant should not provide loan services to guests.

Avoid two-party checks. Do not accept two-party checks; all checks that you accept should name the restaurant as the payee.

Restaurant managers who receive bad checks should learn for future use how to identify those checks judged potentially most troublesome. In university communities, for example, managers might hesitate to honor checks drawn on banks in students' hometowns, checks written by students during the last week or two of the semester, and checks with low account numbers which suggest that accounts were only recently opened. Additional check acceptance policies might include:

1. Not cashing checks for guests who appear to be drunk.

2. Being *most* careful when cashing checks that are more than a few days old.

3. Ensuring that all checks are legible and made out to the correct name of the restaurant.

4. Not cashing checks with erasures, smudges, or other signs of tampering.

5. Not accepting checks marked "For Deposit Only," "For Collection Only," or with similar terms.

6. Stamping checks with "For Deposit Only" immediately after acceptance.

7. Having the guest sign the check in the presence of the cashier, food/beverage server, or bartender.

8. Requiring the presentation of a valid credit card for check acceptance. (Some managers believe that there is a correlation between credit card holders and the worth of checks written by them. They "call in" the credit card number and, if it is valid, they accept a check from the credit card holder.)

Credit Card Acceptance Procedures

Employees accepting credit cards for payment should be trained to use whichever of the following procedures management has set as policy in a property:

Follow authorization procedures. Follow all current rules issued by credit card companies regarding authorization procedures (amount of charge requiring authorization, effective date of card, use of cancellation bulletin, etc.). Naturally, the property will accept only those credit cards that represent a contract between the credit card company and the restaurant.

Use the credit card imprinter correctly. After the card is inserted properly into the imprinter and the voucher is imprinted with the card's information, closely check the hard copy of the voucher to ensure that all card numbers are embossed on it. If they are not legible, either repeat the process, or, with an ink pen, write legible card numbers over the illegible ones.

Request the guest's signature. Have the guest sign the embossed credit voucher. You should also require the guest to sign the guest check(s) to verify that he/she was present and did incur the charge should a future claim arise. Make certain that the credit card is returned to the guest.

Initial or sign credit card vouchers. Employees who complete credit vouchers should sign or initial them. (The management official who checks out employees with cash responsibilities should verify that all vouchers are properly completed. Some properties make the employee responsible for any credit card charges that are not collected because of errors in the credit card acceptance procedures. Managers should check with their attorney or other local authority to determine the legality of charging employees for sales income lost due to improper use of credit card acceptance procedures.)

Refuse credit card loans. Since the operation must pay a discount for all charges on credit cards, under no circumstances should you accept charges in excess of the purchase value. This policy should have no exceptions.

Check the expiration date. Make certain that the credit cards have not expired.

Exhibit 8.5 Confirmation: Receipt of Cash Bank

By signing on the last unsigned line below, I acknowledge receipt of cash in the amount of $ *200.00* to be used as a cash register bank. The total amount is due and payable before checking out at the end of my shift.

Signature of Cash Recipient	Date of Shift	Returned (Signature of Manager on Duty)
D. M. Jones	3/01/00	Janie Smith
Sam Montgomery	3/02/00	

Source: Adapted from Ninemeier, *Food and Beverage Security*, p. 189.

Planning for Cash Income Control

The restaurant manager, at least in small properties, often helps design procedures for handling cash. Let's take a look at some principles that apply to that task.

Cash Banks

Bartenders and cashiers handling cash registers will need an opening cash bank. The employee should count out the opening bank in the presence of the manager. The bank should always contain the same amount of money and the minimum amount of each type of currency required to facilitate change-making tasks. In some operations, employees who receive cash banks sign a receipt (see Exhibit 8.5) to certify that they did, in fact, receive the cash, and they accept responsibility for it during their shift.

In many smaller operations, a management official counts the cash bank at the end of each shift. After the restaurant manager determines the amount of income generated, he/she removes it from the cash drawer. Of course, the amount of currency remaining in the cash drawer should equal the cash bank.

In larger operations which employ several bartenders and cashiers, it may be impractical to count the cash banks at the end of each shift. When this is true, management should assign each register operator a cash bank. Management and/or accounting staff should spot-check the banks frequently (at least once a week). When a cash-handling employee takes a vacation, his/her cash bank should be circulated among other register operators.

Employee IOUs are a major problem in some operations. Many properties refuse to grant employees cash advances. When policy does permit this practice, management should grant only one cash advance per pay period (or other time interval) and should establish a maximum amount for a pay advance (obviously not to exceed the estimated amount of wages owed to the employee).

In some operations, management officials "X" or "Z" the machine in the presence of the register operator to confirm that a specific amount of income has been rung on the register prior to the register operator's arrival. In case of a cash shortage, this procedure makes it impossible for the register operator to claim that the previous operator rang income on the register but did not collect it. (The terms **"X"** and **"Z"** respectively refer to determining the total amount of income rung on the register up to that point in time, then ringing the total register balance to zero. Most registers have a master control meter that cannot be reset, thereby preventing unauthorized interim machine clearings.)

Closing Procedures

Generally, restaurant managers are thoroughly involved in the closing procedures for food servers, beverage servers, bartenders, and cashiers. It is important to note that the manager's very presence during these closing activities functions as an important income control device.

Food Server Closing Procedures

Some of the closing duties for food servers relate to the collection of income. When properties do not use a precheck register, the restaurant manager or another official must account for all guest checks for each server and total them. The total of all the food server's guest checks is the amount of sales income which that employee has generated. Exhibit 8.6 is a form which you can use to tally information from guest checks in a manual (non-precheck register) system. You do not need to complete this form before the food server's shift is over. Rather, clerical staff can fill it out later; you can reconcile any discrepancies with the server during his/her next shift.

When properties use a precheck register, the check-out system is relatively easy. After the restaurant manager accounts for all the server's guest checks, he/she reads the precheck register to determine the amount of sales which the server has generated. He/she then enters this information onto a form such as the one shown in Exhibit 8.7. The total amount of sales on the precheck register should equal the total of all the server's guest checks. When these amounts agree, and they should, the income which the server collected from the guests should equal both totals. However, when the amounts differ, the income collected should equal the precheck register's total. The bookkeeper or controller, using a guest check audit, can then determine the reasons for the difference, make corrections, and notify the manager about the amount that he/she should collect from or pay to the food server.

If your property uses a cashier, sales income collection duties may have an impact on the cashier rather than the server. In that case, food server check-out procedures will normally involve only an accounting of all guest checks that were issued.

Beverage Server Closing Procedures

Closing procedures for beverage servers vary in each operation. Typically, they have at least some relationship to the sales income control system that the property uses. For example, if a property uses a server banking system, the restaurant manager must account for and total all guest checks, then compare this total with precheck register readings if such equipment is available, and collect income from the service staff. If the property uses a bartender banking system, an important first step is still an accounting of all guest checks.

The procedures you use to transfer beverage charges from the lounge to the dining room will complicate beverage server closing procedures. You may need to consult the transfer log which the receptionist maintains to verify that such transfers took place.

If beverage servers also sell food products, they may use separate guest checks for food; you will need to account for all these guest checks and establish sales verification procedures to ensure that the property receives income for all food products issued to the beverage servers.

Exhibit 8.6 Food Server's Daily Report: Manual System

Date: __4/23/00__

Shift: __AM__

Employee: __Spencer Lange__   __042__
        Name   Employee Number

	Guest Checks
Beginning No.:	97650
Ending No.:	97670
Total Issued:	21
No. Returned:	3
No. Used:*	18

Part I—Guest Check Audit:

Check No.	Food (1)	Tax (2)	Liquor (3)	Wine (4)	Beer/ Soda (5)	Total Sales Income (6)
97650	$ 21.75	$ .87	$ 3.85	$ —	$ —	$ 26.47
97651	46.55	1.87	—	18.49	—	66.91
97652	29.50	1.18			3.00	33.68

Part II—
Check Totals: $_____ $_____ $_____ $_____ $_____ $_____
                Col. 1   Col. 2   Col. 3   Col. 4   Col. 5   Col. 6

Part III—Sales Income—Check-out:
Guest Check Total** $_____

Amount Turned In $_____
Cash Over $_____
Cash Short $_____

*Should agree with number of guest checks used for calculations in Part II.
**Calculator total of all used guest checks made by manager at time of food server check-out.

Source: Adapted from Ninemeier, *Food and Beverage Security*,, p. 175.

Exhibit 8.7 Food Server's Daily Report: Precheck Register System

Guest Checks

Date: _6/20/00_

Shift: _PM_

Employee: _Ruth Price_   _96574_
           Name   Employee Number

Beginning No.: _97650_

Ending No.: _97670_

Total Issued: _21_

No. Returned: _3_

No. Used:* _18_

Part I—Guest Check Audit:

Check No.	Food (1)	Tax (2)	Liquor (3)	Wine (4)	Beer/ Soda (5)	Total Sales Income (6)
97650	$ 21.75	$ .87	$ 3.85	$ —	$ —	$ 26.47
97651	46.55	1.87	—	18.50	—	66.92
97652	29.50	1.18	—	—	3.00	33.68

Part II—Totals:

Precheck Register Readings:

$ _____ $ _____ $ _____ $ _____ $ _____ $ _____

Col. 1   Col. 2   Col. 3   Col. 4   Col. 5   Col. 6

Part III—Sales Income—Check-out:

Guest Check Total** $_____

Amount Turned In $_____
Cash Over $_____
Cash Short $_____

*Should agree with number of guest checks used for calculations in Part II.

**Calculator total of all used guest checks made by manager at time of food server check-out.

Source: Adapted from Ninemeier, *Food and Beverage Security*, p. 176.

Bartender Closing Procedures

Closing procedures for bartenders involve accounting for all the beverage guest checks issued and assessing the amount of sales income which they should have collected. Exhibit 8.8 illustrates a form which you could use for this purpose. This form enables you to account for all guest checks (upper right-hand corner) and determine the sales rung on each of four product keys (liquor, wine, beer/soda, and food). You can factor any adjustments and the value of the beginning bank into the amount of sales income collected.

You should generate information about the income rung on the bartender's register by reading the machine using the "X" key, then clearing the machine using the "Z" key. Have the register print the sales journal tape when you perform these tasks.

It is important to verify the accuracy of register ring-ups. For example, if you use only a simple mechanical register with department keys, the sum of the cocktail server's and bartender's completed guest checks should equal the total beverage sales rung on the beverage department key. On the bar operations report illustrated in Exhibit 8.8, the total beverage sales were $311.25. (To calculate, add lines 1, 2, and 3.) Therefore, the total of the guest checks used by the bartender and cocktail server should equal $311.25.

In many operations, especially those using equipment without accounts receivable capabilities, employees use the register only when ringing up sales for which they have actually collected income. Therefore, a bartender would not ring up sales for beverages prepared for food servers since he/she would not collect income for them. In such an operation, you may also have to devise specific procedures to follow when you close out the cashier to ensure that he/she has collected beverage income generated by food servers.

If your property uses a more complex electronic machine, you may have separate department keys for beverage and food sales made by each bartender and beverage server. You can compare these separate totals with the guest check totals which represent the food and beverage sales of the bartenders and beverage servers, respectively.

If beverage servers use a precheck register to print guest checks before bartenders prepare drinks, you can then compare the bar register totals with the totals on the precheck register. You can manually add guest check totals if discrepancies exist.

Regardless of the type of machine and system you use, you should have some way to ensure that department totals printed on the register do, in fact, represent the amount of sales income which you should collect. Likewise, you should have a system that permits a comparison between machine totals and the total of the bartender/beverage server's guest checks.

After you verify the amount of sales income generated by department, you should count all cash, charge vouchers, and checks in the register drawer. Add the amount of sales income taken from the "Z" reading, less any deductions or plus any additions which management has approved, to the amount of the beginning cash bank. This is the amount of revenue which you should have in the register drawer. Record this information on the bar operations report or a similar form.

In many operations, the restaurant manager verifies the sales journal tape before the bartender completes his/her shift. In other operations, the bartender, controller, or other employee deposits the total amount of money from the register's cash drawer into a safety vault at the front desk, in the controller's office, or in some other area. With this plan, someone does the income verification and counting tasks later. In still other operations, the register operator may withdraw the amount of the cash bank from the register's cash drawer and give the remaining funds to a management official. He/she then places the cash bank in a safety box or other safe storage area for future use.

Whenever possible, the restaurant manager should count the money in the presence of the bartender. The manager should record any over-rings or underrings on the bar operations report. It is generally easier to separate sales income from the cash bank by removing all checks and charge card vouchers first. Then remove currency (cash) in an amount necessary to equal the total sales; the remaining cash should represent the value of the cash bank. Often, you will need change (small bills and coins) to replenish the bank and provide sufficient denominations

Exhibit 8.8 Bar Operations Report

Date: 9/15/00

Shift: PM

Employee: J. T. Tower   090
Name   Employee Number

Guest Checks	
Beginning No.:	70000
Ending No.:	70050
Total Issued:	51
No. Returned:	3
No. Used:	48

Lounge Sales
(Product Key Totals: "Z" Readings)

Line 1	Key #1	Liquor	$ 210.50
Line 2	Key #2	Wine	60.25
Line 3	Key #3	Beer/Soda	40.50
Line 4	Key #4	Food*	66.36
Line 5		Total	377.61
Line 6		Add Underrings**	—
Line 7		Subtract Overrings**	—
Line 8		Subtract Promotions**	4.95
Line 9		Subtract Payouts**	—
Line 10	Total Sales with Adjustments		372.66
Line 11	Add Beginning Bank		200.00
Line 12	Total Cash/Checks/		
	Charge Vouchers Due		572.66
Line 13	Total Turned In		$ 571.66

Line 14   *J. T. Tower*
          Bartender Signature

$ _____
Cash Over

$ 1.00
Cash Short

Comments:

*When calculating bar food sales, the ring-ups (P-Key #4) must be divided by a factor to determine food sales *less* sales tax. Difference between food sales (this calculation) and amount rung on P-Key 4 is sales tax due for food sold in the bar. The factor is 1.04 when taxes are 4%, 1.05 when taxes are 5%, etc.
**Must be approved by manager on duty.

Source: Adapted from Ninemeier, *Food and Beverage Security*, p. 169.

to deal with transactions that will occur during the next shift.

Place the completed bar operations report, along with guest checks, register tapes, revenues collected, and any other supporting information, in the controller's office, your office, or other place of safekeeping. Audit guest checks, prepare deposits, and secure monies according to required procedures.

Cashier Closing Procedures

When a property uses a cashier banking system in dining areas, cashiers should put all the guest checks which they have rung for each food server in sequence. The restaurant manager or other official can then quickly account for all the guest checks and undertake an income verification process similar to the one used for bartender closing procedures. (The form shown in Exhibit 8.4 can be used for this purpose.) As with the bartender's register, you should do "X" and "Z" readings with the register tape. Remove sales income to a secure site for later processing into bank deposits and similarly protect cash bank funds.

You should also perform some routine but random audits of guest checks to ensure that the cashier is following all sales income control procedures. When discrepancies occur between register ring-ups, guest check totals, and/or the amount of revenue actually collected, you should conduct a more detailed audit.

Recordkeeping Requirements and Income Control

Someone must put together information about income generated by food and beverage servers and bartenders during each shift. Typically, officials other than the restaurant manager perform this task. Nevertheless, restaurant managers should have a basic understanding of the procedures which these officials use. This knowledge may help the restaurant manager revise cash handling procedures to simplify the task for service, management, and/or other cash-handling staff.

You have already learned that an audit of guest checks is necessary to account for all checks that were issued. Audits can also verify

the prices charged for products and confirm that no arithmetic errors, sales miscalculations, or other problems had an impact on the amount of sales income generated. When employees use precheck and/or cash registers to print on guest checks, audits will confirm that the employees pushed the correct department/product keys.

Personnel can also audit the bartender's and cashier's register tapes when a property uses a cashier banking system. You should do an audit when there is a difference between the amount of sales income actually collected and the amount rung on the register. Generally, the audit starts with the premise that the register reading is correct and the cash/charge vouchers are incorrect. Since a guest check should support every entry in the machine, you can match the guest checks to the register tape to determine the cause of any problems. For example, if the guest checks and tapes are in accord and the cash/charge vouchers are short, you might be able to attribute the problem to an error in making change or the misuse of the cash security system. If the guest checks and tapes disagree, a comparison and reconciliation of the checks with the register tape become necessary to correctly assess the level of sales. You should then compare this level to the amount of cash and charge vouchers which your employees collected.

After you have accounted for all food and beverage guest checks and/or completed the register tapes, you should complete a daily income report (Exhibit 8.9). When completed, this form becomes a source document for daily sales calculations in the accounting department. Information needed to complete the daily income report comes from the bar operations report (Exhibit 8.8), the food server's daily report (Exhibit 8.6 or 8.7), the cashier's department sales record (Exhibit 8.4), or other income reports developed specifically for the property. It should represent the amount of sales income deposited for the day, including any deductions from or additions to the income as a result of the guest check auditing procedures which the manager, controller, or other official performed. The completed daily income report should remain in the office for review by management officials. Attach a duplicate copy of the bank deposit slip to this report.

Information from the daily income reports should be transferred to a monthly income recap form (Exhibit 8.10). The accountant uses this

Exhibit 8.9 Daily Income Report

Date: _____

Information Source	Food*	Tax*	Liquor	Wine	Beer/Soda	Total Sales
	Information is from Bar Operations Report					
Lounge	Key 4		Key 1	Key 2	Key 3	
	Information is from Individual Food Servers' Reports					
Restaurant	Col. 1	Col. 2	Col. 3	Col. 4	Col. 5	
Part I AM:	Amount	Amount	Amount	Amount	Amount	Amount
Lounge Sales						
Restaurant Sales						
Emp. #						
Emp. #						
Emp. #						
Emp. #						
Emp. #						
Emp. #						
Emp. #						
Emp. #						
TOTALS						
PART II PM:						
Lounge Sales						
Restaurant Sales						
Emp. #						
Emp. #						
Emp. #						
Emp. #						
Emp. #						
Emp. #						
Emp. #						
Emp. #						
TOTALS						

Source: Adapted from Ninemeier, *Food and Beverage Security*, p. 181.

Exhibit 8.10 Monthly Income Recap

Date	Food		Tax		Liquor		Wine		Beer/Soda		Total	
	AM	PM	AM	PM	AM	PM	AM	PM	AM	PM	AM	PM
Totals:												

Month: _____

Adapted from Ninemeier, *Food and Beverage Security*, p. 183.

form at the end of the month or other accounting period to process required financial statements. You should retain a copy of this document for management staff to review and analyze.

Finally, all guest checks, reports, precheck and cash register tapes, and the like should be put together in a large envelope which should be sealed, marked with the date, and filed in a secure place for future use.

Security of Income Collected

Obviously, someone must keep secure all cash, checks, credit card vouchers, and other types of income collected from food and beverage servers, bartenders, and cashiers until the funds are deposited in the bank. In large properties, this responsibility rests with the accounting department, rarely with the restaurant man-

ager. In small properties, especially where a general manager performs duties otherwise assigned to a restaurant manager, this responsibility is likely to rest with the latter.

In a server banking system, income collected from each food or beverage server, along with the guest checks which the server has used, is often kept in individual envelopes that are locked in the property's safe. Properties using cashier banking systems should keep all sales information separate from income collected from cashiers and bartenders.

Some properties make one daily bank deposit; others may make several daily deposits. Management officials may transport funds to the bank; or the property may employ an armored car or other service. The point is that a concern for the protection of sales income must extend beyond the time that products are sold to guests. Security and income control procedures must address issues related to the collection of income from employees, the preparation of bank deposits, and the actual transportation of funds to the bank.

Professional restaurant managers understand that income control procedures also extend to the processing of checks to pay the property's bills, the preparation of employee payrolls, the handling of petty cash funds, and more. Dishonest acts by employees can divert money at any point, and managers must establish protective measures for every step that involves the handling, processing, and/or accounting of monies.

Managing Service at the Hotel Columbia
Page Sixteen

"Here it is," Lewis thought. "I'll review this article on sales income control systems to make sure it is current and applicable, then I'll distribute it to the director of restaurant operations and the restaurant managers to use when they design the sales income control systems for their outlets."

Originally an article in a trade journal, the information Lewis had kept on file read as follows:

Designing and Implementing Sales Income Control Programs

There are many ways in which both dishonest employees and guests can steal revenue by taking advantage of flaws in a property's sales income control system. Being aware of problems that can occur in your own property will help you design effective sales income control systems to keep revenue losses to a minimum. How can you do this? Take the following steps:

1. It is reasonable to expect that your employees will turn in the actual income your property generates daily. If you can determine through such means as a shopper's service or close supervision that the amount turned in does not equal the amount actually generated, a problem exists. You need to develop a program that provides for double- or triple-checks on the income that servers should collect.

2. Develop a basic set of income control procedures by using your own experience with a variety of systems and take the best from each.

3. When designing sales income control systems, recognize the need to trace each employee's responsibility for sales income as it is assessed, collected, and prepared for deposit.

4. Involve employees in the redesign of sales income control procedures. Frequently, employees who must work with the system every day will have a variety of good ideas to improve the procedures.

5. Once you develop income control procedures, put them in writing. Written procedures provide a record of the correct way to protect income. They are also useful training aids for new staff.

6. Once you have written sales income control procedures, train all affected employees to use them properly. Explain, from the employees' perspective, why changes in existing operating procedures are necessary (e.g., mention that improved control procedures will help protect the service staff from allegations of theft). You must also provide any additional equipment the employees will need to implement the revised procedures.

7. Continually and effectively supervise your employees to ensure that they consistently use all required sales income control procedures.

8. Even when you think you have developed an excellent sales income control system, regularly ask yourself, "If I were a dishonest employee, in how many different ways could I still steal from the property?" Restaurant managers who can answer that question have identified potential problems and additional operating flaws which they must quickly address.

9. As part of your front-of-house evaluation procedures, continually observe and assess your sales income control methods.

As Lewis reviewed the list of steps, he was aware that they were just as relevant today as they were when they were written. He gave a copy to his executive secretary to duplicate for the director of restaurant operations. After Don Jackson had seen the list, he stopped by Lewis's office to discuss it before it was duplicated for all the dining outlet managers.

Don told Lewis, "I'm going to dictate a memo to accompany it and express my hope that the restaurant managers will work closely with me,

Managing Service at the Hotel Columbia
Page Sixteen, continued

each other, and their colleagues to design effective sales income control procedures. Our procedures have to recognize the unique characteristics of each food outlet and, at the same time, the need to provide efficient service to the guest."

Lewis immediately agreed with Don's suggestion. "After all," Lewis said, "in a property like ours that aims to maximize the guests' dining ex-periences, we can't justify sales income control procedures that would sacrifice effective guest service to ensure collection of every penny of in-come. On the other hand, the property that em-phasizes service without a concern for the income it generates will not exist long in this competitive industry."

Part II
Delivering Dining Service

9
Coffee Shop Service

Many lodging properties offer coffee shop service for their guests. Coffee shops provide faster service and generally offer less expensive and easier to produce menu items than the other food service outlets within the property. In many city hotel coffee shops, breakfast is the important meal of the day from a marketing perspective, followed by late-night snacks. Coffee shops in other locations may be relatively busy all day long. Hotel coffee shops in locations with high pedestrian traffic may do a high volume of business with nonhotel guests. Properties in more remote locations may offer coffee shop service almost exclusively for hotel guests and travelers.

Many self-contained family-type restaurants offer the equivalent of coffee shop service. These facilities often provide both counter and table service. The combination of fast service and relatively low prices set these properties apart from other commercial food and beverage operations.

From the perspective of guests, the key elements of a well-run coffee shop include: a bright, lively informal atmosphere; cheerful and efficient service; well-prepared and well-presented food; and quiet busing of used tableware and dishes.

Although coffee shop menus frequently offer products that are simple to prepare, they may still feature a large variety. Exhibit 9.1 shows two pages from a varied coffee shop menu. Indeed, some California-style menus offer over 100 different food items. (A **California-style** menu provides traditional breakfast, lunch, and dinner items at any time during the property's hours of operation. So, no matter what time it is, guests can order from a variety of egg dishes, luncheon sandwiches, dinner entrees, desserts, and other products.)

In the past, coffee shops offered an atmosphere reflecting the briskness of their service and the economy of their prices. Recently, however, many coffee shops have been designed to reflect the ambience of the hotel. Modern coffee shops are located in main concourses, atriums, lobbies, or other public areas and may feature waterfalls, towering sculptures, fascinating views of the hotel, or even live entertainment. Hoteliers have come full circle from almost hiding their coffee shops in out-of-the-way areas to placing them in prominent positions in the hotel.

Many principles that coffee shop managers must use to direct their operations have already been discussed. For example, they must establish standards, purchase required products, and select, orient, train, and supervise employees. The menu, food production systems, and related factors are just as important to the coffee shop as they are to any other food service operation. In this chapter, we will attempt to focus on some service concerns which are of special interest to the coffee shop manager.

Personnel

The organization of a coffee shop is similar to other food service outlets in the hotel. Exhibit 9.2 illustrates a typical chain of command from the food and beverage director at the "top" to food service attendants at the "bottom" (who with first-rate training and incentives from management may work their way up). Of course, titles of various positions will differ from coffee

Managing Service at the Hotel Columbia
Page Seventeen

Lewis Scott received a telephone call from Don Jackson. "Lewis," he said, "I know you share my feelings about the importance of our coffee shop. I've been hearing a lot of talk lately about how the Tremont's coffee shop operation is slipping. Maybe it would be a good idea to visit it and see what we can learn."

"Great idea." said Lewis, "Why don't you go over within the next week or so? You can fill out that shopper's service report you told me about earlier. I'm interested in seeing how useful it can be."

shop to coffee shop. However, no matter what their titles are, all coffee shop personnel must realize that friendly staff can "make or break" the success of the outlet.

Coffee Shop Manager

Coffee shops are often managed by those who are just beginning their management careers and are striving for promotions to management positions in other food and beverage outlets within the property. Typically, coffee shops require more than one manager to cover all their hours of operation. Service and all other front-of-house concerns in hotel coffee shops are generally the responsibility of the coffee shop manager.

Generally, the chef, or someone on his/her staff, is responsible for the food production aspects of the operation. Although the coffee shop manager's primary concern is service, it is very important for this official and the individual who oversees the outlet's food production systems to communicate and cooperate.

Coffee Shop Cashiers

Cashiers in coffee shops perform many of the same functions that cashiers in other dining outlets do (see Chapter 8). However, since money handling and recordkeeping tasks are important to this job, the food and beverage controller or other official in the accounting department, rather than the coffee shop manager, often supervises these cashiers.

Hosts/Hostesses

At least during busy times, coffee shops frequently use a host or hostess to welcome and seat guests, provide menus, and perform other guest services. Because the host/hostess is usually the first person the guest comes in contact with in a coffee shop, he/she must be aware of the impression he/she makes. As is true with any food service operation, the host's/hostess's friendly greeting and genuine concern for the guest is important. Recognizing guests as soon as they approach, confirming the number of guests in a party, and offering seats in the appropriate section of the coffee shop are all service responsibilities of the host/hostess. (During slow business periods, a sign may invite guests to seat themselves in open areas of the coffee shop.)

Food Servers

As is true in other dining outlets, the role of the food server is to greet the guests, provide menu information, take orders, deliver food, provide other assistance during the meal, and offer the guest check for payment at the appropriate time. However, in some coffee shop operations, the food servers must also help with some food preparation. For example, they may put the dressing on salads, portion soups, and dish up vegetables from serving equipment located behind counters or in server stations.

Exhibit 9.3 is a job description for a coffee shop server and reviews tasks that a staff member in this position must perform. Notice the emphasis on side work. **Side work** comprises service-related tasks performed at various times during a shift. The job description also stresses fast, courteous, and efficient service.

The kind of service required in coffee shops

Exhibit 9.1 Sample Coffee Shop Menu

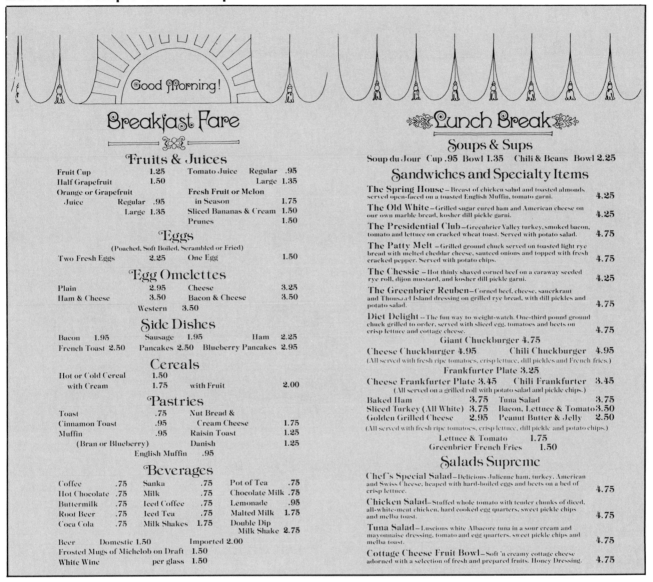

Good Morning!

Breakfast Fare

Fruits & Juices

Fruit Cup	1.25	Tomato Juice	Regular	.95
Half Grapefruit	1.50		Large	1.35
Orange or Grapefruit		Fresh Fruit or Melon		
Juice	Regular .95	in Season		1.75
	Large 1.35	Sliced Bananas & Cream		1.50
		Prunes		1.50

Eggs
(Poached, Soft Boiled, Scrambled or Fried)

Two Fresh Eggs	2.25	One Egg	1.50

Egg Omelettes

Plain	2.95	Cheese	3.25
Ham & Cheese	3.50	Bacon & Cheese	3.50
		Western 3.50	

Side Dishes

Bacon	1.95	Sausage	1.95	Ham	2.25
French Toast 2.50		Pancakes 2.50	Blueberry Pancakes 2.95		

Cereals

Hot or Cold Cereal	1.50		
with Cream	1.75	with Fruit	2.00

Pastries

Toast	.75	Nut Bread &	
Cinnamon Toast	.95	Cream Cheese	1.75
Muffin	.95	Raisin Toast	1.25
(Bran or Blueberry)		Danish	1.25
English Muffin	.95		

Beverages

Coffee	.75	Sanka	.75	Pot of Tea	.75
Hot Chocolate	.75	Milk	.75	Chocolate Milk	.75
Buttermilk	.75	Iced Coffee	.75	Lemonade	.95
Root Beer	.75	Iced Tea	.75	Malted Milk	1.75
Coca Cola	.75	Milk Shakes	1.75	Double Dip	
				Milk Shake	2.75

Beer	Domestic 1.50	Imported	2.00
Frosted Mugs of Michelob on Draft	1.50		
White Wine	per glass	1.50	

Lunch Break

Soups & Sups

Soup du Jour Cup .95 Bowl 1.35   Chili & Beans Bowl 2.25

Sandwiches and Specialty Items

The Spring House – Breast of chicken salad and toasted almonds served open-faced on a toasted English Muffin, tomato garni. **4.25**

The Old White – Grilled sugar cured ham and American cheese on our own marble bread, kosher dill pickle garni. **4.25**

The Presidential Club – Greenbrier Valley turkey, smoked bacon, tomato and lettuce on cracked wheat toast. Served with potato salad. **4.75**

The Patty Melt – Grilled ground chuck served on toasted light rye bread with melted cheddar cheese, sautéed onions and topped with fresh cracked pepper. Served with potato chips. **4.75**

The Chessie – Hot thinly shaved corned beef on a caraway seeded rye roll, dijon mustard, and kosher dill pickle garni. **4.25**

The Greenbrier Reuben – Corned beef, cheese, sauerkraut and Thousand Island dressing on grilled rye bread, with dill pickles and potato salad. **4.75**

Diet Delight – The fun way to weight-watch. One-third pound ground chuck grilled to order, served with sliced egg, tomatoes and beets on crisp lettuce and cottage cheese. **4.75**

Giant Chuckburger 4.75

Cheese Chuckburger **4.95**		Chili Chuckburger	**4.95**

(All served with fresh ripe tomatoes, crisp lettuce, dill pickles and French fries.)

Frankfurter Plate 3.25

Cheese Frankfurter Plate **3.45**		Chili Frankfurter	**3.45**

(All served on a grilled roll with potato salad and pickle chips.)

Baked Ham	**3.75**	Tuna Salad	**3.75**
Sliced Turkey (All White)	**3.75**	Bacon, Lettuce & Tomato	**3.50**
Golden Grilled Cheese	**2.95**	Peanut Butter & Jelly	**2.50**

(All served with fresh ripe tomatoes, crisp lettuce, dill pickle and potato chips.)

Lettuce & Tomato 1.75
Greenbrier French Fries 1.50

Salads Supreme

Chef's Special Salad – Delicious Julienne ham, turkey, American and Swiss Cheese, heaped with hard-boiled eggs and beets on a bed of crisp lettuce. **4.75**

Chicken Salad – Stuffed whole tomato with tender chunks of diced, all-white-meat chicken, hard cooked egg quarters, sweet pickle chips and melba toast. **4.75**

Tuna Salad – Luscious white Albacore tuna in a sour cream and mayonnaise dressing, tomato and egg quarters, sweet pickle chips and melba toast. **4.75**

Cottage Cheese Fruit Bowl – Soft 'n creamy cottage cheese adorned with a selection of fresh and prepared fruits. Honey Dressing. **4.75**

Courtesy of The Greenbrier, White Sulphur Springs, West Virginia

suggests special concerns that managers must address as they select service personnel. For example, coffee shop servers must be able to work quickly, yet carefully. They must be able to do several things during one trip through the dining area, such as carry food to one table, present a guest check to another, and remove used dishes from a third. Since families are likely to be guests in coffee shop operations, service staff must be able to relate well with children and recognize parental needs for assistance with baby seats, high chairs, or cushions.

Servers must know how to show consideration for guests in a hurry by using techniques that demonstrate that they have a genuine concern for guests' schedules. Coffee shop personnel working morning shifts may have to deal with guests who are easily irritated early in the day. A friendly and genuine "Good morning" can really make a difference in a guest's attitude toward the service employee, the coffee shop, and even toward the lodging property itself.

Exhibit 9.2 Typical Coffee Shop Organization

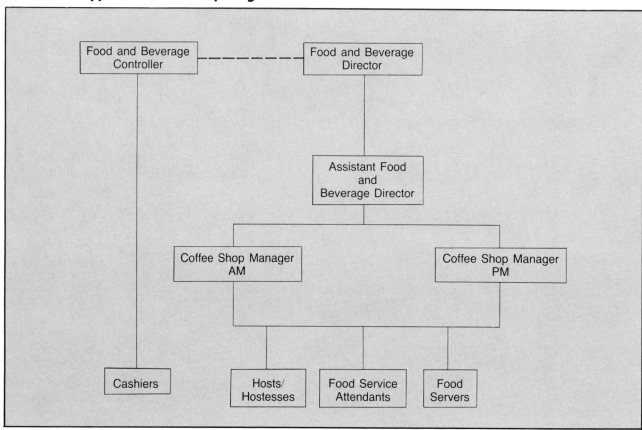

Because guest check averages are usually lower in the coffee shop than in other dining outlets within a hotel, service staff should understand that table turns will probably occur more frequently. Thus the total income generated by one employee can still be high. (The term **table turn** refers to the amount of time that a table or counter seat is occupied. For example, if three separate parties are seated at the same table within a 60-minute period, the table turn rate is three times per hour. Said another way, the average guest occupies a seat/table for approximately 20 minutes; 60 minutes divided by three table turns equals 20 minutes per guest.) Of course, quality service often determines the amount of gratuities received by servers.

The type of suggestive selling used by service employees can also affect guest check totals. Attempts to sell a variety of entree accompaniments, desserts, and/or after-dinner beverages are generally in order and are examples of the special attention that pleases guests and in-

creases profits for the property. In addition, the guest, the coffee shop, the hotel, and the food server all gain from the sale of additional or new food products enjoyed by guests.

Food Service Attendants

Many coffee shops use food service attendants to help food servers. Clearing and resetting tables, pouring water, coffee, and other beverages, and assisting with the service of food during rush periods are typical duties of food service attendants.

Coffee Shop Service Procedures

Coffee shop service begins when service employees perform their pre-opening duties. Employees in all coffee shops need to prepare tables or counters for service and ensure that everything is clean. Greasy or unfilled salt and

Exhibit 9.3 Sample Job Description for a Coffee Shop Server

JOB TITLE: Coffee Shop Server

IMMEDIATE SUPERVISOR: Coffee Shop Manager

JOB SUMMARY:

Waits on coffee shop guests, takes their orders, and serves them immediately when orders are prepared. When guests have departed, quickly cleans and resets tables. Responsible for knowing the menu items, prices, and daily specials. Must perform side work as required.

DUTIES:

Greets guests at assigned tables with coffee shop's required greeting, gives them menus, and pours water for them. When guests are ready, takes order. Places food order with kitchen personnel; portions and serves nonalcoholic beverage order. Serves food order immediately when prepared.

Watches every assigned table carefully to anticipate guests' needs; checks back with guests regularly for additional orders or requests. When guests complete courses, removes used cutlery and dishes. Presents menu so that guests may order dessert; presents check when guests have been served their final orders.

Places dishes and cutlery that have been removed from the guests' tables in respective bus trays.

Wipes table clean and dries it; decrumbs chair seats; resets table with placemats, cutlery wrapped in a napkin, and glassware; places condiments in proper place. In smoking section, cleans and replaces ashtray and matchbook.

Side work such as stocking condiments, filling salt and pepper shakers, and organizing side stands should be done as needed by server during shift. At end of shift all condiments should be completely full.

SPECIFICATIONS AND PREREQUISITES:

Requires a basic knowledge of composition of food and beverage items on menu as well as menu prices.

Requires familiarity with daily specials and proper table cleaning and setting procedures.

EDUCATION:

High school diploma, General Equivalency Diploma (GED), or equivalent.

SKILLS:

Must have the special skills necessary to make guests feel welcome, must have legible handwriting and basic mathematical skills, and must be able to give courteous, efficient service.

PHYSICAL:

Must be neat in appearance, possess a pleasant personality, have correct posture, and be able to carry loaded service trays.

---

pepper shakers, spotty glasses, and improperly cleaned flatware are just as annoying to coffee shop guests as they are to diners in other food and beverage outlets. Guests in a coffee shop are not willing to accept compromises on cleanliness in return for fast service.

The coffee shop manager must carefully plan the exact procedures for setting tables so that all tables are set uniformly. As in other outlets, the manager is responsible for training and supervising food servers and food service attendants to ensure that they consistently follow the procedures.

Greeting and Seating the Guests

Many coffee shops have street, lobby, and other entrances. The host/hostess stand should be located so that he/she can properly meet and greet guests entering from any one of these entrances. Because coffee shops and family-type restaurants do not generally accept reservations, it is difficult for the host/hostess to recognize guests by name. However, experienced hosts/hostesses use such friendly greetings as "It's good to see you again," or "Welcome back," to

Pre-Opening Duties in a Coffee Shop

Regardless of the type of outlet service employees work in, they must perform many of the same tasks before dining areas open. However, because coffee shop service must be very fast and efficient, servers in these outlets must be especially certain to carefully and completely stock counters, food server stations, mini-kitchens, and other areas. All the necessary supplies, food and beverage products, equipment, and tools must be available in sufficient quantities before the coffee shop opens.

In 24-hour operations, service employees stock these areas during slow periods. We have mentioned the concept of *mise en place* throughout this book. Personnel in coffee shop positions must make a special effort to get everything ready before the rush of business. Time wasted looking for items or obtaining them from other storage areas frequently has a negative impact on the service rendered to guests.

let frequent guests know that they are recognized and valuable patrons of the outlet.

When the host/hostess assigns guests to server stations, he/she should consider several key factors. First, whenever possible, guests should be seated in the area they request. For example, many coffee shops offer "no smoking" sections. When these are available, the host/hostess should inquire about which section the guests prefer. Also, some guests may like to sit at a counter, in a booth, or at a table; others may appreciate a window view. Less desirable seats (in high traffic aisles, close to kitchen doors or server supply stations, and others) should be used only after all other seats are occupied. Since the speed of service is important, the host/hostess should attempt to seat guests in sections which are the least busy. If a food server has several four-top tables completely occupied, this station is a poor section in which to seat arriving guests; whenever possible, the host/hostess should select a less busy service station.

Offering the Menu

In many properties, the host/hostess offers the guests menus. This practice helps speed service; guests may decide what to order before the food server approaches them. The host/hostess may also pour water and serve coffee. This latter service is especially important in the morning when many guests want their coffee as soon as possible. (However, in coffee shops that serve alcoholic beverages, the host/hostess who is quick to offer coffee at lunch or dinner may be losing sales on the higher priced beverages.) In

some properties, the host/hostess tells the guests about the daily specials. In addition, when it is the policy of the operation, he/she tells the guests the name of their food server and assures them that they will receive prompt attention from that server.

Acknowledging Guests

The food server should approach the table as soon as possible. If he/she is busy, such words of acknowledgement as, "Good morning, I'll be at your service in just a moment," are in order.

Taking and Placing the Orders

As soon as the food server is able to serve the guests, he/she should ask if they wish to order. In properties that serve alcoholic beverages, the server makes certain that guests know they are available by asking a question such as, "May I bring you a cocktail?" Food servers should be able to answer any of the guests' questions about menu items, daily specials, or foods that can be prepared very quickly. If a guest orders items which take a long time to prepare, the food server should tell the guest about the wait.

Operating procedures often require coffee shop servers to place orders with the kitchen as soon as they receive them. When placing the order, if a food server learns there will be a delay in the food production process, he/she should, of course, inform the guest promptly so that the guest may make an alternate selection if desired.

A coffee shop marketing rule is, "Always give the guest something to do." Some sugges-

Beverage Service

Many self-contained, family-style restaurant operations do not offer alcoholic beverage service. (Frequently, the cost and/or availability of liquor licenses make beverage service impractical.) Liquor, beer, and/or wine is also not available in many hotel coffee shop operations. However, some properties do offer beverage service and place service bars in locations that are convenient for coffee shop food servers, room service personnel, and the dining room service staff. If alcoholic beverages are available, servers must receive the appropriate training so they can serve them correctly (see Chapter 14).

Alcoholic beverage service in coffee shops becomes more necessary if, at times, these food outlets are the only ones available. Some hotels that close their dining rooms during slow periods such as in the mid-afternoon or late evening expect their coffee shops to provide food and beverage service to their guests. The coffee shop managers in such properties recognize that some guests enjoy having a drink with certain meals, so they provide beer, wine, and limited alcoholic beverage service during appropriate times in their outlets.

tions for following this rule include: serving hot coffee immediately after guests are seated; offering newspapers to guests who don't bring in their own; using paper placemats with games or puzzles that children or the whole family can enjoy; serving such items as fresh, warm muffins, croissants, scones, or rolls and a selection of jams to guests who are waiting for their breakfast entrees; and serving such items as breadsticks or crackers, warm breads, and salads to guests waiting for their main courses at lunch or dinner. In some coffee shops, service employees circulate with pitchers of juice during all meal periods. Offering juice as an alternative to other beverages not only adds a special touch, but also provides a means to increase the check average. Note, however, that guests might become uncomfortable if they are not certain whether special foods or services are a usual part of the meal, are complimentary, or whether they will be charged for them later. Such information could be included in the menu, or food servers could explain unique offerings of the coffee shop to guests.

In general, while guests are waiting for the entrees, food servers should periodically check back with them to refill coffee cups and water glasses, take further beverage or other orders, and to let them know that their orders are in process and will arrive shortly. Of course, once the order is ready, the food server should serve it promptly.

Presenting the Check

Since guests may be in a hurry, it is impor-
tant for the food server to have the guest check ready when the guests desire it. Although service must be fast, the food server must also take the time to comply with all the sales income control procedures which the property uses. The use of precheck registers, calculators to total multiple guest checks, sales tax charts, and credit card authorization lists is just as important

Coffee shop server presents menu to guests. (Delphines, Lansing Hilton Inn, Lansing, Michigan)

Exhibit 9.4 Sample Coffee Shop Guest Check

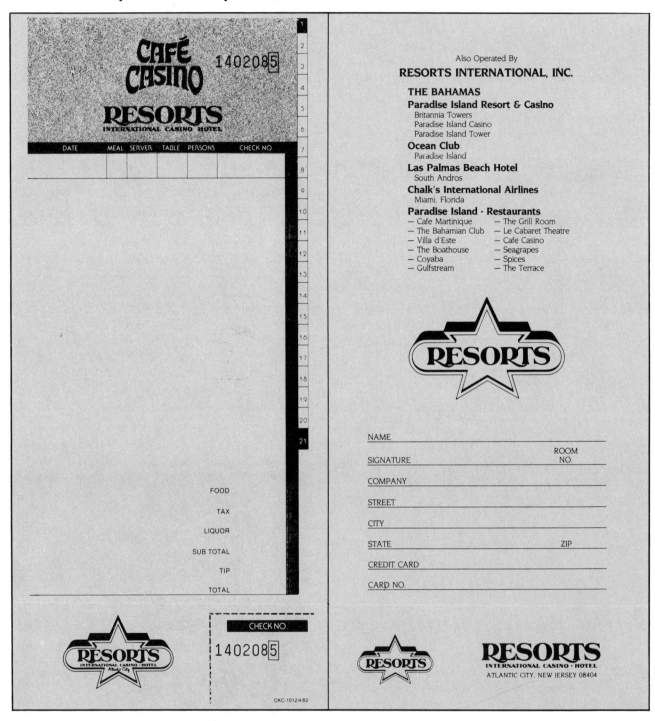

Courtesy of Resorts International, Atlantic City, New Jersey

in coffee shop service as it is in any type of food service operation.

Some coffee shop guests will want to charge their meal expenses to their hotel rooms. Exhibit 9.4 shows a sample hotel coffee shop guest check that can be used for such a purpose. Typically, guests are allowed to do so unless they paid for their rooms when they checked in and the hotel is not extending credit to them, or they have checked out before eating a coffee shop meal. In many properties, the front desk provides the coffee shop and all other outlets with a list of guests who are allowed to charge food and beverages to their rooms. Properties using electronic registers which interface with the front desk may be able to instantly verify authorization for charges to rooms.

In some properties, it is necessary to physically carry guest checks that indicate coffee shop meal charges to the front desk for posting on guest folios. In other properties, modern electronic registers automatically transfer charges from food and beverage (and other) outlets directly to the guest folio. With the use of such procedures, it is becoming increasingly difficult for guests to charge a meal to their rooms, then check out before the front desk has posted these charges to their bills.

Forecasting and Employee Scheduling

It is imperative that the correct number of service employees are available to provide proper service in the coffee shop. If too few staff members are available, service will obviously suffer. Similarly, too many staff members will affect the operation's labor costs. The procedures for forecasting anticipated sales levels and scheduling service staff for coffee shops and other outlets are discussed in Chapter 7.

In many hotels, a direct relationship exists between occupancy rates and coffee shop business, especially during the breakfast period. This relationship is clearly evident in lodging properties which do not have an extensive banquet or convention business, but it is also true in facilities which deduct their banquet breakfast business from their occupancy rate formulas when they forecast their anticipated coffee shop business.

Coffee shops which are open 24 hours a day or provide service during slow periods have a larger percentage of fixed labor costs than coffee shops which are open only when large business volumes warrant service. It is especially impor-

tant that schedule planners consider minimum service needs during slow business times and assign tasks such as filling sugar bowls and syrup containers or folding napkins, which servers can perform when the coffee shop has few guests. Such assignments reduce both the amount of variable labor needed at other times and the negative impact that a large amount of fixed labor can have on labor costs. Coffee shops with a significant amount of business from nonhotel guests will need to use sales history forecasts and estimating procedures to schedule an appropriate number of servers.

Supplies and Equipment

The types of dining service supplies and equipment that a coffee shop needs vary according to the image it desires to project to guests. They can range from disposable placemats, paper napkins, and inexpensive or disposable tableware to tablecloths, cloth napkins, and high-quality tableware. The cost of the serviceware used will, of course, be reflected in the coffee shop's menu prices.

Many hotels view the coffee shop as a legitimate profit center which, when marketed correctly, contributes to the property's financial goals. Since this is the case, the same degree of attention which managers give to decisions about dining service supplies and equipment in other outlets should also be given to the coffee shop operation. What do the guests need and want? The answer to that question can come only from doing market research and considering the role of the coffee shop in the particular lodging property.

Control Procedures

Quality service in the coffee shop must be fast and efficient. But it is still necessary to ensure that the servers do, in fact, collect all income due from the sale of products. Therefore, the coffee shop manager must incorporate effective principles of sales income control into the service procedures which employees use.

As is true in other food service outlets, the possibility that service staff and/or guests may

Clearing and Resetting Tables in the Coffee Shop

Food service attendants must carefully clear and reset tables in the coffee shop. If they don't, unsanitary or unclean conditions may result. Also, if employees do not clear and reset tables properly, they may cause excessive breakage and noise. While the problem of noise is always a major concern, it is especially crucial during breakfast. Excessive noise is among the most frequent coffee shop complaints during the early morning hours.

Guests do not enjoy seeing their own or others' used serviceware while they dine. Therefore, employees should not only remove such items from guest tables as soon as possible, but also quickly and quietly take them out of sight into nonpublic areas. Whenever possible, routes to and from dishwashing areas should be designed to avoid distracting guests. Carts used to transport dishes should be quiet and not travel on any uncarpeted areas. What could be worse than a squeaky cart with dirty dishes moving noisily past guests in a busy coffee shop?

try to steal from the coffee shop exists. The coffee shop manager, working in conjunction with the accounting department and/or other personnel, must develop proper procedures to protect the property. Procedures which ensure that production employees do not prepare menu items without authorization are an absolute must. Typically, authorization takes the form of orders which servers write onto guest checks, enter into precheck registers (if applicable), and/or turn in for production.

Sales income control procedures need to be developed specifically for each operation. In some facilities, improper layout and design may enable guests to exit to other hotel areas or even out of the hotel without passing the host/hostess stand. Frequently, only extensive remodeling, which is very expensive, can correct this design flaw; therefore, closer supervision in such properties becomes necessary.

Special Concerns

The physical design of the coffee shop affects the flow of guests, employees, and food through the operation. Because slow service can be a serious problem in coffee shops, managers should identify and carefully study production and service bottlenecks; they must also determine the causes of such problems and correct them.

The number of employees on each shift also affects the speed of service. Coffee shop manag-

ers should use basic scheduling procedures which meet the quality requirements of service and any anticipated changes in business volume.

Little things count in coffee shop service. Coffee shop managers must consider the speed of service as they develop procedures for setting tables. For example, the number of pieces in the table setting affects the speed with which a food service attendant can clear, clean, and reset a table. It takes longer to set the table with three forks than with two. Laying individual packets of jelly or other condiments in a specific pattern on a plate takes more time than simply placing such items in a basket that is placed in front of the guest.

Before coffee shop managers establish their outlet's hours of operation, they must conduct careful studies. Some properties set operating hours based on the question "When can we make a profit?" However, it is also important to remember that the hotel coffee shop provides a service. If business is sufficient to meet the direct costs of food, labor, and energy, it may be best to remain open even when the income generated does not cover all the fixed costs.

Exhibit 9.5 provides an example of how to analyze operating costs. From 6:00 a.m. to 2:00 a.m. daily, coffee shop sales equal approximately $1,500. Variable costs, such as food, labor, energy, and other costs directly incurred to generate sales income, are approximately $855 (57% of the sales). Fixed costs, such as property taxes, insurance, and telephone charges, which the hotel allocates to the coffee shop and would

Exhibit 9.5 Analysis of Coffee Shop Operating Costs

Assume the following:		
	Hours of Operation	
Economic Factors	6:00 a.m.–2:00 a.m	2:00 a.m.–6:00 a.m.
Sales	$1,500	$125
Variable Costs*	$855	$71
Fixed Costs**	$300	$60
Total Costs	$1,155	$131
Coffee Shop Profit	$345	$(6)

*Food, labor, energy, and other costs directly incurred to generate sales income are the variable costs. While labor and energy costs are really semi-variable (fixed up to a minimum business volume, then variable beyond this level), we will consider them as variable costs to simplify this example.

**Prorated costs such as property taxes, insurance, and telephone rates, which would be incurred even if the coffee shop were closed, represent the fixed costs.

be incurred even if the coffee shop were closed, equal approximately $300 or $15 per hour ($300 divided by 20 hours equals $15/hour). Adding the $855 and $300 produces total costs of $1,155. Based on these calculations, the coffee shop generates a profit of $345 from 6:00 a.m. to 2:00 a.m. ($1,500 sales income minus $1,155 in variable and fixed costs equals $345 in profits).

In the same property during the early morning hours (from 2:00 a.m. to 6:00 a.m.), the coffee shop generates sales income of only $125. Variable costs (57% of the sales) are $71, and fixedcosts for the four-hour period are $60 (four times $15). Total costs are $131. A loss of $6 results.

Upon examining such calculations, the first reaction might be to close the coffee shop during the early morning hours. However, the fixed costs ($60) will be incurred even if the shop is closed. If the coffee shop remains open, it will generate $54 in sales which can offset part of the fixed costs ($125 in sales minus $71 in variable costs equals $54). Given these statistics, the coffee shop should remain open 24 hours a day. Not only will an economic benefit be realized, but the provision of coffee shop service to guests and others may also have spin-off effects on other aspects of the hotel operation. Remember, the guests are the first consideration.

The Coffee Shop—an Asset or a Liability?

A property can benefit in many ways from its coffee shop operation. Some guests may enjoy the coffee shop's food and service so much that they will visit the property's other food and beverage outlets. Other guests may recommend the hotel to out-of-town friends or business associates in part because of their good dining experience in the coffee shop. Still other coffee shop guests may be so impressed that they will try the hotel's banquet department when they are planning a special event.

The reverse of the preceding examples is also true. The lodging property with an inadequate coffee shop operation certainly does not enhance its public image. Because hotel guests enjoy the convenience of a coffee shop for an early breakfast or a late-night snack, they may be very displeased when they find the coffee shop is not open 24 hours a day. Others, who appreciate the low prices which coffee shops typically charge, may become very disgruntled with outlets that charge what they perceive as being an excessive amount for food or beverages. In large convention hotels where many guests rely on the coffee shop for their breakfasts or in motels where the coffee shop is the sole dining outlet, substandard food or service may make a difference in whether or not guests ever stay at the lodging property again. Similarly, a hotel may lose future local, commuter, or travel business if its coffee shop service does not meet the expectations of those who are not guests of the hotel.

Managing Service at the Hotel Columbia
Page Eighteen

Several days later Don decided he needed a break from his routine at the Hotel Columbia and decided it was a good time to visit a hotel that was open and operating even if all was not right in its coffee shop.

Upon reaching the Tremont, Don thought he could see a waiting line inside the coffee shop. (The windows weren't very clean and there was a lot of glare.) As he entered, he realized that he was correct. There was a waiting line even though there were empty tables which had not been cleaned and reset after other guests had eaten and gone. There was also a waiting line at the cashier station but there was no cashier. Fortunately, there was a single stool at the coffee shop counter; Don decided to sit there rather than wait for a table or booth in the main dining area.

"Hi, what can I get you?" was the greeting he received from the counter attendant who arrived almost a moment after he sat down.

"I don't know," said Don, "may I see a menu?"

"Well," said the attendant, "I think I can find one. By the way, we're out of the daily specials noted on the menu board."

As Don waited for his attendant to return, he looked around and noticed pans full of soiled dishes on various shelves and on the floor behind the counter. He also noticed the cashier was now at her stand, and he realized she was also doubling as a food server and hostess. Finally, he noticed the bright sun shining in through the windows which appeared to make dining uncomfortable for guests seated facing the windows.

Don noted relatively few problems with the way his server took his order. The food was served promptly and it was very good. He did, however, have to ask for another fork (the tines on the first were bent) and the plate was chipped.

During his lunch he spoke to the guest seated next to him at the counter. "Sure, I come here often," the guest said, "my office is right across the street. The food is reliably good, but I've noticed lately that they don't seem to be paying attention to details. Service is pretty bad at the tables—that's why I sit at the counter. Their prices are decent here, so I put up with sometimes having to wait in line to pay. They have lost a number of other regular customers though."

Don asked for his check and received it after a few minutes. Fortunately, the cashier was at her station so he didn't have to waste time waiting to pay his bill.

Managing Service at the Hotel Columbia
Page Eighteen, continued

On his drive back to the Hotel Columbia, Don thought about what he had learned. He knew that coffee shops are often overlooked when top-level managers develop their plans. They seem to give more attention to glamorous food service outlets which produce relatively high contribution and profit margins. He would not let that happen at the Hotel Columbia; the Round the Clock coffee shop would reflect the same quality of service given in all other dining outlets.

Upon reaching his office, Don made some notes and filled out his shopper's service report. (A sample form for such a report accompanies this case study.)

The points emphasized in his notes included the following:

1. It is just as important to show attention to service quality in the coffee shop as it is in any other food and beverage outlet.
2. Service staff in the coffee shop need training and close supervision. The development of quality standards dictating "how things should be done" would precede this training.
3. Management staff must recognize that good food alone is not sufficient to help ensure the success of an outlet. Attention to details from the guests' perspective is critical. (Don noted such points as the dirty windows, glare from the sun, and lack of inspection of flatware and dishes coming from the dishroom.)
4. The quality of work and the appearance of the servers reflect the standards of the entire hotel. The coffee shop is not a "second-class citizen" of a hotel; it is an equal partner with full rights.
5. Close attention to staffing requirements is important. Many people go to a coffee shop for a meal because service is quick. Staffing and scheduling plans must recognize this fact, and contingency plans for "no-show" employees must be made. (Don made a note to talk about the problems that are caused when a cashier also is the hostess and has table service and table busing duties.)
6. Value is the "name of the game" in the coffee shop as well as in any other food and beverage outlet. The quality of the food, service, and atmosphere relative to the price that is charged is just as important to guests in the coffee shop as in the gourmet dining room.
7. Production plans must be coordinated with anticipated business volume. It was, of course, very likely that there would be occasional "run-outs" of food products. However, Don had the feeling that daily specials at the Tremont were not managed effectively and that run-outs were common.
8. It is difficult to evaluate objectively one's own property. The use of a shopper's service is a good idea. Don decided that when the Hotel Columbia opened, he would ask someone to act as a shopper in his coffee shop.

Shopper's Service Report

Name of Property (Dining Outlet) _____

Address _____

Date of Visitation _____ Meal Period _____ Time _____

Manager/Supervisor on Duty _____

Shopper's Service Report, continued

ITEMS PURCHASED:

Beverages: Food:

#	ITEM	PRICE	#	ITEM	PRICE
___	___	___	___	___	___
___	___	___	___	___	___
___	___	___	___	___	___
___	___	___	___	___	___
	TOTAL	___		TOTAL	___

Total Price _____

Please respond to each statement using the following scale:
5—Strongly Agree
4—Somewhat Agree
3—Neither Agree nor Disagree
2—Somewhat Disagree
1—Strongly Disagree
NA—The statement does not apply.
To Score: Total all points and compare the actual score with the Standard Point Score. (When statements are not applicable, change Standard Point Score correspondingly.)

TOTAL STANDARD POINT SCORE _____   TOTAL ACTUAL POINT SCORE _____

GREETING

A. You were greeted immediately upon entering the dining area.	5	4	3	2	1
B. The host/hostess moved away from the stand.	5	4	3	2	1
C. The host/hostess asked your name and/or made a friendly/gracious comment.	5	4	3	2	1

D. Comments regarding your greeting: _____

_____

_____

STANDARD POINT SCORE FOR GREETING ___15___   ACTUAL POINT SCORE _____

SEATING

A. You were asked whether you preferred to be seated in the nonsmoking or the smoking section.	5	4	3	2	1
B. When you were ready to be seated, you were immediately led to your table.	5	4	3	2	1
C. The host/hostess was attractively dressed.	5	4	3	2	1

Shopper's Service Report, continued

D. The host/hostess was neat and clean.	5	4	3	2	1
E. The selection of your table location showed good judgment.	5	4	3	2	1
F. The chair/booth was comfortable.	5	4	3	2	1

If uncomfortable, in what way? _____

_____

G. The host/hostess distributed menus when you were seated.	5	4	3	2	1
H. The host/hostess informed you of special or additional menu items.	5	4	3	2	1
I. The host/hostess informed you of the name of your server(s).	5	4	3	2	1
J. The host/hostess left with a pleasant message.	5	4	3	2	1
K. The host/hostess seemed happy about his/her job and interested in you.	5	4	3	2	1

L. Comments regarding your seating: _____

_____

_____

STANDARD POINT SCORE FOR SEATING ___55___   ACTUAL POINT SCORE _____

CLEANLINESS

A. The dining area was clean.	5	4	3	2	1
B. The table was clean and free of crumbs.	5	4	3	2	1
C. The chair/booth was clean.	5	4	3	2	1
D. Dirty dishes were completely cleared from the table as soon as they were empty.	5	4	3	2	1
E. The flatware and dishes were clean.	5	4	3	2	1
F. The glasses were clean.	5	4	3	2	1
G. The carpet was clean.	5	4	3	2	1
H. The restrooms were clean.	5	4	3	2	1
I. Rank the overall cleanliness.	5	4	3	2	1

J. Comments regarding cleanliness: _____

_____

_____

STANDARD POINT SCORE FOR CLEANLINESS ___45___   ACTUAL POINT SCORE _____

ATMOSPHERE

A. The dining outlet was conducive to conversation.	5	4	3	2	1
B. The lighting was appropriate.	5	4	3	2	1

If not, what was wrong? _____

_____

Shopper's Service Report, continued

C. There was no noticeable kitchen noise.	5	4	3	2	1
D. The background music was peaceful.	5	4	3	2	1
E. The following were in agreement with the outlet's theme:					
Decor	5	4	3	2	1
Menu	5	4	3	2	1
Uniforms	5	4	3	2	1
F. The experience was what you expected.	5	4	3	2	1

G. Comments regarding atmosphere: _____

_____

_____

STANDARD POINT SCORE FOR ATMOSPHERE __40____   ACTUAL POINT SCORE _____

SERVICE

A. A server made contact with you within three minutes after you were seated.	5	4	3	2	1
B. The server provided water during his/her first contact.	5	4	3	2	1
C. The server had a pleasant greeting.	5	4	3	2	1
D. The server's hands and fingernails were clean.	5	4	3	2	1
E. The server's posture was good.	5	4	3	2	1
F. The server was cordial, smiled, and created a pleasant atmosphere.	5	4	3	2	1
G. The server was familiar with the menu items.	5	4	3	2	1
H. The server used suggestive selling and was courteous without being pushy.	5	4	3	2	1
I. The server could answer all your questions about the property.	5	4	3	2	1
J. The lady's order was taken first.	5	4	3	2	1
K. The server did not use his/her tray as a writing platform.	5	4	3	2	1
L. Beverage items were served promptly.	5	4	3	2	1
M. Food items were served promptly.	5	4	3	2	1
N. The timing between courses was appropriate.	5	4	3	2	1
O. The server knew which items to serve to each guest.	5	4	3	2	1
P. Beverages were served from the right.	5	4	3	2	1
Q. Food items were served from the left.	5	4	3	2	1
R. The server returned to the table within five minutes to provide additional assistance.	5	4	3	2	1
S. Water glasses were refilled promptly.	5	4	3	2	1
T. Empty dishes were removed promptly.	5	4	3	2	1
U. Dirty dishes were removed from the right.	5	4	3	2	1
V. Dirty ashtrays were properly removed (capped) and replaced.	5	4	3	2	1
W. It was not necessary to summon the server during the meal.	5	4	3	2	1
X. The server seemed to enjoy his/her job.	5	4	3	2	1
Y. The server did an excellent job.	5	4	3	2	1

Z. Comments regarding the service: _____

_____

Shopper's Service Report, continued

_____

_____

_____

_____

_____

STANDARD POINT SCORE FOR SERVICE __125__   ACTUAL POINT SCORE _____

FOOD

(Please indicate suggestions to improve the quality of any item under "Additional comments.")

A. The food items corresponded with their menu descriptions.	5	4	3	2	1
B. All items ordered were available.	5	4	3	2	1
C. The hot foods were served hot.	5	4	3	2	1
D. The cold foods were served cold.	5	4	3	2	1

APPETIZER (Name _____)
E. The appetizer:

looked appetizing,	5	4	3	2	1
was fresh,	5	4	3	2	1
had excellent coloring,	5	4	3	2	1
had an excellent flavor, and	5	4	3	2	1
was seasoned well.	5	4	3	2	1

BREADSTICKS
F. The breadsticks:

were fresh and	5	4	3	2	1
were seasoned perfectly.	5	4	3	2	1

G. Additional comments regarding the appetizer or breadsticks: _____

_____

_____

_____

_____

SALAD (Name _____)
H. The salad:

looked appetizing,	5	4	3	2	1
was neatly plated,	5	4	3	2	1
was appropriately portioned,	5	4	3	2	1
had excellent coloring,	5	4	3	2	1
was fresh,	5	4	3	2	1

Shopper's Service Report, continued

had a dressing that complemented it, and	5	4	3	2	1
was of excellent quality.	5	4	3	2	1

I. Additional comments regarding the salad: _____

_____

_____

ENTREE (Name _____)

J. The entree:

looked appetizing,	5	4	3	2	1
was neatly plated,	5	4	3	2	1
was appropriately portioned,	5	4	3	2	1
had excellent coloring,	5	4	3	2	1
was fresh,	5	4	3	2	1
was seasoned well,	5	4	3	2	1
had an excellent flavor, and	5	4	3	2	1
was of excellent quality.	5	4	3	2	1

K. Additional comments regarding the entree: _____

_____

_____

_____

_____

VEGETABLE (Name _____)

L. The vegetable:

was appropriately portioned,	5	4	3	2	1
had excellent coloring,	5	4	3	2	1
was fresh,	5	4	3	2	1
had the correct texture,	5	4	3	2	1
was seasoned well, and	5	4	3	2	1
had an excellent flavor.	5	4	3	2	1

M. Additional comments regarding the vegetable: _____

_____

STARCH (Name _____)

N. The starch item:

was appropriately portioned,	5	4	3	2	1
was fresh,	5	4	3	2	1
was seasoned well, and	5	4	3	2	1
had an excellent flavor.	5	4	3	2	1

O. Additional comments regarding the starch item: _____

_____

Shopper's Service Report, continued

DESSERT (Name _____)

P. The dessert:

was appropriately portioned,	5	4	3	2	1
was fresh,	5	4	3	2	1
was served at the correct temperature, and	5	4	3	2	1
had an excellent flavor.	5	4	3	2	1

Q. Additional comments regarding the dessert: _____

_____

R. Each of the following items corresponded with its menu description:

Appetizer	5	4	3	2	1
Salad	5	4	3	2	1
Entree	5	4	3	2	1
Dessert	5	4	3	2	1

S. Additional comments regarding the overall food quality: _____

_____

_____

_____

_____

STANDARD POINT SCORE FOR FOOD __220__   ACTUAL POINT SCORE _____

MENU

A. The menu was clean and free from spots.	5	4	3	2	1
B. The menu fit the theme of the dining outlet.	5	4	3	2	1
C. The menu was well organized.	5	4	3	2	1
D. The menu was clearly written.	5	4	3	2	1
E. Descriptions were appetizing.	5	4	3	2	1
F. The number of items available was appropriate.	5	4	3	2	1
G. Specials were available.	5	4	3	2	1
H. Vegetarian menu items were available.	5	4	3	2	1
I. The menu was an effective marketing tool.	5	4	3	2	1

J. Comments and changes you'd like to see regarding the menu: _____

_____

_____

STANDARD POINT SCORE FOR THE MENU __45__   ACTUAL POINT SCORE _____

Shopper's Service Report, continued

GUEST CHECK (BILL) HANDLING

A. The guest check arrived at the appropriate time.	5	4	3	2	1
B. The check was readable.	5	4	3	2	1
C. The check correctly reflected what had been served.	5	4	3	2	1
D. The check was correctly totaled.	5	4	3	2	1
E. The server informed you that he/she would return for your payment when you were ready.	5	4	3	2	1
F. The server said thank you after he/she received your payment.	5	4	3	2	1
G. The server took the payment directly to the cashier.	5	4	3	2	1
H. The server brought your change directly from the cashier.	5	4	3	2	1
I. You received the correct change.	5	4	3	2	1
J. You received the check stub.	5	4	3	2	1
K. The server invited you to return.	5	4	3	2	1

L. Please list restaurant check number _____ Total _____ Tip (if charged) _____

M. Comments regarding check handling: _____

_____

_____

STANDARD POINT SCORE FOR CHECK HANDLING __55__   ACTUAL POINT SCORE _____

10
Room Service

A number of lodging properties provide their guests with the opportunity to order and enjoy food and beverage products in the privacy of their own rooms or suites. Many people, when they see a room service menu for the first time, are surprised at the relatively high prices. Even more surprising is the fact that few room service operations make a significant profit. Why, then, is room service offered? One reason is that guests at many properties desire room service and professional managers have guest satisfaction as their major goal. These managers know that when room service is a well-run operation, it can give the hotel a competitive edge and enhance its image.

From the guests' perspective, the key elements of a well-run room service operation include: the prompt and courteous answering of the room service telephone when orders are called in; the close attention to all details of guests' orders; the efficient and quick delivery of orders to guestrooms; the tact and courtesy displayed by room service attendants when delivering and/or serving orders; strict adherence to rules of safety when using equipment that involves liquid fuels or open flames; the assurance that hot and cold foods and beverages are at the correct temperature when they are served; and the prompt removal of trays and other equipment when guests have finished their meals or snacks.

Some hotels do a large volume of business offering food and beverage service for small group meetings, corporate meetings, organizations entertaining business guests during conventions, and other occasions. They are able to increase the productivity of their room service operations by placing the responsibility for such hospitality suites with room service rather than with the banquet department. Room service then provides all food and beverage services in any hotel room, including suites, for groups of any size. Since food and beverage sales in hospitality suites usually produce a profit, they can help offset losses accrued from the traditional delivery of products and services to transient guests in their rooms.

Several factors have an impact on the relationship between dining rooms and room service. Twenty-four-hour room service is much easier when one or more restaurants are also open around the clock; room service is generally very unprofitable if a separate production facility must be maintained for it. For this reason, some room service ends at midnight. However, some facilities transfer the production responsibilities from a special room service kitchen to a dining room or coffee shop kitchen during slow times.

Personnel

Planning the organization of room service is an important task; Exhibit 10.1 illustrates one way to organize an effective room service operation. Notice the number of different positions needed to provide room service. Other properties may have other titles for the positions or may not have all of the positions listed; however, someone must be able to perform each of the tasks associated with these positions. Details about the duties and responsibilities of room service personnel are included in the following discussions.

Managing Service at the Hotel Columbia
Page Nineteen

Lewis Scott and Don Jackson decided to focus some of their attention on the development of standard operating procedures for room service at the Hotel Columbia. They knew that a number of guests rate a hotel on the quality of its room service, so they felt that investing time to produce a well-functioning department was worth the effort.

Lewis and Don agreed that room service was not a profitable operation in some hotels. "Of course I'm concerned about making a profit, but I'm more concerned about ensuring that room service will address our guest-related goals," Lewis explained to Don.

"Why don't we develop general room service procedures now that our room service manager, when we hire him or her, can use to develop more specific procedures later?" Lewis continued.

"Where do we start?" asked Don.

"Well," Lewis replied, "first we need to identify all the goals that the Hotel Columbia wants to achieve with room service. And I think we need to familiarize ourselves concerning the most common room service problems in other properties—then we can devise ways of keeping them from being problems here."

"Sounds like a good topic of conversation for tonight's Food and Beverage Managers' Association Meeting," Don commented.

"Right," said Lewis, "our colleagues will have plenty of advice. We'll get some answers this evening."

Room Service Manager

The room service manager has a large number of management responsibilities ranging from planning and executing the department's operation to enforcing the department's rules. He/she is responsible for organizing the room service staff and should therefore have a role in selecting, orienting, training, and scheduling staff members. Handling problems with food orders and delivery, controlling costs, and ensuring that service staff collect all sales income due the outlet are additional duties. When guests plan special functions in hospitality suites, the room service manager becomes an important member of the planning team (if room service is responsible for these functions). Furthermore, the room service manager must handle complaints from guests, employees, and others; ensure that room service equipment is properly maintained; and requisition necessary equipment and supplies. Since the department is labor-intensive, supervisory duties are also part of the room service manager's work.

Assistant Room Service Manager

In properties that have an assistant room service manager, this official performs some of the tasks that would otherwise be the responsibility of the room service manager. Frequently, he/she supervises employees, undertakes many of the daily and/or routine decision-making tasks associated with special functions, solves operational problems, and completes required records and reports.

Room Service Captain

During a specific shift, the room service captain is in charge of the order-takers, room service attendants, and buspersons. Captains help the assistant room service manager ensure that employees follow all operating procedures and consistently attain performance standards. They also issue guest checks, ensure that room service supply areas are adequately stocked, and personally supervise functions in hospitality suites. When VIPs order room service, the captains themselves may prepare, deliver, and otherwise render service to these guests in their rooms.

Room service captains may also expedite room service when special problems arise. Rescheduling or reassigning room service attendants is an example of how they could do that. Captains may make inspection rounds to ensure

Exhibit 10.1 Sample Room Service Organization Chart

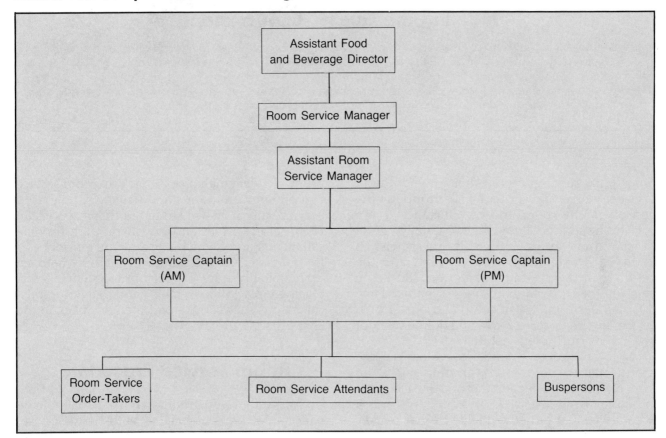

that buspersons remove soiled equipment and supplies promptly from guestrooms and off the floors. The captain may also check incoming orders to ensure that the order-takers are taking them in a timely fashion and the room service attendants are delivering them quickly. When room service attendants leave the kitchen area, captains may also serve as checkers to confirm that equipment and tray orders are correct. Properties such as resorts may assign a captain to a room service office or pantry on each floor; the duties of these captains generally increase substantially. Overall, captains help ensure that the room service operation runs smoothly.

Room Service Order-Taker

The room service order-taker's job begins when he/she receives numbered guest checks, learns about any problems, substitutions, or other concerns related to the menu; and ensures that the room service attendants are on duty as assigned. As guests place room service orders, the order-taker must record their orders according to specific procedures, place the orders with the kitchen, and, in many properties, ring up the check on a precheck register or other data machine.

This staff member may also serve as a food checker to confirm that the orders removed from the kitchen area match the items listed on the guest check. The order-taker's role during initial contacts with the guests is much like that of a food or beverage server. Suggestive selling and knowing the menu are also parts of this employee's job.

Room Service Attendants

Room service attendants accept orders from the kitchen, ensure that all items listed on the guest check are on the food tray or table, permit the order-taker to double-check the order if procedures require it, deliver orders to designated

Meeting the Guests' Expectations

What would you like or dislike about room service if you were a guest in a hotel? Thinking about your own reactions to room service can help you to design plans for room service in a property which you manage. Do you want reasonable variety on the menu? Do you want room service at all hours? Do you want timely delivery and quality food and beverage products? The answers to these questions can provide you with some guidelines for developing and instituting specific room service procedures.

rooms, and serve guests in their rooms. Room service involves more than just dropping the food off in the room. In every instance, room service attendants should knock quietly, greet guests warmly, and ask where the guests wish to be served. Depending on the property and the menu, room service attendants may do some tableside food preparation in guestrooms. They may also perform station setup and breakdown tasks in the room service area and do the work of buspersons during busy shifts.

It is absolutely essential for room service attendants to be totally familiar with the property's floor layout and location of each room and suite. Time lost while an attendant finds a room affects not only the quality of that guest's service, but also the service of subsequent guests who will receive their orders later than expected. Furthermore, the quality of food will deteriorate as the length of time between production and service increases.

In properties such as resorts that are spread over many areas and buildings, room service attendants often deliver orders in motorized vehicles such as golf carts. Room service managers in these facilities must often meet the needs of very demanding guests and often ask for input from room service attendants to help develop creative methods to ensure that those needs are met.

In general, room service attendants function like food and beverage servers; they not only serve food and beverage products to guests following certain procedures, but also ensure that the guests are completely satisfied with the items.

Buspersons

Buspersons may help set up room service stations in the kitchen, assemble items for an order, deliver small orders, pick up room service equipment from rooms and hallways, take used serviceware to dishwashing or other areas, clean room service tables and trays, and perform miscellaneous tasks which increase the efficiency of the room service attendants. They may help set up hospitality suites by performing such tasks as placing tablecloths on tables and delivering miscellaneous serviceware and food supplies to the suites.

Room Service Procedures

Now that you understand the roles of the various positions associated with room service, let's take a look at how room service actually operates.

In well-run room service departments, room service attendants have completed preparation work during slow times or prior to the beginning of the service period so they have only a minimum number of tasks to perform during peak business hours. For example, they will have pre-set room service carts (e.g., they make certain the cart is clean, they place a tablecloth or other table covering on it, and they set it properly with tableware, napkins, and appropriate condiments). Pre-set carts are generally stored in out-of-work aisle areas where room service attendants can conveniently obtain them. To ensure that the attendants have an adequate number of items at the beginning of their shifts, some managers use a checklist of room service equipment and supplies (Exhibit 10.2).

Before room service attendants begin work, they should be briefed about any special functions occurring in the property, the amount of forecasted business, any unavailable menu items, specials of the day, a list of VIPs and

Exhibit 10.2 Checklist of Room Service Equipment and Supplies

Item	Amount Required			
	Day/Shift Weekday (AM)	Day/Shift Weekend (AM)	Day/Shift Weekday (PM)	Day/Shift Weekend (PM)
Service Trays				
Tables				
Tablecloths				
Cloth Napkins				
Paper Napkins				
Bread Baskets				
Placemats				
Coffee Cups				
Saucers				
Juice Glasses				

groups of people staying at the hotel, and any other information that will enable them to provide good service to the guests.

Taking the Order

Order-takers should answer all calls promptly and offer an apology if the phone rings more than a specific number of times (such as five rings). Computerized aids that identify guests' names for order-takers enable them to provide personalized service. Most guests are impressed when an order-taker uses their names without having been told by the guests who they are. An example of a conversation where the order-taker already knows the guest's name might be: "Room service; good evening. May I take your order, Mr. Rhodes?" Some systems use guest lists that are printed up at the front desk and given to the room service department; other systems display the guest's name and room number when the phone rings. When we consider that the order-taker can also automatically send orders to the kitchen with a remote printing device, it is easy to see how fast-paced technology can affect the order-taker's job and improve service.

Order-takers should follow specific procedures as they take orders from guests. For example, as the guest recites the order, the order-taker completes a guest check. Frequently, duplicate guest checks are used. Guest checks are typically pre-numbered and assigned to specific order-takers; all guest checks then must be accounted for at the end of each order-taker's shift. Exhibit 10.3 illustrates the instructions one lodg-

Exhibit 10.3 Room Service Check and Order-Taking System

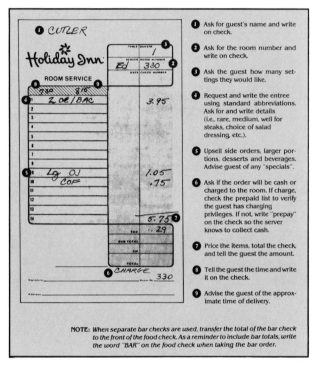

① Ask for guest's name and write on check.

② Ask for the room number and write on check.

③ Ask the guest how many settings they would like.

④ Request and write the entree using standard abbreviations. Ask for and write details (i.e., rare, medium, well for steaks, choice of salad dressing, etc.).

⑤ Upsell side orders, larger portions, desserts and beverages. Advise guest of any "specials".

⑥ Ask if the order will be cash or charged to the room. If charge, check the prepaid list to verify the guest has charging privileges. If not, write "prepay" on the check so the server knows to collect cash.

⑦ Price the items, total the check, and tell the guest the amount.

⑧ Tell the guest the time and write it on the check.

⑨ Advise the guest of the approximate time of delivery.

NOTE: *When separate bar checks are used, transfer the total of the bar check to the front of the food check. As a reminder to include bar totals, write the word "BAR" on the food check when taking the bar order.*

Reprinted with permission from *Room Service* (Memphis, Tenn.: Holiday Inns, Inc.—U.S. Hotel Operations, 1981), p. 20.

ing operation uses for order-taking. When order-takers use manual systems, it is very important that they write legibly since production staff, service personnel, the guest, and, in some cases, a cashier may need to read it. They should also use standard menu abbreviations which no one will misunderstand. Order-takers must include all details about the order on the guest check (e.g., how the guests wish their eggs to be prepared, what type of salad dressing the guest prefers).

Order-takers can sell by suggestion. The same procedures service employees use in the dining room apply here. Informing guests about specials, suggesting high-contribution margin items, and asking questions to which guests cannot answer "yes" or "no," but instead asking such questions as "Which of our two excellent desserts would you like, Mr. Jones?" are techniques which can expand room service sales.

Some properties use a tape-recorded message system for room service; the guest calls the required number and places the order. Other properties use this system only during very slow periods when an order-taker is not on duty. For example, the room service attendant may serve as order-taker; a taped message is then used when he/she is away from the station delivering an order. The impersonal service and the possibility of confusion about the guest's exact needs are two potential disadvantages to this system. The room service manager must ensure that the advantages of faster service and reduced operating (labor) costs offset these potential problems.

Routing the Order

After the order-taker writes the order on the guest check, he/she must route it to the appropriate food and/or beverage production department. Several alternatives for doing so include:

1. The order-taker may hand-carry the guest check to the food production department. This system may work well when a separate room service kitchen is located close to the order-taker's telephone stand or when the order-taker is a cashier or receptionist in the dining room.

2. The order-taker may give the guest check to a room service attendant, who then takes it to the production department.

3. The order-taker may use a precheck register with a remote printer. With this system, the order-taker automatically transmits the order to the production staff as he/she enters the information into the precheck register. He/she must then enter information from the guest check onto a room service order form (Exhibit 10.4). Properties use this form to record such information about each order as the guest's name, the guest check number, the server's name, and the time the order was placed. The order-taker must also complete a room service control form (Exhibit 10.5), which keeps track of all guest checks. It indicates the person responsible for delivering the order, the time required to prepare the order, and the total amount of cash and charge sales generated by room service. However, a properly programmed remote printer could replace the

room service control form since the electronic data machine can maintain all the information related to each order.

Procedures for transmitting room service orders to production personnel become more complicated when order-takers must give copies of orders to both hot and cold food production stations as well as to the service bar. One operation solves this problem by using a five-part order ticket. The order-taker writes the entire order on this ticket; one copy goes to the cashier, another goes to the hot food station, a third goes to the cold food station, a fourth goes to the service bar, and the fifth copy goes to the room service attendant so that he/she can put the order together on a tray or service cart.

Preparing the Order

Room service attendants should be aware of the orders being prepared by production employees so they can do any additional setup work. For example, room service attendants may prepare or portion salads and desserts while production personnel prepare other parts of the order. If appropriate, they should cover these items with plastic wrap or store them in protective containers to help maintain quality. Room service attendants could also obtain beverages. Typically, they obtain beverages from a service bar located close to the room service area. Since the par inventory levels of liquor will be reduced by the number of bottles issued to room service, attendants must give the bartender a copy of the room service order indicating that they require a full bottle.

In properties with a central beverage storeroom, a management staff member issues full bottles of alcoholic beverages from the central storeroom to the room service beverage storage area. (He/she can use a standard issue requisition and then transfer the costs of issued beverages to the room service department.) If guests request full bottles from room service, the attendants can obtain bottles from the room service beverage storeroom.

Standard procedures often require that when food orders are ready, the attendants pick them up, cover them with lids or other insulated material, and present them to the order-taker, food checker, or other staff member for inspection. Some properties put caps or covers on cups

Server (in tuxedo uniform) preparing a table for room service. (Amway Grand Plaza Hotel, Grand Rapids, Michigan)

prevent spills. The entire cart or serving tray should be covered with a washable cloth or dis-

A well-run room service department with one table ready to be checked and other tables ready for meals to be placed on them. (Amway Grand Plaza Hotel, Grand Rapids, Michigan)

Exhibit 10.4 Room Service Order Form

DATE: _____

Room #	Guest Name	Time Order	Delivery Time	Order	Tray	Cart

Courtesy of Hotel du Pont, Wilmington, Delaware

posable clear plastic cover. The food is now ready for delivery to the guest.

Delivering the Order

It is imperative that room service attendants deliver orders as quickly as possible. Following are a number of ways to expedite service: (1) dumbwaiters may be used to move products between floors; this plan may work well when continental breakfasts (coffee, juice, and rolls) are offered to all guests or standard breakfasts are offered to VIPs and guests occupying suites; (2) one or more freight or passenger elevators could be designated for room service use—at least during peak business periods; (3) "flying kitchens"—well-equipped elevators that enable service employees to prepare a limited number of menu items as they move between floors—could be installed; (4) a service attendant can be assigned to one or more floors during busy pe-

Exhibit 10.5 Room Service Control Form

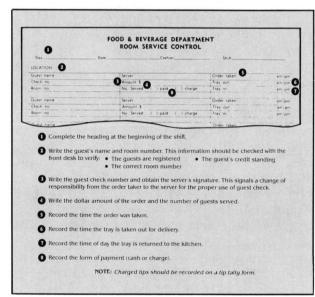

Reprinted with permission from *Room Service* (Memphis, Tenn.: Holiday Inns, Inc.—U.S. Hotel Operations, 1981), p. 30.

The Brisk Breakfast Business

Most room service orders occur during the breakfast hours. Also, many meetings begin at 9:00 a.m. or earlier. Therefore, the kitchen and room service staffs have a great burden placed on them when meeting attendees order breakfast in the dining rooms or through room service at the same time that others are also ordering breakfast. These problems intensify when a group or tour is in the property. Since members of these groups generally depart at the same time, usually in the morning, breakfast periods can be very busy. For these reasons, procedures for dining room as well as room service must be responsive to the rush of early morning business.

riods; after the carts are transported to each floor, the assigned attendant delivers the orders.

Procedures must be developed for delivering room service orders. Such procedures could

Exhibit 10.6 Sample Guest Courtesy Card*

Dear Guest,

We hope you enjoy your meal and would appreciate upon completion a call from you so we may promptly remove your tray.

Tel. 3151

Thank you and looking forward to serving you again.
Room Service Staff

*The hotel which uses this courtesy card reports that approximately 75% of the guests using room service call for tray removal.

include: delivering orders in the approximate sequence in which they are received, using a uniform greeting and method of alerting guests that the order has arrived (e.g., a short knock followed by the statement "Room Service with your order"), and verifying the guest's name and room number when the guest opens the door.

Other procedures could require the room service attendant to ask the guest where he/she prefers the order to be placed—on a table, left on the cart, or elsewhere; and if the order requires tableside preparation, to indicate how long the order will take to prepare and ask if the preparation can begin.

Normally, it is necessary for guests to sign a copy of the guest check indicating that they have received the order. Usually, the guest's signature is sufficient; however, sometimes cash payments are required in certain circumstances. The room service attendant should give the guest a number to dial for additional service or to request tray pickup; this information could be provided on a courtesy card (Exhibit 10.6) left on the tray or cart. Of course, the room service attendant should thank the guest as he/she leaves.

Providing Wine Service and Other Amenities

Guests may order bottled wines from room service; therefore, room service attendants should know the proper ways to uncork both table and sparkling wines. Room service attendants may also be responsible for delivering fruit baskets, cheese trays, and other amenities for special guests; therefore, management must develop procedures for preparing and/or arranging these items. Frequently, a courtesy card accom-

Telephone Etiquette

The following ten suggestions can help order-takers give effective service to guests:

1. Stop previous conversations before picking up the receiver.
2. Answer the telephone promptly.
3. Give a friendly greeting. For example, some properties specify that from 7:00 a.m. to noon the order taker should say, "Room Service, good morning"; from noon to 6:00 p.m., "Room Service, good afternoon"; from 6:00 p.m. to 8:00 p.m., "Room Service, good evening"; and from 8:00 p.m. to closing, "Room Service, may I help you?"
4. Use the caller's name whenever possible.
5. Whenever possible, write the room number down first on the guest check. To help eliminate errors, repeat the order the guest has placed.
6. State the approximate time that the guest can expect the order. Allow some flexibility, depending on the amount of business room service is handling when the order is placed.
7. If you must interrupt the conversation, explain the reason to the guest.
8. Thank the guest for calling.
9. Allow the guest to hang up the phone first.
10. Because guests should not have to hear unnecessary noise and background conversations, order-takers who are not busy should not converse among themselves.

panies such amenities, and the room service attendant is often responsible for ensuring that it is in place. In addition, if special amenities require cloth napkins, flatware, or plates, the attendants must ensure that those supplies accompany the products.

Exhibit 10.7 is an example of a form which a friend, relative, business associate, or hotel official can use to place an order for a special room service amenity. Often, these amenities are a good source of revenue for the room service department. When a hotel official provides a special order for a guest, he/she should credit room service for at least the cost of the item. He/she can charge the cost to the affected department or promotional or other account.

A welcome card (Exhibit 10.8) can accompany a special room service amenity which a hotel official or department orders. This special touch can be instrumental in gaining the favor of a VIP. In cosmopolitan hotels, this card may be available in five or more languages.

Guests frequently order bar setups through room service. Typical items in a bar setup are a pitcher of water, cocktail napkins, stir sticks, glasses, a bucket of ice, and appropriate gar-

nishes. The guest may also order mixers, such as tonic water, club soda, and bottled water. Depending on the room's location, attendants may bring ice to the room from the room service area or from an ice machine located close to the room.

Some properties offer executive coffee service. Guests staying on special VIP floors, specific guests identified by the management, guests paying the full rate for expensive rooms, and others may receive this extra room service amenity. This complimentary coffee service may consist of hot beverages, juice, pastry, and/or a morning newspaper. Exhibit 10.9 illustrates a form that summarizes the information room service employees need to provide this amenity.

Finally, a system must be in place for removing used room service trays and carts quickly. Coordination and effective communication between housekeeping personnel and the room service staff is essential. For example, housekeepers could call room service staff to remove room service equipment from the rooms, or housekeepers could move used room service items to a central location, or a card left on the tray could ask guests to call room service or the

Exhibit 10.7 Special Room Service Order

NR: **1555**

SPECIAL ROOM SERVICE ORDER

FOR MR./MRS.: _____   ROOM: _____

DELIVERY DATE: _____   COST CODE: _____

FROM:

☐ _____   ☐ _____

☐ _____   ☐ _____

☐ _____

☐ $22.50   LARGE DELUXE FRUIT TRAY WITH ONE BOTTLE OF WINE
             (SELECTION OF FRUITS AND CHOCOLATE, PRESENTED ON A SILVER
             TRAY INCLUDING ONE BOTTLE OF WINE WHITE OR RED)

☐ $15.00   LARGE DELUXE FRUIT TRAY
             (SELECTIONS OF FRUIT AND CHOCOLATE, PRESENTED ON A SILVER
             TRAY)

☐ $15.50   SMALL FRUIT MIRROR WITH CHEESE AND ½ BOTTLE OF WINE
             (SELECTION OF FRUIT, CHEESES AND CHOCOLATE, PRESENTED ON A
             SMALL MIRROR WITH ½ BOTTLE OF WINE)

☐ $ 8.50   SMALL FRUIT MIRROR WITH CHEESE AND CHOCOLATE
             (SELECTION OF FRUIT, CHEESES AND CHOCOLATE PRESENTED ON A
             SMALL MIRROR)

☐ $ 5.00   FRUIT ARRANGEMENT IN A WICKER BASKET
             (ASSORTED FRUITS IN A BASKET)

☐ $ 6.00   PRESENTATION OF CHOCOLATE CUPS WITH 2 SMALL LIQUOR BOTTLES
             (PRESENTED ON A BLUE PLATE WITH CHOCOLATE CUPS AND FLOWERS)

☐ $_____   CHAMPAGNE   DOMESTIC _____   IMPORT _____

NAME: _____   TOTAL COST: $_____

Courtesy of Hotel du Pont, Wilmington, Delaware

How Long Will the Order Take?

Guests frequently ask how long the order will take, and the order-taker should be able to answer that question. He/she should know which menu items can be prepared quickly as well as those which take a long time. Based on this information, the order-taker can provide suggestions to guests in a hurry. Similarly, he/she can caution guests who order other items about how long it will take to prepare the order.

When guests order items which require tableside preparation, the order-taker should inform the guest about that fact and indicate whether or not the items can be quickly prepared.

Some order-takers may understate the order's delivery time, especially when guests are in a hurry. They may think that room service attendants, rather than themselves, will have to deal with guests' complaints when orders are delivered late. Of course, this practice should not be permitted. Order-takers should always estimate a realistic delivery time and be able to explain the reasons for the delivery time they quote to the guests.

housekeeping department when they wish room service equipment to be removed.

The Room Service Menu

Room service challenges management to offer a variety of high-quality menu items that will please guests. Some of the options available for developing menus include: offering fewer items that cost more than their dining room counterparts; offering those items from regular menus that can maintain their quality during holding periods and transportation to guest rooms; featuring items not on the standard menus; or using dining room menus as a basis for the room service menu, then supplementing it with other items.

Regardless of the approach used, planners must be sure that the items offered on room service menus will meet the property's quality requirements. Furthermore, designing attractive menus to help sell the products which the operation wants sold—such as those with the highest contribution margin (food income minus food costs)—is just as important to room service as it is to any other food and beverage outlet.

Room service menus should be readily available in guestrooms. Generally, all items available through room service should be included on that menu. However, some room service departments that offer high levels of service sometimes

use their menus to tell guests to inquire about unlisted items. Properties which offer a different room service menu for each meal or other period frequently combine all the menus into an attractive display which is located in a conspicuous place in the guestroom.

Room service menus in cosmopolitan hotels are frequently written in several languages. That feature is important since guests alone in their rooms are more likely to have translation problems than guests in public dining areas who receive assistance from the service staff. Some hotels offer special menus in braille for blind guests.

Uniquely designed room service menus can influence guest purchases in much the same way that dining room menus do. Room service managers should first determine what they want to sell (such as those items with the highest contribution margin), provide good descriptions using boxes, pictures, or other techniques to focus attention on the desired products, and observe all other principles of effective menu design.

In addition to menus, some properties place tent cards on the dresser, television, night stand, or other piece of furniture to promote room service as well as other food and beverage outlets. Some properties offer a nightly turn-down service in which housekeeping attendants prepare the guest's bed, tidy up the room, provide additional linens if necessary, and place a flower, candy, or a cheerful note on the guest's pillow; these employees may also place a breakfast doorknob menu on the guest's pillow. Other

Exhibit 10.8 Welcome Card

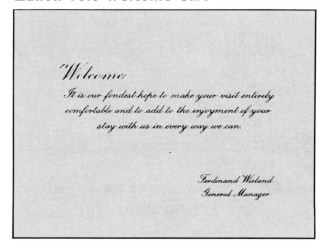

Welcome

It is our fondest hope to make your visit entirely comfortable and to add to the enjoyment of your stay with us in every way we can.

Ferdinand Wieland
General Manager

Courtesy of Hotel du Pont, Wilmington, Delaware

properties may have a doorknob menu always available in the room for the guest to complete and place on the outside of the door. The room service staff then picks up these menus during the early morning hours. The guest not only indicates which items he/she desires, but also the approximate time that he/she would like to be served. (Some flexibility, such as one-half hour, should be built into the delivery time since the time which the guest prefers could be a very busy period for the room service staff.) Exhibit 10.10 is a doorknob menu that one property uses. The doorknob menu expedites room service since guests can place orders and room service staff can prepare and deliver them without involving the order-taker during the breakfast rush.

Because the guest must be able to locate the telephone number for room service easily, the room service number should be in a conspicuous location on the room service menu as well as in other information about guest services. The ho-

Exhibit 10.9 Executive Coffee Service

				FOR MORNING OF _____ (DATE)								
Time	Name	Room	Guest Covers	Beverages				Newspaper				Duplicate Delivery On Stayover Yes/No
				Coffee	Tea	Sanka	Juice	N.Y.T.	Wash. P	Wall St.	Local	

Courtesy of Hotel du Pont, Wilmington, Delaware

Exhibit 10.10 Doorknob Menu for Breakfast

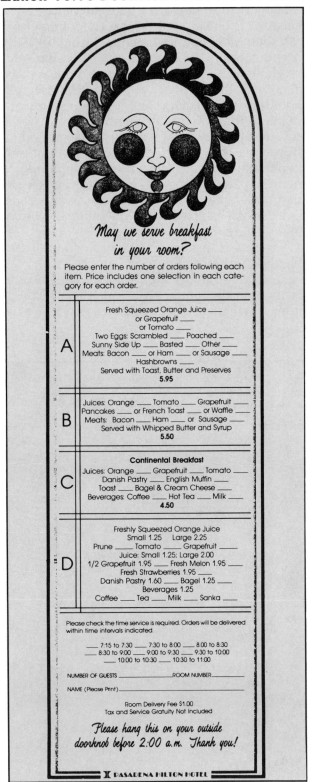

May we serve breakfast in your room?

Please enter the number of orders following each item. Price includes one selection in each category for each order.

A
Fresh Squeezed Orange Juice ____
or Grapefruit ____
or Tomato ____
Two Eggs: Scrambled ____ Poached ____
Sunny Side Up ____ Basted ____ Other ____
Meats: Bacon ____ or Ham ____ or Sausage ____
Hashbrowns ____
Served with Toast, Butter and Preserves
5.95

B
Juices: Orange ____ Tomato ____ Grapefruit ____
Pancakes ____ or French Toast ____ or Waffle ____
Meats: Bacon ____ Ham ____ or Sausage ____
Served with Whipped Butter and Syrup
5.50

C
Continental Breakfast
Juices: Orange ____ Grapefruit ____ Tomato ____
Danish Pastry ____ English Muffin ____
Toast ____ Bagel & Cream Cheese ____
Beverages: Coffee ____ Hot Tea ____ Milk ____
4.50

D
Freshly Squeezed Orange Juice
Small 1.25   Large 2.25
Prune ____ Tomato ____ Grapefruit ____
Juice: Small 1.25: Large 2.00
1/2 Grapefruit 1.95 ____ Fresh Melon 1.95 ____
Fresh Strawberries 1.95 ____
Danish Pastry 1.60 ____ Bagel 1.25 ____
Beverages 1.25
Coffee ____ Tea ____ Milk ____ Sanka ____

Please check the time service is required. Orders will be delivered within time intervals indicated.

____ 7:15 to 7:30   ____ 7:30 to 8:00   ____ 8:00 to 8:30
____ 8:30 to 9:00   ____ 9:00 to 9:30   ____ 9:30 to 10:00
____ 10:00 to 10:30   ____ 10:30 to 11:00

NUMBER OF GUESTS _____   ROOM NUMBER _____

NAME (Please Print) _____

Room Delivery Fee $1.00
Tax and Service Gratuity Not Included

Please hang this on your outside doorknob before 2:00 a.m. Thank you!

⊁ PASADENA HILTON HOTEL ⊁

Courtesy of Pasadena Hilton Hotel, Pasadena, California

tel operators must also know the number for room service. In properties that operate room service out of a room service kitchen during busy hours and out of other preparation facilities at slower times, the operator should know which room service telephone number to give guests: it could be the order-taker's number during busy periods, the dining room cashier's number when the dining room is open, and/or the coffee shop operator's number during still other periods.

Forecasting and Employee Scheduling

Room service managers must plan their staffing needs carefully. Unfortunately, this task is not easy because it is difficult to assess all the factors that have an impact on room service needs. Some of these factors include: (1) occupancy rates that create a derived demand for room service (the experienced room service manager can estimate from the house count the number of guests who will desire room service); (2) the number of guests who are traveling with an expense account; (3) the number of convention and business groups in-house (front desk and catering department personnel can help forecast how many people will require room service based on the number of guests who will attend organized meal functions); (4) the number of guests who have through their room rates already paid for and will automatically receive continental breakfast or similar in-room amenities (obviously there will be a direct correlation between these guest counts and room service needs).

Some properties transfer service staff back and forth between the dining rooms and room service as volume fluctuates in these areas. When this system is used, all service employees must be well trained in all the procedures which apply to each outlet. Properties which do not use this system have a much greater need to forecast accurately the volume of business anticipated for room service since slow service is likely to result if the estimates for room service staff are inadequate.

Room service business that is arranged in advance (such as cocktails and appetizers in hospitality suites or small group dining in guestrooms) is not difficult to plan for. The schedule

What Is Room Service?

Room service can involve activities other than the provision of food and beverage products in guestrooms. For example, in many properties the operation of hospitality suites is under the control of room service. In other facilities, room service employees provide food and beverages to guests in the swimming pool area and/or in recreation and other areas. The provision of fruit baskets and other amenities to VIPs is often a room service duty. In some hotel rooms, metered bars dispense alcoholic beverages, or an inventory of single portion beverages is available (guests pay for the difference between beginning and ending inventory amounts). Frequently, the responsibility to provide this service and the income which is generated is part of the room service operation.

planner will need to study the applicable function sheets which provide detailed information about room service staff needs in those areas. (Function sheets are discussed in greater detail in Chapter 12.)

Supplies and Equipment

Carts are frequently used to transport food to guestrooms and hospitality suites. These carts may be equipped with hot boxes which are either electrically powered or use canned, gel-type fuels. Safety codes, however, prohibit the use of these fuels during the transportation of food items. Some properties use a two-piece pellet system. Service employees place a preheated pellet in a base and put the plate in/on the base; they place a second hot pellet in the cover. For smaller room service orders, some properties use service trays pre-set with a placemat, flatware, napkin, and appropriate condiments.

Normally, a wide variety of equipment and supplies should be available in appropriate quantities in room service areas. While some room service departments may require only a mobile or stationary cart, shelving units, or one or two shelves on a wall, others will require additional square footage of storage space for room service supplies.

Room service volumes will differ by day and shift. For example, if the hotel caters to business travelers, it will have higher occupancy rates and serve more breakfasts on weekdays than on weekends. Therefore, the property will require a different quantity of room service items at different times. The checklist shown in Exhibit

10.2 allows for variations between busy and slow shifts.

Income Control Procedures

Control procedures to collect payment for all orders served through room service begin at the time order-takers write orders on guest checks. They enter information about the order and the amount of income it will generate on the room service control form (Exhibit 10.5). Typically, room service attendants return signed guest checks to the order-takers who then enter information about the payment (cash or charge) into a log. Hotels increasingly use point-of-sale devices in the room service department. When properties use this equipment, charged sale information is electronically transferred to the guest folio at the front desk. In the absence of this system, employees must manually transfer guest checks, representing guest charges, to the front desk for posting into the folios.

Because most guests wish to have their room service charges billed to their accounts, procedures to accommodate this request should be developed. Sometimes, however, charges are not possible. For example, a guest may have paid for the room in advance with cash, or guests may have reached or exceeded pre-established lines of credit. The front office should regularly report guests who are on a cash basis to the room service department so that order-takers can note the need for cash payments on the guest check. In addition, order-takers should inform guests that the room service attendant will require cash when he/she delivers the products. Some properties provide room service attendants with a credit card imprinter and appropriate supplies in anticipation of guests who wish to use their credit cards. Policies and procedures regarding the acceptance of credit cards and checks must comply with those developed by the property for use in other areas of the facility.

Managing Service at the Hotel Columbia
Page Twenty

Lewis Scott and Don Jackson had been reading, thinking, and talking about room service for several days. "I think at this point we have some good background information to help us develop some overall room service operating procedures," Lewis told Don. "First of all, we have confirmed the fact that when some hotels add up all the costs of their supposedly successful room service operations that they discover they have not generated a profit from that department after all."

"I was suprised to discover that some operations that did show a profit were able to only because they allocated to other departments a number of expenses that room service should directly bear," added Don.

Both men saw advantages to the increasingly common practice of having room service provide food and beverages in all guestrooms and hospitality suites. Their decision would not hurt the catering department since food and beverage sales in small function rooms constitute a relatively small percentage of the total catering sales. Furthermore, if the room service manager attended to the details of planning for these functions properly, staff members in the catering and banquet departments would have more time to carry out their mission—providing food and beverages to large groups in public areas.

Assigning to the room service department the responsibility for food and beverage services in guestrooms and hospitality suites would also help Lewis and Don plan the best for both the guest and the property. After all, profits from providing service for small function rooms would help reduce losses in regular room service sales and help keep selling prices for room service menu items at reasonable levels.

Certainly, the Hotel Columbia would not benefit from charging "outrageous" prices for room service items. "Since some guests might select the Hotel Columbia mainly because room service is available, high prices should not dissuade them from using it," Lewis concluded.

Next, Lewis and Don turned their attention to some of the most common challenges confronted by room service. Their goal was to provide guidance to the room service manager so that he/she could develop specific procedures to meet the challenges.

Challenge #1—Serving High-Quality Food. Lewis and Don both realized that the development and use of food purchase specifications would aid in the purchase of high-quality food products. "I'm responsible for and must control food quality," Lewis remarked. "Quality control has to start with the menu. Our manager has to give special attention to placing items on the room service menu that will hold up well during the time between food production and service. Since, in some cases, the time lapse will be 15 minutes or more, our manager will have to test carefully all products considered for the room service menu."

"What is wrong," Don asked, "with preparing some menu items, holding them for 15 minutes under conditions similar to those they would experience en route to the room, and then objectively evaluating them to assess any quality problems which might have arisen?"

"Let's have our room service manager try it," was Lewis's enthusiastic response.

Both men also realized that the type of food transport equipment that the hotel used would have an impact on food quality—especially its temperature. They would ask their room service manager to experiment with preheated electric carts, pellet systems, and other heating devices available.

"While I know that canned gelatin and liquid fuels are often very satisfactory methods for keeping transported foods hot, I'm concerned that some employees might inadvertently use these open fuels

Managing Service at the Hotel Columbia
Page Twenty, continued

on moving carts or trays," Lewis told Don.

"In the interest of safety, we could simply tell our room service manager not to use them," Don replied.

"Either not use them at all, or ensure that our room service manager knows that training in their safe use is an absolute must. I'll make some notes about our various concerns and use these notes when we're interviewing applicants for the room service manager position," Lewis responded.

Food transportation systems would also affect service time. During busy service periods, Lewis and Don thought that room service could take over a passenger elevator so that attendants would not have to wait for elevator service. They would also ask the room service manager to experiment with "partner" plans in which one attendant would take several meals to a floor for subsequent delivery by another attendant.

"This system should work well during rush periods in the morning when room service attendants will serve large numbers of continental breakfasts," Don remarked.

Challenge #2—Delivering Food Quickly.
Lewis remembered from a former job that guests frequently complained about the time required for the delivery of room service orders. He told Don that the procedures designed to address this complaint should begin at the time employees take the order, continue through the process used to communicate orders to the kitchen, and conclude with the process used to pick up, check out, and deliver the order to the room. "Our room service manager will need to carefully consider each of these steps as he or she develops specific room service procedures," Lewis said.

"Fortunately," Don replied, "the room service satellite kitchen is properly designed and adjacent to the order-takers' work station. In addition, order-takers will use remote printing equipment to place orders quickly with production personnel."

Both men were also aware of the need for effective communication between the order-taker and the guest. They would recommend that standard operating procedures require order-takers to indicate the expected delivery time to guests when they placed their orders and that the order-taker would state a *reasonable* time, not an optimistic

estimate to please the guest on the phone. Similarly, they wanted their room service manager or the captains to train order-takers to suggest special items for guests in a hurry and to alert guests to the preparation time required for other items.

Challenge #3—Establishing Good Communication.
When orders are delivered to the wrong room, menu items on the order are incorrect, or orders are incomplete, communication problems may be the cause. To avoid such problems, Lewis asked Don to work with the room service manager to ensure that the order-takers knew how to do their job correctly. Procedures would require these staff members to read back the order to the guest, including the guest's name and room number. Also, the procedures would provide a triple check on plated items; the cook, captain, and room service attendant would all confirm that every item on the guest check was on the plate.

"Problems can still arise," said Lewis, "but we'll ensure that the standard operating procedures minimize the problems which turn *good* room service departments into *bad* ones."

Challenge #4—Training Staff Adequately.
When no one answers room service calls, when room service employees are indifferent or discourteous, and when room service equipment and supplies are not cleaned and effectively managed, inadequate training of personnel may be the source of the problem. Lewis and Don wanted to ensure that careful employee selection, orientation, training, and supervisory procedures were followed. They would require their manager to attend a wide range of management and supervisory courses which could help reduce personnel problems.

Challenge #5—Offering Room Service When Guests Want It.
Since the Hotel Columbia would be a first-class hotel, room service would be available 24 hours a day. The hotel would be able to offer this service, in part, because the coffee shop would be open at all times and it could provide food for room service during slow periods. To make this service practical from the hotel's perspective, Lewis and Don had already decided to offer a limited menu between 2:00 a.m. and 6:00 a.m.

Managing Service at the Hotel Columbia
Page Twenty, continued

Challenge #6—Removing Soiled Food Trays and Other Items Promptly. "Let's use a courtesy card to request that guests telephone room service when they want items picked up," Don remarked to Lewis. "Let's also require our room service manager to train the room service captains, attendants, buspersons, and others to walk the hallways on a frequent basis to observe and pick up these items."

Lewis agreed and also thought that they could make an arrangement with housekeeping employees to telephone room service when rooms in their areas required the removal of room service items.

Lewis and Don knew that room service offered a wide range of other challenges; however, they felt that the ones they had just listed were among the most important. They resolved to ask their room service manager to design procedures that would help meet these challenges satisfactorily. Don concluded their discussion on room service by saying, "I firmly believe we can develop a high-quality room service department comparable to the Hotel Columbia's other fine services."

Lewis said, "I couldn't agree with you more."

11

Dining Room Service

Dining room or table service is a traditional method for providing dining service. Each property must develop its own procedures for dining room service; however, one basic rule is consistency. For instance, whether the dining room manager decides to have servers set the tables with the knife handles a half inch from the edge of the table—or one inch from the edge—all servers should set the table in the same way. (While there is no specific or universal rule that applies to knife placement, flatware handles should be set back from the table edge so that guests do not knock them off while being seated.) Similarly, whether the menu is already on the table when guests are seated or the host or food server hands the menu to the guest, the procedure depends more on the desires of the dining room manager than on a rule of etiquette. The point is that all service procedures should be *consistently* followed and enforced. (We discussed basic types of service styles in Chapter 6.)

A second consideration in the planning and delivery of service in dining rooms is quality. The dining room manager defines the quality standards which service employees must meet as they get ready for service, actually serve guests, and carry out a wide range of duties including the operation of equipment, the performance of sales income control procedures, the placement and pickup of food orders, and interaction with bar staff. Guests react to many factors other than food and beverage products while in the dining room; therefore, close attention must be paid to all details which ensure that the atmosphere, service, and cleanliness in the dining room are harmonious with the quality of the food and beverage products offered. All procedures must recognize and provide for the needs of guests. In other words, service is the successful execution of a wide range of details. The manager is responsible for anticipating and planning all these details and for ensuring that the property's standard operating procedures incorporate its concern for quality service.

Personnel

The following discussions review how to manage dining room service by focusing on the personnel needed and the work which they must perform. Exhibit 11.1 shows one possible organization chart for a dining room. Note that standard titles for dining service employees occupying various positions do not exist. For example, the person in charge of a dining room can be called a dining room manager, maitre d'hotel, headwaiter/headwaitress, receptionist, host/hostess, or another title. It depends on the type of service and degree of formality provided in a dining room.

Dining Room Manager

The manager in the dining room is often the first staff member that the guest sees. Like all other front-of-house employees, this individual must be friendly. Guests can tell when employees are forcing a smile or if a smile is genuine. All service employees must like people and be able to focus on helping the guests, even when they are experiencing job and personal pressures.

Dining room managers perform a wide variety of tasks in dining room operations. Exhibit 11.2 provides a list of these activities. In addition to the duties listed in this exhibit, they may also

Managing Service at the Hotel Columbia
Page Twenty-One

Lewis Scott was pleased about his and Don Jackson's plans for the Eagle Room, the Hotel Columbia's high-check-average, a la carte restaurant. While each dining outlet was very important to the success of the food and beverage department, he recognized that some guests would judge the entire property by their experiences in the Eagle Room.

Two events happened almost at the same time that made him think about operating problems that needed to be resolved through proper planning. First, invoices for the purchase of stemware to be used in the Eagle Room passed over his desk. Of course, he realized that it was necessary to purchase top-quality glassware for this dining outlet. However, the cost of these products made him recall his first job as an assistant beverage manager at a small resort. Glassware costs were high then too—and they continued to grow higher. Lewis remembered well that the resort had to continuously re-order glassware—it was constantly being broken—but he had been able to figure out the reason. There had been so much antagonism between a few members of the dishwashing staff and the service staff that both groups became careless about stacking and handling glassware. Thus, breakage was far beyond normal.

His thoughts about breakage were interrupted by a telephone call.

"Lewis," said Karen Gannon, the caller, "we're looking for a speaker for our next Lodging Association meeting and we'd like you to be the one."

"What do you want me to talk about?" asked Lewis.

"Well, we came across an article you wrote a couple of years ago about improving relations between service staff and production staff. Would you mind reviewing those principles and updating it as necessary? Also, of course, we'd like any up-to-date information you can give us about the Hotel Columbia."

After agreeing to the request, Lewis thought how ironic it was: his early experience with dish breakage and the request for his presentation both centered on people and, more specifically, the relations between front-of-house and back-of-house staff.

be responsible for examining the guests' appearances to ensure that they conform with the required dress code. (For example, when gentlemen are required to wear coats and ties, the manager should have a supply of these garments available to lend to guests. Of course, these items should be dry cleaned after each use.) When municipal ordinances prohibit the service of guests who are without shoes or shirts, the manager may have to explain such laws to guests. Because in many areas guests cannot remove liquor from the building, the dining room manager again may have to communicate such regulations to guests in as tactful a manner as possible. Managers also often have to devise methods to prevent guests from leaving without paying for their meals or from taking property from the restaurant. Alert dining room managers can address these and related issues tastefully and discreetly.

On the positive side, the dining room manager can, through his/her personal interest in guests, be a main reason why guests return to a facility. For example, some professional managers make a note of all local residents' birthday, anniversary, and business celebrations occurring in the dining room throughout the year. As the special event approaches the next year, the manager drops a note to the guest who hosted the previous year's celebration, recalls the previous event (including details such as the flowers that were ordered), and asks if the dining room can again be privileged to make the occasion special for the guest and his/her party. Another way managers take a special interest in guests is by sending those who dine frequently in their outlets a letter thanking them for their frequent reservations and offering them a card for a complimentary dinner or a "two meals for the price of one" discount.

Exhibit 11.1 Organization of One Dining Room Operation

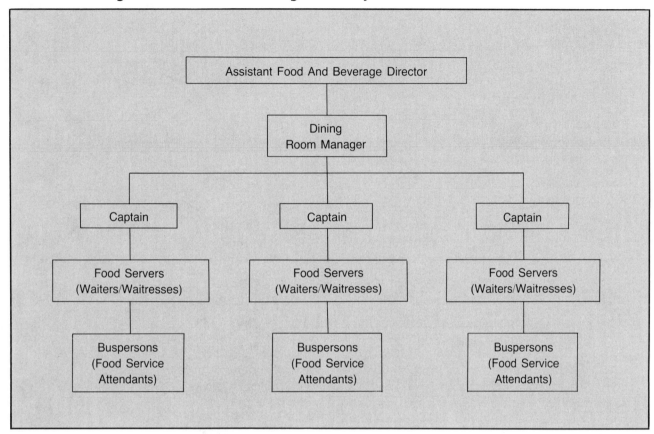

It goes without saying that the guests' last contact with a facility should be as pleasant as the first. The manager or other representative of the property should be on hand to say good-bye and cordially thank guests as they leave. Again, the use of the guest's last name, if known, is important and a hallmark of personalized service. A cordial, well-intended "Thank you" is an excellent way to inform guests that you appreciate being able to serve them and hope that they will return soon.

Captain

Large and formally organized dining rooms use individuals with the title of captain, or sometimes headwaiter/headwaitress, to supervise food servers in individual service stations. As shown in Exhibit 11.1, these individuals report to the dining room manager. While their specific duties vary among properties, captains generally are responsible for a number of procedures.

Before the server station opens for guest service, the captain inspects table settings. He/she checks, for instance, that flowers are fresh and the vase water is clean. If lamps are on the table, he/she confirms that the shades are clean and in a level position and that the bulbs are in working order. He/she also checks tablecloths, napkins, place settings, glassware, condiment containers, candles, and any other tabletop items. The captain confirms that chairs are crumb-free and that the carpet is clean under and around tables. To ensure fast, smooth dining service, he/she must also confirm that the food service side stations are adequately stocked with such items as place settings, required equipment, and food and beverage supplies. To help their captains, some properties provide them with a pre-opening checklist similar to the one shown in Exhibit 11.3.

Captains supervise any food preparation tasks that are the responsibility of dining service

Exhibit 11.2 Duties of a Dining Room Manager

OPENING DUTIES

Make sure the dining room temperature is comfortable.

Check the light level and all light bulbs. (Some properties have a policy that guests should be able to read a newspaper at the table. Other properties have discovered that guests wish for very subdued lighting.) Make sure lamp shades are straight.

Make sure pictures are straight and lighted.

Check table locations and room setup.

Check the condition of china, glassware, and silver.

Inspect the dining room for cleanliness and safety. Check restrooms.

Communicate information regarding reservations (numbers and arrival times) to production personnel. (Put special emphasis on large parties.)

Check the schedule to confirm adequate staffing.

Develop whatever information is possible about guests who are VIPs (Very Important Persons).

Check the menu items and the condition of menus.

Make sure the music level is appropriate.

Check the sound system (if you use one).

Discuss special instructions with the staff.

Plan table arrangements according to group reservations.

Ensure that precheck and/or other registers and/or sales income control equipment are set for the beginning of the new dining period.

Make sure each food server is properly groomed.

Check each food server station's checklist to ensure that the dining room supplies are at proper inventory levels.

Meet with the service staff to discuss special guests, special menu items, daily specials, etc.

OPERATING DUTIES

Greet and seat guests.

Make recommendations and provide information about foods, wines, and spirits.

Ensure courteous and efficient service.

Make sure that the guests are satisfied and follow up on any complaints.

Discreetly take care of intoxicated, disabled, or hard-to-handle guests. (It may be necessary to get assistance from another supervisor.)

Enforce procedures to detect fraudulent guests. (Also, ensure that dishonest service staff cannot steal from guests.)

Enforce safety regulations.

Relay any special instructions to the kitchen.

Maintain a pleasant atmosphere in the dining room.

Maintain the reservation book.

Take appropriate action in the case of an accident to guests or employees.

Follow up on special requests.

Supervise food service.

Exhibit 11.2, continued

CLOSING DUTIES

Inspect for fire hazards (especially waste containers and linen receptacles for lighted cigarettes).

Turn off lights and adjust the air conditioning to the proper level.

Lock all doors.

Leave written information concerning any items requiring correction and any other information that will help the dining room manager who opens the room for the next dining period.

Follow the procedures for processing cash and charge vouchers.

Report any maintenance problems.

Review the next day's schedule and menus if possible.

Be sure to communicate to the appropriate personnel any guest complaints or comments.

Close precheck and other registers; follow required closing procedures.

Inspect for safety and sanitation.

Turn in the required reports to the appropriate officials.

MISCELLANEOUS DUTIES

Conduct training sessions for dining service employees.

Participate in food and beverage, safety, and other meetings.

Plan reservations. (This is a key element in efficient service flow.)

Review menu items for their sales popularity.

Interview prospective employees.

Maintain employee time records.

Develop effective operating procedures for dining service with a special focus on periods of high business volume.

Prepare weekly work schedules according to forecasted guest demand.

Issue maintenance orders.

Adjust work assignments and schedules.

Authorize overtime, vacation time, and time-off for dining room staff according to established practices.

Conduct accident/incident investigations and hold weekly training meetings, monthly safety meetings, and fire drills as required.

Implement and enforce safety regulations and house rules.

Coordinate cost control, purchasing, and maintenance duties with the assistant food and beverage director.

Order and requisition special occasion cakes from the bake shop.

Prepare requisition sheets for operating supplies.

Observe and record employee performance.

Make recommendations regarding employee promotions.

Make complete dining room inspections at least weekly.

Source: Adapted from the *Dining Room Manual* of Hotel du Pont, Wilmington, Delaware.

Exhibit 11.3 Dining Room Pre-Opening Checklist

	Required Quantities						
	M	T	W	TH	F	S	SU
1. Serving Supply Areas A. Prestock with all necessary service supplies:							
tablecloths							
placemats							
napkins							
knives							
forks							
teaspoons							
soup spoons							
cocktail forks							
steak knives							
juice glasses							
water glasses							
coffee cups							
salad plates							
side dishes							
bread/butter plates							
dessert plates							
soup cups/bowls							
coffee pots							
water pitchers							
wine brackets/stands							
candles							
doilies							
bus tabs							
doggie bags							
sanitizing solution (to wipe tables)							
other:							
B. Prestock with food supplies:							
salt							
pepper							
sugar							
sugar substitute							
steak sauce							
ketchup							
mustard							
Worcestershire sauce							
preserves							
butter							
cream							
milk							
sour cream							
crackers (saltine and/or oyster crackers)							

Exhibit 11.3, continued

	Required Quantities						
	M	T	W	TH	F	S	SU
decaffeinated coffee							
horseradish							
tea bags (variety of flavors)							
lemons							
filled ice bins							
other:							
2. Public Areas							
reception area clean							
foyer clean							
public restrooms clean							
entry clean							
exterior areas clean							
dining room areas clean							
other:							
3. Service Staff							
clean and proper uniforms worn							
pre-opening meeting held							
stations assigned							
daily specials reported							
run-outs reported							
out-of-stock items reported							
groups/reservations discussed							
guest checks dispensed							
other:							
4. Dining Room							
table decorations (flowers, candles, etc.)							
lighting							
regular and emergency exits							
air conditioning							
sound system							
no smoking signs							
other:							

Exhibit 11.3, continued

	Required Quantities						
	M	T	W	TH	F	S	SU
5. Service Stations							
tables steady							
tables set							
chairs clean							
napkins folded							
candles lit							
centerpieces fresh looking							
salt/pepper/etc. available							
ashtray/matches available							
table tents available							
table arranged for size of group reservation							
tray stand ready							
other:							
6. Reception Stand							
reservation book							
menus (food/wine/beverage)							
pencils							
flashlights							
credit card authorization books							
other:							

staff. Examples include preparing butter curls, slicing bread, and portioning cakes and pies.

Captains may perform other miscellaneous tasks such as checking that menus are in good order and are not dirty, worn, or torn. Since the menu represents the image, quality standards, and reputation of the property, this task should not be overlooked. They also review their station for safety problems such as loose tabletops, wobbly chairs, and rough spots on furniture which may snag guests' clothing. Monitoring equipment such as bags and carts that hold used linen before removal to laundry areas may be another of their responsibilities.

Of course, captains also supervise dining service employees during the performance of their pre-opening duties; therefore, depending on the specific assignments of the servers in their stations, they can be responsible for a wide range of activities. The captain may make specific table assignments within his/her section and conduct pre-opening meetings to give the staff such information as daily specials, menu changes, and any potential difficulties.

During actual food service, the duties of the captains differ according to the requirements of the property. They may assist the dining room manager in greeting guests, seating them at the proper table, providing them with information about the menus, and informing them about any specials. Captains typically present menus to guests and take orders for beverages and food. In some properties, the dining room captains actually serve orders to guests; in other properties, food servers have this responsibility.

During meal service, the captain makes cer-

Front-of-House Positions Have Much in Common

Front-of-house employees, no matter what their titles are, have much in common. They must be able to portray their concern for the guests and provide them with courteous, professional dining service. They must have an immaculate appearance and wear uniforms that are clean and in good repair.

All front-of-house employees must be attentive and able to anticipate the needs of their guests before they are asked. They must be dependable, report to work on time, and be physically and mentally able to do a good job. They must be creative and able to think of better ways to perform tasks—not only from their own perspective, but also from the viewpoints of guests and management.

Dining service employees must be efficient. In order to be efficient, they must be prepared. That means that they must perform a wide range of duties before the dining room opens and help organize equipment and supplies at the end of the workshift so that the next dining period can begin as smoothly as possible.

Other important traits include honesty, loyalty, and persuasiveness. When necessary, staff members must also be able to suggestively sell desirable products to guests.

Professional dining service employees obviously require a wide range of knowledge, skills, and common sense. Yet, they must be trained to use specific procedures and supervised to ensure that they do the required work according to the desired quality standards. However, some important dining service traits cannot be taught. Therefore, the job requires a very special person—a *people person*—who is sincere about the job and knows that both he/she and the property will benefit from his/her service to guests.

---

tain that service flows smoothly, that ashtrays are kept empty, that water glasses are refilled and, in general, that desires of the guests are anticipated and/or provided for. He/she also ensures that food servers keep their supply areas clean, neat, and well stocked. The captain must know the property's sanitation and safety procedures so that he/she can make certain that staff members follow them.

In properties offering tableside preparation, the captain is frequently responsible for this service. Also, he/she often has the authority to handle guest complaints and resolve most guest-related problems. For example, what should be done for a guest who complains about another guest's smoking? (Move the guest who complains—not the guest who smokes.) What should be done about hard-to-please guests? (Perhaps the captain can satisfy them by providing them with "official" attention.)

After the dining room closes, captains must supervise employees as they perform miscellaneous closing duties. They must ensure that the servers properly set the tables for the next meal period, clean and fill all condiment containers, clean and polish the silverware, and replace used tablecloths. Captains should also inspect server stations and side work areas to ensure that the food servers have properly cleaned and

restocked them. In addition, they should confirm that the dining room tables are in the proper configuration for the next shift. To do this, employees may need to move tables, bring in extra tables, or remove unnecessary tables from the dining area. Finally, the captain should ensure that small items and supplies are properly secured and should check such items as waste cans for smoldering cigarettes.

Typically, captains have had many years of training and experience and have worked their way up in the organization to assume this responsible position. While some operations may not designate individuals as captains, many do employ individuals who are given the supervisory and other responsibilities of this position. Regardless of the size of the dining room operation or its organization, *someone* must perform each of the duties discussed here to ensure that guests receive the proper quality of service.

Food Servers

Some dining service operations that use captains to take food orders use food servers to deliver the food and perform a wide range of other duties before, during, and after the service period. In other operations, the captain may take the order and serve the food; food servers

---

A Professional Image for Dining Service Employees

Experienced front-of-house employees know there is nothing mysterious about projecting a professional image to guests. They know that while they must carry out the duties and responsibilities required by their jobs, they must also remember how important the "personal touch" is to guests. Professional employees always make an effort to:

1. Be clean and neat.
2. Wear the required uniform.
3. Have good poise and posture.
4. Smile.
5. Always be courteous.
6. Practice good manners.
7. Apply rules of etiquette.
8. Cooperate with others as a member of the team.
9. Be dependable.
10. Be honest.
11. Be friendly to guests and co-workers.
12. Smoke only in designated places at designated times.
13. Limit gum chewing to break times only.

In many ways, good service is not overt; it simply requires service employees to pay attention to what guests need and provide it. Often, guests never even notice good service, but they *do* remember poor service.

---

may function only as runners to bring food to service areas. Of course, servers must also perform the many pre-opening and closing duties which have been discussed throughout the chapter.

In many dining service operations, however, the food server performs the bulk, if not all, of the food serving duties, occasionally assisted by buspersons. In addition to getting ready for and cleaning up after service, food servers arrange and set up tables, present menus to guests, provide them with information about menu items, take orders, and serve them. Cleaning and resetting tables for additional service may be the responsibility of food servers or buspersons (or both).

It is difficult to discuss the specific duties of a food server because of the enormous variety of food service operations. For example, even in some informal operations the food server takes the guests' orders but runners deliver them. The advantages of this plan include keeping food servers on the floor in contact with the guests and speeding up service. In other properties,

food servers may take the guests' orders and turn them in to the production staff; however, whoever is available when the order comes up delivers it. In such cases, servers must write order information on guest checks in such a way that "who gets what" is very clear. (See Chapter 6 for tips on writing such information on guest checks.)

Buspersons

The busperson, also known as an assistant food server or food service attendant, has an important role to play in the service of products to guests. First of all, buspersons may initially stock and replenish equipment, food, beverages, and other supplies required in food server stations. They may also perform other pre-opening duties to make the dining room ready for service, including setting tables, filling wine buckets with ice, moving tables, and more.

During the service period, buspersons perform a wide array of tasks designed to help the food server provide better service to the guests.

Making Tables Ready for Service

The job of clearing and resetting tables for guest service is a very important one. Obviously, guests should not be seated at a table that has not been cleared after other guests have left. However, it is very frustrating for both the host and the guest to be unable to use unoccupied tables. Similarly, guests already seated in the dining room do not like to be surrounded by tables with soiled serviceware on them. Management must develop procedures to clear and reset tables quickly so they can be brought back into service as soon as possible.

Buspersons should think of the guest as they clear and reset tables. They should be careful about noise, never haphazardly or noisily place soiled serviceware onto side stands, and never leave unsightly soiled dishes in full view of guests still eating.

Furthermore, buspersons should be careful as they set the tables. Are there holes in or stains on the linen? Do the glasses look spotty or have lipstick smudges on the rims? Is there dried food on cutlery? Is the knife blade bent? Buspersons can resolve these potentially irritating problems as they discover them. If the problem occurs frequently, they can notify the food server, captain, or other dining service employee so that appropriate corrective action can be taken.

Examples include pouring water, refilling coffee and tea cups, taking bread and butter to the table, clearing tables, and even serving food during busy periods. Buspersons must work efficiently. For example, they should pour water and coffee for all tables in a section at the same time and completely clear a table in one trip.

If a property offers tableside food preparation, buspersons may restock the food carts used for this purpose. Cleaning tables, crumbing chairs, and resetting tables with fresh linen, clean serviceware, and glasses are all jobs which buspersons might perform.

After the dining room closes, buspersons can perform a variety of closing duties, such as cleaning and restocking food server supply stations, cleaning and resetting dining room tables, and emptying and cleaning food preparation carts. They may clean such equipment as the coffee urn and the bread warmer, return soiled linen to the laundry, and clean dining room chairs and children's high chairs or booster seats.

The busperson has an entry-level job in many operations. Since this is the case, many buspersons are seeing the property and its staff for the first time and making decisions about whether to remain with the operation. It is important that managers take an active interest in buspersons, show them the possibilities for career advancement, and provide them with training so that they can be ready for new, higher paying, and more responsible positions.

Dining Room Service Procedures

As has been said, an important rule in dining service is consistency. While some general procedures for opening and closing a food service operation, setting tables, serving guests, developing sales income control systems, and placing food and beverage orders have been discussed elsewhere in this text, specific procedures for each dining room or restaurant must be developed and all service employees should be trained to use such procedures consistently. Nothing is wrong with serving guests at dining room tables one way and using other procedures for guests in booths, as long as all service employees consistently follow both procedures *and* the procedures used are acceptable from the guests' perspective. Exhibit 11.4 shows a flowchart being developed by one property that identifies and breaks down service responsibilities in a high-check-average dining room. It names the staff member responsible for tasks, lists guest expectations about service, and points out possible failures to meet guest expectations.

Greeting and Seating Guests

Someone must be available to greet guests at the front door of the dining room and to answer the telephone at all times. Often this person is the dining room manager. However, no matter

Exhibit 11.4 Flowchart Showing Standard Operating Procedures for Guest Service in One Dining Room

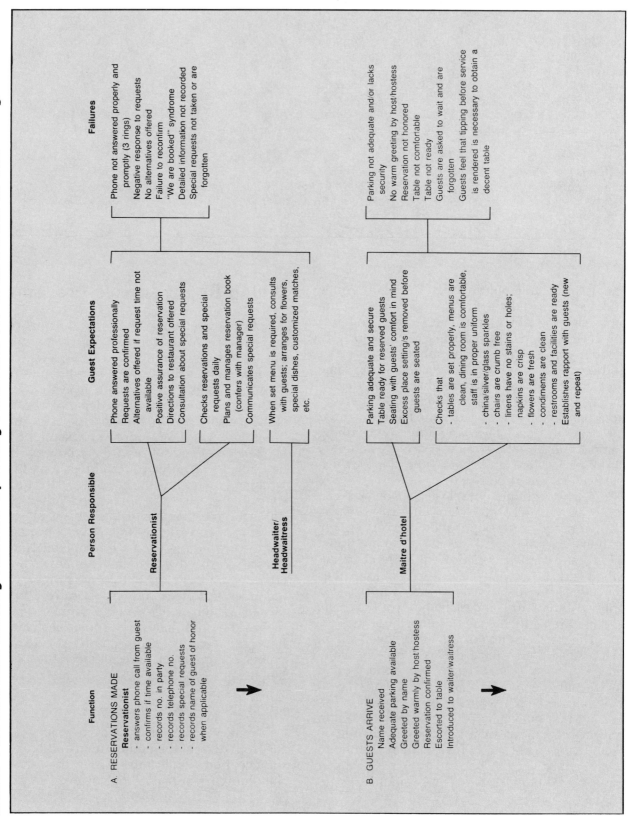

Exhibit 11.4, continued

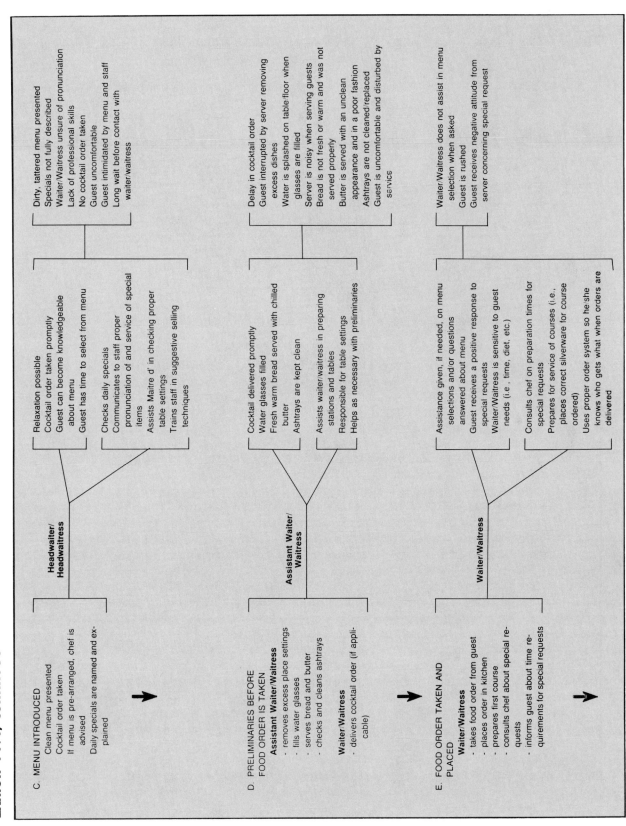

C. MENU INTRODUCED
   Clean menu presented
   Cocktail order taken
   If menu is pre-arranged, chef is advised
   Daily specials are named and explained

Headwaiter/ Headwaitress

Relaxation possible
Cocktail order taken promptly
Guest can become knowledgeable about menu
Guest has time to select from menu

Checks daily specials
Communicates to staff proper pronunciation of and service of special items
Assists Maitre d' in checking proper table settings
Trains staff in suggestive selling techniques

Dirty, tattered menu presented
Specials not fully described
Waiter/Waitress unsure of pronunciation
Lack of professional skills
No cocktail order taken
Guest uncomfortable
Guest intimidated by menu and staff
Long wait before contact with waiter/waitress

D. PRELIMINARIES BEFORE FOOD ORDER IS TAKEN
   Assistant Waiter/Waitress
   - removes excess place settings
   - fills water glasses
   - serves bread and butter
   - checks and cleans ashtrays

   Waiter/Waitress
   - delivers cocktail order (if applicable)

Assistant Waiter/ Waitress

Cocktail delivered promptly
Water glasses filled
Fresh warm bread served with chilled butter
Ashtrays are kept clean

Assists waiter/waitress in preparing stations and tables
Responsible for table settings
Helps as necessary with preliminaries

Delay in cocktail order
Guest interrupted by server removing excess dishes
Water is splashed on table/floor when glasses are filled
Server is noisy when serving guests
Bread is not fresh or warm and was not served properly
Butter is served with an unclean appearance and in a poor fashion
Ashtrays are not cleaned/replaced
Guest is uncomfortable and disturbed by service

E. FOOD ORDER TAKEN AND PLACED
   Waiter/Waitress
   - takes food order from guest
   - places order in kitchen
   - prepares first course
   - consults chef about special requests
   - informs guest about time requirements for special requests

Waiter/Waitress

Assistance given, if needed, on menu selections and/or questions answered about menu
Guest receives a positive response to special requests
Waiter/Waitress is sensitive to guest needs (i.e., time, diet, etc.)

Consults chef on preparation times for special requests
Prepares for service of courses (i.e., places correct silverware for course ordered)
Uses proper order system so he/she knows who gets what when orders are delivered

Waiter/Waitress does not assist in menu selection when asked
Guest is rushed
Guest receives negative attitude from server concerning special request

Exhibit 11.4, continued

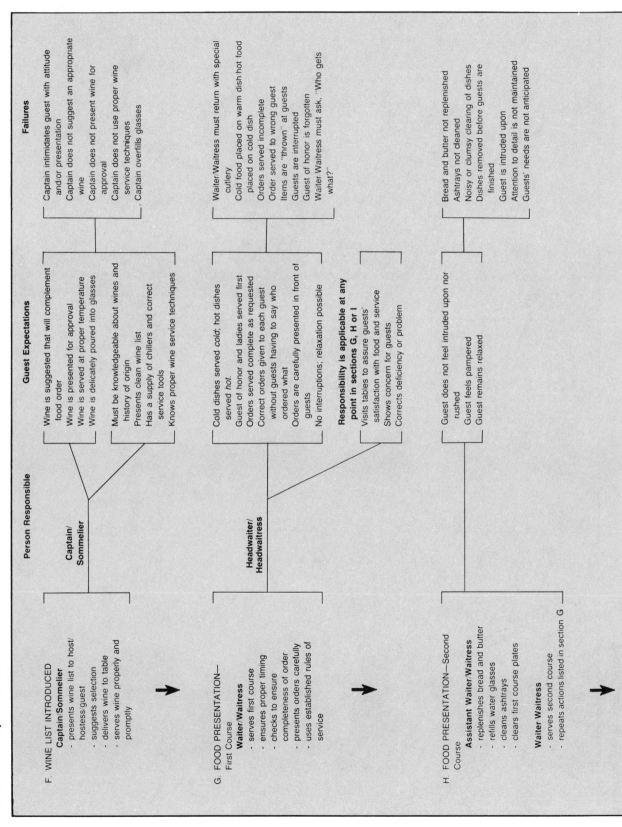

Person Responsible	Guest Expectations	Failures

F. WINE LIST INTRODUCED

Captain/Sommelier
- presents wine list to host/hostess/guest
- suggests selection
- delivers wine to table
- serves wine properly and promptly

Person Responsible: **Captain/Sommelier**

Guest Expectations:
- Wine is suggested that will complement food order
- Wine is presented for approval
- Wine is served at proper temperature
- Wine is delicately poured into glasses
- Must be knowledgeable about wines and history of origin
- Presents clean wine list
- Has a supply of chillers and correct service tools
- Knows proper wine service techniques

Failures:
- Captain intimidates guest with attitude and/or presentation
- Captain does not suggest an appropriate wine
- Captain does not present wine for approval
- Captain does not use proper wine service techniques
- Captain overfills glasses

G. FOOD PRESENTATION—First Course

Waiter/Waitress
- serves first course
- ensures proper timing
- checks to ensure completeness of order
- presents orders carefully
- uses established rules of service

Person Responsible: **Headwaiter/Headwaitress**

Guest Expectations:
- Cold dishes served *cold;* hot dishes served *hot.*
- Guest of honor and ladies served first
- Orders served complete as requested
- Correct orders given to each guest without guests having to say who ordered what
- Orders are carefully presented in front of guests
- No interruptions; relaxation possible

Responsibility is applicable at any point in sections G, H or I
- Visits tables to assure guests' satisfaction with food and service
- Shows concern for guests
- Corrects deficiency or problem

Failures:
- Waiter/Waitress must return with special cutlery
- Cold food placed on warm dish/hot food placed on cold dish
- Orders served incomplete
- Order served to wrong guest
- Items are "thrown" at guests
- Guests are interrupted
- Guest of honor is forgotten
- Waiter/Waitress must ask, "Who gets what?"

H. FOOD PRESENTATION—Second Course

Assistant Waiter/Waitress
- replenishes bread and butter
- refills water glasses
- cleans ashtrays
- clears first course plates

Waiter/Waitress
- serves second course
- repeats actions listed in section G

Guest Expectations:
- Guest does not feel intruded upon nor rushed
- Guest feels pampered
- Guest remains relaxed

Failures:
- Bread and butter not replenished
- Ashtrays not cleaned
- Noisy or clumsy clearing of dishes
- Dishes removed before guests are finished
- Guest is intruded upon
- Attention to detail is not maintained
- Guests' needs are not anticipated

Exhibit 11.4, continued

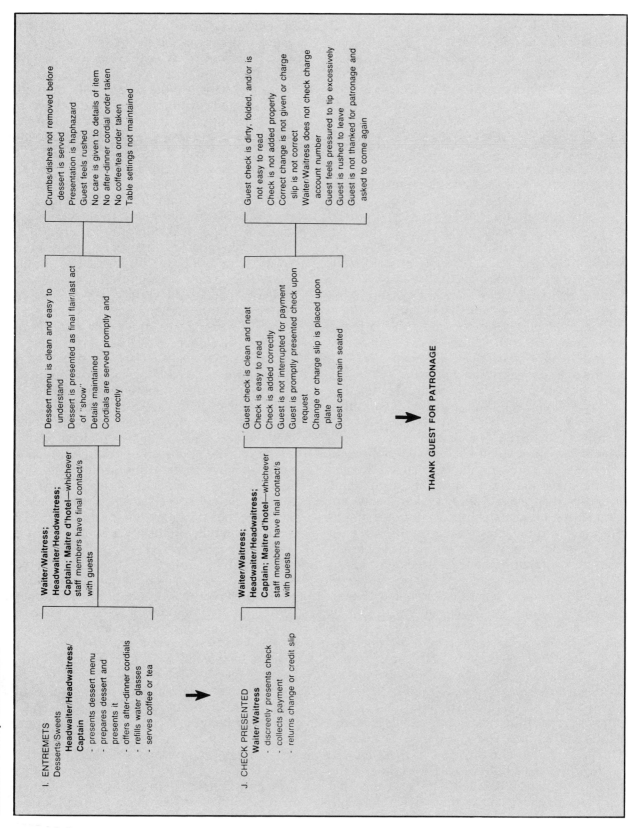

I. ENTREMETS
Desserts/Sweets
Headwaiter/Headwaitress/
Captain
- presents dessert menu
- prepares dessert and
  presents it
- offers after-dinner cordials
- refills water glasses
- serves coffee or tea

Waiter/Waitress;
Headwaiter/Headwaitress;
Captain; Maitre d'hotel—whichever
staff members have final contact/s
with guests

Dessert menu is clean and easy to
  understand
Dessert is presented as final flair/last act
  of "show"
Details maintained
Cordials are served promptly and
  correctly

Crumbs/dishes not removed before
  dessert is served
Presentation is haphazard
Guest feels rushed
No care is given to details of item
No after-dinner cordial order taken
No coffee/tea order taken
Table settings not maintained

J. CHECK PRESENTED
Waiter Waitress
- discreetly presents check
- collects payment
- returns change or credit slip

Waiter/Waitress;
Headwaiter/Headwaitress;
Captain; Maitre d'hotel—whichever
staff members have final contact/s
with guests

Guest check is clean and neat
Check is easy to read
Check is added correctly
Guest is not interrupted for payment
Guest is promptly presented check upon
  request
Change or charge slip is placed upon
  plate
Guest can remain seated

Guest check is dirty, folded, and/or is
  not easy to read
Check is not added properly
Correct change is not given or charge
  slip is not correct
Waiter/Waitress does not check charge
  account number
Guest feels pressured to tip excessively
Guest is rushed to leave
Guest is not thanked for patronage and
  asked to come again

THANK GUEST FOR PATRONAGE

who is the first representative of the property to come in contact with the guest, this person must be hospitable; he/she sets the scene for the remainder of the guests' visits.

If guests are to seat themselves, a simple sign located in a place where guests will easily see it should alert guests to this fact. If a host/hostess is on duty to greet and seat guests, it may be necessary to assign one or more other staff members to welcome guests and inform them that someone will return shortly to seat them. (Receptionists can also handle incoming telephone calls, process beverage transfers from lounge areas, and perform other tasks.)

Name recognition can be very important. If the outlet uses a reservation system, the staff member who is greeting and seating guests should know and refer to guests by name and pronounce the name correctly. He/she can also identify regular guests: "Good evening, Mrs. Jaynes, it's nice to see you again," or, "We have your usual table ready for you, Mr. Smythe. Right this way." If the dining room is busy and this staff member must place names on a waiting list, he/she has another opportunity to call guests by name: "Ms. Black, your table for four is ready." Then, as he/she seats Ms. Black, other opportunities to use her name become possible: "Here is your menu, Ms. Black." If the guest's name is known, it should be relayed to the food server assigned to the table so that he/she can use the guest's name during the meal. Some properties using reservation systems may put place setting tags, matchbooks, and other items imprinted with the guest's name on the table. (If your operation decides to do so, make certain each guest's name is spelled correctly.)

In contrast, some guests do not want their names announced. Regardless of whether their reasons are commercial, political, social, or personal, the guests' desires should always be followed. The politician, entertainer, or sports celebrity may well select dining outlets that exercise discretion in announcing his/her presence.

If, for any reason, guests cannot be seated immediately, they should be informed of the approximate waiting time before a table is ready. Tell the truth. If they must wait for a long period of time, the guests should know so that they can decide whether or not they wish to dine at the property. You can imagine the problem that arises when guests on a time schedule (with

theater tickets or en route to a business appointment) decide to wait based on the estimated time an employee gives them, only to find that the waiting period is longer. After guests are told about the waiting time, they could be referred to the lounge or other areas where their wait will be more enjoyable. (Note that guests without reservations who cannot be served on their first visit to your property will no doubt be impressed with your popularity; they'll most likely return— the next time with a reservation.)

Politeness and common sense are two tools which an effective service employee must constantly use. For example, when service employees do not know the guest's name, they should address the guest as "Sir" or "Ma'am." If possible, guests' requests for a special table should be honored and, of course, the table should be ready (e.g., place settings should be correct, the table shouldn't wobble, the chairs must be free of crumbs), before they are taken to it.

While the guest's choice of a table should be honored whenever possible, the dining room manager often needs to balance server stations. For example, if a table of the appropriate size is available in several stations, a large party is given to the server with the least number of guests. However, managers in some operations feel that they should use a rotation plan so that each server has the opportunity to receive a fair share of tip income. Some dining outlets do not use server stations; if seven food servers are on duty, each server gets every seventh party regardless of where the manager seats the group. While this plan is generally ineffective in many operations, some very famous, well-established restaurants have used it with obvious success. Typically, however, a seating chart should be used to help even out server workloads, but it should be kept flexible to accommodate guests' requests.

Exhibit 11.5 is a sample dining room seating chart with four server stations. Since headwaiters/headwaitresses, food servers, and buspersons all perform specific service tasks during meal periods, the manager can seat a relatively large number of guests within a service station.

After the guests have reached the appropriate table, they are often seated by giving women, the elderly, handicapped, or other special guests priority. If applicable, ladies are provided assistance with their coats. In some properties, the staff member who seats guests may also pick up extra

Exhibit 11.5 Sample Seating Chart with Four Service Stations

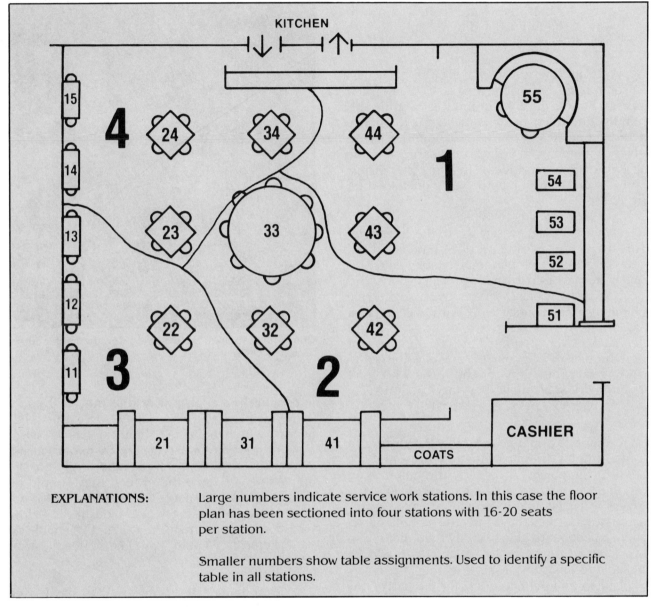

EXPLANATIONS: Large numbers indicate service work stations. In this case the floor plan has been sectioned into four stations with 16-20 seats per station.

Smaller numbers show table assignments. Used to identify a specific table in all stations.

Source: *Food and Beverage Systems Training* (Holiday Inns, Inc., Hotel Group, Training and Development, 1982), p. 15.

place settings, present menus, fill water glasses, or perform other tasks. If it is the policy of the dining room, this service employee also tells guests the name of the food server who will help them. When operating procedures require, the host/hostess checks back with the table after a few minutes to ensure that the food server assigned to the table has acknowledged the guests and begun to provide the required services.

Techniques for Serving Guests

Some procedures that food servers might use from the time the guests are seated until they depart from the dining room are explained in the following discussions. Dining room managers who are in charge of a new operation, or are improving service in an existing one, can find suggestions in this section for developing standard operating procedures. Servers, of course, would then receive thorough training in these procedures so that guests are treated in a uniform way throughout the dining room and on every subsequent visit.

Welcome the guest. Making the guest feel welcome is an important first task for the food server. Food servers should be tactful and friendly, and they should smile. If it is the policy of the property, servers should identify themselves by name even if they are wearing a name tag (which is a good idea). In some properties, food servers bring or pour water on their first trip to the table.

Provide beverage service if the guest desires it. Some dining outlets have cocktail menus. Others use placemats, table tents, or similar devices to list beverage suggestions and specials. If it is policy, servers use a suggestive selling technique, such as, ''We have the best margaritas in town and we make a splendid Manhattan. May I bring you one of these or something else?'' Of course, servers will want to make certain they don't offend those who can't or don't drink alcoholic beverages (because of health, religious, or other reasons).

Present the menu and take the order. In some outlets, the host/hostess presents the menu to the guest. Elsewhere, the menu is on the table when guests are seated. However, food servers must be able to provide detailed information to guests as they study the menu. Guests will need adequate time to study their menus, so they should not be rushed. Servers should be available to answer questions as they arise.

Unless one person orders for the party, it is traditional to begin with a woman and take orders clockwise. Servers should write out the

One dining room's table setting for the first course. (Courtesy of Libbey Glass)

guest check in such a way that they will know ''who gets what'' when they serve the food. Servers who need to ask about the guests' selections at the time of service annoy many guests. Whenever possible, servers stand to the guest's left. As servers take the orders, they should be certain to ask all necessary questions: ''What type of salad dressing would you like?'' ''How would you like your steak?'' ''What vegetable do you prefer?'' ''Would you like coffee now or later?''

Offer wine lists. Some outlets have wine lists on the table when guests are seated. They are then immediately available for those who

Use the Worst Seats Last

Unfortunately, many dining areas have seats/tables which are not as desirable as others. Those located in traffic aisles, next to service stations, and close to the kitchen door are examples. Normally, you should not use these seats until all others have been taken. A guest seated at an undesirable location might look around and wonder, ''Why me?'' If the best tables are occupied, consider giving the guest the choice of being seated at a less desirable table or waiting until a better one becomes available.

Using Telephones and Microphones

Dining room managers and other service staff must frequently answer the telephone. Generally, employees should not receive personal calls while on duty unless they are of an emergency nature. Therefore, most telephone calls will come from potential guests.

A friendly greeting is the first step to a successful telephone conversation. Such a greeting as, "Good afternoon, thank you for calling the Terrace Room. May I help you?" takes only a little more effort than the traditional "Hello," and provides a special touch that the guest will appreciate.

Always stop speaking before you pick up the telephone. If the phone has more than one line and another extension rings, remember that it is annoying for guests who are dining to be disturbed by the sound of a ringing telephone. Excuse yourself to the first party, answer the other line, and ask, "May I put you on hold?" When you finish your business with the first party, return to the second party and say, "Thank you for waiting, may I please help you?" Remember to use the caller's name as frequently as possible throughout the conversation.

When concluding the conversation, a simple "Thank you for calling us, good-bye," is much better than just hanging up. Also, always let the prospective guest hang up first.

Dining room managers or other employees may need to use a public address system to page staff members to a specific area of the restaurant or make general announcements, such as closing calls. (In a well-operated property, guests who are expecting a phone call will leave their names with the dining room manager so that he/she will not need to page them.) When using public address equipment, speak clearly and as briefly as possible. Also, frequently check how the volume of the public address system affects various areas in the dining room.

Before using such equipment, employees should practice speaking into it (before the property opens) and experiment with both the volume of their voices and the distances they hold the microphone from their faces. When speaking over a public address system, employees should be as professional as possible. Systems should be turned off when not in use.

wish to study them. In other cases, it is important to ask guests whether or not they desire wine with their meal. Knowledge of wines is important to help guests make the proper selection, and servers must use the proper techniques to serve wine. (See Chapter 14 for more detailed information.)

Place and pick up the order. Procedures for placing orders vary greatly among properties. Some utilize a precheck register and/or an expediter. In some operations, food servers simply call out orders. In still others, they present guest checks to production personnel or use remote printing devices. It is very important for food servers to know and comply with the specific ordering systems established by management to ensure professional service. Teamwork is critical to effective and efficient service.

The same concern for following procedures consistently is necessary when servers pick up orders. Before going to the table, servers should check the written orders against the food on the serving tray to ensure that the order is correct. They should take the time to look at each plate from the guest's perspective. Is the garnish attractive? Are there food spills on the rim of the plate? Does the food look hot (or cold) and tasty?

Serve the food. Food servers should know how to carry a loaded food tray. For the sake of safety, the heaviest dishes and dishes containing liquids are loaded toward the center of the tray. When trays are being loaded, hot dishes are placed next to hot dishes, cold dishes next to cold dishes. Such items as underliners are stacked toward the outer edge of the tray. When the tray is loaded properly, the server should bend from the knees keeping his/her back straight, lifting the tray with the palm of the hand to shoulder height, and using the other hand for balance. Experienced servers situate the heaviest side of the tray close to their bodies and make certain no items will tip.

Examples of Poor Dining Room Service

Guests frequently complain about some very basic and resolvable problems which occur in many properties. Read the following examples of poor service and guard against them:

1. An inadequate reservation system.
2. Regular guests are not recognized by name.
3. Inappropriate service language, such as "What do you all want?"
4. Service employees are not knowledgeable about the menu, or they use improper service procedures.
5. Long waits for food and beverage servers.
6. Indifference and inattention by service staff.
7. Employees are poorly groomed, improperly dressed, and/or wearing dirty uniforms.
8. Poor housekeeping such as the presence of dust, dirt, or equipment in disrepair.
9. Dining service that appears rushed and disorganized.
10. Dining service employees that talk excessively to each other, smoke, eat food, or otherwise act unprofessionally in public.
11. Hot food served cold and cold food served lukewarm.
12. The following response to a guest: "That's not my job."
13. Errors on guest checks.
14. Long waits to receive guest checks or to have payment collected and change returned.
15. No one at the door to wish the guests a pleasant hello or a courteous good-bye.

The list of possible problems which cause poor dining room service is endless. The point is that you can do many things to improve dining service. Think about what you like and don't like when you are in a restaurant. Many of these same factors will concern your guests. Think about them, then develop operating procedures which will ensure that you would be happy in the dining room you manage.

Managers should select a traffic pattern that servers should always follow, alerting others

Dining service with a flair—the plate covers reflect the theme of the Cygnus Restaurant, named for the swan constellation which can be seen through the glass roof. (Amway Grand Plaza Hotel, Grand Rapids, Michigan.)

when servers are behind them or coming through a door. When swinging doors are involved, servers must be trained to use the correct one. (Dining room managers should establish "in" and "out" doors.)

When serving food, servers follow the procedures required by the outlet. (Basic styles of food service are discussed in Chapter 6.) While traditional service procedures can be modified as necessary, once an operation has established its own standard procedures, servers should always follow them.

Servers should check back with the guests soon after delivering the order. Rather than asking, "Is everything okay?" which suggests that the guests have a problem, servers should ask, "Is everything to your satisfaction?" or a similar question. When approached with a positive question, guests have a chance to make further orders and are fully aware that their servers are available to help them.

Gratuities

Frequently, there is confusion as to the difference between a gratuity and a service charge. Basically, a gratuity or tip is a guest's voluntary payment to a server, while a service charge is a compulsory addition to a guest's bill. The Fair Labor Standards Act (FLSA) established several criteria that distinguish a gratuity from a service charge. To be considered a tip, the guest must have the right to:

• Offer it voluntarily and without direction by any policies or procedures of the employer.
• Detemine the amount without any influence from the employer.
• Determine who should be the recipient of the tip.

If any of these criteria are not met, the amount is considered a service charge. Compulsory service charges are not tip income to servers, but are part of the operation's gross receipts and may be used by the employer in any way it chooses.

The FLSA also makes it clear that tips are the property of employees. This is not intended, however, to discourage the practice of pooling, splitting, or sharing tips among employees who customarily and regularly receive tips. Employees may pool, split, or share tips. Moreover, employers should inform new employees, as part of the hiring procedures, of any tip practices of the operation's employees. However, the sharing of tips among tipped employees must be strictly voluntary. Employers cannot coerce, direct, or intimidate employees to participate in the pooling of tips, but can cooperate, coordinate, and oversee the practice voluntarily agreed to by the employees.

The laws and regulations regarding tipping practices are extensive and subject to change by Congress and the Internal Revenue Service. Managers should check with their attorneys to make certain that their practices are legal.

Also, in 1982, the federal government implemented new procedures that govern the reporting of tips as income for wage and tax purposes. Managers of dining service operations should be fully aware of these procedures.

When several courses are served, the dishes from one course should be cleared before the next course arrives. This principle also applies to the service of drinks; if possible, the empty glassware should be removed as the next round is served. This method provides guests with more tabletop room, does not make them feel uncomfortable about eating too much, brings dishes and glassware back into service more quickly, and helps prevent guests taking serviceware home as souvenirs.

Present the check. Timing the delivery of the check is important. Some guests may be in a hurry. While this is more likely to happen at breakfast and lunch, even dinner guests may sometimes be rushed. Whatever type of income collection system is used, the check should be totaled and ready when the guest desires it. (Sales income control systems are discussed in Chapter 8.) Accurately completing the guest check, double-checking the figures, and assessing the total amount of the bill are also important procedures. If guest check totals must be hand-tallied, servers will find that a calculator with a printing tape is very helpful.

There are two typical "signals" to guests that help them know how to pay the bill. If the check is presented on a plate or tray, generally this means the server will collect the guest's payment and, whether using server banking or cashier banking, will see that the guest gets proper change (or will handle the credit card transaction or charge the bill to the guest's room).

If the check is presented without a plate or tray, this generally signals that guests will pay at a cashier's stand. Many properties also clarify payment procedures for guests by printing them on the bill: "Please pay the cashier" or "Please pay the server." Whenever there is a possibility of the guest being confused, servers could say, "I can take your payment for you when you're ready" or "You can pay the cashier when you're ready."

When presenting the check to groups, the server may already know who will pay the bill. A signal from the guest, an earlier conversation, or a specific request when a host made the reservation may have made this apparent. Servers undecided about who is responsible for the bill's payment often place the check in the center of the table.

The use of separate checks is also relatively

common. While they create a hardship for the food server, many guests prefer them, and every property should consider using them. It is wise to ask at the beginning of the meal whether or not the guests prefer individual checks.

Setup and Cleanup Duties

Typically, servers are paid a base wage supplemented by tip income. Since servers can earn tips only when guests are in the dining room, they frequently view pre-opening and after-closing duties, which are among the most physically difficult tasks to perform, with disfavor. However, these tasks are an extremely important part of a food server's duties and responsibilities.

Managers must develop very specific opening and closing procedures, train food servers and others to do the work, creatively schedule service staff so that the same person does not constantly perform the more difficult tasks, and supervise employees to ensure that they do all the work required to meet the property's quality levels. For example, someone might have to set up the entire salad bar before the dining room opens, which can require a considerable amount of time. Someone else might have to vacuum the dining room after the last guest has gone; again, the job requires a great deal of time and effort. To resolve a situation where the same employee constantly must perform such tasks, the manager could rotate the shifts of service staff so that different employees open and close the dining room each day. The required setup and cleanup work would then rotate among the employees accordingly.

In order to implement a rotation schedule, assign each employee an activity number which correlates with the setup/cleanup duties listed on a *printed*, permanent schedule. Exhibit 11.6 is an example of a format which can be used to list required duties.

The list of required activities will depend on the operation. Turning on such equipment as bread warmers, restocking storage areas, setting up (or checking) tables in the entire dining area or specific work stations, preparing butter and cream servers, making coffee, stocking the salad bar, and portioning salad and/or dessert items are just some of the setup activities which a specific operation might require.

The schedule of setup activities should recognize that the start of different shifts may re-quire different duties. For example, lunch and dinner shifts may have different menus and, therefore, different portioning requirements. When applicable, a schedule of setup activities should be developed for each shift.

When scheduling employees, managers try to ensure that duties are rotated fairly. Review Exhibit 7.9, an employee schedule, to note how staff members are informed about required setup and cleanup duties. (Remember it is important to adhere to union requirements as setup and cleanup duties are scheduled.)

Proper planning for dining service is absolutely critical to the success of the food service operation. Ongoing procedures to keep dining areas sanitary and in good order are necessary to enhance the operation's public image.

Reservation Systems

Some dining outlets do not take reservations. They include restaurants with very fast table turns as well as dining rooms whose tradition of good business has never included having a reservation system.

However, many dining rooms use reservation systems to allow guests the chance to reserve seating at a specific time; such systems guarantee that guests will receive service in an efficient manner. A reservation system also increases the manager's ability to pinpoint slow and busy times and plan for them. In addition, such a system can increase business since many guests desire a formal commitment and guarantee about their dining arrangements and will visit only those properties that accept reservations. The use of a reservation system is a convenience and service to your guests as well as an important management tool to:

1. Increase guest turnover,

2. Help recognize guests by name,

3. Guarantee speed and quality of service, and

4. Promote production efficiency.

In fact, some professional managers believe that a fine dining establishment cannot be operated without a reservation system.

Exhibit 11.6 Required Setup and Cleanup Activities

Activity Number	Standard Time	Description of Activity
1	20 minutes (two people)	Set up salad bar
2	10 minutes	Prepare coffee
3	20 minutes	Chip butter
4	30 minutes	Set up pantry
5	10 minutes	Refill salad dressing containers
6	15 minutes	Stock server stations
7	10 minutes	Check tables in entire dining room
8	15 minutes	Portion pies and cakes
19	20 minutes (two people)	Position tables for next shift
20	30 minutes	Wash tabletops

However, some potential disadvantages accompany the use of a reservation system. For example, difficulties can arise when guests do not arrive at the appointed time (no-shows), are delayed, or indicate that they have a reservation when they really do not. In addition, when tables committed for upcoming reservations do not turn over as planned, problems occur. What happens when a large group, which is using several tables needed for parties with reservations, remains at the table much longer than expected? When a dining outlet decides to offer a reservation system, it is imperative that management develops procedures that will ensure the proper implementation of such a system. Reservation systems require management input

Table Service is Always in Style

Traditional table service is used in operations ranging from very inexpensive, family-type restaurants to the most expensive, gourmet dining rooms. Of course, other alternatives are available; cafeteria lines, fast-food counters, buffets, and room service provide examples. However, most of us, at one time or another, like to have someone seat us at a table and have an efficient, professional dining room server wait on us. After all, we purchase more than just food and beverage products when we dine. The element of service, which is an integral part of the total dining experience offered to the guest, sets apart a successful, ongoing business from a business failure.

Many rules of dining room service apply more to consistency than to specific procedures. Some principles really only require common sense. Others involve making decisions based on what is best from the guests' perspective. Still others relate to the degree of quality which is built into the service that the property provides. Of course, concern for and control of labor, sales income, and the products themselves are also important. The good dining room manager is able to blend concerns for the guest with the goals of the property. This duty is not a problem; it is a challenge.

since a reservation is a commitment to a guest that a table will be available at a specific time.

There are two basic types of reservation systems. One system offers seating at specific intervals during the meal period, such as seatings at 6 and 8 p.m. only. When this system is used, at least 30 minutes must be allowed between serving periods to clean up, reset, and otherwise get ready for the next seating. Potential disadvantages to interval seating include crowd control problems when a large number of guests must be seated or leave the dining room at the same time, and food production problems when a large number of meals must be served simultaneously. Proper attention to these matters is critical to the success of interval seating reservation plans.

A second and more usual type of reservation system provides staggered seating during the entire meal period; for instance, a guest may make a reservation at any five- or ten-minute interval during the evening meal period.

Experienced managers know that in order for a reservation system to work, they must be able to estimate the length of time it will take for guests to dine. For instance, because the experienced manager knows that large groups usually take longer to dine than small groups, he/she factors this knowledge into the reservation plan as he/she considers the mixture of small and large groups which the dining room can accommodate. The environment, service style, and type of dinner served (a quick meal or a dining experience) are also factors the room manager should consider.

As the time required for meal consumption increases, taking reservations at specific intervals only may be more advantageous than staggered seating. However, managers should exercise common sense as they make staggered seating reservations to avoid overloading the kitchen. (Suggesting that a large group consider specific menu items which are easy and/or quick to prepare can also help speed service.)

When properties offer buffet service, either type of reservation system is generally useful. However, if interval seating is used, a gourmet buffet will require some time between seating periods in order to prepare the buffet for the next guests.

Reservation commitments affect production. For example, if three eight-top tables are seated at the same time, there may be a rush of work in the kitchen 30 minutes later when service employees place 24 entree orders. Managers sometimes plan staggered arrival times for large groups so neither they nor other small groups in the dining room are inconvenienced. The reservation taker can frequently suggest an alternate time and emphasize that service will be better for the guest(s) at that time.

Most properties take reservations by telephone. Because of the need for very specific information, telephone efficiency, and courtesy,

Exhibit 11.7 A Reservation Sheet

Date of Service: **May 1**

Table No. and Capacity	No. in Party	Guest Name (Please Print)	Reservation Time	Special Information	Tel. No.	Reservation Taken by (Initials)	Date
#12 (2)	2	Ann Halm	8:00	Single white rose in vase	353-5517	DP	April 19
#33 (8)	8	J. Moore	8:15	Mrs. Moore's Birthday	332-4448	MH	April 20

only a few authorized people should accept reservations.

Typically, reservation information is entered into a reservation book. Exhibit 11.7 illustrates a page in a reservation book and shows the type of information needed when reservations are taken. Reservation takers should ask for the guest's telephone number so that someone can call him/her later to confirm the plan or inquire why the guest chose not to visit the property. Some high-check-average properties call guests the day before the event to confirm reservation information even though, as in the case of business travelers, such a procedure may require long-distance calls. This is especially important when guests place their reservations several weeks ahead of time. The "Special Information" column is used to record special instructions, such as the need for a special occasion cake, a wide aisle for a handicapped person, or a special wine. If the person making the reservation for a group wishes to ensure that he/she receives the check for the entire group at the end of the meal, the reservation taker could make a note of that caller's request in the Special Information column.

Professional managers in operations that offer continuous seating know from experience the maximum number of parties of various sizes that they can seat at any one time. These managers may develop reservation sheets which enable the reservation taker to block off specific tables.

Handling Reservation Problems

What should the dining room manager do when a guest with a reservation does not arrive, comes early or late, brings more or fewer guests than the reservation indicated, or does not wish to sit at the table which has been set aside for his/her group? Obviously, it is always wise to accommodate guests whenever possible. However, when the dining room is full, the situation must be explained to the guest tactfully and courteously.

Some properties have policies that offer an amenity, such as a drink or an appetizer, to guests inconvenienced by having to wait for their reserved table. This strategy may work well in some cases; however, in other instances, such as when guests have severe time limitations, it may not provide adequate compensation for the inconvenience. Explaining to the late arriving guest that his/her table was held for 15 minutes past the reservation time but could be held no longer is a good tactic when accompanied by management's promise to work him/her into the dining room as soon as possible. (The outlet which takes telephone numbers has another tool to help determine whether or not guests with reservations have changed their plans.)

Stated policies and procedures help when handling reservation problems so everyone involved knows what to do. Common sense is also important. As problems arise, affected guests must be told the truth and offered appropriate alternatives; in other words, management must be prepared to find creative solutions so that guests are not frustrated. To help head off potential reservation problems, some managers reserve specific tables by indicating the reservation time and number of guests in the party directly on the seating chart (Exhibit 11.5). They don't assign other guests to that table before a specific time interval has elapsed. These intervals can differ widely according to the shift and type of guests the dining room attracts—intervals can range from 1 to 2 ½ hours.

Computerized seating aids are also available. One type, for use on a personal computer, enables the manager to keep very specific reservation information for several days in a row close at hand. For example, it indicates the number of tables available, the number of guests to be seated, and the service staff needed for any given time period. Other computerized programs provide specific information on the current dining period. While various types of programs are available, many show the status of a table; they indicate if a table is in use, is being cleared and reset, or is ready to sell. Such programs may also indicate, on a by-table basis, when tables are likely to be available. These aids are particularly helpful in large properties, operations with several floors of dining space, or in other situations where the dining room manager or other staff member would have to make several trips to the dining area to ensure that a table was ready for guest use.

The Waiting List

During busy times, the dining room manager may not be able to seat guests without a wait. Guests without reservations should be served on a "first come, first served" basis. When there is a waiting line, it is important that one person—the manager, receptionist, or another greeter—be at the door at all times to take names of arriving guests and to call parties as tables become available.

Names should be recorded on a waiting list. They should be printed very clearly along with the number of guests in the party. In some properties, the time of arrival is also noted. As tables become available, guests should be paged. Some managers have the policy of paging twice, two minutes apart. If, after paging, the guest does not respond, the name is removed from the list and the next party of appropriate size is called.

Typically, large groups should be highlighted or listed separately so that they will not be overlooked. Generally, parties are called in the order in which they appear on the list except that special procedures may be required when there are handicapped, elderly, or other persons requiring special attention.

Policies about door personnel accepting tips from guests who want to reduce their waiting time should be developed and carefully followed. Personnel should *never* accept a gratuity before they render service; a tip before service is really a bribe. Generally, guests do not like to wait for extended periods, and questions such as "We came in first—why were we not seated first?" are likely to arise if late arriving guests without reservations tip an employee and are seated ahead of those who have been waiting.

It is absolutely critical that guests are given the best estimate of the length of waiting time when their names are placed on the waiting list. If guests choose not to wait, they should be thanked for coming and should be invited to return on another occasion.

The Dining Room Menu

One of the most important services food servers perform is to provide information to the guests. They also sell the items the property wants sold. To do this properly, food servers must know the menu and the property's policies and rules about what they can and cannot do. Food servers must memorize the menu and know how to pronounce the name of each item properly. (Exhibit 11.8 is a dining room menu that servers would have to be trained to use effectively.) When applicable, servers must also know the daily specials and their prices. In addition, food servers must be aware of the property's house specialties and the factors that make them special.

Food servers must also know how every item is prepared. Some guests will want to know about the cooking methods and ingredients which the property uses. Others will need to know because of health or nutrition requirements.

Truth-in-menu laws or similar programs in many states prohibit misrepresenting menu items and ingredients. For example, servers should not say that mashed potatoes are made with fresh potatoes if they are not; they should not describe frozen foods as fresh, call margarine butter, or refer to nondairy coffee whiteners as cream.

Guests may want to know about the size of portions, if entrees include any side dishes, and what garnishes the property uses. Does the property allow guests to substitute a specific item on the menu for another one? Does the property charge extra for such substitutions?

Guests who are in a hurry may ask the server which items on the menu can be served quickly. Others will wish to be informed when an item they have ordered will take an excessive amount of time to prepare. (Consider the problems that may arise if one guest in a large party requests a prepared-to-order dessert item such as a vanilla souffle while the rest of the guests order such pre-portioned items as pies and cakes that can be served almost immediately.)

Guests may also ask servers questions about beverages and their prices. For instance, they'll want to know if alcoholic beverages are available and whether the property carries a specific brand. Sometimes they'll ask servers to suggest a wine to complement a specific meal. Therefore, it is important that service employees have some knowledge about food and wine affinities (wines which do and do not go with certain foods), even if a sommelier (wine steward) is available. (Other aspects of wine service are discussed in Chapter 14.)

From the preceding discussion, you can see how important it is for food servers to know exactly what products and services are available. The chef or cook should attend occasional food server training meetings to provide information about food products. Bartenders or service staff from the beverage department can also provide

Exhibit 11.8 Dining Room Menu

CENA/DINNER

ANTIPASTI/APPETIZERS

SPIEDINO DI MOZZARELLA
  (white bread and mozzarella fried with butter,
  parsley, and lemon sauce) XX
COCKTAIL DI GAMBERI
  (shrimp cocktail) XX
PROSCIUTTO E MELONE XX
VONGOLE CAPRI
  (little neck clams in tomato sauce) XX
COZZE IN SALAS BIANCA O ROSSA
  (mussels in white or red sauce) XX
ANTIPASTO PICCANTE PER DUE
  (selection of: baked mozzarella, broiled scampi,
  clams casino, and stuffed mushrooms for two) XX

FARINACEI/FARINACEOUS

PAGLIA E FIENO
  (white and green thin homemade noodles,
  bechamel sauce with peas and ham) XX
FETTUCCINE
  (homemade green or white egg noodles in white parmesan
  cream sauce or tomato sauce) XX
CANNELLONI XX
TORTELLINI ALLA PANNA
  (homemade pasta in white cream sauce) XX
GNOCCHI
  (pasta filled with ground veal, ham, mozzarella, and parsley) . . . XX
LINGUINE ALLE VONGOLE
  (flat spaghetti with clams in red or white sauce) XX
AGNOLOTTI
  (homemade pasta filled with spinach) XX

PESCE/FISH

ZUPPA DI PESCE
  (assorted fish in red lobster sauce) XX
SCAMPI SALTA
  (broiled giant scampi, red sauce) XX
SCAMPI E CAPPESANTE ALLE MANDORLE
  (scampi and baby scallops in almond sauce) XX
COZZE IN SALSA BIANCA O ROSSA
  (mussels in white or red sauce) XX
DOVER SOLE
  (butter, lemon, wine) XX

PIATTI DEL GIORNO/ENTREES

PICCATA DI VITELLO AL LIMONE
  (sauteed veal with butter and lemon and asparagus) . . . XX
SCALOPPINE DI VITELLO
  (veal and breast of chicken with mozzarella,
  tomato sauce and basil) XX
SALSICCIA ALLA CALABRESE
  (sausages with mozzarella, tomatoes and basil) XX
PETTO DI POLLO MIMOSA
  (boneless breast of chicken, ham, mozzarella, and cream sauce) . . . XX
FILET MIGNON
  (broiled filet mignon in Bearnaise sauce) XX
NEW YORK SIRLOIN STEAK XX

LEGUMI/VEGETABLES/SALADS

ZUCCHINE FRITTE
  (thin fried zucchini) XX
FUNGHI
  (mushrooms sauteed in white wine) XX
INSALATA
  (mixed green salad with dressing) XX
INSALATA DI POMODORI
  (fresh tomato salad with olive oil, oregano and basil) . . . XX
RUGOLA SALAD
  (in season) XX

information to food service employees.

Some properties provide taste sessions for service staff. The employees sample food and beverage products available at the property so

Selling by Suggestion

To sell by suggestion, you must:

1. Know your products.
2. Know how to read your guests; be alert to their needs and wants.
3. Be considerate and tactful.
4. Have a sense of humor and timing.
5. Know when you've said enough.

Source: *Profit Motivation: The Key to Waiter/Waitress Training,* (East Lansing, Mich.: Educational Institute of the American Hotel & Motel Association, 1980), p. 19.

they will know, firsthand, how items taste. Wine tasting sessions may help employees explain subtle differences among wines to guests who have questions about them.

Service employees also learn about their products and services by paying attention as they serve items. For example, if the server realizes that in the past, male guests have enjoyed the large cut of steak rather than the small one, he/she can mention that fact to current guests.

The timing of dining service is very important, and the menu affects it in at least two ways: the menu affects the speed with which guests "turn over" and it affects when and how service employees place product orders with production personnel.

You know that dining service managers are concerned about turnover. (They also use the term "table turn" which essentially means the same thing.) If a dining room seats 150 guests, and employees serve 300 guests during a specific shift, the turnover rate is 2 (300 guests divided by 150 seats equals 2). In other words, each chair accommodates an average of two guests. Managers like the turnover rate to be as high as possible but, as rates increase, it is important to ensure that quality standards do not decrease.

It is obvious that the faster guests can be served, the quicker they will complete the meal, and the more likely they are to leave. The speed of dining service—whether fast or at the guests' leisure—is always very important. Breakfast and the businessperson's quick lunch are typical examples of fast service. At dinner, however, guests often desire a leisurely dining experience.

In either event, the timing of dining service is important. Simply put, guests want to receive items at a pace which they, not the server or the manager, set.

What are the implications of the menu on the timing of dining service? If production employees can prepare menu items in advance, they will need only to heat and/or portion them for quick service later. On the other hand, items which require preparation from scratch at the time the food server places the order will slow down dining service. Compare, for example, the "help yourself" salad bar to the chef's salad which the kitchen must prepare before the server can bring it to the guest. Obviously, some menu items take less production and service time than others. Depending on the items made available to and selected by guests, the menu does indeed affect the turnover rate.

The Art of Suggestively Selling Menu Items

Food servers should know how to influence the orders their guests place. The reason that they should exercise such influence is not just to increase their tip income, although as they sell more items, the check average and tip generally increase. Rather, food servers should seek to make the dining experience of their guests a memorable one.

Guests will especially enjoy some menu items more than others. With proper management planning, those items can be among the outlet's most profitable. As service employees sell those products, all parties—the guests, food servers, and the food and beverage operation itself—will benefit.

The most profitable menu items are those with the highest contribution margin (income minus food cost). For example, if a chicken dinner sells for $5 and has a food cost of $2, its contribution margin is $3 ($5 minus $2 equals $3). The contribution margin is used to meet all nonfood expenses and contribute to the operation's profits. As the contribution margin increases, the operation benefits. Wise dining room managers know the contribution margin of each item, take creative steps to make these items popular with the guests, and train their employees to use good suggestive selling techniques.

Suggestive selling is an art. It goes beyond informing the guest, but stops short of being pushy. If it is the property's policy, servers give guests choices rather than ask questions that can be answered "Yes" or "No." For example, "The flaming cheese appetizer is extraordinary and the soup du jour is lobster bisque. Which may I bring you?" is one way a server could use suggestive selling.

Suggestive selling is often used to sell extra items that guests will enjoy. Examples include appetizers, side dishes not included with the meal, salads and salad bars, desserts, and beverages. Servers should give guests a chance to order before-dinner drinks, wine with the meal, and after-dinner beverages as well.

When an operation uses suggestive selling, the manager should make certain that servers don't aggravate guests or inadvertently make them believe that side dishes or appetizers are a usual part of the meal price. If a guest orders a specialty salad thinking it is the meal's side salad, for example, he/she may become disgruntled once he/she realizes the mistake and never return to the property again.

The Menu and Special Guests

All guests are special, of course. However, food servers sometimes find themselves in situations that require special techniques. They should consider the following:

The guest in a hurry. Suggest menu items which production personnel can prepare quickly. Serve the food as promptly as possible. Be pleasant, but don't waste time talking.

Diet-conscious guests. Don't automatically suggest low calorie dishes to overweight guests. Reserve those suggestions for when guests express an interest in them.

Guests with special diet needs. Know which menu items do not contain sodium and which items are available for vegetarians who, in addition to meat, do not eat fish, eggs, or milk products. People with special health concerns may need to speak to the dining room manager or chef to ensure that their concerns are properly addressed.

Senior citizens. Older guests tend to like light meals and eat more slowly than other guests. They may also wish to eat their evening meal earlier than other diners. They may prefer foods that are soft and bland rather than chewy and spicy. Frequently, they are on a limited budget. Know in advance the items that they might enjoy and, if asked, recommend them.

Children. Children like to receive their meals as soon as possible. Giving them crackers or similar items may prevent them from becoming restless before you serve the food. Some children may enjoy a nonalcoholic "kiddie cocktail" (Shirley Temple). If you have a children's menu, make sure that the adults are aware of it. If not, make suggestions according to the age of the child. (Many restaurants have a separate menu for children under the age of 10 or 12.)

Young adults. Young adults tend to spend money freely; don't hesitate to recommend extras and entrees, especially items which are *in* among their age groups.

Foreign guests. Some foreign guests may not understand English or cannot speak English or read it very well; do not speak louder to them, but do speak slowly. Ask if they have any special food preferences. Put yourself in their place and ask, "How would I like to be treated if I were a visitor in another country?" Menus with pictures will help communicate the availability of items.

Supplies and Equipment

An extensive discussion of dining room supplies and equipment is presented in Chapter 5. The dining room manager must know about and handle a wide variety of front-of-house equipment, such as dining room furniture, salad bars, service equipment, items found in server stations, cash registers, precheck registers, and other electronic sales income control equipment. He/she may also require a wide variety of consumable supplies ranging from condiments to tabletop appointments to linens. Managers must have the basic information necessary to purchase, restock, maintain, and control each of these pieces of equipment and supplies.

Special Occasions Can Be Fun and Profitable

Some properties, especially high-check-average restaurants, may be *special occasion operations*; a large number of guests may visit the property to celebrate birthdays, anniversaries, holidays, and similar events. Of course, any type of operation can offer special occasions; for example, consider the birthday party packages which fast-food operations sometimes offer and the availability of separate dining areas in cafeterias. Offering sparkling wines at a variety of prices and training food servers to sing "Happy Birthday to You" and other greetings are examples of what dining outlets could do to make a special occasion extra special.

Marketing personnel frequently speak of the "unexpected extra." Offering a small cake, bottle of wine, a rose for ladies, or a memento from the restaurant can help build a solid repeat business base. The use of special occasion products can be an integral component in management's marketing plans.

Managing Service at the Hotel Columbia
Page Twenty-Two

"Everyone knows," thought Lewis, "that the food service industry is very labor-intensive. Perhaps this is most evident in dining service and food production areas. A large number of employees are required and, even though a cooperative teamwork approach is necessary, problems with interpersonal relationships can evolve."

Lewis was thinking about the dish breakage problem experienced during his first job and was concerned for a number of reasons, including the high cost of glassware, that this experience not be repeated at the Hotel Columbia. He was certain that training programs would emphasize proper handling of these items. Would this be all that was necessary to minimize breakage problems? "No," thought Lewis, "the problem is deeper than that and goes back to the 'people' aspect of the job." He knew job descriptions would specify the "who, what, where, and when" of glassware handling. However, what happens if only the "letter of the policy" is followed? For example, what if a tray being used to transport soiled dishes is full—and more soiled glassware must be placed upon it? What if a food server is responsible for removal of the dishes but a busperson is assigned to transport them to the soiled dish area? What happens if it is the responsibility of the dishwasher to keep the soiled dish counter clear for additional soiled items, but the area is full because of a backup of work? What does the busperson do?

Yes, orientation, training, and supervision could help answer these questions and head off such problems. However, it would take more than that. The staff must want to work as a team and be able to help each other. Poor staff morale could affect dish breakage as well as cause a wide range of other problems.

Lewis immediately thought of examples of such potential problems among staff members. What about "communication" problems between service and production staff as food items were ordered or picked up? What about differences of opinion regarding who is responsible for the quality of food after it is delivered to the guest? What about favoritism being shown when items are produced first for favorite servers? What about the whole matter of tips—and how much, if any, should be shared among service and production personnel? "The list of examples can go on and on," thought Lewis, "but the point is very clear. It is necessary for all staff members in all positions to work very closely together in order to please the guest and to meet the production and service standards of the Hotel Columbia."

Lewis knew that these concerns were real— and problems could regularly occur in his property unless the right people were selected and trained. He knew that his staff needed to provide an environment for employees to meet their own goals while addressing those of the Hotel Columbia. Stated simply, his managers needed to know how to supervise. Some of this information could be taught. Other elements in successful supervision require tact and common sense. He vowed that, even though everyone would be busy in the transitional period of opening, all supervisory staff would become involved in ongoing supervisory development training. The impact of this training program would, he hoped, help prevent such problems as glassware breakage. However, the objective of the training would be much more extensive; the results would spread through the entire food and beverage operation—and would affect all personnel in the department.

12

Banquet Service

Professional catering directors in lodging properties located in or near population centers are quick to realize how having a first-class banquet department can enhance the overall image of the property in the community. For many guests, their first contact with a facility occurs when they attend a banquet. If the guest's reaction to the occasion is good, he/she may very well return with family and/or friends to enjoy additional evenings in other outlets. Banquet guests may also be the future organizers of similar functions for other groups. When they've already experienced banquets that meet all their expectations, they may simply return to the hotel where those events were held and ask for the same kind of menu and service that appear to be the usual offering of the catering department. Groups that typically comprise the banquet market are discussed in the following section.

Banquet Business Markets

Convention and association groups may include fewer than a hundred to many thousands of attendees. They feature simultaneous meetings, exhibit space, and a wide range of food and beverage services, such as coffee breaks and hospitality suites.

Business and corporate groups are composed of business associates, ranging from a limited number of people to many hundreds. They may require food and beverage services for meals and coffee breaks. These groups produce the best revenue for many hotel banquet departments.

Social groups are usually private parties arranged by individuals for such family events as weddings, anniversaries, and graduations. Again, these groups can range from fewer than twenty guests to several hundred. Civic and political events, awards and testimonial meetings, and fund-raising events are other examples of social group meetings which require banquet services.

Organization of a Banquet Department

Successful banquets require an extensive amount of planning, organization, communication, and coordination. Banquet employees must perform many different tasks, typically within different departments. No rules for banquet service apply to every operation. However, regardless of the exact organizational structure and the number of positions involved in a banquet department, management must carefully coordinate all the personnel and activities required to make a banquet event successful.

Exhibit 12.1 shows a sample organization chart of a banquet department in one hotel. While most properties probably do not use this organizational scheme or the exact titles of each position listed, it does provide an excellent overview of the functions, relationships, and activities which must exist within an effective banquet department. The general manager is the official with responsibility for all the activities within the property. A food and beverage director administers the food service operation. Note that the food and beverage director supervises two officials with direct banquet/catering responsibilities. First, an executive chef has responsibility

Managing Service at the Hotel Columbia
Page Twenty-Three

Lewis Scott believed that the Hotel Columbia would have a large amount of banquet business. "We'd better," he thought, "since we're putting tens of thousands of square feet of group function space in the building and will heavily market our services to businesses, associations, and social groups."

"I know we're going to have a first-rate banquet sales department that will focus on selling events and services to clients. Our catering department will also effectively focus on the production and service needs of special events."

Lewis realized that repeat business would be critical to the continued success of the catering department. "Our sales representatives must constantly generate new business and work with clients to ensure that their event is extra-special in every way," he thought. He also understood the importance of delivering what was promised; to do that, the banquet manager, assisted by the banquet chef, would have to carefully plan and consistently produce high-quality products and services at a fair price.

Lewis knew that, at a minimum, the Hotel Columbia's catering department would provide these elements. However, did additional issues exist that, if ignored, could hurt the prospects for repeat business? He decided to drop in on Carolyn White, his recently hired catering director, and talk with her about his concerns.

---

for all food production activities in the hotel. The executive chef supervises an executive sous chef who, in turn, supervises the banquet chef.

In Exhibit 12.1, the food and beverage director supervises the catering director, who is the immediate supervisor of the catering sales manager (who is responsible for those food and beverage events not requiring guestrooms), and the banquet manager (who is responsible for all banquet events). Since the banquet chef is responsible for food production and the banquet manager is responsible for food service, there must be a functional relationship between these two officials. (This relationship is shown by the dotted line.)

Exhibit 12.1 also shows the role of the marketing and sales department in catering and banquet services. Personnel in this department typically sell banquet events which involve other services of the hotel (e.g., attendees at a convention or other large group meeting may require overnight accommodations in guestrooms or they may use food and beverage services in regular outlets). Again, someone in the marketing and sales department will be required to coordinate these activities.

There are two additional relationships shown in Exhibit 12.1. First, there is an obvious need for close communication and coordination between the catering director and the director of marketing and sales. (This relationship is illustrated with a dotted line in Exhibit 12.1.) Also, there should be close coordination between the convention services director and the head houseperson in the banquet department to ensure that all function rooms are properly set up on time for required functions. Again, this relationship is illustrated in Exhibit 12.1 with a dotted line.

Special mention should be made of the banquet manager and his/her assistant banquet manager. These officials are responsible for three basic functions: (a) setting up function rooms as required (housepersons are used for this task); (b) serving meals (the banquet captain, banquet servers, and banquet buspersons are required for meal service); and (c) serving beverages at banquets (the banquet bartenders, beverage servers, and beverage runners are used for this activity).

An Overview of Banquet Duties and Responsibilities

A large number of people in different positions in separate departments must perform a wide range of duties and responsibilities to pro-

Exhibit 12.1 Organization of Catering and Banquet Services in a Large Hotel

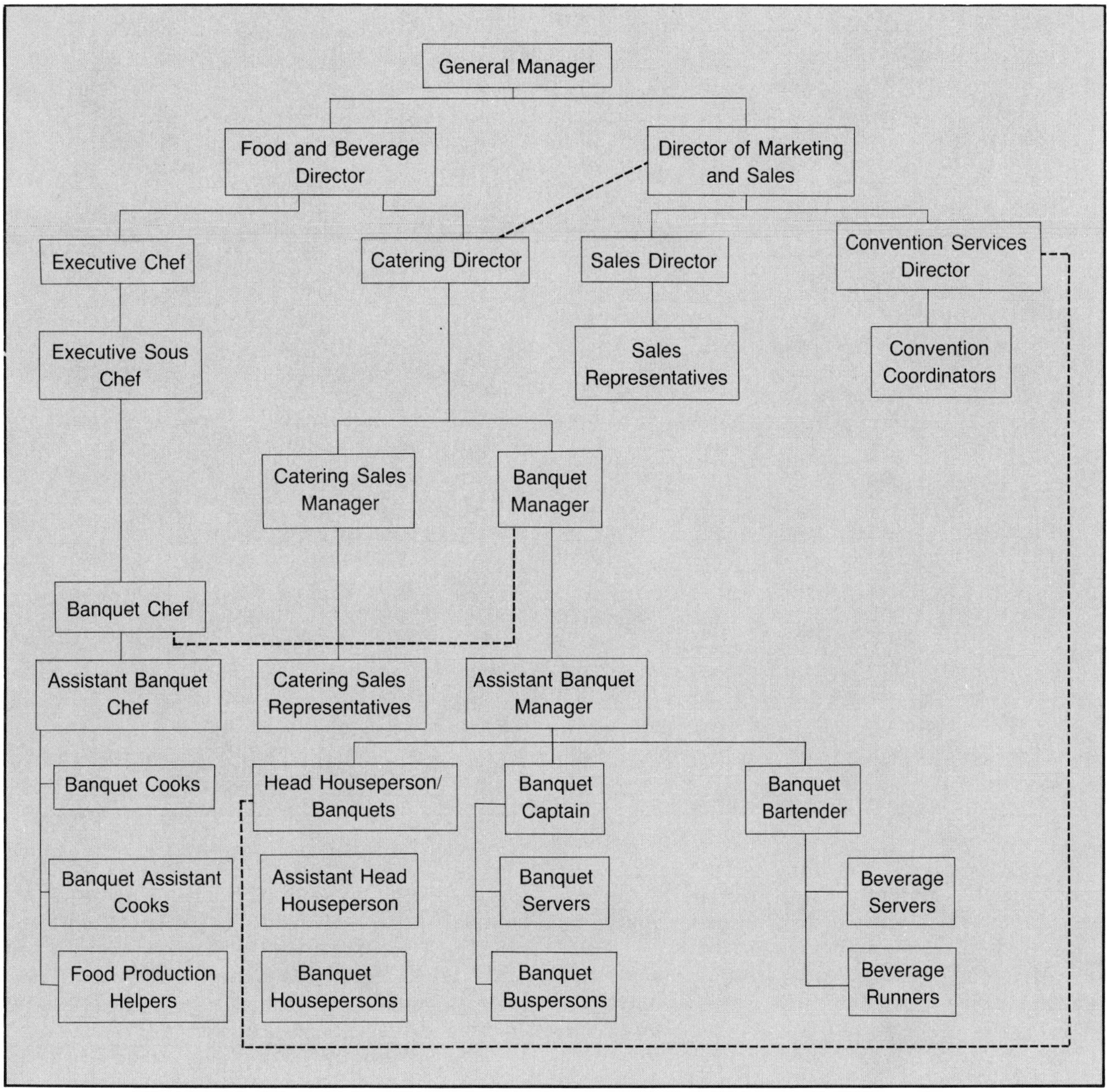

vide banquet services. These activities are reviewed in Exhibit 12.2.

The first task shown on the flowchart is selling the event. Depending upon the size of the property and the titles used, the person responsible may be the general manager, the food and beverage director, the director of sales (catering), or a catering executive.

During negotiations with a potential client and after the property sells the event, other employees must make plans to accommodate the client's desires regarding the food, beverages, service, and special arrangements for the event. These employees organize and coordinate banquet activities and schedule employees to produce food, set up the room, prepare for bev-

Exhibit 12.2 Essential Banquet Duties and Responsibilities

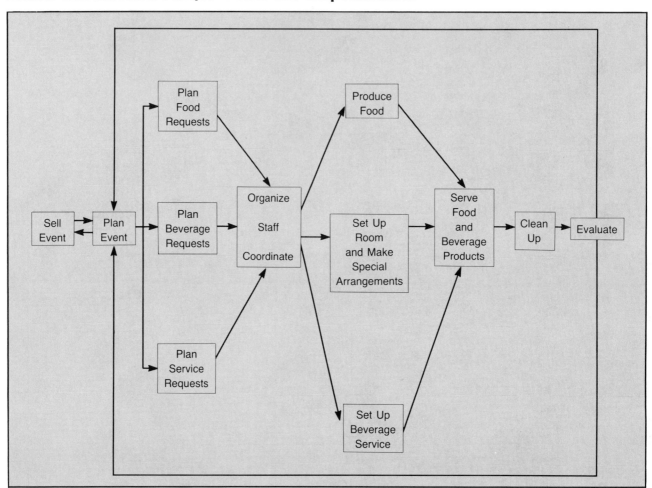

erage service, and otherwise meet the client's needs. These activities lead to the actual event: the service of food and beverages.

After the event is over, employees must undertake cleanup activities. It is also important to evaluate the effectiveness of the banquet plans. The experience gained from each event can help with the planning of other events.

As employees perform each of these activities, control, accounting, and contractual efforts must also occur to ensure that both the guests and the property attain the goals established for the event.

Selling the Banquet

In order to be competitive, hospitality operations must aggressively market their banquet

services. While details of procedures for selling banquets are beyond the scope of this book,[1] the principles are the same whether a specialized sales department sells banquet services or the catering manager or other official in the food and beverage department performs that task.

To sell banquets effectively, catering executives must know what the segments of the marketplace are, what potential guests want, how the hospitality operation can best provide for those wants and needs, and how to negotiate a contract for the right products and services at the right price. In short, catering executives must be

---

[1] Interested readers are referred to Derek Taylor, *How to Sell Banquets: The Key to Conference and Function Promotion*, 2nd ed. (Boston: CBI, 1981) and Arno Schmidt, *The Banquet Business* (Boston: CBI, 1980).

CONTINENTAL BREAKFAST ($4.50 per person)

Chilled Fresh Orange Juice		Chilled Tomato Juice
1 each Danish Pastry	1 each Croissant	1 each Brioche Roll
Jam	Butter	Marmalade
Coffee/Sanka	Tea	Milk

MEETING BREAKS

	Price per person
Coffee, Tea, Sanka, Milk (1½ cups per person)	XX
2 each Assorted Danish Pastries OR	XX
2 each Blueberry Muffins OR 1 each Doughnut OR 1 each Sliced Nut Bread	XX
Chilled Fresh Orange Juice	XX
Chilled Tomato Juice OR Chilled Grapefruit Juice	XX
Coca Cola OR Diet Tab OR Diet Fresca	XX
Fresh Fruit Salad Bowl (Minimum 20 guests)	XX
Assorted Cheeseboard, Fruit Center, Crackers	XX
Doublemint Chewing Gum (approximately 2 pkgs. -7 sticks for every 5 guests)	XX
Beechnut Spearmint Candy (approximately 2 rolls for every 5 guests)	XX

VIP COFFEE SERVICE ($ xxx per person)

Coffee, Tea, Sanka (Milk by request) approximately 1½ cups per person
2 each Assorted Danish Pastries OR 1 each Doughnut OR 1 each sliced Nut Bread
                                                OR
2 each Fresh Macaroons OR 2 each Assorted Cookies
Doublemint Chewing Gum (2 pkgs. - 7 sticks for every 5 guests)
Beechnut Spearmint Candy (2 rolls for every 5 guests)

Additional Suggestions (VIP Coffee Service)   Price per person

Coffee, Tea, Sanka,(Milk by request) approximately 1½ cups per person	XX
Chilled Grapefruit Juice OR Chilled Tomato Juice	XX
Chilled Fresh Orange Juice	XX
Coca Cola, Diet Tab, OR Diet Fresca	XX

* * * * * * * *

Where applicable, waitress service is $5.00 per hour (3 hour minimum)

Prices do not include customary gratuity charge of 15%

NOTE: For Retirement Receptions and/or Economy Coffee Service, contact
            Grill Cafeteria Supervisor, 524-3160 or 524-3164

Prices Subject to Change September, 19XX

Established menus for continental breakfast, meeting breaks, and VIP coffee breaks.

Advantages of Banquet Business

Banquets can be very profitable. In addition, successful banquets have an impact on a property's community relations and can influence the number of rooms it sells to corporate and association accounts. When properties place banquet food orders with orders for their other dining outlets, overall food costs can decrease.

Banquets allow great flexibility in pricing. Typically, per person sales are greater for banquets than for dining rooms. High-volume food preparation helps save money; properties can reduce food costs through high-volume purchasing and minimize labor costs by using employees more effectively. Inventory costs are also low for banquets. Properties can purchase food on an "as-needed" basis; therefore, excessive funds are not tied up in the inventory.

Beverage income also adds to the profitability of banquet sales. Contribution margins (beverage income minus beverage costs) for beverage service can have a significant impact on the property's profits.

Production forecasting and planning are relatively easy when properties serve a pre-established number of guests. Finally, banquets bring many guests into the property who might become repeat business at other banquets, in the dining rooms, for room rentals, and for beverage service.

---

good salespeople. (In dining rooms, the food server is the salesperson; in catering, the responsibility for sales rests with the catering staff.)

One of the most effective sales tools in banquet service is a catering department's tradition of excellence. It is much easier to sell banquets to people who are aware of the department's fine reputation, or better yet, to those who have had previous excellent experiences at banquets, than to people who know nothing about the property. Catering executives who work in facilities with a less than desirable reputation or try to sell banquet services to prospective clients who have had problems with past events will have a difficult task.

Prospective clients may inquire about the hotel's banquet services by telephone or letter. Prompt attention to these requests provides a foundation of concern upon which the catering executive can build during the evolution of a relationship between the department and its client. A catering executive's genuine concern for a client will also lead to a properly executed banquet.

On the other hand, catering executives may initiate contact with prospective clients through telephone calls, direct mail letters, "sales blitzes" (personal visits to prospective clients), or interaction with the local Chamber of Commerce, community organizations, and tourist and convention centers. Whether management or the prospective client makes the initial contact, *the most important step is to let clients know that the property is interested in their business.* When a catering executive contacts a client to secure a booking, he/she may show the prospective client the facilities, provide supplemental information to help the client make appropriate plans for the event, and provide complimentary food and beverage services and lodging accommodations during the client's visits. All of these activities are useful tools for selling a special function.

Many catering departments have established banquet menus that give prospective clients an indication of what is available within specific price ranges. Examples of various kinds of established banquet menus appear in several places in this chapter. Most clients find established menus very acceptable; otherwise, you can use them as a base from which to design the specific menu which the guest desires. Of course, the catering executive should discuss proposed menu changes with the chef to ensure that the revised menu is practical from production, service, and financial standpoints.

In addition to established menus, many catering departments use presentation books which illustrate the possible room/table arrangements in the group function space, provide sample menus from past events, display photographs of buffets, offer possible table settings, and more. Floor plans for each room can also be included in presentation books. The books serve to showcase past favorable events and provide useful ideas to clients planning other special functions.

Catering executives can negotiate price and other factors with clients, depending on the extent to which the property desires the business. For example, if the facilities are available and would otherwise remain unused, the catering representative may offer an additional service or upgrade a menu without additional cost. In these cases, the catering executive should work with the client to establish a price that is beneficial for both the client and the property. Facilities doing an extensive banquet business can offer prospective clients a wide range of other equipment, supplies, and services. Exhibit 12.3 illustrates the types of amenities which banquet departments can provide to clients.

As discussions about specific events evolve, the catering executive may help answer questions and resolve special problems for the guests. Certainly, if the plans involve more than selecting from the property's established menus and procedures, it is important for catering sales executives to confirm that the ideas which the client is considering are possible to execute. Once the arrangements are finalized, the client and the property's representative should sign a contract or letter of agreement, outlining everyone's responsibilities. (Contracts will be discussed in more detail later in the chapter.)

Planning the Banquet

Coordination is critical to the success of any banquet. Typically, representatives from each department meet frequently, sometimes daily, to discuss the details of banquets occurring that day

Exhibit 12.3 Miscellaneous Equipment, Supplies, and Services Available from the Banquet Department

35 MM Slide Projector: (2 projectors)	
Kodak Model AF-2 with Zoom Lens 4 to 6 inches	
(Own projectionist—Banquet Department Inventory—1 Projector)	$15.00 per day
Overhead (Transparency) Projector: (2 projectors)	
Buhl Supreme 600	
(Own projectionist—Banquet Department Inventory—1 Projector)	$15.00 per day
3M Wollensack Tape Recorder:	
Audio-Visual Model 1520-AV Speed 7-½ or 3-¾	
(Own operator—Banquet Department Inventory—None)	$15.00 per day
Tapes for Recorder:	$12.00 per day
1800 ft. Mylar Tape—90 minutes each side	$ 7.00 per day
(Lighted Pointer)	
16 MM Movie Projector: (2 projectors)	
Bell & Howell—Auto Load—Film & Sound	
(Own projectionist—Banquet Department Inventory—1 Projector)	$15.00 per day
Movie Screen:	
Extra-large 8' × 10'	
(Charge includes delivery, set up, and removal)	$50.00 per day
Projectionist:	
Professional projectionist—minimum fee up to 3 hours	$66.00
—after 5:00 PM and weekends	$99.00
(Includes reasonable projector requirements)	
Electrician:	$22.00 per hour
For setting up additional electrical requirements (by Work Order only)	
PA Technician:	$22.00 per hour
To set up and operate PA system, if more than 3 mikes in use	
(by Work Order only)	

Exhibit 12.3, continued

Theatrical Spotlight: (1 set)	$35.00 per day
Requires operator (by Work Order only)	$22.00 per hour
Police Officers:	
Plain-clothes City Police, minimum 3 hours @ $11.00 per hour, + 10%	
Security:	
$6.00 per man (unarmed) per hour—3 hour minimum, + 10%	
Music:	
See separate listing of bands—Fee + 10%	
Piano Tuning:	
1 week notice	
(All pianos tuned every 2 months by contract)	$36.00
Typewriters:	
All types	$15.00 per day
Court Stenographer:	
Usual Fee + 10%	
Flowers:	
See separate listing of florists—Fee + 10%	
Fashion Show Runaway: (with gold carpet and gold pleated skirting)	
Ballroom	$35.00
du Barry	$25.00
Photographers:	
See separate listing—Fee + 10%	
Valet Parking:	
Fee + 10%	
Canopy—Social Entrance:	$350.00
With lights and carpet across sidewalk	(approximately)
(By Work Order only—Subject to weather conditions)	
Baby-Sitting:	
Service for up to 3 children, $2.50 per hour	
More than 3 children, $2.75 per hour	
(3 hour minimum + 10%)	
Gathering Permit:	$15.00
To serve alcoholic beverages after 1:00 AM	
(See Banquet Manager)	
TVs:	$30.00 per day
(Includes delivery, set up, and removal)	
TV—Closed Circuit:	
1 Camera, 4 Monitors	$125.00 per day
Requires projectionist (by Work Order only)	$22.00 per hour
Bars:	
Cash Bars:	
$24.00 per bartender regardless of service hours	
Minimum requirement—1 bartender for every 75 guests	
Self-Service Bar:	
$25.00 Bar Service Charge—No Gratuity	
Maximum 20 guests	

Setup for a banquet buffet. (Courtesy of The Greenbrier, White Sulphur Springs, West Virginia)

or during the coming week. For very large and other special affairs, detailed planning may begin months prior to these final sessions. The sales director, food and beverage director, catering director, convention services manager, banquet service manager, banquet beverage manager, banquet chef, and/or function room arrangements manager (or their representatives) may attend these banquet planning sessions. Many functions are annual events, so detailed planning that leads to a successful banquet can help to secure repeat business.

Exhibit 12.4 is a special function sheet listing all the details that apply to the function. The

catering executive who books the event completes this form. He/she then makes as many as 40 copies of the form to distribute to the banquet office, the banquet service manager (who schedules staff), the beverage department (which schedules staff and orders the necessary products), the accounting department (which prepares the billing), the function room arrangements manager (who arranges the room setup), the kitchen storeroom, the kitchen banquet staff, the kitchen's pantry area, the kitchen commissary, and the kitchen's bakeshop.

Participants in the banquet planning meeting study the special function sheets in detail to

Orchestrating Banquet Service

Banquet planners must have the organizational talent and leadership capabilities of orchestra leaders and theater directors. They must be able to assign and lead the service brigade to ensure a smooth running operation and, ultimately, guest satisfaction. As in the theater, the guests should enjoy themselves and never see any difficulties that occur behind the scenes.

Successful banquets need a prelude similar to the practice session of an orchestra. Employees should rehearse and perform the steps of service according to the signals given by the captain or headwaiter/headwaitress. Close coordination with the kitchen, host, and banquet planners themselves is an absolute must.

Successful banquets are the result of a very detailed planning system which draws upon the property's past experiences. Every banquet requires creativity when planners organize it to make it a special event.

ensure that the time, products, service, space, and other requirements are clearly understood, and to forestall potential problems. With such study of detailed function sheets, communication problems should be at a minimum.

Frequently, banquet space must have a special layout to accommodate the parties planned. Exhibit 12.5 shows the layout for the space required to set up the banquet specified on the special function sheet in Exhibit 12.4. Note the

LUNCHEON SUGGESTIONS
(Private Dining Rooms)
Prices include Vegetable and/or Potato, Salad, Dessert, and Beverage
(Appetizers are optional at additional cost.)

			Price
BEEF:			
	L-1	SKEWER OF BEEF TENDERLOIN, Pepper Sauce	XX
	L-2	(6 oz.) CHOPPED PRIME STEAK, Toast Round, Sauteed Mushrooms	XX
	L-3	(4 oz.) TENDERLOIN TIPS, STROGANOFF in Rice Ring	XX
	L-4	(4 oz.) LONDON BROIL, Madeira Sauce	XX
	L-5	(6 oz.) BROILED FILET MIGNON, Sauteed Mushrooms	XX
	L-6	(7 oz.) BROILED U.S. PRIME SIRLOIN MINUTE STEAK,	XX
		Toast Square, Herb Butter, Fried Onion Rings	XX
POULTRY:			
	L-7	SAVORY CREPE A LA REINE	
		(Chicken with Mushrooms & Wine in Crepe)	XX
	L-8	MEDALLION OF TURKEY "DIVAN," Mornay Sauce	XX
	L-9	(6 oz.) TURKEY SCALLOPPINE "CORDON BLEU," Chasseur Sauce	XX
	L-10	BONELESS BREAST OF CAPON "AUERSBERG"	
		(Duxelles of Mushrooms, Mornay)	XX
	L-11	BONELESS BREAST OF CHICKEN "KIEV," Marsala Butter	XX
	L-12	SKEWER OF SHRIMP & CHICKEN NUGGETS, Fricassee Sauce	XX
SEAFOOD:			
	L-13	SEAFOOD EN COCOTTE (Shrimp, Scallops, Red Snapper in Wine)	XX
	L-14	POACHED FILLETS OF DOVER SOLE "FLORENTINE"	
		(over Spinach, Mornay Sauce)	XX
	L-15	FILLETS OF FRESH FISH (Season), Meuniere	XX
	L-16	(2 each - 3 oz.) BACKFIN CRABCAKES, Tartare Sauce	XX
	L-17	SAUTEED SCALLOPS A LA PROVENCALE EN COCOTTE	XX
	L-18	OPEN FACE CRAB AND CHEESE SANDWICH	XX
VEAL:			
	L-19	(2 each - 3 oz.) MEDALLION OF VEAL A LA CREME,	
		(Cream Sauce w/Mushrooms)	XX
	L-20	(2 each - 3 oz.) MEDALLION OF VEAL, topped with Artichoke Puree	XX
LAMB:			
	L-21	(8 oz.) BROILED DOUBLE LAMB CHOP, Mint Jelly Garnish	XX
	L-22	POLYNESIAN SKEWER OF SPRING LAMB & SHRIMP, Toasted Almonds	XX
MISCELLANEOUS:			
	L-23	QUICHE DES TROIS LEGUMES-PIE SHAPED WEDGE (Broccoli, Spinach,	XX
		Carrots)	
	L-24	QUICHE LORRAINE - PIE SHAPED WEDGE WITH	
		GRILLED CANADIAN BACK BACON	XX
	L-25	ENGLISH MIXED GRILL (Beef Filet, Lamb Chop, Calf's Liver, and Bacon)	XX
	L-26	OMELETTE PAYSANNE (Diced Sausage, Peppers, Pimiento, Mushrooms,	
		Onion, and Parsley)	XX

Prices Subject To Change September, 19XX

Established banquet luncheon menu from which clients can select the entree around which the meal will be created.

Exhibit 12.4 Special Function Sheet

HOTEL DU PONT

FUNCTION No.   DATE

NAME OF ENGAGER AND ADDRESS   CHARGE

FUNCTION	FROM TO	ROOM	GUARANTEE	SET FOR
Reception	6:00 PM - 8:30 PM	Gold Ballroom	500 - 550	

MENU-TIME   6:00 PM (Special Uniforms)   **PRICE PER COVER**

OTHER SERVICES

BUFFET A: (1 Swan Ice Carving)

- 4 oz. per person Roast Sliced Tenderloin of Beef
  (Carved in room by 1 Chef)
  Sauce Bearnaise
  2½ inch Petite Halved French Finger Rolls
- 6 oz. per person Crown Roast of Spring Lamb,
  Provencale (Carved by chef)
  Sauce Taragon
- 4 oz. per person Seafood Newburg
  (Shrimp, Lobster, Crabmeat)
  Petite 3" Oval Patty Shells
- 1 each Crepe (individual) a la Reine, Mornay
- 2 each Oysters Rockefeller, Rocksalt
- 2 each Clams Casino, Rocksalt

BUFFET B: (Large Floral Centerpiece)

BUFFET C: (1 Eagle Ice Carving)

- 2 oz. per person Pate Maison - Sauce Cumberland
- 2 oz. per person Duckling Galantine - Sauce
- 2 oz. per person Salmon Galantine - Sauce
- 2 oz. per person Pheasant Terrine - Sauce
- 2 oz. per person Turbot Terrine - Sauce
- 2 oz. per person Mousse de Poisson (Fish Mousse) Fume
- 2 oz. per person Lump Backfin Crabmeat in ice block
  (On Side)   Sauce Calypso - Cocktail Sauce
  (Attractively arranged on mirrored trays)
  (Name Plates for all mirrored food items)

ROOM ARRANGEMENTS

Reception Style
White Linen - Pleated

TUXEDOS

6:00 PM - 8:30 PM: (Ballroom)
(4) OPEN BARS W/(2) BARTENDERS EACH
(6) Additional Waitresses to take and
serve cocktail orders among guests
Bar To Serve Premium Brands Only

----

(2) WINE BARS WITH (1) BARTENDER EACH
Serving Premium Brands
Red, Rose & White Wines
Chateau Montdespic (House Red),
Le Payrie Blanc de Blanc (House White),
Gratien Brut (House Champagne),
Chateau

Music: Hotel to arrange
"Paul Kauriga" 6 PM - 8:30 PM
(7) Pieces including violins

Flowers: Hotel to arrange
"Martines - Isabelle"
(Trees, Bushes, Small Garden, and
Bandstand)

----

(4) Cloakroom Attendants - "No Tipping"
5:30 PM - 8:30 PM

Ladies/Gentlemens Lounges:
(1) Maid on duty 5:30 PM - 8:30 PM
"No Tipping" (Special Uniform)
(1) Butler on duty 5:30 PM - 8:30 PM
"No Tipping" (Tuxedo)

Special Valet Parking:
(Own Arrangements)
(6-8) Men on duty 5:30 PM - 8:30 PM

HOTEL DU PONT

No.   DATE

NAME OF ENGAGER AND ADDRESS   CHARGE

FUNCTION	FROM TO	ROOM	GUARANTEE	SET FOR
...ption	6:00 PM - 8:30 PM	Gold Ballroom	500 - 550	

...ME   6:00 PM   **PRICE PER COVER**

OTHER SERVICES

BUFFET D: (1 Fish Ice Carving)

- Clams on Half Shell (with chef to assist)
  Cocktail Sauce - Horseradish Sauce -
  and Lemon Wedges

BUFFET E: (1 Fish Ice Carving)

- Oysters on Half Shell (with chef to assist)
  Cocktail Sauce - Horseradish Sauce -
  Oyster Crackers - Lemon Wedges

BUFFET F: (Large Floral Centerpiece)

- Domestic and Imported Cheeses
  (Blocks and Wheels)
  Actively arranged on 2 round silver trays and
  Square silver tray with Grapes Garni -
  Assorted Loaves of Bread display
  English Water Crackers
  Sliced Petite French Bread

BUFFET G: (Center of room-72" Table)

- Large Hotel du Pont, Shrimp Pyramid
  Calypso Sauce - Dandeloin Sauce -
  Cocktail Sauce
  Petite Coconut Wedges filled with King
  Crabmeat Salad

HOTEL DU PONT

FUNCTION No.   DATE

NAME OF ENGAGER AND ADDRESS   CHARGE

FUNCTION	FROM TO	ROOM	GUARANTEE	SET FOR
Reception	6:00 PM - 8:00 PM	Ballroom Foyer	500 - 550	

MENU-TIME   6:00 PM   **PRICE PER COVER**

OTHER SERVICES

BUFFET H:

- Medium-Size Special Fruit Pyramid, Sunflower Decor
- (2) Chocolate Fondue
- (2) Caramel Fondue

BUFFET I:

- Assorted Viennese Pastries
  (Bienenstich, Spitzbuben, Schillerlocken, and
  Napoleon)
  (Attractively arranged on square silver trays)
- Assorted Viennese Tortes
  (Sacher Tore, Linzer Torte, Esterhazey Torte, etc.)

BUFFET J: (Coffee Table)

- (200) Demitasse Coffee (Silver Urn)
- (100) Sanka - Tea (Silver Urn)
  Including: Cubed Sugar
  Cream
  Lemon Peels
  Sweet n' Low

6:00 PM - 8:30 PM: (Ballroom Foyer)

(1) OPEN BAR WITH (2) BARTENDERS
Premium Brands

Social Entrance Canopy:
(Hotel to arrange)

To be set-up on _____ (date)
8:00 AM - 12:00 Noon
To be removed on _____ (date)
8:00 AM - 12:00 Noon

Hotel to arrange: Special Doorman
(1) Doorman on duty (canopy)
5:30 PM - 8:30 PM

ROOM ARRANGEMENTS

Reception Style (See Diagram)
White Linen - Pleated (See Diagram)
(3) Registration Tables - Upper Foyer

Exhibit 12.5 Layout for a Banquet Function

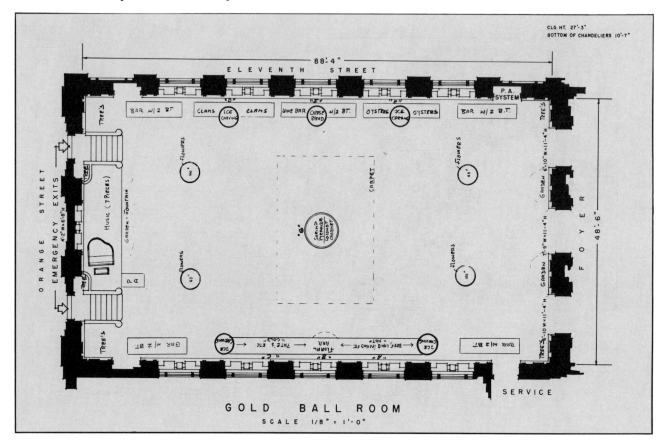

Banquets and Special Community Activities

Want to make money and become an integral part of the community at the same time? Most hotel managers will answer yes to that question. Then why not develop special banquet functions and other activities to complement community events? Or, you can create a special event with community-wide implications, such as the celebration of a sports victory or the recognition of the population growth cited in the last census. Parties highlighting the French, Italian, Mexican, or other heritage of the community are also very popular.

Start with a menu and add a little adventure, such as atmosphere and entertainment. If possible, use items from the regular menu. Sales may be generated by offering early seating to accommodate guests before the community event is to occur. A function featuring dinner, desserts, and beverages after the community event might also be profitable.

Perhaps a complete package including dinner as well as admittance and transportation to the event will help guests and serve as an incentive for their participation in the special function. Such a package may include hotel room accommodations, especially on nights with slow business.

Featuring the special event in your advertisements will also help all parties involved. Not only can food service and lodging properties be involved in events that can enhance their community image and generate increased revenues, they can also help ensure the success of such events for the community organizers.

location of the bars, food buffet stations, ice carvings, garden and tree decorations, and the bandstand with a piano. Paying close attention to the details listed on the special function sheet and illustrated on the layout is just as important for small events as it is for large, elaborate events like the one illustrated.

Generally, the client is responsible for any seating charts which the event may require. However, the banquet manager can assist the client with that task and indicate the property's preferences regarding seating arrangements.

Reserving the Banquet Room

The space reserved for a banquet is very important to both the property and the guests. The property views this space as a profitable commodity. Unused space represents lost banquet income. As a catering executive, what would you do if a client wished to use a specific room that could seat 50 guests for a party of only 20? Obviously, if the client is booking the event two years in advance, you would make serious efforts to convince him/her of the benefits of a smaller room so that you could put the larger room to its optimal use with a future booking. However, if the client is booking a party which will occur within two weeks, you might be more likely to satisfy the guest's request. (Most hotels set a minimum number of covers for each banquet room, but if a client requests a larger room that is not booked, often it will be released. Of course, management must consider heating, air conditioning, and other indirect costs as they establish minimum covers for their banquet rooms.)

Catering executives use a daily function room diary to determine if space is available for a particular banquet. They also use the diary to reserve the room after they sell an event so that no one else will commit it for another function. (See Exhibit 12.6 for a sample sheet from a daily function room diary.)

The daily function room diary lists all the function space a property has available for sale and divides it into various intervals during the day for the sale of different events. The books vary according to the size of the operation and the number of available function rooms. Some properties need less information in their daily function room diaries than others do.

Catering executives may make a tentative entry in the diary to hold space for a potential client until the client has made a definite commitment for a particular room on a particular day. Exhibit 12.7 is a function room reservation form that can be used to inform the coordinator of the daily function room diary about a tentative hold on a room.

When the catering executive confirms the entry, the diary's coordinator will officially enter the event into the appropriate time slot. An actual copy of the guest-signed confirmation letter or a function room diary entry form may serve as official authorization for the event. Here again, remember that hotels vary their operation and procedures according to what best suits their needs.

Typically, *one person* is responsible for the maintenance of the daily function room diary. This individual must notify sales and/or catering executives of any duplicate bookings, conflicts, or overdue holds on space in the diary.

Most hotels will permit clients to hold space on a tentative basis for up to two weeks. (Never trust oral agreements. Draft a proposal letter outlining your decisions/understandings for the

```
                    BANQUET OFFICE PRICE LIST
                     Hot and Cold Hors d'Oeuvres


ITEM:                                                         PRICE/EACH

Alaskan King Crab Claws, Hot Butter                              XX
Assorted Finger Sandwiches                                       XX
Belgian Endive Hearts filled with King Crab Salad               XX
Chicken Livers in Bacon                                          XX
Chicken Nuggets in Beer Batter, Pineapple and Mustard Sauce     XX
Clam Balls, Hot Cocktail Sauce                                   XX
Clams Casino                                                     XX
Clams on Half Shell, Cocktail Sauce                             XX
Crabmeat Balls, Hot Cocktail Sauce                             XX
Deep Fried Scallops, Tartare Sauce                             XX
Deep Fried Shrimp in Beer Batter, Hot Cocktail Sauce           XX
Egg Roll                                                         XX
Gougeres (Cheese Puffs)                                          XX
Ham and Pickle in Bacon                                          XX
Iced Shrimp, Cocktail Sauce                                      XX
Miniature Pizza                                                  XX
Mushroom Caps, Stuffed with Beef                                XX
Mushroom Caps, Stuffed with Crabmeat                            XX
Mushroom Turnover                                                XX
Deep Fried Mushrooms, Tartare Sauce                            XX
Mushroom Caps, Stuffed with Sausage                            XX
Mushroom Caps, Stuffed with Snails                             XX
Open Face Canapes, "Executive Style"                           XX
Open Face Crab and Cheese Canapes                              XX
Oysters on Half Shell (October - May)                          XX
Oysters "Rockefeller" (October - May)                          XX
Petite Potato Balls with Sour Cream and Caviar                 XX
Pigs in Blanket, Mustard Sauce                                 XX
Pineapple Cubes in Bacon                                        XX
Potato or Liver Knishes                                         XX
Quiche Lorraine - Mushroom Quiche - Spinach Quiche - Vegetable Quiche  XX
Roquefort Beignets, Apple Sauce                                XX
Stuffed Bouchees (Meat or Fish)                                XX
Stuffed Celery Hearts with Cream Cheese                        XX
Stuffed Cherry Tomatoes with Mousse                            XX
Sushi (Smoked Salmon, Abalone, Shrimp, etc.)                  XX
Swedish Meatballs, Brown Sauce                                 XX
Tenderloin Tips, Bearnaise (½ oz.)                            XX
Watercress and Cream Cheese Pinwheels                         XX


               Prices Subject To Change September, 19XX
```

An established banquet or reception hors d'oeuvres menu that gives clients a wide range of choice for their functions.

Exhibit 12.6 Sample Sheet from a Daily Function Room Diary

Date: May 12, 19XX

	ROOM	7:00 a.m.–11:00 a.m.	11:00 a.m.–4:00 p.m.	4:00 p.m.–Midnight
Grand Ballroom	ROOM A	Group: AFSIA By: PF Function: Breakfast Mtng. File # 107-C Max: 50	Womens Club By: AS Luncheon (Request this room) 109-F Max: 70	By: Max:
	ROOM B	Group: By: Function: File # Max:	By: Max:	By: Max:
	ROOM C	Group: By: Function: File # Max:	By: Max:	By: Max:
CARIBOU		Group: Lions Club By: DP Function: Breakfast Mtng. File # 1001-D Max: 300	By: Max:	By: Max:
ESSEX		Group: By: Function: File # Max:	By: Max:	Acme Book Co. By: JN Awards Dinner/Dance 1007-F Max: 350

client. Written agreements help eliminate communication problems which could affect the success of the event.) At the conclusion of that period, the coordinator should update the diary regarding the spaces on hold. Because the daily function room diary controls the flow of business through public function rooms in a hotel, good judgment must be used when entries are made in it to maximize the catering department's revenues.

From the guest's standpoint, selection of the banquet room is very important because the atmosphere it provides must complement the event and its size must accommodate the number of people expected. Exhibit 12.8 illustrates the type of information which catering executives make available to prospective clients. A tour of the property, particularly at a busy time when rooms under consideration are set for another special event, can often affect the client's final decision to contract with the property.

In making banquet room assignments, the following factors should be considered:

1. Is space available for all the support services, entertainment, and other equipment? In addition to a specific number of guests, it may be necessary to provide space for portable bars, buffet tables, entertainment bandstands, dance floors, and other items.

2. Does the event require the seating of guests? The room may easily accommodate many more people for a stand-up reception than a sit-down banquet. (A rule of thumb is 10 square feet per person if guests sit, 9 square feet if they stand.) Similarly, the space requirements for theater-style and schoolroom or classroom-style seating vary significantly. Exhibit 12.8 provides information about the number of guests you can serve in a room set up in theater, schoolroom, banquet and reception styles. You should develop seating charts that illustrate the exact seating requirements of each room and provide the function room arrangements manager with them.

Exhibit 12.7 Tentative Function Room Reservation

Sheraton Washington Hotel
2660 WOODLEY ROAD, N.W. WASHINGTON, D.C. 20008, TELEPHONE (202) 328-2000

☐ DEFINITE   ☐ TENTATIVE

_____
DATE TODAY

NAME OF GROUP_____

PERSON IN CHARGE/TITLE_____

ADDRESS_____

_____ PHONE: A.C. _____ NO. _____

DAY-DATE-HOUR	ROOM	FUNCTION	ATTENDANCE	RENTAL

DATE								
ROOM BLOCK								

_____   _____
CUSTOMER SIGNATURE   HOTEL REPRESENTATIVE

3. Are any events planned for the space immediately before and/or after the special function under consideration? For example, if you must tear down a room that held a meeting with exhibits before you can set up the next activity, you will need much more time to prepare the room for the next function than if the room were set up for a theater-style meeting or a stand-up reception.

4. What municipal codes and ordinances affect room assignments? Fire or other codes may limit the number of people that can occupy a room. In addition, you must never block fire escape doors.

Exhibit 12.8 Summary of Special Function Room Information

SUMMARY OF PRIVATE DINING/MEETING ROOMS

	LOCATION	CAPACITIES				DIMENSIONS		PA SYSTEM	EXHIBITS	ELECTRICAL	
		Theater Style	Schoolroom Style	Banquet Style	Reception	Length and Width	Ceiling Height		# of Booth	Floor Outlets	Wall Outlets
Foyer	Ballroom	150	50	120	250	48'4" x 33'8"	14'	YES	12	2	12
Ballroom	1st Floor	400	150	440	500	48'6" x 88'4"	27'3"	YES	34	5	30
du Barry	Mezzanine	200	100	200	250	48' x 53'	14'	YES	18	1	19
Delaware Suite	11th Floor	50	30	50	75	12' x 49'8"	11'	YES—PORT. UNIT	—	—	9
New Castle	2nd Floor	40	30	40	50	14'3" x 37'	10'	★	—	—	6
Kent		20	—	18	30	21' x 11'5"	10'	★	—	—	2
Suite 214–218		20	—	16	30	14' x 22'1"	10'	★	—	—	4
Suite 210–212		14	—	14	20	14'11" x 19'4"	10'	★	—	—	3
Suite 208		16	—	12	20	15'2" x 17'10"	10'	★	—	—	2
Seaford Room		10	—	8	10	9'8" x 13'11"	10'	★	—	—	1
Yorklyn Room		10	—	10	10	11'6" x 14'6"	10'	★	—	—	1
Georgetown		40	30	40	50	17' x 34'9"	10'	★	—	—	6
Sussex		30	—	32	40	22'6" x 22'9"	10'	★	—	—	6
Dover		—	—	26	26	12' x 28'	10'	★	—	—	2

10 Smaller Conference Rooms and Suite Parlors

Rentable Equipment
Projectors —35 mm slide
—16 mm sound
—overhead
—opaque
Screens up to 7½' by 20'
front or rear surface

Video—camera, monitor and
related equipment (color)
Audio—cassette and reel-to-reel
recorder and playback
Some multi-image devices such
as programer and dissolve
units available
Special equipment available with
prior notice

Set up
Portable Stage 24' x 8'
Lecterns with Light—3
Chart pads and easels
Blackboards—3' x 5' and 5' x 8'
Projectionists and Electronic
Technicians available upon request.

★Portable unit available
upon request

Courtesy of Hotel du Pont, Wilmington, Delaware

5. Is the room easily accessible to both the guests and the service staff? Rooms accessible only by stairs might be undesirable; you should use them only when no other appropriate space is available.

6. What are the sizes of the tables, chairs, and other equipment that you plan to use for the event? While this may seem like a minor point, tables or chairs that are just a few inches larger than others can significantly reduce the number of guests that you can accommodate. For example, 900 chairs placed theater style, which are just two inches wider than necessary, will require 25 square feet more than their smaller counterparts.

Setting Up the Banquet

Based on the number of special functions scheduled each day, the banquet manager or his/her representative must schedule employees to set up and tear down the rooms, as well as perform all the front-of-house service and related tasks. Exhibit 12.9 is a sample schedule of special function room activities for each day. The special function sheets for banquets (see Exhibit 12.4) were used to compile this schedule.

Procedures for setting up each banquet

Exhibit 12.9 Sample Schedule of Special Function Room Activities

DATE	TIME	FUNCTION	# PERSONS	ROOM	BEO/FILE NUMBER*	GROUP
Tues. 3/22/XX	9:00 AM–6:00 PM	Refreshments LH/RS	300/400	Cotillion	1576 C-236	Texaco, USA
	12:30 AM–3:00 PM	Buff. Lunch LH/RS	375/400	Green	1577 C-236	Texaco, USA
	11:30 AM–1:30 PM	Lunch JC	60/70	Le Palais	1194 B-144C	Rotary
	7:00 PM–8:00 PM	Reception LH/RS	350/400	Cotillion P.F. and Foyer	1578 C-236	Texaco, USA
	8:00 PM–11:00 PM	Dinner LH/RS	350/400	Superstar	1578 C-236	Texaco, USA
Wed. 3/23/XX	4:30 PM–5:30 PM	Rec/Mtg. CS/JC	65	Derbyshire	1585 B-200B	R.I.C.H. Dept. Heads
	7:00 PM–8:00 PM	Reception JC	50	Green	1249 B-200	Intertel
Thurs. 3/24/XX	10:00 AM–2:00 PM	Mtg/Lunch RS	25/30	Derbyshire	G-69	Government Information Mgmnt. Assn.
Fri. 3/25/XX	8:45 AM–5:00 PM	Coffee JP/RS	250	Cotillion	1181 C-300	Nuclear Medicine
	9:00 PM–1:00 AM	Reception JP/RS	300	Green	1184 C-300	Nuclear Medicine

*BEO = Banquet Event Order

room will vary according to the needs of the special function. The following is a partial list of activities involved in setting up banquet rooms:

1. Place runways, carpets, and pianos.
2. Place dinner tables, meeting tables, and head tables.
3. Place chairs, sofas, and other seats.
4. Place bars, buffets, and cake tables.
5. Place the registration, gift, and display tables.
6. Place the movie screen, projector table, projectors, and extension cords.
7. Place blackboards, chartboards, easels, etc.
8. Place microphones, lecterns, and flags.
9. Place linens, ashtrays, sugar bowls, salt and pepper shakers, etc.
10. Place candle holders, fountains, flowers, cakes, etc.
11. Place table numbers on each table, if necessary.

Prior to opening the banquet room, the banquet service manager, captain, or other official assigned to the function must perform specific tasks to ensure that the room setup is complete. Exhibit 12.10 is a checklist of possible pre-opening duties. Whenever practical, the official in charge of a special function should meet with the client to ensure that no changes have occurred in the guest counts, seating arrangements, or timing of the event.

Preparing Banquet Foods

Banquet managers must be sensitive to the concerns of the banquet chef and other production personnel who produce, portion, and otherwise prepare banquet food for service. Management must never overlook the fact that the chef or his/her representative is an integral member of the banquet planning team. When the input of the food production staff is used to develop banquet menus in advance of events, few, if any, operating problems should arise as production employees prepare these menus within the specific quantity limits required by each event.

Hospitality operations that handle a large banquet business may use an automated assembly line to portion banquet meals. More typically, however, properties with a large volume of banquet meals use a manual plating and setup process. Exhibit 12.11 shows one arrangement of people, equipment, supplies, and food products which can be used to plate and set up banquet meals.

As illustrated in Exhibit 12.11, one person carves and places roast beef slices on plates, then passes (actually slides) them along the table to a second employee who portions the green beans amandine. A third employee portions the potatoes au gratin and slides them across the table to a fourth employee who places sauce on the meat. A fifth employee puts plate covers on the dishes and inserts them in a rack or onto a mobile cart. Using this system, five employees can portion food for 300 people in approximately 45 minutes.

If the catering department had requested a plate garnish, the process would have required another employee. You can see how communication and coordination ensure that the guests get what they want, *and* the chef is able to meet back-of-house quality and cost requirements.

What should the catering executive do if the client requests special diet foods or other menu items for selected banquet guests? Unless the hotel has previously established policies, it is generally necessary to discuss these requests with the banquet chef before a commitment is made. When a guest orders melon balls, for example, the chef can point out how labor-intensive, and thus how expensive, they will be. The chef may suggest using melon cubes instead. (See Chapter 4 for further discussions of banquet food production.)

Some Words of Advice About Banquets

Communication between the banquet chef and the banquet manager is critical. For instance, any time that established menus are modified, the chef must know and agree to the change. Because the guest wants a definite menu, including the exact appetizers which will be served, a menu listing "chef's choice" should be avoided. Even if the guest finds such a menu item as an "assorted appetizer tray" acceptable, someone must decide what to put on it and how to plate and serve it.

If the prospective client imposes requirements on the property which prohibit the function from being perfect, management should try to explain the problems which the client's desires would create. If the client remains unconvinced, turn the event down. Catering executives should remember that when food, beverage, service, or other problems occur, guests become angry at the property—not the function's host/hostess. Highlight any of the client's special concerns on the special function sheet, review them in the banquet planning meetings, and carefully recall them during banquet service. Be certain to take care of every agreed-upon requirement of the client, whether it is a centerpiece on every table or ice carved in a special design.

Kosher food functions provide an excellent opportunity for properties to increase their banquet business since many operations do not understand or cater to this market. Detailed information about catering for kosher functions is in Appendix B.

Exhibit 12.10 Sample Checklist of Pre-Opening Duties for Special Functions

☐ Obtain a copy of the function order to familiarize yourself with the client's requirements.

☐ Check room for the proper number of tables and chairs, table numbers, etc.

☐ Check room to ensure that the proper equipment is in place, such as microphones, spotlights, easels, projectors, flags, and other miscellaneous items requested on function order.

☐ Check room to ensure that the proper items are in place, such as linens (proper color), lace cloths, candelabras, cakes, flowers, etc.

☐ Check room for proper cleanliness, light level, air conditioning, heating, unusual noise.

☐ Check room for potential safety hazards, such as damaged chairs, tables, sofas; tripping hazards, such as carpets, extension cords, microphone cords; or the unsafe use of candles in connection with flower arrangements or other combustible decor.

☐ Check the restroom facilities to ensure that they are operational and clean.

☐ Assign staff to specific stations/tables in the room (maximum 20 guests per service staff member).

☐ Assign cart numbers to staff.

☐ Make sure all employees are on time, in proper uniform, and familiar with their assignments.

☐ Hold a meeting with the staff and discuss the plan of action as well as pertinent safety matters.

☐ Check to see that the cloakroom attendant, if any, is present and aware of his/her specific duties.

☐ Greet the host, introduce yourself, and discuss such matters as the final objectives of the function, the timing of it, and the specific course of action.

Other duties (specify)

_____

_____

_____

_____

Source: Adapted from Hotel du Pont, Wilmington, Delaware

Exhibit 12.11 Possible Setup for Plating Banquet Meals

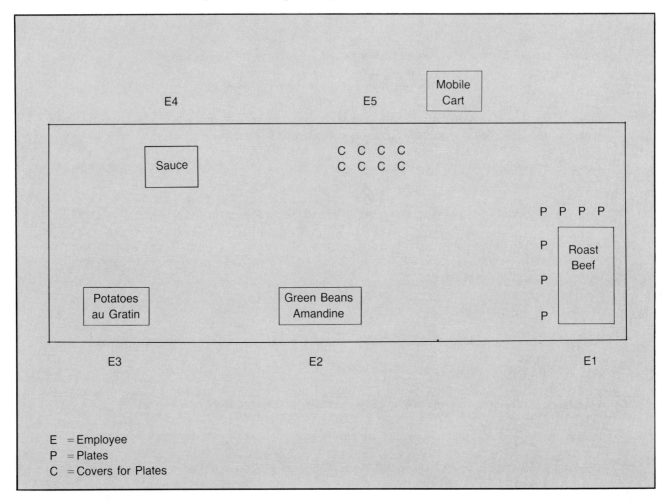

E = Employee
P = Plates
C = Covers for Plates

Providing Service for the Banquet

Banquet managers must develop rules for serving guests at banquets. Frequently, many of these rules also apply to service in public dining rooms. Generally, such similarities occur because the rules established in dining areas were developed for a purpose: to meet the needs of guests. Also, properties often use employees from the dining rooms in banquet service; their jobs are less difficult to learn if the same rules apply to both service areas. A list of basic banquet service rules used in one property follows. These rules were developed by a manager with a great deal of experience in banquet service; they are based on the premise that guests should experience as little inconvenience as possible while enjoying a banquet meal. (See Chapter 6

for a discussion of buffet service requirements.)

General Rules for Banquet Service: An Example

1. All servers must carry a napkin/side towel at all times.

2. All food must enter the room on a tray with a cart unless otherwise specified.

3. All liquids (hot or cold) must be on trays with spouts facing inward.

4. When placing plates in front of guests, servers must place them so the property logo is at the top.

5. Used plates, glasses, and flatware must leave on properly stacked trays.

6. Leftover foods must be placed on a tray and set under the cart.

7. Servers should **always** pick up glasses by the base, flatware by the handle, and plates by the rim.

8. Serve all plated food from the right. Serve anything that is actually passed by the guests from the left.

9. Serve all beverages from the right.

10. Serve the head table first.

11. Serve ladies first.

12. Clear all dishes and glasses from the right.

13. Do not stack dishes or scrape plates in front of guests.

14. Place appetizers on the tables before service begins, unless they are hot items which must be served after the guests are seated.

15. Set salads on tables unless they are served as a separate course.

16. Clear the empty appetizer plates.

17. Serve the main course.

18. Serve coffee and/or wine.

19. Serve more water if needed.

20. Change ashtrays if needed.

21. Clear entree plates, bread and butter plates, butter, melba toast, rolls, salt and pepper, and any flatware not needed for dessert.

22. Serve the dessert.

23. Serve more coffee if needed.

24. Clear dessert plates, empty wine glasses, empty coffee cups, and remove napkins. If a meeting follows food service, leave water glasses and partially filled coffee cups on the tables.

Upon completion of service, the banquet official in charge of the specific function must perform several after-banquet tasks. One task is the supervision of banquet service employees to ensure that they complete their duties. Exhibit 12.12 provides a checklist for many of these required practices.

Banquet Beverage Service

Banquet beverage service—including the art of selling and serving wine—is covered in detail in Chapter 14. It is important to note here, however, that applicable liquor laws must be observed as plans for special events are developed and implemented. Legal hours for beverage service and age limits for minors are among the most important beverage laws which may have an impact on banquet service. In some localities, you may have to obtain permits to serve liquor to private groups in banquet facilities during hours other than those stated by law. If this is the case, the property must make this known to guests and tell them how to obtain the special approvals/ permits. In addition, you may need to curtail beverage service on election days in some states.

The property is responsible for ensuring that guests adhere to minimum age drinking laws; you cannot delegate this responsibility to the client. Because of this responsibility, it is wise for a banquet official to closely monitor

This established banquet dinner menu features many gourmet entree selections at a variety of prices.

Exhibit 12.12 Checklist for After-Banquet Duties

Banquet Service Staff
- [ ] Clear all tables of china, glass, silverware, and ashtrays.
- [ ] Remove all linens.
- [ ] Straighten legs on all tables.
- [ ] Rearrange all chairs around tables neatly.
- [ ] Store salt and pepper shakers, sugar bowls, ashtrays, water pitchers, etc.
- [ ] Clear all remaining carts and lock them.
- [ ] Remove candles and any melted wax from candelabras and return to storage.
- [ ] Pour several pitchers of water into garbage cans in kitchen to prevent possible fire hazard.
- [ ] Check out with supervisor on duty.

Banquet Supervisor
- [ ] Supervise the banquet service staff.
- [ ] Turn off public address system.
- [ ] Collect microphones and cords and return to proper storage area(s).
- [ ] Collect projectors and other audio-visual equipment and return to storage.
- [ ] Search area for valuable items left behind.
- [ ] Check cloakroom and restroom areas.
- [ ] Secure any items found and turn in to Lost and Found the following day.
- [ ] Inspect for fire hazards.
- [ ] Turn off lights.
- [ ] Lock all doors. (If a band is moving out, alert front desk personnel.)
- [ ] Leave written information regarding any maintenance problems or items helpful to the supervisor who will open the room the next day.
- [ ] Leave written information on the banquet manager's desk regarding any guest complaints or serious employee relations problems.
- [ ] Lock, secure, and turn off lights and air conditioning units in all other banquet rooms.

beverage service when underaged guests are present.

Food and Beverage Services for Conventions and Annual Events

Conventions. Selling food and beverage services for conventions is different from selling them for social events (e.g., wedding receptions, holiday banquets). Convention planners generally base their budget for food and beverage products on the previous year's costs—often with a small increase to cover inflation. This is a mistaken approach, for they are overlooking such variables as cost-of-living variances in different geographic locations. (Many conventions are held in a different location each year.) So that convention planners will not arrive at their property with a predetermined budget, experienced catering executives contact them many months ahead of time, before they determine their budgets.

If a convention that is booked several years ahead will require large quantities of food and beverage products, the director of catering could try to attend the convention the previous year. Not only will his/her attendance at the convention enable him/her to meet the planners, but he/she can also observe details about food and beverage needs and book all the functions connected with the convention for the next year. Guests always prefer to deal with people who take the time to understand their needs. They

SHERATON WASHINGTON HOTEL

T.2 AMERICA THE BOUNTIFUL RECEPTION
Minimum of 1,000 guests.
CAN BE TAILORED BY FEWER GUESTS
APPROXIMATELY 15-16 PIECES HORS D' OEUVRES PER PERSON

America's abundance is exemplified as we conduct a food fantasy flight from its heartland to its
four far-flung geographical corners. As a people, we have been shaped as much by the foods we have
eaten as by democratic ideals; we are taller, stronger, healthier than our ancestors.
We are, in a sense, a nation that food has made possible.
Join us now, gastronomic traveler, as we enjoy an exciting tour of regional foods.
Elevated in the center of the room, we will place a huge replica of the symbol of our American freedom
and independence—the Liberty Bell—and surround it with the flags of all 50 states.

From the Nation's heartland,
we will present a Mid-America cheese and bread display to consist of
an elaborate selection of Domestic Cheeses in large wheels and chunks, garnished with Fresh Fruit
and accompanied by baskets of whole Bread of all varieties, Lavoche and Assorted Crackers,
complemented by a toast to California: serving Cabernet Sauvignon, Chablis and Grenache Rose
wines of California vintage charged as consumed.

The New England States will feature:
Fresh Clams and Oysters shucked to order, served with Cocktail Sauce, Horseradish, Tabasco,
Lemon Wedges and Oysterettes

Crab Claws, Cold Jumbo Shrimp, garnished with Lemon Stars and Parsley,
accompanied with Remoulade Sauce and Cocktail Sauce

Large round chafing dishes of:
Clams Casino on Rock Salt, Oysters Rockefeller on Rock Salt, Scallops wrapped in Bacon

Deep Fried Maine Potato Skins served with Sour Cream

Steamship Round of Corned Beef,
carved in room and served on New York-style Rye Bread with Horseradish, Mustard and Mayonnaise

From the South, we will serve:
Ham and Buttermilk Biscuits, Country Style Sausage and Biscuits, Southern Style Fried Chicken Drumettes

Half Ears of Corn placed on a popsicle stick, heated in the room in large boiling pot, and Drawn Butter

Fried Catfish Pieces with Tartar Sauce

The Crepe au Crab station, individual Crabmeat Crepes
prepared to order, flambed in the style of New Orleans with a taste of the Gulf Shores

Farmer's Market of Fresh Whole Vegetables displayed in old crates and baskets and accompanied with
Sliced Fresh Vegetables served on crushed ice and to include: Zucchini, Cauliflower, Carrots,
Cherry Tomatoes, Celery, Mushrooms, Green Beans, Broccoli with Dill, Sour Cream and Cheese Dips

(CONTINUED)

SHERATON WASHINGTON HOTEL

T.2 AMERICA THE BOUNTIFUL RECEPTION
(CONTINUED)

From the Great Southwest,
A station for the preparation of Tacos made to order by attendant in costume
Mini Barbecued Texas-style Spare Ribs, Bowls of Guacamole Dip with Tostadas

From the West Coast,
We present the flavor of San Francisco's Oriental population, Peking-style Duck,
prepared in the room by attendant in costume. Duck is wrapped in Mandarin Pancakes with Plum Sauce
and a sprinkle of Scallions and Chinese Parsley

Whole Poached Kennebec Salmon presented on mirrors with Troncons of Salmon en Bellevue

Crabmeat Won Ton with Selection of Sauces, Oriental mixture of Crabmeat and Vegetables
captured in a Flaky Pastry Shell

Spinach Quiche a la San Francisco, a delightful contemporary treatment of a popular French creation
Oriental Egg Rolls, English Mustard and Sweet and Sour Sauce

For the Sweet Side of the Evening

Presented in creatively sculptured ice socles, an elaborate display of Fresh Fruits
to include:
Pineapple, Assorted Melon, Blueberries, Strawberries, Kiwi and Mangoes,
accompanied by Brown Sugar and Whipped Cream,
Petite chafing dishes of Chocolate Fondue

Shuckers $55.00 each (3 hours)
Carvers $55.00 each (3 hours)

Special banquet reception menu for a minimum of 1,000 guests that emphasizes regional and ethnic foods. (Courtesy of Sheraton Washington Hotel, Washington, D.C.)

also appreciate working with one hotel representative from the beginning to the end of the banquet event.

Annual Events. Annual events are the foundation of a good banquet operation. After a property has scheduled all its annual events, the catering department can then solicit other accounts and additional convention business to round out the schedule for the year. Exhibit 12.13 lists potential markets, their lead sources, and possible functions that could be organized and catered for them. Effective catering executives solicit annual events from other hotels on a daily basis. Visiting the competition and looking at their bulletin or function boards are good ways to see "who goes where."

The annual banquet business is very competitive. A cost of 50 cents or less per guest can make the difference between a planner's choosing one property over another. Imagine, a property can lose a dinner for 2,000 people due to the price of a garnish or salad.

Don't assume that annual business functions will stay with your property forever. If their events are not handled properly, clients will move quickly to another property. One of the fastest ways to lose an account is to take it for granted. It is always important to make an extra effort to help the guest whenever possible. Build a personal relationship and when clients phone, take their room reservations personally, don't switch the call. Whether they are from political, religious, union, or social groups, annual banquet clients not only run their own affairs but usually serve on committees for other events. The more involved the banquet staff is with the clients, the more the clients will generate new business leads for the property. Exhibit 12.14 is an example of a form used to summarize infor-

Exhibit 12.13 Examples of Potential Banquet Markets

Markets/Submarkets	Lead Source	Possible Functions
Hospitals		
Auxiliary	Public Relations or Administrative Office	Luncheon fashion shows, evening fund-raisers, art auctions, etc.
Medical Staff	Medical Staff Secretary	Quarterly or annual dinners/dances graduation dinners (interns)
Volunteer Functions	Director of Volunteers	Lunches
Employee Recreation Club	Personnel Office	Christmas parties, seasonal parties dinner/dances
Employee Awards Dinner	Personnel Office	Usually midweek dinners
Credit Union	President of Credit Union	Annual dinner/dance or meeting
Colleges & Universities		
Alumni	Alumni Office, University Affairs Office, or individual schools	Recruiting parties, annual dinner dance, class reunions, fund-raisers, alumni functions related to athletic events
Sororities and Fraternities	Panhellenic or Inter-Fraternity Council or social chairperson of each sorority or fraternity (University Affairs Office)	Founders day luncheons, formal installations, dinner/dances
Ceremonial Events	University Affairs Office	Groundbreaking, dedication events
Athletics	Athletic Department, Business Manager, Athletic Director	Awards dinner/alumni events
Department Functions (e.g., math, physics, or English department)	Department Head	Dinner meetings
Graduation Parties	Affairs Office for graduating classes/schools	Weeknight & weekend dinner functions
Faculty & Staff Functions	Faculty Club President, Personnel or Business Office	Dinners
High Schools		
Proms	School Office for names of class officers	Friday night dinners
Reunions (past years) 10 year, 25 year, etc.	School Office	Weekend dinner/dance

Exhibit 12.13, continued

Markets/Submarkets	Lead Source	Possible Functions
Athletic Dinners	Athletic Office	Awards banquets
Faculty Events	Faculty Club President	Annual banquet
Churches/Synagogues		
Anniversary Events	Pastor's Office, Rabbi's Office, Church or Temple Business Manager	Annual dinner, usually weeknights
Women's Council or Auxiliary	Church Office	Fashion show luncheon
Choir	Musical Director or Church Office	Annual dinner
Budget Finance Committee	Church Office	Dinner meetings
Banks		
Employee Clubs (25/50 yr.)	Personnel Office	Midweek dinners, holiday parties
Stockholders Meeting	Administrative Office	Annual meeting, various meal functions
Friends of the Bank	Corporate Development Office	Dinners/meetings
Local Corporations		
Long-Term Employee Clubs	Personnel Office	Dinners & dinner/dance
Retirement Dinners	Personnel Office	Weekday dinners
Credit Unions	Credit Union Office	Annual meeting or dinner/dances
Employee Groups	Personnel Office	Holiday parties
Charitable Groups, Service Clubs, & Miscellaneous Organizations		
Charitable Groups (e.g., American Heart Assn., Cerebral Palsy)	Chamber of Commerce, Public Library	Fund-raising banquets
Men's Club, Women's Assn. (e.g., Rotary, Lions, etc.)	Chamber of Commerce	Midweek luncheons, evening functions
Professional Associations		
State/Local Bar Assn., Medical Assn., Home-builders Assn., etc.	Chamber of Commerce, Public Library	Monthly luncheon or dinner meetings, annual dinner/dance
Miscellaneous Markets		
Weddings	Newspapers	Receptions & dinners, rehearsal dinners

Exhibit 12.13, continued

Markets/Submarkets	Lead Source	Possible Functions
Bowling Leagues	Secretary of League, Manager of Bowling Alley	Weeknight awards dinner (low budget)
Political Organizations	Local Party Chairman	Dinners
Major Department Stores, (Long-Term Employee Clubs, Store Anniversaries)	Personnel Office	Midweek/weekend dinner functions, holiday parties
Cultural/Musical Organizations (Opera, Ballet Society, etc.)	Chamber of Commerce	Weekend evening dinners
Local Youth Sports Groups (e.g., Little League, Adult Softball Leagues)	Little League Regional Headquarters (for names of local groups); County, City or Town Recreation Dept. (has names of all leagues)	Awards dinner (low budget)

Courtesy of Resorts International Hotel and Casino, Atlantic City, New Jersey.

mation about lost business. Careful study of this information, especially for several lost events, can help catering and banquet departments revise sales strategies to minimize future business losses.

Pricing Banquets

Many banquet departments do not objectively consider the relationship between profit and price when they make pricing decisions. Information to be used in establishing a pricing structure should be obtained from an operating budget developed specifically for the banquet department. The operating budget is a profit plan. Once you determine the profit you expect the banquet department to generate, you can use the costs expressed by the budget to establish both a base selling price for each function and a foundation against which you can monitor the banquet department's operations.

Hypothetically, if the banquet department's budget projects income of $100,000 and food costs of $25,000, you could develop a simple base markup for food; banquet food income

Exhibit 12.14 Sample Report of Lost Business Form

Courtesy of Sheraton-Washington Hotel, Washington, D.C.

Keep Banquets Profitable

Labor costs can be the largest single expense in many operations. In fact, in some metropolitan hotels, labor costs represent approximately 40 to 50% of all sales income.

Consider labor costs when you sell banquets. Do you want to offer Cornish game hen, which has a very low food cost, but requires such labor-intensive tasks as boning and stuffing? Or, should the catering executive attempt to sell filet mignon or prime rib of beef, which has a higher food cost but requires less food preparation resulting in very low labor costs? The answer to these questions depends on the specific situation. However, banquet officials must at least be aware of the impact that labor costs can have on their profits.

($100,000) divided by banquet food costs ($25,000) equals a base markup of 4.0. In this example, you could mark up the food costs an average of four or five times to arrive at a selling price, depending on what your clients will pay and what the competition charges. However, this is only an example; it is up to each property to determine its own pricing system. You may want to use a smaller markup to generate business during slow periods or a higher markup when business is more ensured or less desirable. You could use a menu markup factor to price both established menus and special menus developed for a specific function. You could also use these basic procedures to price beverages.

In addition, you can use budget information to monitor the banquet department's performance. In the previous example, you can establish a standard (potential) food cost percentage; budgeted food costs ($25,000) divided by budgeted banquet income ($100,000) equals 25%. Said another way, banquet officials can study monthly income statements knowing that the banquet food cost percentage should be approximately 25% in order for the department to attain its budget plans.

Generally, you also mark up miscellaneous services, such as flowers, music, valet parking, candy and cigars, and special equipment, especially when the property does not provide them, to yield a reasonable profit for the property. For example, if your property contracts with a flower shop to provide decorations or with an entertainment group to provide music, you might charge the client more than the price of the flowers or entertainment to cover the costs of securing these services.

Banquet Contracts

After the catering executive and client have agreed on the exact terms of the special function, they should confirm the terms in a contract. Exhibit 12.15 is a contract that one property uses. Every detail which the two parties have discussed and agreed upon should be written on the contract. The client should also be alerted to the requirement of a guaranteed number of guests (paragraph three).

It is important to determine an approximate guest count at the time the contract is signed. However, since the special event itself may be held months or years from the date that the contract is signed, the catering representative cannot require a definite guest count at that time. Some operations contact the client approximately two weeks before the event to get an update on the expected number of guests. Of course, if the event is large or requires special purchases, the property will make this contact a month or more in advance of the function. In some cases, ticket sales fluctuate so much from the original proposal that the client may need a larger or smaller room. Generally, two days before the event, the client must state the final number of guests expected.

Banquet contracts typically address minimums and guarantees. Sometimes, the guarantee becomes the minimum; the property will charge the client for a minimum number of guests but will serve an additional specified percentage should more guests attend the function.

Other operations apply a guarantee to either side of a base. For example, if the guarantee is set at 240 guests with a 5% variance factor, the client

Exhibit 12.15 Sample Banquet Contract

CONFIRMATION (STANDARD FUNCTION CONTRACT) — HOTEL DU PONT Wilmington, Delaware 19899 656-8121 — GS 10755 REV. 10-79

TENTATIVE ☐ DEFINITE ☐

NAME OF PATRON — CHARGE TO
ADDRESS — ADDRESS
FUNCTION — PHONE NO. — ROOM(S) ENGAGED
TIME: FROM — TO — SERVING TIME — GUARANTEE — SET FOR — PRICE PER PERSON

PLEASE NOTE: FINAL ARRANGEMENTS REQUIRED TWO WEEKS BEFORE DATE OF FUNCTION.

MENU — OTHER SERVICES

_____ deposit required to reserve facilities. Refundable if Patron cancels function in writing at least 90 days prior to date.
Total estimated cost

FOR HOTEL DU PONT

FOR YOUR SIGNATURE
(please approve within 30 days and return one copy with your deposit)

NOTE: This agreement includes the terms listed on the reverse side of this form.

1. The Patron hires and the Hotel agrees to furnish the services herein set forth in accordance to the terms hereof.

2. The Hotel reserves the right to require additional payments or full payment at any time prior to the scheduled date of the function.

3. Patron agrees to advise the Hotel at least 48 hours in advance of the function of the definite number of guests. This figure will be used as the guaranteed minimum. Hotel shall not be responsible for service or accommodations to more than 5% increase over minimum guaranteed attendance.

4. Unless the Hotel is provided with satisfactory credit references for Patron and explicitly waives its right to advance payment, seventy-five percent (75%) of the total estimated cost for the function must be paid by Patron at least two weeks prior to the date of the function and the remainder must be paid within thirty (30) days after the function. The Hotel reserves the right to cancel this agreement and the function to which it pertains within ten (10) days prior to the function if the required advance payment is not received. Furthermore, in the event of any failure to make any payment due the Hotel, the Patron hereby agrees to be personally liable for such payment.

5. No food or beverage of any kind can be permitted to be brought into the Hotel by the Patron or any of the Patron's guests or invitees.

6. Patron assumes responsibility for any and all damages caused by it or any of its guests, invitees, or other persons attending the function, whether in rooms reserved or in any other part of the Hotel.

7. Patron shall not put up any displays within the Hotel without the permission of the Hotel.

8. Patron agrees not to enter into any contracts for music or other forms of entertainment or other service or accommodation in connection with this function, without prior consent of the Hotel.

9. In the event that the Hotel, at request of Patron, furnishes any food, beverages, or any other services not provided for in this contract, Patron agrees to pay Hotel the charges thereof.

10. In the event this agreement is signed in the name of a corporation, partnership, association, club, or society, the person signing represents to the Hotel that he has full authority to sign such contract, and that in the event that he is not so authorized, he will be personally liable for the faithful performance of this contract.

will have to pay for at least 234 guests and the property will prepare for a maximum of 246 guests. The variance factor is the difference between the maximum number of guests for whom the property prepared and the minimum number of guests for whom the client must pay.

The difference in this case is 12 guests, which is 5% of 240. Six guests are on either side of the guaranteed 240 guest base. Of course, if the menu is unusual or difficult to prepare, the guarantee plan may not be as flexible.

If possible, the catering department should

Sell a Wine Centerpiece

A magnum of white wine or champagne can substitute for other table decorations and serve two purposes at one time—it is both decorative and drinkable. (In addition, it most likely will be profitable.) The bottle can be placed in an ice-filled container that is elevated in the center of the table by being placed on an inverted soup plate. To hide the soup plate, cover it with a napkin that is either the same color as the tablecloth or a contrasting color.

The Spin-Off Effects of Banquets

Quality banquet service can be an excellent source of revenue for a hotel. In addition to the income generated by the banquet itself, consider the following possible benefits:

1. Additional guestrooms are often sold.
2. Room service business increases because of the additional room sales.
3. Special receptions in hospitality suites may be booked before or after the banquet.
4. Meal service at dining periods other than the banquet may increase because guests attending the special function may stay at the property.
5. Flower sales increase. (Flowers are often sold by the hotel or the hotel florist; if it is the latter, the hotel often gets a commission.)
6. Limousine service, hotel photography studios, and related guest services (which frequently pay commissions to the hotel) may enjoy increased business.
7. Receipts from parking lot fees may increase.
8. Hairdresser and barber shops may enjoy increased business. (Contracts which establish rental rates plus a percentage of the sales from these services benefit the hotel.)
9. Gift certificates and weekend or other packages custom-made for banquet attendees may influence these guests to stay over. (Such marketing activities as free champagne breakfasts for guests who stay over can also generate increased revenues.)

make the final arrangements for the menu, beverages, required services, and price for large functions several months prior to the date of the event. After all the arrangements have been made, the confirmation (standard function contract) is sent to the client for acceptance.

Unless the property receives satisfactory credit references from the client, he/she often needs to pay a specific portion or as much as 100% of the estimated cost of the function at least two weeks in advance of the event's date. Typically, the client must pay any remainder within 30 days of the function. Catering departments generally reserve the right to cancel any function if the client has not established proper credit or made the required advance payment.

The contract must indicate the exact products/services which will be provided. The food, beverages, labor, and other direct costs incurred to produce and serve the items required by the contract are included in the price. But what about rental of the special function rooms? Some properties require a payment if the cost of the event does not exceed a specific amount. Other operations require a room rental payment for events without dinner. Typically, hoteliers do include the following services in room rental rates:

1. Setup labor for normal meetings (tables, chairs, tablecloths, ice water, and ashtrays).
2. Movement of large furniture in the room to other locations.
3. Removal of carpets.
4. Public address system and microphones (without special attendants during the event).
5. Movie screen, table for projector, easels, chartboard, and extension cords.

The following services are often not included in rental rates but are charged for separately:

1. Electrical layouts for exhibits.
2. Movie projector, slide projector, overhead projector, tape recorder, etc. (These items may be available from the property for an additional charge, or the hotel might obtain them for a markup fee. See Exhibit 12.3.)
3. Table decorations.
4. Dance floor.
5. Service staff.

Determining the Client's Budget

Catering sales representatives must learn the amount of money which the prospective client wants to spend early in the negotiation process. In order to develop the budget, it is necessary to know exactly what the client desires and the number of guests the catering department is expected to serve.

The property should try to accommodate the client by providing the highest possible value for the dollars the client wishes to spend. If the client has used the hotel's services previously, the catering representative can review past records to assess the price range which will most likely interest the potential guest. Alternatively, the representative can show the client established menus and tactfully suggest items that might be of interest. Selecting menus for discussion and heeding comments from the client will help eliminate the need to ask, "How much do you want to spend?" The effective salesperson has good culinary training and/or experience and is able to suggest creative food and beverage items which fall within the prospective client's budget.

Protocol for Banquets

Banquet service staff must always be courteous and exercise common sense to make the guests' experiences as enjoyable as possible. They must demonstrate an appreciation for the opportunity to serve guests. In addition, they should understand protocol—the formal rules of etiquette used for ceremonies of state, military functions, and other special events.

While the details of protocol are beyond the scope of this book,[2] banquet organizers should understand that there are rules which dictate the proper way to do things when very special guests are served. Not only should the banquet management staff know protocol, but the service employees who come in direct contact with special guests must also understand and be able to practice principles of protocol.

A few of the rules that typically apply to special functions are discussed in the following section. (When planning special events which are to be attended by heads of state or other very special officials, you should review the refer-

ences cited on this page for more specific information.)

Seating at the Head Table

At formal events, the seat of honor at the head table is to the **right** of the host. The second seat of honor is to the **left** of the host. If another seat of honor is required, it is the second seat on the right of the host. The balance of seats at the head table should be allocated according to the rank or prominence of the guests. These guests should be assigned to seats by going from the right and the left of the host out from the center of the head table. Exhibit 12.16 illustrates seating arrangements at the head table.

Flag Display in the United States

Flags are also important concerns in protocol. For example, in America, at a cocktail party, standing gathering, or theater-style seated event where flags must be positioned before the guests arrive, the United States flag is placed on the guests' **visual left** when they enter the room.

If a five-place arched flag stand is used, the U.S. flag takes the center (highest) position. Other flags are placed to the left and right of the U.S. flag in order of importance. As illustrated in Exhibit 12.17, the second most important flag is placed in the next hole on the audience's visual left, then on the visual right, etc.

When flags are used behind a podium, the national colors are placed on the physical right of the speaker as he/she addresses the audience.

---

2   More detailed information about protocol is found in: Virginia Depew, ed., *The Social List of Washington, D.C.* (Kensington, Md.: Jean Shaw Murray, 1980); Mary Jane McCaffree and Pauline Innis, *Protocol: The Complete Handbook of Diplomatic, Official, and Social Usage* (Englewood Cliffs, N.J.: Prentice-Hall, 1977); and Elizabeth Post, *Emily Post's Etiquette* (New York: Funk & Wagnalls, 1969).

Exhibit 12.16 Protocol: Seating Guests

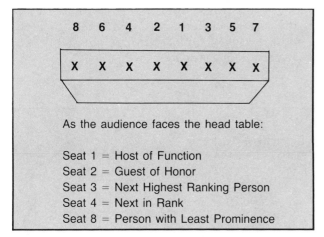

As the audience faces the head table:

Seat 1 = Host of Function
Seat 2 = Guest of Honor
Seat 3 = Next Highest Ranking Person
Seat 4 = Next in Rank
Seat 8 = Person with Least Prominence

Exhibit 12.17 Five-Place Arched Flag Stand

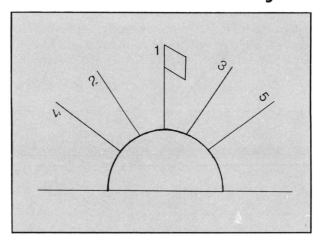

When displayed behind a speaker's platform without a staff, the flag must be placed flat and horizontally, directly behind and slightly above the podium. The union of stars is always placed to the observer's upper left. When displaying flags on crossed staffs, the flag of the United States is placed on the visual left (flag's own right) and its staff is placed in front of the other flag.

Do not decorate with the American flag. You cannot use the American flag for table covers, as a drape, as rosettes, or as any other type of decoration. To decorate with bunting that has the national colors, place the color blue uppermost, then white, and finally red as the lowest of the three colors.

Banquet Income Control

Normally, sales income is not collected from guests at the time of the banquet. Rather, the contract specifies the payment terms to which the catering department and the sponsor/host agree. However, after the banquet occurs, the catering representative must accurately assess the number of guests served to determine if payment is due for guests served in excess of the minimum.

How do you determine the number of guests for pricing purposes? If you provide a buffet where no one goes back for seconds or uses more than one plate, take a plate count. (The number of plates on the buffet line at the beginning of service minus the number of plates on the buffet line at the end of service equals the number of guests served.)

At buffets where guests go through the line more than once or at table service events, the primary responsibility for determining the number of guests served rests with the captain or other banquet official in charge of the function. He/she must count the number of dinners served. Typically, the captain takes a count which he/she confirms with separate counts taken by other officials in charge of specific areas of the dining room and/or counts of meals served by individual food servers. Frequently, someone counts the number of empty seats and subtracts it from the total number of chairs set up to arrive at the number of guests served. In some properties, the guests receive tickets from their host which they turn in either as they enter the banquet room or after they are seated.

At stand-up receptions, a representative of the property could be stationed at the entrance of the reception area to count guests as they arrive. To avoid re-counting guests who leave and return, the ticket system discussed above could be used; the count of guests served is based on the number of tickets turned in.

At coffee breaks and similar functions, the price is based on the volume of products used to set up the affair, such as gallons of coffee or dozens of pastry. If, however, the price of these functions is determined by the number of people served, a property official should count the number of guests seated in the meeting immediately before the start of coffee service.

Regardless of the procedures used to establish the number of guests served, it is always best to involve the client or his/her representative. If the client wishes to monitor these tallies, allow him/her to do so. The catering department does not wish to have any disagreement over pricing. When the client is involved in determining the count, a difference of opinion is not likely to occur. (Sales income control in banquet bars is discussed in Chapter 14.)

Banquet Guests Deserve Privacy

All staff members must understand the need to protect the privacy of banquet guests. They should not answer any questions posed by members of the press about lavish banquets or special functions sponsored or attended by politicians, influential community members, those in sports or entertainment fields, or any others. It is up to the sponsor, not the property, to publicize fund-raisers. Staff members who come in direct contact with the guests should be discreet; discretion is the key to all activities. They should not discuss any business overheard at a table, repeat details about the cost of the banquet, or mention anything else about what went on before, during, or after an event. Service personnel should refer any requests for information about a special function to top management in the banquet, food and beverage, and/or sales departments. Management, of course, should know when the banquet host/hostess desires publicity. Then staff members likely to receive phone calls from the press can be alerted about this desire and will know who to contact for press releases and conferences.

Managing Service at the Hotel Columbia
Page Twenty-Four

Lewis had worked carefully with Carolyn White, the catering director, to develop selling procedures for banquet sales representatives and planning and delivering procedures for banquet staff. Now they could turn their attention to extra touches that could promote repeat business at the Hotel Columbia. Working together, Carolyn and Lewis developed the following procedures that employees would routinely practice to promote repeat business:

1. The banquet sales representative who worked with the client during the initial planning for the event should personally greet the host/sponsor on the day of the event. If that is not possible, another sales representative should meet and greet the client, express appreciation for the business, and provide information about whom he/she can contact should any problems evolve during the event.

2. Immediately after the function, someone from the executive staff (e.g., the president of the Hotel Columbia or the vice president for food and beverage) should contact the client while he/she is still in the property. The purpose for this interaction is to obtain the client's view of the event, show him/her that everyone at the Hotel Columbia really cared about the event, and thank the client very sincerely for his/her business.

3. On the morning after the event, the sales representative should contact the client to again inquire about the event, handle any last-minute details, and thank the client once more for the opportunity to host the event.

4. Within a week of the event, someone should send a thank-you letter to the client. It should not be a form letter. (At this point the catering director and Lewis couldn't decide whether the property's president and managing director, the catering director, the banquet sales representative, or all three should sign the letter—or whether separate letters should be sent from each.)

Managing Service at the Hotel Columbia
Page Twenty-Four, continued

5. When an association or business with a recurring need for food and beverage-related events sponsors a particular event, the sales representative involved should send another letter approximately six weeks after the event to indicate a willingness to work again with the client to meet all of his/her banquet needs creatively. If the event is an annual one, the sales representative could also use the letter to request permission to establish a tentative booking for the next event. (The Hotel Columbia would use an internal tracing and follow-up system to maintain contact with the client.)

6. Whenever the property revises established banquet menus, the banquet sales department should send sample copies to all prospective clients—including those who had recently done business with the Hotel Columbia.

7. The banquet sales department should establish a schedule for occasional telephone calls to stress, "We would like you to consider us for your banquet needs."

8. At an appropriate time, a sales representative should invite the client to the hotel for a personal discussion about how the Hotel Columbia could help with his/her special function needs.

Lewis knew that developing and maintaining a banquet business required a great deal of effort. However, he also knew that the profits generated by the banquet department could easily make the extra effort cost-effective. He and Carolyn vowed that generating new banquet business would not take a back seat to planning previously booked events. Obviously, both are necessary for banquet success, and both would receive high priority at the Hotel Columbia.

Lewis was pleased about the pre-opening plans of his entire department. The Hotel Columbia would open in two weeks and all the planning, policies, and procedures would be put to the test. He was confident that he and his staff would be ready and that the guests would be pleased.

13

Other Dining Services

Food and beverages can be sold in a wide variety of outlets not discussed in the previous four chapters. The professional restaurant manager must know how to plan, control, and evaluate service in these outlets as well as in coffee shops, room service, dining rooms, and banquet rooms. This chapter gives an overview of managing service in operations that range from vending and fast food services to club and show operations.

Vending Machine Services

Many lodging properties use vending machines to dispense food and beverage products. Such machines are placed in or near the lobby, on guest floors, and in other public areas. They are also used in employee dining rooms and other back-of-house areas. Vending machines may be owned or leased by the property or operated by a vending service company. Regardless of whether the hotel owns or leases vending machines, management must have some knowledge about this mechanical service.

Advantages and Disadvantages

Vending services are efficient; they can offer a number of products around the clock, and can provide a service to employees and guests at little or no cost to the property. (Commission rebates to the property are even a possibility when another company operates the machines.) The use of vending services also helps control the time that service must be available in the coffee shop, dining room, and elsewhere.

Of course, vending services do have some disadvantages, the main one being that the service is impersonal. While during times of heavy use in some large vending machine operations an attendant is available to restock machines, keep the area clean, and provide information to machine users, usually vending service offers no contact with food service employees. Another

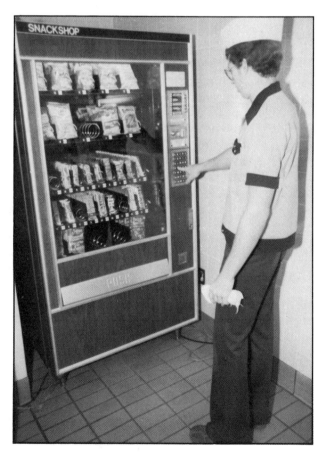

Employee using vending machine. (Amway Grand Plaza Hotel, Grand Rapids, Michigan)

Managing Service at the Hotel Columbia
Page Twenty-Five

At last! The Hotel Columbia had opened, and what a hectic several weeks they had had. However, the planning efforts and training programs had paid off. While a number of problems did arise, many more had been anticipated that obviously had been forestalled. Lewis Scott was satisfied with past efforts but also ready to confront new situations as they arose.

Lewis had known that the Hotel Columbia needed to offer entertainment on a regular basis in one or more of its lounges and possibly in the Eagle Room and La Terrasse. He wanted to please the guests, but at the same time it was necessary to attain the property's economic goals. How could he match the guests' desires for entertainment with the property's economic concerns?

Lewis and Don Jackson had trained their various managers in techniques that could help them assess the various financial implications of offering entertainment. The managers could use the procedures to conduct feasibility studies and make operating decisions about this important subject.

disadvantage is that vending machines generally cannot offer a wide variety of quality products. In some cases, guests are wary of vending machines because of past experiences with them—they may have received stale or even moldy products previously, or they may have lost money in vending machines. A final disadvantage of vending machines is the increase in service costs if special equipment is required (such as microwave ovens) so that hot foods can be offered.

Typically, guests recognize the drawbacks of vending machines, but they find that well-run vending services have these key elements: the machines function well mechanically, they are well stocked, they do not run out of change, they are in top sanitary condition and, when applicable, they serve high-quality coffee.

Management should consider all the costs and benefits of purchasing or leasing vending machines for the hospitality facility. Since it is unlikely that technicians will be available on-site for the maintenance and repair of the machines, such costs should be considered. If the property is planning to operate its own vending machines, the cost analysis must indicate that the savings or profit resulting from self-operation, less all the applicable direct and indirect costs, will be greater than the possible commissions from the vending machine company.

Unfortunately, many hospitality operations pay little or no attention to vending services. Not only does this attitude reveal a lack of concern for marketing details, but it also leads to decreased profits and increased costs.

Cafeteria Food Service

An American is credited with inventing the cafeteria. During the California Gold Rush days in the nineteenth century, John Krueger designed a commercial food outlet patterned after the Swedish smorgasbord. Before the turn of the century, New York City's first cafeteria had opened.

As the end of the twentieth century approaches, lodging properties continue to offer cafeteria operations. Cafeterias provide fast, low-check-average service, they allow food service in facilities that cannot hire a large number of service employees, and they lend themselves to increased lunch business from nonhotel guests working or visiting near the hotel. (Generally, an external entrance to the cafeteria is needed to realize the benefits of external business.)

From the guests' perspective, the key elements of a well-run cafeteria are (1) the constant availability of trays that are clean and dry, (2) an orderly and efficient traffic flow and speed, (3) well-trained counter attendants and cashiers, (4) appealing food presentation, (5) a reasonable number of food and beverage choices, and (6) efficient and quiet busing.

Exhibit 13.1 shows some popular cafeteria

Exhibit 13.1 Alternative Cafeteria Layouts

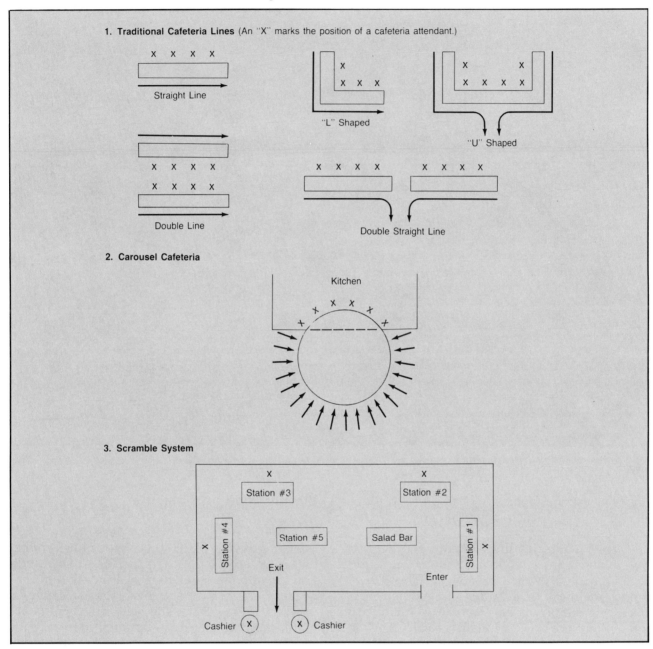

layouts. While traditionally guests obtained trays, walked alongside a stationary serving counter, and requested and received items from attendants working behind the counter, modern cafeterias offer many variations. Some of these are carousel cafeterias, scramble systems, and "help yourself" lines.

Carousel cafeterias feature a rotating counter similar to a very large lazy Susan. Guests may stand in one place while the food moves in front of them, and make their selections as the food items pass by.

Scramble systems offer guests the opportunity to move between a number of serving stations. For example, if they do not wish a salad, they do not have to stand in line while other

Exhibit 13.2 Well-Designed Modern Buffet/Cafeteria

Courtesy of Bishop Buffets, Inc., Cedar Rapids, Iowa

guests select this item; they can walk to other service stations which offer the products that they desire.

"Help yourself" lines require very few, if any, cafeteria line attendants. Rather, the guests portion the items which they desire. This plan is almost identical to a buffet line, although it places less emphasis on elaborate presentation and centerpieces. Occasionally, a cafeteria line attendant may be needed to portion the most expensive items for the guests.

In the past, cafeterias featured stainless steel islands that looked rather institutional and provided little if any atmosphere or ambience. Increasingly, however, cafeteria serving lines are made of materials such as wood, plastic, and chrome and feature nontraditional paintings, designs, and other amenities which make the cafeteria look anything but drab. Exhibit 13.2 illustrates a modern buffet/cafeteria.

Placing Food on Cafeteria Lines

Optional items, such as desserts and side salads, are often placed on cafeteria lines so that guests pass by them first; then the more traditional components of the meal follow (entrees, vegetables, breads, and beverages). Managers use this strategy with the belief that guests are more likely to select the optional items if they cannot see how full their trays will be after they have selected the other meal components. Also, since guests are likely to be hungry, they may select the first items that they see. These optional items need to be attractive and suitably garnished, the products themselves must look delicious, and the serving dishes used must enhance their appearance.

Well-designed posters, promotional information on the cafeteria line, and advertising buttons on employee uniforms are examples of

Cafeteria Locations

Many people associate cafeterias with such settings as schools, colleges, hospitals, nursing homes, and manufacturing plants. However, cafeteria service can also be found in large department stores, office complexes, airports, and even in supermarkets. A number of hotels offer their employees cafeteria programs, and some—such as those connected with office buildings or airports—offer cafeteria services to both in-house and walk-in guests. In addition, some self-contained restaurants use cafeteria rather than table service systems.

internal advertising devices that can be used to draw the guests' attention to certain items. Announcements on outdoor signs, advertisements in newspapers, and word-of-mouth recommendations from satisfied guests are external marketing methods.

When scramble cafeteria systems are used, such devices as signs over specific stations (e.g., salads, entrees, desserts) may be needed to inform guests quickly about the system's operation and the location of specific foods.

Unlike table service, in which guests do not see items until after they order them, cafeteria guests have a first-hand look at the products they can order. Thus, foods must be attractive and creatively presented. Neat and well-garnished arrangements of portioned items in serving counter pans and portioned salads on beds of shaved ice help create a visual effect that will help whet guests' appetites. It is also important to keep the serving counter areas clean. The cafeteria manager will do well to walk down the public side of the cafeteria line before opening (as well as frequently during service), and ask the question, "If I were a guest, how would the serving area look to me?" Often, surveying the serving area from the public's viewpoint can alert him/her to food presentation and related problems.

Cafeteria Personnel

While one of the advantages of cafeteria service is that it generally requires fewer service personnel than table service, some service staff will be required. Following is a brief discussion of their duties and responsibilities.

Line Attendants. When cafeteria line attendants

portion the foods that guests order, they serve as salespeople representing the operation to the guest. Guests may expect the attendants to inform them about available items, make suggestions about accompaniments for entrees, and take care of miscellaneous problems which arise. As is true for any dining room food server, cafeteria line attendants should be very neat, well groomed, and clean; be able to serve the public tactfully; know about the operation and the menu; and be professional and competent.

In some operations, the cafeteria line attendant must supply the line. For instance, the attendant may have to walk to the kitchen or other preparation area, fill the cafeteria line pans, and/or roll carts of portioned food items to the line. In other, perhaps more properly designed facilities, food needed to replenish the line is held close to it in reach-in or roll-in hot and cold food cabinets that are built into the walls separating the cafeteria from the preparation area. When some properties set up cafeteria lines in remote locations, they use heated and chilled mobile food carts that keep food at the proper serving temperature until attendants place it on the serving line.

In some properties, especially those with brief periods of guest service, cafeteria line attendants perform other functions. They may prepare food before the serving line opens, and/or clean up the dining room and dishes after service has ended. When cafeteria line attendants perform duties before the service period begins, it is important that they are given time to freshen up, change their uniforms, or otherwise prepare for their work which is in public view.

Other Cafeteria Positions. Cafeteria operations often have two other kinds of employees—cash-

Exhibit 13.3 Cafeteria Income Calculation Form

	Number of Portions Sent to the Serving Line								
ITEM	Opening	Add'l.	Add'l.	Add'l.	Total	Number Left	Total Sold	Selling Price	Total Potential Income
Swiss Steak	35	15	10	—	60	5	55	$3.15	$173.25
Mashed Potatoes	60	25	—	—	85	3	82	$.65	$53.30

iers and dining room attendants.

Most operations use a cashier at the end of the cafeteria line or at the dining area exit. Regardless of whether the cafeteria has a cash or guest check collection system (or both), income control procedures must be developed to help ensure that all the income the cashier should collect *is collected*. Some operations keep a count of the number of food portions brought to the serving line. The number of portions left at the end of service is subtracted from this total; the difference represents the number of portions that the cashier should have sold and rung on register preset keys (if available), or accounted for in some other manner to compare to the total sales income generated.

Exhibit 13.3 is a sample of a form used to develop information about standard (potential) cafeteria income. Record the number of portions of each product placed on the line at the beginning of the service period. As service progresses, note the number of any additional portions brought to the line. Adding these quantities yields the total number of portions available for sale. Deduct the number of portions left at the end of the service period from this total to yield the total number of portions sold. That amount, multiplied by the item's selling price, yields the total income expected from the sale of that item.

Use the total income from the sale of all the items to establish the standard income which can be compared to the actual amount of income rung on the cashier's register.

Many of management's methods to reduce employee theft can be adapted for use in cafeterias (see Chapter 8). For instance, rules for operating the cash register become very important in the cafeteria manager's plan to minimize the theft of income by the cashier.

Dining area attendants can perform a wide variety of tasks in cafeterias. They may assist guests (such as elderly people, guests with children, and others) by carrying their trays to tables. They may also perform busing activities, such as clearing and cleaning tables and replacing the necessary tableware on them. Pouring water and coffee are other tasks that dining room attendants perform in some cafeteria operations. When a guest's order will take time to complete, an attendant may bring the order (that the guest has paid for) to the table. In addition, managers may assign to these attendants a wide range of pre-opening and after-closing duties in supply stations and the dining area itself.

Cafeterias that offer salad bars or private rooms for group dining create additional work for someone—perhaps a dining room attendant. Usually, at least one attendant needs to constantly resupply and clean "help yourself" counters. When a cafeteria offers group dining accommodations, the manager often assigns an attendant to arrange tables and provide some table service.

Alcoholic Beverage Service in Cafeterias

As the cafeteria manager develops operating plans for a facility, the question of serving alcoholic beverages may arise. If the facility will serve beer, wine, and/or liquor, the manager must then decide on how such beverages will be served. (Of course, cafeterias must comply with local liquor laws if they offer alcoholic beverage service.) Some options available include using sections of the existing service counter to place containers of beer and wine in beds of shaved ice (guests passing through this part of the cafeteria line can help themselves to these products); making these products available in beverage stations; and offering draft beer and bulk wine by the glass, pitcher, or carafe. Cafeterias have an excellent opportunity to merchandise draft beer and wine with dispensing units.

Employee Dining Arrangements

While many of us think of employee food service as a modern development, its birth has been traced back to 1815. However, it was not until 1902 and 1906—when Illinois Bell and Sears Roebuck, respectively, began providing employee food service—that it started to become "big business."

Employee meals are generally thought of as a convenience to the employee, but the employer also derives a number of benefits from employee meal programs. For example, if employees must work long hours, applicable laws may and common sense does require that they be given a break with food. (Usually managers plan one meal per eight-hour shift.) When employees leave the property for a meal, they may return late to their work stations or gain access to alcohol or drugs which could impair their work performance. Experienced managers also consider the implications of guests and others seeing employees of a hospitality operation carrying a lunch box to work. They also wish to avoid the implications of their uniformed employees eating at a fast-food establishment down the street from their own property.

Of course, employees also benefit from such programs. For instance, nutritious and wholesome meals may be available to them at a very reasonable price. (Sometimes, they are free.) Employees do not need to waste time or spend money on transportation to visit another site for a meal. Because the pressure to get back to the property on time doesn't exist when employees are on-site during their breaks, they can relax during their meals.

Vending for Employee Food Services

Lodging properties can design vending machine programs for employee dining that fit their own needs. Benefits to employees can even be factored into contract negotiations. For instance, when management contracts with another company to provide vending machines, it can forgo commissions in favor of lowered prices for products offered. Or management could use the proceeds from employee vending machines to sponsor events of interest to the employees. (When this is the case, employees should know how the proceeds are being used.) As a third alternative, management can subsidize vending machine operations by offering products at very low costs to employees and, to compensate for the losses, pay the difference to the vending machine company.

Details about the development, negotiation, and administration of contracts for vending services are beyond the scope of this book.[1] However, the following questions illustrate the details that must be considered when vending machine contracts are developed: What are the exact specifications for the vending machines? What are the exact specifications for the vending operation itself? What responsibilities will the hospitality operation handle? What responsibilities will the vending contractor handle? What information must be agreed upon regarding records, payments, and special notices? What general provisions must be specified in the con-

---

[1] Interested readers are referred to Herman Zaccarelli and Jack Ninemeier, "Food Management Contract for Vended Services," *Cost Effective Contract Food Service: An Institutional Guide* (Rockville, Md.: Aspen System Corporation, 1982), pp. 157-168; 263-272.

tract? What legal requirements and specifications should also be considered? After selecting a company, how should the agreement for vending services be monitored? This brief list of questions is a reminder that there is more to making a vending machine decision than just signing a contract.

Other Employee Meal Options

Many large hotels provide separate dining rooms for their employees' meals—sometimes in a traditional cafeteria line arrangement. Employees in these properties enter the employee dining area, pass through a serving line, show required identification, and make their selections from among the available food and beverage items. These operations may prepare special meals for the employees, or they could be the same meals as those served in outlets that guests visit.

Another option available is allowing employees the opportunity to order directly off guest menus; possibly the employee will receive a discount on the established selling price(s). Food products left over from an earlier food production period or banquet can also be served to employees if the items are held under proper sanitary conditions. The quality and variety of such products can provide excellent dining opportunities for employees. Occasionally, special dining events are held for employees, perhaps to promote new items on the menu, to celebrate a major holiday, or to observe a community occasion. Such events are opportunities for management to do something special for employees. Unfortunately, staff in some hotel kitchens are allowed to "eat as they go"; they do not get break time because an employee eating policy is not in effect. Of course, this is a very poor practice for a number of reasons including sanitation, potential illegality, cost, and productivity.

An employee food service that is used by at least one hotel is an outside contractor who is hired to provide meals for the staff. The hotel's management reports that using an outside contractor helps eliminate problems encountered when meals for guests and employees must be prepared simultaneously. Finally, some large properties provide managers with credit cards, which they use to charge products to their respective departments.

Whenever practical, managers assess the costs of employee meals, whether consumed in front- or back-of-house areas, and deduct those costs from the property's food costs. This amount is then added to the employee benefits or other labor costs.[2] Because state, local, or other laws and regulations may govern such activities as employee breaks and the calculation of employee meal costs, management must be fully aware of such laws and follow them carefully when developing specific policies relating to employee breaks and meals.

Make Employee Dining Areas Special

The atmosphere of employee dining areas is not a problem when employees eat in the public dining room during slow periods or after business hours. However, when employees eat in back-of-house areas, special thoughts about the area's ambience are in order. Cheerful, clean, and bright employee dining areas are a welcome relief from many work stations in hospitality operations. Employees like to rest and relax on their breaks; unfortunately, this is not possible in some employee dining areas.

Management needs to look at the employees' dining room from their perspective. If management's answer to the question: "Would I like to eat in and spend breaks there?" is, "I wouldn't," it is highly likely that the employees who must spend time in these areas feel the same way.

Employee breaks give management an additional opportunity to develop teamwork and build a cooperative spirit among the employees. In some operations, the restaurant managers often eat in the employee dining areas. At least they should visit these areas frequently and take time to converse with and get to know the employees.

The atmosphere of employee dining areas is important. After all, it reflects the image of the property to the employee. How do you think employees feel when a property treats guests lavishly, but does not even give the employees the courtesy of a clean and pleasant place to eat?

---

[2] Interested readers are referred to Jack D. Ninemeier, *Planning and Control for Food and Beverage Operations* (East Lansing, Mich.: Educational Institute of the American Hotel & Motel Association, 1982).

Exhibit 13.4 Calculation of Weekly Employee Meal Credits

Employee Name	Mon.			Tues.			Wed.			Thurs.			Fri.			Sat.			Sun.			Total Meals			Meal Credit			Total Meal Cost			Total Wage Credit
	B	L	D	B	L	D	B	L	D	B	L	D	B	L	D	B	L	D	B	L	D	B	L	D	B	L	D	B	L	D	
Bill																						1	2	2	$1.20	$1.60	$2.00	$1.20	$3.20	$4.00	$8.40

Recordkeeping for Employee Meals

Federal wage and hour laws allow employers a credit on (reduction of) the minimum wage which they must pay to employees when they provide their meals. Typically, states develop their own maximum allowances for meal credits and, assuming that the actual cost of the meal is equal to or more than the amount of the meal credit, restaurant managers can deduct the amount of the credit from an employee's wages. For example, if the minimum wage is $3.35, and an employee works eight hours, he/she must receive cash or its equivalent of $26.80 ($3.35 per hour times eight hours). However, if the employee received two meals in a state which allows a credit of two dollars per meal, he/she needs only to receive actual cash wages of $22.80 ($26.80 total minimum wages minus two meals at $2 each equals $22.80).

Exhibit 13.4 shows a form which can be used to record and assess employee meal credits. To complete such a form, record the number of breakfasts, lunches, and/or dinners consumed by each employee each day during the week. Tally the total number of each meal type, then multiply those figures by the applicable meal credit to arrive at the total credit for each meal period. To assess the total wage credit, add together the total meal credits for breakfast, lunch, and dinner.

Bill is a minimum wage employee whose meals during a week are summarized in Exhibit 13.4. He received a lunch on Monday, a dinner on Tuesday, a breakfast on Wednesday, a dinner on Thursday, and a lunch on Friday. He did not work or receive meals on Saturday and Sunday. During the week, therefore, he received a total of one breakfast, two lunches, and two dinners. The state in which Bill works allows a meal credit of $1.20 for breakfast, $1.60 for lunch, and $2.00 for dinner. Since Bill had one breakfast at a meal credit of $1.20, his total meal credit for breakfast is $1.20. Bill had two lunches with a meal credit of $1.60 each; therefore, his total lunch credit is $3.20 ($1.60 x 2 = $3.20). His total dinner meal credit is $4.00. (Two dinners at a meal credit of $2 each equals $4.) The total wage credit is then $8.40 (breakfast meal credit of $1.20 + lunch meal credit of $3.20 + dinner meal credit of $4.00). According to these calculations, the employer can pay Bill $8.40 less than the actual minimum cash wages due him if the employer can prove that the actual cost of the meals equaled or exceeded the maximum credit allowed.

In order to keep records of employee meals that are sold at rates lower than food costs or

Exhibit 13.5 Calculation of Weekly Employee Meal Costs

Dept/Name	Total Meals			Estimated Meal Cost			Total Meal Cost			Cost of Employee Meals
	B	L	D	B	L	D	B	L	D	
Steward/Elizabeth	1	2	2	$1.50	$1.90	$2.25	$1.50	$3.80	$4.50	$9.80

provided at no cost, managers must calculate the cost of employee meals, subtract the amount from the total food costs, and add it to the labor costs (employee benefits). Such recordkeeping helps management match the income generated from the sale of food items with their associated costs. Since discounted meals served to employees generate reduced or no income, the cost of food used for these meals is considered a separate expense.

Typically, most operations base the cost of employee meals on food costs alone; except when managers assign special staff to this task, managers of dining outlets do not attempt to allocate labor and other related expenses to the costs of the employee meal. However, when properties have a separate employee dining room, it does become easier to allocate at least the direct labor costs for serving meals to the employee benefits account.

Exhibit 13.5 illustrates a recordkeeping procedure to determine the total cost of employee meals. That total is deducted from the property's total food costs as part of the accounting-bookkeeping process. As shown in Exhibit 13.5, Elizabeth received one breakfast, two lunches, and two dinners during the week. At an estimated meal cost of $1.50, $1.90, and $2.25, respectively, the total meal cost is $1.50 for break-

fast plus $3.80 for lunch plus $4.50 for dinner. The total cost of the employee's meals which would be deducted from the cost of food is $9.80 ($1.50 + $3.80 + $4.50).

It may appear that the recordkeeping procedures for tracking employee meal costs are rather cumbersome. Some properties use an automated system to more easily and practically maintain a record of these credits and costs. However, no matter what procedures are chosen, they must comply with applicable laws.

Off-Site Catering Operations

Some food service and lodging operations cater food and beverage services at locations other than the food service or lodging property itself. Management must consider the service aspects of these catering operations.

Off-site catered events may range from simple picnics to very lavish and elegant gourmet meals. For example, Exhibit 13.6 shows a variety of box lunch menus that could be used for off-site catering to groups of 5 to 5,000 people. The staff and service requirements will vary according to the type of function which is catered. Typically, the responsibility for delivering the

Exhibit 13.6 Special Lunch Menus

SHERATON WASHINGTON HOTEL

On The Go With Style!...

Is the Sheraton Washington Box Lunch Program, offering five different package menus. The box lunch is designed to facilitate bus movement, boost exhibit hall traffic or provide quick meals for people on the go. For groups of 5 to 5,000, our box lunch may be the answer to your requirement for quick!

Cole Slaw
Fried Chicken
(3 pieces)
Biscuit with Butter
Red Apple
5" Chocolate Chip Cookie
12 oz. Soft Drink
$10.00

Pasta Salad
Roast Beef Sandwich
on an Onion Roll
Crisp Crudite
Banana
5" Oatmeal Raisin Cookie
12 oz. Soft Drink
$10.00

Tomato and Mozzarella
with Basil Vinaigrette
Ripe Pear
Sliced Tenderloin
served on Petite Baguette
Dijon Mustard
Chocolate Mousse
Champagne
$15.00

Pate Maison
Brie Cheese
Port Salut Cheese
Red Apple
Croissant and Biscuits
Grape Cluster
8 oz. Red Wine
$10.00

Fresh Fruit Cup
Ham and Swiss
on Pumpernickel Roll
Corned Beef
on Petite Rye Roll
Potato Chips
Chocolate Brownie
12 oz. Soft Drink
$10.00

TAX AND GRATUITY ADDITIONAL

Courtesy of Sheraton Washington Hotel, Washington, D.C.

food and beverage products rests with the hospitality operation; hence, a driver is needed. (Often, the driver will also help set up, serve, and/or tear down.) Properties serve many catered events buffet style in either an informal or formal setting (e.g., at a tailgate lunch in a parking lot or at a supper or breakfast in a decorated hall after a prom). When buffets are used, service employees may need to portion food as guests pass through buffet lines. Alternatively, guests may help themselves, and the role of service staff becomes one of supplying the line, clearing tables, and setting up and tearing down the buffet line.

Some catered events feature table service; at such events, service employees perform duties similar to those of banquet service employees. At still other catered events, service employees may circulate among the guests with trays of appetizers and other food items. They may also take and serve drink orders, which are prepared by bartenders who may or may not be employees of the catering operation.

It is difficult to generalize about the duties of employees at off-site catered events because of the wide range of guest services which can be provided. However, fundamental rules of good service such as properly representing the operation, knowing and using guest-relations skills, practicing safe and sanitary food handling methods, and being professional and competent are just as important for service employees working at off-site catered events as they are for any other food service employees at any other time.

It is very important to pay close attention to all details when negotiating with clients, planning for the event, and actually catering the occasion. A lack of pre-planning often correlates with the number of problems that occur which jeopardize the success of the event. Frequently, the catering executive who sold the event will provide additional assistance before, during, and after the function. He/she may coordinate activities of the kitchen (which produces the food), the employees who deliver the food, and the service staff required to set up the event and provide guest services during the event.

VIP Dining Rooms

Some noncommercial (institutional) food service operations offer VIP (Very Important Person) dining service to top-level administrators and invited guests. They offer very elegant gourmet meals with appropriate serviceware, table linens, furnishings, and decor. Similarly, some commercial operations may have VIP dining rooms or other special areas set aside to serve influential people and/or special meals. Again, the elegance of the table appointments and the quality of food products set these dining areas apart from other outlets within the facility.

While basic principles of dining service management are important in VIP areas, the elegance of the special touches which VIP areas often feature sets them apart. For example, when "white glove" service is provided, employees wear tuxedoes as uniforms, a large number of service staff in proportion to the guests are present, very expensive glassware and other service supplies are used, and a sorbet is served to refresh the palate before the entree is served.

Because VIP areas frequently serve special meals unavailable from the facility's regular menus, employees often need special training to serve these items effectively. Servers must also be able to appropriately answer questions posed by the guests. Since normally all VIPs should be addressed by name, service employees must know who the guests are and where to seat them.

The timing of the meal's service is also very important. Sometimes, government or other protocol requirements must be observed. Frequently, fine wines and special beverages (e.g., after-dinner liqueurs) are served; therefore, again the service staff must be very well informed about them.

While it is true that every guest is a VIP, extraordinary procedures for very special people in unique, well-appointed dining areas are an important part of a number of food service operations.

Club and Show Operations

Many commercial food and beverage operations offer entertainment. Large hotel or casino properties may feature musical groups in their lounges and/or big-name stars in theaters which seat 1,000 or more people. Dinner-theaters located in lodging properties may offer package attractions consisting of a meal, before- and after-dinner drinks, and a stage production. Small properties often offer entertainment such as classical music ensembles, pianists, or strolling musicians in their lounges. Principles for managing these club and show operations are discussed in some detail in the following pages.

Financial Aspects of Entertainment

Managers in a number of commercial food and beverage operations believe that after paying all the direct costs associated with entertainment, their net profit is greater when they offer entertainment than when they don't. In contrast, operations such as casinos in Las Vegas and Atlantic City may consider that offering en-

tertainment is a marketing tool more than a profit center. Management staff in many of these properties believe that entertainment is necessary because guests expect it, and good entertainment helps attract people to a property. Sometimes, properties charge their casino operations for the costs incurred from providing free entertainment packages to their most preferred gamblers ("high rollers"). Many of these properties desire or expect only to break even on entertainment, particularly when they feature big-name entertainers who charge large fees.

Just because a manager thinks that entertainment will make a profit for his/her outlet does not make it so. Professional managers make careful studies to assess the impact that the proposed entertainment will have on the property. Exhibit 13.7 illustrates a simple process that can be used to help gauge whether or not the proposed entertainment will be financially viable. It essentially outlines a process to conduct a break-even analysis both in terms of the number of guests and the amount of additional income needed to pay for associated entertainment costs. In Step 1, the restaurant manager calculates the direct costs for a dinner/entertainment event. In this case, let's assume that a band (or other entertainment) will cost $800, and advertising and additional labor will cost $300 and $100, respectively. If no other costs exist, the total direct cost for the entertainment is $1,200.

In Step 2, let's assume that 10% of all food sales represents the bottom line, or net profit, and 20% of the beverage sales yields net profit. Let's further assume that the average food check is $14 and the average guest consumes two drinks at $2 each. We can then estimate the net profit per guest. Ten percent of a $14 average food check equals a profit of $1.40 for each meal. Since the beverage profit equals 20% of sales, $.80 ($4.00 x .20) represents the beverage profit. The total profit per guest is $2.20 ($1.40 + .80).

It is now possible in Step 3 to calculate the number of guests needed to break even: total direct costs of $1,200 divided by $2.20 net profit per guest yields 545 guests required to break even. Profit, therefore, will accrue to the property only if it can sell the dinner/entertainment package to more than 545 guests.

It is also possible to estimate break-even statistics in terms of dollars rather than guests.

Exhibit 13.7 Financial Aspects of Entertainment

Part A: Break-Even Concerns (Number of Guests)

Step 1—Calculate Direct Costs for Event

a. Band (or other entertainment)	$800.00
b. Advertising	300.00
c. Additional Labor (arrange room, cleanup, etc.)	100.00
Total Direct Costs	$1,200.00

Step 2—Estimate Net Profit per Guest

a. Food Sales	= 10% Net Profit
b. Beverage Sales	= 20% Net Profit
c. Average Food Check	= $14.00
d. Average Drink Sales	= 2 @ $2.00 = $4.00

Net Profit per Guest is:

e. Food Profit	= $14.00 × .10 = $1.40
f. Beverage Profit	= $ 4.00 × .20 = .80
Net Profit	= $2.20

Step 3—Calculate Number of Guests to Break Even

$1,200	÷	$2.20	=	545
Total Direct Costs		Net Profit per Guest		Number of Guests Needed to Break Even

Part B: Break-Even Concerns (Additional Income)

Step 1—Calculate Income per Guest (See Step 2 of Part A)

Food Income	$14.00
Beverage Income	4.00
Income per Guest	$18.00

Step 2—Estimate Number of Guests Needed

From Step 3 of Part A = 545 Guests

Step 3—Determine Break-Even Level for Sales Income

545	×	$18.00	=	$9,810.00
Number of Guests (Step 2)		Income per Guest (Step 1)		Approximate Income Needed to Break Even

---

Entertainment Doesn't Have to be Live

While part of this chapter focuses on live entertainment, food and beverage operations can offer other forms of entertainment as well. Examples include big-screen television sets which attract guests to the property to view athletic and other special events, jukeboxes and their modern counterpart—video-jukeboxes—which entertain guests in many lounge operations, and discotheques in which extravagant lighting, sound systems, and disc jockeys playing records help provide the atmosphere for dancers. Food and beverage operations also use sound systems to provide background for guests in dining and lounge areas.

Each outlet must decide on the type or types of entertainment, if any, that it will provide. Entertainment can be popular and profitable—it all depends on the ability of the management staff to discover and meet the requirements of their guests.

Part B of Exhibit 13.7 shows how this is done. The income per guest is approximately $18 (food income of $14 plus beverage income of $4). Since the property needs 545 guests to break even, break-even income can be estimated by multiplying 545 guests by the $18 per guest income level. The property requires approximately $9,810 of income to break even; thus the property will make a profit only after ticket sales for the entertainment exceed that amount. Obviously, in order for managers to decide whether or not they should offer entertainment packages, they should carefully assess the anticipated costs and estimated income by using procedures shown in Exhibit 13.7.

Must the property make a profit or at least break even on every event? If a property plans a program for a week, must the program make a profit each day? The answers to these questions depend on the property. Experienced managers realize that they may need some time to advertise, to get the word out, so that the operation can gain a reputation for providing quality entertainment of a specific type.

Some properties offer entertainment packages for their derived demand effect. The concept of "derived demand" suggests that a relationship exists between different revenue centers in a property. For example, as a hotel sells additional rooms, the potential for food and beverage sales increases. A lounge offering entertainment may similarly attract additional dining room business.

Some outlets offer entertainment because their guests expect it. They recover many of the costs of entertainment by charging higher prices for products consumed. Other properties consider entertainment as a cost of enticing guests from a specific market into the property. The point here is simple: managers of food and beverage operations must understand the financial implications of their decisions concerning whether or not to offer entertainment and, if they decide to do so, what type of entertainment they should feature.

How to Select Entertainment

Managers of food and beverage outlets may regularly receive unsolicited letters, telephone calls, and visits from prospective entertainers. Unfortunately, many of these people do not have the professional expertise to please guests. Therefore, some experienced managers visit their competition in an effort to discover good entertainment that will meet their needs.

Alternatively, management may secure the services of a talent agent. Since the agent receives fees from the entertainer, the property incurs no cost. Good talent agents are able to help management match the needs of the property with desirable entertainment. In order to do this, however, the talent agent must have details about the property's market and the total funds it can spend on entertainment.

Regardless of who secures the entertainment, it should be considered from the guests' perspective. Do the performers dress appropriately? Will the entertainment appeal to the guests the property serves? Are the entertainers

Copyright Music Performance in Hotels and Motels
or
Dealing with ASCAP, BMI and SESAC

A summary of American Hotel & Motel Association advice to owners/managers

As a general rule, the owner of a copyrighted musical composition has the exclusive right to control public performances of that work. Under U.S. statutes, no person can give a public performance of a copyrighted work without permission of the owner.

Thus, a hotel or motel which performs live music or background music by means of records or tape recordings, or rebroadcast of radio music, must have an agreement with the owner to perform his or her works, or the hotel may be liable for copyright infringement regardless of intention or knowledge of the infringement. There are a few very narrow exceptions but in general they are immaterial where hotels and motels are concerned, except to jukeboxes as noted later in this article.

To facilitate collection of performance fees for the use of copyrighted materials the owners generally have banded together in associations or corporations which "license" the users, for a fee, to perform their works. Thus, hoteliers quickly learn that ASCAP (American Society of Composers, Authors and Publishers), BMI (Broadcast Music, Inc.) and SESAC (Society of European Stage Authors and Composers) are the usual representatives which issue license agreements and collect a fee depending on how the performances are handled by a hotel or motel. These three organizations control practically all copyrighted music.

The license agreements provided by ASCAP, BMI and SESAC are similar in that they charge an annual fee based upon the hotel's total entertainment expenditures for the year.

They may differ slightly in areas noted as live, mechanical or recorded music only, or where no dancing, admission, or cover charges are made. Discotheques may be treated differently but in general are included in all agreements.

Jukeboxes

The revised Copyright Act contains a jukebox exemption which permits the "operator" of the jukebox to be licensed by the Register of Copyrights, pay an annual royalty fee, and affix a certificate provided by the Register of Copyrights to each jukebox where it can be readily examined by the public. Playing of a musical composition on such jukeboxes will not be considered a public performance *unless a fee is charged for admission to the place where the jukebox is heard*.

The American Hotel & Motel Association negotiates the license rates charged by ASCAP and BMI for all hotels. SESAC negotiates its own rates with hotels. All of these organizations generally issue license agreements for a term of five years, paid for quarterly on an annual basis.

NOTE: Included in each agreement is a clause which permits these organizations to examine, if necessary, a property's books to determine if the contract is in the proper financial category. This agreement is limited to those areas which pertain to the use of live music or entertainers, background music, discotheques, etc., as covered in the license agreements and, if necessary, should be enforced by the hotel.

friendly and able to relate well with the guests? If the act involves music, will it create undesirable noise levels?

Marketing Aspects of Entertainment

Hotels have a particular problem in considering entertainment alternatives. Should they attempt to appeal only to the guests of the property, or should they attempt to generate business from the community?

Well-known acts are expensive; in-house guests may not be able to support the costs associated with such entertainment. Therefore, in order to inform the community about the package, the property may need to advertise

Taxes for Entertainers

Unless entertainers are specific employees of the food and beverage operation, they are independent contractors or contract labor. The operation does not have to withhold payroll taxes or make contributions toward social security taxes for such entertainers. Lodging, meals, and related expenses incurred to support entertainers are expenses for the employer and will show up as such on the property's income tax statement.

heavily, which can be expensive. The size of the room in which entertainment can be offered must also be considered. Is the room large enough to accommodate the number of guests needed to recover expenses incurred? If the room is relatively small, is it possible to offer several performances in order to increase guest counts? What is the most that the guest is willing to pay for a certain act? You can see how the decision to select a specific type of entertainment depends on many very closely related concerns.

Laws and Entertainment

Local and other laws have an impact on the entertainment decision. Laws mandating maximum occupancy, emergency lighting, and exit requirements are of obvious concern whether or not a property provides entertainment. Laws concerning alcoholic beverages may have an impact on the hours that a property can offer entertainment and even on the *type* of entertainment it can feature. For example, ordinances may forbid nudity (however it is defined) in places which serve alcoholic beverages.

Managers must also consider music and/or entertainment taxes when they plan for entertainment. Some states claim dancing is entertainment; others levy taxes on dinner guests who remain in the dining room after the music begins.

In addition to applicable laws, restaurant managers in properties offering live entertainment must often deal with unions. For example, the American Federation of Musicians (AFM) requires its members to work under a standard union contract. Exhibit 13.8 is a union contract that illustrates the legal relationship which exists between a food and beverage operation and an entertainer. Other unions also represent enter-

tainers; however, most entertainment unions function like the AFM.

Service Procedures for Entertainment Operations

Few, if any, changes in operating procedures are necessary to accommodate many types of entertainment. (Collecting cover charges, which is an operating procedure change, is discussed later in this chapter.) For example, when lounges offer entertainment, procedures for taking drink orders, serving drinks, and collecting payments from guests should remain the same for the beverage servers except when entertainment taxes are involved.

At many dinner-theaters, the meal precedes the show. As a result, the procedures which employees use to provide service during specific dinner times are very likely to be the same as those used for a sit-down banquet. Beverage service may be available before the meal at portable bars located throughout the dining area; however, it is more likely that beverage service will occur at the table, just as it does in the dining rooms of most food service operations.

Managers of theaters or showrooms usually develop and follow specific procedures that they have learned work well in their kind of operation. For example, the manager assigns beverage servers to a particular work station and gives them a specific time interval to set up. (They may need to place table linens, napkins, candles, wine and other beverage price lists, and table tents on the table.)

At a specific time before the theater opens, the servers are required to be ready in their work stations. As guests are seated, the servers take beverage orders. One major property uses, as a rule of thumb, one showroom captain for each

Exhibit 13.8 Typical Union Contract for Entertainers

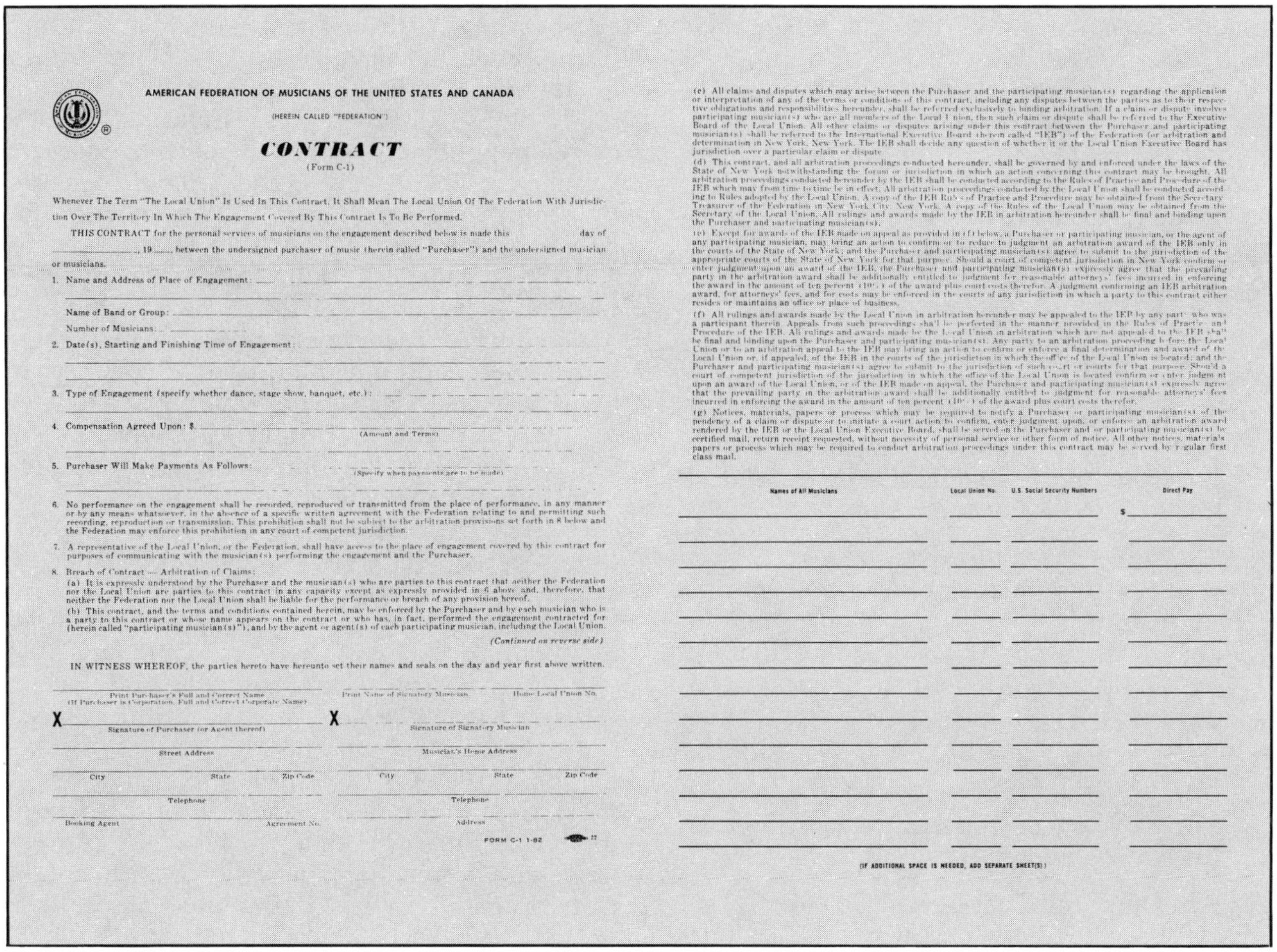

AMERICAN FEDERATION OF MUSICIANS OF THE UNITED STATES AND CANADA

(HEREIN CALLED "FEDERATION")

CONTRACT

(Form C-1)

Whenever The Term "The Local Union" Is Used In This Contract, It Shall Mean The Local Union Of The Federation With Jurisdiction Over The Territory In Which The Engagement Covered By This Contract Is To Be Performed.

THIS CONTRACT for the personal services of musicians on the engagement described below is made this ______ day of ______, 19____, between the undersigned purchaser of music (herein called "Purchaser") and the undersigned musician or musicians.

1. Name and Address of Place of Engagement: ______

   Name of Band or Group: ______

   Number of Musicians: ______

2. Date(s), Starting and Finishing Time of Engagement: ______

3. Type of Engagement (specify whether dance, stage show, banquet, etc.): ______

4. Compensation Agreed Upon: $ ______ (Amount and Terms)

5. Purchaser Will Make Payments As Follows: ______ (Specify when payments are to be made)

6. No performance on the engagement shall be recorded, reproduced or transmitted from the place of performance, in any manner or by any means whatsoever, in the absence of a specific written agreement with the Federation relating to and permitting such recording, reproduction or transmission. This prohibition shall not be subject to the arbitration provisions set forth in 8 below and the Federation may enforce this prohibition in any court of competent jurisdiction.

7. A representative of the Local Union, or the Federation, shall have access to the place of engagement covered by this contract for purposes of communicating with the musician(s) performing the engagement and the Purchaser.

8. Breach of Contract — Arbitration of Claims:

   (a) It is expressly understood by the Purchaser and the musician(s) who are parties to this contract that neither the Federation nor the Local Union are parties to this contract in any capacity except as expressly provided in 6 above and, therefore, that neither the Federation nor the Local Union shall be liable for the performance or breach of any provision hereof.

   (b) This contract, and the terms and conditions contained herein, may be enforced by the Purchaser and by each musician who is a party to this contract or whose name appears on the contract or who has, in fact, performed the engagement contracted for (herein called "participating musician(s)"), and by the agent or agent(s) of each participating musician, including the Local Union.

(Continued on reverse side)

IN WITNESS WHEREOF, the parties hereto have hereunto set their names and seals on the day and year first above written.

Print Purchaser's Full and Correct Name (If Purchaser is Corporation, Full and Correct Corporate Name) | Print Name of Signatory Musician | Home Local Union No.

X Signature of Purchaser (or Agent thereof) | X Signature of Signatory Musician

Street Address | Musician's Home Address

City | State | Zip Code | City | State | Zip Code

Telephone | Telephone

Booking Agent | Agreement No. | Address

FORM C-1 1-82

(c) All claims and disputes which may arise between the Purchaser and the participating musician(s) regarding the application or interpretation of any of the terms or conditions of this contract, including any disputes between the parties as to their respective obligations and responsibilities hereunder, shall be referred exclusively to binding arbitration. If a claim or dispute involves participating musician(s) who are all members of the Local Union, then such claim or dispute shall be referred to the Executive Board of the Local Union. All other claims or disputes arising under this contract between the Purchaser and participating musician(s) shall be referred to the International Executive Board (herein called "IEB") of the Federation for arbitration and determination in New York, New York. The IEB shall decide any question of whether it or the Local Union Executive Board has jurisdiction over a particular claim or dispute.

(d) This contract, and all arbitration proceedings conducted hereunder, shall be governed by and enforced under the laws of the State of New York notwithstanding the forum or jurisdiction in which an action concerning this contract may be brought. All arbitration proceedings conducted hereunder by the IEB shall be conducted according to the Rules of Practice and Procedure of the IEB which may from time to time be in effect. All arbitration proceedings conducted by the Local Union shall be conducted according to Rules adopted by the Local Union. A copy of the IEB Rules of Practice and Procedure may be obtained from the Secretary-Treasurer of the Federation in New York City, New York. A copy of the Rules of the Local Union may be obtained from the Secretary of the Local Union. All rulings and awards made by the IEB in arbitration hereunder shall be final and binding upon the Purchaser and participating musician(s).

(e) Except for awards of the IEB made on appeal as provided in (f) below, a Purchaser or participating musician, or the agent of any participating musician, may bring an action to confirm or to reduce to judgment an arbitration award of the IEB only in the courts of the State of New York; and the Purchaser and participating musician(s) agree to submit to the jurisdiction of the appropriate courts of the State of New York for that purpose. Should a court of competent jurisdiction in New York confirm or enter judgment upon an award of the IEB, the Purchaser and participating musician(s) expressly agree that the prevailing party in the arbitration award shall be additionally entitled to judgment for reasonable attorneys' fees incurred in enforcing the award in the amount of ten percent (10%) of the award plus court costs therefor. A judgment confirming an IEB arbitration award, for attorneys' fees, and for costs may be enforced in the courts of any jurisdiction in which a party to this contract either resides or maintains an office or place of business.

(f) All rulings and awards made by the Local Union in arbitration hereunder may be appealed to the IEB by any party who was a participant therein. Appeals from such proceedings shall be perfected in the manner provided in the Rules of Practice and Procedure of the IEB. All rulings and awards made by the Local Union in arbitration which are not appealed to the IEB shall be final and binding upon the Purchaser and participating musician(s). Any party to an arbitration proceeding before the Local Union or to an arbitration appeal to the IEB may bring an action to confirm or enforce a final determination and award of the Local Union or, if appealed, of the IEB in the courts of the jurisdiction in which the office of the Local Union is located; and the Purchaser and participating musician(s) agree to submit to the jurisdiction of such court or courts for that purpose. Should a court of competent jurisdiction of the jurisdiction in which the office of the Local Union is located confirm or enter judgment upon an award of the Local Union, or of the IEB made on appeal, the Purchaser and participating musician(s) expressly agree that the prevailing party in the arbitration award shall be additionally entitled to judgment for reasonable attorneys' fees incurred in enforcing the award in the amount of ten percent (10%) of the award plus court costs therefor.

(g) Notices, materials, papers or process which may be required to notify a Purchaser or participating musician(s) of the pendency of a claim or dispute or to initiate a court action to confirm, enter judgment upon, or enforce an arbitration award rendered by the IEB or the Local Union Executive Board, shall be served on the Purchaser and/or participating musician(s) by certified mail, return receipt requested, without necessity of personal service or other form of notice. All other notices, materials, papers or process which may be required to conduct arbitration proceedings under this contract may be served by regular first class mail.

Names of All Musicians	Local Union No.	U.S. Social Security Numbers	Direct Pay
			$

(IF ADDITIONAL SPACE IS NEEDED, ADD SEPARATE SHEET(S))

100 to 150 guests expected; therefore, if the property expects 1,500 guests for a performance, it schedules 10 to 15 showroom captains to show guests to their reserved tables.

After recording the orders on guest checks, the servers place the orders at the service bars. Procedures dictating the exact responsibilities of the bartender and the beverage server vary among properties. Frequently, a server needs to enter guest check information on a precheck register before presenting an order at the service bar. Often, bartenders will have to prepare a very large number of drinks for many servers within a relatively short time period, in which case great detail is necessary regarding the exact procedures they should use. Some properties specify the precise way that servers should write orders on guest checks, ring them through precheck registers, and/or call them to the bartender. Service bars frequently use expediters (with tasks similar to food expediters) to help coordinate drink orders with drink preparation. Beverage servers and bartenders must be able to work very quickly without error in a very high-pressure situation.

Some properties require beverage servers to collect payments from guests as they are served. Immediately after they serve the orders, they collect the payment and return any change to the guests. Servers must also consistently follow all policies regarding the acceptance of credit cards and/or personal checks.

After the beverage attendants serve all the drinks on their trays, they should turn over the guest checks, along with applicable income, to a cashier. After verifying that the check totals equal the income turned in, the cashier stamps a slip or otherwise provides a stub for the beverage servers. (Beverage servers should retain their check stubs for 30 days in case of questions.) Beverage servers can then return to their service stations to take additional drink orders.

Standard operating procedures in some properties may require servers to follow certain steps when guests wish to charge drink purchases to their rooms or credit cards. As required by the property, servers use the following procedures:

1. If the guest wants the bill charged to his/her room or credit card, he/she signs the back of the guest check and includes his/her room number. (Frequently the guest also must show his/her room key.)

2. The server takes the room card (or key) or credit card to the cashier who then verifies that credit is approved and processes the charge using specific procedures adopted by the property. (If credit is not approved, a supervisor, not the beverage server, may need to resolve the problem with the guest.)

3. The beverage server then returns the card (or key) to the guest.

4. After the initial processing of the charge, the beverage server may serve additional rounds without involving the cashier. At the end of service, the beverage server should present the guest check to the guest for his/her signature. After the guest has added a tip if he/she chooses to, checked the total, and signed the voucher, the beverage server takes the guest check and voucher to the cashier for settlement.

Casino operations may give guests a complimentary slip which they can present when a server requests payment for food and/or beverages. Typically, the guest will need to sign the "comp" slip and the beverage server will take it, along with the guest check, to the cashier. This official will need to verify the comp slip, stamp the guest check, and otherwise process it.

Sometimes, comp guests who are high rollers will order products not routinely carried in service bar inventories. The server typically checks with his/her supervisor to assess whether or not these special requests should be honored.

Beverage servers may serve additional rounds after they have verified the comp slip up to any limit imposed by the supervisor or noted on the slip itself. When guests indicate that they do not require more drinks, the beverage servers should present the guest check for the guest's final approval—frequently, they need the guest's signature. Then servers take the comp slip and guest check to the cashier for final settlement. Normally, high rollers pay for the tip.

Exhibit 13.9 summarizes the actual procedures one casino operation uses to collect payment from beverage servers working in a theater seating 1,700 guests. Exhibit 13.10 illustrates a sample of a form which the same operation provides to guests eligible for free food and beverages. After reviewing these forms, you can understand the detail which they require and the procedures that must be developed to ensure that employees can efficiently serve a very large number of guests within a reasonable time.

After the performance ends and guests leave, beverage servers must perform cleanup duties and related work.

Before servers can check out, management must account for all guest checks and reconcile them with the precheck register, service bar register, and/or readings on other equipment in cashier areas. In many operations, service personnel must also pick up the charged tips which are due them. (For a discussion of general sales income control procedures, see Chapter 8.)

Reservation Procedures

Procedures for taking reservations for special entertainment packages are carefully developed by experienced managers. Perhaps reservations are available on a "first-come, first-served" basis. Alternatively, especially in casino operations, a specific number of seats may be committed to a mini-reservation system within the overall reservation system for the operation. For example, Exhibit 13.11 shows the theater seating arrangement in a large casino hotel. The theater can seat approximately 1,600 people. However, the property allows the casino to reserve seats, as required, in the area closest to the stage. If, after a specific date, the casino operation has not reserved all of these seats, the remaining seats are opened for sale to the general

Exhibit 13.9 Payment Collection Procedures for One Casino Operation

COLLECTING PAYMENT

Payment **must** be collected from **each party when drinks are served**.

For Cash Transactions:

1. Present the guest check to the guest and state the total saying, "Sir/Madam, your check totals_____."

2. Upon receiving payment, indicate the amount tendered by stating, "That's $17.50 out of $20.00."

3. Write the amount tendered at the top of the guest check.

4. Give the guest his/her change by counting it out and stating, "Your change is $2.50. Thank you."

5. Repeat steps 1-4 for each party you have served, then proceed to the cashier station to pay the guest checks. You may take additional orders for parties as they are seated *before* returning to the service bar to pay your guest checks; however, pay your guest checks at the cashier station *before* ordering these drinks at the bar.

6. At the cashier station, make sure that you receive your cashier-stamped stub.

7. Return to your station to continue service.

For Charge Transactions (Room Charges, Credit Cards):

1. Present the guest check to the guest and state the total.

2. When given the room card or credit card, immediately ask the guest to sign the back of the guest check where indicated, by saying, "Sir/Madam, may I please have your signature on the back of the check?" (For room charges, also ask the guest to list the room number where indicated.) Say, "Thank you," after the guest has signed.

3. Proceed to the cashier station where he/she will verify credit by initialing the top of the guest check.

4. If credit is approved, return the room card or credit card to the guest without delay.

5. If credit is not approved, **immediately inform the supervisor on duty who will handle the situation**.

6. For credit card charges, the cashier will prepare the appropriate voucher and staple it to the guest check.

7. Add additional rounds to the same guest check for valid charges. (Remember to invert the guest check in the imprinter when ringing additional rounds.)

8. At the end of service, when the guest indicates that no further rounds are needed, present the guest check for the guest's final approval. For credit card transactions, write the total amount of sale (top line only) on the voucher; ensure that the guest takes his/her copy of the voucher after he/she has signed and totaled it.

9. Take the guest check, with the voucher attached if it is charged to a credit card, to the cashier for settlement.

For Complimentary Drinks:

1. Present the guest check to the guest and state the total.

2. When given the comp slip, immediately have the guest sign the back of the guest check using the standard phrase, "Sir/Madam, may I please have your signature on the back of the check? Thank you."

3. Take the guest check and comp slip to the cashier. He/she will affix the comp slip to the guest check, verify the comp, and stamp the guest check with "Complimentary, Gratuity Not Included."

4. Obtain the supervisor's approval in instances when the guest requests wine (or champagne) that is not on the wine list.

5. Also obtain the supervisor's approval when the guest wishes to exceed the comp limit.

6. Serve additional rounds **up to the limit of the comp;** remember to invert the guest check in the imprinter when ordering additional rounds.

7. Remember to circle each round's **total** on the guest check.

8. Have the cashier settle the comp check as soon as the guest indicates that there will be no more rounds or when the comp limit has been reached, AFTER you have presented the guest check for the guest's final approval.

9. Let the **supervisor** handle any discrepancies, problems, or guest questions on comps.

Source: Adapted from *Superstar Theater Server's Handbook* (Atlantic City, N.J.: Resorts International Hotel Casino), no date.

Exhibit 13.10 "Comp" Slip for In-House Entertainment

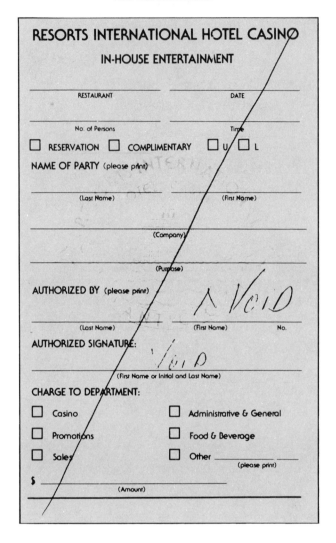

RESORTS INTERNATIONAL HOTEL CASINO

IN-HOUSE ENTERTAINMENT

RESTAURANT _____ DATE _____

No. of Persons _____ Time _____

☐ RESERVATION ☐ COMPLIMENTARY ☐ U ☐ L

NAME OF PARTY (please print)

_____ (Last Name) _____ (First Name)

_____ (Company)

_____ (Purpose)

AUTHORIZED BY (please print) ∧ Void

_____ (Last Name) _____ (First Name) No.

AUTHORIZED SIGNATURE: Void

_____ (First Name or Initial and Last Name)

CHARGE TO DEPARTMENT:

☐ Casino ☐ Administrative & General

☐ Promotions ☐ Food & Beverage

☐ Sales ☐ Other _____ (please print)

$ _____ (Amount)

public. The best seats often go to the most preferred gamblers and others who are frequent guests of the casino; casino personnel often give such guests a ticket and a comp slip.

Nonhotel guests must purchase tickets that guarantee seats. Frequently, the procedures used for these guests involve showroom seating. Other properties use tickets with assigned table numbers printed on them; the ticket purchase guarantees at which table guests will be seated; guests who arrive first are given their choice of the best seats.

The showroom captains, who escort guests to their seats, may have additional responsibilities which include inspecting their assigned areas before opening to ensure proper station setup, walking their designated areas during the show to assess whether service is adequate, and noting any problems and referring them to a supervisor.

Special Problems in Entertainment Operations

While some operations eliminate cover charges and do not increase product prices with the hope that increased business will result from the entertainment, others increase the price of products to cover entertainment costs.

When a cover charge (an "entertainment tax") is levied in an entertainment operation, management has several options for collecting it from guests. The most simple process involves stationing an employee at the entrance to collect cover charge payments from guests as they enter. Obvious problems include reconciling the amount of cover charge income collected with the number of guests who entered and the possibility that the employee will not collect income from all guests (especially if he/she receives tips). A variation of that plan involves the use of a turnstile to count the guests as they enter the facility.

Another option is to give guests numbered tickets at the time they pay the cover charge; they then present the ticket to the beverage server for a free drink. Each of these alternatives contains elements of inconvenience to the guest.

A final alternative is to have guests pay the cover charge after they are seated. In properties that use this method, servers enter the charge on the guest check and collect it when they receive payment for drinks. With this plan, a beverage server would use numbered guest checks; management must then account for all guest checks at the time the beverage server's shift ends. Most guest checks would have a cover charge recorded on them; the supervisor would have to investigate any discrepancies. The number of guests who paid a cover charge can be easily reconciled with a separate count of guests taken at the door.

The sale of products during the show can also be a problem. When a musical group performs in a lounge or dining room, for instance, guests usually expect to order and receive drinks while the entertainers perform. In some operations, the policy is to sell all the drinks possible;

Exhibit 13.11 Theater Seating Plan in Large Casino Hotel

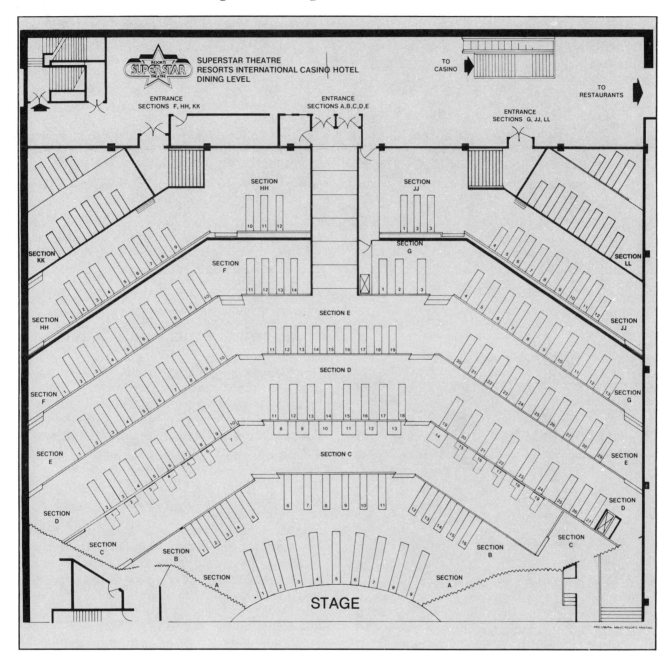

the guests understand that beverage sales support the show. At the other extreme is the policy that curtails all beverage sales during the show—a policy some entertainers demand. Sales then resume during intermissions. A third and relatively common alternative requires servers to remain in the theater area, but they must not block any guest's view. They pay attention to

their guests, watch for signals from them that indicate the desire for additional service, and perform their duties as quickly and inconspicuously as possible. Managers obviously must determine policies and procedures for serving beverages during the show; they must consider all guests—those desiring service and those interested primarily in the entertainment.

Common Guest Complaints During Club and Show Operations

Many managers indicate that among the most frequent complaints of guests in club and show operations are sight lines (the view that the guest has of the stage), slow beverage service, and staff rudeness.

Problems with the guest's view may partially be due to design problems in the facility. Seating priorities also affect one's view. At any rate, seating problems are probably neither the fault nor the responsibility of the service staff.

The remaining complaints—slow beverage service and staff rudeness—are not unique to club and show operations. Inadequate selection, training, and supervision of employees can cause problems of this nature in any department of a food service operation. Devising specific procedures to provide drinks efficiently can help reduce some of the problems. Training servers in guest relations frequently helps them put the proper emphasis on guests as they perform their work. Management must always look at procedures and personnel from the perspective of the guest; supervision is necessary to ensure that employees consistently use the required procedures and courtesies. Management may find that the frequent use of a beverage shopper service to pinpoint problems and suggest solutions to them is in order. Exhibit 14.3 could be adapted to suit a club or show operation's beverage service.

Exhibit 13.12 Tower Club

TOWER CLUB

For the special needs of many of our guests, we have created the Tower Club, a warmly intimate enclave where our very special guests are pampered with the ultimate in service and style.

At the Amway Grand Plaza Hotel.
Pearl at Monroe Grand Rapids, MI 49503
Telephone 616 774 2000

Tower Club accommodations feature the extra touches of a private lounge, accessed by special elevator keys, luxurious guestroom amenities and VIP registration at a separate area of the Front Desk.

The exclusive TOWER CLUB LOUNGE on the 25th floor of the Amway Grand Plaza West tower features:

- A complimentary Continental Breakfast Buffet from 6:30-10:00 am, Monday through Friday; and 7:00-11:00 am, Saturday & Sunday
- Complimentary soft drinks, coffee and tea
- Honor bar from 12:00 noon daily (self-serve with our guest's signature)
- Complimentary cocktails and hors d'oeuvres 5:30-6:30 pm daily
- A telescope offers close-ups of the already breathtaking view

A wide selection of magazines, books and parlor games (backgammon and chess), as well as the warmth and intimacy of a fireplace make the lounge a true oasis of luxury.

Special GUESTROOM AMENITIES separate our Tower Club guests from the usual fine standards of excellence enjoyed by guests of the Grand Plaza:

- Remote control television set
- Built-in AM/FM stereo clock radio
- Built-in hair dryer
- Shower massage unit
- Complimentary morning paper delivered to your door daily
- Use of exclusive Tower Club terry velour bathrobes

Our TOWER CLUB CONCIERGE, located in the lounge, is readily available to meet our guest's every need with personalized service. (Telex, dictaphone, typing, photocopying and other secretarial services available.) Our GUEST SERVICE MANAGER will also be happy to assist in any way with your traveling needs.

We invite you to discover the Tower Club at the Amway Grand Plaza for a modest premium charge over and above our regular rates for these special rooms. Simply indicate your Tower Club preference when making your reservations. We would love to pamper you.

Miscellaneous Food Services

Depending on the specific needs of their clientele, hotels can offer a wide variety of other types of food services not discussed in any detail in this text. For example, special suites or entire floors of the property can be set aside for special guests and complimentary breakfasts, beverage service, or hors d'oeuvres may be offered to them. Exhibit 13.12 illustrates the food, beverage, and other services which one large hotel offers to its guests.

Some properties provide retail pastry shops or "take-out deli bars." Typically, the pastries and/or other food products sold in such outlets are also served in one or more of the property's regular dining outlets. The products offered for retail sales thus require little additional production time and may be very profitable.

Some resorts may offer morning coffee, afternoon tea, or similar services. Elegant French pastries, petits fours, assorted tea sandwiches, English scones, canapes of all types, and, perhaps, entertainment by a music ensemble make this type of service extra special. High teas are popular in some metropolitan hotels as well as in resorts. Business people often make use of such events in hotels; they are more social in nature at resorts. The availability of high teas often helps enhance the status of the property.

A genuine smile from the server in the deli lets the guests know that the property cares about them. (Amway Grand Plaza Hotel, Grand Rapids, Michigan)

Some hotels offer stand-up (or "swim-up") snack and/or cocktail bars in swimming pool areas. Snack bars in game rooms, public rooms, and other areas provide another possibility for food and/or beverage service. Hotels may use portable bars in lobby areas on a regular basis or at least when a large number of guests are using the facility. Concierges in some hotels provide a variety of refreshments to guests waiting in check-in lines or for tour buses. Other hotels offer free coffee service in the lobby or other areas for guests catching early morning flights.

Managing Service at the Hotel Columbia
Page Twenty-Six

"It's great," thought Lewis Scott, "our managers are using the right procedures to determine the economic feasibility of offering entertainment." He was reviewing a memo he had received from the Log Cabin Lounge manager concerning offering live entertainment in that lounge during Homecoming weekend (see accompanying memo).

After reading through the proposal, Lewis picked up his phone and dialed her extension.

"You've done your homework well, Jackie," he said after greetings were exchanged. "I agree that we should offer country music to our guests in the Log Cabin Lounge during Homecoming weekend."

"I'm glad you agree, Lewis," replied Jackie. "I honestly don't think we can miss. I first heard The Country Three a month before starting work here and I not only liked *them*, I liked the way the crowd behaved."

"I'll try to stop by while they're performing," Lewis said. "And let me know how it all went when the weekend is over."

After the conversation between the two was completed, Lewis decided to talk to other outlet managers about live entertainment possibilities. "Now that our opening festivities have calmed down," he thought, "it's time to think of other ways to attract guests. The upcoming winter holidays provide the perfect chance for us to please guests with live entertainment in various food and beverage outlets in the Hotel Columbia."

MEMO

TO: Lewis Scott, Vice President for Food and Beverage
FROM: Jackie Monsoon, Manager of the Log Cabin Lounge
SUBJECT: Feasibility of entertainment in the Log Cabin Lounge during the weekend of 11/18/XX
DATE: 10/04/XX

   I have calculated the feasibility of entertainment in the Log Cabin Lounge for Homecoming weekend and think we can pull it off. What do you think? What additional information would you like?

Direct Costs for Event

a.	The Country Three (group)	$600.00
b.	Advertising	200.00
c.	Additional Labor (arrange room, cleanup, etc.)	100.00
	Total Direct Costs	$900.00

Estimated Net Profit per Guest

a.	Food Sales	=	12% Net Profit
b.	Beverage Sales	=	24% Net Profit
c.	Average Food Check	=	$13.00
d.	Average Drink Sales	=	2 @ $2.25 = $4.50

Net Profit per Guest is:

e.	Food Profit	=	$13.00 × .12	=	$1.56
f.	Beverage Profit	=	$ 4.50 × .24	=	1.08
	Net Profit	=			$2.64

Estimated Number of Guests to Break Even

a.	$900.00	$2.64		341
	Total Direct Costs (÷)	Net Profit per Guest (=)		Number of Guests Needed to Break Even

Recap of Estimated Income per Guest and Number of Guests to Break Even

Food Income	$13.00
Beverage Income	4.50
Income per Guest	$17.50

Break-Even Level for Sales Income

341	$17.50		$5,967.50
Number of Guests (×)	Income per Guest (=)		Approximate Income Needed to Break Even

   The above calculations show that approximately 341 guests spending a total of $5,967.50 will be necessary to break even. Considering past weekend sales it would not be a problem. Recognizing that the weekend in question will be extra busy, I think the plan is a wise one; not only should we break even, but we should generate additional income.

Part III
Supportive Functions for Dining Service

14

Beverage Service

As anyone who has ever taken a course in American history knows, the Declaration of Independence was written in 1776. Few people know, however, that 1776 may also have heralded the birth of the cocktail. As one version of the story goes, that year Betsy Flanagan, a tavern barmaid in New York State, served a customer a mixed drink decorated with a tail feather from a rooster. The drink was dubbed a "cocktail." From these humble origins, the term not only came into the English language but could certainly be said to have been heard around the world. Since then, the cocktail has continued to be considered "American"—for most well-known cocktails were invented in America. Within 100 years of Betsy Flanagan's invention, both the martini and Manhattan had been introduced—the latter, in fact, by Winston Churchill's mother at the Manhattan Club in New York City.

The tavern was a major part of early American life and has been called a forerunner of today's hotels and motels. In fact, it was so important to such people as the Massachusetts colonists that in the mid-1600s, any town in the colony that did not have a tavern was fined. Of course, as Americans began moving west, the tavern, roadside inn, and saloon went with them. Those that did not provide lodging were generally called taverns or saloons; the more spectacular inns started calling themselves hotels.

While prohibition, which lasted nearly 14 years in America, closed down some restaurants such as Delmonico's and a number of grand hotel barrooms and dining rooms, it produced some very famous free-standing restaurants.

Some of these are Club "21," Lindy's, and El Morocco—all former speakeasies.

Many lodging properties today again offer beverage service both in the dining room and in separate lounge areas. Some hotel coffee shops and cafeteria operations provide a separate section or station to serve alcoholic beverages. These products are an important part of club and show operations (Chapter 13) as well, and room service often provides alcoholic beverages.

While the typical restaurant may generate 30% or more of its total sales from beverage products, in a lodging property's food and beverage department, the percentage of the total sales representing beverages can be even higher. Beverage operations can also make sizable contributions to the profit of the food service operation. The contribution margin (income minus product cost) is greater for the beverage dollar than the food dollar.

Beverage service is also important to the guests. They demand value (quality relative to price) from all the products which they purchase. It simply is not possible to emphasize the food service operation and ignore beverage service because it is an integral part of the overall operating philosophy and standards of well-run properties.[1] As management develops a marketing focus to attract business, the entire package of products and services offered, including beverages, must be considered.

---

[1] For an overview of the origin, history, and service of alcoholic beverages, see Donald A. Bell, *The Spirits of Hospitality* (East Lansing, Mich.: Educational Institute of the American Hotel & Motel Association, 1976).

Managing Service at the Hotel Columbia
Page Twenty-Seven

Lewis Scott recognized that alcoholic beverage service was an important complement to the food provided in a number of the Hotel Columbia's dining outlets. Guests in La Terrasse, the Eagle Room, the three lounges, at banquets, and those who ordered meals from room service could all be served alcoholic beverages if they wanted them.

Lewis was very familiar with the procedures required to design beverage menus, select wines for wine lists, suggestively sell beverages in dining rooms, and develop in-house marketing programs using table tents and menu clip-ons. He had made certain his managers and service staff had received training both in marketing alcoholic beverages and serving them properly.

Lewis was also aware that a significant portion of total beverage sales could accrue from room service sales. Several large, multi-unit lodging operations priced alcoholic beverages sold in guestrooms at retail sales levels rather than marking them up. Similarly, Lewis and his room service manager had decided to use the retail price method for beverages sold in the Hotel Columbia's guestrooms. They believed that the sale of soft drinks,

beverage accompaniments, and appetizers would increase significantly if guests felt that prices charged for beverages ordered from room service were reasonable.

Since banquet operations are another great source of revenue from beverage sales, the hotel's banquet sales representatives would routinely inquire about the need for wine at each banquet they would handle. Lewis had encouraged the representatives to alert potential clients about the availability of either cash or host bars as a part of their special event.

While the sale of alcoholic beverages is important in many commercial operations, Lewis wanted the Hotel Columbia to provide beverage service in a highly professional and socially responsible way. He had recently read several excellent articles dealing with dram shop laws (pertaining to third party liability), and he planned to train his dining outlet managers and beverage service staff about this issue. "After all," Lewis thought, "the socially responsible management of beverage operations is the single most important issue affecting all hospitality operations—including the Hotel Columbia."

Personnel

The number of beverage service personnel needed and the kinds of tasks they will perform depends, of course, on the size and organization of the lodging property. The following discussions identify various personnel generally involved with beverage service.

Beverage Manager

Large food service operations may employ a beverage manager who is responsible for beverage services in the total operation. He/she generally reports to the food and beverage director or his/her assistant. Smaller operations may assign many of the beverage manager's *and* the bartender's tasks to a head bartender.

What does a beverage manager do? Functioning as a department head or section supervisor, the beverage manager may be involved in

personnel administration (selecting, orienting, supervising, scheduling, and evaluating employees). Because he/she frequently plans the beverage service for banquets and other special functions, the beverage manager is often on the banquet planning team.

Many of the beverage manager's duties involve day-to-day management activities. For example, the tasks of purchasing supplies, controlling inventory, standardizing recipes (especially for new promotions), and designing and constantly improving sales income control systems may be the responsibility of the beverage manager. Working with the food and beverage controller and/or the food and beverage director, the beverage manager frequently determines standard beverage costs and develops and uses an operating budget for his/her department. Issues related to the design of beverage service areas and necessary equipment are also important to the beverage manager.

The Beverage Manager and the Bartender

The beverage manager is typically the bartender's boss. Perhaps this relationship is never more obvious than when the bartender first comes on and leaves a shift. Much of the bartender's start-of-shift work involves preparing products and getting ready for service. However, some tasks involve sales income control. The beverage manager may need to issue guest checks and/or cash banks to the bartender, count bar inventories of liquors and wines, and, in the presence of the bartender, clear the register.

Many end-of-shift bartender duties involve cleaning and restocking. However, the beverage manager and the bartender must work together to perform sales income control duties. For example, the beverage manager must determine the amount of sales income which the bartender *should* have collected. He/she must also assess the amount of income *actually* collected and determine the amount of income due from beverages sold in the dining areas. The beverage manager must ensure that the bar inventory is intact and issue beverage products to restock low inventories. He/she must also account for all guest checks, ready the cash bank for its next use, and complete any financial forms that the operation's bookkeeper/controller requires.

Most opening and closing duties are the responsibility of the beverage manager and bartender rather than the restaurant manager. However, procedures that the beverage manager develops must also provide for efficient beverage service in dining areas. The restaurant manager might also have some good ideas about sales income control systems, which have a direct bearing on many aspects of opening and closing procedures for beverage service.

Because the beverage manager's job involves supervising and controlling the production and service of beverages throughout the property, the beverage manager and the restaurant manager must develop a close working relationship. In the same way that the chef is responsible for food production and food-related concerns in the dining room, the beverage manager is responsible for the beverage production and beverage-related concerns in dining service areas. However, because the quality and presentation of beverages, the speed of beverage production, and the appearance and conduct of beverage production and service personnel have an impact on guests' experiences in the dining room, the restaurant manager also has an ongoing interest in the management of beverage service.

How do properties handle this duplication of concern? The secret lies in effective cooperation and communication among all management staff members. Constant communication, which may occur during informal conversations or at formal meetings, ensures a smooth-flowing beverage operation that can be the pride of the property.

Bartender/Mixologist

In addition to performing necessary open- ing and closing procedures related to sales income control, beverage production, and cleanup duties, the bartender/mixologist may also perform a service function. In a public lounge, this staff member may serve guests at the bar. In some lounge operations, especially during slow business periods, the bartender may also serve guests seated at tables. Because bartenders perform such guest services and often are constantly on public view for many hours at a stretch, they must not only know the proper procedures for beverage service and participate in many of the same training sessions that food and beverage servers attend, but they must be very alert to their personal appearance and hygiene.

Because good bartenders/mixologists are often psychologists, innovators, and entertainers, they can make a cocktail lounge or bar famous and draw guests back repeatedly. Such bartenders are not only willing to listen to guests but occasionally will lighten the conversation with a new joke (or change the subject deftly). Even though one partron tries to monopolize their attention, professional bartenders constantly make certain that no one waiting to be served is ignored. They often have to do several tasks at once, yet, of course, must be able to prepare each

The Beverage Manager and the Server

The use of proper motivational and other supervisory techniques should make beverage servers understand the importance of their role in the organization. We have already expressed this concern when we talked about food servers; it also applies to beverage servers. In many operations, the beverage server has an entry level job which can grow into a long-term, professional position. The career ladder in Chapter 2 (Exhibit 2.6) illustrates a possible route by which beverage servers could advance up through the organization.

Authors have written entire books on techniques to supervise entry level employees. The basic principles of supervision apply to beverage servers as well as all other dining service staff and food service employees.

Beverage and restaurant managers should recognize the significant amount of assistance which beverage servers can provide. For example, if operational problems need to be resolved, it is very likely that the beverage servers, who deal with the problems on a constant basis, may have some excellent ideas about how to identify the source of the problems and resolve them. Wise managers involve their staff when making decisions about an operation; they solicit advice from staff members and use their suggestions whenever possible.

patron's drink efficiently, expertly, and seemingly effortlessly. They may invent new drinks and/or garnishes (both alcoholic and nonalcoholic) or think of new ways of marketing traditional ones. Some bartenders, like the nineteenth century's Professor Jerry Thomas (inventor of the Tom and Jerry and other cocktails), are akin to actors. Thomas concocted a drink called the Blue Blazer which amazed his customers. It consisted of hot water and whisky—he set fire to the latter—and, making a stream of flame, poured the liquor into the hot water. He continued to pour the drink back and forth—to the astonishment and peril of all who gathered to watch the spectacular sight.

Bartenders, like chefs, must be knowledgeable about the products they are responsible for preparing. They must know how alcoholic beverages should taste, the ingredients necessary to make them, and the various standard recipes available.[2] While experienced bartenders know that fashions in mixed drinks come and go, they generally have in their repertoire methods for making and garnishing the traditionally popular drinks such as the martini, Manhattan, Scotch and soda, Rob Roy, Bloody Mary, gimlet, old fashioned, Margarita, whisky sour, screwdriver,

gin and tonic, Tom Collins, and vodka versions of some of these. Finally, a bartender's memory should be good enough so that when regular guests, who always order the same drink, return to the bar, he/she should be able to ask simply (and impressively), "The usual?"

Unlike in food production areas, an expediter does not serve as a liaison between the beverage production staff and service personnel. Therefore, the manager must develop procedures to minimize operating problems that can occur, especially during peak business times. He/she must also ensure that the beverage employees consistently follow those procedures.

Because a wide variety of procedures to order, prepare, and provide drinks can be used, each property must develop its own procedures based on such factors as the facility's design, available equipment, and the number of available bartenders and beverage servers. The beverage manager and restaurant manager can work together to develop the best procedures for the property, selecting from those such as the following: (1) The bartender is responsible for preparing the complete drink. He/she obtains the glass, fills it with ice, adds the liquor and other ingredients, provides the garnish, and helps the beverage server with such supplies as swizzle sticks and cocktail napkins. (2) Beverage servers physically present orders to the bartender and wait for him/her to prepare them. (3) A call or

---

[2]   Standard recipes can be found in references such as *Mr. Boston Deluxe Official Bartender's Guide* (Boston: Mr. Boston Distiller Corp., 1979).

timing system indicates when drinks are ready for service. (4) Beverage servers use a remote printing device so they can place orders without going into the beverage production area.

Beverage Server

What do beverage servers do? In many ways, their work is similar to the duties of food servers. For example, beverage servers must typically carry out a required list of opening and closing duties, follow sales income control procedures, and adhere to guest-courtesy standards. They must know how to suggestively sell products, cash checks, accept credit cards, and more. Sometimes, because of their personalities and genuine concern for their guests, beverage servers attract their own clientele. Guests may visit a property primarily because of the charisma of such service staff members. The restaurant manager who is able to make efficient use of beverage servers will have a labor force of trained and qualified dining service employees available constantly.

Procedures for Beverage Service

While each property must develop its own procedures for beverage service, some basic principles are important. Following is a discussion of some of them.

Beverage Service in the Lounge

Either the beverage server or the bartender can serve guests in lounge areas. However, since the bartender may prepare orders for beverage servers, food servers in the dining room, and guests seated at the bar, he/she generally should not leave the behind-bar area. As was explained in Chapter 8, many beverage service procedures directly relate to sales income control. For example, a property may require beverage servers to take drink orders and pay for drinks received from the bartender out of their own cash banks. They then replenish their cash banks with payments from guests. Other properties require beverage servers to present to the bartender both the guest's payment and a guest check, which they may have previously rung through a precheck register. No matter which system is used in a property, management officials must de-

velop and consistently use a process to minimize the possibility that dishonest beverage servers and/or bartenders pocket sales income.

A number of lounges feature food service as well as beverage service. Some of the ways of doing so include: providing snack foods on a continual basis; offering appetizers, especially when lounges are "holding areas" for guests awaiting food service in dining rooms; or serving food items during the cocktail hour. When lounges serve food, and especially when they receive payment for it, management must develop additional sales income control procedures. Developing procedures which are in close harmony with those used to order and serve food in dining areas can help avoid confusion.

Managers or other officials must also develop policies about beverage servers running tabs for guests (serving several rounds of drinks and not receiving payment until just before the guests leave). They must also draft policies about transferring charges for beverage service in the lounge area to the dining room for later payment by guests. Beverage service staff must know how to complete guest checks, use service equipment, and perform all other tasks which the property requires of them.

Beverage Service at the Bar

While in public bars the bartender may serve guests seated at the bar, bartenders in service bars provide drinks to food and/or beverage servers, who then serve them to guests. Because management needs to determine the amount of sales income which bartenders generate during their shifts, bartender service requirements are developed. Bartenders may be required to use numbered guest checks, operate the cash register in certain ways, and write all guest orders on guest checks. Since the bartender is also a salesperson, he/she must be able to interact with guests, suggestively sell products, and otherwise represent the management to the guest.

Beverage Service in Dining Rooms

Most food and beverage operations require food servers to take and serve beverage orders. Frequently, servers use the back of guest checks to record beverage orders. In many operations, the order must go through a precheck register to record sales information for later use by management. (See Chapter 8.) Some operations connect a remote printer to the precheck register; as servers record sales information in the precheck register, the remote printer automatically transfers the information to the bartender who prepares the drinks which appear on the printed slip.

These procedures have several variations. For example, in some operations, food servers use a separate guest check for each round of beverages ordered. They keep *all* the guest checks in a wall slot rack by table number and later combine them for one total bill when the guest wishes to leave.

Some properties use a separate employee to take beverage orders in the restaurant. In effect, this staff member is a beverage server, not a food server, and typically follows the procedures required of beverage servers in lounge areas.

If a property uses a service bar, it becomes relatively easy to calculate the total sales which beverage servers generate in lounge and/or restaurant areas. Calculations are especially easy when the property uses separate cash register keys to record the sales generated by each server. If this equipment is not available, the operation should at least use separate register keys to record the sales generated by food service and beverage service employees.

Cocktail Service. Many procedures used to serve beverages relate to suggestive selling, guest relations, and sales income control. There are, however, traditional rules for beverage service that should be discussed. Food and beverage managers will want to study procedures used in outlets similar to their own and select those that will best suit their own operations.

In some properties, servers prepare drinks at the table. For cocktails, this generally means that the server brings the required glassware filled with ice and mixer (tonic, soda, water, etc.) to the table. (Alternatively, an opened split of the mixer could be carried to the table.) He/she places the glass in front of the guest and then pours the liquor from the jigger or other standard measurer into the glass. The drink is generally served to the guest from the right side. Preparations of after-dinner drinks such as Irish coffee or cafe diable at tableside require special

training to be effective.[3] In the more typical property, bartenders prepare drinks at the public or service bar. (The food or beverage server might also perform some tasks such as adding ice or garnish at the bar.) When this system is used, properties usually develop specific procedures which they expect their servers to follow. For example, servers might be instructed to perform the following tasks:

1. Greet guests; ask if they are ready to make a cocktail order. If there are daily specials, this is the time to tell the guests.

2. When guests order, number guest checks in some way so that you will know who ordered what. Be certain to write down exact directions you are given including the guest's choice of garnish and whether the drink should be "up" or "on the rocks." When the guest requests a call brand, be certain to write it down (e.g., Cutty Sark rather than Scotch; Gordon's rather than gin).

3. When writing checks, stand straight and rest guest checks in your hand, never on the guests' table.

4. When carrying drinks or glasses to the table, always use a cocktail tray.

5. The cocktail tray should rest in one hand while drinks are served with the other; it should never rest on the table.

6. Drinks are typically served from the right.

7. Clear cocktail glasses as soon as they are empty; ask if guests would like a refill when glasses are approximately one-quarter full.

8. Change ashtrays as often as necessary by capping the soiled ashtray with the clean one.

Wine Service Wine sales in the United States are increasing at a fast pace. Many guests already know a great deal about wine; others are interested in knowing more. Therefore, it is impor-

---

[3] Interested readers are referred to Raymond J. Goodman, Jr., *The Management of Service for the Restaurant Manager* (Dubuque, Iowa: Brown,1979), and The Foodservice Editors of CBI, *The Professional Host* (Boston: CBI, 1981).

Exhibit 14.1 Selection of House Brands

When purchasing house brands, consider the following:

1. Supplier services
2. Supplier discounts (if any)
3. Opportunity buys
4. Availability of product
5. Type (reputation) of establishment
6. Price structure of operation
7. Owner preference
8. Liquor proof
9. Testing results
10. Brands used by competitive operations
11. Suggestions from competent individuals
12. Supplier payment plans (if laws permit variations)
13. Reputation of label
14. Clientele preference

Source: Adapted from Jack D. Ninemeier, *Beverage Management: Business Systems For Hotels, Restaurants, and Clubs* (New York: Lebhar-Friedman, 1982), pp. 150-151.

tant for dining service staff to at least know the basics of wine service.

As in so many other situations, when managers select wines to be served in their outlets, they focus first on their guests. Because many guests recognize the most popular wines, managers must decide if their operations will offer them. They also realize that sophisticated guests in a high-check-average property might find it inconsistent to be offered an inexpensive product or an unknown brand name. Similarly, serving a very expensive product to guests in a low-check-average property would also seem inconsistent.

The sale of house or "jug" wine by the glass or carafe is gaining popularity in many food and beverage operations. (In some areas, state and local laws apply to these sales.) In many respects, procedures to select house wines are similar to those used to select house liquors (Exhibit 14.1) in that the reputation of the food and beverage operation and the kind of clientele it plans to serve are primary considerations. Simply stated, a high-check-average property would probably not serve the least expensive (and lowest quality)

house wines, and properties appealing to price-conscious guests would not purchase high-priced wines for sale by the glass or carafe.

Beverage managers should recognize that the sale of house wines by the glass and carafe is an excellent merchandising method, but, in some cases, it may reduce the sale of bottled wines. Therefore, experienced managers confirm that guests desire the sale of wine by the glass/carafe and that such an alternative will increase wine sales beyond the level of income lost from declining bottle sales. Some operations offer relatively expensive bottled wines by the glass as a signature item to enhance the reputation of the property. This practice can also be profitable for the operation because it will receive more revenue by selling the wine glass by glass than it would receive by selling the entire bottle. Clearly, managers of food and beverage operations must consider both marketing/guest-related concerns and the income/profit objectives of the facility as they make decisions about purchasing and selling wines.

Rules of thumb about matching wine with food products are popular. For example, many

Capping an ashtray. (University Club, Michigan State University)

guests believe that they should order white wine with seafood, red wine with meat, and rose wine when both seafood and meat have been chosen as entrees at the same table. While in general, lighter wines complement lighter foods and heavier wines suit heavier foods, many properties recognize that whatever the guest desires is appropriate for him/her. Therefore, while the servers can make suggestions, the final decision is really up to the guest. (Many properties develop wine lists with specific recommendations or make wine suggestions on the food menu.) Dining service staff should, of course, be trained not to react negatively to any wine orders which guests place.

Managers generally develop procedures for their servers to follow while opening and serving wine from corked bottles. The following principles are typical and can be adapted as necessary:

1. Servers should suggestively sell wine. A question or comment about wine by the server can provide a strong incentive for some guests to order the product (e.g., "What wine did you wish to be served tonight?" or "We're featuring the new Beaujolais this week.").

2. Because the names of foreign wines intimidate some guests, include a bin number on the menu so guests can order wine by number rather than name.

3. The server should bring the bottle of wine to the table before opening it. (Older red wines should be carried carefully to avoid disrupting sediment.) He/she should present the bottle by holding it in a food service towel or napkin and showing the person who ordered it the label so that the guest can confirm that he/she did order the product.

4. After the guest has approved the wine, the server opens it by following the steps illustrated in Exhibit 14.2. First, holding the bottle with both hands, cut the foil below the top bulge on the bottle neck and peel it off. Wipe the cork and exposed glass rim with the food service towel and twist the corkscrew into the cork until it is almost through the cork. Then, hooking the lever on the bottle rim, draw the cork out. It may be necessary to slightly wiggle the cork for the last inch; however, do not pop out the cork. Remove the cork from the corkscrew and place it on the right side of the host. He/she may wish to examine the cork to see if the wine has "turned" due to poor storage and/or mishandling in the wine cellar.

5. After the cork is removed, the bottle rim is wiped again.

6. The server should allow the host to sample a small amount of the wine. (Servers should allow uncorked vintage red wines to "rest" or "breathe" before they offer them to guests.) After the host approves, the beverage server can fill the wine glasses of all the guests. Frequently, wine service is counter-clockwise starting with the guest on the host's right. As a courtesy, many properties serve female guests first, then male guests.

7. The server should fill the glass according to the property's procedures—usually a "full" glass is no more than two-thirds full. (Guests who are wine connoisseurs may request the server to fill the glass no more than one-third full.) Some properties like to use very large wine glasses for presentation purposes.

Exhibit 14.2 Opening a Bottle of Wine

1. Present the wine to the guest. 2. Cut the foil below the top bulge of the bottle neck. 3. Wipe the cork and exposed glass rim with a food service towel. 4. Twist the corkscrew into the cork until it is almost through, and hook the lever on the bottle rim. 5. Draw the cork out without making a "popping" sound and remove it from the corkscrew. 6. Place the cork to the right of the host. (Kellogg Center, Michigan State University)

The server should place a bottle of red wine to the right of the host's wine glass—the label should face the host. When white wine has been served, the remaining wine is placed in an ice bucket to the host's right. Some properties use wine bucket stands so that they can keep the wine off the table. The bucket is draped with a clean food service napkin and the food server refills glasses as needed.

The basic procedures for serving sparkling wine are similar to those for serving wine. However, the process for opening the bottle differs. First, the beverage server must remove the wire twist by holding the thumb on the cork, breaking or untwisting the wire, and removing the foil. He/she should hold the cork under a towel, grip the cork firmly, and twist the bottle to loosen the cork. While doing this, he/she should hold the bottle at a 45-degree angle and point it away from all guests and other service staff. The secret to opening sparkling wine is to hold the cork and twist the bottle—*not* the reverse. When done correctly, the cork is not forcibly expelled from the bottle; the server always has the cork in his/her hand so that no damage or injury results. After the cork is removed, the server wipes the rim of the bottle and pours the wine carefully so that the effervescence is not lost.

When properties serve wine in the dining room, food and beverage servers often serve the wine. However, some properties, especially high-check-average outlets, use a wine steward or "sommelier" (an expert in wine).

Staff members must know what to do when the host rejects the wine after he/she has tasted it. In many properties, servers simply return inexpensive wines to the bar, and production employees use it later for cooking or other purposes. However, pre-established policies dictate the return of high cost wines. If the wine is bad, it can probably be returned to the supplier for credit. If, in the judgment of the beverage manager, it *is* acceptable, it could be offered as a "special" for sale by the drink. Unusually expensive wines may require a statement on the wine list indicating that guests are obligated to make at least partial payment if they return a wine which is of acceptable quality to the wine steward. This latter policy has many negative marketing implications, however, and managers should carefully consider the consequences of such a policy before they implement it.

Restaurant managers should understand that they need to develop consistent procedures for their property which are in line with commonly accepted practices. They must then communicate these procedures to the affected dining service staff through effective training programs and supervise them to ensure that they consistently follow the procedures.

Beverage Shopper Service

Shopper services are discussed in the case study in Chapter 9. Properties not only use such services to evaluate various aspects of food service and production but also for beverage service. Exhibit 14.3 is a sample of a shopper's evaluation form for overall beverage service. It would be especially useful in evaluating servers in lounges and bars but could also be used in dining rooms and coffee shops that offer alcoholic beverages. This form can be adapted as necessary to suit a specific property. If the shopper will also be evaluating sales income control methods, other applicable items can be added to the form, such as "The bartender wrote each order on a guest check" or "The bartender did not make change out of the tip jar" or "The server totaled the guest check properly."

Exhibit 14.4 illustrates a sample form a shopper could use to evaluate wine service. It would often be used in dining rooms in conjunction with food service shopper forms and, perhaps, the beverage service form shown in Exhibit 14.3.

Note that Exhibit 14.4 reflects the specific procedures used in a property. For example, the consistent practice in the property that uses this form is that red wine should be poured so that glasses are no more than half full and white wine so that no more than three-fourths of the glass is full.

As with Exhibit 14.3, this form can be adapted as necessary to suit a specific property's needs. Most properties that use shopper services not only use the evaluation forms as training tools but also explain to employees that they do occasionally use shopper's services to evaluate training methods.

Exhibit 14.3 Beverage Service Evaluation Form

	5	4	3	2	1
A. The beverage item corresponded with its menu description (if applicable).	5	4	3	2	1
B. The liquor ingredient(s) was (were) of acceptable quality.	5	4	3	2	1
C. The mixer was acceptable.	5	4	3	2	1
If not, what was wrong? (too strong, sweet, sour, salty, bitter, or other) _____					
D. All drinks ordered were available.	5	4	3	2	1
E. The presentation of the drink was appropriate.	5	4	3	2	1
F. There was a variety of specialty drinks.	5	4	3	2	1
G. Your call brand was available.	5	4	3	2	1
H. The garnish appeared fresh.	5	4	3	2	1
I. The drinks were of overall excellent quality.	5	4	3	2	1
If not, what was the problem? _____					
J. All beverage items were served at the proper temperature.	5	4	3	2	1
K. The glasses were appropriately sized.	5	4	3	2	1
L. The ice was appropriately sized.	5	4	3	2	1
M. The drinks were consistent in quality.	5	4	3	2	1
N. The overall quality of the product was excellent.	5	4	3	2	1
O. Comments regarding your beverage service: _____					

STANDARD POINT SCORE FOR BEVERAGE SERVICE _70_   ACTUAL POINT SCORE _____

Beverage Service for Banquets

Banquet guests frequently enjoy alcoholic beverages before, during, and/or after the meal. Many properties use one or a combination of the following popular beverage plans to provide banquet beverage service.

Cash Bar. At a cash bar, guests pay cash to the bartender or purchase tickets from a cashier to pay for drinks prepared by the bartender. With this latter plan, the cashier may be issued numbered tickets of different colors, which represent different drink prices. The guest pays the cashier the cost of the drink he/she desires and is given a color-coded ticket which he/she presents to the bartender. The beverage manager generally sets the sales price, which can be the same as or different from normal selling prices. Frequently, management will reduce the price from the normal lounge rate in order to attract additional business.

Host Bar: Charge by the Drink. The host bar uses a system to keep track of the number of each type of drink served (e.g., the presentation of a ticket, a ring-up on the register, or a mark on a tally sheet). Guests are not charged; rather, the host pays according to a pre-set drink selling price which is assessed for the number of drinks served. Again, the drink sales price will frequently be reduced from the normal charge to attract special events to the facility.

Host Bar: Charge by the Bottle. This plan involves charging for beverages consumed on the basis of the number of bottles used or opened.

Exhibit 14.4 Wine Service Evaluation Form

A. The food server suggested a wine to complement the meal.	5	4	3	2	1
B. The wine was properly presented before opening.	5	4	3	2	1
C. The wine was opened properly (e.g., the server used a knife to cut the foil just below the bulge).	5	4	3	2	1
D. The glass selection was an excellent choice for the type of wine served.	5	4	3	2	1
E. The host was poured a sample of the wine.	5	4	3	2	1
F. The bottle was twisted at the completion of the pour.	5	4	3	2	1
G. The wine was filled to the proper glass level (e.g., no more than half full for red wine; three-fourths full for white).	5	4	3	2	1
H. The wine was served at an appropriate temperature (e.g., white wine chilled—50°F (10°C); red wine at cellar temperature—65°F (18°C).	5	4	3	2	1
I. Comments regarding your wine service _____					

STANDARD POINT SCORE FOR WINE SERVICE ___40___   ACTUAL POINT SCORE _____

The difference between the number of bottles of each type of liquor, beer, etc., in the "beginning inventory" and "ending inventory" behind the bar represents the number of bottles used. An agreed-upon price *for each bottle opened* is assessed to the event's sponsor (who is, in effect, purchasing any liquor, wine, or nonalcoholic beverage that remains in open bottles).

Charge by the Hour. This beverage pricing plan involves establishing a fixed beverage fee per person per hour. The effective use of this plan involves estimating the hourly number of drinks guests will consume. While such estimates are not easy to make for all groups (e.g., health- or weight-conscious groups will probably consume less than fraternities or other groups), a rule of thumb used by some major food and beverage departments is three drinks per person during the first hour, two the second, and one and a half the third. Beverage managers who want to price drinks for special events on a per person per hour basis can use this formula to estimate the number of drinks to be served per person. Then they must multiply the number of drinks per person by an established drink charge to arrive at the hourly drink charge per person. As manag-

Established wine menu for banquet service. (Courtesy of the Hotel Du Pont, Wilmington, Delaware

ers use the hourly charge system they will obtain their own specific information that will assist them in setting hourly charges for future events.

Wine Service. When banquets in some properties include wine, service employees circulate with bottles of several wines (red and white, dry and semi-dry) so that they can offer guests a choice. Of course, banquet department employees must be trained to practice proper wine service. So they will be knowledgeable about the wines they serve, they should be told about them during the employees' briefing session prior to the actual event.

When properties serve beverages at banquet tables, managers must carefully plan procedures for providing drinks to the guests. Perhaps a portable bar can be set up in a nearby area so that bartenders can prepare drinks as needed. White or rose wines (which should be chilled before service) could be moved to refrigerated units in the banquet serving kitchens close to the time of service; could be maintained for small groups with ice in tote or other boxes; or could be chilled in remote walk-ins and quickly transported to the banquet site when needed. The point is that beverage, catering, and banquet staff members must initially work together to develop procedures that suit different sized groups in different dining areas within the property.

Portable beverage service equipment makes the task of providing beverages much easier. Exhibit 14.5 pictures a portable bar. Most portable equipment is on wheels; it can be stored in remote areas and wheeled to the point of use as needed. Some of the options for stocking the bar include: assigning the bartender who will work at the event the responsibility for stocking the portable bar, requiring a beverage storeroom attendant to stock it, or having bar backs (assistant bartenders) receive beverage products from the inventory to transport to portable bars which are already in use. Some operations make available only the minimum quantity of beverage products required to open service; runners then bring additional beverage products as needed.

Wine Sales for Banquets

Wine sales can contribute significantly to the banquet department's profits. Since consumption of wine is dramatically increasing in the United States, an important question to ask is,

Exhibit 14.5 A Portable Bar

(Kellogg Center, Michigan State University)

"How can I increase wine sales in the banquet department?"

First of all, the wines on the banquet list should be carefully selected and available in the quantities needed. They must complement the food items offered and have an acceptable price. Overpriced wines may cause clients to delete them from their event and, as well, question the value of the other products and services they purchase from the property. Therefore, some relationship between the prices charged for food and the wine which accompanies it should be established. For example, it doesn't make sense to serve an $8.00 per glass wine with a meal costing a total of $10.00.

Generally, you do not need to offer a large selection of wines for banquets. If a client desires a specific wine, it can usually be ordered for the event. Sometimes an extensive wine list only confuses clients. Many banquet departments simply work from the hotel's general wine lists since special wines are rarely required for banquets. While this is a practical approach, some guests may turn down wine entirely when they see the high prices attached to rare wines on a general wine list. (Such wines are often high priced because they are available in the property's gourmet restaurant.)

APERITIFS AND PORTS

Dubonnet Red	$31.00
Harvey's Bristol Cream	$38.00
Dry Sack	$38.00
Cockburn's No. 25 Port	$38.00

VERMOUTH

Included in Bottle Prices

BEER

Budweiser Light, Coors	
Budweiser, Miller, Miller Lite	$ 2.50
Heineken, Michelob	$ 3.00

MIXERS

Included in Bottle Prices

BARTENDERS

First three (3) hours	$55.00
Each hour thereafter	$18.50

CASHIERS

First three (3) hours	$45.00
Each hour thereafter	$15.00

SCOTCH

Chivas Regal	$46.00
Johnnie Walker Black	$46.00
J&B Rare	$42.00
Cutty Sark	$42.00
Dewar's White Label	$42.00
House Scotch (Litre)	$38.00

BOURBON

Wild Turkey	$46.00
Jack Daniels Black	$46.00
I.W. Harper	$42.00
Old Grand-Dad (86°)	$42.00
Early Times	$42.00
Old Forester (86°)	$42.00
House Bourbon (Litre)	$38.00

BLENDED WHISKEY

Seagrams 7 Crown	$42.00
House Blend (Litre)	$38.00

CANADIAN WHISKEY

Seagrams Crown Royal	$46.00
Seagrams V.O.	$42.00
Canadian Club	$42.00

GIN

Gordons	$42.00
Beefeater	$42.00
Tanqueray	$46.00
House Gin (Litre)	$38.00

Consider Cordials with Coffee after your meal.

VODKA

Stolichnaya	$46.00
Smirnoff (80°)	$42.00
House Vodka (Litre)	$38.00

RUM

Bacardi Gold Reserve	$46.00
Bacardi Silver	$42.00
House Rum (Litre)	$38.00

BRANDIES & CORDIALS

Courvoisier V.S.	$46.00
Hennessy Bras-Arme	$46.00
Kahlua	$46.00
B & B	$46.00
Drambuie	$46.00
Grand Marnier	$46.00
Frangelico	$46.00

DRINK PRICES (Select One Choice)

Open Bar

House Brands	$2.95 per drink
Call Brands	$3.40 per drink
Premium Brands	$3.75 per drink
Cordials	$4.25 per drink

Cash Bar
(House Brands Only)

Highballs	$3.00 per drink
Cocktails	$3.00 per drink
Imported Beer	$3.00 per drink
Domestic Beer	$2.50 per drink
Wine	$2.50 per drink
Soft Drinks	$1.50 per drink

All receptions with a minimum of food service will require a waiter charge of $55.00 per waiter for three (3) hours and $18.50 each hour thereafter. One (1) waiter required for each one hundred guests. All beverages MUST be purchased from the hotel. Gratuity and D.C. City Sales Tax not included, except in cash bar prices.

PRICES ARE SUBJECT TO CHANGE WITHOUT NOTICE

PRICES DO NOT INCLUDE D.C. CITY SALES TAX AND GRATUITY

Banquet and reception beverage menu including drinks ranging from cocktails and aperitifs to brandies and cordials. Note details concerning service personnel. (Courtesy of Sheraton Washington Hotel, Washington, D.C.)

A well-informed and well-trained banquet sales staff is an absolute must. When catering executives in a number of lodging properties talk to prospective clients, they emphasize wine and assume that the clients will include it in their banquets. (There are a few obvious exceptions to this statement. A catering executive would not bring up the subject at all to a client organizing an Alcoholics Anonymous function, for example, nor would he/she mention alcoholic beverages to representatives of certain religious groups.) The catering department should also mention wine service in any promotional material it develops. Since every banquet is a special occasion, the material should note that special occasions are not complete without wine.

The catering staff should be very familiar with the department's wine selection. Management can make brief descriptions of each avail-

able wine to the sales staff and prospective clients. Training seminars and tasting sessions can also help employees become familiar with the wines.

After a banquet with wine service has been booked, it would be very annoying to both the catering representative and the client to learn that the wine is no longer available or has increased in price. Thus, management needs to develop effective and cooperative relationships with wine wholesalers/buyers. Suppliers should be alerted when a banquet wine list includes some of their products. The suppliers' assistance should be requested when management is making these products available on a continual basis. If a supplier cannot guarantee price stability, their wines should be removed from the banquet wine list.

Wine needs should be coordinated with the

Pricing Banquet Wines

Many hotels price banquet wines at three to four times their cost. With this plan, a bottle of wine which costs $3 will sell for at least $9. More expensive wines are typically priced at a declining markup rate and therefore are not priced at the above rate. When a catering department applies volume principles, the more bottles of wine ordered by the client, the less the catering department needs to mark up the wine. When guests purchase wine by the glass, its price is frequently the same as wine sold by the glass over the bar; the banquet department *may*, however, give the guest a discount of 25 cents a glass.

Catering executives can also use wine to help close the sale on a large function which requires guest rooms, meeting space, and other banquet services at a time when business is normally slow. In this case, the wine profit might be reduced; however, the property would still make a significant profit by virtue of the total sale. Of course, catering executives should make these decisions in cooperation with the food and beverage director and/or sales director. The client can be told that the significant discount is available because of the special circumstances surrounding the group.

purchasing department. In large properties, purchasing personnel can monitor and expedite wine purchases from suppliers. The expediting is necessary because it often takes a long time for delivery when a large volume of wine is ordered. If quantity discounts and/or other price reductions are possible, a wise purchasing department can help provide these benefits to the property.

When wine is not a part of the banquet contract, it can sometimes be sold on a cash basis. Attractive displays of available wines at the entrance to the banquet room can help sell wine. A limited list of readily available wines could also be placed on each table. A beverage server can ask guests if they desire wine by the glass, carafe, bottle, or magnum. The circulation of wine carts also provides a tremendous opportunity to increase wine sales. Finally, consider using a bottle of wine in a dish decorated with fruits and nuts instead of flower decorations. You may attract banquet attendees to the display, and wine sales can result. (Be sure you can justify these costly displays with increased wine sales.)

Income Control in Banquet Bars

Sales income control is just as important in managing cash bars at banquets as it is to the ongoing sales of beverage products in dining and lounge areas. In some respects, however, you can simplify the procedures since fewer liquor products are generally available. For example, if only two types of liquor (house and call) are available, catering or beverage management staff can easily reconcile the amount of liquor sold with the amount of income collected. The amount of liquor issued to the portable bar (both initially and during service) can be recorded on a form similar to the one in Exhibit 14.6. By conducting an ending inventory, the amount of each product actually used can be assessed. The amount of income which the servers should have generated from a particular liquor can be calculated by expressing the figure from the farthest right column on 14.6—"Net Use"—in standard portion sizes. Exhibit 14.7 illustrates the process. The form works reasonably well when the same price for all drinks of one type (house or call) is charged. However, if different prices are charged for drinks of the same type but with different amounts of liquor (e.g., a double), the average number of ounces of liquor per drink must first be calculated.[4] The calculation must also be adjusted when different prices are charged for different drinks of the same type. For example, a martini containing two ounces of house gin might be sold for $3 and a gin and tonic containing $1\frac{1}{2}$ ounces of gin for $2.

You can see the difficulty in assessing standard income per bottle that arises as you develop

---

4   Jack D. Ninemeier, *Planning and Control for Food and Beverage Operations* (East Lansing, Mich.: Educational Institute of the American Hotel & Motel Association, 1982), pp. 210-216.

Exhibit 14.6 Portable Bar Setup Sheet

Function Order Number __*1007-F*__   Name __*Anne Helmstead*__   Number of People __*25*__

Room __*Blue*__

Date __*5/2/xx*__

Time __*5:00 - 6:00 p.m.*__

Number of Bottles or Drinks

Name of Item	Size	Setup	Add'l.	Add'l.	Add'l.	Total	Returns			Net Use
							Full	Empty	Partial	
House Scotch	liter	5	3	1	1	10	1	8	.5	8.5
House Bourbon	liter	3	1			4	1	3	0	3.0
Call Scotch	liter									
Call Gin	liter									
Vodka	liter									
Rum	liter									
Sherry	liter									
Vermouth	750 ml									
White Wine	750 ml									
Beer	12 oz.									
Bloody Mary Mix	½ liter									
Orange Juice	½ gal.									
Coke	2 liters									
Bitter Lemon	1 liter									
Diet Soda	1 liter									
Soda	1 liter									
Tonic	1 liter									
7-Up	2 liters									
Ginger Ale	1 liter									

Exhibit 14.7 Sample Calculation of Potential Income

For Scotch:

8.5 liter bottles (Net amount used)	×	33.8 oz. per liter (Ounces/Bottle)	=	287.3 (Total oz. used)
287 (rounded) (Total ounces used)	÷	1.5 oz. (Average portion size)	=	191.33 (Number of drinks sold)
191 (rounded) (number of drinks sold)	×	$2.00 (Average sales price)	=	$383.00 (Potential income)

Typically, bartenders pour (measure) liquor on the basis of ounces; however, they purchase liquor bottles in metric units. Managers can calculate potential income from sales of a particular beverage as follows:

1. Calculate the number of ounces actually used. (In Exhibit 14.6, you will note that 8.5 one-liter bottles of scotch were used at the banquet. Since each liter contains 33.8 ounces, approximately 287 ounces of scotch were actually used.)

2. Determine the approximate number of drinks sold. (Divide the total ounces used by the portion size: 287 oz. ÷ 1.5 oz. = approximately 191 drinks sold.)

3. Estimate the potential income. (Multiply the number of drinks sold by the selling price: 191 drinks × $2.00 selling price = $382.)

calculations of potential income within these varying circumstances. Many beverage managers resolve the problem by tracking drink sales, ounces used, and income generated in order to arrive at average rates which they can easily include in the calculations in Exhibit 14.7. The same process is used to reconcile the amount of beverages sold with the income generated by all other types of beverages listed on the setup sheet in Exhibit 14.6.

Purchasing Beverage Service Supplies and Equipment

You know that you must consider the guests' wants and needs as you purchase supplies and equipment for the food service operation. It is just as important to address marketing concerns when you select beverage service products.

Beverage Products

Many operations classify their liquor into "house," "call," and "premium" categories. House liquor is served when the guest does not order a drink using a special brand of liquor; call liquors are specific brands of liquor which guests often request by name. Premium liquors are very costly call brands. (Properties price them at a higher rate than call brands.) Typically, many food and beverage operations purchase house liquors which are less expensive and presumably of somewhat lower quality than their call brands; they are usually less expensive for guests too. Exhibit 14.1 lists some of the factors which should be considered when decisions are being made about these products.

Attitudes of beverage managers about house brands can range from "Don't use anything you wouldn't be proud to display on the back bar," to "Use the least expensive; let people pay extra for premium brands." Many managers use neither the least nor the most expensive brands; rather, they shop for value with an emphasis on what the guest desires. Input from the restaurant manager (who generally has a great deal of knowledge about the clientele) can help. After all, dining service employees must serve the products which the property purchases. Guests will ask the servers, "What is your house brand?" Both beverage sales and the property's reputation will be enhanced if the answer to that question is compatible with the interests of the guest. As an oversimplified example, one would obviously not serve the least expensive liquor available in a high-check-average property where drinks sell for $4.00 each. It is a marketing decision which is best made when dining service employees work with beverage management personnel.

Marketing concerns are also important when you purchase call brands. It is not generally possible nor, for that matter, desirable to offer every available brand of liquor. A much better approach is to have available those call brands which guests most frequently request. If a specific brand is not available, most guests will order another. Obviously, if guests frequently order an unavailable call brand, it should be added to the property's product list. This is another example of how dining service staff can help beverage managers. After all, food and beverage servers know what the guests order. Such information is invaluable to managers who make the purchase decisions. (Servers should use great care to serve exactly what guests order or fines, lawsuits, and even the loss of a property's liquor license could result. For example, if a guest orders "Pepsi" or "Jim Beam" and is served another cola or bourbon without being told that the property does not have the name brand, the server may get the property into a great deal of trouble.)

The procedures for purchasing beverage products are the same as those used to purchase dining service supplies (Chapter 5). In many ways, however, the purchase of beverage products is less difficult. For example, you generally purchase beverage products by brand—which then becomes the purchase specification—and you usually cannot purchase a specific brand from more than one local supplier. Also, in some states you can purchase beverage products only from state-controlled facilities; the state agency

dictates many of the purchasing procedures which the property normally develops.

Typically, many beverage suppliers offer deals, such as case discounts, when a property purchases a specific number of units. Also known as "post-offs," case discounts are usually seasonal. These discounts can effectively reduce your beverage costs. Sometimes, suppliers have a family plan in which they offer special prices if properties purchase all or most of their house brands in predetermined quantities. Beverage managers should carefully consider these deals but temper their interest in reducing beverage costs with the marketing concerns discussed previously.

Beverage Service Equipment

The typical beverage operation needs far less equipment than the food service operation. However, in order to minimize equipment-related problems which have an impact on guests, beverage serving equipment must be properly selected and used.

In recent years, a wide variety of automated beverage equipment has become available. Metered equipment counts the number of ounces of liquor that runs through the metered lines. This equipment helps to account for the liquor sold, making it easier to reconcile the beverage income generated by the products. More sophisticated equipment actually prepares the drinks which guests order. For example, some equipment can automatically add mixers, two or more liquors, juices, and more. Generally, such equipment is interfaced with a cash register that prints the guest check, records sales information, and enables the manager to review almost any required statistical information.

Automated equipment is neither *right* nor *wrong* for all operations. Managers must make decisions based on the specific needs of their facilities. They should consult with their dining service staff and consider not only the marketing implications of the equipment's use but also the maintenance, operational, and repair costs of such equipment. Some key points to consider are: automated systems reduce bartender errors and increase sales income control; they reduce training time, storage space behind the bar (since liquor can be stored in remote areas), and purchasing costs (since larger bottles, which frequently have lower cost-per-unit prices, can be used).

However, if the equipment breaks down, time will be lost while supplies are brought in, and bartenders (who may be untrained) will have to hand-pour drinks and work out of a nonoperative cash drawer. Therefore, when a property uses automated equipment, management will have to develop procedures for use if and when the automated equipment fails. In addition, some guests may become concerned that they are not receiving the quality or amount of liquor which they have ordered because they cannot see the bartender prepare the drinks nor see their favorite label on the bottle from which their drink is made. Finally, managers should know that automated equipment often instills negative attitudes in bartenders; such negative attitudes might be conveyed to guests.

Many properties have resolved the problem of guest concerns by using automated systems in service bars (which the public does not view) and retaining manual systems in public bars. Because lounges and dining areas have literally hundreds of seats from which guests cannot see the bartender preparing drinks, managers must be careful not to make decisions about beverage equipment based solely on the fact that a few guests seated at the bar can observe the equipment in use.

Cash registers and data machines are other pieces of beverage service equipment which managers may have to purchase. Some properties have replaced yesterday's cash registers with modern, high technology, electronic registers (electronic data machines) which do much more than ring up a sale and hold the money collected. Precheck registers, which record sales information on a by-server basis and print required information on guest checks, were discussed in Chapter 8.

Other necessary beverage service equipment includes refrigerated units, frozen drink machines, sinks, glass storage areas, blenders, and hand tools such as shakers, corkscrews, and bar strainers. Bartenders must have adequate equipment to serve guests efficiently. When equipment is in public bar areas within view of

guests, it must be compatible with the property's atmosphere. Noisy, rusty, dented, and dirty pieces of equipment are simply not compatible with any atmosphere and do not exhibit a concern for sanitation. Remember that health officials can close down bars and lounges that are not absolutely clean at all times.

Bar Design

The design of the bar area is very important. Exhibit 14.8 shows one possible layout/design for a combination public and service bar as well as the placement of equipment in it.[5]

Professional bartenders and servers know that bar design and available equipment affect their productivity and performance, which, in turn, affect service to guests. Thus, when bar areas are designed, those responsible should consider the sequence of the activities necessary to prepare drinks, properly locate equipment required for these tasks, design work stations so that employees can share expensive and/or space-consuming equipment, and provide ample space for drinks that are ready to be picked up.

A server working from this bar has ample room to place a serving tray on the pick-up area (location 14). In fact, several servers who will need drinks at the same time would be able to place their trays in this area. The layout also allows the service staff to perform several production tasks (e.g., placing ice in glasses, adding garnishes, filling glasses with soda). Note that one electronic data machine is behind the bar (location 2) while a second one is located near where the bartender prepares/provides drinks to servers; these locations will help make this bar's sales income control system work efficiently.

---

5 For further discussion of this subject, see Jack D. Nine-meier, *Beverage Management: Business Systems for Restaurants, Hotels, and Clubs* (New York: Lebhar-Friedman, 1982), pp. 70-78.

Exhibit 14.8 Combination Public/Service Bar

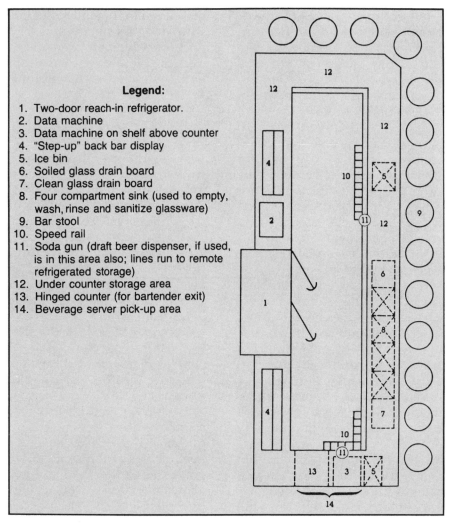

Legend:
 1. Two-door reach-in refrigerator.
 2. Data machine
 3. Data machine on shelf above counter
 4. "Step-up" back bar display
 5. Ice bin
 6. Soiled glass drain board
 7. Clean glass drain board
 8. Four compartment sink (used to empty, wash, rinse and sanitize glassware)
 9. Bar stool
10. Speed rail
11. Soda gun (draft beer dispenser, if used, is in this area also; lines run to remote refrigerated storage)
12. Under counter storage area
13. Hinged counter (for bartender exit)
14. Beverage server pick-up area

Source: Jack D. Ninemeier, *Beverage Management: Business Systems for Hotels, Restaurants, and Clubs* (New York: Lebhar-Friedman, 1982), p. 74.

Managing Service at the Hotel Columbia
Page Twenty-Eight

The Hotel Columbia's president and managing director dropped by Lewis Scott's office with materials he had just received from the Educational Institute of the American Hotel & Motel Association.

"Lewis," he said, "this may be exactly what you've been looking for—a complete training course about the responsible service of alcoholic beverages."

Lewis and his supervisor looked at the leaflet describing the *Serving Alcohol with Care* program (a copy of it accompanies this case study).

"I'm going to do just as the leaflet suggests

and order the training package today," said Lewis. "We need 300 servers' manuals to cover our beverage service staff plus any new employees we hire during the year. I think we'd better order seven manager's manuals: one each for our beverage director; director of restaurant operations; the managers of La Terrasse, the Eagle Room, room service, and banquets; and, of course, I want one too."

The Hotel Columbia's president concluded their conversation by saying, "I agree entirely. I'm also going to check with our insurance agent and see if we can get a reduction in our liquor liability insurance premium."

Promote the Proper Use of Alcohol

You can't afford not to. . .

Extend your hospitality to patrons by encouraging proper dispensing and use of alcoholic beverages. At the same time, protect your property's interests – be aware of the importance of responsible alcohol service.

The Educational Institute of the American Hotel & Motel Association has developed a complete new training package specifically for the hospitality industry: **Serving Alcohol with Care.** Available in a convenient handbook and/or seminar format, this low-cost, easy-to-use training tool has two primary components which provide important information for both managers and servers.

The Manager's Manual:

* suggests policies and information on procedures followed by other managers with regard to alcohol service
* suggests possible alternatives to traditional "happy hours" and "two-for-one" promotions
* explains in simple terms the liability associated with Dram Shop Laws
* offers tips for the instruction/training component, including role playing ideas to better prepare employees

The Servers' Manual:

* helps servers understand the physical and psychological effects of alcohol
* offers tips for observing patrons' alcohol consumption
* points out behavioral patterns to watch for
* explains how to use discretion in serving
* discusses when to consider discontinuing service of alcohol to a patron
* suggests tactful ways to discontinue service of alcohol to a patron

Your employees may learn the material by reading it themselves, by participating in an in-house group setting, or through a state association-sponsored seminar. No matter what the format, **Serving Alcohol with Care** gets the message across quickly and effectively.

By participating in this program, you show your patrons and your community that you care enough to make yourself and your employees aware of alcohol service related problems. Participation helps show a responsible management attitude which could be important to your property in helping to prevent unfortunate accidents.

Please join us in promoting safe, responsible, and enjoyable use of alcohol. Order your training package today! Cost: $15.00 per participant (group discounts available). This fee includes a Servers Manual, final test, grading of the final test, and a Certificate of Completion from the Educational Institute of AH&MA. The Manager's Manual charge is $49.95. Simply complete the attached order form and mail it with your check made payable to:

Order Form

Yes! We want to promote safe, responsible, and enjoyable use of alcohol.

Name _____ Title _____

Property _____

Address _____

City, State, Zip _____

Telephone (_____) _____

Please fill my order as follows:

Servers' Manuals:

1-9 copies at $15.00 ea.	#_____	$_____
10-49 copies at $13.50 ea.	#_____	$_____
50-99 copies at $12.00 ea.	#_____	$_____
100-199 copies at $11.00 ea.	#_____	$_____
200 or more copies at $10.00 ea.	#_____	$_____

Manager's Manual(s):

$49.95 ea.	#_____	$_____

Subtotal: _____
U.S. and Canada add 10% to subtotal for shipping and handling: +_____
Other countries add 30% to subtotal for shipping and handling: _____
Michigan residents add 4% sales tax: +_____
TOTAL: _____

☐ Enclosed is my check

☐ Please bill my credit card

☐ Visa   ☐ Mastercard
☐ American Express   ☐ Diners Club

Account #

☐☐☐☐☐☐☐☐☐☐☐☐☐☐☐☐

Expiration Date _____

Signature _____

Detach and return in the postage-paid envelope, **or call 1 (517) 353-5500**

You Should Know About. . .

Alcohol and "Third Party Liability"

Society is placing increasing responsibility upon the *sellers* of goods. Third party liability presupposes that servers become responsible for controlling the amount of alcohol consumed by patrons. Twenty-three states have passed legislation which hold liquor licensees liable for injuries to third parties caused by intoxicated persons. More states are expected to follow suit.

Alcohol and "Common Law Liability"

A person who is injured by the acts of an intoxicated individual may also have the common law right to bring suit against the owners of a restaurant or bar where the person causing the injuries was served intoxicating beverages. Such suits may be based on a common law theory of negligence that a barkeeper, for example, has a duty not to serve a known "drunk."

The Educational Institute of the American Hotel & Motel Association
1407 S. Harrison Road, #310
Stephen S. Nisbet Building
East Lansing, Michigan 48823
(517) 353-5500

Protect Yourself and Your Patrons. . .

SERVING ALCOHOL WITH CARE

an important program for owners, operators, and employees in the hospitality industry from

a nonprofit educational foundation

15

Sanitation, Safety, and Security

All dining service personnel must pay close attention to sanitation, safety, and security procedures; they have a responsibility to protect the guests whom they serve. While local and state laws can require dining operations to follow such procedures as storing food products in certain ways, installing sneeze-guards on buffets, limiting occupancy of a dining room to a certain number, and installing fire extinguishers, such mandates should be only the beginning of dining service employees' concerns. Professional dining service employees know that they must do all that is possible to ensure that their guests' visits to their facility are enjoyable. That obligation includes provision for sanitation, safety, and security measures that are far beyond the dictates of the law.

Correct procedures in all three of these important areas not only affect the reputation of a particular dining outlet in a lodging property but also the reputation of the entire property. No manager would want headlines about a food-related illness that had been traced back to his/her outlet in the hotel. Experienced managers know that a kitchen or dining room fire or other emergency that results in property damage or worse—human injury or death—will adversely affect a property's business. Thus, such managers ensure that sanitation, safety, and security measures are major parts of their standard operating procedures for dining service employees. Each of these three concerns are discussed in detail in this chapter.

Sanitation

Sanitation and cleanliness are important influences on a guest's attitude about a property.[1] Exhibit 15.1 reviews characteristics which guests view as important when they choose a restaurant. You will notice that in quick- and moderate-service properties, cleanliness is the number one priority of guests. In full-service facilities, cleanliness is still very important; it ranks number two. Note that cleanliness is more important to many people than price, menu variety, portion sizes, or nutritional content of foods. Another nationwide survey of restaurant patrons yielded similar results which are listed in Exhibit 15.2. As the exhibit illustrates, overall cleanliness ranked second to tasty food in the requirements of frequent restaurant patrons when they dine out. Exhibit 15.2 also shows that three of the top five characteristics which restaurant patrons consider most important in choosing a restaurant relate to sanitation and cleanliness.

Guests often believe that if public areas such as restrooms and dining rooms as well as dining service supplies such as tableware and glassware are not clean, it is very likely that back-of-house

---

[1] Interested readers are referred to Ronald F. Cichy, *Sanitation Management* (East Lansing, Mich.: Educational Institute of the American Hotel & Motel Association, 1984).

Managing Service at the Hotel Columbia
Page Twenty-Nine

Lewis Scott knew that all managers of food and beverage outlets must provide ongoing attention to sanitation, safety, and security as they develop training programs for dining service employees and supervise them. Both employees and guests must be protected.

In spite of efforts to protect guests, unfortunate incidents did still occur. Lewis was, at the moment, reviewing an accident investigation report submitted by the hotel's security department.

Since he had received a phone call from the victim's attorney, he was already familiar with the problem (a guest in the dining room had fallen down some steps). Lewis had, of course, referred the attorney to the hotel's legal counsel. Because he did not know the exact legal implications of the problem, he knew that the referral was best.

"What can we do to help prevent accidents in dining areas?" he asked himself.

areas in which the property stores and prepares food are also dirty—and they are probably right. Most food outlets wish to present the best possible image to their guests. If they don't care about sanitation in areas with public access, why would they care about areas out of public view?

On the other hand, managers in some food service operations recognize guest concerns and use a dual standard; they keep front-of-house areas meticulously clean but give less attention to nonpublic areas. Of course, their approach is very shortsighted because proper sanitation ex-

Exhibit 15.1 Consumer Reactions Toward Restaurant Practices/Responsibilities

	Characteristics Important in Choosing a Restaurant		
	Type of Property		
Rank Order	**Quick Service**	**Moderate Service**	**Full Service**
1	Cleanliness	Cleanliness	Food quality/preparation
2	Food quality/preparation	Food quality/preparation	Cleanliness
3	Price	Menu variety	Menu variety
4	Location	Price	Courtesy/friendliness
5	Courtesy/friendliness	Courtesy/friendliness	Type of atmosphere
6	Speed of service	Speed of service	Price
7	Menu variety	Location	Nutrition of meals
8	Nutrition of meals	Nutrition of meals	Location
9	Type of atmosphere	Type of atmosphere	Speed of service
10	Choice of portion sizes	Choice of portion sizes	Individual preparation of meals
11	Individual preparation of meals	Individual preparation of meals	Choice of portion sizes
12	No-smoking section	No-smoking section	Reservations
13	Reservations	Reservations	Liquor
14	Liquor	Liquor	No-smoking section

Source: A consumer attitude survey prepared for the National Restaurant Association, 1977. Reprinted in *Sanitation Operations Manual* (Chicago: National Restaurant Association, 1979), p. iii.

Exhibit 15.2 Results of Nationwide Survey of Restaurant Patrons

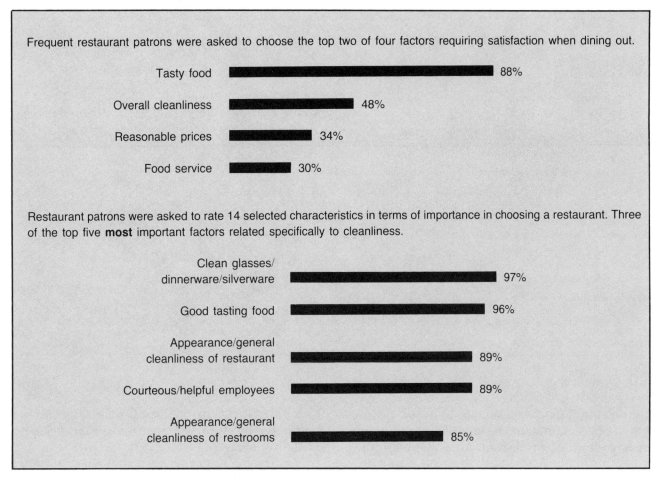

Frequent restaurant patrons were asked to choose the top two of four factors requiring satisfaction when dining out.

- Tasty food — 88%
- Overall cleanliness — 48%
- Reasonable prices — 34%
- Food service — 30%

Restaurant patrons were asked to rate 14 selected characteristics in terms of importance in choosing a restaurant. Three of the top five **most** important factors related specifically to cleanliness.

- Clean glasses/dinnerware/silverware — 97%
- Good tasting food — 96%
- Appearance/general cleanliness of restaurant — 89%
- Courteous/helpful employees — 89%
- Appearance/general cleanliness of restrooms — 85%

Source: Lebhar-Friedman Research. Printed in *Nation's Restaurant News*, September 28, 1981.

tends beyond public concerns. The procedures which production and service employees use to handle food must be correct regardless of whether or not the guest is looking.

Personal Hygiene of Service Staff

Personal cleanliness is very important in preventing food-borne illnesses (sicknesses caused by food which has become contaminated by germs). Each dining service employee must develop good personal sanitation habits to help avoid such problems.

A good personal hygiene program includes regular physical examinations by a physician. States and/or local communities may have specific requirements about health examinations for food service personnel. For example, some states require a physical examination immediately

upon employment and at least every few years thereafter. Requirements may include chest x-rays and blood and stool tests. Some people who do not feel sick themselves can carry diseases such as tuberculosis. Physical exams can help identify such "carriers," who should not work in food service establishments.

A physical exam can tell you about the status of a person's health only at the time of the exam. That person could become ill the next day. Service employees who are ill should not work around food; they could easily contaminate it. Employees with open cuts or even soiled bandages can also contaminate food products.

Personal hygiene habits such as those listed in Exhibit 15.3 are especially important for dining service personnel to practice. Dining service employees should also know and practice sani-

Guests Do Care About Sanitation and Cleanliness

Percentage of respondents "agreeing strongly" with selected observations about restaurants:

An unsanitary restroom in a restaurant makes me wonder about the cleanliness of the kitchen 73

I lose my appetite, no matter how good the food, when a restaurant's dishes and silverware are not clean 63

The personal hygiene of a waiter or waitress influences the way I feel about the food in a restaurant. 62

Even if the food is good, I will not eat at a restaurant that does not appear to be clean 56

I can excuse a restaurant for slow service but not for poor quality food 56

I don't mind paying more for a meal when the service is good 56

Even if the prices are high, I will eat at a restaurant if the food is good 34

Napkins and tablecloths don't bother me if they are slightly worn as long as they are clean......... 33

If I have to wait a long time to be seated, I won't go back to that restaurant...................... 26

If a restaurant serves good food, then the dining atmosphere does not matter.................... 14

Sometimes fast service is more important to me than good food................................ 10

Source: Lebhar-Friedman Research. Printed in *Nation's Restaurant News*, September 28, 1981.

tary work habits. For instance, they should not chew gum or smoke in any storage, preparation, serving, dining, or cleanup areas. Those practices not only look unsightly but can also cause sanitation problems, for as one's hands come in contact with the mouth, germs spread from the mouth to the fingers. Another special concern related to smoking is the smell of tobacco which lingers on one's hands and breath. This odor can offend nonsmoking guests whom the employee serves. Employees should always wash hands well with soap and hot water after smoking. Unless employees wash their hands each time after they touch their mouths, they can easily contaminate food, flatware, table surfaces, or any other equipment or supplies.

If dining service staff need to cough or sneeze, they should move away if possible, avert their faces, and use a tissue. They should use disposable tissues and throw used ones away. It is both unsightly and unsanitary to carry used handkerchiefs in one's uniform pocket.

Service personnel should not undertake any personal grooming in public areas. This includes filing their nails, applying makeup, or combing hair in the dining room or at server stations close to dining areas.

Employees should keep their hair properly restrained with a hairnet, cap, or other hair covering to prevent it from dislodging. Hair in food is among the most offensive and most frequent sanitation problems. All dining service employees should wash their hands frequently with soap and hot water. Proper facility design and layout make that task easier; employees are more likely to wash their hands if they have a convenient place to do it. They should use handwashing basins, not food preparation or dishwashing sinks. They should be supplied with disposable towels or a blow dryer to dry their hands. Of course, it is not proper for them to dry their hands on dish towels, aprons, or uniforms. Dining service employees should always wash their hands before beginning work and before beginning each food handling operation. They should also wash their hands after using the toilet, touching their faces or hair, or handling soiled articles, including money.

Exhibit 15.3 Personal Hygiene Habits for Dining Service Staff

1. Bathe daily and use a deodorant.

2. Brush your teeth several times daily; practice good dental hygiene.

3. Shampoo your hair regularly to keep it clean and healthy; wear your hair in a simple and easy-to-manage style. You may need a hair covering which hides the hairline. (Generally, hair spray is not a substitute for a proper hair covering.)

4. Keep fingernails clean, well-trimmed, and free of nail polish.

5. Do not wear excessive makeup or perfume.

6. Dress properly for the job; wear a clean uniform daily.

7. Wear clean, low-heeled shoes which fit properly. You need nonskid soles. The heel and toe should be completely enclosed. Women should wear white or neutral hose only.

8. Do not wear jewelry other than unadorned wedding bands.

Sanitation Practices for Dining Service Staff

The service employees' concern for sanitation does not end when they meet personal hygiene requirements. Also included in the sanitation program are the way that service employees handle food and beverage products and dining equipment and supplies and the way that they set up, work within, and clean up dining service areas.

Unfortunately, food service personnel sometimes use unsanitary procedures in dining rooms. Examples include service employees who wipe tabletops with obviously soiled food service towels, those who handle glassware or cups by their drinking surfaces or pick up flatware by the tines, and those who place clean dishes and flatware on vacant seats while they reset tables. The point is that it is very easy and common to thoughtlessly practice poor sanitation habits.

If service employees first understand why they should practice sanitary work habits, then are taught the specific procedures which they should use, they should be able to incorporate sanitation practices into all their work.

One of the basic sanitation practices which food service employees should consistently follow is cleaning dining room tables with a clean, sanitized cloth. Whenever possible, they should place flatware on a clean napkin or tablecloth or use another method of table setup to avoid setting flatware directly on the tabletop. They should hold flatware by the handles rather than by the eating surfaces. They should hold glasses by the stems or bases and cups by the handles to avoid bringing their fingers in contact with drinking surfaces, and they should use trays to transport clean tableware to tables. They should also wash their hands frequently, especially after handling soiled eating utensils and completing cleanup activities.

Dining service employees must be particularly careful when serving food. Properties should store potentially hazardous foods (those of animal origin or which contain large amounts of a product of animal origin) at temperatures out of the danger zone—from 45°F (7°C) to 140°F (60°C). Service employees do their part by promptly serving food so that it is at the correct temperature. When practicing this basic sanitation principle, the server also helps make the food more palatable for guests.

While in some operations, service employees slice cheese, chop or tear salad greens, and prepare other items for guests, such preparation should take place only if servers are able to wash their hands before doing so (as during pre-preparation). Service employees should, of course, use clean knives and cutting boards and practice other principles of sanitary food preparation. When beverage service employees provide drink

Cleaning and Maintaining Dining Service Equipment and Facilities

Keep moist cloths or sponges used to wipe dining room equipment clean; rinse them in a sanitizing solution and store them in the solution when not in use. Clean the dining room floor and equipment during slow service periods when a minimum amount of food is exposed to the dust and dirt particles which are raised. Whenever possible, use dustless methods of cleaning floors; for example, vacuum cleaners or sweeping compounds which reduce dust. Keep service stations neat, clean, and free of food particles. Do not store personal medication, cleaning supplies, pesticides, etc., in any areas in which food is stored, processed, or otherwise handled.

garnishes, fill glasses with ice, and provide swizzle sticks or other items, they must also follow sanitation rules.

Service staff in some facilities may help clean and sanitize serviceware. If the proper equipment and supplies are available, the sanitary washing of dishes and flatware is easy. In some municipalities, the health department issues laws and regulations which govern this activity. Where there are no laws or regulations, knowledge of basic sanitation principles can help management design proper procedures. Small operations may use a sink with at least three compartments to wash dishes, flatware, pots, and pans. One sink is used to wash, a second to rinse, and a third to sanitize. A proper and clean drainboard is also necessary so that items can air dry. (Sanitized dishes can be recontaminated when they are dried with food service towels.) Sink compartments should be large enough to completely immerse the largest item that must be washed. Sanitize serviceware either by applying heat—over 180°F (82°C) for specific time periods or using chemicals in the concentrations required by local regulatory agencies. Many facilities find chemical sanitizing agents more practical since food service employees cannot immerse their hands in water hot enough for proper sanitizing.

Larger food service operations make use of automatic dishwashers and/or pot-washing machines. A wide range of equipment is available—from small under-the-counter units to larger door-type machines to very large and expensive flight-type units. When proper cleaning supplies are used, machines are kept in good working order, and thermometers are constantly checked for the proper water temperature, machine washing of serviceware is economical, sanitary, and requires few personnel.

Cleaning Dining Service Areas

Dining service employees must perform such tasks as cleaning tables, crumbing chairs, and removing products from and cleaning self-service food areas. Additional activities may be part of their task of keeping dining areas clean; for example, service employees remove crumbs and other food particles from carpeted areas at the end of each shift (or at least daily). However, what about thoroughly cleaning and shampooing carpets on a routine basis? Servers may routinely dust wall decorations, but what about the actual washing of walls, ceilings, and light fixtures? Employees may routinely clean refrigerators, ovens, and other food production and serving equipment at the end of each shift or day, but what about removing and cleaning filters in ventilation filtering systems? A large amount of nonroutine cleaning is necessary to keep dining service areas clean for guest use.

Far too many operations have major types of cleaning activities done when someone gets around to them. Then they establish other priorities that do not permit time for these unpopular, dirty jobs. However, the tasks are very important. The public notices how clean dining areas really are; employees notice cleanliness too. Is it reasonable to expect employees to consistently practice good sanitation habits when they work in an environment which is itself less

Exhibit 15.4 Sample Major Cleaning Schedule for Dining Areas

Dining Area: _____

Cleaning Activity	Month:	Jan.				Feb.				March				April				May				June			
	Week:	1	2	3	4	1	2	3	4	1	2	3	4	1	2	3	4	1	2	3	4	1	2	3	4
Thoroughly Clean Server Refrigerator																									
Thoroughly Clean Carpets																									
Dry-Clean and Fireproof Draperies																									
Clean Host/Cashier Stand																									
Wash Walls and Ceilings																									
Thoroughly Clean Light Fixtures																									

than optimally clean? While service employees rarely handle major cleaning tasks, managers of dining outlets must be aware of all the cleaning jobs that must be done.

Exhibit 15.4 illustrates a form that can be used to list and monitor major cleaning activities in specific dining areas. To use this form, the outlet's manager and employees concerned would first of all list nonroutine cleaning activities that are needed in their dining outlet. Then, using Exhibit 15.4, these major cleaning activities would be scheduled for some time during a six-month period. For example, if someone needs to clean the server station refrigerator weekly, the manager would note that task on the form. If the property has dining room draperies cleaned only once a year in January, the manager would set one week aside during that month to do the job.

After developing a cleaning schedule, the manager must consider carefully the procedures employees should follow as they perform cleaning activities. Assigned employees cannot simply be allowed to clean things any way that they like. Rather, they must be provided with specific written instructions, as well as cleaning supplies, correct tools, and related items. Supervision is also necessary to ensure that employees properly carry out the cleaning schedule and to confirm that the completed cleaning activity meets the sanitary standards that the food service operation has established.

Additional Sanitation Issues

Some guests judge a facility's cleanliness by its public restrooms. When restrooms are built into a hotel's restaurant, the restaurant manager is often charged with developing procedures to maintain the restrooms' supply levels and keep these facilities clean throughout the day. They must then supervise employees to see that the procedures are correctly carried out. Exhibit 15.5 illustrates a form which can be used to inform the public about the property's concern for sanitation; it enables guests to notice the frequency of inspections. When employees are responsible for keeping these facilities clean and are required to sign or initial their names on such a form to indicate that the facility is in good order, the

Exhibit 15.5: Sanitation Inspection Sheet for Public Restrooms

To Our Guests:

We care about the cleanliness of our facilities and the protection of your health while you are visiting us. Employees inspect this restroom hourly to ensure that it meets both our high standards and yours. If you have any concerns about these facilities, please let us know so that immediate steps can be taken to improve the situation. Thank you for your cooperation.

Time	Inspection By:	Time	Inspection By:
7:00 am		6:00 pm	
8:00 am		7:00 pm	
9:00 am		8:00 pm	
10:00 am		9:00 pm	
11:00 am		10:00 pm	
12:00 noon		11:00 pm	
1:00 pm		12:00 am	
2:00 pm		1:00 am	
3:00 pm		2:00 am	
4:00 pm		3:00 am	
5:00 pm			

Date	Time	Condition(s) Requiring Action	Time Action Taken	Employee's Initials	Supervisor's Initials

likelihood is increased that the restroom facilities are actually clean.

Hotels which offer room service, banquet service, and/or off-site catered events must give special attention to their food transport equipment. For instance, such equipment must be able to provide proper holding temperatures for prolonged periods. Service staff using such equipment should report repair and/or maintenance problems to the appropriate official.

Management must decide who will clean food transport equipment. Often, dining service employees believe that cleaning personnel in the steward's department will maintain such equipment. They, in turn, believe that the responsibility should rest with the service staff. Thus, this assignment must be made and specified in the appropriate job description. Management, of course, must then ensure that the right person—using the right procedures and the right supplies—actually does clean and maintain the food transport equipment.

Dining Service Sanitation Checklist

Developing a written sanitation checklist can help employees learn the principles and procedures of sanitation and ensure that they consistently emphasize them. Exhibit 15.6 reviews many basic sanitation procedures which apply to dining service in a number of outlets. If you use the checklist, consider your specific outlet and question whether or not the recommended procedure applies. Sessions with other management staff and interested employees can yield a final checklist which is appropriate for your property.

Following the initial development of a checklist, and on a routine but random basis thereafter, conduct a self-inspection of those areas under your control. Use the format shown in Exhibit 15.6 to note any problems which you observe. Ongoing supervision of employees reinforces management's concern for proper sanitation and allows management to note when corrective measures are required.

Safety

The restaurant manager must be concerned about the safety of both employees and guests. Some aspects of safety actually relate to the property's ongoing security program. In this chapter, **safety** means preventing accidents which can harm both employees and guests. **Security** relates to other emergencies and methods to handle them.

Accidents are caused by someone's carelessness; they are unplanned or unforeseen events. Many accidents can be prevented by using basic safety principles. The restaurant manager's most important concern when developing and implementing safety programs is to protect human resources. However, these programs will also reduce the possibility of losses in revenue, equipment, and even the facility itself.

Earlier in this chapter, we noted that an important step in developing sanitation programs is to instill in both management and employees an attitude or philosophy about sanitation. The same rule applies here: both management and the food service employees must make a commitment to regard safety programs as important. Managers can:

1. Help develop work procedures that recognize safety concerns.

2. Train employees to use safe work procedures.

3. Conduct continuous inspections of food service areas to ensure that the equipment and facilities lend themselves to safe work practices.

4. Complete accident reports, assist in accident investigations, and do all that is necessary to quickly correct problems causing accidents.

5. Seek medical assistance for injured employees and guests, and, if qualified, administer first aid.

6. Report needed repairs, maintenance, changes in work procedures, or other conditions which can potentially cause accidents.

7. Conduct regularly scheduled safety meetings and other programs for dining service staff.

Dining service employees can:

1. Closely observe and follow all required work procedures.

2. Keep their work areas in safe conditions.

3. Report any problems requiring repair or maintenance as soon as they observe them (e.g., a burned out light bulb, a rip in the carpet, a loose step or banister.)

4. Notify their supervisors of any accidents, regardless of how minor, as soon as they occur.

Many safety rules which dining service employees should follow apply to all employees of the food and beverage operation. Exhibit 15.7 provides examples of these general safety rules,

Exhibit 15.6 Checklist for Serving

Personnel

1. Servers understand the operation's standards for quality, cost, and sanitation.

2. Service standards are developed based on the menu, personnel skill levels, hours of service, the size of the operation, and its sales volume.

3. Servers see themselves as public relations agents for the establishment.

4. The appearance and health of servers is evaluated before each meal period.

5. Servers are friendly, calm, confident, alert, dependable, and honest. In addition to professional skills, they possess initiative and a willingness to adhere to the establishment's procedures and standards.

6. Prior to service, servers prepare themselves and their stations for service.

7. Servers clean and restock their stations and complete closing duties before leaving the property.

8. Servers adhere to standards of personal hygiene covering:

    a. bodily cleanliness

    b. posture

    c. hair and hair restraints

    d. handwashing

    e. uniforms

    f. jewelry

9. Supervisors of service conduct an employee line-up and inspection of the facilities immediately before the meal period begins.

10. Servers adhere to standards of cleanliness covering:

    a. handwashing

    b. gum chewing, smoking, and eating

    c. disposing of food that has left the plate or dropped on the floor

    d. replacing dropped tableware

    e. touching food with hands

    f. touching tableware with hands

    g. maintaining service towels or napkins

    h. maintaining service trays

11. Servers load their trays neatly and safely.

12. Servers know the operation's procedures for handling guests' complaints about sanitation or any other concern.

13. Servers are trained to maintain the operation's standards of sanitation.

Equipment

1. Personnel regularly clean and sanitize equipment and utensils used in the service of food and beverage products.

2. Cleaned and sanitized utensils and equipment are stored in a way that prevents recontamination.

3. Tableware is handled so as to prevent contamination.

4. Stations and sidestands are kept restocked with adequate supplies of tableware and other necessities.

5. Food products at stations and sidestands have minimum contact with the temperature danger zone (TDZ).

6. Tables, chairs, floors, and windows are regularly cleaned and maintained.

Source: Adapted from Ronald F. Cichy, *Sanitation Management* (East Lansing, Mich.: Educational Institute of the American Hotel & Motel Association, 1984), pp. 319-323.

Exhibit 15.6, continued

7. Condiment and spice containers are regularly cleaned.

8. Care is exercised in the handling of all equipment used in service.

Inventory

1. Potentially hazardous foods have minimum exposure to the TDZ during display and service.

2. Ice is dispensed by employees with ice-dispensing equipment or by guests if an automatic dispensing machine is available.

3. Condiments, seasonings, and dressings are available in individual serving packages or approved self-service containers.

4. Dispensing utensils are stored in a safe and sanitary manner.

5. Re-service of packaged food is limited to items that are unopened, in sound condition, and are not potentially hazardous.

6. Food on display is protected from contamination.

7. Tableware (except beverage cups and glasses) is not reused by self-service guests.

8. Acceptable quality levels defined in terms of appearance, texture, color, odor, and temperature are known to servers and checked before an order is delivered to the guest.

Facilities

1. Facilities are routinely cleaned, maintained, and repaired.

2. Restrooms are regularly inspected and cleaned.

3. Facilities are clean, dry, and odor-free.

4. Adequate lighting levels are maintained.

5. The supervisor conducts a facility inspection immediately before the meal period.

6. Menus are inspected to remove all dirty, soiled, or spotted menus from circulation.

Banquet and Buffet Food Service

1. Correct time-temperature controls are practiced.

2. Station setup is checked before service begins.

3. Menu items are chosen for the ease, safety, and speed with which they can be served.

4. The necessary equipment and utensils are available to maintain product temperatures.

5. Food and beverage products are free of contamination.

Off-Premises Catering

1. Special equipment and transportation vehicles are available in sufficient quantity.

2. Product time-temperature controls are closely monitored.

3. Food is protected during storage and transportation.

Room Service

1. Room service standards are established based on guest satisfaction and the resources of the property.

2. Product quality and time-temperature controls are assessed.

3. Servers are trained to adhere to the property's standards.

4. Menus are limited to those items that the operation can successfully prepare and deliver to the guestrooms.

5. Soiled tableware, linen, and equipment is promptly removed from the guestrooms or hallways.

Exhibit 15.7 One Property's Safety Rules for Dining Service

The following rules and regulations are essential to the safety of the individual employee and to the safe operation of the property. They are of major importance; read them attentively and follow them in every detail.

1. Walk, do not run. The few minutes saved by rushing could result in an injury to yourself or another employee.
2. Do not engage in horseplay.
3. Report all accidents and injuries to your supervisor immediately.
4. Report faulty equipment immediately; don't leave it for someone else to report.
5. Inspect equipment before you use it; never use a machine that needs repair.
6. Do not operate machinery unless you have the authorization and training to do so.
7. Do not operate equipment tagged "out of order."
8. Unplug electrical equipment before cleaning it.
9. Use all safety guards on equipment; don't bypass them.
10. Use the proper equipment for the job.
11. Be alert to the task you are performing.
12. Be sure you know how to do a job; if in doubt, *ASK.*
13. Look where you are going, not where you have been.
14. Turn on the lights before entering a dark room.
15. Open all doors with caution.
16. Keep all desk and file drawers closed.
17. Maintain good housekeeping in all areas.
18. Show caution in special work areas; observe restrictions on entry and use protective equipment.
19. Use handrails on stairs.
20. Never carry so much that you obscure your vision.
21. When carrying coffee pots and teapots on a tray, turn the spouts toward the center of the tray.
22. Empty all ashtrays into a metal container.
23. Exercise care when handling knives and forks.
24. Limit stacks of dishes on carts to a height that will not topple if you make a sudden stop.
25. When carrying a tray, place the heavy load toward the body.
26. Use care in handling glasses and dishes.
27. Use a pan and broom to sweep up pieces of glass or china.
28. Do not use glasses as ice scoops.
29. Do not polish glasses by forcing a towel inside the glass.
30. Keep all knives in proper storage when not in use.
31. When drawing hot water or coffee from an urn, turn the spigot slowly.
32. Never carry more than six to eight plates per tray.
33. "Flag" spills in public areas by dropping a towel over the spot until it's cleaned up; alert guests to the hazard so they can avoid the area.
34. Do not rush while carrying trays to and from the dining room.

Source: Adapted from *Safety Manual* (Wilmington, Del.: Hotel du Pont, undated), p. 1-10, IV-5.

Exhibit 15.7, continued

35. Use care in ascending and descending stairs.
36. Watch out for guests' wraps, purses, and other belongings that may fall or be placed on the floor.
37. Always warn guests if plates are hot.
38. Handle hot plates with a side towel.
39. Follow the correct procedures for handling sterno in the dining room.
40. Never place bottles of liquor near a flame or pour directly from a bottle into a pan.
41. Flambe items at an appropriate distance from the guests' tables.

which can be adapted for use in a specific property. They form the foundation of rules which should be explained in training and supervision programs as well as incorporated into standard operating procedures.

Restaurant Managers and Guest Safety

Injuries to guests not only have an impact on the reputation of a food service operation but also can result in massive insurance settlements. Restaurant managers should know exactly what to do in the event of an accident; better yet, they should know how to prevent them from happening.[2] They must also effectively inform their employees about required safety procedures.

If a guest is injured, contact your insurance company as soon as possible and follow the company's instructions carefully.

Falls

Approximately one third of all guest claims arise from falls.[3] This fact emphasizes why aisles should be kept free of obstructions, floors should be clean and dry, interior and exterior areas should be well lighted, and snow and ice should be removed from outdoor walkways. Most falls occur from slips or trips at floor level, not from

---

[2] Readers can find further information about liability and other legal concerns relating to guest and employee injuries in Jack P. Jefferies, *Understanding Hotel/Motel Law* (East Lansing, Mich.: Educational Institute of the American Hotel & Motel Association, 1983).

[3] *Safety Operations Manual* (Chicago: National Restaurant Association, 1981), p. B-8.

high places. The following suggestions are used in some properties to help prevent falls:

1. Keep floors clean and dry at all times. Wipe up spills immediately.

2. Keep floors free from all hazardous objects.

3. Use a sturdy stepladder to remove items from high places.

4. Require employees to always walk, never run; train them to use caution when going through swinging doors.

5. Require employees to wear properly fitting shoes with low heels and nonskid soles. Do not allow them to wear thin soles or broken-down, open-toed, tennis, or related shoes. Train them to keep shoestrings tied to prevent slipping.

6. Remove snow and ice from entrances and walkways.

7. Clean such areas as side entrances. Keep floor mats or other protective devices in good, clean condition.

8. Use slip-resistant floor waxes.

9. Use "Caution" or "Wet Floor" signs when appropriate.

10. Replace cracked or worn stair treads.

11. Provide adequate lighting in stairwells and in other places—whether few or many guests go to these areas.

Successful Sanitation Programs

Formal and informal methods can be used to monitor the effectiveness of dining service sanitation programs. Using a sanitation/safety inspection checklist is a formal method that should be undertaken on a routine basis. Many operations would benefit from a self-inspection at least monthly.

Restaurant managers can also use informal techniques such as asking the following questions about their facilities and adding others to them as necessary:

1. How often do we receive guest complaints about food quality? Do any of them relate to the temperature or palatability of food products?
2. Do serviceware items have spots or streaks? Does glassware have an off-odor?
3. Are any serviceware items dirty, chipped, or cracked?
4. How does the dining area look? (The restaurant manager can look at the facility from the perspective of the guest and note whether the windows are streaked, the carpets are clean, the dining room furniture is in good condition, and more.)
5. Do service employees appear to practice principles of personal hygiene? Do they report to work in clean uniforms?
6. How do service employees handle serviceware and food and beverage products? Do they appear to consistently practice principles of sanitation? What happens to food products that someone drops on the floor? Do employees ever eat food products that come back from guest service?

As managers supervise employees and note problems, they will probably identify needs for closer supervision, greater employee motivation, and more intensive training programs. Through both formal and informal monitoring of the effectiveness of a sanitation program, managers become aware of problems and then can take steps to resolve them.

---

12. Repair loose or upturned floor tiles as soon as possible.

13. Do not run electrical or other cords across traffic aisles; keep carpet in good repair.

Safe floor mopping procedures can prevent many falls:

1. Post "CAUTION - WET FLOOR" signs at all entrances to area.

2. Use two buckets, one containing cleaning solution and the other, rinse water.

3. Rinse area thoroughly after mopping to avoid leaving a sticky or slippery residue.

4. If practical, block off access to the area being mopped.

5. While mopping, never leave the area, buckets, or mops unattended.

6. Warn anyone passing through the area of wet floors.

7. Do not use excess water or allow any puddles to form on the floor.

8. Use extreme care when walking across the wet area yourself.[4]

Correct Lifting Procedures

Proper lifting procedures help prevent lifting injuries:

1. Place your feet a comfortable distance apart; make sure that your footing is firm and your body well-balanced.

2. Bend your legs; keep your back straight.

3. Grasp the object you want to lift.

4. Keeping a firm grip on the object and your back straight, push up with your leg muscles.

---

[4] Adapted from *Safety Manual* (Wilmington, Del.: Hotel du Pont, undated), p. IV-13.

To prevent an injury when lifting:

1. Do not lift with your body in a twisted or awkward position.

2. Do not lift with a jerk.

3. Do not lift too heavy a load.

4. Do not twist your body while carrying a load.

5. Do not lift objects too bulky to grasp correctly.

6. Do not lift objects weighing more than 50 pounds (for men) or 25 pounds (for women).[5]

Electrical Equipment

Various kinds of electrical equipment can cause accidents in dining service areas. The following practices can help prevent these accidents:

1. Instruct dining service employees in the proper way to disassemble, reassemble, and operate all electrical equipment.

2. Have a qualified electrician inspect all electrical equipment, wiring, and switches on a regular basis as part of the preventive maintenance program.

3. Ensure that all electrical equipment is properly grounded.

4. Carefully follow manufacturer's instructions whenever operating electrical equipment.

5. Never allow dining service personnel to touch metal sockets or electrical equipment while their hands are wet or when they are standing on a wet floor. They could be electrocuted.

6. Do not use an electrical cord if it is worn through to the wire.

7. Remove the electrical plug from an outlet before cleaning any piece of electrical equipment.

8. Never use unauthorized extension cords; never overload circuits.

9. Always use water resistant cords.

Accident Inspection Programs

Even when safety education programs are in effect and employees use safe work practices, some accidents may still occur. Restaurant managers should train all personnel to know what to do when an accident occurs. They should also learn from accidents to help ensure that they do not recur, and they must thoroughly understand the legal complications associated with accidents.

While state laws differ, regulations related to workers' compensation and federal Occupational Safety Health Administration (OSHA) standards require the reporting of a number of accidents. OSHA has issued regulations designed to provide for safe working conditions in many workplaces in America. If you are interested in specific, current information about OSHA regulations, contact the federal and/or state Department of Labor office in your area.

Exhibit 15.8 illustrates the type of information which employers must report for workers' compensation in one state. Employers send copies of the form to the insurance company and the employee; they should also retain a copy for their records. As a result of this report and follow-up investigations by state labor officers and/or insurance company representatives, the employer and employee may reach a settlement. State compensation laws normally apply. This form should be completed carefully and accurately.

Restaurant managers can learn much from accidents which can help prevent their recurrence. In addition to the information which must be provided for workers' compensation purposes, employee accident reports and reports of guest injury are useful tools to evaluate accidents. (See Exhibits 15.9 and 15.10.)

An accident investigation, perhaps conducted by the property's safety committee, should help the manager assess exactly what happened, why it happened, and what can be done to prevent its recurrence. In some properties, top management follows up on all accident investigation reports to ensure that employees have taken the necessary actions to prevent the recurrence of an accident.

---

[5] *Ibid.*, p. IV-10.

Exhibit 15.8 Employer's Basic Report of Injury for Workers' Disability Compensation

SM03337

13?371

127905

Form 100
Rev. 9-84

OSHA
Case or File No. _____

THIS FORM MUST BE TYPED

DEPARTMENT OF LABOR

Bureau of Workers' Disability Compensation
P.O. Box 30016
LANSING, MICHIGAN 48909

EMPLOYER'S BASIC REPORT OF INJURY

COPIES TO BE DISTRIBUTED

Yellow and Green — Bureau of Workers'
Disability Compensation, Lansing, Mich.
Blue — Insurance Company
Pink — Employer File
White — Employee

Employers must report to the Bureau on Form 100 all injuries, including diseases, which arise out of and in the course of the employment and cause: 1. Seven(7) or more days of disability not including Sundays or the day of injury. 2. Death. 3. Specific Losses. In case of DEATH also file immediately an additional report on Form 106.

1. **INJURED EMPLOYEE** _____ Soc. Sec. No. __/__/__
2. Address _____ Telephone No. _____
3. Birthdate - Month _____ Day _____ Year _____ If under 18, date working permit issued _____
4. Sex: ☐ Male ☐ Female   Number of injured employee's children under age 16 living with injured _____
5. Marital status: ☐ Married ☐ Single   If married male, is wife living with him? ☐ Yes ☐ No
6. Number of other family members or relatives at least 50% supported by injured _____
7. **DATE OF INJURY** _____ Last day worked _____ Did employee die? ☐ Yes ☐ No   If yes, date _____
8. Location of Injury   City _____ State _____ County _____
9. Was place of accident or exposure on employer's premises? ☐ Yes ☐ No
10. Name and address of physician _____
11. If hospitalized, name and address of hospital _____

12. DESCRIPTION OF ALLEGED INJURY (Complete and specific information needed for each category)
   A. Describe the injury or illness
      Examples: Amputation, Burn, Cut, Fracture, Sprain, etc.

   B. Part of body - The part of body directly affected by the injury or illness.
      Examples: Head, Arm, Leg, Circulatory system, etc.

   C. Describe the events that caused the injury. Examples: Fell, Operating machinery, Exposure to chemicals, etc.

   D. Name the object or substance which directly injured the employee.
      Examples: Knife, Band Saw, Acid, Floor, Oil, Punch Press, etc.

13. Occupation of injured employee (be specific) _____
14. Department _____ Foreman or supervisor _____
15. Total Gross Wages - Highest 39 of 52 weeks preceding date of injury.   Total value of fringe benefits $ _____
   Total Gross Weekly Wages $ _____ No. of weeks used in calculation _____ Value of discontinued fringe
   benefits $ _____ Average weekly wage (including value of discontinued fringe benefits) $ _____
16. Complete the following only if the injured employee received wages from a second employer.
   Name of second employer _____
   Mailing address _____
17. Date returned to work _____ or estimated lost time from work _____

18. IS EMPLOYEE CERTIFIED AS VOCATIONALLY HANDICAPPED?   ☐ Yes   ☐ No

19. IS EMPLOYEE RECEIVING UNEMPLOYMENT INSURANCE BENEFITS?   ☐ Yes   ☐ No

20. **EMPLOYER**   MESC. No. _____
   A. _____   Federal ID No. _____
   B. _____
21. Location (if different from mail address) _____
22. **TYPE OF BUSINESS** _____
23. **INSURANCE COMPANY (Not agent)** _____ Carrier ID No. _____
24. **HAS WHITE COPY OF THIS REPORT BEEN GIVEN TO EMPLOYEE?**   ☐ Yes ☐ No
      Questions or errors should be immediately reported to the employer representative indicated below

Date of Report _____   Prepared by _____
      Signature (in ink) **Employer** or Representative   Tele.#

Source: State of Michigan, Department of Labor, Bureau of Workers' Disability Compensation, Lansing, Mich.

Exhibit 15.9 Employee Accident Report

Establishment: _____	Address: _____
Supervisor: _____	Name of Injured: _____
Department: _____	Position: _____
Date of accident: _____	Time of accident: _____
Place of accident: _____	
Nature of injury: _____	

☐ None   ☐ First aid   ☐ Medical doctor   ☐ Ambulance
☐ Hospital   ☐ Other (specify) _____

Medical attention necessary: _____
Action of injured at time of accident: _____
_____
_____

Conditions in the environment contributing to the accident: _____
_____
_____

Corrective action necessary to prevent further accidents: _____
_____
_____

Date corrective action taken: _____
Employee's signature: _____   Supervisor's signature: _____
Date: _____   Date: _____

Source: Cichy, *Sanitation Management*, p. 425.

Procedures similar to those used to develop and implement sanitation inspection programs can be used to develop accident prevention programs.

First Aid Is Important

Immediately after an accident occurs, first aid provided by someone trained in the proper procedures is the primary concern. Training in cardiopulmonary resuscitation (CPR) is especially important for service personnel. People without proper training should normally not attempt to give first aid beyond clearly needed procedures, such as making the person comfortable. Untrained people may also provide necessary information for accident reports and urge an accident victim to visit a physician when a less serious accident has occurred.

The American Red Cross provides excellent first aid training programs throughout the United States. Restaurant managers should encourage staff members at all organizational levels to avail themselves of these and similar educational opportunities which provide them with helpful information for both their professional and personal lives. If possible, someone with first aid training should be in the food service operation at all times.

First aid equipment and supplies should also be available on-site. Frequently, state departments of labor, municipal regulatory agencies, insurance companies, and/or other groups require specific first aid equipment for food service operations. Because cuts, burns, sprains, and bruises are the leading injuries in most food service properties, first aid supplies should be available for treating those injuries.

First aid equipment and supplies should be located in convenient areas. Large properties and those with more than one floor require several first aid kits. Various types of medical and first aid

Exhibit 15.10 Report of Guest Injury

INJURY-ACCIDENT REPORT

Note: Use reverse side for
      additional information

CASE NO. _____
DATE _____
SECURITY
OFFICER _____

INJURED PERSON (Name) _____ SEX _____ DATE OF BIRTH _____
    Address: (Street) _____ Phone ( ) _____
        City, State, Zip code _____
DATE OCCURRED _____ TIME _____
REPORTED BY _____ TIME _____ DATE _____
    Address _____ Phone _____
WHERE OCCURRED (exact location) _____

REASON PERSON WAS AT LOCATION _____

DETAILED DESCRIPTION OF ACCIDENT _____
_____
_____
_____

INJURY _____
CLOTHING: Street-length dress _____ Floor-length dress _____ Shorts _____
           Swimsuit _____ Shirt/blouse & trousers _____ Other _____
SHOES: Regular _____ Sandals _____ Barefoot _____ Platform shoes _____
           High heels _____ Tennis or running shoes _____ Other _____
WEARING GLASSES: Yes _____ No _____ Prescription glasses _____ Sunglasses _____
               Required to wear glasses Yes _____ No _____
PHYSICAL CONDITION PRIOR TO ACCIDENT: No physical defects _____
    Handicapped (describe) _____
      On crutches _____ Uses cane _____ Uses wheel chair _____ Had been drinking _____
    Other _____
INJURED TAKEN TO _____ TAKEN BY _____
PHYSICIAN'S NAME _____ PHONE _____
WITNESSES (Name, phone and local address) _____
_____
_____

SIGNATURE OF PERSON FILLING OUT REPORT _____

Source: Adapted from Donna M. Paananen, *Condominiums and Timesharing in the Lodging Industry* (East Lansing, Mich.: Educational Institute of the American Hotel & Motel Association, 1984), p. 42.

posters are also available from several sources. (See Exhibit 15.11.) These can serve as helpful reminders to practice safe work procedures.

Safety Inspection Programs

Safety programs must begin with an aware

ness of and a concern for protecting the health and well-being of employees and guests. Training programs to teach employees safe work practices are also necessary. Managers of dining service outlets have the further obligation to develop procedures for safety inspection pro-

Exhibit 15.11 First Aid for Choking

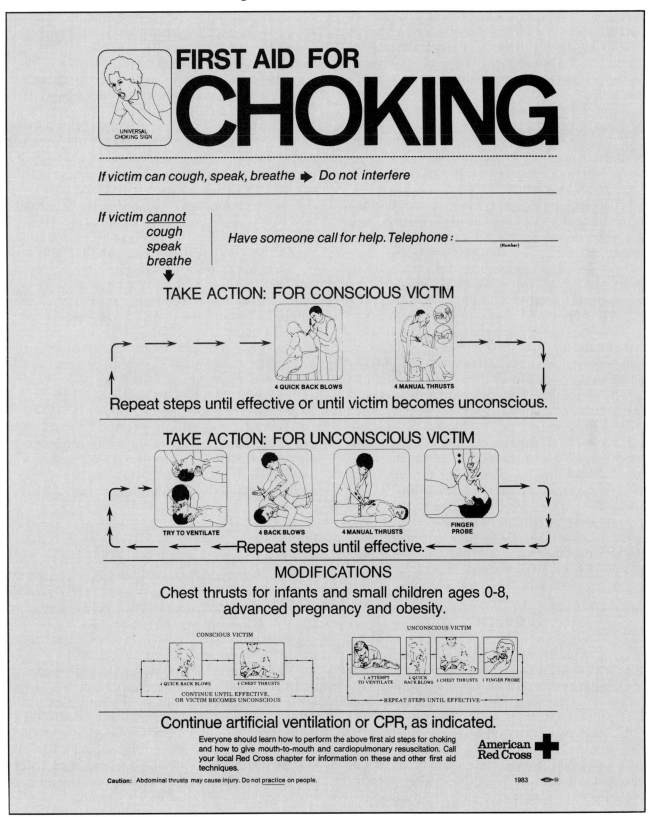

grams that ensure both that employees practice safe work habits and that the equipment and facility itself are not likely to contribute to accidents. The objectives of inspection activities include determining how safe the existing facility, equipment, and procedures are and what methods the property needs to develop to make them more safe.

How often should you conduct safety inspections? In part, that will depend on how well your property measures up during the first inspection. You should make a complete inspection at least once a month. However, daily inspections of specific work stations, equipment, and facilities are also generally necessary. It may be possible for department heads to inspect their own areas using previously developed inspection report forms. Top management of the property can also make inspections on a routine but random basis. A sample safety checklist to protect guests is included with the case study at the end of this chapter.

Problems identified during safety inspections should be promptly corrected. However, managers cannot simply assume that employees will automatically follow through when told to correct something. Management must ensure that someone actually does take the necessary corrective action.

Professional managers retain self-inspection report forms. Not only do they provide some indication of the long-range effectiveness of safety inspection programs, but if any safety problems occur, such as lawsuits or inspections by OSHA or other safety representatives, the report forms are also evidence of an operation's interest and effectiveness in maintaining a safe food and beverage operation.

Security

Ongoing safety programs help prevent many accidents, and those which do occur provide lessons so that the chances of repetition are less likely. Expanding this concern for safety into an effective security program can help protect people and property from external threats, including fires, terrorist attacks, and robberies.

Every food service operation should develop plans and procedures that address exactly what affected personnel should do in the event of an emergency. The proper time to develop these procedures is *before* an emergency occurs— not during or after. The likelihood of injury or property damage is greatly reduced when staff members act according to a rational plan at a time when every second counts.

The best way to develop procedures for handling emergencies is to get ideas from each department head and other top-level managers. Large properties usually have a security department; the official in charge of that department might serve as the chairperson of the security planning efforts. Because smaller properties do not have the luxury of such specialized positions, the general manager or a designate usually develops security plans. Properties of any size can make use of a safety committee to help design, implement, and evaluate a security program.

You must design procedures for emergencies on a specific, by-property basis. You cannot pick up a book and adopt the procedures found within it. After you have developed security procedures, employees at all organizational levels must know about them. These procedures can be the topic of staff training programs. Alternatively, you may want to offer special training sessions designed to present, explain, and clarify the prescribed procedures.

Security precautions should be part of a property's standard operating procedures or employee handbook. Newly hired employees will need to study the procedures to use in the event of an emergency and other employees will need reminders.

Food Service Fires

Many fires in food service facilities occur when the operation is closed; some are caused by arson (the willful burning of a property). Unfortunately, other fires occur when guests are in the facility. These fires are of special concern to dining outlet managers as well as all other management and submanagement staff members.

Municipal codes often regulate the number of people that can occupy dining areas. Other laws may require automatic fire sprinklers, fire extinguishers, emergency lighting, and related protection equipment. Such regulations may also specify the number, type, and location of emergency exits, as well as the width of aisles. They may address special concerns about interior walls, ceilings, stairwells, and elevators, as well as utility requirements. The point is that government regulatory agencies are concerned about protecting guests from fires and other emergencies.

Managers of food service operations must comply with existing laws when they design and remodel buildings and/or as inspections reveal violations of these laws. Fire department officials can provide good advice as management helps design buildings or conducts training programs. If these representatives visit the property frequently, they will be more familiar with it and will be better able to help if an emergency arises.

Employees must know how to determine if a fire exists. Visible flames are obvious; however, the presence of smoke or even unexplained odors can also suggest the presence of a fire. Various types of fire detection devices are available which, when a fire is present, can summon employees and even the local fire department. Such devices include many different types of smoke detectors and heat detectors.

Restaurant managers must determine when a fire is potentially serious enough to disturb diners. Should you alert guests when there is a fire in a garbage can in the parking lot? What about a smoldering linen bag caused by a lighted cigarette thrown in with a tablecloth? What about sparks from an electric motor on a trash compactor? You might be able to resolve these and related or potential fires without interrupting the production of food or the service of guests. On the other hand, a grease fire in the kitchen or the outbreak of fire in the dining area itself could be very serious; policies should be developed regarding notifying the employees and guests about these incidents. (Since grease fires are a common problem in food service operations, ventilation and fire extinguishing equipment or systems that meet local fire codes are an absolute must.)

If an actual fire occurs, employees should know both where to find the fire alarm switches and what to do after sounding the alarm. Employees should be trained to remain calm and help direct the exit of guests, who should be told to leave in a quick, but orderly fashion. Fire alarms should not be turned off until it is determined that a fire does not exist.

The fire department should be telephoned first; then guests and employees should be alerted about a fire. (Emergency phone numbers should be posted by all back-of-house telephones.) The employee making the phone call should give the exact name and address of the facility, along with any other information the fire department may require.

Dining service and all other employees should know the classes of fires that available extinguishers can put out. To help ensure performance when necessary, have this equipment serviced regularly. The type of fire most likely to occur in a specific area will determine the type of extinguisher needed in that area. Exhibit 15.12 identifies the three classes of fires and shows the type of extinguishers that can be used for each.

Place dry chemical extinguishers in kitchen areas where grease and oil fires are most likely to occur. (Never use water on an electrical or grease fire.) Water extinguishers are generally located in dining areas where paper, wood, and cloth fires are more likely. Managers should contact their local fire departments for assistance when selecting fire extinguishers for specific areas in their facilities. Fire department officials can also help managers select the best location for each extinguisher.

Employees should never attempt to extinguish a fire if they will jeopardize their own personal safety. While fire extinguishers can typically put out small fires if used properly, they should not be used for large fires which require professional firefighters and equipment.

An informed employee must be available when firefighters arrive in order to direct them quickly to the exact fire location. Naturally, employees should follow all instructions that fire department personnel give them.

Bomb Threats

Restaurant managers must be prepared for anything. Only intensive preparation can help ensure that they will handle emergencies in a professional manner with a minimal threat to both employees and guests. The possibility of bomb threats is real; restaurant managers have the responsibility to develop written procedures for handling these threats.[6]

The number of bombs or other potentially

---

6   Jack D. Ninemeier, *Food and Beverage Security: A Systems Manual for Restaurants, Hotels, and Clubs* (Boston: CBI, 1982), pp. 142–143.

Exhibit 15.12 Identification of Extinguishers

KIND OF FIRE		APPROVED TYPE OF EXTINGUISHER							HOW TO OPERATE
DECIDE THE CLASS OF FIRE YOU ARE FIGHTING...	...THEN CHECK THE COLUMNS TO THE RIGHT OF THAT CLASS →	MATCH UP PROPER EXTINGUISHER WITH CLASS OF FIRE SHOWN AT LEFT							FOAM: Don't Play Stream into the Burning Liquid. Allow Foam to Fall Lightly on Fire.
		FOAM Solution of Aluminum Sulphate and Bicarbonate of Soda	CARBON DIOXIDE Carbon Dioxide Gas Under Pressure	SODA ACID Bicarbonate of Soda Solution and Sulphuric Acid	PUMP TANK Plain Water	GAS CARTRIDGE Water Expelled by Carbon Dioxide Gas	MULTI-PURPOSE DRY CHEMICAL	ORDINARY DRY CHEMICAL	
CLASS A FIRES — USE THESE EXTINGUISHERS — ORDINARY COMBUSTIBLES • WOOD • PAPER • CLOTH ETC.		foam	X	soda acid	pump tank	gas cartridge	multi-purpose	X	CARBON DIOXIDE: Direct Discharge as Close to Fire as Possible. First at Edge of Flames and Gradually Forward and Upward
CLASS B FIRES — USE THESE EXTINGUISHERS → FLAMMABLE LIQUIDS, GREASE • GASOLINE • PAINTS • OILS, ETC.		foam	carbon dioxide	X	X	X	gas cartridge	ordinary dry	SODA-ACID, GAS CARTRIDGE: Direct Stream at Base of Flame
CLASS C FIRES — USE THESE EXTINGUISHERS → ELECTRICAL EQUIPMENT • MOTORS • SWITCHES ETC.		X	carbon dioxide	X	X	X	gas cartridge	ordinary dry	PUMP TANK: Place Foot on Footrest and Direct Stream at Base of Flames
									DRY CHEMICAL: Direct at the Base of the Flames. In the Case of Class A Fires, Follow Up by Directing the Dry Chemicals at Remaining Material That is Burning

Source: Centers for Disease Control, Public Health Service, U.S. Department of Health, Education, and Welfare, *Health and Safety Guide for Hotels and Motels*, 1975.

dangerous devices which are found as a result of threats is much less than the actual number of threats. Nevertheless, experienced managers treat bomb threats as real announcements of potential death, injury, and extensive damage.

If threats are received by mail, they should immediately be referred to the local police. In addition, since the United States mail service is involved, post office inspectors and the Federal Bureau of Investigation (FBI) should be notified.

Many bomb threats are communicated by telephone. Therefore, management must train employees in advance to solicit as much information as possible from the threatening caller.

For example, if it is the policy of the property, the employee who receives a bomb threat should:

1. Attempt to keep the caller talking. If possible, alert another employee who can listen on another telephone.

2. Attempt to discover when the bomb will explode, where it is located, what type of device it is, and what it looks like.

3. Listen to the voice. Is the person male or female, sober or drunk, rational or irrational, or someone you know? Does the

Don't Forget the Local Fire Department

You are aware that someone should telephone the fire department as soon as a fire is suspected. However, don't forget the fire department when you develop fire prevention and security procedures. Staff members from the fire department are experts and will provide many good ideas applicable to your property. Call them in; don't be afraid that they'll spot code violations. Rather, consider their visit as a way to become prepared for any fire emergencies.

speaker have an accent or speech impediment; is the voice that of a child, teenager, older person, etc.?

4. Listen for any identifiable noises in the background (e.g., factory, night club, street sounds indicating a phone booth).

5. Note any additional information, such as an explanation of why the caller placed the bomb and if the caller has any demands.

6. Note the time the call was received and the time the caller hung up.

7. Attempt to recall the exact words the caller used.

8. Notify local police immediately.

Frequently, if a caller is serious, he/she will provide information to help find the bomb. If the caller is incoherent, clearly intoxicated, or sounds as though he/she thinks it's all a joke, the call is probably a hoax. Even so, the employee who notifies the police should carefully follow any advice they provide.

If the restaurant manager did not take the call, someone should notify him/her. Large properties have an internal security department; someone must also notify its staff members according to a pre-arranged sequence.

If a policy regarding bomb threats is developed before a property receives a threat, the call's receiver (normally a management official, receptionist, office worker, or someone else from a relatively small number of employees) will know what to do. Regardless of the procedures developed and implemented, all employees should know that time cannot be wasted when a property has a bomb threat.

Police inspection personnel, perhaps with the aid of volunteer employees who know the work areas and would more readily notice anything out of the ordinary, should inspect the facility to either ensure that no bomb is present or locate the device. If the police allow employees to make a preliminary search before the police arrive, then volunteer employees and management personnel should do so. However, only trained police or other qualified personnel should retrieve any bomb that might be discovered.

Management personnel and employees must not panic when they receive a bomb threat; advance training in security procedures can help calm personnel. Whenever possible, department heads should allow employees from their own work areas to review the specific plans and procedures developed for a search. Management should draw up these plans and procedures in advance of need.

If police and managerial personnel consider the threat a hoax, they may not order the evacuation of guests. In fact, panic and the rush of crowds to emergency and other exits can, by themselves, cause bodily harm to guests. However, a search of the facility is still in order to confirm the absence of a bomb. Conduct such a search in public areas discreetly to avoid unduly alarming the guests.

Personnel familiar with individual areas within the building can help search for a bomb when a property receives a threat. They can note whether or not anything out of the ordinary is present such as a bag, box, case, or package which should not be in the area. If anyone notices an abnormal item which cannot be explained, no one should attempt to move, touch, examine, or in any other way disturb it. Rather, all personnel should leave the area, and the police should be notified about its exact location.

Flaming Foods in Dining Areas

The flaming of drinks, desserts, and entrees is forbidden in some parts of the United States because of the risk of fire. Accidents occasionally occur which cause personal injury to guests and employees and property damage to the facility. Municipal codes may regulate whether or not a property can flame foods, or they may specify the type and minimum amount of fuel which properties can use.

If your property does flame food items, your employees must know what they're doing. Required procedures must incorporate fire safety concerns. For instance, because the transportation of flaming items from kitchen areas to guests is especially dangerous, properties develop rules forbidding such a procedure in crowded dining areas. Professional managers also make certain the proper types of fire extinguishers are readily available in all parts of the dining area.

While the factors surrounding every situation are unique, many authorities suggest that it is generally unwise to evacuate the facility before a search confirms that a bomb or suspicious device is present. However, if you have strong feelings that the threat is real, an immediate, calm evacuation is in order. Again, closely follow the advice of police officials regarding the need to evacuate the premises.

Generally, guests evacuating a building during a bomb threat should leave through the fire exits. Employees should exit according to plans that enable property officials to account for them. All evacuation plans should ensure that absolutely no one remains in the building.

If an evacuation plan is in order but no imminent danger exists, management staff should lock all equipment containing cash. Doors should remain unlocked in order to facilitate the search for the bomb. If police do not object, equipment can be turned off and other precautions can be taken to protect the facilities.

After an evacuation is complete, personnel should not return to the building and grounds until the police declare them safe. Employees should then return to their assigned work areas to await instructions from their department heads.

Robberies

Food service operations are special candidates for robberies; a thief may confront an employee or a guest and demand money or other valuables.

Managers need to carefully think about and develop procedures to follow during robberies. As a property considers robbery precautions, its paramount concern should be the safety of human beings. While sales income is obviously important, concern for personal safety has a much higher priority.

In some properties, employees are instructed to follow procedures such as the following when a robbery attempt is made:

1. Cooperate in every respect with all requests made by the criminal. Do not do or say anything that would jeopardize your safety.

2. Give the robber cash, food, beverages, or anything else that he/she demands.

3. Do not attempt to deceive, lie, resist, or be uncooperative in any way.

4. Do not volunteer unsolicited information.

5. Attempt to observe everything possible about the criminal, including:

   - height (Are the criminal's eyes above or below your line of vision?)

   - skin color (If it's not obvious, look around the eyes and collar.)

   - eye color

   - hair (Length? Color? Any facial hair?)

   - facial characteristics (Size of nose? Facial scars?)

- weight (Is the criminal heavier or lighter than you are?)

- voice (Is it male or female, high or low pitched, etc.? Does the criminal talk fast or slow, with an accent, etc.?)

- right- or left-handedness (In which hand is the weapon?)

- the kind of weapon used

- clothing (Is it new or old? What color, type, and style is each item of clothing? Is the criminal wearing any unusual item such as a special belt buckle or designer's logo?)

- miscellaneous items (Any distinctive personal characteristics, such as earrings in a man's ears, elaborate rings or other jewelry, tattoos, scars, etc.?).

6. Do not follow the criminal out of the building. If the property has a window or other safe viewing place, you may be able to note the criminal's mode of transportation. If he/she is using a car, note the license plate number, the color and type, and any rust, dents, or other special characteristics which the vehicle might exhibit.

7. Try to determine the direction the robber took when he/she left the property.

8. As soon as the criminal leaves, notify the police; relate all required information. Then, notify the manager if he/she is not available on the site. Even before the police arrive, employees should begin to write down all that they can recall about the criminal and his/her personal characteristics. Each employee should make notes without talking to the others. Items that were touched by the robber should not be moved or handled.

9. Encourage guests who were witnesses to remain until the police arrive.

10. Give police your full cooperation as they attempt to obtain relevant information about the robbery.[7]

A dining outlet could use several procedures to reduce the impact of robberies. For example, the facility's manager could remove large sums of money from the cash register(s) during each shift and place them in a safe or other secure place. This procedure reduces the amount of sales income that someone can take during a robbery since most robbers would not know how to open a safe on the premises. In some instances, properties use silent alarms, bullet-proof cashier cages, and on-site guards. Frequent bank deposits or trips to bank depositories can also help reduce the amount of cash on the premises. Finally, closed circuit television is used to monitor cashier areas; the obvious presence of a camera may deter some robbers.

Additional precautions are necessary to protect sales income that is in transit to the bank for deposit. Operations with large amounts of sales income should consider the use of an armored car or bonded messenger service. Managers should also eliminate routines. Personnel making deposits should go at varying times and leave the building through different exits. A few trusted employees can take turns making deposits. If employees use their own cars to make bank deposits, they should park them as close as possible to the building exit. When management officials make night deposits after the facility closes, they should exit through doors within the public's view rather than through back doors which may not be visible to passing cars or pedestrians. Finally, contact local police for additional, specific suggestions that can help reduce the possibility and magnitude of losses from theft.

---

[7] This discussion is taken in part from L. Gottlieb, "Protection Measures in the Event of a Robbery," *Restaurant Business*, Vol. 79, No. 8, June 1, 1980; and Ninemeier, *Food and Beverage Security*, pp. 139-140.

Managing Service at the Hotel Columbia
Page Thirty

Lewis Scott was still thinking about the injured guest and had worked with his management staff to develop a program to resolve (or, at least, minimize) safety-related problems. To identify potential safety problems, each manager of a food and beverage outlet (or his/her designated representative) would use a safety checklist specially designed for the outlet. (A sample hotel safety checklist that managers can adapt to suit their own facilities accompanies this case study.) Each manager would also review his/her assigned outlet daily and would take immediate corrective action as soon as a problem was identified.

Lewis liked to use checklists when they were practical. It occurred to him that guest safety checklists could help his managers develop standard operating procedures around which they could build training programs designed to make all employees "partners" in guest safety efforts. They could also use the checklists to help ensure that the employees helped to identify potential problems.

"It is unfortunate," Lewis thought, "that dining service employees don't pay more specific attention to the safety of their guests. Here at the Hotel Columbia, we're going to have a philosophy about safety that will give it a very high priority in everything that we do. After all, the guests expect that and we do not want to let them down."

Safety Checklist

Date of Review: _____

Review by: _____

Check (   ) to indicate that you observed no problem.

☐   1.   Parking lots and sidewalks are well-defined, well-lighted, and well-maintained.

☐   2.   Outdoor lighting at ground level is protected with grills or other devices to prevent children and trespassers from getting burned.

☐   3.   Signs, lights, or other devices are used to alert guests to steps or ledges in areas between parking lots and the building.

☐   4.   Tree limbs that hang over parking lots or sidewalks are not in danger of falling.

☐   5.   Snow is removed promptly; salt or sand is spread over shoveled sidewalk areas to prevent slipping and falling.

☐   6.   Exterior light fixtures and building ornaments are firmly attached.

☐   7.   Steps, ramps, and other passages leading to exterior doors and well-marked, well-lighted, and in good repair.

☐   8.   Steps have nonskid strips or other devices to prevent slips and falls.

☐   9.   Banisters and rails are available and well-secured.

☐   10.   Mats, abrasive strips, or other devices are used in entrance areas where water may be tracked in during inclement weather; they are in good repair.

☐   11.   Safety decals, draperies, or other devices/materials clearly indicate large panels of glass.

☐   12.   All interior steps are clearly marked/lighted.

☐ 13. All light fixtures, other ceiling attachments, pictures, and other wall decorations/attachments are securely fastened and in no danger of falling.

☐ 14. Ceiling and wall attachments are located to prevent/minimize the possibility of guests bumping heads on the attachments.

☐ 15. No items stick out of floors or carpets (nonflush nails, wooden splinters, improperly laid bricks, etc.)

☐ 16. Carpeting is not frayed or torn; any exposed edges are secured to prevent slipping and falling.

☐ 17. Nothing is placed either permanently or temporarily on steps or in guest traffic aisles.

☐ 18. Coat racks are in no danger of collapse and/or are securely fastened to the wall or other support.

☐ 19. All furniture is in good condition; tables, chairs, and stools are checked frequently for damage; chairs are checked for loose legs, arms, and backs; damaged seating equipment is not used.

☐ 21. Emergency door-opening devices are in good working order.

☐ 22. Fire alarms, emergency lighting, fire extinguishers, and similar equipment are in good working order.

☐ 23. Elevators are routinely checked and properly maintained.

☐ 24. Aisles between tables, booths, or counters are wide enough to prevent accidents from employees/guests running into each other.

☐ 25. Food server tray stands are placed in areas where guests cannot bump into them and where spillage and dropping will not affect guests.

☐ 26. Food/beverage servers are trained in proper service procedures to minimize the possibility of spilling food and beverages on guests.

☐ 27. No equipment has damaged or frayed electrical cords or is otherwise unsafe to operate.

Source: Adapted from Jack D. Ninemeier, *Food and Beverage Security: A Systems Manual for Restaurant, Hotels, and Clubs* (Boston: CBI; 1982), pp. 152-153.

16

Dining Room Design, Decor, and Maintenance

A total dining experience comprises not only food and beverages but also the atmosphere of the dining area and the service provided. The design and decor must harmonize with the cuisine and the service. As designers and planners view the operation from the guests' perspective and develop plans and procedures to meet guests' needs, they must consider such elements as noise, lighting, color coordination, and space in their outlets.

Those who are responsible for designing dining areas must be aware of government regulations concerning safety. These laws may govern such factors as the maximum number of occupants that public areas can accommodate and emergency lighting and exits.

Design also affects service. If dining areas are laid out properly, for instance, guests will be comfortable and service employees will not have to waste time traveling long distances unproductively.

Maintenance of the dining area requires constant attention. Facilities that are unclean and/or in disrepair negatively affect guests' attitudes about the property. An effective preventive maintenance program for the dining room is an important element in the property's ongoing safety program. Such a program also helps minimize operating and capital equipment costs which some properties incur due to inattention to their furniture, equipment, and fixtures.

Planning an Effective Design

Properly designed dining areas necessitate a complex planning process to ensure that:

1. Completed dining areas have the proper appeal and ambience.

2. A minimal investment for dining service space is made.

3. A maximum return on the investment in space is realized.

4. There is a practical layout to ensure an efficient flow of guests, employees, products, and equipment within dining areas.

5. Simplified procedures for performing required tasks are possible.

6. Dining areas provide safe work space for employees and public access space for guests.

7. Dining areas adhere to the high sanitation standards which the property requires.

8. Dining areas lend themselves to efficient employee work.

9. Dining areas lend themselves to low maintenance costs.

10. Dining areas are energy-efficient.

Managing Service at the Hotel Columbia
Page Thirty-One

Lewis was aware of the significant amount of money used to purchase the equipment, furniture, and fixtures for the Hotel Columbia's dining service outlets. He also understood that if these items were properly cleaned, maintained, and repaired there would be a positive impact upon the total dining experience of the guests. The conscious effort to do all that was possible to please guests required that Lewis and his entire management team pay constant attention to every detail, including the maintenance and repair of dining service equipment.

About six months after the hotel opened, Lewis was having lunch in the Round the Clock coffee shop, and he noted that the dinner rolls were not warm. When he asked the server why, she commented, "Oh, I guess the bun warmer is not working today; sometimes it does work—and sometimes it doesn't. I'm sorry about this; I'll ask our chef to warm some rolls 'specially for you."

"Why especially for me?" thought Lewis, "I'm no more—and, in fact, I'm *less*—important than our guests. Do we have a problem with our preventive maintenance program?"

---

11. The design makes the supervision of dining service employees and other management activities easy.

12. The design provides guests with the "comfort zone" they desire.

Effective planning of dining areas takes time and generally requires the specialized knowledge of several people as the process evolves. These people form a dining room planning team. The owner/manager, of course, should always be on the planning team, and the restaurant manager should help make decisions affecting front-of-house design. In many instances, an architect needs to work on the planning team. Unless the owner/manager is thoroughly familiar with the complex task of designing interior space to meet the identified characteristics of the property, the team may also require a food service facility consultant, interior decorator, and/or other designers. People with backgrounds and experiences ranging from managing operations to designing them are needed to develop the best design plans for dining areas.

One of the first steps in the planning process is to develop the concept of the outlet by determining just what the completed design needs to accomplish. A high-check-average dining room will obviously be designed much differently from a low-check-average outlet. A high-check-average dining room must have a luxurious ambience; the costs of this ambience are included in the high charges which guests pay in these outlets. While the atmosphere of the low-check-average outlet must be pleasant in order to enhance the dining experience, it would not require elegance. Obviously, both outlets must feature a design which meets the specific needs of the clientele served.

One method the dining room planning team can use to understand the needs of guests is market analysis—a detailed study of potential guests and their wants and needs. Because in commercial operations economic viability depends on profit, a feasibility study is needed to ensure that the property's design is cost-effective. Properties base their estimated income on the anticipated turnover of guests and the expected check average. Of course, seating capacities in dining areas affect the number of guests that can be served, and, therefore, potential income.

The planning team must also assess cost estimates for dining room plans. Not only is the dining area space itself expensive, but the furniture, fixtures, and equipment necessary to furnish it properly also add significantly to the expense.

In addition, the planning team must identify each activity and task which someone must perform to meet the food service operation's objectives; then they must determine the space and equipment required to perform those activities. In part, the task involves an analysis of the

Selecting a Designer

How does a dining room manager select a designer? Among the factors that should be considered are the following:

Membership in the American Society of Interior Designers (ASID). A member of ASID has a formal, accredited education, professional experience, and has successfully completed a comprehensive two-day examination. Likewise, this association stresses high standards of ethical conduct.

Education. Inquire about the degrees which the designer holds, the institution(s) which granted the degrees, and the designer's major fields of study.

Experience. Does the designer have experience in hotel and/or restaurant design? With what properties has he/she worked? Ask for references and contact them.

Portfolio. Look at his/her portfolio. Professional designers generally have many photographs, drawings, and other information illustrating their creative skills. Do you like what he/she has done?

First Impressions. What are your feelings about the designer? Does he/she seem to be professional? Can the two of you communicate with each other? Does it appear that the designer understands what you want, and do you believe that he/she can do the job?

Contacts. With which suppliers does the designer work? What services will the designer provide and what additional work will others need to do? Do you have any problems using the suppliers suggested by the designer?

Budget. Does the designer think that he/she can deliver the necessary design within the allowable budget?

Design Fees. What will the designer charge for his/her services? What additional fees will you need to pay to others as a result of the designer's contacts?

It is not easy to find a good designer; you must allow ample time for this task. Since you want to hire a professional, you should be willing to accept many of the concepts which he/she offers.

You need to be very candid with the designer about all details of the operation. What are the property's menu and marketing concepts? What are its economic concerns? What are the elements that the owner/manager does and does not like in design work? Very effective communication is important both when you select a designer and as various design activities evolve.

flow of guests and employees through the dining facility.

Preliminary layout and equipment plans help the team allocate available space. Such floor plans show the proposed arrangement of equipment, traffic flow aisles, and the relationship of each area to the other. When the team is at the point of examining preliminary floor plans, the members can assemble basic cost estimates and, if necessary, adjust the preliminary plans to accommodate the available funds.

When members of the planning team have reviewed, modified, and approved all preliminary information, they can draw up final blueprints for the space and prepare specifications for the necessary equipment. They use these documents to request price quotations and select contractors and suppliers to work on the project. Construction and installation tasks follow according to a schedule which meets the needs of all parties.

From this brief description, you should realize that the planning process involves many steps and many people. Since a commitment of capital funds is generally great, a great deal of planning is required to ensure that the project goals are met without surprises.

Space Requirements

Determining space needs for dining service is always difficult since such requirements depend on many factors which are unique to the specific operation. Examples of unique factors include the number of meals the property plans to prepare, the exact tasks the employees must perform in dining areas, the equipment service staff will use, and the amount of dining space needed for guests. The facility must also have space for storing dining service supplies, exercising sales income controls, and carrying out other front-of-house activities.

Planners of food service operations often obtain an estimate of the total size of the facility by building up from the number of seats they wish to provide. They need to make this estimate because income and profit levels, both of which relate to the number of meals that will be served, determine the feasibility of the property's design.

Food service managers in schools, colleges, universities, businesses, and industries are able to estimate the number of meals they will serve with relative ease. They base their estimates on past history, or, if they are new operations, on a percentage which similar facilities have calculated as their average. The number of dining periods which the operation will offer will then affect the dining room's seating capacity. For example, if a school has an enrollment of 1,000 students, 80% of whom eat three meals a day, and it offers four specific dining periods for each meal, then it must design a seating capacity of 200 for the dining room (80% of 1,000 students = 800 per meal; 800 students divided by 4 meal periods = 200 seats per period).

Lodging property managers plan sizes of dining areas according to estimates of room occupancy, the extent to which the community will use their dining room services, and the number of banquet functions they expect to schedule. To determine the dining space required for any type of operation, consider the number of guests that will be seated at one time and the total square feet allowed per seat. Exhibit 16.1 is a base from which specific calculations can be made. The actual number of square feet that must be allowed is determined by the amount of comfort guests desire and by any applicable governmental regulations which dictate aisle width and space requirements (such as the amount of unobstructed space in front of emergency exits). Design and placement of cashier stations, host stands, food server stations, and salad bars also affect the number of square feet a specific facility needs; you must add additional space to the estimates in Exhibit 16.1 for them.

You already know that "seat turnover" means the number of guests who will occupy a seat during a specific time period (such as an hour). You have also learned that the turnover of seats is a useful way to determine the estimated sales volume for a specific property. Exhibit 16.2 shows how to use seat turnover information to calculate estimated income. If an owner plans a dining room with 150 seats and expects a 2.5 seat turnover rate for the dinner period, he/she can easily determine the estimated annual sales for dinner. However, properties rarely have every seat occupied at any one time. For example, three people may sit at a four-top table, or one person may sit at a deuce (table for two). The occupancy factor is used to determine the number of guests whom you can reasonably expect to be seated at one time.

Once you know the estimated guests served per meal, you can calculate the daily income per meal period by multiplying the estimated guests times the dinner check average. You can then arrive at the estimated annual sales for dinner by multiplying the daily dinner income times both the days per week and the number of weeks per year that the dining room is open.

Using similar calculations, you can estimate annual sales for other meal periods. You also need to estimate income from banquet sales and beverage sales at the bar in order to arrive at an anticipated total annual income for the property. You could then use that information as a base for a feasibility study to assess the economic worth of the proposed design project.

The property's service method, type of menu, guests, and dining atmosphere all affect actual turnover rates. For instance, tableside food preparation, a one-course versus a five-course meal, a diner desiring a quick lunch, or another wishing to have a leisurely social experience would all influence turnover. Exhibit 16.3

Exhibit 16.1 Range of Estimated Square Feet for Dining Area Space

Facility	Dining Area Space (Square feet per person)
Table Service	12–18
Counter Service	16–20
Booth Service	12–16
Cafeteria Service	12–16
Banquet Service	10–12

Source: Edward Kazarian, *Food Service Facilities Planning*, 2nd ed. (Westport, Conn.: AVI, 1983), p. 183.

Exhibit 16.2 Calculation of Annual Estimated Income for One Meal Period Based on Seat Turnover

Number of Dining Room Seats	(×)	Average Seat Turnover per Meal	(×)	Occu-pancy* Factor	(=)	Estimated Guests Served per Meal	(×)	Check Average	(=)	Estimated Daily Income per Meal Period	(×)	Days/ Weeks Meal is Served	(×)	Annual Weeks Open	(=)	Estimated Annual Sales for Meal Period
150	(×)	2.5	(×)	80%	(=)	300	(×)	$5.75	(=)	$1,725.00	(×)	6	(×)	52	(=)	$538,200

*The "occupancy factor" indicates that not all dining room seats are occupied at one time.

Exhibit 16.3 Typical Turnover Rates

Facility	Hourly Turnover Rate
Commercial Cafeteria	1.5–2.5
Industrial/School Cafeteria	2.0–3.0
Counter Service	2.0–3.5
Combination Counter/Table Service	2.0–3.0
Regular Table Service	1.0–2.5
Leisurely Table Service	.5–1.0

Source: Kazarian, p. 184.

shows the range of hourly turnover rates in some types of food service operations. Facility planners may use this information to determine specific turnover rates for the properties they are developing.

Basic management and dining service practices can also influence the speed of turnover. Examples of factors which can affect seat turnover include:

1. The amount of processing which menu items must undergo after servers place the order. (Compare a cooked-to-order item such as a tournedos bearnaise with a bulk item such as chili, which an employee must only portion.)

2. The number of production personnel, the amount of space, and the equipment required at peak serving times. (A rush of business may back up kitchen production and delay the service of orders.)

3. High levels of illumination and light colors, which are not as conducive to leisurely dining as lowered lights and subdued colors.

4. Dining tables in close proximity to each other, which are less conducive to leisurely dining than tables that are further apart.

5. The quantity of available service staff, which relates directly to the level of service provided.

6. The speed with which employees can clean and reset tables after guests leave. (The more quickly they can clean and reset them, the more quickly the next guests can be seated.)

7. The sale of before- or after-dinner drinks, wine, menu items requiring tableside preparation, and desserts. (The more your employees sell these items, the slower the turnover.)

8. Entertainment in the dining area, which slows turnover.

9. The size of group served. (Large groups generally take longer to dine than small groups.)

10. Meal periods. (Diners generally want fast service for breakfast and lunch but more leisurely service for evening meals.)

The preceding list, while not complete, does suggest the wide range of factors affecting turnover which should be considered when specific turnover rates are established for a property. Turnover statistics are obviously important when you plan new operations since such information is used to determine estimated income when planners conduct feasibility studies. Since turnover affects the levels of income generated during the actual operation of a property, restaurant managers should understand the factors which affect turnover and attempt to influence them so that the property can increase its sales without sacrificing the established serving quality standards.

Traffic Flow Concerns

The term "traffic flow" refers to the movement of employees, guests, products, and supplies through the food service operation. The manager of dining service must address issues related to the movement of people in both front- and back-of-house areas.

Exhibit 16.4 represents a preliminary, schematic drawing developed during the early planning stages of a food service facility. It is not drawn to scale. Instead, it is the kind of preliminary drawing which planners make to help them decide how to locate various spaces relative to each other. In the design represented in this exhibit, guests would typically enter the property through the main entrance (#1). The property may find a separate entrance (#2) helpful for banquet guests only. The location of the emergency exit (#3) will be dictated by local ordinances. Parking areas should be situated on the side of the building where the entrances are located.

When guests use the main entrance, they can either go to the lounge or register with the host/hostess for dining service. Many people do not like to go through a lounge area to get to the dining rooms; therefore, a separate entrance to the lounge area is useful. You could even design an outside lounge entrance; however, such an entrance may cause problems with sales income control. To avoid the potential problem of guests

Exhibit 16.4 Schematic Layout of Front-of-House Areas

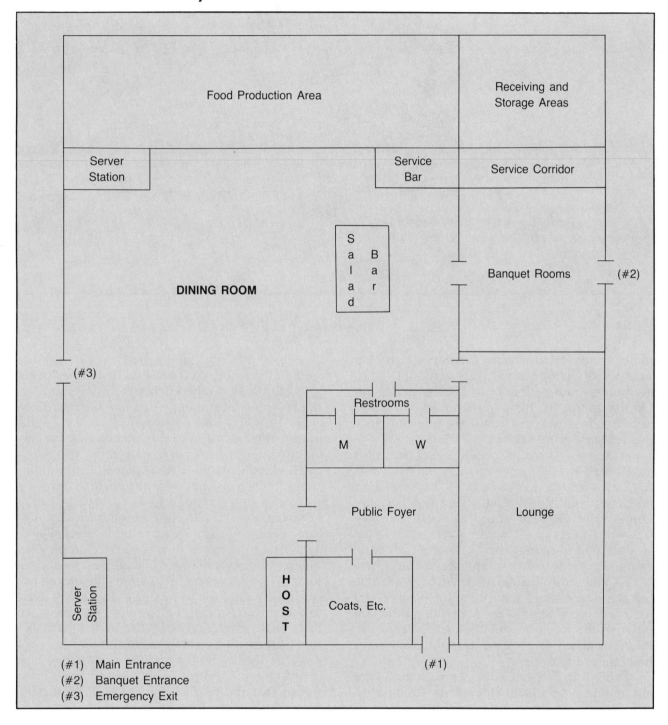

who drink and dash, the property can be designed so that guests must enter and exit the lounge through a public foyer. Upon entering the facility, guests have access to an area to check coats and use telephones. The property could also locate restrooms in this area.

The designer placed the salad bar so that both dining room guests and, when practical,

Perception of Space

Our distance from an object influences our perception of that object. Edward T. Hall defines distance in terms useful to design:

Public distance	12′ or more
Social	4′ to 12′
Personal	18″ to 4′
Intimate	Touch to 18″

Ethnic background also influences our perception of space. In Paris, people are comfortable in crowded conditions—indeed, prefer them. Hence, the popularity of the cozy French cafe. In Japan, by contrast, people seek a sense of serenity and spaciousness. Thus the design of the Japanese teahouse.*

Most Americans do not like to eat in crowded dining rooms. Except in some fast-food operations, crowding is generally unacceptable. Thus, the more American guests require leisurely dining, the more the amount of square feet allowed per guest should increase.

*Adapted from Regina Baraban, "A Psychological Primer on Restaurant Design," *Lodging*, April 1984, p. 96.

small groups of diners in the banquet rooms could use it. The restrooms are accessible from the dining room so that both sets of diners can also use them. (If this plan complies with municipal codes, you can reduce significant non-revenue-producing space.)

A service corridor provides service staff quick access to banquet rooms. The service bar is in an area which accommodates the service of diners in both the dining room and banquet rooms. (The property could also use portable bars when necessary.) Server stations are in areas designed to reduce the distance which servers must walk to get to dining service supplies.

As you study Exhibit 16.4, you may be able to make suggestions to improve the design. The point is that you should put something down on paper so that members of the design team can react and make improvements before they have final blueprints drawn.

Exhibit 16.5 focuses on service employees and the tasks they must perform in back-of-house areas. The property may require service employees to enter order information on a guest check before they enter the food pickup area. The location of a precheck register (#1) or similar piece of equipment should then be in the server's traffic flow to the kitchen area.

Upon entering the kitchen, servers can unload soiled dishes in the soiled dish area, which is located close to the kitchen's dining room entrance. Planners using a similar design, however, must consider noise control factors so that guests at tables close to the kitchen door are not inconvenienced. Service staff may also move clean glasses, flatware, and plates to the dining room. However, they will not need to transport clean dishes as frequently as they will need to remove soiled dishes from serving areas; therefore, the clean dish area can be located slightly away from the traffic flow of service employees. The clean dish area in Exhibit 16.5 is close to the food serving line so that responsible employees can move clean plates, bowls, and other items to the line as needed, but service employees still have reasonable access to the area when they must transport clean dishes to the dining room.

The facility might use an expediter (#2) to coordinate the ordering and plating activities of the service and production staffs. This official is placed in front of the serving line.

Cold items such as salads or desserts might be available from a pantry area. Perhaps a production employee gets such foods when servers place orders. Alternatively, service employees may help themselves to these items. If the latter

Exhibit 16.5 Traffic Flow Patterns in Back-of-House Areas

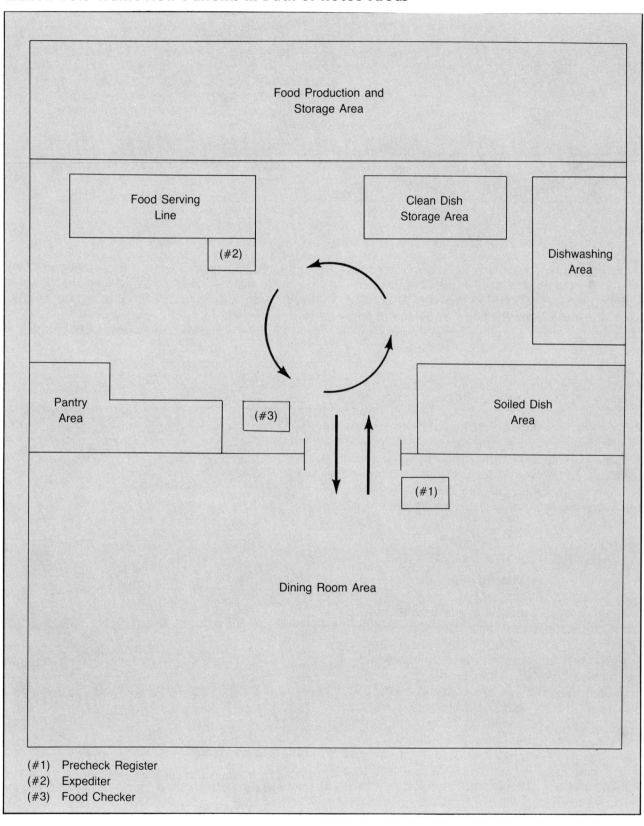

(#1) Precheck Register
(#2) Expediter
(#3) Food Checker

The Location of the Host/Hostess is Important

It may seem obvious that the host/hostess area should be close to the dining room's guest entrance. However, the reason for selecting this location is more than just the ease of meeting and greeting guests. For example, many properties allow guests to transfer beverage charges incurred in the lounge area to the dining area for payment at the end of the meal. Some properties might do this electronically. (Point-of-sale systems in some hotels transfer charges to the guest's folio as soon as they incur them; restaurants use precheck registers and similar equipment to automatically carry lounge charges forward to a master account.) However, most properties handle beverage transfers manually, which is why the host stand should be as close to the lounge area as possible.

In many respects, the host stand is the command post of the entire dining room. It should be easily accessible to service employees as well as guests.

method will be used in an outlet, the pantry area should be placed close to the dining room exit.

The planned procedures for income control might require a food checker (#3). This official might confirm that items ready for service have been entered properly on guest checks; he/she might also review plate presentation. Food checkers are usually located close to the kitchen's exit to the dining area.

The schematic drawing of the back-of-house food server flow illustrated in Exhibit 16.5 can help the planners of a food service facility consider the impact of locating different work areas in specific locations. We cannot overemphasize the analysis and study of such schematic drawings in the early planning stages of a facility.

Dining Room Decor and Ambience

Dining areas must be compatible with a property's menu and service style. All too often, owners think yesterday's steak house can become today's pizzeria by simply hanging up a few pictures of the Italian landscape, or they think that their old English pub can become an 1890s bar just by changing the uniforms the service employees wear. While extreme, these examples point to the frequent inattention given to the atmosphere created in a dining area. Successful managers do not overlook the fact that details such as fixtures and equipment make their own contribution to dining room decor and

ambience. For example, stainless steel and glass no more fit into an Early American theme than heavy wooden furniture fits into a twenty-first century motif.

Service personnel themselves contribute to the dining room atmosphere. Guests in a gourmet dining room find it appropriate, for in-

Dining room reminiscent of family-style restaurant in The Netherlands. (Amway Grand Plaza Hotel, Grand Rapids, Michigan)

stance, that the manager is wearing a morning suit consisting of black jacket and vest, pin-striped trousers, and a gray tie. The ambience of a dining room with a German or other ethnic theme is enhanced when servers wear colorful national costumes.

While creating the perfect environment, managers should not neglect proper function. (See Chapter 5 for details about purchasing dining service equipment.) Furniture, fixtures, and equipment must be easy to clean and long-wearing. Concerns about costs and whether or not replacement products can be purchased in the future must be addressed. Typically, products of commercial, not household, quality should be purchased in order to withstand the wear and tear to which guests and employees will expose them. Very delicate or rare decorative items should not be used unless they are out of reach and well anchored. (It is a fact of life that guests may take for souvenirs decorations which are not vandal-proofed.) Unfortunately, many people do not treat furnishings in public areas the same way that they do in their own homes; therefore, furnishings must wear well to withstand employee and/or guest misuse or mischief.

When managers plan dining room atmosphere, they must also consider safety factors. Problems can occur when:

1. Entry floors are made of materials which are slippery on rainy or snowy days.

2. Rug edges are exposed (they can trip guests).

3. Furniture and equipment are highly flammable.

4. Wooden furniture has splinters; metal furniture has sharp edges.

5. Glass windows are not covered or marked to prevent people from thinking that they are open doors.

6. Steps are not lighted and there are no railings.

7. Areas are so dark that people cannot see as they move about.

8. Furniture tips easily.

9. Floor coverings catch the high heels on women's shoes.

10. Fixtures or hanging decorations are too low for tall people.

11. Swinging doors are in traffic aisles.

12. Emergency exit traffic flow pattern is obstructed.

The list of examples could continue. However, the point is that when atmosphere is being planned, safety cannot be overlooked.

Colors Affect Atmosphere

The colors used in dining areas obviously affect the atmosphere portrayed. As is true with most decisions the restaurant manager makes, the important consideration is, "What do the guests want?" The answer to that question may be far different from the feelings he/she has

Well-designed lounge in a hotel lobby. (Amway Grand Plaza Hotel, Grand Rapids, Michigan)

The Psychology of Lighting

More than any other design element, lighting creates the mood of a space. (It can also obviate the effectiveness of all other design elements.) Here are some rules of thumb for lighting:

1. Sparkle enhances the appetite and encourages conversation. Chandeliers or multiple pin lights can achieve sparkle. Light also bounces off mirrored surfaces, wet-looking finishes, and shiny serviceware to create sparkle.
2. Dark shadows appear hostile; small patterns of light appear friendly.
3. Brightly lit architectural surfaces tend to move people and are therefore good for high-volume facilities.
4. Direct lighting must be counteracted with indirect lighting to avoid a boring look and achieve environmental comfort.
5. Candles (or equivalent soft illumination) between people will draw them together.
6. Strong down-lighting is unbecoming to people.
7. If lighting makes flesh tones look good, it also tends to make food look good. (Light should always flatter people.)
8. Surround people with light rather than spotlighting them (thus making them look onstage).
9. Design lighting in transition zones so guests won't feel blinded when they enter from sunlight or disoriented when they exit into darkness.
10. Use a dimming system in food rooms to permit mood changes:
    - Brightness and cheer for breakfast.
    - Restfulness for lunch.
    - Animation for cocktails.
    - Romance for dinner.

Source: Adapted from Regina Baraban, "Lighting and Color in Hospitality Design," *Lodging*, May 1984, pp. 17-19.

about specific colors and combinations of colors. Interior designers use a wide range of rules for selecting colors. For this and many other reasons, it is often wise to involve a professional interior decorator in the design of dining areas and to depend on him/her for color coordination ideas.

Violets, blues, and light greens are cool colors and tend to make guests feel relaxed. Facilities emphasizing leisurely dining may want to use these colors or combinations of these colors. In contrast, warm colors, such as reds, yellows, and oranges, are stimulating; they encourage activity. Therefore, these colors could encourage fast table turnover.

Many of us are aware that rooms which receive little sunlight should have light and warm colors, while those receiving a lot of sunlight should utilize cool, dark colors. Colors also have an impact on perceived room size. Light colors make the room appear large; dark colors tend to make a room look small. Dark colors also make ceilings look lower than they are. When one wall is a very bright color, the other wall should be more neutral, perhaps in the same shade or tint.

Small pictures, wall hangings, and other decorations should be used in small rooms. Larger items should be used with care, even in large rooms. When decorations from various periods or with differing styles are selected, a unified effect can be created if their colors are coordinated. Such decorations should be selected carefully if they are to help portray a theme. For example, various items that could be chosen to portray a nautical theme include models of ships, anchors, oars, buoys, fishing nets, and shells. To add to an Old West theme, such items as copper cooking utensils, saloon signs, whiskey barrels, and branding irons might be appropriate. Careful thought and often considerable expense are necessary to decorate dining areas effectively.

Exhibit 16.6 Typical Cleaning Tasks Performed by Nonservice Personnel

1. Vacuum carpeted floors.

2. Mop uncarpeted floors.

3. Clean such surfaces as window ledges and tops of partial walls.

4. Spot-clean walls, floors, and other areas requiring special attention.

5. Clean floor, wall, and ceiling air vents.

6. Clean decorations and lighting fixtures.

7. Clean table bases and chair legs.

8. Dust and polish metal chairs; polish and oil wooden chairs.

9. Wash vinyl booths, bar stools, etc.

10. Clean bar and counter fronts.

11. Polish foot rails, metal trim, and other applicable parts of bars.

12. Wash, wax, or otherwise care for the host/receptionist stand.

13. Empty wastebaskets in public areas.

14. Clean public areas such as restrooms, coatrooms, and foyers.

Maintenance of Dining Areas

Restaurant managers must monitor the routine maintenance of furniture, fixtures, and equipment in dining areas. They must also develop and use effective preventive maintenance programs.

Of course managers know that dining room areas should be cleaned routinely to meet sanitation standards, but they should realize that the frequency and method of routine cleaning affects the life span of dining service supplies. Furthermore, cleanliness is important from the guests' perspective.

Who should perform cleanup and maintenance activities? Typically, service employees should clean tabletops, the interiors of service station refrigerators, and dining service supplies. But what about vacuuming floors, washing table bases, cleaning window ledges, and other jobs? The restaurant manager, working closely with the executive steward, executive housekeeper, or other management official who handles the cleaning of the facility, should make these decisions. Job descriptions should indicate the specific tasks which employees in each position are to perform, and cleaning and mainte-

nance schedules should be developed with these activities in mind.

Exhibit 16.6 provides examples of difficult and/or time-consuming cleaning activities which nonservice personnel may perform and which must be incorporated into the facility's ongoing maintenance activities.

Management must also decide who should clean, set up, and tear down banquet rooms. Frequently, housekeeping personnel, not dining service employees, handle those tasks. Specialized and very expensive equipment is available to clean banquet and meeting room areas.

Cleaning Procedures

Managers would be wise to consider maintenance and cleaning requirements when they select furniture, fixtures, and other equipment for dining areas. They should also consult with manufacturers and/or suppliers of products to solicit their recommended maintenance and cleaning procedures. Properties can use a wide range of exotic chemicals and specialized equipment. Because differences of opinion often occur, over which cleaning procedures are best, properties should obtain specific advice from experts, both about the cleaning and mainte-

Exhibit 16.7 Overview of Basic Hard-Floor Cleaning Techniques

Time	Wood	Linoleum	Rubber Tile	Vinyl Asbestos
Initially	Sanding, vacuuming, filling, sealing, buffing, and waxing/polishing.	Don't scrub for 4–5 days after installation. Damp mop. Apply polish recommended by manufacturer/supplier.	Do not wash with water for 4–5 days after installation. Sweep. Damp mop.	Do not scrub for 5 days after installation. Sweep.
Daily	Buffing, waxing, buffing again. Use wax-treated dust mop. Damp mop only if necessary.	Sweep with non-oily, specially-treated mop. Damp mop. Buff lightly.	Sweep or dry mop. Damp mop. Scrub lightly to remove soiled spots.	Sweep or dry mop. Damp mop. Scrub lightly to remove soiled spots.
Periodically	Buff with steel wool or nylon pads, or use glossy solvent-soluble chemicals specially developed for wood floors.	Scrub lightly, wax. Strip when necessary with recommended chemicals.	Strip floor to remove built-up wax or polish. Rewax or polish.	Strip floor to remove built-up wax or polish. Rewax or polish.

Time	Terrazzo	Quarry Tile	Asphalt Tile	
Initially	Seal thoroughly. Mop daily for first several months.	Scrub with nonalkaline detergent, rinse well. Seal floor.	Do not wash with water for 5–10 days after installation. Sweep frequently.	
Daily	Sweep. Buff.	Sweep. Damp mop. Wet mop.	Sweep or damp mop. Buff.	
Periodically	Wet mop or machine scrub.	Polish or wax.	Touch up with water-based polish. Strip, rinse, and repolish.	

Source: Adapted from Georgina Tucker and Madelin Schneider, *The Professional Housekeeper*, 2nd ed. (Boston, CBI, 1982), pp. 128-134.

nance of products and the materials that should be used.

Exhibit 16.7 presents a brief list of cleaning activities which properties should perform initially, daily, and periodically for different types of floors. (You can consult the reference cited in Exhibit 16.7 for more detailed information.)

Floor mats or other coverups used at entrances and runners used in heavy traffic areas are good ways to keep carpets clean. They also

---

Care and Maintenance of Dining Room Areas

There is a wide range of supplies, equipment, and recommended techniques to clean and maintain dining room areas and furniture, fixtures, and equipment. The following advice comes from experts in the care and maintenance of dining rooms:

1. Talk with the supplier and/or manufacturer of the products the food service operation uses. Take their advice about recommended cleaning procedures.
2. Develop written procedures for when and how employees should clean dining room areas.
3. Train cleaning personnel in the proper procedures.
4. Supervise employees as they undertake cleaning activities.
5. Using a written checklist, routinely confirm that employees are performing all cleaning and maintenance tasks on a regularly scheduled basis.

Managers should understand how important well-maintained dining room areas are to guests and the effect operating and capital replacement expenses have on the budget. Cleaning and maintenance tasks should not be done only when someone can get around to them. Rather, they should be an integral and ongoing aspect of service, housekeeping, and/or other staff members' jobs.

---

prevent wear, control noise, and reduce the possibility that a guest may slip or trip. Routine duties for carpet care include daily vacuuming, thorough weekly vacuuming, periodic shampooing, and regular cleaning with steam or another method.

Heavy traffic areas and dining spaces where spills occur frequently may require vacuuming after each meal and shampooing with a dry foam chemical each night. As is true with hard floors, a wide variety of supplies and equipment is available to clean carpets. Contact experts in carpet cleaning to obtain specific information about the best procedures to use.

Because walls in dining areas can be covered with paint, tile, wallpaper, wood, foil, cork, or a wide variety of other products, managers must be aware of the correct methods to clean them. Before washing walls covered with any of the above products, it is usually wise to dry-dust them. Of course the wall washing solution recommended by the manufacturer should be used, but before using any chemical, a weak solution of it should be tested on a small part of the wall. Generally, a water-based cleaning solution—strong enough to be effective without damaging the wall covering in any way—should be used.

Badly soiled areas may need to be saturated

with the proper solution. Heavily soiled areas should be rinsed and wiped immediately. Experts recommend washing and rinsing from the lower half of the walls as far up to the ceiling as is possible, and going from one corner of the room to the other. Finally, they recommend that the upper portion should be carefully cleaned to minimize drips and streams of solutions which can leave stains. Washing marble, ceramic, plastic, metal, acoustic, and papered walls requires special procedures. Again, advice from an expert is best.

It is difficult to keep windows clean on the inside; it is virtually impossible to keep the outside surfaces clean. New properties sometimes install windows which can be removed or pivoted to clean outside surfaces easily. While a wide range of chemicals and other supplies is available to clean windows, a mild liquid detergent and water works effectively. Lint-free materials such as sponges and squeegees should be used to clean windows. Normally, window screens, shades, and blinds should be removed before windows are cleaned. Those items should also be cleaned before re-installing them.

Most drapery materials should be vacuumed regularly and dry cleaned at least once annually. Some materials such as fiberglass can be washed.

Exhibit 16.8 Sample Work Order

WORK ORDER No. _____
Requested Service: _____
_____
Person Requesting: _____
Nature of Problem: _____
_____
Work Performed: _____
_____
Person Completing Work: _____
Date Performed: _____
Maint. Supervisor's Signature: _____

Source: Energy Technical Center, *Energy Maintenance Manual*, Vol. II (San Antonio, Texas: Hospitality, Lodging, and Travel Research Foundation, Inc.), no date.

Repairs

Purchasing the best equipment and using an effective preventive maintenance program will not exempt dining service equipment from needing occasional repairs. If the engineering or other internal-property department does the repairs, a work order system can be implemented. Exhibit 16.8 illustrates a work order form. If repair work is necessary, the form is completed and routed to the appropriate department. Upon completion of the work, the service person fills out the form which the accounting department then uses to bill the incurred costs to the appropriate department. Exhibit 16.9 is a sample of a repair log that properties use to keep records on specific appliances or machines.

Smaller properties, in which repairs by employees are not practical, will need to hire someone outside the property to repair equipment. If the equipment is under warranty and/or a preventive maintenance contract is in effect, the restaurant manager should know whom to contact. However, it is unwise to wait until something breaks, then shop around for a repair person. A new dining outlet manager can get recommendations from the food and beverage department head or other management employees to learn from their past experiences which local supply/repair company could best do the necessary work.

Frequent repairs of a specific piece of equipment or fixture may be a sign that either the equipment was an unwise purchase or the preventive maintenance program is not being effectively carried out. (Exhibit 16.10 is a sample preventive maintenance schedule.) If a record is kept of such repairs, it can be consulted when future purchasing and maintenance decisions are made. Because employees themselves can be hard on equipment, supervision is always in order to ensure that they do not use incorrect operating procedures, which contribute to excessive repair problems.

Managing Service at the Hotel Columbia
Page Thirty-Two

Lewis had asked Don Jackson, the director of restaurant operations, and Jamie Walker, the coffee shop manager, if they could meet with him in his office. Lewis was concerned about the preventive maintenance program in the coffee shop: could the cold dinner rolls caused by an inoperative bun warmer be indicative of other problems?

"Let's start by reviewing our operating procedures for the ongoing preventive maintenance program," he said to them.

1. Managers of each food and beverage outlet should meet with the chief engineer to identify items in their dining areas which should be included in the property's preventive maintenance program.
2. Each manager should consult operating instructions and other written information from the manufacturer that dictate when and how employees in each outlet should perform routine cleaning and maintenance activities.
3. An engineering department representative should summarize information on a maintenance and repair record (see Exhibit 16.9). This record, revised as necessary, provides a source of information for scheduling preventive maintenance.

4. A preventive maintenance schedule (see Exhibit 16.10) should be used. This form, developed for a six-month interval, indicates the week during which each item of equipment in the program should receive preventive maintenance.
5. All managers are responsible for developing and monitoring preventive maintenance schedules for their own outlets.
6. Whenever practical, a service employee should be trained to perform routine preventive maintenance on some equipment. If this is not practical and it is not possible for maintenance staff to perform the work, then the manager of the food and beverage outlet should consult with the appropriate director (department head) to consider the possibility of entering into a service agreement with a local supply company.
7. Regardless of whether or not preventive maintenance work is performed by someone on the property's payroll, the manager of each food and beverage outlet should assume full responsibility for ensuring that all necessary preventive maintenance schedules are followed.

As Lewis reviewed the procedures and forms

Exhibit 16.9 Repair Log

Service	Type Machine	Equipment No.
Location	Serial No.	Model No.
Make	Date Purchased	Purchase Cost

Preventive Maintenance Procedures

Function	Interval

Special Instructions

Specifications

Voltage	Drive
Amperage	Belts
Phase	Fuse
Pressure	Lubrication
RPM	Filter
Fluids	

Spare Parts Required

Part	Mfr. Part No.	Hotel Stock No.	Quantity

Repair Log Record   Equip. No.

Date	By	Work Performed		Hours	Mat'l.	Labor	Cost To Date

Source: Adapted from Jack D. Ninemeier, *Principles of Food and Beverage Operations* (East Lansing, Mich.: Educational Institute of the American Hotel & Motel Association), p. 424.

Exhibit 16.10 Preventive Maintenance Schedule

Location of Work	Description of Work	No. Items	Month	January	February	March	April	May	June
			Week	1 2 3 4	1 2 3 4	1 2 3 4	1 2 3 4	1 2 3 4	1 2 3 4

with Don and Jamie, he discovered that the coffee shop manager had delegated preventive maintenance duties to each shift supervisor. Over the past two or three months, less follow-up was being done to see whether procedures were being followed. (A call to the engineering department indicated that somehow the coffee shop bun warmer had been dropped from the preventive maintenance program when new maintenance schedules were developed.)

At the suggestion of Don Jackson, Lewis agreed that a training session on preventive maintenance would be given to all management staff members responsible for equipment maintenance. (The chief engineer would be asked to conduct it.) There would be a re-emphasis on the importance of the maintenance program and the need for managers to assume the responsibility for the program in their own outlets. Managers would also be reminded to instruct their employees to inform supervisors when problems occur. "Yes, there are lots of details to look after," thought Lewis, "but details do count when we're trying to provide the highest quality products and services to our guests."

Appendix A
Selecting Table Linens

Every food service outlet should have some type of covering on every table for health and cleanliness purposes. If you have ever watched a food server in a coffee shop wipe the top of the table with a dirty rag, using some of the water spilled from the glass of the previous guest, and then reset the table with clean tableware, you know how unsanitary a table without some kind of covering is. Every manager of dining service should attempt to alleviate a potential health hazard by furnishing table coverings, even if they are paper, in his/her outlet.

Table coverings also can be used to enhance ambience and guest comfort. Nothing presents the character of a dining room more dramatically than beautifully laundered, crisp-looking tablecloths draping each table. Fine linens provide guests with an attractive association with the dining room.

While sanitation, ambience, and guest comfort are each valid reasons for using table linens, together they add up to one overall motive—value. If you charge your guests for spending time in your dining outlet, you are obligated to justify the cost to them by offering embellishments with the meal commensurate with the price charged.

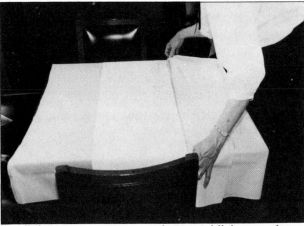

The dining room manager needs to establish procedures so that servers can change tablecloths consistently and unobtrusively when guests are in the dining room. (Kellogg Center, Michigan State University)

Types of Fabrics

Table linen is a generic term that refers to any fabric used for napkins and to drape a table. (Today, the word **napery** is often used interchangeably with table linens.) The fabrics used to make table linens represent many different fibers, weaves, and textures. We will concentrate on several basic constructions which are most applicable to our purpose.

Linen

Linen is among the most popular fibers from which tablecloths and napkins are woven. Linen

is a natural vegetable fiber grown as flax. After harvesting, the flax is dried and treated before it is spun into the linen yarns used to weave fabrics. The advantages of linen tablecloths and napkins come from the following qualities of the flax fiber:

1. It is strong, thereby affording long wear to the resultant woven products.

2. It has a long staple (fiber from which yarns are spun) which is responsible for the smooth texture of the fabric and the natural lintless character of the material. (When you select a fabric for your table linen, it should be lint-free. Guests often complain when their dark wool suits or dresses take on the appearance of a snow-covered field because a cheap napkin has left lint.)

3. It has a luxurious luster.

4. It is absorbent, an important characteristic for napkins.

5. Under proper conditions, it launders beautifully, producing a crisp, clean look.

This appendix was written and contributed by Leonard R. Weiss, President, James G. Hardy & Co., Inc., New York, New York.

6. The flat, shallow flax fiber allows the fabric to dry relatively fast.

Cotton

Cotton, like linen, is a plant fiber, but it does not have as long a staple and therefore is not as long-wearing or lustrous. It also requires special finishes to limit its tendency to lint. The process of **mercerizing** eliminates most of the short fibers on the surface of the cotton fabric by singeing and flattening the yarns. The procedure reduces the fabric's tendency to lint. Although mercerization adds to the cost of table linens, it results in a better looking, more serviceable product. If you buy your linens on the basis of price alone, you may eventually face more costly problems than had you purchased better quality products.

Polyester

The development of man-made fibers has added to the choice of materials available for commercial table linens. The most important of these fibers is polyester, a petroleum derivative.

Among its attributes, polyester has strength. In addition, it does not absorb water; thus, fabrics woven out of polyester require less processing time when laundered. However, polyester requires cooler wash water than linen or cotton; and the temperature of irons should be lowered so the resins added to establish polyester's "memory" aren't destroyed. Actually, one of the prime advantages of polyester is its memory, which enables fabrics woven out of it to return to their previous shape with little or no ironing.

A major objection to polyester fabrics is their "hand"—the way they feel to us. Pure, untreated polyester feels slippery and slimy. In addition, due to its lack of absorbency, polyester is not very practical for napkins. It also has a tendency to lose its crisp look and become limp after washing, which makes it difficult to fold napkins into decorative shapes.

Fabric Blends

To offset the disadvantages of fabrics made from just one fiber, manufacturers have developed fabrics that blend two or more fibers with some success. These blends highlight the more beneficial qualities of each of the components. For example, a polyester-cotton blend yields a fabric with more strength than a fabric made of 100% cotton, yet it is more absorbent and more pleasing to the touch than a fabric of 100% polyester.

However, while polyester and cotton combinations decrease the need for ironing, repeated launderings wash out the weaker cotton fibers, leaving all the polyester fibers and their undesirable characteristics.

Repeated washings do not have the same effect on fabrics which are blends of linen and cotton. Although the cotton fibers will wash out, the remaining linen fibers have more natural advantages. The most important benefit derived from combining linen with cotton is the cost savings. In recent years, the availability of flax has declined, while the desire for linen has enjoyed an upturn; consequently, the price of linen has increased. To moderate the effect of higher prices, the spinners and weavers have developed fabrics which combine flax with less expensive and more plentiful cotton. These fabrics, known as **union**, can be woven to resemble their all-linen counterparts, but they still retain many of their functional qualities.

Types of Weaves

Now that we have considered the more common and most practical fibers used to produce table linens, let's take a look at the types of weaves from which we can choose.

Crash Fabrics

The simplest materials are woven in a basic one-over-one construction. The weft yarns (those running the width of the material) simply cross the warp yarns (those running lengthwise) in an over-one, under-one sequence. These materials are called crash fabrics, and, although they are simply woven, they can be varied in many ways by using yarns of differing thicknesses and textures.

Crash fabrics and their blends create an atmosphere of superior quality. They are versatile, look dignified, and are less austere than other fabrics. Many fine European restaurants use crash fabrics for their table linens; therefore, sophisticated, well-traveled Americans appreciate their use in the United States.

Dobby Cloth

Another type of cloth used for table linens is known as dobby. This cloth is woven on dobby looms and is distinguished by constantly repeated geometric designs or insignia woven throughout the material. The best known of all the dobbies is **momie cloth**. (The name originates from the fabric's earliest use as the shroud in which the Egyptian mummies were wrapped.) Momie-weave table linens are the most widely used table coverings in the United States. They are durable, launder well, and offer a cloth table covering at a reasonable cost. Since they are so common, more expensive properties seeking distinctiveness often select other fabrics for their table linens. However, a printed momie or crash can help create a unique, if informal, atmosphere.

Damask

A third type of cloth which food service operations use is damask. Although damask fabrics were originally woven of silk, the term now refers to any cloth of any fiber which is woven in a certain pattern. The damask technique allows artisans to weave a name or crest into the fabric to make the tablecloths unique.

Two types of damask (single and double) are woven on Jacquard looms. Although double damask designs are more intricate and more expensive, the construction of the cloth makes it less durable than single damask. Most people define single damask as a five leaf twill; a satin field results from floats of warp passing over and under four weft yarns. The design is the result of a plain or taffeta weave that creates less luster than the satin areas.

Damask table linens are formal, elegant, and usually seen in high-check-average dining rooms and banquet facilities. They are durable and can withstand repeated launderings. Pure linen damask is probably the epitome of all fabrics in terms of dignity, appearance, launderability, and durability; however, linens made from pure linen damask are very expensive.

Colors

Many food service operations use colored table linens for their decorative appeal. It is essential that the dyestuffs used to color tablecloths and napkins are fast to laundering and, in some instances, to the sun.

To ensure that your property's table linens are colorfast, select only those items that are **vat dyed**, although even with the best of dyestuffs most dyed natural fibers do not retain their exact color after several washings. By purchasing tablecloths and napkins which have been dyed in a vat solution, you reduce the risk of having to use variously shaded table linens.

Recently, the textile coloring industry has introduced a category of dyes called "fiber-reactive" for blended fabrics. If you do not have an on-site laundry which could follow special laundry instructions, you may wish to avoid such fabrics because these dyes are extremely sensitive to chlorine bleach, which commercial laundries use to remove stains.

Accepting the superiority of vat colors over other dyeing formulas, we must now examine when and how these vat dyes are used.

Yarn Dyeing

Yarn dyeing—a process in which yarns are vat dyed *before* the cloth is woven—ensures longer lasting color and a more even shade in the fabric. Dyeing the yarns allows the color to penetrate better because a greater surface area is exposed to the dyeing solutions than woven fibers expose. In addition, evenly dyed yarns make the resulting cloth less streaked than cloth which is dyed after it is woven.

Piece Dyeing I

Piece dyeing is by far the most prevalent method of adding color to cloth because it is less expensive than yarn dyeing. After the fabric has been woven in the greige (the rough, unfinished loom state), the hundreds of yards of cloth are fed through a series of solutions to apply color. Because these large rolls of fabrics are called pieces, the dyeing procedure is known as piece dyeing. As long as the fabric is woven of good quality yarns and the dyestuffs are vat, piece dyeing can produce satisfactory products.

Piece Dyeing II

Trouble does ensue, however, when it is necessary to vat dye material that has already been cut and sewn into tablecloths and napkins. This technique is also called piece dyeing; however, in this case, the term actually refers to the tablecloths and napkins. This kind of piece dyeing is used when a property orders a special color, but the order is too small to warrant mill processing.

So that the dye can penetrate the fibers, the finish that the factory applied to the fabric (to prevent lint or add luster) must be removed. The process tends to weaken the fibers and, since it doesn't always completely or evenly remove the finish, the dye may not react consistently, causing the fabric to blotch or streak.

Furthermore, after being dyed in this fashion, the linens must be laundered. Since the fabric's original finish cannot be restored, you end up with an old-looking set of linens. If your napery requirements are too modest to require processing at the mill, rather than ordering a special color that will be produced by this method, choose a standard color and fabric for your linens.

Prints

Another method for adding design and color to table linens is through prints. You may create your own design or you may choose an existing pattern to which you can adapt your own crest, logo, or name.

Since printed designs are applied only to the surface of the cloth and the dyes do not penetrate the yarns fully, printed table linens do not hold their color as well as dyed fabrics, even though they may be printed with vat colors. Constant launderings cause this surface application to gradually abrade and the color tones to lighten.

Most of the printed table linens used in food service outlets are produced with screens because they permit working with small quantities. (Roller printing requires large quantities to justify the cost of engraving a roller.) The designs are drawn on a nylon screen and chemically etched out; when the dyes are spread along the length and breadth of the screen, only the etched out areas allow the dye to go through to the cloth. A separate screen is usually needed for each color and each size of tablecloth or napkin since only special areas are etched out on each one.

Although screens are not as expensive as the copper rollers used in mass production printing, they are costly. It is usually wise to minimize the number of colors in your pattern. Often, properties use one to four colors; in rare cases, some have used as many as seven. At $200 to $300 or more per screen, per color, and per size, you can see how quickly the cost of prints can rise.

Other Factors Affecting Table Linens

Here are just a few more specifications to consider when you select table linens.

Thread Count

As we previously explained, all woven fabrics have warp yarns (running lengthwise) and weft or filling yarns (running the width). The total number of yarns used in both directions, per square inch, comprise the thread count of the fabric.

Usually, the higher the thread count, the better the fabric, but we must also take into account the size or thickness of each yarn. Two fabrics with the same thread count can look entirely different from each other because while thin, light yarns will give one fabric a sleazy, loosely woven look, heavier yarns will make the other fabric more opaque. Conversely, two fabrics with different yarn counts may appear similar to each other because one has a few heavy, coarse yarns compared to the other which has many finer yarns.

Thread count comes into play only when you are considering two or more fabrics of the same type, such as two cotton damask cloths or two crash linen fabrics. It is not practical to compare a high-thread-count cotton damask with a high-thread-count linen crash or any other "apple-orange" combination.

Fabric Weight

Weight is also a factor when you choose one fabric over another in any given category. While you may prefer a fine looking material, you have to consider its durability. A heavier fabric will withstand repeated washings better than a delicate fabric.

We have all heard the expression "threadbare." A fabric's surface is constantly abraded until the yarns become worn down to thin, fibrous strands. Naturally, it will take a longer period of time before heavier yarns look threadbare.

Tensile Strength

Determining a fabric's thread count and weight is not always enough; you must also examine how those totals are derived. A 160-thread-count damask woven with 100 yarns in the warp and only 60 in the weft would not be as durable as a 160-thread-count fabric with 80 yarns in each direction. (In this example, all the yarns are the same size and quality.) The unequal construction affects the durability of the cloth because the fabric's tensile strength (the number of pounds of pull per inch required to tear the material) is reduced.

Tensile strength becomes a factor only during repeated launderings when cloths are constantly pulled through a flat-work ironer. The chain, so to speak, is as strong as its weakest link, and the life of a cloth will be reduced by the early failure of an inferior construction.

You can compensate for the effect of unequal thread count by using heavier yarns in the low-count direction which will produce a textured appearance. Texture is often desired in a crash fabric and can be produced by weaving yarns of different sizes and appearances into one piece. Heterogeneous yarns are not necessarily a disadvantage as long as they compensate for one another in terms of appearance and durability. However, when choosing damask, homogeneous yarns are important to the smooth, satiny look that is one of the fabric's main attributes.

One of the most important factors which contributes to the life and look of all table linens is the length of the staple or fiber from which the yarns are spun. Long staple fibers will lint less and wear better.

Sewing and Stitching

Most of the fabrics that we have discussed are customarily woven in standard widths. However, recent innovations in the manufacture of weaving equipment have revolutionized the industry. Instead of weaving single widths of fabric on a loom, modern machinery permits the same loom to weave multiple widths at one time. After the cloth is woven, it is split lengthwise to create two or more narrower widths. The new widths obviously have raw edges which require hems.

While it is not always necessary to hem the original outside edges, or selvages, because they are usually woven with extra strength to obviate the need for sewing, it is a good idea to hem them for aesthetic reasons. It is more attractive to hem tablecloths and napkins on two or four sides to close up all the cut edges from the bolt of cloth than to leave raw edges. To be hemmed properly, the material should be turned under twice before stitching.

The quality of ordinary hemming varies according to the number of stitches used per inch. The more, the better, but nine or ten stitches to the inch are usually adequate to hold the hem fast during the life of the cloth. The four corners of every piece used in food service operations should be backstitched (a return over the completed sewn edge) to lock in the previous stitches so that the hem will not unravel.

It would be wise to inquire about the type of hemming thread used on the napery you are considering. The hemming thread must shrink at a rate consistent with the cloth, or the material will pucker and be difficult to iron. If the fabric is all linen, all cotton, or union, cotton thread should be used for hemming. Fabrics containing a large proportion of polyester should be hemmed with polyester thread.

Cloths can be finished in a variety of ways. An expensive but attractive finish is a wide hem of about a half to one inch and mitered corners on napkins, and somewhat wider hems on the tablecloths. You should use this finish only on better quality materials, or the cost of the hem could outweigh the cost of the cloth.

A merrowed edge offers a more distinct look for your dining room. This finish overlocks the outside edges of the tablecloths and napkins in a special way. Using a narrow or wide stitch, a merrowed edge should contain at least 24 stitches to the inch to ensure full coverage of the edges. As a rule, merrowing does not last as long as a regular hem but, if it is done properly, it will wear well and is very attractive.

Other methods for adding a special touch to your table linens include scalloping the edges, and/or adding unusual embroidered stitches along the hems. Dealers of better quality napery can demonstrate the details of these methods.

Selecting Sizes

One of the most important decisions you will make when purchasing tablecloths and napkins is selecting correct sizes.

A common error which some managers commit when they plan dining facilities is giving little or no consideration to the number of different table sizes purchased and, consequently, the variety of tablecloth sizes needed to cover them.

It is more important for the property's layout to include as few table size variations as possible than to utilize every square foot of space. Make architects and interior designers aware of the practical considerations you will have to deal with once their creation emerges as a flourishing food service outlet. For example, if you use a variety of table sizes, laundry personnel and food servers will have difficulty keeping the various tablecloth sizes properly separated so that the wrong-sized covering is never placed on a table.

To help you and your designer use your space most efficiently and economically, Exhibit 1 illustrates the various tablecloth sizes which accommodate the most commonly used table sizes in restaurants. Alternate cloth sizes are also listed to allow you to duplicate one cloth size on tables of slightly different dimensions.

Over the years, manufacturers have produced tablecloth fabrics in standard widths by the quarter yard (9 inches). The standards are 36, 45, 54, 63, 72, 81, 90, and 108 inches. Of course, not every fabric is woven in every one of these widths, so you will have to adapt to the availability of your chosen cloth.

For the most part, damask designs can be available in most of the standard widths with slight variations from mill to mill and design to design. However, the design restrictions of damask cloths effectively limit the possibility of cutting small tablecloths out of wider ones. Crash and dobby (momie) fabrics do not pose this problem because there are no symmetrical patterns to cut through. If you require large banquet tablecloths, you will discover that only a limited number of sources supply the 108 x 108-inch size.

Most dining tables are about 29 inches high. While a high-check-average restaurant may wish to create a luxurious look by using tablecloths with a deep drop at the sides, the size of the cloth should not create a corner drop that touches the floor. You can use a rather simple formula to determine the corner drop of a square tablecloth on a square table and adapt it to calculate the corner drop of a square cloth on a round table. Exhibit 2 illustrates this formula.

Commonly preferred and acceptable drops range from about 9½ inches to 13 inches at the sides; however, in order to use one size cloth on two different tables, it is necessary to compromise at as little as 7½ inches and up to 15 inches.

Occasionally, when restaurateurs insist on a very deep side drop, they may need to round the corners of the cloths to prevent them from touching the floor. This procedure is costly, though.

Sometimes, after you make your calculations, you discover the cloth's corners just touch the floor anyway. Launder the cloth before its first use; the shrinkage should correct the problem. Shrinkage allowances for most fabrics of natural fibers average about 8% in length and about 4% in width. Crash fabrics may slightly exceed those figures. Fabrics woven in polyester and natural fiber blends shrink less, usually about 2 to 3% in length and a negligible factor in width; 100% polyester has virtually no shrinkage.

Determining Quantities

Among your most important tasks when buying table linens is the determination of correct quantities. Overbuying is a costly mistake, and if you buy too few linens you will constantly strain to have enough on hand for each meal.

You must allow for breakdowns at the laundry, whether you use an outside laundry or one on your own premises. You should also consider

Exhibit 1 Table and Tablecloth Sizes

Table Size (inches)	Tablecloth Size (inches)	Side Drop (inches)	Corner Drop (inches)
24 x 30	45 x 45	7 ½ x 10 ½	12.9
	54 x 54	12 x 15	19.2
27 x 30	45 x 45	7 ½ x 9	11.7
	54 x 54	13 ½ x 12	18.1
30 x 30	54 x 54	12 x 12	17.0
	63 x 63	16 ½ x 16 ½	23.3
36 Rd	54 Rd	9	—
	54 x 54	9	20.2
36 x 36	54 x 54	9 x 9	12.7
	63 x 63	13 ½ x 13 ½	19.1
40 Rd	63 Rd	11 ½	—
	63 x 63	11 ½	24.5
42 Rd	63 Rd	10 ½	—
	63 x 63	10 ½	23.5
42 x 42	63 x 63	10 x 10	14.8
	72 x 72	15 x 15	21.2
48 Rd	72 Rd	12 x 12	—
	72 x 72	12	26.9
36 x 36	63 x 63	13 ½ x 13 ½	19.1
Opening to			
51 Rd	72 x 72	10 ½	25.4
60 Rd	81 x 81	10 ½	27.3
	90 Rd	15	—
	90 x 90	15	33.6
72 Rd	90 x 90	9	27.6
	102 Rd	15	—
	102 x 102	15	36.1
30 x 36	54 x 54	12 x 9	15.0
	54 x 63	12 x 13 ½	18.1
30 x 42	54 x 63	12 x 10 ½	15.9
	63 x 63	16 ½ x 10 ½	19.6
30 x 48	54 x 72	12 x 12	17.0
30 x 60	54 x 90	12 x 15	25.6
30 x 72	54 x 96	12 x 12	17.0
30 x 96	54 x 120	12 x 12	17.0
36 x 48	54 x 72	9 x 12	15.0
	63 x 72	13 ½ x 12	18.1

Exhibit 1 Table and Tablecloth Sizes, continued

36 x 72	54 x 96	9 x 12	15.0
	63 x 96	13 ½ x 12	18.1
36 x 96	54 x 120	9 x 12	15.0
	63 x 120	13 ½ x 12	18.1

the possibility that a holiday weekend could disrupt your normal flow.

To arrive at the most efficient number of table linens you need to purchase for each table size, try this method: determine the number of turnovers you expect at each table during each meal on each day. If you expect 2½ turnovers at breakfast, 2 at lunch, and 1 at dinner, your daily turnover is 2½ + 2 + 1, or 5½. Next, determine your laundry factor. If you operate 7 days a week, but the laundry operates only 6 days, you will need an extra day's complement of linens to compensate. You will also need to make allowances if the laundry makes deliveries only two or three times a week.

Let's take a hypothetical dining room which operates at 5 turnovers per day, 7 days a week, but the laundry services it only 5 days a week. Let's assume that we have 20 tables, all the same size, and that we seat a total of 80 people at each turn. We need 5 tablecloths per table for today, plus 5 on the shelf for tomorrow, plus 5 that are in the laundry. In addition, we must buy enough tablecloths to cover the 2 extra days when the laundry is closed. Therefore, we must initially purchase 5 sets (5 tablecloths in a set) of linens for each table to ensure that we do not run short.

The formula, then, for arriving at the correct quantity of table linens to purchase is as follows: the number of tables per size multiplied by the daily turnover rate multiplied by the number of sets needed on hand each day. In our example, we need 5 turnovers x 5 sets x 20 tables, or 500 tablecloths.

Napkins require a slight modification, although the formula is essentially the same. Use the number of seats as the guide, instead of the number of tables; however, keep in mind that two contradictory factors distort the numbers.

1. Although the turnover rate may accurately reflect table usage, not every seat at these tables will be occupied. This factor could reduce the number of sets of napkins you need to purchase.

2. Napkins are often abused and/or stolen. Guests frequently require a second one. These factors increase your napkin needs.

Exhibit 2 Formula for Calculating Corner Drops on a Tablecloth

To find the corner drop of a 72" square cloth on a 54" square table:

Cloth size 72" square x .707	= 50.90"
Table size 54" square x .707	= 38.18"
Difference is drop at corner of the cloth	12.72"

To find the corner drop of a 72" square cloth on a 54" (in diameter) round table:

Cloth size 72" square x .707	= 50.90"
The radius (half the diameter) of the table	= 27.00"
Difference is the drop at corner of the cloth	23.90"

The latter factor probably has the greatest influence, so the proper number of sets of napkins you will need should be six or seven.

Placemats and Runners

An individual place setting (placemat) is often used as an informal, inexpensive table covering. However, placemats and table runners are also acceptable in properties which feature beautiful, costly tables to enhance the decor of the dining room. They not only allow the tables to be displayed, but add the decorative touch of fresh linens and accommodate the sanitary requirements of the patron.

Placemats come in standard sizes ranging from 12 x 18 inches to about 14 x 20 inches. These dimensions accommodate most service plates and cutlery. When choosing a mat, which may be available in only one size, make sure that the mats will not overlap each other on the table. Such a practice is not only unsightly, but also impractical.

You can use runners in a variety of ways. Most runners are 17 inches wide and should be cut lengthwise to allow a drop over the table edges of 7 to 12 inches.

While placemats are available in a limited number of damask patterns, runners do not offer a complete damask design. If you plan to use runners, you should use a fabric other than damask for your table linens.

Silence Cloths

When setting up any dining table, you need a liner of some kind under the tablecloth to soften both the surface of the table as well as the sounds of dinnerware being placed on it. You may not always require liners if both tablecloths and placemats are used together, but in the event that you place only one cloth on the table, you should put something under it.

Most food service operations use one of two common "silence cloths." The first is a heavy cotton felt material which can be draped over the top of the table; it is usually sold with overlocked or tape-bound edges. When it gets soiled, it can be laundered. (Allow 10 to 15% for shrinkage.) Because this type of finished underliner can be expensive, it is usual to budget for them.

The second material widely used for silencers is a very thin layer of vinyl laminated to a base of polyurethane (a soft, spongelike material). It is usually sold by the bolt and can be cut with scissors and left unfinished at the edge because it does not ravel. This product does not shrink or support bacteria; it needs only to be wiped clean to prevent decaying bacteria from causing unpleasant odors. It is marketed under the name of Curon. However, Curon does not drape as well as felt, and because it is very lightweight, it has a tendency to lift off the table when the tablecloth is removed unless it is tacked in some way to the underside of the table.

Appendix B
Preparing for Kosher Service

Many hotel food and beverage operations enjoy extensive kosher catering and banquet operations. Other facilities could expand into this market if they knew more about kosher laws and how they apply to menu planning and other aspects of food and beverage operations. The following questions and answers provide background information on this subject.

What is the definition of kosher? Kosher is a term which means "fit or proper"; it applies to foods that meet the specifications and requirements established by Jewish dietary laws. These laws are extremely rigid, do not permit deviation, and mandate many aspects of the purchase, preparation, and service of food.

What meat, fish, or poultry are edible by kosher law? Meat from those animals which have split hooves and chew their cud may be eaten. Pigs have split hooves but do not chew their cud; that is why pork is not eaten. (Some people erroneously believe that health reasons prohibit the consumption of pork; this is not correct.) Specifically, those animals that may be eaten are cattle, sheep, goats, and deer (Leviticus 11:10). Only fish that swim and have easily removable scales and fins may be eaten. Shellfish and mollusks are forbidden, which eliminates lobster, shrimp, crab, clams, oysters, and mussels from the menu. Only domestic birds, such as chicken, duck, goose, turkey, and Cornish hen, can be eaten. Neither birds of prey, nor scavenger birds, nor those used in the *hunt* are permitted. Only specific portions of permitted animals and food may be consumed. There are, for example, certain nerves, veins, and fats which cannot be eaten and must be removed before eating.

Are there restrictions on eating certain fruits and vegetables? No. There is no prohibition against anything that grows on the land. All

fruits, vegetables, and edible grasses (e.g., oats, wheat) are permitted by kosher law.

What rituals are involved in the preparation of kosher food? The rituals of preparation basically apply to the slaughter of animals and how they must be treated immediately after slaughter *before* being prepared for eating. Meat for any kosher food production must be slaughtered and "kashered" by an authorized "shocket." Meat and poultry are "kashered" by the following process: within 72 hours of slaughter, the meat or poultry must be soaked in cold water for one-half hour in vessels kept specifically for soaking purposes. The meat is then rinsed with cold water, sprinkled with coarse (kosher) salt, and placed upon a grooved board which is tilted to allow the blood to flow from the meat. The meat must then remain on the board for one hour at which time it is again washed and finally readied for use. Meat may not be frozen for future use unless it is first kashered. Only meat from the forequarters may be eaten. The hindquarters may be used *only* if certain textured fat and all the veins have first been removed. (Unfortunately, the process of removing those veins and fat is entirely too labor-intensive to make it commercially feasible.) After meat is prepared according to this procedure, it may be ground, frozen, or processed in any desired manner.

Are there any exemptions to this rule? Yes. Meat used for broiling need not be kashered *if* it is used within 72 hours of slaughter. Livers need not be kashered and may be frozen for preparation later. However, when livers are ready to be processed, they must be completely thawed, washed, sliced, broiled, sprinkled with salt while broiling, rinsed and prepared for eating.

Are there other regulations governing kosher food? Yes. All meat and meat products may not be cooked with any dairy product or dairy derivatives. For instance, you cannot serve chicken a la king or creamed chipped beef at a kosher function. Dairy food may not be served at

---

Some of this material is adapted from Marianna Desser, "Kosher Catering: How and Why," Cornell Hotel and Restaurant Administration Quarterly, Vol. 20., No. 2., (August, 1979), pp. 83-91.

a meal where meat is being used. For example, butter may not be served at a steak dinner. In addition, coffee may not be served with cream; however, a nondairy substitute may be used. The pots and pans in which meats have been cooked and the dishes upon which they are served may only be used for meat products. The same is true of pots, pans, and dishes used for dairy food preparation and service. If these utensils are used incorrectly, they must be discarded. Drinking glassware need not be changed as service moves from meat to dairy products; however, glass dishes used for service of hot food require a separation of meat and dairy items.

Do fish have to be kashered? No. Fish may be used in its entirety and requires no salting after cleaning. Fish dishes may be combined with dairy foods, but must not be combined with meat dishes. Fish may, however, be eaten separately at a meat meal as an appetizer (separate forks should be set).

Do vegetables require special handling or ritual? Vegetables and fruits may be combined with either dairy or meat dishes. If the vegetables are used with meat dishes, they must be cooked in pots and pans used for meat service. All fruits and vegetables, including vegetable oils, and all cereals and derivatives, as well as eggs, are called parve.

What is meant by milchik and fleshik? "Milchik" refers to milk-containing foods, including milk, milk derivatives, and any product that contains milk in any proportion. "Fleshik" refers to meat products and includes any item containing meat, its by-products, or derivatives.

Is there a term used to denote forbidden foods? Yes. "Trefe" is used to denote all forbidden foods.

Do these rules apply all year? Are there times when they may be relaxed or modified? These rules are never relaxed. They become even more stringent during the eight days of Passover. During Passover, for instance, unleavened bread is the only bread which may be eaten. Also, the separate cooking and serving of meat and dairy products is done with special pots, pans, and china set aside for use only during Passover. Specific utensils are also used only for Passover and are stored for the remainder of the year.

What are the rules for the preparation of kosher foods? Since it is not possible to mix meat and milk, separate sets of utensils become necessary. Most kosher caterers prepare only meat dinners and eliminate the need to maintain two sets of utensils. Some hotels with extensive kosher business maintain two separate kitchens, one for the preparation of meat and one for dairy products, and use color codes to distinguish the utensils used in each unit.

Kosher regulations prohibit the cooking of kosher food in nonkosher equipment; similarly, kosher food cannot be served in nonkosher serving utensils. (The reason is that hot food can absorb traces of nonkosher food from a nonkosher dish even if the utensil is clean.) Therefore, utensils used in hot food preparation and subsequent service must be used for kosher purposes only.

In contrast, since cold foods do not absorb food traces from utensils used to handle them, solids which contain kosher ingredients can be eaten from nonkosher dishes.

Utensils, equipment, and flatware can be made kosher even if they were previously used for handling nonkosher items. Techniques include immersing them in boiling water, passing them through a flame, or putting them into the soil. However, these techniques must be performed with a mashgiach (a trained supervisor) or rabbi in attendance.

Utensils made of porcelain, enamel, and earthenware cannot be made kosher since they are porous and absorbent. Solid flatware made of a single metal piece can be made kosher; items made with a plastic or bone handle or with uncleanable crevices or grooves cannot.

Is supervision required during preparation, service, and cleanup? Since some kosher laws are very technical and complex, the supervision of a mashgiach is required. The food service operation offering kosher food must ensure that all aspects of the function are in accordance with kosher dietary laws.

What are alternatives for kosher catering in the hotel? Hotels make various provisions for kosher catering. For example, as previously mentioned, some properties maintain separate kosher kitchens in which personnel from the property prepare the food. In contrast, others contract with an external kosher caterer who does catering exclusively for kosher functions at the property. Still other hotels rent their kitchen facilities to one or more kosher caterers. The subcontracting of facilities for kosher events is frequently justifiable due to the extensive amount of thorough cleaning required to render utensils and equipment items kosher.

Sometimes kosher food is ordered only as needed for a specific function; no separate storage areas for meat are then required. In contrast, dry products can be stored in a central storeroom as long as they do not come into direct contact with nonkosher products.

Exactly how is kosher food preparation undertaken? Under the supervision of a mashgiach, the kitchen area must be thoroughly cleaned and then koshered. Ovens and stoves can be koshered by sterilizing the interior surfaces with a propane torch. Or, salt can be spread inside an oven which is then heated to its highest temperature for 30 minutes.

Hotels with extensive kosher business frequently purchase dishes especially for this business. Since solid flatware made of one metal piece can be koshered, it is not generally necessary to purchase separate flatware for kosher functions. However, since items to be koshered cannot be used for 24 hours prior to the koshering process, a larger supply of silverware may be needed. The koshering process for flatware involves immersing it in a pot of boiling water, removing it, and then rinsing it in cold water.

Sometimes, the hotel supplies kosher caterers with all the necessary equipment; in other instances, caterers provide their own utensils. It is necessary to mark all utensils with an identifying feature when the caterer and the hotel mix equipment so that each property can identify its own utensils.

Dishwashing machines can be made kosher; the soaps used should be of vegetable or chemical origin. All areas in the immediate vicinity of the kosher preparation, even if they are not used by the kosher caterer, must be covered with paper or aluminum foil. Exact procedures may vary with the particular equipment and should be done only by rabbinic authority and under the careful supervision of a mashgiach.

Should a contract be used when an external caterer uses the hotel's facility? Yes. Typically a formal agreement is necessary to ensure that misunderstandings do not arise. Frequently, revenues are split according to an agreed upon formula between the hotel and the caterer. In addition, the hotel includes the costs of the foods it provides. They may, for example, prepare such parve foods as melons and fruit cups, raw vegetables, salads, and coffee. Typically, the hotel is responsible for liquor service but, because of restrictions placed upon wine, wine service is frequently the caterer's responsibility.

The hotel should charge for the space used, the dishwashing costs, and the labor expenses. Most often, service personnel are provided by the hotel; members of the kitchen staff are provided by the kosher caterer.

The menu is conceived jointly by the caterer and the hotel. While menus are starting to reflect a trend toward lighter and more healthful foods, traditional products are still very popular. Typically, the hotel will establish the selling price of the kosher event. Occasionally, the caterer will bill the guest and reimburse the hotel for the prearranged costs; however, it is generally more advantageous for the hotel to contract with the caterer, add its costs and profit margin, then bill the client directly.

How can kosher functions be classified? There are two basic types of kosher functions: commercial activities, such as fund raising events and awards programs, and social or family functions, such as weddings and bar mitzvahs.

Is the kosher catering business seasonal? Generally, kosher catering is not seasonal, but that depends in part on the scheduling of community activities. Usually, there are no catered kosher functions during Jewish holidays or during brief periods which are designated as times of mourning. Cooking is prohibited on the Jewish Sabbath (from sunset on Friday until after sunset on Saturday). Therefore, most kosher functions are not routinely scheduled for Saturday evenings during the summer months since the Sabbath ends late in the evening.

What conditions are necessary for the success of a kosher catered event? In order for kosher catering to be successful, all individuals participating in the catered affair must be aware of their specific responsibilities. Trust is also important. Clients trust the caterer to provide the kosher meals which have been arranged. Likewise, the caterer trusts that the mashgiach and the hotel will provide necessary services.

Index

A

Advertising, radiation, 107-108
Accidents, 333
  from electrical equipment, 339
  from falls, 337
  from lifting, 338
Accident inspection programs, 339
A la carte
  definition of, 7
  example of (exhibit), 9
Alcoholic beverages. See Beverage
    service; Wine
Ambience, 353-364
American Federation of Musicians
  (AFM), 292
American (plate) service, 95
American Red Cross, 341
Annual events, service for, 265
Ashtray, how to cap, 310
Assistant food server, 220
Audits, 164

B

Banks, cash, 158
Bank deposits, 349
Banquet(s). See also Catering
  beverage service, 263-264, 313-315
  charge by hour, 314
  client's budget for, 272
  community activities and, 254
  contracts, 269
  guarantees, 269
  how to plan, 249
  how to price, 268-269
  income control, 273
  labor cost, 269
  minimums (guest counts), 269
  protocol, 272
  rooms, 255-258
  service, 252, 262-263
  setting up, 258-260
  side effects of, 271
  wine service, 315
Banquet business
  advantages of, 248
  markets for, 243-244

Banquet chef, 244
Banquet contract, sample of (exhibit),
  270
Banquet department, organization of,
  243
Banquet duties and responsibilities
  (exhibit), 246
Banquet food
  plating of, 62
  preparing, 260
Banquet guests, privacy for, 274
Banquet kitchen, 61
Banquet manager, 244
Banquet operations, 13
Banquet wines, how to price, 317
Bar operations report (exhibit), 163
Bars, design of, 321
Bartender role of, 305
  procedures for, 144
Beverage manager
  bartender and, 305
  role of, 304
  server and, 306
Beverage operations, shopper service
  for, 312
Beverage products, 319-321
Beverage servers
  procedures for, 143
  role of, 307
Beverage service, 228, 303-322. See
  also Wine
  at bar, 307
  for banquets, 263-264, 313
  for dining rooms, 307
  equipment, 320
  in lounge, 307
  marketing of, 320
  personnel, 304-307
  procedures, 307-319
Beverage service equipment, automated, 320-321
Beverage service evaluation form (exhibit), 313
Bomb threats, 345
Breakage, 74, 91
Budget, operating, 115
Buffet service, 102-106
Buspersons, role of, 220-221
Butler-style service, 101

C

Cafeteria(s), 278-283
  alcoholic beverage service in, 283
  employee, 86, 284
  food service, 278
  income, 282
  income calculation (exhibit), 282
  layouts (exhibit), 279
  lines, food placement on, 280
  personnel for, 281
Captain, dining service, 213, 218-219
Call liquor, 320
Cardiopulmonary resuscitation (CPR),
  340
Carousel cafeterias, 279
Career ladder, 34-35
Carriers, as health concerns, 327
Cash banks, 158
Cash bar, at banquets, 313
Cash handling equipment, 140-142
Cash income control, 158-159
Cash registers, 141, 321
  operating procedures (exhibit), 146,
    148
Cashier(s)for cafeteria, 282
  procedures for, 145
  theft by, 153
Cashier banking system, 142
Cashier's department sales record (ex-
  hibit), 149
Casino operations, 288, 294-297
Catering. See also Banquet(s)
  director, 244
  executive, 255
  off-site, 286-287
  of kosher foods, 395
Central kitchens, 59
Check(s), accepting as payment, 156
Check, guest. See Guest check(s)
Checklists
  dining room pre-opening (exhibits),
    216-218, 261
  for after-banquet duties (exhibit),
    264
  for serving (exhibit), 334-335
  of dining room accessories (exhibit),
    264
  safety (exhibit), 350-351
  sanitation, 333

Chef, 105, 244
Chef de rang, 98
China
    patterns of, 70
    selection, 73-75
    specifications for, 76
Cleaning schedules, 331
Cleaning tasks (exhibit), 365
Cleanup duties, dining room 232
Closing procedures
    for bartender, 162
    for beverage server, 159
    for food server, 159
Club and show operations, 288-298
"Club 21," 303
Cocktails, service of, 307-308
Coffee shop, 173-184
    cashiers, 174
    control procedures, 181
    food attendants, 176
    food production in, 60
    food servers, 174
    forecasting for, 181
    guest check (exhibit), 180
    guest orders in, 178
    host/hostess, 174
    manager, 174
    menu (exhibit), 175
    operating costs (exhibit), 183
    organization (exhibit), 176
    server, job description (exhibit), 177
    service procedures, 176
    shopper's service report (exhibit), 186-191
    supplies and equipment, 181
    tables, 182
Combination public/service bar (exhibit), 322
Commis de rang, 98
Commissary, 59
Communication, 33, 64-65
Complaints, 18, 298
"Comp" slip for in-house entertainment (exhibit), 296
Concierge, 299
Confirmation, receipt of cash bank (exhibit), 158
Consumer reactions (exhibit), 326
Contribution margin, 106
Control, as management task, 111
Conventions, service at, 264-265
Copyright music performance, 291
Corrective action plans, 135
Cotton, as dining room fabric, 373
Crash fabrics, 374
Credit cards, acceptance of, 157

D

Daily function room diary, sample of, (exhibit), 256

Daily income report (exhibit), 165
Damask, as type of weave, 375
Delivery invoice, 87
Delmonico's, 3
Designer, how to select, 355
Dessert cart, mobile, 84
Dining area attendants, for cafeterias, 282
Dining areas, maintenance of, 365-372
Dining room(s)
    accessories, checklist of (exhibit), 85
    areas, cleaning and maintenance of, 330-331, 365-369
    decor and design, 353-362
    equipment, repair of, 368
    furniture, 84-86
    manager, role of, 211
        duties of (exhibit), 214-215
    menu, 236-240
        example of (exhibit), 237
    pre-opening checklist for (exhibit), 216-218
    supplies and equipment for, 240
    service procedures for, 221-232
Dining service(s)
    elements in, 10
    manager, 14-17
        qualifications and responsibilities of (exhibit), 15
    methods and procedures, 95-108
    miscellaneous types of, 277-299
    sanitation checklist for, 333
    sanitation issues in, 331
    space requirements for, 356
    supplies, control of, 89
Dining tables, silence cloths for, 391
Dinnerware, 70
Director of marketing and sales, 244
Director of service, definition of, 7
Discipline, 37-38
Dobby cloth, 374
Dress code, 212
Dyeing, of linens, 375

E

Economy of scale, concept of, 115
El Morocco, 303
Electronic data machines, 141
Emergencies, how to handle, 344
Employee(s)
    accident report (exhibit), 341
    dining areas, design of, 284
    dining methods for, 283
    dining rooms, 284
    food services, vending for, 283
    front-of-house, 219
    how to schedule, 120
    lockers, 153
    meals, recordkeeping for, 285-286
    schedule, 123

(exhibit), 127
    time log(s), 130, 134
        (exhibits), 131-132
Employer's basic report of injury (exhibit), 340
English (family) service, 101-102
Entertainment financial aspects of, 288
    how to select, 290
    laws and, 292
    marketing aspects of, 291
    reservation procedures for, 294
Entertainment operations
    service procedures for, 292
    special problems of, 296
Entertainers, taxes for, 292
Equal Employment Opportunity Commission (EEOC), 22
Equipment, 69-89, 249-250, 330
Escoffier, Auguste, 3, 6
Estimated income based on seat turnover (exhibit), 357
Estimated square feet for dining area (exhibit), 357
Evaluation, procedures for, 34-37
Executive coffee service (exhibit), 205
Executive council, 71
Expediter, 63

F

Fabrics, 373-391
Facilities, cleaning of, 330
Falls, 337
Federal Bureau of Investigation (FBI), 345
Financial aspects of entertainment (exhibit), 345
Fire. See also Safety
    department, 347
    extinguishers, dry chemical, 345
    extinguishers, identification of (exhibit), 346
    in food service outlets, 344
First aid, 341
    for choking (exhibit), 343
Fish, and kosher laws, 384
Fixed labor, 112-115
Flag display, 272
Flag stand, five-place arch (exhibit), 273
Flaming foods, in dining areas, 348
Flatware, 78-81
Fleshik, 384
Floors, cleaning techniques for, (exhibit), 336
Food and beverage operations
    commercial, definition of, 7
    in hotels, 10-14
    other, 13
Food carts, mobile, 75
Food checker, 362

Food covers and beverage revenue (exhibit), 122
Food orders, placing and picking up, 229
Food preparation rules, kosher, 385-386
Food, procedures for serving, 229
Food production planning worksheet (exhibit), 119
Food production systems, 59
Food server(s). See also Employee(s); Personnel
    daily report: manual system (exhibit), 160
    daily report: precheck register system (exhibit), 161
    procedures for, 142
    role of, 219-220
Food service attendant, 220
Food service outlets
    coffee shops, 10
    family-oriented operations, 10
    first-class dining rooms, 11
    gourmet dining rooms, 11
    specialty (theme) dining rooms, 11
Food services, institutional, definition of, 7
Food, transportation of, 59
Forecasting, 116-120
French (cart) service, 97
Furniture, dining room, 84-86

G

Glassware, 76-80
Grand Hotel National, 3
Gratuities, 231
Gueridon, 74, 99
Guest check(s), 64
    in coffee shops, 179
    how to issue, 142
    number log (exhibit), 141
    presentation of, 231
    procedures, manual, 139
    rules for, 140
Guest counts, hourly, 126, 129
Guest courtesy card (exhibit), 201
Guest, definition of, 7
Guests
    greeting and seating, 221; 226-227
    serving, 227-232
Guest safety, 337
Guest service, standard operating procedures (exhibit), 222-225

H

Haute cuisine, 10
Head table, 272

Headwaiter/headwaitress, definition of, 7
Health and menu planning, 51-52
Horwath & Horwath International, 4
Hospitality, definition of, 6
Host bar, 313
Host/hostess, location of, 362
Hotel, definition of, 7
Hotel garni, definition of, 7
House brands, 309, 320

I

Income, noncash, 156-157
Income control
    in banquet bars, 317
    procedures for, 142-145, 181, 207, 273, 317
    security of, 166, 167
    systems, 140
Inventory, par, 69
Issuing
    procedures, 88
    requisitions, 88
    requisition form (exhibit), 90

J

Job breakdown, 28
    sample of (exhibit), 29-30
Job description, 22
    for banquet headwaiter/headwaitress (exhibit), 23
Job list, 28
    for food server (exhibit), 29
Job performance standards, sample of (exhibit), 31
Job specifications, 22
Jukeboxes, 291

K

Kosher food and service, 383-385
Kitchen, banquet, 61

L

Labor costs, control of, 111-135
Labor staffing guide, 112, 121
Laws, and entertainment, 292
Layout for banquet function (exhibit), 254
Leadership styles, 31
Lifting, procedures for, 338
Lighting, psychology of, 364
Lindy's, 303

Line attendants, for cafeterias, 281
Linens, 83, 373-391
Liquor. See Beverages, Beverage

M

Maitre d'hotel, definition of, 7
Managers, qualities of, 33
Manhattan Club, 303
Market analysis, 354
Marketing and sales department, 244
Marketing aspects of service, 17-18
Marketing, definition of, 17
Menu(s). See also Menu planning a la carte, 46
    and costs, 43
    and cost control, 54
    and service plan, 54-55
    and special guests, 239
    and staffing needs, 52
    banquet, 50
    basic types of, 46
    buffet, 49
    California style, 47, 173
    coffee shop, 47-48
    design, 55-58
    effects on operation, 52-54
    engineering, 107
    how to present, 228
    room service, 48-49
    server knowledge of, 237
    table d'hote, 46
Menu planning
    and health, 51-52
    considerations in, 46-50
    constraints in, 50-57
    objectives, 41-44
    procedures for, 44-46
Microphones, in dining service, 229
Milchik, 384
Mise en place, 88, 178
Miscellaneous food services, 298-300
Modern buffet/cafeteria (exhibit), 280
Momie cloth, 374
Montagne, Prosper, 7
Morale, 32-34
Motivation, 32-34

N

Naisbitt, John, 6
Name recognition, of guests, 226
Napery, 373
National Restaurant Association, 5
Nationwide survey of restaurant patrons (exhibit), 327
Nutrition, 43, 51-52

O

Occupational Safety Health Administration (OSHA), 339
Opening a bottle of wine (exhibit), 311
Operating budget, 115
Operations, self-contained, 13-14
Organization of catering and banquet services (exhibit), 245
Organization of dining room operation (exhibit), 213
Orientation programs, 24-27
Orientation program outline (exhibit), 26

P

Par inventory for china, 70
Par level(s), 71
Payment collection procedures for one casino operation (exhibit), 295
Payroll taxes, 130
Performance reviews, 34, 36
Performance standards
    development of, 36
    establishment of, 111-112
Perpetual inventory record (exhibit), 89
Personal hygiene, 327-329
Personnel. See also Employee(s)
    beverage, 304-307
    coffee shop, 173-176
    dining service, 211-221
    room service, 193-196
Personnel management, quality concerns, 32
Physical examinations, 327
Placemats and runners, 390
Planning, pre-production, 119
Plates, service, 75
Plating banquet meals, setup for (exhibit), 262
Polyester, 374
Potentially hazardous foods, 329. See also Sanitation
Portable bar (exhibit), 315
Portable bar setup sheet (exhibit), 318
Portion-control, 62
Position performance analysis, 112
    form (exhibit), 113
Position prerequisites, 22
Potential banquet markets (exhibit), 266-268
Precheck registers, 141
"Precious room," 87
Preventive maintenance schedule (exhibit), 371
Price, and purchase decisions, 78
Productivity, definition of, 130
    measuring, 128-134
Productivity rates, 12

Professional image, 220
Purchase record, 73, 86
Purchase requirements, 72
Purchase specifications, 71, 86
Purchasing
    centralized, 71
    definition of, 69
    of dining room items, 69-86

Q

Quality, 111, 114
    definition of, 18
    purchase decisions and, 71-72
    in service, 211
Quality assurance programs, 18

R

Radiation advertising, 107-108
Recordkeeping requirements and income control, 164-166
Receiving and storing, 86-88
Rechaud unit, 99
Recruitment procedures, 21-24
Repair log (exhibit), 370
Repairs, of dining room equipment, 368
Report of guest injury (exhibit), 342
Report of lost business form (exhibit), 268
Reservation sheet (exhibit), 235
Reservation systems, 232-235
Restaurant manager, definition of, 7
Restaurant managers and guest safety, 337
Restrooms, public, 331
Ritz, Cesar, 3, 6
Robberies, in food service, 348
Room service, 12-13, 193-208
    assistant manager, 194
    attendants, 195
    buspersons, 196
    captain, 194
    check and order-taking system (exhibit), 198
    control form (exhibit), 200
    doorknob menu for breakfast (exhibit), 206
    equipment and supplies, checklist for (exhibit), 197
    forecasting employees for, 206
    food production for, 60-61
    income control procedures, 207
    manager, 194
    menu, 204
    order form (exhibit), 200
    order routing, 198

    order-taker, 195
    organization chart (exhibit), 195
    procedures, 196-204
    scheduling employees for, 206
    special order (exhibit), 203
    supplies and equipment, 207
    telephone etiquette, 202
    timing of order, 204
    wine and amenities, 201
Runners, as server system, 95
Russian (platter) service, 100

S

Safety, 325, 333-344
    buffet service and, 106
Safety checklist, 350-351
Safety inspection programs, 342
Safety rules for dining service (exhibit), 336-337
Sales, forecasting, 116-120
Sales history record, 117, 118 (exhibit)
Sales income control 139-168
Sales tools, for catering department, 248. See also Banquet(s); Catering; Marketing
Salesmanship, in dining room, 106
Sanitation, 325-333
    buffet service and, 105
Sanitation inspection sheet for public restrooms (exhibit), 332
Schedules, employee, 123, 126
Schedule worksheet (exhibit), 124
Schematic drawings, 358
Schematic layout of front-of-house areas (exhibit), 359
Scramble system, 103
Seating chart with four service stations (exhibit), 227
Seating guests, protocol (exhibit), 273
Seat turnover, 356
Security, 325, 344-352
    definition of, 333
Selection procedures, employee, 21-24
Selling the banquet, procedures for, 246
Server banking system, 142
Server. See Employee(s); Food server(s); Personnel
Service. See also Banquet(s); Beverage service; Coffee shop; Dining room; Room service
    at annual events, 264-265
    for conventions, 264
    definition of, 7
    marketing aspects of, 17-18
Service corridor, 360
Service stations, 91, 97 (exhibit), 213

Serving pieces, guide to (exhibit), 82
Setup and cleanup activities (exhibit), 233
Setup duties, in dining room, 232
Side work, definition of, 174
Silence cloths, 391
Silverware, 78-81
Sommelier, 98
Space, perception of, 360
Special function(s)
    pre-opening duties, checklist of (exhibit), 261
    room activities, schedule of (exhibit), 259
    room information, summary of (exhibit), 258
Special function sheet, 251
    example of (exhibit), 253
Special lunch menus (exhibit), 287
Special occasions, marketing for, 240
Specifications, purchasing, 71
Staffing guide, 115
Standards, labor, 111-112
Suggestive selling, 107
    of menu items, 238
Supervision, principles of, 28-34
Supplies and equipment, 69-91

T

Tab, in bar, 144
Table covering, placemats, and runners, 390
Table d'hote, definition of, 7
Table d'hote menu, example of (exhibit), 8
Table linens, 373-391
    determining quantities of, 378
    factors affecting, 376
    how to select, 373

sewing and stitching, 377
    sizes of, 377-378
Table and tablecloth sizes, 379-380
Tables, clearing and resetting, 21
Tabletop appointments, 99
Table turn, definition of, 176
Tableware, definitions of, 77
Taste sessions, 237
Tavern, 303
Telephones, in dining service, 229
Ten-day volume forecast: food (exhibit), 121
Tentative function room reservation (exhibit), 257
Theater seating plan in large casino hotel (exhibit), 297
Theft. See also Income control
    by bartender, 145
    by employee, 152
    by guest, 154
    of dining supplies, 91
    of income, 145
Timeclock, automatic, and print-out (exhibit), 133
Time records, employees, 130
Timing of food orders, 63-64
Toffler, Alvin, 6
Tower Club (exhibit), 298
Traffic flow, concerns about, 358
Traffic flow patterns, back-of-house (exhibit), 361
Training programs, 27-28
Truth-in-menu laws, 43
Turnover, guest, 358
Typical turnover rates (exhibit), 357

U

Uniforms, 81-83
Union contract for entertainers (exhibit), 293

Unions, employee, 115
Utility serving cart, mobile, 84

V

Variance analysis, 134
Variable labor, 112-114
Variable labor staffing guide, 114 (exhibit), 115, 134
Vending machines 277-278, 283
VIP dining rooms, 287

W

Waiting lists, for reservation systems, 236
Warehousing, of supplies, 74
Weaves, types of, 374
Weekly employee meal costs (exhibit), 286
Weekly employee meal credits (exhibit), 285
Weekly labor hour report, 125 (exhibit), 134
Welcome card (exhibit), 205
Wine, 308-312
Wine lists, 228
Wine sales
    for banquet, 270, 315
    how to prorate, 316
Wine service, at banquet, 315
Wine service evaluation form (exhibit), 314
Work order, sample (exhibit), 368

The Educational Institute Board of Trustees

The Educational Institute of the American Hotel & Motel Association is fortunate to have both industry and academic leaders, as well as allied members, on its Board of Trustees. Individually and collectively, the following persons play leading roles in supporting the Institute and determining the direction of its programs.

Caroline A. Cooper, CHA
Department Chair
Hospitality/Tourism
Johnson & Wales University
Providence, Rhode Island

Arnold J. Hewes
Executive Vice President
Minnesota Hotel & Lodging Association
St. Paul, Minnesota

Edouard P.O. Dandrieux, CHA
Director
H.I.M., Hotel Institute Montreux
Montreux, Switzerland

Howard P. "Bud" James, CHA
Hotel Consultant
Steamboat, Colorado

Robert S. DeMone, CHA
President, Chairman & CEO
Canadian Pacific Hotels & Resorts
Toronto, Ontario
Canada

Richard M. Kelleher, CHA
President & CEO
Guest Quarters Suite Hotels
Boston, Massachusetts

Ronald A. Evans, CHA
President & CEO
Best Western International, Inc.
Phoenix, Arizona

Donald J. Landry, CHA
President
Manor Care Hotel Division
Silver Spring, Maryland

Robert C. Hazard, Jr., CHA
Chairman & CEO
Choice Hotels International, Inc.
Silver Spring, Maryland

Bryan D. Langton, CBE
Chairman & CEO
Holiday Inn Worldwide
Atlanta, Georgia

Lawrence B. Magnan, CHA
President & CEO
Select Asset Management
Mercer Island, Washington

Gene Rupnik, CHA
General Manager/Partner
Days Inn
Springfield, Illinois

Jerry R. Manion, CHA
Executive Vice President - Operations
Motel 6
Dallas, Texas

Charlotte St. Martin
Executive Vice President
Operations & Marketing
Loews Hotels
New York, New York

John A. Norlander, CHA
President
Radisson Hotel Corporation
Minneapolis, Minnesota

William J. Sheehan, CHA
Vice Chairman
Omni Hotels
Hampton, New Hampshire

Michael B. Peceri, CHA
Chairman
Marquis Hotels & Resorts
Fort Meyers, Florida

William R. Tiefel
President
Marriott Lodging Group
Washington, D.C.

Philip Pistilli, CHA
Chairman
Raphael Hotel Group
Kansas City, Missouri

Paul E. Wise, CHA
Director
Hotel, Restaurant
  & Institutional Management
University of Delaware
Newark, Delaware

The
Educational Institute Fellows

Respected experts dedicated to the advancement of hospitality education

Scott W. Anderson, CHA
President & CEO
Callaway Gardens Resort, Inc.
Pine Mountain, Georgia

W. Anthony Farris, CHA
President & CEO
Rank Hotels N.A.
Dallas, Texas

Edward W. Rabin
Executive Vice President
Hyatt Hotels Corporation
Chicago, Illinois

Michael J. Beckley, CHA
President
Commonwealth
   Hospitality. Ltd.
Etobicoke, Ontario
Canada

Creighton Holden, CHA
President, Hotel Division
Encore Marketing
   International
Columbia, South Carolina

John L. Sharpe, CHA
Executive Vice President
Four Seasons Hotels
   & Resorts
Toronto, Ontario
Canada

Stephen W. Brener, CHA
President
Brener Associates, Inc.
New York, New York

Michael W. Jalbert
Vice President
National Sales & Marketing
   Non-Commercial Accounts
Pepsi-Cola Company
Somers, New York

Melinda Bush, CHA
Executive Vice President,
   Publisher
Hotel & Travel Index
Hotel & Travel Index/
   ABC Int'l. Ed.
Secaucus, New Jersey

Allen J. Ostroff
Senior Vice President
The Prudential Realty Group
Newark, New Jersey